TEXAS
WILDLIFE ENCYCLOPEDIA

— AN ILLUSTRATED GUIDE TO —

BIRDS, FISH, MAMMALS, REPTILES, AND AMPHIBIANS

SCOTT SHUPE

Skyhorse Publishing

Skyhorse Publishing books may be purchased in bulk at special discounts for sales promotion, corporate gifts, fund-raising, or educational purposes. Special editions can also be created to specifications. For details, contact the Special Sales Department, Skyhorse Publishing, 307 West 36th Street, 11th Floor, New York, NY 10018 or info@skyhorsepublishing.com.

Skyhorse® and Skyhorse Publishing® are registered trademarks of Skyhorse Publishing, Inc.®, a Delaware corporation.

Visit our website at www.skyhorsepublishing.com.

10 9 8 7 6 5 4 3 2 1

Library of Congress Cataloging-in-Publication Data is available on file.

Cover design by Rain Saukas and David Ter-Avanesyan
Cover photographs courtesy of the author

Print ISBN: 978-1-5107-7723-1
Ebook ISBN: 978-1-5107-7724-8

Printed in China

ACKNOWLEDGMENTS

The author gratefully acknowledges the following individuals and organizations who contributed to the completion of this book. They are, in no particular order:

Dr. Robert Dowler, Professor Emeritus of Biology, Angelo State University, for supplying papers on skunk species in Texas.

John R. MacGregor for supplying a number of excellent mammal and reptile photos.

John Hewlett, who accompanied the author in the field and helped locate and collect fish and reptile specimens for photography.

James Kiser for several excellent bat photos.

Tim Johnson for photo of Feral Hog.

John Williams for photo of Eastern Woodrat.

Greg Schechter for photo of Southern Short-tailed Shrew.

Florida Fish and Wildlife Conservation Commission for permission to download and use photos from their Flickr site.

Don Martin, Don Martin Bird Photography, for several exceptional bird photos.

Will Bird and Phil Peak for allowing the author to photograph False Map Turtles in their possession.

U.S. Fish and Wildlife Service for photo contribution.

Alan Cressler for photo of Cuban flat-headed Frog.

Dave Frymire for allowing the author to photograph reptile specimens in his possession.

National Oceanic and Atmospheric Administration/Department of Commerce/NOAH Library and SEFSC Pascagoula Laboratory and collection of Brandi Noble for several fish photos.

Bret Albanese, Georgia Department of Natural Resources for photo contributions.

Brian Zimmerman for providing several fish photos.

Matthew R. Thomas for providing several fish photos and for help in identifying fish species in the author's photo library.

Dave Neely for contributing a large number of fish photos.

Konrad Schmidt for numerous fish photo contributions.

Corey Raimond for photo contributions.

Peter Paplanus for photo contributions.

Dr. Edmund Zimmerer for photo contributions.

Margaret Novak for photo contribution.

Julie Whitsett, Giddyup Art Studio.

Candy McNamee for guiding the author on bird photography trips in Texas and the southwestern US, and for providing several of her bird and wildlife photographs.

Allison Holdorf for photo contribution.

John Dickson for providing the largest number of bird photo contributions, other than those of the author.

Tim Leppek for contributing photos.

Pete Siminski for contributing photos.

C K Kelly for contributing photos.

Cyrus Allen for photo contributions.

Bureau of Land Management for the use of photos.

American Society of Mammalogists for the use of public domain photographs.

National Park Service for the use of public domain photographs.

Robby Deans for supplying a large number of photos.

Romey Swanson for supplying a large number of photos.

Dean Hendrickson, Adam Cohen, and the Fishes of Texas Project Staff for allowing the use of photos downloaded from the Fishes of Texas Team site on iNaturalist.

Rob Mottice, Senior Aquarist at the Tennessee Aquarium in Chattanooga, TN for help in identifying freshwater fish species photographed at that facility.

David Wilkins, Curator at the South Carolina Aquarium in Charleston, SC for his help in identifying freshwater fish species photographed at his facility.

Larry Warner – North Carolina Aquarium on Roanoke Island, NC for his help in identifying freshwater fish species photographed at his facility.

The staff of the North Carolina Aquarium at Pine Knoll Shores, NC for help in identifying freshwater fish species photographed at that facility.

The staff at the Georgia Fish Center for helping identify minnow species photographed at that facility.

The staff at the Texas Fresh Water Fish Center for help in identifying minnow species photographed at that facility.

Amy Berry-Clay, Hill Memorial Forest and Nature Center, for providing fish & amphibian specimens for photography.

Dr. Gordon Weddle, Campbellsville University for providing fish & amphibian specimens for photography.

Dr. Richard Kessler, Campbellsville University for help collecting fish specimens for photography.

Jim Harrison and Kristin Wiley of the Kentucky Reptile Zoo for allowing the author to photograph snake species at their facility and for their many years of friendship.

Judy Tipton for allowing me to photograph birds in her yard.

Matt Wagner and John Hardy from the Mississippi Museum of Natural History for helping to ID fishes photographed in aquariums at that facility.

Karen Finch for guiding the author in a search for migratory birds in south Florida.

Dr. Tim Spier, Murray State University for his help in collecting fish specimens for photography.

John Hewlett, who accompanied the author in the field and helped locate and collect fish and reptile specimens for photography.

The Staff of the Appalachicola National Estuarine Reserve for helping to identify fish species photographed at their facility.

The Staff of the Guano Tolomota Matanzas National Estuarine Reserve for helping to identify fish species photographed at their facility.

Kyle S. Shupe for being the author's eyes and ears during wildlife photography excursions across the southeastern United States.

North American Native Fish Association (NANFA) website which hosts many of the fish photographers whose photos appear in this book.

iNaturalist website which hosts many many wildlife photographers from around the world, some of whose photos appear in this book.

The staff and management of Reptile Gardens who have provided this author with myriad professional opportunities through the years and more importantly close personal friendships; most specifically Joe Maierhauser-CEO, Tom Lang-Manager, Terry Phillips-Curator, Virginia Garrigan-Human Resources and the late Bill Texel-Curator Emeritus.

Scott Wahlberg for some Texas herp photos.

Clint Guadiana for some Texas snake photos.

Micheal Price for his reptile photo contributions.

Sophia Osho for providing the photo of the author.

The following are recognized for their contributions to Wikimedia Commons, which has provided a source of additional photographs. The Wikimedia user name (or photographer name) and link to the license are shown.

American Society of Mammalogists-License Link: American Society of Mammalogists Grasshopper Mouse

https://upload.wikimedia.org/wikipedia/commons/2/2e/Chihuahuan_grasshopper_mouse.jpg

Bob Johnson-CC BY-SA 4.0 <https://creativecommons.org/licenses/by-sa/4.0>, via Wikimedia Commons

Connor Long-CC BY-SA 4.0 <https://creativecommons.org/licenses/by-sa/4.0>, via Wikimedia Commons

Alex Borisenko-CC BY-SA 3.0 <https://creativecommons.org/licenses/by-sa/3.0>, via Wikimedia Commons

Mario Suarez Porras-CC BY-SA 3.0 <https://creativecommons.org/licenses/by-sa/3.0>, via Wikimedia Commons

Hector Bottai-CC BY-SA 4.0 <https://creativecommons.org/licenses/by-sa/4.0>, via Wikimedia Commons

Dominic Sherony-CC BY-SA 2.0 <https://creativecommons.org/licenses/by-sa/2.0>, via Wikimedia Commons

Sapphosyne-CC BY-SA 3.0 <https://creativecommons .org/licenses/by-sa/3.0>, via Wikimedia Commons

Llussier-CC BY-SA 4.0 <https://creativecommons.org/ licenses/by-sa/4.0>, via Wikimedia Commons

Clinton & Charles Robertson—https://commons.wiki media.org/wiki/File:Etheostoma_grahami.jpg and

https://commons.wikimedia.org/wiki/File:Percina_ apristis_(3628005726).jpg

Nick Loveland—https://commons.wikimedia.org/wiki/ File:Plateau_Shiner_imported_from_iNaturalist_ photo_187972116_on_24_October_2023.jpg no rights reserved, CC0, via Wikimedia Commons

I would also like to thank my editor, Jason Katzman of Skyhorse Publishing. Jason has shown patience and a willingness to compromise, not to mention great faith in this author. He has also exhibited extraordinary entrepreneurial courage in taking on a huge project for which this book represents the eight installment in a series of wildlife encyclopedias for individual states.

Last and certainly not least, this book is dedicated to the three best things in my life, my three sons. Haydn, Ken (Denham), and Kyle Shupe. Although now grown men, as youngsters their keen eyes, youthful enthusiasm, and unflinching companionship were responsible for many of the photographs that appear in this book. More importantly, their presence in this world has provided this author with the incentive to repeatedly take on challenges at the limit my abilities.

PHOTOGRAPHERS

Most of the 1000 plus wildlife photographs that appear in this book were taken by the author. However many of the photographs were contributed by other wildlife photographers from across the USA. Those individuals were crucial to the completion of this book and their remarkable photographs add much to its content. The names of each of those photographers and the number of photos each contributed appears below.

Robby Deans—35
John Dickson—27
Dave Neely—15
Matthew R. Thomas—12
C K Kelly—10
Romey Swanson—7
Tim Leppek—7
Candy McNamee—7
John R. MacGregor—6
Konrad Schmidt—6
Fishes of Texas Project Team—6
Peter Paplanus—5
Don Martin Bird Photography—5
Brian Zimmerman—4
Florida Wildlife Commission—4
Clint Guadiana—3
Scott Wahlberg—3
Michael Price—3
Dr. Edmund Zimmerer—2
James Kiser—2
Pete Siminski—2
Corey Raimond—2
Cyrus Allen—2
U.S. Fish and Wildlife Service—2
Alan Cressler—1
NOAH Library and SEFSC Pascagoula Laboratory: collection of Brandi Noble—1

Bret Albanese, Georgia Department of Natural Resources—1
Margaret Novak—1
Allison Holdorf—1
U.S. Fish & Widlife Service, Bill Shreve—1
U.S. Fish and Wildlife Service, Micheal Sealy—1
U.S. Fish and Wildlife Service Lisa Hupp—1
Nicole Montoya BLM NM—1
American Society of Mammalogists—1
National Park Service—1
NPS White Sands National Park—1
Alex Borisenko, Biodiversity Institute of Ontario—1
Bob Johnson—1
Tim Johnson—1
John Williams—1
Greg Schechter—1
Connor Long—1
Mario Suarez Porras—1
Hector Bottai—1
Dominic Sherony—1
Sapphosyne—1
sai_silish—1
Barbod Safae—1
Johnyochum—1
Llussier—1
Nick Loveland—2
Clinton & Charles Robertson—1
Sophia Osho—1

TABLE OF CONTENTS

INTRODUCTION

Wildlife has always played an important role in the human history of Texas. For at least ten thousand years, Native Americans living in the region sustained themselves largely by harvesting mammals, birds, and fish for sustenance, as well as fashioning clothing from fur and hides. Bone and antler were made into tools, and sinew provided string and bindings. But the first humans in the state had relatively little impact on wildlife populations. Their small numbers and primitive weaponry combined to ensure that theirs was largely a sustainable harvest.

However, beginning almost with the first European settlement of Texas and continuing well into the mid-1900s, untold millions of birds and mammals were hunted and killed for personal sustenance, for sport, and for commercial harvest. By 1885, the Bison had disappeared from the plains of Texas, followed by the extirpation of the Pronghorn from most of its range in the state. By the late 1890s, even Whitetail Deer populations had reached perilously low numbers.

The large carnivores fared even worse than their prey species. The last wild Jaguar seen in the state was killed in 1943. And the last Gray Wolf was killed in west Texas in 1970, followed within a short time by the extirpation of the Red Wolf in the eastern part of the state.

For many years in America there was little consideration given to the fact that all resources can be finite. As a result, all the forests were felled, wetlands were drained, and the prairie was plowed or converted to pasture. Even the remote and rugged regions of the western tip of Texas have not escaped the impact of modern humans, as overgrazing significantly changed fragile arid landscapes. These man-made alterations to natural habitats have impacted wildlife populations even more than unregulated hunting.

The story of wildlife conservation in America began in response to dwindling wildlife populations, and as early as the 1920s, the first efforts to conserve wildlife began to take shape. It is worth noting that these early efforts were often lead by sport hunters. By mid-century the conservation movement had evolved into a new scientific discipline that became known as "Wildlife Conservation and Management." In today's vernacular, it is more often called simply "Wildlife Biology." With the advent of the conservation movement and its new scientific discipline came the formation of state and federal agencies like the Texas Parks and Wildlife Department and the U.S. Fish and Wildlife Service.

Funded mainly by the sale of hunting and fishing licenses and employing thousands of dedicated and highly trained professionals, America's wildlife agencies have done a remarkable job of protecting, managing, and enhancing wildlife populations. Some species have responded so well to wildlife management practices that today there are probably more Whitetail Deer in Texas than there were when Davy Crockett fought his last battle at the Alamo. And recent efforts by conservation organizations may even result in magnificent and long gone species like the wolf and the Jaguar someday returning to protected wilderness enclaves in the state.

Texas's wildlife has always been an important resource for the state's trappers, hunters, and fishermen, but wildlife is also increasingly important for its intrinsic, aesthetic value. Though the age-old practice of hunting and fishing is the most obvious example of how wildlife can enrich our lives, for many the opportunity to simply observe wildlife and experience nature also serves to enhance our existence.

In more recent history, the pursuit of wildlife has evolved to encompass more benign activities such as bird watching, wildlife photography, etc. In fact, the numbers of Americans who enjoy these non-consumptive forms of wildlife-related recreation today exceed the numbers of those who hunt and fish. These interests and activities have broadened so considerably that the U.S. Fish and Wildlife Service, in a recent assessment of the economic impact of wildlife in America, lists a broad category labeled "Wildlife Watching." The economic impact of wildlife watching in America today actually exceeds the impact that hunters and fishermen have on the economy.

With interest in wildlife and nature continuing to grow in Texas, the need for a single, simple reference to the state's wildlife has become evident. There are available a number of excellent books that deal specifically with the state's birds, reptiles, mammals, fishes, etc. But there are none that combine all the state's wildlife into a comprehensive, encyclopedic reference. This volume is intended to fill that niche. It is hoped that this book will find favor with school librarians, life science teachers, students of field biology classes, and professional naturalists as well as with the general populace.

As might be expected with such a broad-spectrum publication, intimate details about the natural history of individual species is omitted in favor of a format that provides more basic information.

In this sense, this volume is not intended for use as a professional reference, but instead as a usable layman's guide to the state's wildlife. For those who wish to explore the information regarding the state's wildlife more deeply, a list of references for each chapter appears in the back of the book which includes both printed and reliable internet references.

Embracing the old adage that a picture is worth a thousand words, color photographs are used to depict and identify each species. Below each photograph is a table that provides basic information about the biology of each animal. This table includes a state map with shaded area showing the species' presumed range in the state, as well as general information such as size, habitat, abundance, etc.

The taxonomic classification of each species is also provided, with the animal's Class, Order, and Family appearing as a heading at the top of the page.

The range maps shown in this book are not intended to be regarded as a strictly accurate representation of the range of any given species. Indeed, the phrase "Presumed range in Texas," which accompanies each range map should be literally interpreted as a presumption only. The ranges of many species in the state are often not well documented and the range maps for some species in this book may be regarded at best as an "educated guess."

Furthermore, many wide-ranging species are restricted to regions of suitable habitat. Thus an aquatic species like the Beaver, while found nearly statewide, would not be expected to occur in the middle of the desert, except perhaps along a river or permanent stream.

Some species that may have once been found throughout a large geographic area may now have disappeared from much of their former range. Other species may be expanding their range. Further complicating the issue of species distribution is the fact that animals like birds and bats, possessed with the ability of flight, are capable of traveling great distances. Many species of both birds and bats are migratory and regularly travel hundreds or even thousands of miles annually. It is not uncommon for these migratory species to sometimes appear in areas where they are not typically found. The mechanisms of migration and dispersal of many animals is still a bit of a mystery and the exact reason why a bird from another portion of the country (or even from another continent) should suddenly appear where it doesn't belong is often speculation. Sometimes these appearances may represent individuals that are simply wandering. Other times it can be a single bird or an entire flock that has been blown off course by a powerful storm or become otherwise lost and disoriented. Whatever the cause, there are many bird species that have been recorded in the state that are not really a part of the state's regularly occurring fauna and their occasional sightings are regarded as "accidental." On the other hand, some bird species may appear somewhere in the state once every few years dependent upon weather conditions or availability of food in their normal habitat. Although these types of "casual species" could be regarded as belonging among Texas's native bird fauna, their occurrence in the state is so sporadic and unpredictable that deciding which species should be included becomes very subjective. The point is that the reader should be advised that while all the bird species depicted in this volume can be considered to be members of the state's indigenous fauna, not every bird species that has ever been seen or recorded in the state is depicted in this book.

For readers who wish to delve into more professional and detailed information about the vertebrate zoology of Texas, the list of references shown for each chapter should adequately provide that opportunity.

The pages that follow are intended to introduce Texans to the remarkable diversity, wondrous beauty, and miraculous lives of the state's wildlife species. It is hoped that this introduction will lead to a greater awareness, concern, and appreciation for the state's natural heritage. It is further hoped that acquiring that awareness and appreciation will lead to a better stewardship of the living things with which we share this planet. And more importantly, the natural ecosystems upon which both they and we ultimately depend.

CHAPTER 1

THE FACE OF THE LAND

— NATURAL REGIONS OF TEXAS —

Defining and understanding the natural regions of Texas is the first step in understanding the natural history of the state. Man-made political boundaries such as county lines and state borders are meaningless to wildlife, whereas natural features like rivers, mountains, or plains can be important elements in influencing the distribution of the state's wildlife.

The major considerations used in determining and delineating natural regions are such factors such as elevation, relief (topography), drainages (rivers and streams), geology (rocks and soils), and climate. All these are important elements that can determine the limits of distribution for living organisms. It follows then that some knowledge of these factors is essential when involved in the study of the state's wildlife. The study of natural regions is known as Physiography, which means "physical geography" or literally "the face of the land." While the terms geography and physiography are closely related and sometimes used interchangeably, geography is a broader term which includes such things as human culture, resource use, and man's impact on the land, while physiography deals only with elements of geography created by nature.

The term most often used to define a major natural region is "Physiographic Division." There are eight of these physiographic divisions across the conterminous United States. Among those eight there are three that impact the state of Texas. They are the *Interior Plains Division*, the *Atlantic Plain Division* and the *Intermontane Plateaus Division* (See Figure 1 on the next page). Note that in the map shown in Figure 1 the gray shaded area depicting the Atlantic Plain Division extends into the Atlantic Ocean to encompass the Continental Shelf of North America.

Each of the eight Physiographic Divisions of North America can be subdivided into smaller units known as Physiographic Provinces. The three Physiographic Divisions that impact the state of Texas are divided into Provinces as follows:

In eastern and southern Texas, the Atlantic Plain Division is divided into the *Coastal Plain* (on land) and the *Continental Shelf* (offshore). Both these are huge provinces that range from southern Texas around the coast all the way to New England.

In central Texas and the Panhandle, the Interior Plains Division is divided into the *Great Plains Province* and the *Interior Lowland Province*. The Great Plains Province extends northward from Texas well into Canada. Meanwhile the Interior Lowland Province extends north into Canada and eastward to the Great Lakes.

In westernmost Texas, the portion of the Intermontane Plateaus Division that occurs in Texas is known as the *Basin and Range Province*. The Basin and Range Province is the largest subdivision of the Intermontane Plateaus and extends westward through southern New Mexico and Arizona well into southern California. It also extends northward and encompasses the entire state of Nevada as well as parts of southeastern Oregon, western Utah and southern Idaho.

The map of the United States shown in Figure 2 on the next page shows how the major divisions are divided into provinces across the country. Meanwhile Figure 3 on page 6 shows where these provinces occur in the state of Texas.

These physiographic divisions and provinces sometimes exhibit a parallel relationship with wildlife species. For instance, the Attwater's Prairie Chicken and the Gulf Coast Toad are native only to the Coastal Plain Province, while the range of the Pronghorn is restricted to the Interior Plains and the Basin and Range Provinces.

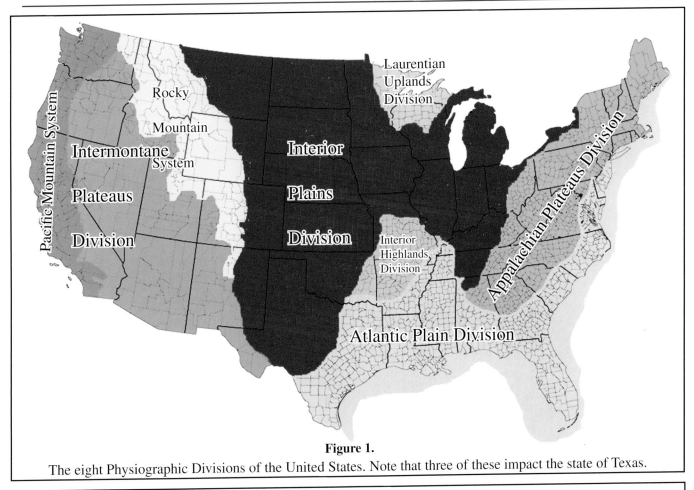

Figure 1.
The eight Physiographic Divisions of the United States. Note that three of these impact the state of Texas.

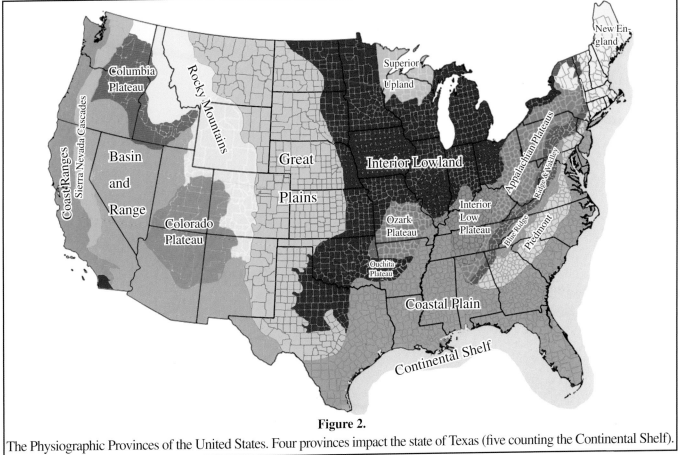

Figure 2.
The Physiographic Provinces of the United States. Four provinces impact the state of Texas (five counting the Continental Shelf).

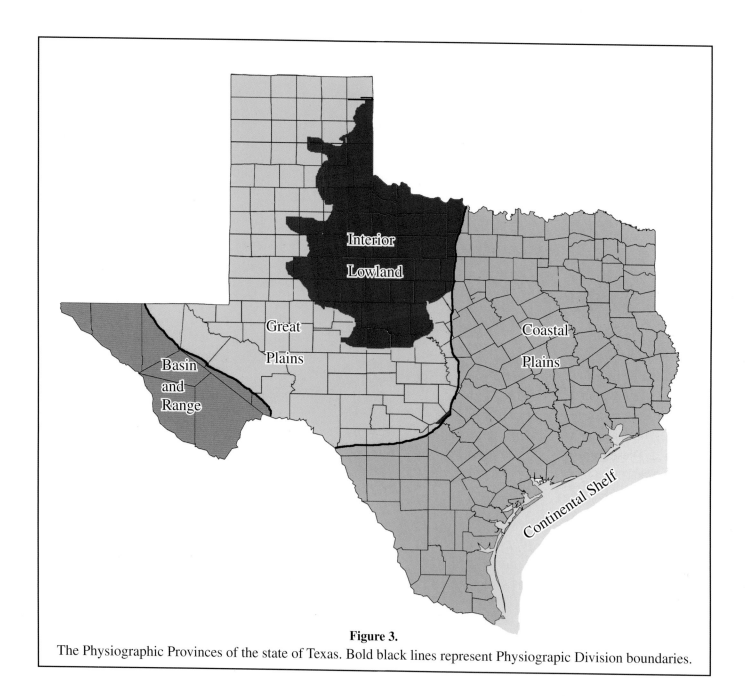

Figure 3.
The Physiographic Provinces of the state of Texas. Bold black lines represent Physiograpic Division boundaries.

CHAPTER 2

ECOREGIONS & WILDLIFE HABITATS OF TEXAS

— PART 1—ECOREGIONS —

The designation of the different landscapes is just one of many tools scientists use to understand nature and natural systems. For wildlife biologists a more important model is the designation of "ecoregions." While ecoregions have much in common with physiographical regions, an ecoregion also takes into account not only landforms but also factors such as climate, soil conditions, and the assemblage of plant and animal species that are found within that region.

The US Environmental Protection Agency publishes a series of maps of the various ecoregions of North America. These maps begin with the broad based "Level I Ecoregions" that encompass large areas. These Level I Ecoregions are then refined in a hierarchy of smaller and smaller units designated as "Level II Ecoregions," "Level III Ecoregions," etc.

Unlike the physiographic divisions and province shown in Figures 1 through 3, the ecoregions are not always contiguous. The Northern Forests and the Northwestern Forested Mountains in particular consist of several widely separated units that may be surrounded by and embedded in larger, more continuous regions like the Eastern Temperate Forests or the Great Plains. Figure 4 on the following page shows where the Level I Ecoregions of the conterminous US occur.

Of the ten Level I Ecoregions in the conterminous US, only four impact the state of Texas. Those four are the *Great Plains*, the *Eastern Temperate Forests,* the *North American Deserts*, and the *Temperate Sierras*. The Temperate Sierras region barely enters westernmost Texas from New Mexico in the area of the Guadalupe Mountains. Figure 5 on page 8 shows where these Level I Ecoregions occur in the state of Texas.

The next level of designation in the ecoregion units hierarchy are of course the Level II Ecoregions. At level II their are twenty ecoregion divisions across the conterminous US. Figure 6 on page 9 shows where the Level II Ecoregions occur on a map of the conterminous United States. Six of the Level II/Ecoregions impact Texas. Those six are listed below.

The Great Plains Level I Ecoregion has five Level II Ecoregions. Three of those occur in Texas. They are the *Tamaulipas-Texas Semi-arid Plain*, the *South Central Semi-arid Prairies,* and the *Texas-Louisiana Coastal Plain.*

The American Deserts Level I Ecoregion is split at Level II into *Cold Deserts* and *Warm Deserts*. The Level II portion of the American Deserts that affects Texas is a part of the Warm Deserts ecoregion.

The Temperate Sierra Level I Ecoregion (which occurs mostly in Mexico) has a total of six Level II Ecoregions, with only the *Upper Gila Mountain*s occurring in the US (with a tiny portion in Texas).

Finally, all of the Eastern Temperate Forest Level I Ecoregion that occurs in Texas is a part of the Level II Ecoregion known as the *Southeast US Plains.*

Figure 7 on page 9 shows approximately where these level II ecoregions occur in the state of Texas.

In addition to the Level I and Level II ecoregions there are additional designations at levels III and IV that represent much more refined ecoregion designations. There are eighty-five level III ecoregions in the conterminous US. Of these there are twelve that occur in Texas. Figure 8 (page 10) shows the Level III Ecoregions of Texas.

Finally, an even more refined level of ecoregion designations exists at the Level IV Ecoregion specification. The total number of Level IV Ecoregions in the

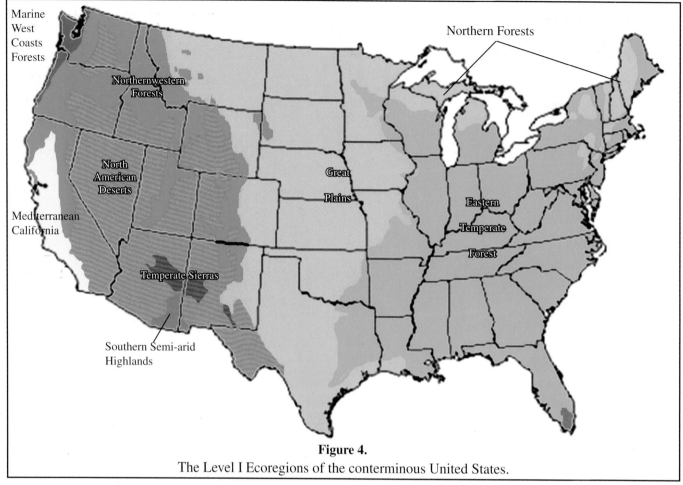

Figure 4.
The Level I Ecoregions of the conterminous United States.

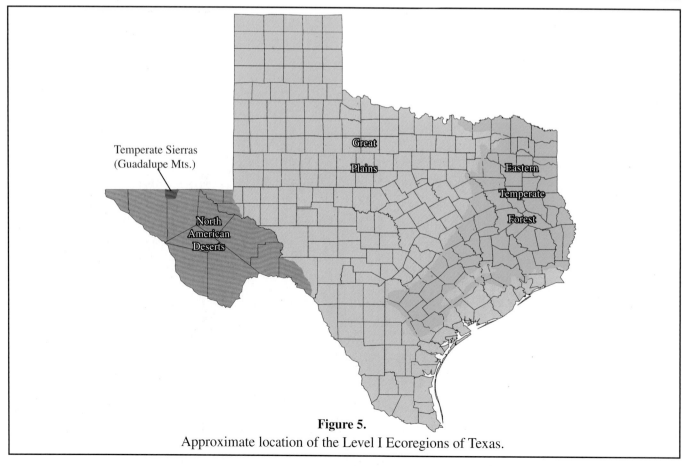

Figure 5.
Approximate location of the Level I Ecoregions of Texas.

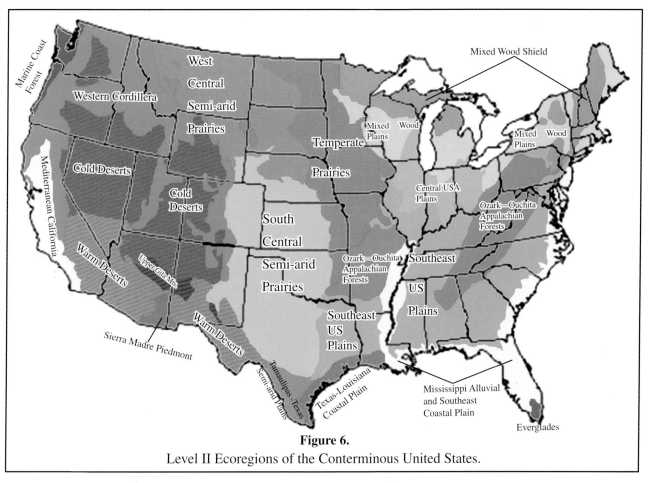

Figure 6.
Level II Ecoregions of the Conterminous United States.

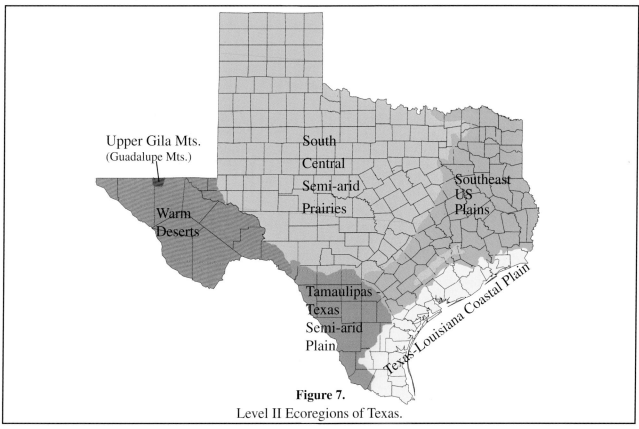

Figure 7.
Level II Ecoregions of Texas.

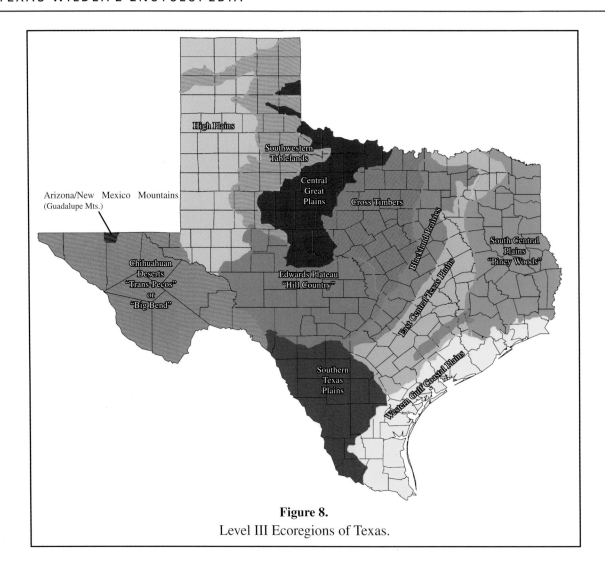

Figure 8.
Level III Ecoregions of Texas.

conterminous US is 967. Of these, there are fifty-six that occur in Texas. The maps for Level IV Ecoregions are extremely detailed and are not depicted in this book. For those interested in exploring the more refined level of ecoregions designations, maps of the Level IV Ecoregions of the US can be found online at the US Environmental Protection Agency's website, or by simply googling "Level IV Ecoregions of Texas."

It should be acknowledged that the nomenclature used in the ecoregion maps shown in Figures 7 and 8 may not correspond with names used in other models of the natural regions of Texas. For instance, in many popular models the Edwards Plateau level III ecoregion shown in Figure 8 above is often referred to as the "Texas Hill Country." Likewise the Chihuahuan Deserts region often goes by the name "Big Bend Region" and the High Plains and Southwestern Tablelands are regularly referred to as

"the Panhandle." In eastern Texas the South Central Plains is largely synonymous with the region frequently called "the Piney Woods." Ecologists and biologists use different models based on different criteria to designate natural regions and there can be differences between these designations. In this book, the author has chosen to follow the model adopted by the US Environmental Protection Agency.

Maps of the various ecoregions of the US and of individual US states can be found online at ecological regions.info. Additionally, the Texas Parks and Wildlife Department's website features a "Texas Ecoregions" page which provides in-depth descriptions of the ecoregions of Texas shown in Figure 8; but the ecoregion model and nomenclature used by TPWD may differ slightly from what is used in this book.

— PART 2—HABITATS —

In many discussions about the natural environments of America, the terms habitat and ecoregion are sometimes used interchangeably. But strictly speaking, there are differences between the two. The term "ecoregion," as defined by the World Wildlife Fund, means "a large unit of land or water containing a geographically distinct assemblage of species, natural communities, and environmental conditions." A habitat, meanwhile, is usually defined simply as "where an organism lives." Moreover, many habitat types can be embedded in an ecoregion unit. For instance, the Eastern Temperate Forest Level I Ecoregion (which is characterized mainly by forests), may also contain within its boundaries habitats such as wetlands, savanna, and grassland as well as the forests which give the ecoregion its name.

All the natural habitats in America can be divided into two all inclusive habitat types, *Aquatic* and *Terrestrial*. Within these two broad categories there are numerous habitat types, each of which can be further categorized based on a variety of factors. For instance, a forest habitat can be described by the types of trees present, as in the Mixed Pine-Hardwood Forest habitat. Other localized factors such as soil moisture may result in the same habit being differentiated between xeric (dry) or mesic (moist) forest.

It should be noted that all habitat types usually exist in a mosaic pattern rather than in a large contiguous block. Thus a forest may contain patches of wetland or grassland. A grassland can have ribbons of forests following river valleys or have patches of savanna. Likewise, a wetland marsh may become a meadow during droughts or seasonal dry spells. Finally, different agencies or organizations may have different criteria for habitat types. The habitat designations used in this book are this authors designations and may not parallel those used by other agencies or individuals. The definitions below describe the most common habitats referred to in this book.

Terrestrial Habitats of Texas

Grasslands

First, it is important to note that while grassland habitats are dominated by the presence of grasses, other plant types occur within a grassland habitat. The most common of these non-grass plant species are annual and perennial forbs and wildflowers. Woody plants like shrubs and occasional tree species can also be found in the grassland habitat. Prairies are perhaps the most iconic and best known type of grassland habitat. But there are other habitat types in Texas with plant communities consisting mostly of grasses. The other two grassland habitats in Texas described in this book are Meadows and Desert Grasslands.

Historically, grassland habitats were common and widespread in Texas. Indeed it was the lush grasslands of the state that were so attractive to early settlers who saw in these lush pastures the state's great potential for farming and ranching. Today, most of the prairie native to the eastern half of the state has been converted to croplands, while the grasslands of the western half of the state are widely used for livestock grazing. Although controlled grazing by livestock has only a limited impact on grasslands, early settlers often overgrazed the landscape and significantly changed the character of the grassland habitat. Row cropping has essentially eliminated all but tiny fragments of the original Tallgrass Prairie grassland habit once found in the eastern half of the state. In the Blackland Prairies ecoregion it is estimated that less than 1 percent of the original Tallgrass Prairie remains intact.

Descriptions of the three main types of grassland habitats of Texas appear below:

Prairies

Prairies are regions where trees are either absent or present only along stream courses or moist soil areas such as river valleys. Grasses are the dominant plant species in prairies along with a variety of forbs and sometimes woody shrubs. Prairies tend to occur in regions where soil type, moisture, and frequent wildfire inhibits the growth of trees. In this book, there are three types of prairies recognized based on the types of dominant grass species present. The first is the Tall Grass Prairie that is characterized by grasses such Big Bluestem, Indiangrass, and Switchgrass. Tallgrass Prairie historically occurred in the Coastal Plain, East Central Texas Plains, and in the Blackland Prairie level III ecoregions (see Figure 8). In the more arid western part of the state, grasses like Little Bluestem, Sideoats Grama, and Buffalograss make up the Short-grass Prairies. These Short-grass Prairies were typical in the High Plains level III ecoregion of the Texas Panhandle. Sandwiched in between these two is the Mixed Grass Prairie that hosts both short and tall grass species.

Meadows

The term meadow and prairie are often used interchangeably and generally the same types of plants (grasses and forbs) dominate in both habitats. The biggest difference between a meadow and a prairie is that meadows are usually transitional and temporary habitats. A prairie, on the other hand, is a more permanent form of grassland habitat. Additionally meadows are typically rather small parcels of grassland usually occurring within and surrounded by another habitat such as a forest. Meadows can occur in regions where soil types and rainfall amounts readily support the growth of trees, but some other factor such as forest fire or human clearing of forests eliminates the trees which are replaced by grasses and forbs. In some instances, excessively wet soils can keep trees that are not wetland adapted from growing. Meadows tend to occur more in the eastern parts of North America where forests are common and in high mountain swales and valleys.

Desert Grasslands

Desert Grasslands have much in common with the Shortgrass Prairie and in many ways they are synonymous. But Shortgrass Prairies can extend well to the north of Texas along the eastern slope of the Rocky Mountain uplift, occurring throughout the colder climates of the northern great plains all the way into Canada. The Desert Grassland may be best described as a Shortgrass Prairie existing in an especially arid and seasonally hot region. Desert Grasslands usually harbor desert plant species such as cacti and a variety of thorn bushes. In Texas the Desert Grasslands historically occurred in the Chihuahuan Desert level III ecoregion (commonly known as the "Big Bend" or "Trans-Pecos" Region). Much of desert regions in North America today were originally Desert Grasslands. Where livestock overgrazing by early ranchers eliminated the grasses (and their all important root systems) soil exposed to the baking effects of direct sunlight hardened and became

impervious to water, changing the soil structure enough so that "true desert" plants such as cactus often now dominate in regions where grasses once proliferated. Even in the total absence of further grazing the short grasses of the original desert grassland often fail to reclaim the landscape.

Forests

Forests need no introduction. Everyone has a image of the forest. In the simplest terms, a forest is a region characterized by the dominant presence of trees. The terms "forest' and "woodland" are used interchangeably, but in most instances a forest is understood to encompass a large area of land where trees dominant. A woodland, on the other hand, may be just a small patch of trees constituting an "island" of forest surrounded by otherwise open lands such as croplands or grassland. When considering the forest habitats of America, there are two main categories which need consideration. The first of these is the *condition* of the forest. Forest conditions are determined by factors that have the power to create changes to existing forests (such as fire or logging); or environmental conditions that determine whether the forest is dry or moist (i.e. rainfall amounts, topography, and soil type). The second category is the *type* of forest. Forest types are usually determined by the types of plant species that are present, with the most common tree species often lending their name to the forest type. Listed below are the definitions of forest conditions, followed by a list of the types of forest found in Texas.

Forest Conditions

All forest *conditions* listed below can occur in all *types* of forests.

Climax Forest

A climax forest is a forest that is in an undisturbed and fully mature state of existence. In climax forests many of the trees present are at or near the maximum age attainable by the species. In most cases that will be an age of at least several hundred years. At one time, most of the entire eastern United States was home to mature, climax forest (also called Virgin Forest). The forests of America today are but a shadow of their former glory. Nearly all of America's (and Texas's) forests today are regrowth forest with few trees more than a century old. There are only a few isolated, widely scattered enclaves of Climax Forests remaining in protected areas in the eastern half of Texas. They are tiny remnants of what once was, and usually encompass no more than a few hundred acres. By contrast much of the woodlands in the Cross Timbers Ecoregion can be defined as Climax Forest with many trees that are hundreds of years old.

Regenerative Forest
This forest condition is the opposite of a climax forest. Regenerative forests are forests that are in a stage of regrowth following logging, fire, or fierce windstorms and tornadoes. Nearly all the forest in the eastern US today are regenerative forests. This is also true of the once great Pine-Hardwood Forest that covers much of eastern Texas.

Mesic Forest
These are forests with moist soils. Mesic forest conditions can be the result of high annual precipitation or soil conditions such as high organic content that acts as a sponge to retain moisture, or that have clay and silt soils that prevent rainfall from percolating through the soil surface. Heavily shaded slopes facing north or east in deeply dissected landscapes can also produce mesic forests, as can lowland regions and bottomlands where streams are present.

Xeric Forest
The xeric forest is a forest where soil moisture is low. Xeric forests tend to occur in upland areas of high rainfall runoff, south or west facing slopes, areas of shallow rocky soils or areas of sandy soils that allow rainfall to rapidly percolate underground.

Forest Types
In the state of Texas most of the true forests are found in the eastern third of the state in the South Central Plains Ecoregion (a.k.a. Piney Woods). Westward from this region most of the woodlands occur in a mosaic with other habitat types like savanna or brushland habitats. But "forests" of a type can be found in many regions of the state. The forest types described next are the most common forest types in Texas.

Mixed Pine-Hardwood Forest
Pines of three species are the dominant trees in most of this forest type in Texas. In fact, the easternmost region of the state where this forest type occurs is often referred to as the "Texas Piney Woods." In places, these forests can be almost exclusively pines. But in many areas dozens of species of hardwoods also occur (oaks, hickories, etc.) along with many species of shrubs, vines, weeds, and wildflowers. These forests may be either xeric forest in upland regions or areas of sandy, well-drained soils; or mesic forests in river bottoms or regions where the soil moisture is high for much of the year.

Post Oak Forests
This forest type occurs in east central Texas between the South Central Plains Ecoregion and the Cross Timbers Ecoregion. Hardwood trees like oaks and elm are the main tree species.

Crosstimbers Woodlands
These forests occur in the Crosstimbers Ecoregion. The definition of forest is here is arguable, as the region is a mosaic of woodlands, savanna, and prairie. However there are abundant trees here and many of the trees are quite old, some as much as four hundred to five hundred years. Trees are mostly oak species and junipers with a few other hardwoods such as elm and hickory. In sharp contrast to the forests of the eastern United States, the trees in the Crosstimbers Woodlands do not reach great heights and tend to have canopies that are as wide as they are tall.

Oak-Juniper Slope Forests
Also known as "Cedar Brakes Forests" this forest type features mostly Ashe Juniper and a variety of evergreen oaks and is the classic tree aggregation of the Edwards Plateau Ecoregion. It is a decidedly xeric forest type and characteristically occurs on poor, rocky soils.

Mountain Forests
Occurring in the higher elevations (above five thousand feet) of the mountainous areas in the Chihuahuan Desert Ecoregion in the westernmost portion of Texas. Junipers, oaks, and hackberry are characteristic trees in these dry mountains; some scrub species such as yucca and agave are also common, especially on sunlit western and

southern slopes. Pines appear in the highest elevations and on shaded northern or eastern slopes; while cotton-wood and ashes may exist in canyons and along waterways.

Savanna

Savanna habitat is best described as a habitat that is "in between" forest and grassland. In savanna habitats there are trees but they are widely spaced and are never close enough to each other to create a closed canopy. Thus, in savanna habitats there is a significant amount of sunlight that reaches the ground. Grasses are found throughout and carpet the ground in savanna habitats. In fact, some ecologists consider savanna to be a type of grassland habitat. Much of south Texas is considered by some to be a type of savanna called the Tamaulipan Savanna Grassland (also sometimes called the South Texas Brushlands). Others may consider savanna to be a type of open forest habitat, as in the case of the woodlands of the East Central Texas Plains Ecoregion, where occurs the Post Oak Forest type; which is also sometimes referred to as "Post Oak Savanna." Likewise, the Cross Timbers Ecoregion, which harbors the "Cross Timbers Woodland" forest type is also to home savanna habitats which exist in a mosaic with both forest and grasslands. In conclusion, Savanna is a habitat type that is intermediate between forest and grassland. In some cases, Brush/Scrub habitats may also have Savanna-like characteristics.

Brush/Scrub Habitats

This habitat type consists of stunted trees or bushy tree species such as Mesquite, along with a variety of shrub species. Thorny bushes like Acacia and yuccas are important components in brush/scrub habitat in more arid regions. Mesquite is one of the most widespread plant species in Texas and ranges throughout all of the state except the eastern one-third. Brush/ scrub habitats can also be widespread and occur in a mosaic pattern among other habitats such as Savanna or Grassland. Brush/scrub habitat is most common in southern and western Texas but can occur statewide. and in some places may be created by the natural succession of habitats (such as a fallow field becoming overgrown with briers, shrubs, and saplings).

Riparian Habitats

Riparian habitats are associated with rivers. The classic example of a riparian habitat would be the ribbon of lush vegetation that grows along the banks of rivers in desert or prairie regions. Stream courses with a profusion of trees and shrubs along the bank meandering through cropland, pasture or otherwise open landscapes can also be regarded as riparian.

Universal Habitats

These are habitats that may occur anywhere within the other habitat types (i.e. Forest, Grassland, Savanna, etc.)

Successional Habitats

Successional habitats are universal and found in all habitat types and ecoregions. A successional habitat occurs when one type of habitat is being naturally transformed into a different habitat. Such as a grassland that is slowly being taken over by tree saplings on its way to becoming a forest; or a fallow crop field reverting to a natural grassland, Another example would be a marsh that is slowly filling and drying to become a meadow. Likewise a meadow flooded by Beavers can become a marsh. Nature is never static and with a few exceptions habitat types are constantly undergoing change.

Ecotones

Ecotone habitats are places where two or more habitat types meet. A classic example would be where a forested upland meets a lowland swamp. In ecotone areas, wildlife from two or more habitat types can often be found, usually making ecotone habitats richer and more productive any single habitat alone.

Man-made Habitats

Human altered habitats are not usually considered in discussions of wildlife habitat. But most of the landscape in America today has been altered by man to some degree and some of these altered habitats have become important to wildlife. The most obvious are croplands which provide a food source for many herbivores and seed eating mammals and birds. Rice fields are used as a replacement for natural freshwater marsh by many wetland loving species. Man-made pastures are also used as a substitute for natural meadows. Even urban neighborhoods can be wildlife habitat. Everyone is familiar with a Robin plucking worms from a well manicured lawn, or Rock Pigeons wandering city streets and Gray Squirrels foraging in the trees of city parks.

Micro Habitats

All the terrestrial habitats thus far discussed are what ecologists refer to as "Macro-habits." So called because they encompass large areas of the landscape. The opposite of a Macro-habitat is the "Micro-habitat" (or small habitat). One example of a micro-habitat might be a fallen dead tree that becomes home to a small animal like a lizard. The fallen tree is a micro-habitat within the much larger macro-habitat of the forest. All Macro-habitats contain within them an almost infinite variety of Micro-habitats.

Aquatic Habitats of Texas

Wetlands

The definition of a wetland can vary depending upon the organization or agency defining it. Some definitions of wetlands included ephemeral, seasonally flooded lands such as river floodplains or vernal (wet season) ponds and pools. In this book the definition of a wetland is simplified to mean an area where water is present on the land year-round. Using that definition, there are two types of wetland habitats in Texas. They are found mostly in the South Central Plains and Western Gulf Coastal Plain Ecoregions.

Swamps

A swamp is best defined as a wetland area in which the dominant plants are trees. Most of Texas's swamplands have always been found in eastern part of the state, especially in low lying areas adjacent to rivers and streams. Baldcypress, willows, Red Maple, and Water Tupelo are the common tree species of Texas swamps. Generally speaking swamps are permanently flooded, but some habitat models may include seasonally flooded bottomland forest. Swamps are important areas of biodiversity and are critical to the survival of many vertebrate wildlife species. Swamps are sometimes categorized by the dominant tree species present (as in Baldcypress Swamp, Gum-Tupelo Swamp, etc.).

Marshes

Marshes are wetlands in which the main plant species are grasses, sedges, and shrubs. Some small trees like willows may be present, but they are never dominant. Some marshes may be only seasonally flooded, while others have permanently standing water. As with swamps, marshes enjoy significant diversity and are vital habitats to many of the state's vertebrate wildlife species. There are several distinct types of marshes in Texas. Freshwater marshes occur in inland regions and coastal saltwater marshes in coastal areas. Cattails, Pickerel Weed, Buttonbush, Rose Mallow, and Water Lily are common plants in freshwater marshes. Throughout the gulf coast region saltwater marshes make up one of the state's most important wildlife habitats. These marshes are dominated by salt tolerant grasses. As you move inland from the coastline, saltwater marsh is often replaced by freshwater marshes in the lowlands of the "coastal prairies." Where these two types of habitats meet are the "brackish marshes" characterized by the mixing of fresh and salt waters. The importance of the coastal salt marshes is hard to overstate. They are the "nursery of the seas" and many marine fish species spawn in the salt marsh.

Streams

The stream habitats of Texas are familiar to everyone and need no introduction. Everyone knows what a river looks like and that a creek is a smaller version of a river. What should be noted about streams is that ecologists studying this type of aquatic habitat have a variety of systems for classifying streams. One of the simplest classifications is based on the amount of water present in the stream and the duration of time in which water is present. This simple method uses three basic classification which are self explanatory. Those classifications are *Ephemeral*, *Intermittent*, and *Perennial*. A more complete discussion of this aquatic habitat can be found in Chapter 9 "Rivers and Streams of Texas" along with maps of the state's major streams and their respective watersheds.

Estuaries

Estuaries are regions where rivers meet the sea. Here, fresh waters mingle with salt water producing what are known as "brackish waters." Estuaries are extremely rich in aquatic species and will contain both freshwater and saltwater fish species.

Lakes & Ponds

In Texas, most of the lakes are man-made impoundments on rivers and streams. Man-made lakes of course provide habitat for many fish species. They are also used by migratory waterfowl, shorebirds, turtles, amphibians, water snakes, and a few aquatic mammals such as Beaver, Otter, and Muskrat. There are a few natural lakes in the form of small "oxbow" lakes formed by horseshoe bends in a river that has been cut off from the main channel. These Oxbow Lakes are usually a product of larger rivers and being a natural occurrence and often associated with nearby wetlands, they can be very important to a wide variety of aquatic and semi-aquatic species.

"Playas" are a type of seasonal lake occurring in low lying areas in arid plains and deserts. During periods of rainfall these shallow depressions fill with water and become temporary lakes. Generally, playa lakes are not important as wildlife habitats, but they can be important to some waterfowl and shore bird species. Small man-made impoundments producing ponds are widespread and these small aquatic habitats can be especially import-ant as breeding habitats for the state's amphibian species.

CHAPTER 3

WILDLIFE CONSERVATION IN TEXAS

The history of the wildlife conservation effort in Texas mirrors that of most of the rest of the United States. Following many decades of irresponsible exploitation of natural resources and wanton destruction of wildlife populations by early settlers and pioneers, the science of wildlife management and conservation ethic began to emerge in the early part of the twentieth century. Controlled hunting regulated by seasons and limits, coupled with the requirement of hunting licenses, permits, and excise taxes on hunting and fishing equipment are today the backbone and the pocketbook for wise wildlife management and conservation principles.

Early conservationists realized that just regulating the harvest would be inadequate to rejuvenating America's wildlife populations. A successful plan for restoring abundant wildlife resources also required the protection and restoration of America's wildlife habitats.

The formation of the U.S. Fish and Wildlife Service in 1940 was one of the most important events in the history of wildlife conservation in America. In addition to providing a federal framework for wildlife protection, today that agency manages 576 National Wildlife Refuges with nearly 150 million acres of protected wildlife habitats across America. Twenty-one of these refuges are found in the state of Texas.

As the fledgling science of wildlife management began to blossom in the mid-twentieth century, mistakes were made. Early efforts at protecting America's wildlife resources often lacked a good science-based ecological model and were often misguided. One of the biggest oversights was a lack of understanding of predator-prey relationships. Thus predators were not included in early conservation efforts. In fact, predator populations were targeted for extermination as means of promoting an increase in game species such as deer and elk. Over time, wildlife biologists came to understand the important role of predators in population dynamics and today sound wildlife management aims to restore entire ecosystems rather than just promote population increases of a few selected species.

The first statewide efforts to regulate harvesting of fish and wildlife by the state of Texas go back over century, but today's Texas Parks and Wildlife Department (TPWD) was not fully formed until 1963. This agency has evolved over the decades into a modern science-based organization that not only strives to protect the state's wildlife resources with approximately five hundred game wardens across the state, but also oversees fifty wildlife management areas encompassing nearly 750 thousand acres. Additionally, the TPWD oversees 89 state parks and natural areas totaling an additional 640 thousand acres.

To those dedicated to wildlife conservation and management and well versed in wildlife science, many of the wildlife-related laws in Texas seem to rely mostly or entirely on the good will of private landowners. In this respect, those charged with welfare of the state's wildlife would seem to face some unusual challenges when engaged in the study and assessment of the Texas wildlife populations. For instance, Texas is the only state in the US having a breeding population of Mountain Lions that lacks a conservation program for this magnificent species. Additionally, some state laws relating to wildlife research projects in the state seem to be aimed more at appeasing landowners than protecting and managing the state's wildlife resources.

However, there are more than three thousand dedicated and conservation minded individuals today working for TPWD. Many are wildlife biologists, ecologists, fisheries biologists, naturalist-educators and other individuals who are "in the trenches" of the conservation effort.

In addition to the TPWD, there are many private organizations and individuals involved in wildlife conservation efforts in Texas. Most of the larger cities and many of the small towns in Texas protect wildlife habitat in parks and preserves. Outside of these urban centers there still remains large areas of natural wildlife habitats in Texas. Most of this rural landscape is privately owned. As such, the responsibility for preservation and protection of wildlife habitats lies largely in the hands of private individuals and corporations. While the many game ranches in the state make a point of being good stewards of the natural environment, most of the state's private lands are not managed for wildlife or for the maintenance of wildlife habitat.

The pages that follow are intended to introduce Texans to the remarkable diversity, wondrous beauty, and miraculous lives of the state's wildlife species. It is hoped that this introduction will lead to a greater awareness, concern and appreciation for Texas's natural heritage. It is further hoped that acquiring that awareness will lead to a greater concern for and a wiser stewardship of not only the state's wild inhabitants, but the environments and ecosystems upon which both they and we ultimately depend.

CHAPTER 4

THE MAMMALS OF TEXAS

TABLE 1

— THE ORDERS AND FAMILIES OF TEXAS MAMMALS —

(in order of appearance)

Class—**Mammalia** (mammals)

Order—**Didelmorphia** (opossums)

Family	**Didelphidae** (opossums)

Order—**Cingulata** (armadillos)

Family	**Dasypodidae** (armadillos)

Order—**Carnivora** (carnivores)

Family	**Ursidae** (bears)
Family	**Procyonidae** (raccoon family)
Family	**Mustelidae** (weasel family)
Family	**Mephitidae** (skunks)
Family	**Canidae** (canines)
Family	**Felidae** (felines)

Order—**Artiodactyla** (even toed ungulates)

Family	**Cervidae** (deer family)
Family	**Bovidae** (cattle, sheep, goats)
Family	**Antilocapridae** (pronghorn)
Family	**Suidae** (pigs)
Family	**Tassysuidae** (peccaries)

Order—**Lagamopha** (rabbits, hares, pika)

Family	**Leporidae** (rabbits & hares)

Order—**Rodentia** (rodents)

Family	**Sciuridae** (squirrel family)
Family	**Castoridae** (Beaver)
Family	**Muridae** (rats, mice, voles)
Family	**Dipdidae** (jumping mice)
Family	**Geomyidae** (pocket gophers)
Family	**Heteromyidae** (kangaroo rats)

Order—**Soricomorpha** (shrews & moles)

Family	**Soricidae** (shrews)
Family	**Talpidae** (moles)

Order—**Chiroptera** (bats)

Family	**Vespertilionidae** (typical bats)
Family	**Molossidae** (free-tailed bats)
Family	**Mormoopidae** (leaf-chinned bats)
Family	**Phyllostomidae** (new world leaf-nosed bats)

Class—**Mammalia** (mammals)

Order—**Didelmorphia** (opossums)	Order—**Cingulata** (opossums)
Family—**Didelphidae**	Family—**Dasypodidae**
Virginia Opossum *Didelphis virginiana*	**Armadillo** *Dasypus novemcinctus*

Size: About 2.5 feet from nose to tail tip. Males can weigh up to 14 pounds, females are smaller.

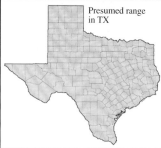
Presumed range in TX

Variation: Variable. In most the fur is grizzled gray (as in photo above. All white or all black individuals can occur, along with a cinnamon color.

Abundance: Very common. In fact this is one of the most common medium-size mammals in America.

Habitat: Virtually all habitats in the state are utilized except for more arid deserts. May be found in suburban or even urban areas where there is enough vegetative cover. They are more common in areas disturbed by humans such as farmlands and in the vicinity of rural homesteads and small rural communities. They are less common in true wilderness areas.

Breeding: This is America's only member of the mammalian subclass Marsupialia. Young opossums are born as embryos only twelve days after conception. The Newborn babies are just over 0.5 inch in length. At one month they are about the size of a mouse. Litters are large (up to 13) and two litters per year is not uncommon.

Natural History: Opossums are one of the most successful medium-size mammals in America, which is somewhat surprising given that they are slow moving, somewhat dim-witted animals that rarely survive beyond two years in the wild. They are mainly nocturnal and eat most any palatable plant matter (seeds, grains, fruits, berries) and any type of meat they can catch or scavenge. They are known to kill and eat venomous snakes and have a strong resistance to pit viper venoms. They are well-known for faking death (playing possum) when stressed. They have strong nocturnal tendencies but are sometimes abroad during the day, especially when breeding. When hard pressed they will climb to escape. In trees they use their prehensile tail to compensate for their somewhat clumsy climbing. They will forage for road kills along highways and their greatest enemy today is the automobile.

Size: About 30 inches from snout to tail tip. Adult can weigh up to 17 pounds. Females are smaller than males.

Presumed range in TX

Variation: There is no variation in Armadillos in Texas. The sexes look alike but males are somewhat larger than females.

Abundance: Very common in much of Texas but apparently absent from the westernmost counties of the state.

Habitat: This wide-ranging animal's habitat includes everything from tropical rain forest to arid semi-desert, grassland, and temperate forests. Moist or sandy soils are preferred as they facilitate easier digging of denning burrows as well as rooting for soil invertebrates. Absent from the western portions of the High Plains and Chihuahuan Desert ecoregions.

Breeding: Females always give birth to four identical twins, all derived from a single fertilized egg that divides in two, then divides again to form four zygotes before beginning to then develop into individual embryos. The young are well developed at birth which reduces mortality among immatures. One litter per year is typical.

Natural History: Armadillos first began their northern expansion into the US from Mexico about 150 years ago. One hundred years later, they were found as far north as west Tennessee. By the 1980s they were in western Kentucky and the first documented sighting in southern Indiana was in 2003. How far north they will spread is unknown. Lacking in fur and unable to hibernate, they are vulnerable to prolonged, severe cold snaps. Cold climates may be a limiting factor to their spread northward, but they may be benefiting from a warming climate. Surprisingly, Armadillos are capable of swimming and they are also known to hold their breath and "bottom walk" short distances across small streams. They are known to sometimes carry the ancient disease of leprosy and have been used in leprosy research. Their food is mostly invertebrates. There are 21 species in the family (Dasypodidae) in Central and South America. Only one ranges into North America.

Class—**Mammalia** (mammals)

Order—**Carnivora** (carnivores)

Family—**Ursidae** (bears)	Family—**Procyonidae** (raccoon family)

Black Bear
Ursus americanus

Raccoon
Procyon lotor

Black morph

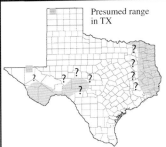
Cinnamon morph

Size: Four to five feet in total length. Males can weigh up to 400 pounds; females are smaller, averaging about 200.

Variation: Despite their name Black Bears may be black, brown, blond, blue-gray, cinnamon, or even white.

Presumed range in TX

Abundance: Rare in Texas. Found mostly in the mountains of the Chihuahuan Desert Ecoregion but recently increasing in the South Central Plains Ecoregion and the Edwards Plateau.

Habitat: Throughout their range in North America Black Bears utilize a wide array of habitats. In the deep south they use swamplands and forests; in the far north they are found in boreal forests. They are widespread across the west and in Texas they are found mostly in desert mountain ranges.

Breeding: Breeds in summer but development of the embryo is delayed until fall. One to three cubs are born in January or February. Twins are common. Newborn cubs will weigh only about a pound. Females will typically breed only every other year. Young stay with the female for about a year.

Natural History: Prior to the European invasion of North America the Black Bear was a common large carnivore ranging across nearly all the continent. Overhunting and deforestation led to their complete disappearance in many regions. By the 1800s and they were regarded as extinct in Texas. Bears from Mexico have re-populated the mountains in the Big Bend and more and more sightings are taking place in east Texas and in the Hill Country. Young male bears will disperse for sometimes hundreds of miles, and are the first individuals to colonize a new area. A variety of plant and animal matter is eaten. Acorns and nuts are an important food item in the fall along with berries. All types of animal matter is also consumed including carrion. The home range is quite large, as much as 120 square miles for males, less for females (about 10 to 20 square miles). The home ranges may overlap. Bears enjoy a keen sense of smell and rely more on the sense of smell and hearing than on eyesight.

Size: Up to 2.5 feet in length. Weights of 15 to 30 lbs. Record 62 pounds. Females are smaller than males.

Variation: Several subspecies nationwide and three in Texas. Rare individuals are nearly solid black. Photo above is a typical Raccoon.

Abundance: Very common in the eastern half of the state, especially in the South Central Plains and the Western Gulf Coastal Plains. Least common in arid west Texas.

Habitat: Found in virtually every habitat in the state, but wetlands, forests, stream courses, and lake shores are favorite haunts. In the arid regions of west Texas they are nearly always found along river valleys and stream courses or in forested areas, avoiding the harshest desert areas.

Breeding: Breeds in late winter with an average of 4 (maximum of 8) young born two months later (April or May). Young begin to accompany the mother on foraging trips at about 2 months. They are usually on their own by 5 months but they may stay in the mother's territory for up to a year.

Natural History: Raccoons are omnivores that feed on a wide variety of crustaceans, insects, amphibians, reptiles, small mammals and eggs as well as grains, berries, fruits, acorns, weed seeds, and some vegetables. Although they are mainly nocturnal, they are often active by day, especially in morning and late afternoons. Summer dens are often tree hollows while underground burrows may be used during the winter. In much of America the Raccoon is an important game animal harvested for its fur and to a lesser extent as food. Like other mammals, Raccoons are subject to an interesting phenomena known as "Bergmann's Rule," which states that the body size of mammals tends to be larger the farther north the species is found. Larger bodies have less surface area in relation to body mass and are capable of retaining more heat. Natural selection favors larger bodies in colder climates and smaller bodies in warm climates. A big male Raccoon from cold climates may top the scales at 40 pounds.

Class—**Mammalia** (mammals)

Order—**Carnivora** (carnivores)

Family—**Procyonidae** (raccoon family)

White-nosed Coati *Nasua narica*	Ringtail *Bassariscus astutus*

Size: Total length of up to 36 inches includes a 20 inch tail. Weighs up to 11 to 16 pounds.

Variation: At least four subspecies. *N. n. molaris* is the Texas subspecies. There is no significant variation among Texas individuals except males are a third larger.

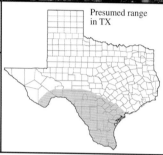

Presumed range in TX

Size: Total length of up to 32 inches, half of which is tail. Weighs up to 3.5 pounds.

Variation: Apparently there is no variation in Texas's Ringtail populations. Some experts recognize several subspecies elsewhere in its range. Males attain a larger size.

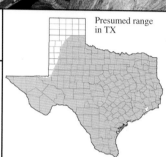

Presumed range in TX

Abundance: Threatened. This is a rare animal in Texas, but there are indications that they may be increasing in the state.

Abundance: Fairly common. Can occur in rural neighborhoods and towns but rarely observed due to nocturnal habits.

Habitat: The White-nosed Coati ranges from the southwestern US to Peru. In the arid and semi-arid regions inhabited in Texas they seem to favor riparian habitats. Elsewhere in their range they are found in tropical forests and savanna.

Habitat: Ringtails love rocky habitats. Canyons, steep ridges with cap-rocks, cliffs, and stream courses through rugged regions. They favor brushy, vegetated habitats or woodlands and tend to avoid open lands.

Breeding: Pregnant females seek a secure nesting site that is often a tree hollow. There may be up to 7 young that wean in about 4 months. By 5 weeks they will follow their mother who may join with other females and young to form a "band."

Breeding: Two to four young are born in late spring. Young Ringtails are weaned at about two months and begin to forage with the mother at that time. By four and half or five months they are on their own.

Natural History: The White-nosed Coati is also commonly called Coatimundi, which is a name that is applied to all four species of Coati (the other three of which live in South America). White-nosed Coatis exhibit an unusual social structure among carnivores. The social construct consists of groups of adult females and immatures of both sexes. These groups will roam and forage together and a "band" can contain up to three dozen individuals. When two bands meet they may exchange members, helping to diversify their genetics. By contrast, adult males are solitary except when breeding. Food items for this omnivorous species includes mainly invertebrates and in tropical regions a wide variety of fruits. A love of nectar makes them important pollinators of some plant species. The diet of the larger males may include large amounts of small vertebrate prey. In an interesting oddity in the annals of wildlife law, the state of Texas has allowed for the breeding of Coatis in captivity for sale as pets. These animals possess long claws and powerful forelegs which are an adaptation for digging in the soil for invertebrates. They also have enormous canine fangs. Thus they are not a good choice as a household pet.

Natural History: Also known as the "Ringtail Cat," they are actually not related to felines but rather are close relatives of the Raccoon and Coati. Like the Raccoon they are omnivorous in diet, but mostly carnivorous and as much as 75 percent of their diet is made up of small animals and invertebrates. Among the vertebrate animals consumed are small mammals (mostly rodents) and birds. Fruits are the major item among the vegetative foods consumed. Ringtails are unusually vocal animals and females in estrous will call to attract males. The sound they produce has been described as "chirping" or "barking." They are secretive, nocturnal animals that are not often observed and are more common than sight observations would indicate. The best way to see this species is probably to drive rural roads at night through the rocky canyons and wooded hill country. They are most common in Texas in the Edwards Plateau and the Chihuahuan Desert. Their range is nearly statewide but they are absent from the High Plains Ecoregion. Although they can be found in eastern and southern Texas they are less common there. In captivity they can become quite tame and have a reputation for being a good pet.

Class—**Mammalia** (mammals)

Order—**Carnivora** (carnivores)

Family—**Mustelidae** (weasel family)

Long-tailed Weasel *Mustela frenata*	Mink *Vison vison*

Size: 12 to 19 inches from snout to tail tip. Weighs up to 17 ounces. Females are slightly smaller

Variation: Males are twice the size of females. Specimens in the north of their range turn white in winter, but not in Texas.

Presumed range in TX

Size: Males are 22 to 27 inches in length and weigh 2 to 3 pounds. Females are as much as 50 percent smaller.

Variation: Varies from light brown to nearly black. Darkest specimens are in the far north. Southern mink tend to more brownish in color.

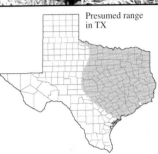
Presumed range in TX

Abundance: Widespread in distribution throughout most of the state but generally uncommon to rare in Texas.

Abundance: Uncommon in Texas. Apparently the Mink is in decline in Texas, possibly due to increased drought conditions.

Habitat: Weasels use a wide variety of habitats but seem to favor mesic meadows, marshes, and riparian areas. They also can be found in ecotones where woods and grassland meet and in desert areas, but always in proximity to water.

Habitat: Mink are a semi-aquatic mammal that is nearly always found in association with aquatic habitats. Swamps and marshes are the favorite habitat. They do occur in uplands where there are creeks, rivers, or lake shores.

Breeding: Nest is on the ground. Sometimes in underground burrows abandoned by other animals but often under the roots of old stumps or in hollow logs. They may also use rock crevices or rock piles. Four to five young is average.

Breeding: Three to six young are born in an underground den that is often an old muskrat house. Young, called "kits," are born blind and helpless but grow rapidly and begin to hunt with mother at about 2 months.

Natural History: Weasels are known for being, on a pound-per-pound basis, one of the world's most ferocious predators. Although their prey includes animals as small as insects, they will also take prey the size of a grown Cottontail Rabbit. Mice, voles, and other rodents, along with shrews and small birds, make up the bulk of their non-invertebrate diet. Voles are a favorite prey and in some regions may make up as much as a third of the diet. They have also been known to scavenge the dead bodies of large animals such as deer. These highly active mammals have a high metabolic rate and are active by both day and night, consuming up to a third of their body weight daily. When an animal is killed that is too large to consume at one meal, they will cache the remains and return to finish it later. The Long-tailed weasel is one of three weasel species in America and is the only weasel found in Texas. Generally speaking, weasels are a northern animal and only the Long-tailed Weasel ranges as far south as Texas. They are sporadically distributed in the state and may be absent from many areas of their range. They are nocturnal and secretive and distributional data for this species in Texas is minimal.

Natural History: Mink are well known for their luxurious fur. Most mink fur sold in America today is from captive, farm raised mink. But trapping of wild Mink still occurs in the northern United States and in Canada (and to a much lesser degree in Texas). Mink are excellent swimmers and their thick fur seals out water while swimming. They have some webbing between the toes of the hind feet and can swim well enough to catch fish in stream pools. They are strict carnivores that feed heavily on frogs, fish, and crayfish during the summer. In winter their diet turns to mammal prey such as rabbits and rodents. Muskrats are a favorite winter food of the large males who kill their formidable prey with a bite to the back of the neck. As with other members of the Mustelidae family, mink have well developed musk glands that produce a distinct musky odor when the animal is excited, breeding, or marking territory. They are solitary animals except when the female is rearing young. The males will fight viciously over territory and fights often result in the death of the loser. The range of the mink extends from the southeastern United States all the way to Alaska, and also includes most of Canada.

Class—**Mammalia** (mammals)

Order—**Carnivora** (carnivores)

Family—**Mustelidae** (weasel family)

River Otter *Lutra canadensis*	Badger *Taxidea taxus*

Size: Length 35 to 45 inches. Up to 25 pounds. Average weight is probably around 15 to 20 pounds.

Variation: There is no significant variation among River Otters except that males are generally larger than females. Above specimen is typical.

Presumed range in TX

Size: To 30 inches. Males to 24 pounds; females are smaller and average about 15 pounds.

Variation: Males average slightly larger than females. Several subspecies are known but no significant variation in pelage color is seen in Texas.

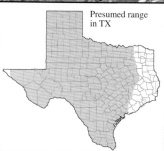
Presumed range in TX

Abundance: Generally uncommon but may be locally common along the major rivers in the easternmost part of Texas.

Abundance: Fairly common but less common in most regions of the state today than in pre-settlement times.

Habitat: River Otters are nearly completely aquatic and although they may roam overland their permanent home is always associated with aquatic habitats. Rivers and large creeks are the main habitat but they also use swamps, marshes, and lakes including man-made impoundments.

Habitat: The Badger is primarily an animal of the prairie. Their historical range mimics that of their favorite prey which are the many species of ground squirrels native to North America. In wooded regions they will frequent open pastures and grassy areas in search of ground squirrels, voles, mice, etc.

Breeding: Two or three young are born in an underground den often dug in a stream bank. Old beaver lodges are sometimes used for dens. Births are usually in the spring or summer. Males are known to fight each other during breeding.

Breeding: Breeds in mid-summer with young born in early spring. Average number of young is two or three but can be as many as six or seven. Young are born in an underground den dug by the female. Young wean at about 8 weeks.

Natural History: River Otters are near fully aquatic mammals that possess fully webbed toes and waterproof fur. They are excellent swimmers that prey on fish, frogs, crayfish, turtles, and small mammals. Their fur was once highly valued, a fact that led to their extirpation from most of the eastern United States by the late 1800s. Restocking programs by state wildlife agencies throughout the Midwest have been successful and today these endearing animals can once again be found in much of their former range. In Texas, however, their range has probably shrunk by as much as 50 percent from pre-settlement times. They can still be found in eastern and southern Texas, mostly in the South Central Plains, East Central Texas Plains, and the Western Gulf Coastal Plains. On rare occasions they will visit small farm ponds, especially if they contain fish, and they can be an enemy to catfish farmers. In addition to fish, they consume many crayfish and frogs and in coastal areas crabs are added to the diet. They are handsome and playful animals that often endear themselves to humans. They may live 20 years.

Natural History: The Badger is a digging machine. It possess long claws, powerful forelegs, and a specialized structure of the eye known as a "nictitating membrane" which keeps dirt from entering the eye sockets. Badgers feed mostly by digging small mammals from their underground burrows. Ground squirrels, gophers, and Prairie Dogs are the favorite prey, but almost any type of animal may be eaten, including carrion. In the western US, Badgers have been observed hunting cooperatively with Coyotes. The Coyote guards the escape holes (and catches a few fleeing animals), while the Badger benefits from having the Coyote blocking the escape route long enough for the Badger to dig out a hapless ground squirrel or gopher. Abandoned Badger dens are utilized by a wide variety of other animals and they are an important animal in the local ecosystem. The large excavations they make when digging out rodents can pose a hazard to those on horseback, but they also control rodents in pastures. Badgers seem to be invading more of eastern Texas as forests have been cleared for pastures.

Class—**Mammalia** (mammals)

Order—**Carnivora** (carnivores)

Family—**Mephitidae** (skunks)

| **Striped Skunk** *Mephitis mephitis* | **Hooded Skunk** *Mephitis macroura* |

Size: Length 23 to 27 inches. Weighs about 8 to 10 pounds. Very fat individuals up to 14 pounds.

Variation: Varies in the amount of white. Stripes can be narrow, very wide, or absent resulting in nearly all white or all black individuals.

Presumed range in TX

Abundance: Common to very common. Found statewide and easily the most common skunk species in Texas.

Habitat: Striped Skunks are found in all habitats in Texas, but they are most common in semi-open habitats, successional areas, and edge areas. They adapt well to human activities and are known to sometimes den beneath outbuildings or houses.

Breeding: Breeding occurs in late winter and may be signaled by the sudden appearance of dead skunks on roadways. Litter size averages three or four but can be as many as ten. Weanlings follow the mother in single file while foraging.

Natural History: The Striped Skunk's distinctive black and white color is almost as well known as its primary defense, which of course is to spray an attacker with its pungent, foul smelling musk. The musk can burn the eyes and membranes and its odor is remarkably persistent. They can effectively project the musk up to about 15 feet and the odor can be detected hundreds of yards away. A direct hit to the face from the musk glands can cause debilitating nausea and temporary blindness. Striped Skunks dine mainly on invertebrates and as much as three-fourths of their diet consists of insects and grubs. They possess well developed front claws for digging and a powerful sense of smell for locating buried grubs, worms, turtle eggs, etc. They will also eat baby mice, eggs, and the young of ground nesting birds. They regularly den in abandoned burrows of Armadillos, Groundhogs, Badgers, etc. In rocky landscapes they will use rock crevices. They are capable of acquiring great amounts of subcutaneous fat which they will live on during periods of cold weather, but they are not true hibernators and are active all winter during milder weather.

Size: Length up to 28 inches, at least half of which is tail. Can weigh up to 2 pounds but usually smaller.

Variation: 3 basic color phases. Black dorsally with two lateral white stripes and white dorsally with or without lateral white stripes.

Presumed range in TX

Abundance: Very rare. Of the five skunk species in Texas this is the rarest. Absent from most of the area on map above.

Habitat: Little is known about the habitat of this species in Texas. It is only found in the Big Bend region where it seems to always be in the vicinity of streams. Canyons with rocky cliffs and dense streamside vegetation seems to be favored.

Breeding: As with Texas's other skunk species, the Hooded Skunk breeds in late winter and the gestation period is about two months. At least three young and up to eight have been reported for litter size.

Natural History: Very similar to the Striped Skunk but has longer fur, especially noticeable on the tail. The name "Hooded" Skunk is derived from the long hairs present on the back of the neck giving it a hooded appearance. Food items are similar to other skunk species and includes both invertebrates and small vertebrates as well as some plant material such as cactus fruits. Although these skunks are quite rare in Texas they are fairly common throughout much of Mexico and range all the way into northern Central America. They are also found in Arizona and New Mexico. Like other skunks they are nocturnal and not frequently observed. These small skunks are today one of the rarest mammals in Texas. But they do appear to be hanging on in parts of the Big Bend Region. The most recent verified reports of the species are from Big Bend National Park, with a much older record (1999) from the Davis Mountains. By contrast some sources list that populations of Hooded Skunks are increasing in some areas of their range in the southwestern US. But that does not seem to be the case for Texas populations. Most recorded observations of this species in Texas have come from camera traps or road kills.

Class—**Mammalia** (mammals)

Order—**Carnivora** (carnivores)

Family—**Mephitidae** (skunks)

Hog-nosed Skunk *Conepatus leuconotus*	Prairie Spotted Skunk & Desert Spotted Skunk *Spilogale interrupta & Spilogale leucoparia*

Desert Spotted Skunk

Size: Maximum length about 28 inches. Average weight about 6 pounds.

Variation: Less variable than the Striped Skunk but some variation in the amount of white on the back. Most are all white dorsally and resemble the photo above.

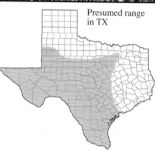
Presumed range in TX

Abundance: Generally uncommon and in decline. Probably most common today in the Edwards Plateau Ecoregion.

Habitat: In the Chihuahuan Desert Ecoregion Hooded Skunks show a preference for mountain foothills and wooded canyons. Semi-open savanna-like habitats and brushy habitats are also favored over dense forests.

Breeding: Breeds in late winter and following about 2 months of gestation, young are usually born in April or May. Little else is known about the reproductive cycle of these rare skunks.

Natural History: Hog-nosed Skunks root like hogs for soil invertebrates which make up the bulk of their diet. Small lizards and snakes along with a few small mammals are also consumed. Vegetative material is also consumed with berries and Prickly Pear Cactus listed as food items. Populations of Hog-nosed Skunks in Texas have been declining for several decades and they have disappeared from some areas of their former range in the state. Even more disconcerting is the fact that there are indications that the species may be declining throughout its range in North America. The reasons for this decline are unknown at this time. The range of the Hog-nosed Skunk extends southward throughout Mexico and into northern South America. It is unknown whether population declines are occurring in the Latin American parts of its range. However, the International Union for Conservation of Nature (IUCN) lists it as a Species of Least Concern, indicating that those populations to the south of the US are probably stable. It should be noted that IUCN only lists as threatened or endangered those species whose populations have been scientifically evaluated. Life span is less than 10 years.

Size: Prairie species about 1.75 pounds. Desert species about 1.25 pounds.

Variation: In both species males are larger than females. The Desert species shows more extensive white striping with more white on the face. Prairie is darker overall.

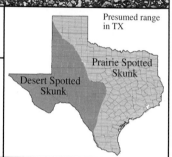
Presumed range in TX
Prairie Spotted Skunk
Desert Spotted Skunk

Abundance: Prairie Spotted Skunk is rare and apparently in decline. Desert species is uncommon and also declining.

Habitat: Prairie Spotted Skunks inhabit woodlands and tall-grass Prairie regions. Desert Spotted Skunks favor rocky canyons and bluffs and in desert areas in the vicinity of mountain streams.

Breeding: The two species of Spotted Skunks in Texas may owe their status as distinct species in part due to the fact that they breed at different times. This prevents interbreeding and helps keep their DNA isolated.

Natural History: These two species are very similar in most aspects of their natural history. Both are omnivores that prey heavily on invertebrates but include small vertebrates and plant material in the diet. Unlike other skunk species, spotted skunk species are good climbers. Young Spotted Skunks are born with the eyes closed and little fur. At about one month the eyes open and they will wean at about two months. Even as adults these are small mammals. As such they have many enemies the greatest of which is probably the Great Horned Owl. When threatened, they will stand on their front legs and arch the back into a U-shape, pointing their anal glands toward the attacker. They can spray up to 15 feet. The decline in both these species is well documented. The cause of the decline is still unknown but some believe the widespread use of insecticides may be to blame. Both these species have undergone a recent taxonomic re-classification resulting in their being elevated from subspecies status to full species. The range map shown above is based on a research paper describing the analysis of DNA of spotted skunk populations (McDonough, et al 2020).

Class—**Mammalia** (mammals)

Order—**Carnivora** (carnivores)

Family—**Canidae** (canines)

Kit Fox *Vulpes macrotis*	**Swift Fox** *Vulpes velox*

Size: Total length 31 inches. Maximum weight about six and a half pounds.

Variation: Slight seasonal variation in pelage color. Long-haired winter foxes are more grayish tan and shorter summer coat is more reddish or tan.

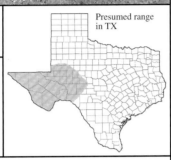

Presumed range in TX

Size: Total length 31 inches. Maximum weight about six and a half pounds.

Variation: Seasonal variation in pelage color. Long-haired winter foxes are more grayish tan and shorter summer coat is more reddish or tan.

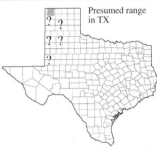

Presumed range in TX

Abundance: Uncommon and limited in distribution in Texas, but perhaps rebounding and more common in recent years.

Abundance: Rare and limited in distribution. Several states offer full protection, but oddly not in Texas.

Habitat: This is a desert species that inhabits all the major desert regions of North America. In Texas they are restricted to the Chihuahuan Desert Ecoregion where they prefer desert valleys and low hills with sparse vegetation.

Habitat: The Swift Fox is the prairie/grassland counterpart of the desert dwelling Kit Fox. Their historical range closely coincided with the Great Plains Physiographic Province shown in Figure 2 on page 5.

Breeding: Breeding can occur throughout the winter and the young are born in late winter or early spring. Four or five young is typical. After about four weeks pups will emerge from the den and may be seen loitering at the entrance

Breeding: Young are born in March or early April in an underground den. At about four weeks they will emerge to play and loiter around the den entrance. Three to six pups is typical and both parents will care for the young.

Natural History: Very similar to the related Swift Fox and some mammalogists regard them as sibling subspecies, a conclusion supported by the fact that they can apparently interbreed. Both are about the size of a house cat and are the two smallest canines in North America. Mostly nocturnal in habits but also active at dawn and dusk. These handsome little foxes do no damage at all to man and help control rodent populations. Unlike most wild animals they are somewhat tolerant of humans. Ironically, they were nearly exterminated by the use of poison baits in predator control programs of the past that were aimed at the wolf and coyote. The food of the Kit Fox includes birds, insects and mammals such as Kangaroo Rats, Ground Squirrels, Desert Cottontails and Black-tailed Jackrabbits. Coyotes are reported to be one of the main enemies of these small foxes. Kit Foxes are hardy little animals that are adapted to the harsh environments of the desert. They can obtain most of their moisture requirements from the bodies of the small animals they consume and are thus able to go for long periods without drinking. Their underground burrows provide a cool refuge during the hot days.

Natural History: The Swift Fox is very similar to the Kit Fox and some regard them as the same species with two subspecies. The most noticeable morphological difference between the two are the smaller ears of the Swift Fox. Ecologically, the Swift Fox is the prairie/grassland counterpart of the desert loving Kit Fox. Like the Kit Fox, Swift Fox populations experienced a severe decline throughout the twentieth century. Poison bait predator control programs aimed first at wolves and then at coyotes are blamed by most experts for the decline in Swift Fox populations. The use of poison baits as a means of predator control are ecologically disastrous because they kill so indiscriminately. Thus that practice should be unanimously discouraged. Today there are indications of population rebounds of the Swift Fox in some areas where habitats are intact. Re-introduction programs have been instigated in Canada, Montana, and South Dakota. All these re-introductions were on tribal lands or national parks. In Texas the Swift Fox once roamed most of the Texas Panhandle. Surveys conducted in 1997–98 detected Swift Foxes in only two Texas counties in the northwestern tip of Texas.

Class—**Mammalia** (mammals)
Order—**Carnivora** (carnivores)
Family—**Canidae** (canines)

Red Fox *Vulpes vulpes*	**Gray Fox** *Urocyon cinereoargenteus*

Size: Length 33 to 43 inches. Weight up to 15 pounds. Most Texas specimens are 10 pounds or less.

Variation: Texas specimens are invariably the classic red phase, but several other color morphs occur.

Abundance: Fairly common, but less common in Texas than in other regions of the US.

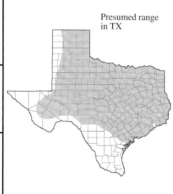

Presumed range in TX

Size: Length 32 to 45 inches. Averages 8 to 12 pounds, maximum of 15 pounds.

Variation: There are 16 subspecies throughout North America. Possibly 3 in Texas.

Abundance: Common. Found statewide but most common in forested areas.

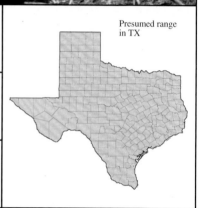

Presumed range in TX

Habitat: Although habitat generalists, Red Foxes show a preference for open and semi-open country over deep woods. May occur in agricultural regions.

Habitat: Primarily woodland animal that is more common in forested regions of the state. Also uses brushlands. Tends to avoid expansive open regions like farmlands and prairies.

Breeding: About four to five young are born underground, often in an old groundhog burrow, but they will dig their own hole.

Breeding: Dens in a burrow, hollow log or rock cave. Four pups is usual but up to seven is known.

Natural History: The Red Fox is one of the world's most widespread mammals and is found in Europe, Asia, north Africa, and Australia (introduced) as well as throughout most of North America. They are less common in Texas than in other regions of North America and are outnumbered in Texas by the Gray Fox. They are adaptable, opportunistic omnivores that will eat everything from grasshoppers to grapes. A variety of small mammals like mice and voles are eaten along with birds, snakes, and lizards. Cottontail rabbits are probably the largest prey animal hunted. Scavenging carrion is also common. Their fur is such a good insulator that they can sleep atop a snow bank without melting the snow beneath their body. These are important fur-bearing animals and are today often reared in captivity on "fur farms." Red Fox populations in Texas have increased since European settlement and the species has been introduced into some areas by houndsmen for the sport of fox hunting. The short, summer coat is paler than the luxurious winter fur. Three distinct color phases are the Red, Silver, and Cross Fox. All color phases have a white tail tip.

Natural History: The Gray Fox is the only American canine with the ability to climb trees. They will ascend trees to raid bird nests and have been recorded resting in trees or denning in hollows above ground. Insects are important food items in summer with mice and rabbits becoming more important in winter. When grapes, persimmons, and other fruits are ripe they will eat them almost exclusively, and in fact this is the most omnivorous canine in America. Home range can vary from a few hundred acres to over a square mile, depending upon habitat quality. Unlike the Red Fox that can be found as far north as the arctic circle, the Gray Fox is a more southerly animal and ranges southward throughout Mexico into South America. Gray Foxes have lived for up to fourteen years in captivity, but the average lifespan in the wild is only a few years. Contrary to popular belief, Gray Foxes never interbreed with Red Foxes. The biggest enemy of the Gray Fox is probably the Coyote and populations of both the Gray Fox and the Red Fox may decline where Coyotes are common. Conversely, the Coyote's main enemy is the Gray Wolf, and foxes benefit in regions of America where wolves still roam.

Class—**Mammalia** (mammals)

Order—**Carnivora** (carnivores)

Family—**Canidae** (canines)	Family—**Felidae** (felidae)

Coyote
Canis latrans

Cougar (Mountain Lion)
Felis concolor

Size: Length up to 49 inches. Average about 35 pounds. Maximum weight can be up to 45 pounds.	**Size:** Males can be 7 feet from nose to tail tip and weigh 200 pounds. Females 30 percent smaller.

Presumed range in TX

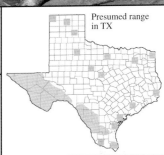

Presumed range in TX

Variation: Some variation in pelage color. Can vary from pale gray to very dark. Reddish or brownish specimens are know to occur.

Variation: There is no variation in this species in Texas. At least six subspecies exist across the entire range from Alaska to South America

Abundance: Very common. Originally they were native mostly to the Great Plains Ecoregion and absent from eastern Texas. Today they are probably most common in the more productive ecosystems of the eastern half of the state.

Abundance: Rare. Originally found statewide but extirpated from most of the state by predator control programs. There has been some resurgence in populations in recent years, but overall the species remains uncommon to rare.

Habitat: Coyotes have adapted to all habitats in Texas. They can even thrive in and around urban areas. Their original habitat was mostly in the Great Plains and their expansion into the rest of the continent was checked by wolves.

Habitat: Cougars are remarkably adaptable animals that can thrive in virtually all habitats in the western hemisphere. In Texas, hunting and predator control activities eradicated them from all but the most remote desert mountains.

Breeding: Coyotes are able to breed before their first birthday. Litter size (two to ten) varies with availability of prey. While pups are nursing the male will provide the female with most of her food. Pups wean at four to six weeks.

Breeding: Due to a rather long development period for juveniles, females will breed only about every two years.
Two young is typical but can be as many as four. Kittens are marked with black spots which fade as the kitten grows.

Natural History: The home range may be as small as 4 square miles in good habitat, but will be at least twice that size in less favorable ecosystems like deserts. The Coyote is a relative newcomer to eastern Texas, having begun their invasion from the west with the clearing of forests and decimation of the Red Wolf in east Texas. Today they range throughout all of the US. They are the top predator in much of the eastern US today, occupying a niche once held by the wolf and the Cougar. They are extremely intelligent, adaptable canines that quickly learn to thrive in almost any environment. In rural areas where hunters abound they are extremely wary, but in urban areas or protected lands they may become quite bold around humans. The characteristic yipping and howling of these vocal canines has become a common sound throughout rural America and at times in suburban areas as well. They are mostly nocturnal, but also active by day. The longevity record is eighteen years for a specimen in captivity, but the average life span in the wild is usually less than ten years.

Natural History: In Latin America it goes by the name Puma. These big cats are strict carnivores. In Texas the diet is mainly deer (both Mule Deer and Whitetails). Javalina and feral hogs are also eaten as are small mammals like jackrabbits, porcupines, and even skunks. They sometimes prey on livestock as well, especially sheep and goats. These large predators have a very large home range and are thus highly vulnerable to habitat loss and development. In Texas the Cougar has suffered greatly from unregulated hunting and trapping and was heavily targeted by predator control programs encouraged by ranching interests. It is still treated as a non-game species in Texas and afforded no protection or wildlife management strategy. As such they may legally be killed at any time by any method. In this regard, Texas is the only state in America having breeding Cougar populations that refuses to regulate and manage the species. Although populations in Texas seem to be attempting to rebound, their status as an unprotected and unmanaged species ensures that they will remain uncommon.

Class—**Mammalia** (mammals)

Order—**Carnivora** (carnivores)

Family—**Felidae** (felines)

Bobcat *Lynx rufus*	**Ocelot** *Leopardus pardalis*

Size: Length up to 3 feet. Typically weighs 15 to 20 pounds. Maximum of about 40 pounds.

Variation: Several subspecies in America. Little variation but some specimens have more pronounced spotting. Males are about a third larger than females.

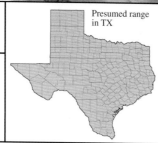

Presumed range in TX

Abundance: Fairly common. Populations declined during the high fur price days of the 1970s but they have recovered.

Habitat: Occupies a wide variety of habitats and is increasingly seen in suburban regions as development encroaches into natural habitats. Favorite haunts are all types of woodlands, swamps and dense thickets of shrubs and brush.

Breeding: In Texas Bobcats breed from late fall through early spring. Up to four young are born about two months after breeding. Young Bobcats begin to forage with the mother in about two months may stay with her for up to a year.

Natural History: Strictly a meat eater, the Bobcat's food items range from mice to deer. Cottontail Rabbits are a favorite prey as are squirrels, young turkeys and songbirds. Bobcats hunt by ambush or stalking to within close range and making an explosive attack. Although mainly nocturnal, they can be abroad at any time of day. Their home range can be from one to several square miles and males have larger ranges than females. Scent marking territory with urine and feces is common. In captivity, Bobcats have lived for over twenty years, but the estimate for wild cats is twelve to fourteen years. This species has just begun to return to many areas of the Midwest after being extirpated decades ago. In Texas the species has always maintained populations where suitable habitat has persisted. As with most wild animals, mortality is highest among the young of the year. Young predators are especially vulnerable as they must lean to perfect their hunting skills to survive. They must also establish a territory, learn the habits of the local prey species, game trails, contend with conflict when wandering into the established territory of an adult, etc. Survivability increases significantly after their first year.

Size: Total length 43 inches. Male can weigh up to 35 pounds, females to 22 pounds.

Variation: The pattern of spots and stripes are different on each individual Ocelot. Researches use pattern recognition to identify individual cats.

Presumed range in TX

Abundance: Very rare in Texas. Listed as an Endangered Species by both the USFWS and the TPWD.

Habitat: Thick brush with a nearly complete canopy is required for this species in Texas. Elsewhere it inhabits a wide variety of habitats ranging from desert mountain ranges to tropical rain forest.

Breeding: In Texas breeding occurs in the fall. Ocelots living in south Texas choose a dense thicket of thorny shrubs for denning sites. Litters are quite small; only one or two young is typical but can be as many as four.

Natural History: Ocelots once ranged across southern Texas from the Chihuahuan Desert Ecoregion to the South Central Plains, including the southern portions of the Edwards Plateau, Blackland Prairies and East Central Texas Plains. They were also found throughout the South Texas Plains and the Western Gulf Coastal Plains ecoregions. Today it is estimated that no more than 80 to 120 of these handsome cats are hanging on in the southernmost tip of the state. The main culprit in the disappearance of the Ocelot from Texas has been over hunting and the loss of habitat as brush lands were converted to agriculture. The small breeding populations of Ocelots still managing to hang on in southernmost Texas are cut off from the larger contiguous populations of northern Mexico. In most of the Rio Grande Valley today the habitat has been converted to agriculture, creating a barrier to most of the remaining populations of Texas Ocelots north of the valley. The range map above shows the region of Texas where dispersing Ocelots may possibly occur. Some conservation organizations working to save the Ocelot believe there are at present only two breeding populations left in the state

Class—**Mammalia** (mammals)

Order—**Artiodactyla** (even-toed ungulates)

Family—**Cervidae** (deer family)

Whitetail Deer *Odocoileus virginianus*	**Mule Deer** *Odocoileus hemionus*

Size: Texas Whitetails are smaller than their northern cousins, and males average about 150 pounds.	**Size:** Males can weigh up to 300 pounds but average about 225. Females are smaller, 100 to 150.
Variation: Four subspecies were originally native to Texas. The most common and widespread subspecies today is the Texas Whitetail (*O.v. texana*). [Presumed range in TX]	**Variation:** There are two subspecies in Texas. The Rocky Mountain Mule Deer (*O. h. hemionus*) and the smaller Desert Mule Deer (*O.h. crooki*). [Presumed range in TX]
Abundance: Very common. TPWD estimates there are over five and half million Whitetail Deer in Texas.	**Abundance:** Fairly common in westernmost Texas but populations can plummet during extreme droughts.
Habitat: Found in virtually every habitat within the state and increasingly common in urban areas. Favorite habitats are successional areas and a mix of woodland, brushy areas, and weedy fields near crop fields.	**Habitat:** Mule Deer are animals of the wide-open spaces of western North America. They inhabit grasslands, deserts, foothills, and mountains. In Texas they occur in the Panhandle and Big Bend regions.
Breeding: Breeding begins in early fall and may continue into the winter, with the peak breeding season occurring in November. One to two (rarely three) young are born in the spring or early summer following a six and a half month gestation.	**Breeding:** Breeding is mostly in the fall, but any unbred does will re-enter estrous every month until late winter. Bucks will fight fiercely over does in estrous. Fawns are born about 210 days after breeding, as early as June or as late as early August.
Natural History: Bucks shed their antlers each year in late winter and regrow a new set by fall. Growing deer antlers are among the fastest growing animal tissue known. While growing, the antlers are covered in a spongy, fuzzy skin called "velvet." Antlers grow larger each year up to about six or seven years of age, when they begin a gradual decline. Whitetail Deer are browsers and they feed on a wide variety of forbs, leaves, twigs, buds, crops, and mast (especially acorns). At present, the population in North America averages around 30 million deer. Although they are sometimes destructive to farm crops like corn or soybeans, they provide food and sport for millions of hunters in America. In Texas, as in the rest of the country, the Whitetail Deer is an important game animal and over half a million are harvested in the state annually. The maximum life span is twenty years, but most are dead by age ten. In recent years these animals have begun to invade urban areas where deer hunting is restricted. In towns and cities they can become a nuisance as they feed in suburban gardens and devour landscape plants. Still, many urban dwellers enjoy their presence and the economic importance they have as a game animal is hard to overstate.	**Natural History:** Mule Deer feed on a wide variety of plant species. Sagebrush, juniper, mesquite, and many types of forbs are eaten, and in areas where there are agricultural fields they will consume forage such as alfalfa. In desert areas cactus flowers and fruits are eaten. Sagebrush is probably the most important winter food source. They are most active at dawn and dusk and at night, but they may be active in the day during winter months if extreme cold forces them to feed more often. Bucks shed their antlers in late winter and begin to grow the next year's antlers within a few days. Mule Deer antlers differ from those Whitetail Deer. In Whitetails the tines branch from a main beam, while in Mule Deer the antlers are forked. In many areas of the west, including in Texas, Whitetail Deer are outcompeting Mule Deer and increasing while Mule Deer populations are declining. In Texas the Mule Deer is much less important to hunters than the Whitetail, but Mule Deer hunting is allowed throughout the species' range in the state. A fleeing Mule Deer runs with a high leaping gait known as a "stot." Their bouncing gait can be as high as six feet and cover over 20 feet in a bound, easily clearing boulders, bushes, cactus clumps, and ditches or gulleys.

Class—**Mammalia** (mammals)

Order—**Artiodactyla** (even-toed ungulates)

Family—**Cervidae** (deer family)

Elk *Cervus canadensis*	Fallow Deer *Dama dama*	Axis Deer (Chital) *Axis axis*
 Male		
Size: A large Bull Elk can weigh between 700 and 1100 pounds and be 5 feet tall at the shoulder.  Presumed range in TX	**Size:** Males can weigh 225 pounds. Females are smaller, rarely reaching 90 pounds.  Presumed range in TX	**Size:** Males can weigh up to 250 pounds. Females are smaller, rarely exceeding 100 pounds.  Presumed range in TX
Variation: Several subspecies of Elk range across North America. The native Elk of Texas is extinct. Todays Elk are from New Mexico or South Dakota.	**Variation:** Four color morphs. May be very dark (nearly black) to solid white. Typical color is tan or rust with a profusion of white spotting.	**Variation:** There is no significant variation in color and pattern. Like all deer, sexual dimorphism is exhibited by the presence of antlers in the male.
Abundance: Wild herds are rare in Texas. But they are common on game ranches throughout the state.	**Abundance:** Introduced. Common on game ranches and fairly common in the wild on the Edwards Plateau.	**Abundance:** Introduced. Fairly common where they have been introduced. Also widespread on game ranches.
Habitat: Elk use grassland areas such as mountain meadows or prairie habitats for feeding. They use forests or savanna areas for resting and hiding during the day. They will move seasonally from high mountains to lower slopes.	**Habitat:** In Texas these deer live mostly on the Edwards Plateau where they use a mosaic of woodland and grassland. In their native range in southwestern Asia they inhabit deciduous woodlands, grasslands, and savanna.	**Habitat:** Savanna and open woodlands are the preferred habitat for these exotic deer. Abundant shade and a permanent water source seem to be requirements. In Texas, wild populations are mostly in central and south Texas.
Breeding: One calf is typical. Twins are rare.	**Breeding:** Breeds September to January. One or two young are produced.	**Breeding:** Can breed year-round. Only one fawn is produced.
Natural History: Elk are highly gregarious animals that will travel in large herds. In summer the cows and their young form large groups while the older males segregate themselves in smaller bands or as solitary individuals. In fall the males return to the herd for breeding. At one time Elk may have roamed over much of Texas, but by the early 1900s the only place in the state where wild Elk could be found was in the Guadalupe Mountains. Those animals were the now-extinct subspecies known as the Merriam's Elk, which was native to the arid regions of the southwest. Elk in Texas today are a different subspecies imported from northern regions. In addition to the herds found in the desert mountain ranges, Elk are widespread on hunting ranches across the state.	**Natural History:** Unlike the introduced Axis Deer which may outcompete native Whitetail Deer, wild populations of Fallow Deer don't usually thrive as well as those on managed game farms and probably don't pose a significant threat to Whitetail populations. These deer feed both on grasses and items such as forbs and the leaves of various tree and bush species. In Texas the wild habitat is primarily the xeric woodlands and savannas of the Edwards Plateau. Native range is southwestern Asia. They were one of the first "exotic" species to be transported to other regions to establish huntable populations. They were introduced to England over a thousand years ago and are now found throughout Europe and populations exist on every continent.	**Natural History:** The Axis Deer is one of several species of Artiodactyla introduced into Texas. Also known as Chital Deer, they are originally from India and they are probably the most common exotic species in the wild in Texas. Like the Elk, they are gregarious animals that often form large herds. They are mainly grazers but also will eat some browse items. Interestingly, these deer are capable of breeding nearly year-round. Both males and females may become sexually active at any time of year and sexual receptiveness in both sexes is an individual event. Thus some males and some females in a large herd may sexually receptive at any given time with individual animals alternating their sexual activities. Most members of the deer family are seasonally sexual.

Class—**Mammalia** (mammals)

Order—**Artiodactyla** (even-toed ungulates)

Family—**Bovidae** (cattle, sheep, goats)

Blackbuck *Antilope cervicapra*	**Bison** *Bison bison*	**Bighorn Sheep** *Ovis canadensis*

Size: Males average about 85 pounds with a maximum of 125. Females average 50 to 60 pounds.

Presumed range in TX

Size: A mature bull can weigh over a ton. Females are smaller but can weigh nearly a half ton.

Presumed range in TX

Size: Mature males can exceed 200 pounds. Females are smaller, up to 140 pounds.

Presumed range in TX

Variation: Only the adult male is black. Juvenile males and females are brownish. Males have long spike like horns that grow in a corkscrew fashion.

Variation: As many as three subspecies are recognized by mammalogists. The Texas population is the Southern Plains Bison (*B. b. bison*).

Variation: There are three subspecies of Bighorn Sheep. The Desert subspecies is native in Texas but may be replaced with Rocky Mountain Bighorn.

Abundance: Introduced. Common on high fence game ranches and rare as a free roaming species.

Abundance: Very rare as a wild animal in Texas but common on many private ranches around the state.

Abundance: Rare in Texas. Presently existing on only about a dozen mountain ranges in westernmost Texas.

Habitat: Native to India and Pakistan where it inhabits grasslands and savanna. Requires water and is intolerant of extreme cold weather. Range in Texas is mostly in the Hill Country. A very common species on game ranches.

Habitat: The Plains Bison is an animal of open grasslands. One subspecies in Canada and Alaska exists in boreal forest regions and a now extinct species was found in the Eastern Temperate Forest Ecoregion.

Habitat: Bighorn Sheep are grazers and thus prefer grassland habitats. They are wide ranging across the west and utilize prairies, desert grasslands and mountain meadows. In arid regions a variety of brush and cacti are eaten.

Breeding: Only one young is produced. Young may wean in a month.

Breeding: Calving takes place in the spring and one calf is typical.

Breeding: Breeding takes place in November. One or two young are born.

Natural History: Females and juveniles band together in small herds. Males are mostly solitary. Like many of the exotic species now living in Texas, the Blackbuck has experienced severe population declines in its native range. In this regard, the many game ranches of Texas may serve as a reservoir for many of the world's vanishing ungulate species. In addition to the exotic species depicted thus far in this book, several other wild ungulates have been established on Texas game ranches. Among the more common of those exotic species seen on Texas ranches are: Greater Kudu (Africa), Thompson's Gazelle (Africa), Sable Antelope (Africa), Scimiter Horned Oryx (Africa, now extinct in the wild), Common Eland (Africa), and the Red Deer (Europe).

Natural History: The story of the Bison is one of the most egregious examples of the wanton slaughter and shameless exploitation of America's wildlife resources. Thanks only to a few far-sighted and conservation-minded individuals, this iconic American species was saved from extinction. The Bison native to the west Texas Plains is believed to have constituted a unique population. A few hundred of these Southern Plains Bison have been re-established in the Texas Panhandle at Caprock Canyons State Park. Bison are herd animals and original herds numbered in the tens of thousands. In many respects the behavior of the Bison mirrors that of domestic cattle. Today, semi-tame herds are common on ranches throughout the state.

Natural History: The native wild sheep of Texas were the subspecies known as the Desert Bighorn Sheep. That population was subjected to overhunting and disease from domestic sheep and disappeared from Texas in the middle of the twentieth century. Re-introduction programs by TPWD have been successful in re-establishing these magnificent animals to parts of their original range in the Chihuahuan Deserts Ecoregion, where they now roam several desert mountain ranges. Original Bighorn herds in west Texas would traverse the wide desert basins and move between mountain ranges. Man-made changes to the landscape now largely prohibit migration and herds are restricted to the mountains where they have been re-introduced.

Class—**Mammalia** (mammals)
Order—**Artiodactyla** (even-toed ungulates)
Family—**Bovidae** (cattle, sheep, goats)

Barbary Sheep (Aoudad) *Ammotragus lervia*	**Nilgai** *Boselaphus tragocamelus*	Additional exotics that are found as rare free-roaming species in Texas

Male

Thomson's Gazelle
Eudorcas thomsonii

Size: Large males reach 300 pounds. Smaller females rarely reach 150 pounds.

Presumed range in TX

Size: Mature males can weigh 650 pounds. Females about 300 to 400 pounds.

Presumed range in TX

Sika Deer
Cervus Nippon

Variation: Males are larger and have larger, heavier horns. Juveniles lack the long hair present in the throat, chest, and front legs of mature adults.

Variation: Males are darker (grayish brown to nearly black), females and young more brownish or tan. Females and young lack horns.

Abundance: Introduced. Fairly common. Large wild herds roam Palo Duro Canyon and the Big Bend Region.

Abundance: Introduced. Fairly common. One of the most common introduced ungulates in Texas.

Scimitar-horned Oryx
Oryx dammah

Habitat: This is a desert-adapted species that inhabits foothills and steep mountain slopes in desert areas. In Texas found in the Panhandle, Big Bend and the Edwards Plateau.

Habitat: Nilgai are native to the foothills and lower slopes of the Himalaya Mountains in India and Pakistan where they prefer drier regions with grasslands and savanna habitats.

Breeding: Most breeding is in the fall. Females may breed as young as eight months.

Breeding: Females frequently give birth to twins. Females and young live apart from males when not breeding.

Common Eland
Taurotragus oryx

Natural History: These sheep are native to north Africa where they live in desert mountain ranges. As is the case with many non-native species, the existence of the Barbary Sheep in Texas is ecologically problematic. Large herds may negatively impact Mule Deer and Bighorn Sheep populations. Food consists of grasses, forbs and shrubs/browse. This species is regarded as declining in its native range but introduced populations are thriving in west Texas and in New Mexico. They are also quite common on game ranches across the state. Despite the threat posed to Texas's native Bighorn Sheep and Mule Deer populations, the only efforts to control Barbary Sheep populations in Texas are through limited harvest by hunters.

Natural History: These are the largest antelope species native to Asia. They are usually seen in small groups of a dozen or so animals but they may congregate into larger herds. They are a popular game species on the game ranches of Texas but also exist as free roaming populations outside of high fence ranches. Their native habitat is in tropical climates and they are unable to withstand prolonged periods of cold weather. Severe cold snaps have negatively impacted populations in Texas in the past. Like the other exotic species of Texas, the Nilgai is a popular game species for hunters from all over the US who pay several thousand dollars for the privilege of killing a Nilgai. The economic impact of the hunting of exotics in Texas would be hard to overstate.

Class—**Mammalia** (mammals)

Order—**Artiodactyla** (even-toed ungulates)

Family—**Antilocapridae** (Pronghorn)	Family—**Suidae** (pigs)	Family—**Tayassuidae** (peccaries)
Pronghorn *Antilocapra americana*	**Feral Hog** *Sus scrofa*	**Collared Peccary (Javalina)** *Pecari tajacu*

Size: Males are about 100 to 120 pounds, females are slightly smaller, about 100 pounds.

Presumed range in TX

Variation: There are two subspecies of Pronghorn in Texas, the Prairie subspecies (*A. a. americana*) and the Desert race (*A.a. mexicana*).

Abundance: Uncommon in Texas today. Occupies less than fifty percent of its original range in the state.

Habitat: Open country. Prairies and desert grasslands, intermontane valleys and desert basins.

Breeding: Breeds in late summer to early fall. Produces one or two young.

Natural History: Adapted for life in the wide open spaces, Pronghorn have large eyes for surveying the landscape for predators at great distance. They also possess enlarged hearts, lungs, and windpipes to enhance their running abilities. They are the fastest land animal in America and can reach speeds of 40 miles per hour. They also have remarkable endurance and have been known to run for miles before stopping. The Desert subspecies has the ability to go for long periods without drinking. They are thus one of the most highly specialized members of the native wildlife assemblage of Texas. They are curious animals that will often investigate unidentified objects on their range. Native Americans used this trait to lure them to within killing range. In spite of their overall athleticism they don't like to jump and will crawl under a barbed wire fence rather than leap over it.

Size: Large males may reach 400 pounds but most are half that. Females are smaller.

Presumed range in TX

Variation: Highly variable, many colors and patterns depending on the breed stock. Typical "wild" morphs resemble the European Wild Boar.

Abundance: Common. Found nearly statewide but most common in eastern, central and southern Texas.

Habitat: They occupy virtually all habitats in Texas except the most arid regions. Favors areas near water.

Breeding: Average six per litter, but can be up to twelve. Usually one litter per year.

Natural History: Today's wild hog population in Texas are mostly descendants of escaped domestic hogs but many are hybrids with the introduced European Wild Boar. Hogs are omnivorous in diet and will eat virtually any type of plant or animal matter. They are mostly diurnal or crepuscular in activity. They tend to thrive best where there is a source of permanent water. Feral Hogs in Texas are regarded as a non-game species that may be hunted year-round. Wild hogs are prolific breeders and females can breed as young as eight months. The babies of the European Wild Boar and hybrids are reddish brown with black stripes. Wild hogs can be highly destructive to native plants and animals as well as being a significant pest in croplands. They can also be a vector for disease transmission to other wildlife and livestock. Lifespan is five to eight years in the wild.

Size: Adults are 35 to 65 pounds and up to 40 inches. Males are slightly larger than females.

Presumed range in TX

Variation: Biologists recognize ten subspecies of Collared Peccary. The subspecies found in Texas is *angulatus,* the Texas Collared Peccary.

Abundance: Fairly common is west Texas and southern Texas. Declining in the rest of its range in the state.

Habitat: Arid and semi-arid brushlands, deserts, and desert mountain ranges. Favors rocky canyons.

Breeding: Females can breed at nine months of age. Litters number one to five.

Natural History: The Peccary family is well represented throughout Latin America where they go by the name Javalina (pronounced Hav-a-leena). There are three species in the Tayassuidae family. The Collared Peccary is the most common and widespread member of the family and the only one found in North America. It ranges from the southwestern US to southern South America. Prickly Pear Cacti are an important food item but a wide variety of plant and animal matter is eaten. They will eat the hard seeds the Mesquite plant and are able to crush the rock-like beans with their teeth. The range of the Collared Peccary in Texas has shrunk from pre-settlement times and they are likely negatively impacted by wild hog populations. Today they are most common in Texas the Chihuahuan Desert and Southern Texas Plains Ecoregions as well as the southernmost Coastal Plain.

Class—**Mammalia** (mammals)

Order—**Lagamorpha** (rabbits, hares & pika)

Family—**Leporidae** (rabbits & hares)

Eastern Cottontail *Sylvilagus floridana*	**Desert Cottontail & Davis Mts. Cottontail** *Sylvilagus audubonii & Sylvilagus robustus*	**Swamp Rabbit** *Sylvilagus aquaticus*
	Desert Cottontail	

 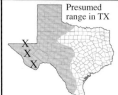 

Size: Adult length about 17 inches. Weight 2.25 to 3.25 pounds. Maximum 4 pounds.

Presumed range in TX

Size: Desert Cottontails can reach 3 pounds. Davis Mountains Cottontails are slightly larger.

Presumed range in TX

Size: Largest of the "Cottontails." May reach 21 inches and weigh as much as 5 or 6 pounds.

Presumed range in TX

Variation: At least 12 very similar subspecies are recognized in the United States and three in Texas, but only a mammalogist can tell them apart.

Variation: These two very similar species are indistinguishable to the non-expert. Locality is probably the best determining factor in the field.

Variation: Some experts recognize two subspecies but not all agree with that. Regardless, all Texas Swamp Rabbits are similar in appearance.

Abundance: Very common but subject to cyclical population fluctuations. Least common in the panhandle.

Abundance: The Desert Cottontail is common, while the Davis Mts. Cottontail is rare except in a few locations.

Abundance: Fairly common in wetland habitats but never reaches the population density of the Eastern Cottontail.

Habitat: May be found in virtually any habitat within the state except for permanent wetlands. Most common in overgrown fields and edge areas. Fond of briers, honeysuckle, and tall weeds.

Habitat: Desert Cottontails are found in arid deserts and desert grasslands. The Davis Mountains Cottontail lives in the higher elevations of the Davis, Chisos and Guadalupe Mountains.

Habitat: Swamps, marshes and bottomlands in the eastern portion of the state. Probably most common in the Western Gulf Coastal Plain Ecoregion where wetlands are more abundant.

Breeding: This is the most prolific of the several rabbit species in America, producing up to seven litters per year with as many as five young per litter.

Breeding: Desert Cottontail breeds at least twice a year and produces three or four young. Little is known about breeding in the Davis Mountains Cottontail.

Breeding: Breeds January through August. Three young is typical after a 37-day gestation period. Averages two litters per year.

Natural History: In the spring and summer Eastern Cottontails feed on a wide variety of grasses, legumes, and herbaceous weeds. Briers, sapling bark, and other woody materials may make up the bulk of the diet in winter. These rabbits are prey for many predators including foxes, coyotes, bobcats, and hawks and owls, especially the Great Horned Owl. The life expectancy for a Cottontail is not high, and only about one in four will live to see their second birthday. Populations are known to fluctuate and during years when their numbers are highest there may be as many as nine rabbits per acre in good habitat. The three subspecies in Texas are *alacer* in eastern Texas, *chapmani* southern and western Texas and *llanensis* the panhandle. All look very similar.

Natural History: On the range map above the X's mark the location of the mountain ranges where the Davis Mountain Cottontail can be found. That species lives in the higher elevations at about 6000 feet and above. The Desert Cottontail is a much more common and widespread animal found throughout the region shaded in gray on the map. All cottontails are very similar in appearance and can be difficult to distinguish in the field. The best way to tell the difference between the Eastern and Desert Cottontails is by ear size. The slightly smaller bodied Desert Cottontail (shown above) has a larger ear, an adaptation for life in the hot desert. The best way to identify the Davis Mountains Cottontail is by location. Any cottontail observed above 6000 feet is likely that species.

Natural History: An excellent swimmer, the Swamp Rabbit will elude hunters' hounds by diving into water and swimming for a long distance. This is the largest of the "true" rabbits in America (not including jackrabbits and hares). They are nearly twice as large as the Eastern and Desert Cottontails. The range of this species has diminished with the loss of wetlands both in Texas and throughout its range in the southeast. The occurrence of the Swamp Rabbit in wetlands is easily detected by the presence of droppings on floating logs within the swamp. Bobcats and Great Horned Owls are probably their biggest predator but they are also preyed upon by Gray Foxes and many other opportunistic predators. Populations are declining in Texas.

Class—**Mammalia** (mammals)

Order—**Lagomorpha**	Order—**Rodentia** (rodents)	
Family—**Leporidae** (rabbits & hares)	Family—**Sciuridae** (squirrels)	
Black-tailed Jackrabbit *Lepus californicus*	**Southern Flying Squirrel** *Glaucomys volans*	**Eastern Gray Squirrel** *Sciurus carolinensis*

Black-tailed Jackrabbit

Size: Adult length about 24 inches. Weight about 7 to 8 pounds. Maximum 9 pounds.

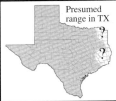
Presumed range in TX

Variation: There are three subspecies recognized in the state but the differences are so slight as to be indistinguishable to the average observer,

Abundance: Common in west Texas. Least common in the eastern and southeastern part of the state.

Habitat: Inhabits semi-open brushy country, mesquite brush, pastures, grasslands, and desert.

Breeding: Breeds year-round. Multiple litters per year are common. Up to six young per litter.

Natural History: The large ears of the Jackrabbit are an adaptation for living in hot environments like deserts. The ears act to radiate heat from the body. On hot summer days these hares will lounge in the shade beneath a thick shrub, often excavating a shallow depression in the soil to lower their profile. They are active at night and during early morning or late afternoon. They feed on a variety of grasses and forbs as well as cactus and shrubs. They can become a problem for ranchers if populations get too high. Ironically, land owners who instigate predator control programs on their property inadvertently protect populations of Jackrabbits and rodents. As these herbivores increase, they decrease the available forage for livestock. Jackrabbits are capable of speeds up to 40 miles per hour and their bouncing gait can cover 10 feet in a leap.

Southern Flying Squirrel

Size: America's smallest tree squirrel. Total length 10 inches. Weighs only 2 to 3 ounces.

Presumed range in TX

Variation: There is little variation, and the sexes are alike. Some biologists recognize as many as eight subspecies nationwide. Only one occurs in Texas.

Abundance: Uncommon but may be more common than sightings would indicate due to secretive habits.

Habitat: These little squirrels are totally dependent upon trees and make their home in woodlands and forests.

Breeding: One litter per year with up to six young. Nest is usually within a hollow in a tree or a man-made nest box.

Natural History: Lives in tree hollows and old woodpecker holes. Texas's only nocturnal squirrel. Leaps from tree to tree and glides using flaps of skin between front and hind legs like a parachute. Flattened tail serves as a rudder while gliding. Feeds on nuts, seeds, fruits, fungi, lichens, tree buds, insects, bird eggs, and nestling birds as well as mice. Flying Squirrels are gregarious animals and several may share a den. Southern Flying Squirrels can live up to ten years and will become quite tame in captivity, making reasonable pets. Wild squirrels in rural areas sometimes invade homes and attics where they can become a noisy nuisance as they scramble about in the wee hours. Favored habitat is primarily hardwoods but also in mixed pine-hardwood forests. They will live in suburbs and urban areas if sufficient mature trees are present. Availability of mast is a requirement.

Eastern Gray Squirrel

Size: Total length about 19 inches, of which half is tail. Weight about 18 ounces.

Presumed range in TX

Variation: At least six subspecies are recognized and some are quite variable. Melanistic and albino populations can be found in some areas of the US.

Abundance: Very common in the eastern portion of the state. Can be quite common in urban parks ands lawns.

Habitat: Prefers mature deciduous forests but also found in mixed coniferous forests and second growth areas.

Breeding: Breeds December through February and again in June and July. Four to six young per litter.

Natural History: Feeds on nuts, seeds, fungi, tree buds, and the inner bark of trees as well as bird eggs and hatchlings. May sometimes eat carrion. Like most rodents they will gnaw bones or shed deer antlers for calcium. Well known for burying and storing nuts. Frequently calls with a raspy "bark," especially when alarmed. Builds summer nests of leaves in tree crotches. Winter dens are in tree hollows. During severe weather may be inactive for several days. Poor mast years may produce mass migrations in the eastern deciduous forests. In Texas these squirrels are most common in lowland forests and swamps, but they will also occupy drier upland woods. They nest in tree hollows and construct nests of leaf clumps for summer use. Introduced into cities and towns well outside their natural range and today are in at least one city as far away as the Panhandle.

Class—**Mammalia** (mammals)

Order—**Rodentia** (rodents)

Family—**Sciuridae** (squirrel family)

Fox Squirrel	Rock Squirrel
Sciurus niger	*Otospermophilus variegatus*

Size: Total length 23 inches from snout to tail tip. Weighs 2 to 2.75 pounds.

Variation: There are three subspecies in Texas but all are very similar. Shown above are subspecies *S. n. ludovicianus* above left and subspecies *S. n. limitis* (right).

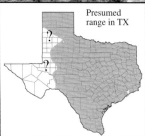

Presumed range in TX

Size: Total length about 19 inches from snout to tail tip. Weighs about two pounds.

Variation: Most are brownish with gray mottling. In parts of the Edwards Plateau dark specimens with a solid black head and anterior body are common.

Presumed range in TX

Abundance: Common. This is the most common tree squirrel in Texas. They range well outside the forested regions in the state, but in prairie and arid habitats they occupy riparian habitats, parks, and towns where trees are present.

Habitat: Prefers open forests with trees widely spaced. Can be common in swamps. Prefers edge areas, overgrown fence rows, etc., over extensive woods. Uses both deciduous and coniferous forests. Riparian habitats are used in open country and arid habitats.

Breeding: Produces four to six young twice annually, breeding in winter and again in summer. Nest is usually in a tree hollow. Young squirrels emerge from the nest at about two months and a few weeks later they are on their own.

Natural History: Fox Squirrels are less arboreal than their Gray Squirrel cousins. They will wander frequently into open areas and spend more time on the ground than Gray Squirrels. Their home range may be ten times larger. Average home range is about ten acres but can be several times that. They are generally less common than the Gray Squirrel, never reaching the population densities of their smaller cousins, but their overall range in the US is much larger. They feed on the same foods of nuts, seeds, buds, berries, etc., but the diet of Fox Squirrels also often includes the seeds of pine cones. During the growing season they will eat leaf buds and the seeds of trees like maples and elm. Dark morph specimens frequently occur in some areas of their range, especially in the eastern United States. In Texas the favorite foods are the nuts of hickory trees and acorns from Southern Red Oaks, Bluejack Oak, and Overcup Oak, Pecans are also relished and they will peel the cones of pine trees to access the seeds. Like the Gray Squirrel they are an important small game species.

Abundance: Common throughout their range in Texas and very common in prime habitats in the Edwards Plateau. Unlike many wildlife species that have suffered at the hands of man, the Rock Squirrel seems to be thriving.

Habitat: The name Rock Squirrel is appropriate as this squirrel species loves rocky habitats. Rocky canyons with steep walls are a favorite habitat in Texas. They also use boulder piles and talus slopes. Their range in Texas is limited to regions where rocky substrates have reached the surface.

Breeding: Breeding takes place in March and April. As many as six or seven young or as few as one may be produced. Usually only one litter per year is produced. Males will wander widely in search of females during the breeding season.

Natural History: Although Rock Squirrels resemble the tree squirrels they are probably most closely related to the marmots (genus *Marmota*). In spite of their name, they are good climbers and are frequently seen in trees. They will climb to top of dead snags or high boulders to bask in the warm in sun on cool mornings or at times perhaps just to survey their surroundings. They sometimes will den in tree hollows but usually live in a rock crevice or a burrow dug by themselves. Unlike the tree squirrels that remain active all winter, Rock Squirrels in colder climates will hibernate. This species shows a tendency for social behavior and they often live in small groups. Groups consist of females, young squirrels, and a dominant male that expels young male squirrels from the group as they mature. They are omnivorous feeders and although most of their diet is plant material they will eat insects and even a few small animals or eggs and young birds on occasion. They are well adapted to living in arid regions and can go for long periods without access to water.

Class—**Mammalia** (mammals)

Order—**Rodentia** (rodents)

Family—**Sciuridae** (squirrels)

Texas Antelope Squirrel *Ammospermophilus interpres*	**Thirteen-lined Ground Squirrel** *Ictidomys tridecemlineatus*	**Rio Grande Ground Squirrel** *Ictidomys parvidens*

Size: Total length including tail about 9 inches. Maximum weight of about 4 ounces.  Presumed range in TX	**Size:** 12 inches in length and weighs 5 to 8 ounces on average. Males are slightly smaller.  Presumed range in TX	**Size:** 12 inches in length and weighs 5 to 8 ounces on average. Males are slightly smaller. 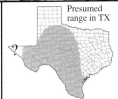 Presumed range in TX
Variation: This is a monotypic species with no significant variation among specimens in Texas.	**Variation:** Mammalogists recognize two subspecies in Texas but differences are imperceptible to the lay observer.	**Variation:** This is a monotypic species with no significant variation among specimens in Texas.
Abundance: Uncommon to rare in Texas.	**Abundance:** Common in the Panhandle but has declined in some areas.	**Abundance:** Common. Can be very common in ideal habitat.
Habitat: Antelope Squirrels are a desert species. In Texas they inhabit the entire Chihuahuan Desert Ecoregion and the western portion of the Edwards Plateau.	**Habitat:** Inhabits prairies and sandy grasslands. Today pastures, golf courses, cemeteries, lawns, and even highway right of ways are often utilized. Prefers areas of short, sparse grass.	**Habitat:** The Rio Grande Ground Squirrel is essentially the arid lands counterpart of the prairie loving Thirteen-lined Ground Squirrel. Desert grasslands are the preferred habitat.
Breeding: Breeding begins in late winter. Large litters of up to fourteen young are reported.	**Breeding:** Mating takes place soon after emerging from hibernation. Average of six to eight young born blind and naked.	**Breeding:** Breeding activities commence almost immediately after emerging from hibernation in early spring.
Natural History: A desert-adapted species, the Antelope Squirrels can survive without access to drinking water. They are able to extract enough moisture from the plant material they consume to meet their requirements. However, they will drink regularly if a water source is available. They are diurnal animals that remain active even very hot summer days, though their activity is interrupted by frequent resting and cooling under the shade of bush or cactus. These are very shy animals that are difficult to approach. They always run with the tail held over the top of the back, a character that is common among all species of Antelope Squirrels. They live in underground burrows and spend most of their time on the ground. But they will climb into bushes and cacti to forage. Food is a variety of desert plants and plant seeds or fruits. Insects are also consumed and possibly small vertebrates and carrion.	**Natural History:** In some regions known by the nickname "Striped Gopher," but the Thirteen-lined Ground Squirrel is a member of the Squirrel Family and not very closely related to the true gophers that inhabit much of America. In the Midwest this species may have expanded its range from pre-settlement days. Cutting of forests and clearing of land for agriculture and other human uses seems to have benefited this open country species. They are confirmed burrowers that may excavate several tunnels which can be six feet in length and over a foot deep. Below ground hibernation begins in early fall and can last over 6 months. In addition to grasses, forbs and clovers they will eat seeds and some insects. In regions where there is intensive agriculture they are likely to experience population declines. But they can adapt and exist in urban parks and golf courses.	**Natural History:** These ground squirrels are very similar in appearance to the Thirteen-lined Ground Squirrel and where the ranges overlap it can be difficult to tell them apart in the field, but this species lacks stripes between the rows of spots. Like the preceding species, they live in burrows which they dig themselves and in most respects they mirror the Thirteen-lined Ground Squirrel in habits, foods and behavior. They may be more inclined to feed on insects in drier regions where vegetative foods are less available and are known to prey on small reptiles and scavenge on road kills. Where the range overlaps that of the Thirteen-lined Ground Squirrel the two similar species may hybridize, making positive identification difficult even for experts. In the cooler regions of their range they will hibernate but in warmer regions they might be active in warm weather during the winter.

Class—**Mammalia** (mammals)
Order—**Rodentia** (rodents)
Family—**Sciuridae** (squirrels)

Spotted Ground Squirrel *Xerospermophilus spilosoma*	**Gray-footed Chipmunk** *Tamias canipes*	**Black-tailed Prairie Dog** *Cynomys ludovicianus*

Size: Total average length is about 8 inches. Weighs on average about 4 ounces. 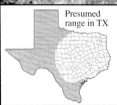 Presumed range in TX	**Size:** Total average length is about 9 inches. Weighs on average about 2.25 ounces.  Presumed range in TX	**Size:** Average length is about 14 inches. Weighs on average about 2 to 3 pounds.  Presumed range in TX
Variation: Some mammalogists recognize as many as three subspecies in Texas but the differences in subspecies are so slight as to be insignificant.	**Variation:** Specimens from the Guadalupe Mountains in Texas average a bit smaller than those from the nearby Sacramento Mountains in New Mexico.	**Variation:** There are two subspecies in Texas, but throughout their enormous range they actually show very little variation and all resemble photo above.
Abundance: Generally uncommon. May be fairly common in some areas.	**Abundance:** Very rare in Texas. Only in the Guadalupe and Sierra Diablo Mts.	**Abundance:** Generally uncommon but they can be fairly common in preserves.
Habitat: An arid land species, the Spotted Ground Squirrel occurs in Texas only in the western and southern portions of the state.	**Habitat:** Endemic to the high elevations of the Sacramento Mts and Guadalupe Mts in the Arizona/New Mexico Mountains Level III Ecoregion.	**Habitat:** Once inhabited Short Grass Prairies of the Great Plains from Mexico to the Canadian border. Now eradicated from all but a fragment of original range
Breeding: Little is known about the reproduction of this species in Texas.	**Breeding:** One litter per year. Four young on average.	**Breeding:** Litter size varies from four to eight. Young are born blind and hairless.
Natural History: The Spotted Ground Squirrel is the easternmost representative of the *Xerospermophilus* genus of ground squirrels. Often called "Pygmy Ground Squirrels," they are among the smallest of the ground squirrels and the genus consists of four species. These little ground squirrels prefer dry, sandy soils and they thrive in desert environments. The Spotted Ground Squirrel also ranges well to the north into the Great Plains as far as Nebraska and South Dakota. These are diurnal rodents but during hot weather they are most active in early morning and late afternoon. Their food is mostly green plants and seeds but they also eat insects and some small vertebrates. They live in burrows which they dig. Burrow is often situated at the base of a shrub. In cooler climates like the Great Plains they hibernate during winter and in warm deserts they will aestivate during the hottest times of the year.	**Natural History:** Gray-footed Chipmunks are a diurnal species that is most active in the mornings. They are a classic example of a "Sky Island" species. Prior to the end of the last ice age the southwestern US was much cooler and wetter. Forests and savanna dominated the region. About fifteen thousand years ago the climate changed and low elevation basins and valleys become hot, dry deserts. The surviving Gray-footed Chipmunks retreated higher into the mountain tops where cooler, wetter conditions and trees still remained. Today they are isolated on the tops of several desert mountain ranges and separated by expansive desert basins. Thus they exist isolated in a mountain-top "island" surrounded by a "sea" of desert. Foods of the Gray-footed Chipmunk include green plants, seeds, grains, nuts, flowers, and fruits. Insects are eaten as well and provide a bolus of high protein food. They will hibernates in winter.	**Natural History:** Among the ground squirrels colony behavior is common, but the prairie dogs take this social conduct to the extreme and live in large colonies called "Prairie Dog Towns." Historical accounts by early pioneers tell of encountering prairie dog towns that covered the land from horizon to horizon. The largest of these "towns" was reportedly in the Texas Panhandle and is believed to have covered as much as 25,000 square miles and contained up to 400 million Prairie Dogs! Populations today are estimated to be less than one percent of the original pre-settlement populations. There has been a resurgence of Prairie Dogs in many areas in recent years as wildlife agencies and conservation organizations have recognized the value of this species to the overall health of the plains. They are regarded as a "Keystone Species," providing food for a wide variety of predators and homes for scores of prairie species.

Class—**Mammalia** (mammals)

Order—**Rodentia** (rodents)

Family—**Erethizontidae** (porcupine)	Family—**Castoridae** (Beaver)	Family—**Echimyidae** (Nutria)
Porcupine *Erethizon dorsatum*	**Beaver** *Castor canadensis*	**Nutria** *Myocastor coypus*

 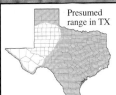

Presumed range in TX

Size: Adult males up to 32 inches in length. Weight about 20 pounds, maximum 25 pounds.

Size: Up to 43 inches in total length. The largest adults can weigh up to 65 pounds.

Size: 3 feet in average total length. Maximum of 42 inches and 24 pounds.

Variation: Females are as much as a third smaller than males. Several subspecies are recognized but all are very similar.

Variation: There are several subspecies. Re-introduction programs led to inter-breeding and dilution of pure strains.

Variation: No known variation in Texas populations. Several subspecies occur in South America.

Abundance: Uncommon but increasing within most of its range in the state.

Abundance: Common. Most common in the eastern part of the state.

Abundance: Introduced. Fairly common and expanding its range in Texas.

Habitat: Prefers forested regions. Can persist in prairies and arid regions in riparian habitats or in mountains. Fond rocky, rugged landscapes.

Habitat: Beavers are thoroughly aquatic mammals that to a great extent create their own wetland habitats by damming streams. They will also inhabit lakes.

Habitat: Nutria are thoroughly aquatic mammals always found in aquatic habitats. Probably most common in salt and brackish marshes but also in fresh water.

Breeding: During the fall breeding season males will wander extensively and will fight over receptive females. Only one or two young are produced.

Breeding: Mating takes place in mid-winter with the young being born about four months later. There is only one litter per year.

Breeding: Breeds year-round and can produce two or three litters per year. A maximum of eleven young has been recorded but five or six is probably average.

Natural History: The porcupine's unique defensive quills are legendary and provide adequate protection from most predators. Domestic dogs often exhibit remarkable stupidity when encountering porcupines and will frequently repeat their attacks until the jaws and face are literally covered in hundreds of quills. Such calamities require medical intervention to save the dog, but more often than not the dog will again attack the next porcupine seen! Porcupines are effective climbers but move slowly in trees. In summer months they feed mostly on the ground on herbaceous plants. In winter they switch to the inner bark of trees and shrubs. These animals are relative newcomers to most of the state. In the last century they have expanded their range eastward from the Panhandle and Big Bend regions and now may be found throughout the western two thirds of Texas.

Natural History: Beavers are primarily nocturnal in habits. In remote locations where human intrusion is absent, they are observed active during the day as well. They feed mostly on the inner bark of trees, with willow being a dietary mainstay. They will also consume sedges and other aquatic vegetation, but in winter live exclusively on bark. The dorsal-ventrally flattened tail is hairless and scaly and along with the webbed hind feet provide these animals with powerful swimming tools. They also possess enlarged incisors which grow continually throughout life and are used to gnaw through trunks and fell trees. Most trees cut by Beavers are small saplings which are used as food, but they will also cut large trees to open the canopy and promote the growth of new food sources. They are famous for their dam building abilities and are a keystone species, creating wetland habitat.

Natural History: The Nutria is one of many introduced species that has become established in Texas. They were first brought into Louisiana in 1938 for fur production. Today they have spread across much of the southeastern United States. They can become quite common in certain areas of prime habitat where they are unmolested by humans. Nutria are strict vegetarians and will consume a wide variety of plant materials. Most food is aquatic plant species and includes roots and tubers as well as stems and foliage. They will den in burrows dug into banks or build platforms of vegetation. Muskrat homes are also sometimes used. Most wildlife biologists regard the Nutria as an overall detrimental species in the ecology of Texas. They can have a negative impact on the native Common Muskrat, and they are known to destroy aquatic plants that are food for native wetland species.

Class—**Mammalia** (mammals)
Order—**Rodentia** (rodents)
Family—**Muridae** (old world rats & mice)

Norway (Brown) Rat *Rattus norvegicus*	**Black Rat** *Rattus rattus*	**House Mouse** *Mus musculus*

Size: Total length as much as 17 inches and can weigh as much as a pound.  Presumed range in TX	**Size:** Total length about 11 inches with a maximum of 14 inches. Weighs up to 7 to 8 ounces. 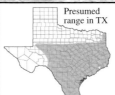 Presumed range in TX	**Size:** About 6.5 inches in length including tail and weighs about 0.75 ounce.  Presumed range in TX
Variation: None in wild populations. Captives are variable. The well-known laboratory rat is an albino form of this species.	**Variation:** Black Rats can be black, gray or brownish. But generally they are darker than the similar Norway Rat or the Eastern Woodrat.	**Variation:** No variation in wild specimens but domestic version known as laboratory mice come in a variety of colors and patterns.
Abundance: Introduced. Very common, especially in urban areas and around dumps, sewers, refuse, etc.	**Abundance:** Introduced. Very common on the Gulf Coast. Less common inland but may be common in cities.	**Abundance:** Introduced. Very common, especially in urban areas. Also quite common around farms and ranches.
Habitat: This highly adaptable rodent can live virtually anywhere, including as a stowaway on ships, which is how it immigrated to America from Europe. Thrives in both cities and in wilderness.	**Habitat:** Black Rat is more common in the coastal lowlands. This rodent is closely tied to human habitations and invades attics and roof crawl spaces. It climbs more often than the Norway Rat.	**Habitat:** A highly successful rodent that usually associates with human habitations and man-made structures, but can also thrive in wild environments. Probably in all habitats in Texas.
Breeding: The fecundity of the Norway Rat is legendary. From 6 to 8 litters per year with up to a dozen young per litter.	**Breeding:** Probably breeds year-round in Texas. Produces 4 to 8 young and can breed 4 to 6 times annually.	**Breeding:** Broods can number from 5 to 12. Young females begin breeding at 6 weeks and produce 14 litters per year.
Natural History: Also commonly called the Brown Rat and less commonly known as the Wharf Rat. This species has followed man to every corner of the globe. They are responsible for an almost unimaginable degree of human suffering. Throughout the history of human civilization these rodents have destroyed crops and stored foods while spreading devastating diseases, most notably Bubonic Plague. Though less of a threat to modern societies, these rats still shadow the human species and are common in both urban and rural settings. The common laboratory rat is a domestic version of this animal that has somewhat redeemed the species for humans, having been used as an experimental animal for medical and scientific research for over a century. They can outcompete native rodents.	**Natural History:** This rodent's other common name is "Roof Rat." It is an appropriate moniker as this species is an adept climber. In natural habitats it shows arboreal tendencies and in urban areas it lives well off the ground in attics, roofs, and walls. Unlike America's other two introduced Eurasian rodents (Norway Rat and House Mouse), this species does not thrive in wilderness and is largely dependent upon human structures (or at least human-altered habitats). They do not tolerate cold weather well and are restricted mostly warmer climates. They also have a strong propensity toward coastal areas and ports. They will invade urban and suburban neighborhoods in coastal areas where they are generally regarded as vermin. Like the preceding species they are disease vectors.	**Natural History:** The House Mouse has adapted to living in close proximity to humans and today they are found wherever there are people throughout the world. As their name implies they regularly enter into houses where they can become both a pest and a health hazard. They live both in cities and farmlands. Like the Norway Rat the House Mouse originated in Eurasia and traveled around the world as a stowaway on sailing ships, eventually populating the entire globe. These mice are primarily nocturnal and their food includes nearly everything eaten by humans plus insects and fungi. They may be able to outcompete native mice species in Texas. Domestic populations of this species are the familiar laboratory mice or "white mice," so called because most are albinos.

Class—**Mammalia** (mammals)

Order—**Rodentia** (rodents)

Family—**Cricetidae** (new world rats & mice)

Common Muskrat	Yellow-nosed & Hispid Cotton Rats	Coues's & Texas Rice Rats
Ondatra zibethicus	*Sigmodon couesi & Sigmodon hispidus*	*Oryzomys texensis & Oryzomys couesi*

 Hispid Cotton Rat

Size: Reaches 20 inches in length and average about 2.5 pounds. 3 pounds max.

 Presumed range in TX

Size: 10 inches in length and about six ounces for *S. hispidus*. Slightly smaller for *S. ochrognathus*.

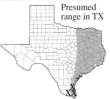 Presumed range in TX

Size: Texas Rice Rat up to 9 inches in length and weighing about 2 ounces. Coues's slightly larger.

Presumed range in TX

Variation: As many as sixteen subspecies range across North America. There are three in Texas but there is no discernible difference to the lay observer in Texas animals.

Variation: Two very similar species in Texas. The Hispid Cotton Rat, *S. hispidus* (statewide) (photo above) and the Yellow-nosed Cotton Rat, *S. ochrognathus* (X's on map above).

Variation: Two species of Rice Rats occur in Texas. On the map above the range of the Texas Rice Rat is in light gray. The X's indicate where the range of the Coues's Rice Rat overlaps.

Abundance: Generally uncommon but fairly common in some areas of east Texas, especially in the northern part of the Gulf Coastal Plain.

Abundance: The Hispid Cotton Rat (shown above) is probably one of the most common small mammals in Texas. The Yellow-nosed is uncommon to rare.

Abundance: The Texas Rice Rat *O. texanus* is very common in coastal marshes. The Coues's Rice Rat *O. couesi* is a Threatened Species.

Habitat: Aquatic. Prefers marshland but also inhabits swamp, ponds, and lakes; even roadside ditches. Rarely in rivers or large streams. Often occurs sympatricly with the Beaver.

Habitat: Old fields, especially in upland areas. Most common in fields dominated by rank grasses. Hispid Cotton Rat is found statewide. Yellow-nosed in the Big Bend region.

Habitat: Prefers to be near water. Wet meadows, marsh, and the edges of swamps. Can also be found in upland woods but this species is most common in coastal lowlands and marshes.

Breeding: Prolific. Capable of multiple litters annually and may produce as many as six young per litter. Young are weaned in about a month.

Breeding: Hispid Cotton Rat is one of the most prolific mammals in Texas. Several litters per year (six to eight babies) and young are weaned in less than a week!

Breeding: A highly fecund rodent that may breed several times per year and will produce up to seven young per litter. Reaches sexual maturity in two months.

Natural History: Primarily nocturnal but often active during daylight hours in the spring. With webbed hind feet and a laterally flattened tail muskrats are excellent swimmers. They feed on a variety of aquatic vegetation. The name comes from the presence of well developed musk glands. These rodents are an important fur-bearer and in the recent past millions were trapped annually. Life span is only three to four years in the wild. The Mink may be the most important predator on muskrats, especially of the young. Adults build lodges similar to the Beaver, but use grasses rather than sticks. The entrance to the Muskrat lodge is below water level. They will also dig burrows into banks.

Natural History: An abundance of grasses seems to be a habitat preference. They are active day and night. These are one of the easier to identify of the mouse-like rodents due to the coarse appearance of the fur. They can attain very high population densities. Cotton Rats are a primary prey for a wide variety of predators including snakes, carnivorous mammals, and birds of prey. Their surface runways through overgrown fields are easy to see following a burn, as are the surface nests consisting of a ball of grasses. Populations fluctuate from year to year. Feeds mostly on grasses, herbs, and grass seeds. These rodents are preyed upon by a wide variety of predators, especially the Bobcat.

Natural History: The name Rice Rat comes from the prevalence of these rodents in rice fields throughout the southeast. In addition to rice they consume several other types of seeds and plants but also eat large amounts of animal matter. In fact, this is one of the most carnivorous rodents in America. The list of animal prey includes insects, crustaceans, fish, and baby birds and bird eggs to name a few. They are accomplished swimmers and will dive and swim underwater to escape a predator. They are strictly nocturnal in habits. As with most other rodents, they are preyed upon by a wide variety of raptors, carnivorous mammals, and especially snakes.

Class—**Mammalia** (mammals)
Order—**Rodentia** (rodents)
Family—**Cricetidae** (new world rats & mice)
Genus—*Neotoma* (Woodrats) 4 species in Texas

Size: Total length 12 to 16 inches. Weighs from 6.5 to 12 ounces. Eastern Woodrat and Southern Plains Woodrat are the largest.

Abundance: All four species can be common. The Southern Plains Woodrat is probably the most common in Texas.

Variation: Although there are four species of Woodrat in Texas, are all very similar in appearance and will resemble the Eastern Woodrat shown in the photo below. The names of Texas's four Woodrat species and their respective ranges are also shown below.

Habitat: Eastern Woodrat inhabits a wide variety of habitats within its range. White-toothed Woodrat and Mexican Woodrat favors desert habitats and rocky canyons. Southern Plains Woodrat lives in both arid deserts and semi-arid woodland and brush country.

Breeding: At least two litters per year is possible with two or three young being typical. Litters of up to six young have been recorded. Development is rapid and most females are ready to breed within a few months.

Natural History: Woodrats eat both plant and animal matter. In some areas of their range they go by name "Packrat" a reference to their tendency to gather human refuse and use it in the construction of a den that is made mainly from a pile of sticks and small stones. Their stick nests, called Middens, are usually constructed at the base of a shrub or cactus clump. In rocky areas they will use crevices or rock piles but will still build middens of sticks and cactus stems. Some middens may be used for many years by several generations and grow to several feet across. In most species, populations never becomes exceptionally high, and in some regions they can be uncommon. Middens constructed in rock crevices and beneath rock ledges in arid regions can persist for hundreds of years. Ecologists have studied ancient midden sites to look for evidence of historical environmental conditions by examining cached seeds and petrified feces.

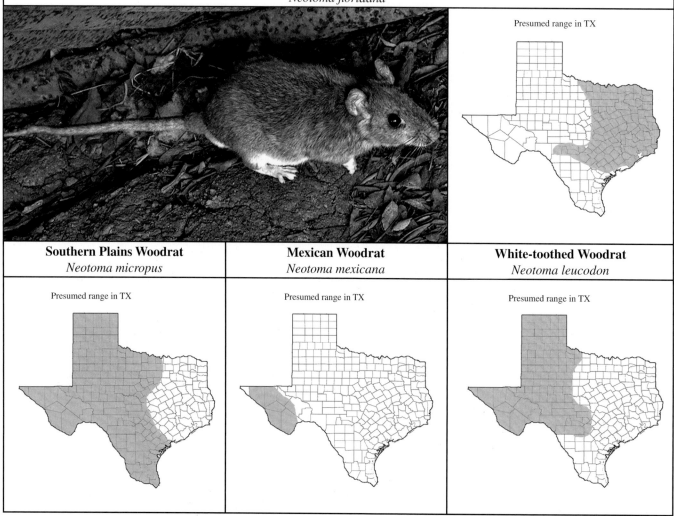

Eastern Woodrat
Neotoma floridana

Presumed range in TX

Southern Plains Woodrat
Neotoma micropus

Presumed range in TX

Mexican Woodrat
Neotoma mexicana

Presumed range in TX

White-toothed Woodrat
Neotoma leucodon

Presumed range in TX

Class—**Mammalia** (mammals)
Order—**Rodentia** (rodents)
Family—**Cricetidae** (new world rats & mice)
Genus—***Peromyscus*** (Deermice)—9 species in Texas

Size: The total length of adult Deermice is on average 6 to 8 inches. Weights are 0.75 to 1.5 ounces.

Variation: The photos of three of the more common species shown below provide a good illustration of the similarity in appearance of the mice in this genus. Even trained mammalogists can experience difficulty in distinguishing between species. For the average observer, referencing range maps is one of the easiest ways to determine species. Where ranges overlap it becomes much more difficult to distinguish species.

Abundance: Northern Rock Deermouse and Pinyon Deermouse are both uncommon. All other species are common within their respective ranges in Texas. The White-footed Deermouse and the North American Deermouse may be the most common.

Habitat: Collectively the *Peromyscus* species inhabit virtually every terrestrial habitat type in Texas.

Breeding: Most *Peromyscus* mice are prolific breeders that are capable of breeding year-round. A typical litter is four or five young, but can be more. The young mice develop rapidly and some are ready to breed themselves when only two months old.

Natural History: These common mice serve as prey for a variety of predators, from coyotes and bobcats to weasels, snakes, and birds of prey. All species are primarily nocturnal. They feed on a wide array of seeds, nuts, and grain as well as berries, insects, snails, centipedes, fungi, and occasionally other mice. They will cache large stores of seeds and nuts in the fall and they remain active throughout the winter. They can become a nuisance as they will regularly enter human dwellings, often nesting in a little used drawer or cupboard. Several species of *Peromyscus* mice are vectors for tick-borne Lyme's disease and in some regions of the southwestern United States some species can harbor the deadly Hanta Virus. Humans who experience close contact or prolonged exposure to their feces and urine may be at risk. Some species can be arboreal and they may den or nest well above the ground, or they may live beneath a rotted log or stump. Most are adaptable, successful native rodents. The Deermice are found in virtually every habitat type in America and they range from near sea level to the high mountains. For more information on each *Peromyscus* species the reader is referred to the book *The Mammals of Texas* by Schmidly and Bradley. This comprehensive volume is also available online through Texas Tech University at www.depts.ttu.edu/nslr/mammals.

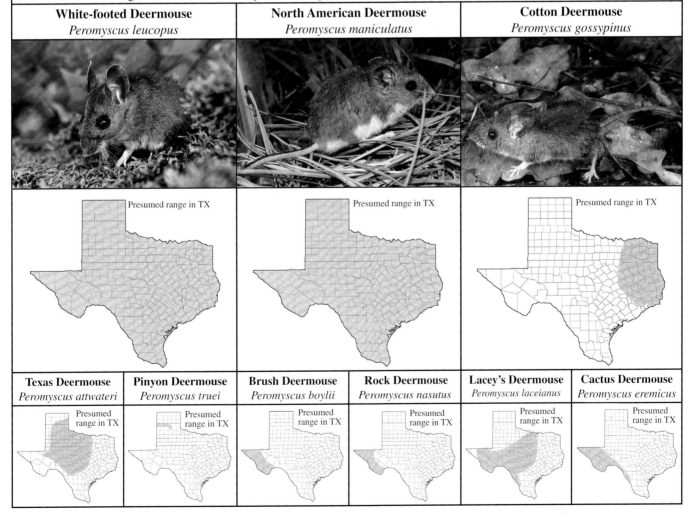

White-footed Deermouse	**North American Deermouse**	**Cotton Deermouse**
Peromyscus leucopus	*Peromyscus maniculatus*	*Peromyscus gossypinus*

Texas Deermouse	**Pinyon Deermouse**	**Brush Deermouse**	**Rock Deermouse**	**Lacey's Deermouse**	**Cactus Deermouse**
Peromyscus attwateri	*Peromyscus truei*	*Peromyscus boylii*	*Peromyscus nasutus*	*Peromyscus laceianus*	*Peromyscus eremicus*

Class—**Mammalia** (mammals)
Order—**Rodentia** (rodents)
Family—**Cricetidae** (new world rats & mice)
Genus—***Reithrodontomys*** (Harvest Mice) 4 species in Texas

Size: These are small mice. The average total length is only 4.5 to 6.5 inches. Weights are from 0.33 of an ounce to 1 ounce. The Fulvous Harvest Mouse is the largest and the Plains Harvest Mouse is the smallest.

Abundance: The Eastern Harvest Mouse is rare in Texas. Both the Western and Plains Harvest Mouse are regarded as uncommon in Texas. Only the Fulvous Harvest Mouse can be said to be a common species in the state.

Variation: Although there are 4 species of Harvest Mouse in Texas, all are very similar in appearance and resemble the Western Harvest Mouse shown in the photo below.

Habitat: Grassy areas and successional habitats overgrown with weeds and brush seemed to favored by Harvest Mice. Collectively they probably occupy most habitats are their collective ranges encompass the entire state.

Breeding: Breeding can occur throughout the year with at least two litters annually but some species can produce up to six litters in a year. The average number of young is probably three or four. Young Harvest Mice are born naked and blind and are tiny, weighing only about one gram. They grow rapidly and are sexually mature in about eight weeks.

Natural History: The diet of Harvest Mice includes some insects, but they are mostly vegetarian, feeding largely on seeds and grains. They will nest both in underground burrow and on the surface. Surface nests consists of a woven ball of grasses about the size of a baseball. They are also known to remodel birds' nests in bushes and shrubs a few feet off the ground. Unlike the introduced House Mouse and the widespread Deermice, both of which can be problematic animals for humans, the Harvest Mice are seemingly innocuous little mammals. They are important in local ecosystems as prey species for many types of predators including raptors, snakes, weasels, foxes, etc. Like many small mammals they are mainly nocturnal. They apparently do not hibernate and are active year-round. The home ranges of Harvest Mice can be quite small and their populations can be vulnerable to loss of habitat from road construction, row-crop agriculture, and urban development.

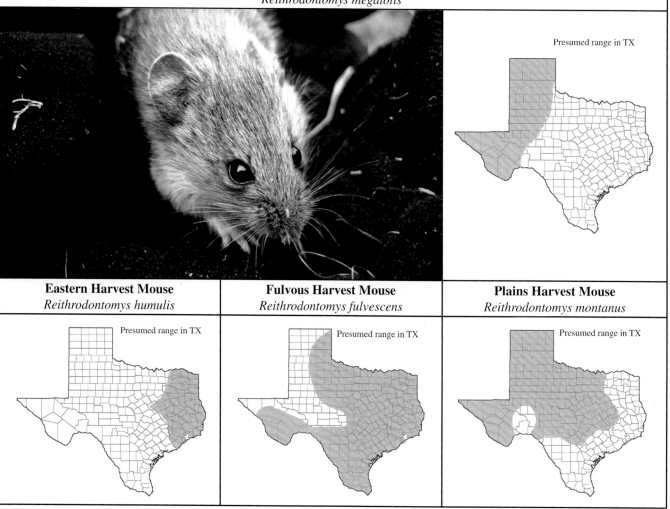

Western Harvest Mouse
Reithrodontomys megalotis

Presumed range in TX

Eastern Harvest Mouse
Reithrodontomys humulis

Fulvous Harvest Mouse
Reithrodontomys fulvescens

Plains Harvest Mouse
Reithrodontomys montanus

Presumed range in TX

Presumed range in TX

Presumed range in TX

Class—**Mammalia** (mammals)
Order—**Rodentia** (rodents)
Family—**Cricetidae** (new world rats and mice)

Golden Mouse *Ochrotomys nuttalli*	**Prairie Vole** *Microtus ochrogaster*	**Woodland Vole** *Microtus pinetorum*

Size: A small mouse. Averages about 6.5 inches and three-quarters of an ounce. 	**Size:** Adults average about 6 inches and 1.5 ounces. Maximum size up to 1.75 ounces. 	**Size:** Average total length is about 5 inches. Weighs about 1 ounce, maximum of 1.5 ounces. 
Variation: No variation in Texas except that young mice are slightly grayer in color. Adults are golden brown.	**Variation:** Two subspecies in Texas. *M. o. taylori* in the panhandle of Texas, *M.o. lucovicianus* in southeastern Texas.	**Variation:** Although there are two subspecies in Texas they are indistinguishable to the lay observer.
Abundance: Uncommon to rare in Texas. Possibly declining.	**Abundance:** Rare. The subspecies from SE Texas is probably extinct.	**Abundance:** Very common in the southeastern US but rather rare in Texas.
Habitat: Mainly a forest species but also uses overgrown fields. Favors lowland forests and swampy areas in the eastern end to the state. Probably most common in the "Big Thicket" region.	**Habitat:** This species generally avoids the woods and prefers open, grassy habitats and overgrown fields. Primary habitat is Tallgrass Prairies and this is an uncommon to rare species in Texas.	**Habitat:** Primarily deciduous and mixed pine/deciduous woodlands. Occurs in pine dominated woodlands throughout the southern US and in fact often goes by the name "Pine Vole."
Breeding: Breeds from early spring through fall, producing several litters per year. Two to four young is typical.	**Breeding:** Unlike most rodents, Prairie Voles are monogamous. Probably breeds all year. Three to five young is typical.	**Breeding:** Breeds spring through fall with up to four litters per year. one to four young per litter.
Natural History: Mainly nocturnal, Golden mice have strong arboreal tendencies. They will forage for seeds among vines and in bushes and trees. The nest is usually in a thicket of vines several feet off the ground. Acorns are also eaten as are invertebrates and these mice are decidedly omnivorous. As much a half their diet may be animal matter. These are handsome little mice with fine, golden fur. Unlike many other mice species, the Golden Mouse rarely enters human habitations, preferring a more natural habitat. One captive individual was reported to have lived for eight years, a very long life-span for a mouse. The average life-span in the wild is probably less than a year. The range of this species in Texas is restricted to the South Central Plains Level III Ecoregion (a.k.a. Piney Woods). Resembles the Deer Mice but easily distinguished by its golden color.	**Natural History:** Coarse, grizzled gray fur and shorter tail distinguish this species from the Woodland Vole. Although insects are eaten, these voles feed mostly on vegetation. Including but not limited to grasses, roots, herbaceous weeds, seeds, leaves, stems, etc. Like other voles they will create a system of shallow burrows. The North American range of this species approximates the occurrence of the original American prairies. In much of its range it is probably less common today than in historical times. The voles are preyed upon by nearly every type of predator in Texas. Snakes, capable of entering their burrows, are one of their major enemies. Especially rat snakes, kingsnakes, and the Bullsnake. The Long-tailed Weasel is also an adept predator of many types of small mammals including voles. Hawks and owls are a major threat when they emerge from their burrows.	**Natural History:** Woodland Voles create networks of tunnels just below the ground or "runways" that are near the surface but beneath the leaf litter on the forest floor. These tunnel systems are utilized by other small mammals such as shrews. They rarely venture far from these tunnels, but do emerge to glean seeds, grasses, and mast. They also eat roots, especially roots of grasses, and root crops like potatoes are also eaten. Along with the Prairie Vole they can be destructive to young orchard trees, by eating the bark at the base of the tree. Active both day and night. Their subterranean habits render them less vulnerable to many predators, but they are prey for a wide variety of carnivores, raptors, and especially snakes which are able to enter the burrow systems. Young exhibit a dark gray color. Adults are more chestnut. This species may be declining in Texas.

Class—**Mammalia** (mammals)

Order—**Rodentia** (rodents)

Family—**Cricetidae** (new world rats and mice)

Northern Pygmy Mouse	Chihuahuan Grasshopper Mouse	Northern Grasshopper Mouse
Baiomys taylori	*Onychomys arenicola*	*Onychomys leucogaster*

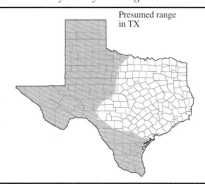

Presumed range in TX

Northern Pygmy Mouse — *Baiomys taylori*

Resembles a tiny Deer Mouse.

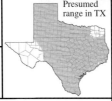
Presumed range in TX

Size: Total length is about 4 inches. Weighs 0.33 ounces.

Variation: Although mammalogists recognize two subspecies in the state, they are indistinguishable to the lay person.

Abundance: Common. Found nearly statewide. Recently expanding its range in Texas.

Habitat: Predilection for grassy areas and successional fields overgrown with rank grasses and weeds.

Breeding: Breeds year-round. Can produce eight or nine litters per year. Litter size is one to five but the average is probably three.

Natural History: This is one of the smallest native rodents in Texas. Unlike many other small mammals in Texas this species seems to be thriving and has actually expanded its range in the state in recent decades. They are found nearly statewide but are absent from the Chihuahuan Desert Level III Ecoregion. They are also absent from the extreme NE corner of the state but they may expand their range into that region in years to come. They feed on seeds and other plant material such as cactus fruits and green grasses. Insects and some small vertebrates are also eaten opportunistically. This is a southern, tropical mammal that ranges northward from Mexico into Texas. It is also found throughout northeastern Mexico east of the Sierra Madre Oriental. The longevity record in captivity is just over three years but few in the wild survive beyond a year.

Chihuahuan Grasshopper Mouse — *Onychomys arenicola*

Size: Average total length about 6 inches. Maximum weight about 1 ounce. Females smaller.

Presumed range in TX

Variation: No variation in Texas specimens except that females are slightly smaller than males. Photo above is typical.

Abundance: Fairly common but does not exhibit high population densities common in many other rodent species.

Habitat: This is Chihuahuan Desert endemic. Lives in low desert with sparse vegetation.

Breeding: Females can produce a litter at four months of age. Probably breeds twice a year and produces two to seven young per litter.

Natural History: This species also goes by the name Mearn's Grasshopper Mouse. But the name Chihuahuan Desert Grasshopper Mouse seems more appropriate as this species is endemic to the Chihuahuan Desert region. Grasshopper mice are vocal animals and will emit sounds that are often described as "howls." These vocalizations are believed to be territorial. These tiny predators feed on a wide variety of invertebrate prey including venomous scorpions and they have evolved a resistance to scorpion venom. They will also kill and eat venomous centipedes but their is no evidence of any resistance to centipede venom. They are able to out maneuver the centipede and kill it without being bitten. Other mice species and even small reptiles may sometimes be included in the diet of this fierce little mouse.

Northern Grasshopper Mouse — *Onychomys leucogaster*

Nearly identical to the preceding species

Size: Total length is about 6.5 inches. Weighs 1.25 ounces. Maximum of 1.75 ounces.

Variation: The two Grasshopper Mouse species in Texas are nearly identical in appearance are best separated by range.

Abundance: Fairly common but does not exhibit high population densities common in many other rodent species.

Habitat: They range from northeastern Mexico to southern Alberta, Canada. Grasslands are the preferred habitat.

Breeding: Reaches sexual maturity as early as three months. Multiple litters per year may be produced with as many as six young per litter (one to six).

Natural History: The name Grasshopper Mouse is an appropriate moniker for this species. One of the their favorite foods is grasshoppers. They will also eat other insects, scorpions, and even other mice. In fact, the *Onchomys* mice are mainly carnivorous in their diet. They do eat some plant material but animal matter makes up as much as 90 percent of their diet. These mice can be quite vocal and can emit a whistling sound. These mice usually have a rather small home range but they will wander widely within their territory. They will use the runways and burrows of other neighboring rodent species including prairie dog and kangaroo rat burrows. This is the most cold tolerant member of their genus and they are mainly found in arid and semi-arid regions. They range throughout much of the western half of United States.

Class—**Mammalia** (mammals)
Order—**Rodentia** (rodents)
Family—**Geomyidae** (pocket gophers)
Genus—***Geomys***—9 species in Texas

Size: The largest species is the Texas Pocket Gopher which reaches 12.5 inches and can weigh up to 14 ounces. Other species average 8 to 10 inches in length.

Variation: The nine species of *Geomys* Pocket Gophers in Texas are so similar that most people could not distinguish between species. In fact, until relatively recently the Hall's, Jones's, and Llano Pocket Gophers were considered to be the same species as the Plains Pocket Gopher; and the Strecker's was regarded as the same species as the Texas Pocket Gopher.

Abundance: Texas, Plains, Attwater's and Baird's Pocket Gophers are common. Llano, Jones's, and Strecker's are uncommon. Hall's and Desert Pocket Gophers are rare in Texas but are more common in other parts of their range.

Habitat: This genus prefers friable soils with a high amount sandy or loamy content which facilitates easier burrowing. This group of pocket gophers are animals of lower elevations and they are replaced in mountainous regions by other genera.

Breeding: Some species may breed multiple times per year. Two or three young seems to be typical but litters of up to six may occur. Hybridization is known to occur in some species whose ranges overlap.

Natural History: To most Texans, the pocket gophers are probably the least understood mammals in the state. Most rural residents are familiar with the mounds of earth the pocket gophers pile up on the surface as they dig their burrows, but few people realize the diversity of the group. To most lay people, there is just one species known as the "Gopher." In fact there are at least thirty-five species in North and Central America ranging from Canada to Panama. Nine species are found in Texas. The name Pocket Gopher is derived from the fact that these rodents have cheek pouches (i.e. "pockets") in their cheeks that serve to collect food. They also have powerful front legs equipped with long claws for digging and use their incisors for chewing through tough patches of earth. Their tunnels average several hundred feet in total length.

Plains Pocket Gopher
Geomys bursarius

Presumed range in TX

Desert Pocket Gopher *Geomys arenarius*	**Baird's Pocket Gopher** *Geomys breviceps*	**Attwater's Pocket Gopher** *Peromyscus attwateri*	**Hall's Pocket Gopher** *Geomys jugossicularis*
Jones's Pocket Gopher *Geomys knoxjonesi*	**Strecker's Pocket Gopher** *Geomys streckeri*	**Llano Pocket Gopher** *Geomys texensis*	**Texas Pocket Gopher** *Geomys personatus*

Class—**Mammalia** (mammals)
Order—**Rodentia** (rodents)
Family—**Geomyidae** (pocket gophers)

Botta's Pocket Gopher *Thomomys bottae*	**Yellow-faced Pocket Gopher** *Cratogeomys castanops*

Size: Up to 10.75 inches in total length. Maximum weight about 9 ounces. Most are a bit smaller.

Variation: There are a total of 10 subspecies in Texas. As with most small mammals the differences in the subspecies are imperceptible except to experts.

Presumed range in TX

Size: Maximum length nearly a foot. Maximum weight about 11 ounces. Most are a bit smaller.

Variation: Mammalogists recognize 7 subspecies in Texas but all are very similar in appearance and resemble the specimen in the photo above.

Presumed range in TX

Abundance: Generally common but there are indications that some populations may be in decline.

Abundance: Common. Within its range it is one of the most common pocket gophers in the state.

Habitat: Utilizes a wide variety of habitats within their range. Can be found in mountain meadows and in desert basins. Unlike some other pocket gophers that require special soil conditions, the Botta's Pocket Gopher uses everything from sandy soils to clay based soils.

Habitat: This species is a resident of short grass prairies and arid grasslands from central Mexico to southwest Kansas and southeastern Colorado. They enjoy drier regions than many other pocket gophers. Their range includes most of the western third of Texas.

Breeding: Breeds year-round. Two litters per year are produced. Average litter is four or five young.

Breeding: Breeds mostly in the spring. Litter size averages only two young. At least one litter per year and maybe more.

Natural History: This species rarely ventures out of the burrow. Schmidly and Bradley in their book *The Mammals of Texas* states that Botta's Pocket Gophers spend 90 percent of their lives underground. The main foods are roots and tubers encountered during burrowing. They may also excavate beneath a desired plant and pull the entire plant down into the burrow. Like other pocket gophers these are solitary animals that live alone in the own burrow when not engaged in breeding or rearing of young. Taking into account side tunnels branching off the main tunnel the total length of their tunnels can exceed 400 feet. The side tunnels are mostly used for foraging but other specialized side tunnels may be used for a latrine, a nest chamber and one for a food cache. The depth of the tunnels varies according to use. Foraging tunnels are near the surface to provide access to plant roots. Main tunnel and nest chambers may be considerably deeper. The diameter of the tunnels matches with width of the gophers body. In regions where pocket gophers become extremely numerous they can be injurious to crops and have even been known to damage underground telephone cables. Poisoning campaigns can be effective but are environmentally devastating.

Natural History: Apparently soil type can affect the body size of populations in this species. Animals living in sandy soils grow larger than those living in regions where heavier, more dense soils occur. Presumably, it is more difficult and requires more energy expenditure to live in heavy soils and thus smaller bodies are favored by natural selection. Availability and quality of food items can also impact body size. For example, one study has shown that gophers living in alfalfa fields with unlimited access to high quality forage grew significantly larger (Patton and Brylski 1987). These gophers live a maximum of two years in the wild, with females living longer than males. These gophers can tolerate more arid conditions than many other pocket gophers. They are thus able to outcompete many pocket gophers of the *Geomys* genus. During periods of extended drought they will maintain or increase in population at the expense of other sympatric pocket gopher species. These are solitary animals and each individual inhabits it own burrow system. Their subterranean habits make them immune from many predators, but Badgers are capable of digging them out and snakes can enter their burrows. Their worst enemy is probably the aptly name Gopher Snake.

Class—**Mammalia** (mammals)

Order—**Rodentia** (rodents)

Family—**Heteromyidae** (kangaroo rats & pocket mice)

Genus—*Dipodomys* (kangaroo rats) 5 species in Texas

Size: Range in size from a total length of 9 inches to a total length of 14 inches. Maximum weights vary from 1.75 ounces to just over 4 ounces. The largest is the Banner-tailed Kangaroo Rat and the Texas Kangaroo Rat (12.5). The smallest is the Merriam's Kangaroo Rat. Gulf Coast Kangaroo Rat, Ord's, and Texas Kangaroo Rats are medium-size (about ten inches total length).

Variation: The Banner-tailed and Texas Kangaroo Rats have white tail tips. Gulf Coast, Ord's, and Merriam's Kangaroo Rats have black tail tips. Ord's and Gulf Coast Kangaroo Rats have five toes on the hind foot. The fifth toe is very small and not evident unless the animal is in hand. All other Kangaroo Rats in Texas have only four toes on the hind foot.

Abundance: Gulf Coast, Merriam's, and Ord's Kangaroo Rats are all common. The Banner-tailed Kangaroo Rat is generally uncommon but can be fairly common in places. Texas Kangaroo Rat is a rare animal listed as a threatened species.

Habitat: Kangaroo Rats are animals of arid and semi-arid regions and several species occur in some of the harshest deserts in North America. Most habitats utilized are in regions with sparse vegetative ground cover. The Ord's Kangaroo Rat favors sandy soils. By contrast the Texas Kangaroo Rat inhabits a region with clay soil which is much more difficult for burrowing. Merriam's Kangaroo Rat inhabits a wide variety of soil types. The Banner-tailed avoids loose soils.

Breeding: Some species have distinct breeding seasons while others can breed year-round. In all Kangaroo Rats the young are altricial but they develop rapidly and some may be sexually mature within two months.

Natural History: These secretive rodents are probably familiar to anyone who has driven a remote rural road in western Texas after dark. In some regions they can be easily observed on roadways at night. They are strictly nocturnal, so much so that some species will not even be active during a full moon. When observed they are easily recognized by their kangaroo-like gait and their long tails with pronounced hair tufts on the tip. Their hind legs are more than twice the length of the forelegs giving them their classic kangaroo-like appearance. They dig extensive burrow systems and will have several burrows within their territory. One burrow serves as a "full-time" home and maternity den while others are used mainly as quick escape tunnels scattered throughout their territory. The main burrow is often at the base of a bush and will have well a worn and highly visible path leading from the burrow and will have several visible paths that branch from the main path. Kangaroo Rats have cheek pouches for storing seeds to be carried back to the den burrow, a trait shared with the Pocket Gophers and Pocket Mice. Although they will drink water when it is available most Kangaroo Rats are highly adapted to living in dry environments and can obtain all their moisture requirements from the plant material they consume. In this manner they can survive without drinking. Their food is mostly seeds but they also eat some green plants. In periods of food scarcity they may eat some insects. Kangaroo Rats are prey for all types of predators and some herpetologists report that they are the favorite food of the Western Diamondback Rattlesnake. They use their extraordinary leaping ability to escape from predators. They can cover up to 9 feet in a leap and will make several leaps in different directions to confuse a predator.

Merriam's Kangaroo Rat
Dipodomys merriami

Presumed range in TX

Banner-tailed Kangaroo Rat
Dipodomys spectabilis

Presumed range in TX

Ord's Kangaroo Rat *Dipodomys ordii*	**Texas Kangaroo Rat** *Dipodomys elator*	**Coast Kangaroo Rat** *Dipodomys compactus*
Presumed range in TX	Presumed range in TX	Presumed range in TX

Class—**Mammalia** (mammals)
Order—**Rodentia** (rodents)
Family—**Heteromyidae** (kangaroo rats & pocket mice)
Genus—***Chaetodipus*** (pocket mice) 4 species in Texas

Size: The Rock Pocket Mouse is the smallest at only about 4 inches total length and weighing barely over a half an ounce. Others are 7 to 8 inches in length and weigh 0.75 to 1.5 ounces.

Abundance: All can be common species. The Hispid Pocket Mouse is the most widespread and is generally common but may be uncommon in some areas of its range.

Variation: Although there are 4 species of Pocket Mice in Texas, are all very similar in appearance except that the Hispid Pocket Mouse has fur that is a little coarser in texture than the other Pocket Mice.

Habitat: The Rock Pocket Mouse, as its name implies, likes rocky areas, a preference shared with the Nelson's Pocket Mouse that inhabits much of the same region in westernmost Texas. The Hispid Pocket Mouse likes grasslands, fallow fields, and overgrown fence rows. The Chihuahuan Desert Pocket Mouse is a species of the low desert, inhabiting desert basins and valleys.

Breeding: Breeding is in the spring for the Desert Pocket Mouse with two to six young produced. The Hispid Pocket Mouse may breed year-round and produce about six young per litter. Rock Pocket Mice produce three to six young. Nelson's breeds from February to March with average litter size of three.

Natural History: Similar in many respects to the related Kangaroo Rats. They are strictly nocturnal species that dig a burrow. Burrows may have several entrances and they will usually plug the entrance with soil during the day. Longevity is only about three years but few survive beyond a year and the annual mortality rates can be as high as 95 percent. Some may experience torpor during cold weather, but they are not true hibernators. The main food item of Pocket Mice is seeds. They will eat seeds of grasses, herbaceous plants, Mesquite, Creosote Bush, prickly pear cacti and many others. In agricultural areas the Hispid Pocket Mouse is sometimes a pest for farmers as it will raid recently planted fields for seeds. But the overall impact of these mice on humans is probably quite negligible.

Hispid Pocket Mouse
Chaetodipus hispidus

Presumed range in TX

Chihuahuan Desert Pocket Mouse
Chaetodipus eremicus

Presumed range in TX

Rock Pocket Mouse
Chaetodipus intermedius

Presumed range in TX

Nelson's Pocket Mouse
Chaetodipus nelsoni

Presumed range in TX

Class—**Mammalia** (mammals)

Order—**Rodentia** (rodents)

Family—**Heteromyidae** (kangaroo rats & pocket mice)

Genus—*Perognathus* (silky pocket mice) 3 species in Texas

Size: Merriam's Pocket Mouse reaches 4.5 inches in total length and weighs only 0.33 of an ounce. Silky Pocket Mouse has a total length of 4.5 inches, weight of less than 3 oz. Plains Pocket Mouse reaches 5 inches and weighs 0.5 ounce.

Abundance: All the *Perognathus* Pocket Mice in Texas are fairly common within their respective ranges.

Variation: There are three very similar species of *Perognathus* Pocket Mice in Texas. All three are very similar in appearance and are nearly the same size. All have soft, silky fur and small ears. The tail is only sparsely furred and about equal in length to the head/body length.

Habitat: Merriam's Pocket Mouse exists on a variety of soil types where ground vegetation is sparse. Silky Pocket Mice are also tolerant of varied soil conditions and its range in Texas includes the Chihuahuan Desert Ecoregion as well as the High Plains Ecoregion in the Panhandle. The Plains Pocket Mouse on the other hand is an obligate of sandy soil conditions.

Breeding: Merriam's breeds during warmer months with two litters of three to six annually. Breeding in the Silky Pocket Mouse is probably similar. Little is known about the breeding habits of the Plains Pocket Mouse.

Natural History: In spite of their name these rodents are more closely related to the Pocket Gophers than they are to the true mice. They are most closely related to the *Chaetodipus* genus of mice shown on the previous page. They resemble the Kangaroo Rats (genus *Dipodomys*) in appearance but have smaller hind legs and smaller feet. Although they don't hibernate they will stay in the burrows and enter periods of torpor during cold weather. Food items are mainly grass and weed seeds. They are mainly nocturnal but are sometimes abroad during daylight. The small hole of the burrow entrance is about the diameter of a man's finger. Burrow openings are plugged with dirt during the day.

Merriam's Pocket Mouse
Perognathus merriami

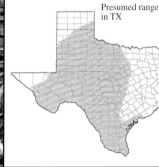

Silky Pocket Mouse
Perognathus flavus

Plains Pocket Mouse
Perognathus flavescens

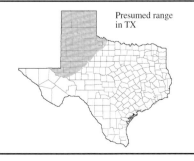

Mexican Spiny Pocket Mouse
Liomys irroratus

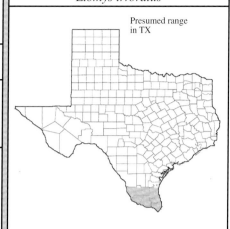

The Spiny Mice are mainly found in Latin America. They are best identified by their coarse fur made up of long, stiff hairs on the entire back. Thus the name "Spiny" Pocket Mouse.

Size: Maximum total length of 9.5 inches. Weighs about 2 to 2.25 ounces.

Abundance: Uncommon.

Habitat: Mainly a Mexican species that ranges into the southern tip of Texas.

Variation: No significant variation in Texas.

Breeding: There is very little information available on the reproduction of this species in Texas. But studies in Mexico where the species is more common indicate it probably breeds year-round. The litter size is probably an average of four with a maximum of eight.

Natural History: This is mainly a Mexican species whose range extends northward into the southern tip of Texas. Although a rare species in Texas it is quite widespread and common in Mexico. Mexican Spiny Pocket mice are strictly nocturnal. Like the other "Pocket" mice, they have fur-lined pouches on the outside of the cheek for storing foods to be carried back to the burrow. Food items are mostly seeds of trees and shrubs as well weeds and grasses. It reportedly lives in dense shrub thickets and palm forest in upland ridges in south Texas.

Class—**Mammalia** (mammals)

Order—**Soricomorpha** (shrews & moles)

Family—**Soricidae** (shrews)

Southern Short-tailed Shrew *Blarina carolinensis*	Least Shrew *Cryptotis parva*	Crawford's Desert Shrew *Notiosorex crawfordi*

  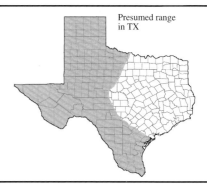

Presumed range in TX

Southern Short-tailed Shrew

Size: Average length of about 3.5 inches and weighs about 0.75 ounce to a maximum of 1 ounce.

Presumed range in TX

Least Shrew

Size: Tiny. One of the world's smallest mammals. Three inches and 0.25 ounce.

Presumed range in TX

Crawford's Desert Shrew

Told from the Least Shrew and the Southern Short-tailed Shrew by its longer tail.

Size: Length of about 3.25 inches and weighs about 0.33 of an ounce.

Variation: There are eleven known subspecies. All appear identical to lay persons. Two subspecies are known to occur in Texas.

Variation: Summer pelage is brownish, turning to slate gray during winter. There are two identical subspecies in Texas.

Variation: Slight variation in the shade of gray from fray with brownish above to pale, ashy gray. No known subspecies in Texas.

Abundance: Very common. Probably the most common shrew species in much of its range.

Abundance: Common. More common than most people realize. Their tiny size allows them to go unnoticed.

Abundance: Fairly common. Ranges throughout the western half of Texas and into southern Texas.

Habitat: Fond of damp woodlands and in fact can't tolerate excessively dry conditions. Avoids saturated soils however.

Habitat: Prefers early successional habitats and grassy areas and overgrown fields, but also rare in woodlands.

Habitat: This is a species of arid regions. Inhabits the Great Plains and North American Deserts Ecoregions.

Breeding: Breeding is believed to occur in spring and fall. Up to four litters of four to six young annually.

Breeding: Several litters per year is common averaging four to five young per litter. Young mature in about five weeks.

Breeding: Three to five young per litter. More than one litter annually is possible. Nest is made of grasses and fur.

Natural History: This species is easily confused with the Least Shrew, from which it can be distinguished by examining the teeth with the aid of a magnifying glass or dissecting microscope (Least Shrews have three visible unicuspids, Short-tail Shrews have four). Short-tail Shrews are primarily nocturnal animals and have very high metabolic rates. They are hyperactive animals that will eat as much as one-half their body weight daily! This species is known to have periods of intense activity followed by periods of lethargy. Food is a variety of insects, snails, earthworms, millipedes, etc. as well as much larger prey including mice that are as large as themselves. The Short-tailed Shrews are known to possess venomous saliva with which kills its prey. It has tiny eyes and its vision is quite poor. Known to utilize echolocation. Forages in runways beneath the leaf litter.

Natural History: Possessing an extremely high metabolism, this tiny mammal can consume its own weight in food daily. Like many other shrews they are known to cache food items. Although these shrews are rarely seen due to their diminutive size and reclusive habits, they are probably more common than generally perceived. Owls are a major predator and in fact the presence of these tiny shrews in a given area is often confirmed by examining owl pellets for skeleton remains. Known food items are caterpillars, beetles, other insects, snails, spiders, and earthworms. The local abundance of these small shrews is often difficult to determine because they are so small they often fail to trigger the capture mechanism on small mammal traps used to capture small mammals during biological surveys. Unlike most shrews this species commonly shares habitat with others of its kind.

Natural History: Like other tiny mammals the Crawford's Desert Shrew has a very high metabolic rate and will consume about 75 percent of its body weight daily. Food items are mostly invertebrates (worms, arachnids, insects) but some smaller vertebrates may also be eaten. They are adapted to living in dry regions and can persist without available drinking water. Their rapid metabolism requires a high activity level so they are probably active day and night. During daylight hours they probably stay in areas of heavy cover. They are capable of entering a state of torpor to conserve energy. Although this species is considered to be fairly common in Texas they are regarded as a threatened species in Mexico. Arid land habitats are especially fragile and easily damaged by human activity. Once destroyed deserts and arid plains are slow to recover to the natural state.

Class—**Mammalia** (mammals)

Order—**Soricomorpha** (shrews & moles)

Family—**Talpidae** (moles)

Eastern Mole
Scalopus aquaticus

Size: Six inches total length and weighs up to 3.75 ounces.

Abundance: Common in most areas of its range in the state with friable soils. May be increasing in the panhandle region of Texas.

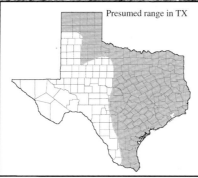

Presumed range in TX

Variation: As many as 6 identical subspecies in Texas

Habitat: Except for wetlands, these moles can be found in any habitat where soils are suitable for burrowing. They can be especially common in coastal regions, barrier islands and other areas where the soils are mostly sandy. They can be common in residential lawns and gardens.

Breeding: One litter per year, two to five young per litter.

Natural History: The most wide-ranging mole in America. Although considered a pest in suburban lawns and rural gardens, Eastern Moles actually perform some helpful tasks. The tunnels they dig help to aerate the soil and allow rainfall to penetrate more easily. The mounds of soil pushed to the surface from the burrow returns soil nutrients to the surface. They also prey heavily upon destructive grubs such as the Japanese Beetle. The pelage of the Eastern Mole is "reversible" and will lie smoothly against the skin whether mole is moving forward or backward in tight tunnels. The powerful forelegs allow this animal to burrow at an astonishing pace, and the webbed toes help move dirt aside. The eyes are tiny and covered with skin, and there are no external ears. This is a completely fossorial mammal that rarely appears above ground. They are superbly adapted to a subterranean lifestyle and Eastern Moles will spend 99 percent of their lives below ground. They can be sometimes be seen above ground when excessive rains flood the burrows and force them to the surface. They are most common in places where the soil is friable and they may be absent from harder clay-based soils.

Order—**Chiroptera** (bats)

Family—**Molossidae** (free-tailed bats) 4 species in Texas

Brazilian Free-tailed Bat
Tadarida brasiliensis

Size: Maximum 3.75 inches. Up to 0.5 ounce.

Abundance: The Brazilian Free-tailed Bat (shown above) and the Pocketed Free-tailed Bat are both common. Western Bonneted Bat and the Big Free-tailed Bat are rare.

Presumed range in TX

Variation: There are four species of Free-tailed Bats in Texas. Brazilian Free-tailed Bat, Western Bonneted Free-tailed Bat, Big Free-tailed Bat and Pocketed Free-tailed Bat.

Breeding: Females give birth to a single pup in late spring.

Natural History: Unlike most Texas bats, the free-tailed bats actually have a distinctly visible tail. The Brazilian Free-tailed Bat is a widespread species that ranges across the southern half of North America from coast to coast. In most areas of its range it uses caves both for roosting and hibernating. Roosts in caves and man-made structures in Texas can number in the millions. At least 20 million of the these bats roost in Bracken Cave in the Edwards Plateau. These bats have a distinctive musky odor and biologists familiar with the species can often detect the presence of large colonies just by using their nose. They are known to travel over 25 miles a night on their feeding forays. Three other similar species of Free-tailed Bat can also be found in Texas. Those ranges of those three species are shown below.

Big Free-tailed Bat *Nyctinomops macrotis*	**Western Bonneted Bat** *Eumops perotis* & **Pocketed Free-tailed Bat** *Nyctinomops femorosaccus*

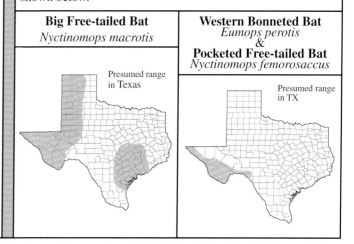

Presumed range in Texas

Presumed range in TX

Class—**Mammalia** (mammals)

Order—**Chiroptera** (bats)

Family—**Vespertilionidae** (vesper bats)

Hoary Bat *Aeorestes cinereus*	**Pallid Bat** *Antrozous pallidus*	**Big Brown Bat** *Eptesicus fuscus*

Size: Maximum 5.5 inches. Weight about 1 ounce.

Presumed range in TX

Variation: Males are slightly smaller.

Abundance: Widespread and presumed to be common.

Habitat: Primarily a forest species but ranges throughout the state and also inhabits deserts and grasslands where trees are present.

Breeding: Averages two pups born in mid-May to mid-June.

Natural History: This is one of the largest bat species in Texas. The wingspan of the Hoary Bat can be up to 16 inches. Its name comes from the white-tipped hairs of the fur on its back. Hoary Bats have the greatest distribution of any American Bat. They summer as far north as Canada and winter in the coastal plain of the southeastern United States. They are a migratory species and oddly, the sexes segregate themselves following breeding and most of those seen in the eastern US in summer are females. Males summer farther west in the great plains, Rocky Mountains, or west coast. In spring and fall both sexes can be found in Texas. Most probably winter in southern regions but some may stay in cooler regions and hibernate. In warm weather these bats will roosts in trees that are in edges of woodlands. They may roost in a clump of leaves or by clinging to the trunk.

Size: Maximum total length is just under 5 inches.

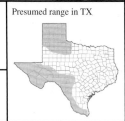
Presumed range in TX

Variation: Two identical subspecies in Texas.

Abundance: Common. Especially common in the Chihuahuan Desert.

Habitat: Favors rugged regions with rocky outcrops. Caves, abandoned mine shafts, man-made structures and deep crevices in rock faces are used as roosts.

Breeding: Breeds in the fall with two to four young born in late spring.

Natural History: Pallid bats exhibit a feeding behavior unique among Texas bats. They have been observed flying a few inches off the ground and pouncing on ground dwelling insects like crickets and scorpions. They may also catch flying insects on the wing in typical bat-like fashion. These bats are well-known to bat biologists for their distinctive odor which has been likened to the musk of skunk. They range across most of the western United States from extreme SE British Columbia in Canada to central Mexico. Throughout their range they occur in many desert and arid grassland regions. But here they are found in proximity to permanent water sources. These are rather large bats with a wingspan of 15 inches. They are a pale-colored bat (yellow brown above with whitish belly) with very large ears, (but not as large as those of the Big Eared Bats on the next page).

Size: Maximum total length 4.5 inches.

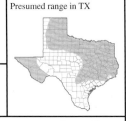
Presumed range in TX

Variation: Two identical subspecies in Texas.

Abundance: More common in southeastern and western parts of Texas.

Habitat: A forest species but also uses open fields, vacant lots, in both rural and urban areas. Sometimes seen hunting insects around suburban streetlights.

Breeding: Breeds in fall. Delayed fertilization. One or two born in late spring.

Natural History: Summer roosts are usually associated with human structures (buildings, eaves, bridges). Also known to use hollow trees and abandoned mines or caves. The primary food is reported to be beetles. This is perhaps one of the most recognizable bat species in much of their range. They are the large, brown bats that are common around human habitations and they range throughout most of the US and Canada in summer. In Texas they are oddly absent from the Edwards Plateau and south Texas. Roosting bats seen alone during warm weather are nearly always males. Females congregate into "maternity colonies" of up to several dozen adults to rear their young. These bats seem to tolerate cold fairly well and they remain active well into the fall. They may even be seen flying around by day in winter during prolonged warm spells.

Class—**Mammalia** (mammals)

Order—**Chiroptera** (bats)

Family—**Vespertilionidae** (vesper bats)

| Genus—*Corynorhinus* (big-eared bats) 2 species in Texas | Tricolored Bat *Perimyotis subflavus* |

Rafinesque's Big-eared Bat
Corynorhinus rafinesquii

Tricolored Bat
Perimyotis subflavus

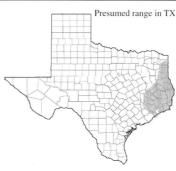

Presumed range in TX

Size: Maximum length 4 inches and weight of four tenths of an ounce.

Variation: There is no significant variation in this species in Texas.

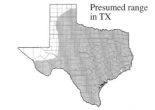

Presumed range in TX

Abundance: The Rafinesque's Big-eared bat is a rare animal in Texas.

Habitat: This is a forest species. In Texas it is found in the Piney Woods region and in the northernmost portion of the Western Gulf Coastal Plain. Uses natural cavities such as hollow trees or beneath loose bark for roosting. Also frequently roosts in man-made structures.

Breeding: Breeds in fall and gives birth to a single baby in spring.

Natural History: Like many bats this is a migratory species. It is seen in Texas mostly during warmer months but some may winter along the coast. In some regions of the US such as Florida it is found year-round. It may roost communally or singly, and like many bats it will sometimes roost among other species. Northern populations use caves, but in Texas it uses hollows in trees or under loose bark and in modern times it has taken to using man-made structures such as old barns or abandoned buildings. Food is mostly moths (as much as 90 percent). More nocturnal than many bats, these bats do not fly at twilight, instead waiting for full darkness. Females congregate in "nursery roosts" in the spring to give birth. Young bats can fly at about three weeks and may live up to ten years (Gonzales and Demere 2018). This bat occurs rather sporadically throughout its range and it is a very rare species in Texas. It is regarded as a Threatened Species by TPWD. Commercial logging in the Piney Woods region may posed a threat.

Townsend's Big-eared Bat
Corynorhinus towsendii

Size: Maximum length 4 inches and weight of four tenths of an ounce.

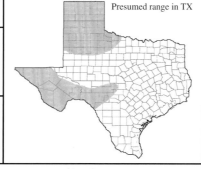

Presumed range in TX

Variation: Although there are two subspecies recognized in Texas, the differences between them are apparent only to a trained mammalogist and are imperceptible to the lay observer.

Abundance: Uncommon to rare in Texas. Apparently this species has declined in recent decades and it is now considered to be a species of concern by TPWD. Although widespread it seems nowhere common.

Size: 3.5 inches. Weight about 0.25 of an ounce,

Variation: Two identical subspecies occur in Texas

Abundance: Fairly common throughout its range in the state

Habitat: Woodlands, stream courses, and edges of fields bordering woodlands are favorite hunting areas. Caves and old buildings are used.

Breeding: Females give birth to one or two babies (pups) in May or June.

Natural History: Tricolored Bats are widespread and common throughout the eastern US. In fall they will migrate short distances to hibernacula. They sometimes emerge in warm weather during winter. Food is tiny airborne insects. They will leave the roost before dark and are often seen hunting at dusk. Hibernating bats may lose as much as 30 percent of their body weight. This species was formerly known as the Eastern Pipistrelle, (*Pipistrellus subflavus*).

Habitat: This is a widespread species that is found in many types of habitats but the presence of caves seems to be an important factor in its distribution. It will also use abandoned mine shafts which are common within its range throughout much of the western US. It can also be found in disjunct populations in the Ozark-Ouchita-Appalachian Forests Level II Ecoregion.

Natural History: Like the Rafinesqe's Big-eared Bat the Townsend's exhibits geographic sexual segregation of adults following breeding. Males then lead solitary lives while females form maternity colonies that can number several dozen (rarely hundreds) of individuals.

Class—**Mammalia** (mammals)

Order—**Chiroptera** (bats)

Family—**Vespertilionidae** (vesper bats)

| Genus—*Dasypterus* (yellow bats) 3 species in Texas | **American Parastrelle (Canyon Bat)** *Parastrellus hesperus* |

Size: Total length 4 inches to 5.75 inches. The Western Yellow Bat is the smallest at barely over 4 inches total length. The Northern Yellow Bat is the largest of the three.

Abundance: Southern Yellow Bat and Northern Yellow Bat are both uncommon in Texas. The Western Yellow Bat is the rarest and only a handful of specimens have been recorded from the Chihuahuan Desert Ecoregion.

Variation: There are three species of Yellow Bats in Texas and all are very similar in appearance. Experts identify species by close examination of things like teeth or by making measurements of the length of the ear or the length of the forearm.

Habitat: These bats roost in trees and are thus associated with regions where trees are present. The Southern Yellow Bat favors palm fronds for roosting and in Texas is found only in the southern tip of the state. The Western Yellow Bat is a desert species but usually associates with riparian habitat where trees like the Cottonwoods and oaks are present. Northern Yellow Bats in Texas inhabit the Coastal Plain.

Breeding: The Western Yellow Bat will have two young. Northern and Southern Yellow bats will produce two to four young annually.

Natural History: The Yellow Bats are primarily neotropical species whose ranges extend northward into the southern and western parts of Texas. They are very similar in many respects to the Red Bats (genus *Lasiurus* shown on the next page) and they were once regarded as belonging to that genus. They are also close relatives of the Hoary Bats (genus *Aeorestes*). Interestingly, the range of one species (the Northern Yellow Bat) coincides with the range of Spanish Moss and they are known to favor clumps of moss for roosting. As is implied by the common name the Yellow Bats all have a decidedly yellowish coloration. Male Yellow Bats are solitary animals, but the females come together in colonies when rearing young. Food is a wide variety of flying insect prey.

American Parastrelle (Canyon Bat)
Parastrellus hesperus

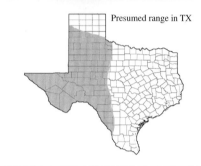

Presumed range in TX

Size: Small. Total length less than 3 inches.

Abundance: Common in west Texas.

Habitat: Found in western Texas where it inhabits rocky canyons and arroyos where streams are present.

Variation: There is no variation in this species in Texas.

Breeding: Two young is typical but may have only one pup. Young are born in late spring or early summer following spring breeding. By late summer the young are mature enough to fly.

Natural History: These small, grayish bats are easily recognized by their black face and ears. This species also goes by the name Canyon Bat, a reference to its preferred habitat in rocky canyons. It is more diurnal than many bat species and can be seen flying in late afternoon and well into the morning hours. Wildlife watchers and bat enthusiasts will know this species by its former name, the Western Pipistrelle (*Pipistrellus hesperus*). The change in name is the result of recent advances in DNA studies. They hunt swarms of small flying insects and when they locate a swarm they will gorge themselves, eating as much as one fifth of their body weight.

Northern Yellow Bat
Dasypterus intermedius

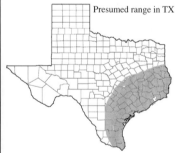

Presumed range in TX

Southern Yellow Bat *Dasypterus ega*	**Western Yellow Bat** *Dasypterus xanthinus*

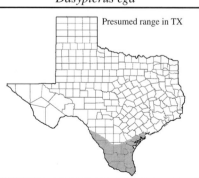

Presumed range in TX

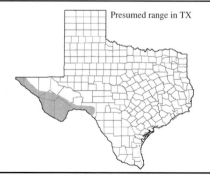

Presumed range in TX

Class—**Mammalia** (mammals)

Order—**Chiroptera** (bats)

Family—**Vespertilionidae** (vesper bats)

Eastern Red Bat *Lasiurus borealis*	**Seminole Bat** *Lasiurus seminolus*	**Silver-haired Bat** *Lasionycteris noctivagans*

Eastern Red Bat	**Seminole Bat**	**Silver-haired Bat**
Size: Maximum total length of 5 inches. Weighs up to 0.5 ounce. **Variation:** Males red, females frosted with white.  Presumed range in TX	**Size:** 4.75 inches and weights of up to 0.5 of an ounce. **Variation:** Some individuals show a "frosted" appearance. 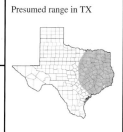 Presumed range in TX	**Size:** Maximum total length 4.5 inches weighs about an ounce. **Variation:** Two identical subspecies occur in Texas.  Presumed range in TX
Abundance: Fairly common in the eastern and central portions of the state, less common in west Texas.	**Abundance:** This is a fairly common species in forested regions of eastern Texas.	**Abundance:** A fairly common year-round resident. More common in southeastern and western parts of Texas.
Habitat: Woodlands and edge areas in both rural and urban regions. This is a forest species that shows a preference for deciduous woodlands.	**Habitat:** Found throughout the southeastern US in a variety of forested habitats. Often uses clumps of Spanish Moss as a roosting site.	**Habitat:** A forest species but also uses open fields, vacant lots, in both rural and urban areas. Sometimes seen hunting insects around suburban streetlights.
Breeding: Litter size is one to four with the pups born in late May or early June.	**Breeding:** Large litters for a bat with one to four pups are born in May or June.	**Breeding:** Breeds in fall. Delayed fertilization. One or two born in late spring.
Natural History: In summer this species usually roosts in trees by hanging from a limb. Usually solitary but sometimes more than one bat will roost together. Roosting bats resemble dead leaves. Trees chosen for roosting are often at the edge of a woodland bordering an open field. This is a migratory species that summers in the northern US and winters farther to the south. Eastern Red Bats in the coastal plain and in south Texas are probably year-round residents. The range is quite large and includes most of the United States east of the Rocky Mountains and in summer much of southeastern Canada. Hibernation takes place in hollow trees or beneath leaf litter on the forest floor, a very unusual tactic for a bat! Though mainly nocturnal, this species often flies in daylight.	**Natural History:** In Texas this bat inhabits the Piney Woods region and the northern portions of the Western Gulf Coastal Plain. They appear to be extending their range westward in the state. They are widespread across the southern United States but populations in more northerly regions migrate south in winter and swell the local populations in the deep south. As with most other bats they feed on the wing, eating flying insects of all variety. They are commonly seen around street lights catching insects drawn to the light. As with other *Lasiurus* bats they are mostly solitary animals that roost and forage singly. Their populations are regarded as secure, due in part to the fact that they are solitary animals that do not congregate in large colonies where the spread of disease can become a problem.	**Natural History:** Summer roosts are usually associated with human structures (buildings, eaves, bridges). Also known to use hollow trees and abandoned mines or caves. The primary food is reported to be beetles. This is perhaps one of the most recognizable bat species in much of their range. They are the large, brown bats that are common around human habitations and they range throughout most of the US and Canada in summer. In Texas they are oddly absent from the Edwards Plateau and south Texas. Roosting bats seen alone during warm weather are nearly always males. Females congregate into "maternity colonies" of up to several dozen adults to rear their young. These bats seem to tolerate cold fairly well and they remain active well into the fall.

Class—**Mammalia** (mammals)
Order—**Chiroptera** (bats)
Family—**Vespertilionidae** (vesper bats)
Genus—***Myotis*** (myotis bats)

Southeastern Bat *Myotis austroriparius*	Western Small-footed Bat *Myotis ciliolabrum*	Southwestern Little Brown Bat *Myotis occultis*
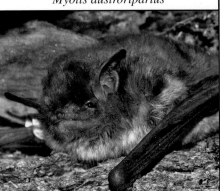		
Size: Total length about 3.5 inches with a wingspan of about 10 inches. Weighs 0.25 ounce. 	**Size:** Total length just over 3 inches with a wingspan of about 9.5 inches. Weighs 0.2 ounce. 	**Size:** Total length 3.5 inches wingspan 9 inches. Weighs 0.33 ounce. 

California Bat *Myotis californicus*	Yuma Bat *Myotis yumanensis*	Long-legged Bat *Myotis volans*	Cave Bat *Myotis velifer*	Fringed Bat *Myotis thysanodes*

Size: All *Myotis* are small bats, ranging in size from 3 to 3.5 inches and weighing from 0.2 to 0.33 of an ounce. The Long-legged Bat is the largest *Myotis* in Texas (3.75 inches), while the Western Small-footed Bat and the California Bat are among Texas's smallest bat species (barely 3 inches in length and about 0.2 of an ounce).

Abundance: The *Myotis* Bats found Texas range in abundance from common to rare. The rarest species is the Little Brown Bat. The Southeastern Bat and the Western Small-footed Bat are also rare or uncommon. The California Bat, Fringed Bat, and Long-legged Bat are all probably common within their respective ranges in Texas. Nearly all these bats were until recent times fairly common in America but they have been hard hit by the deadly fungal disease known as "White-nosed Syndrome."

Variation: Most bats present an identification problem for the average person, but the *Myotis* Bats can be especially confusing. Confirming the exact species requires looking very closely and usually means having the bat in hand.

Habitat: Some *Myotis* species may hibernate in caves but they will also use other places such as hollow trees or buildings for summer-time roosts. Some species are sometimes seen roosting in clumps by day beneath the shelter of roof overhangs, roofs of picnic pavilions, inside old barns, etc. A wide variety of habitats are utilized by these bats during warmer months including forests, fields, wetlands, and especially stream courses.

Breeding: Mating occurs in the fall with fertilization delayed until early spring. Young are born in late spring or early summer and all species form "maternity colonies" of females with young which may be in caves, buildings, hollow trees, or other structures. *Myotis* bats produce a single baby annually, except for the Southeastern Bat which can give birth to twins.

Natural History: Some *Myotis* Bats are migratory, moving south during winter months. Most feed in flight on flying insects but one species may feed by gleaning insects from leaves while hovering. Some like to forage primarily over water above ponds, creeks, and wetland areas. Throughout America, many bat species are in steep decline and many once common species have been hard hit by a fungal disease known as "White Nose Syndrome." The Little Brown Bat, once perhaps the most common *Myotis* in America, has been especially hard hit by this disease. All bats are remarkable little animals that consume untold numbers of injurious insect species, including many millions of mosquitoes. They are thus a valuable friend to man.

Class—**Mammalia** (mammals)

Order—**Chiroptera** (bats)

Family—**Mormoopidae** (leaf-chinned bats)	Family—**Phyllostomidae** (new world leaf-nosed bats)

Ghost-faced Bat
Mormoops megalophylla

Mexican Long-tongued Bat & Mexican Long-nosed Bat
Choeronycteris mexicana & *Leptonycteris nivalis*

Size: Total length just over 3.5 inches. Can weigh a little over 0.5 of an ounce. Wingspan 14 to 15 inches.	 Presumed range in TX	**Size:** Both average about 3.5 inches total length. The Mexican Long-tongued may be slightly larger.	 Mexican Long-tongued Bat (squares) / Mexican Long-nosed Bat (shaded)
Variation: No significant variation in Texas populations.		**Variation:** The Mexican Long-tongued Bat has an elongated muzzle.	
Abundance: Uncommon to rare in Texas.		**Abundance:** Both are rare but Long-tongued is rarest.	

Habitat: Inhabits a wide range of habitats from the desert southwest of the US to tropical rain forests in Central America. They do use montane habitats in warmer climates up to 7000 feet. The main habitat requirement appears to be a warm or mild climate. Uses caves, old mines, or derelict buildings for daytime roosts.

Habitat: These are warm climate animals that seem to be moving northward from Mexico into Texas. The Mexican Long-nosed Bat is found in two mountain ranges in the Big Bend region while the Mexican Long-tongued Bat is seen in Texas mostly in the southern tip of the state. Both species will use caves for roosting.

Breeding: Breeds in winter and gives birth to a single pup in spring or early summer. Females with young form maternity colonies separate from males and non-breeding females.

Breeding: Little is known about breeding in Texas. Most reproductive information available comes from AZ, NM, or Mexico. Birthing of a single pup occurs in spring.

Natural History: The Leaf-chinned Bats are a small family consisting of ten species most of which are found in tropical Central and South America. The Peter's Ghost-faced Bat is the only species that reaches the US. The name "Ghost-faced Bat" comes from the peculiar shaped ears and fleshy protuberances on this species' face, which give it a bizarre, somewhat "creepy" appearance. Like others in the Mormoopida family these are mainly tropical species that inhabit warm climates. In hotter regions they are non-migratory and they do not hibernate. In Texas some seasonal movement to warmer regions may occur in winter. Colonies of this bat in Latin America can contain a half million individuals. Though they will roost in caves containing other bat species, they will partition the cave habit into a segregated colony. Their primary food is believed to be large moths which they catch on the wing. Other types of flying insects are also consumed in smaller quantities. Favorite hunting areas are in canyons. They will also forage over creeks and rivers and can be seen in Texas along the Rio Grande River.

Natural History: The Phyllostomidae family is best known for being the group that contains the western hemisphere's three species of vampire bats. The members of this family that reach the US however are not the blood feeding bats of horror movie fame (although at least one species of vampire bat was recorded from Val Verde County Texas). The two more benign members of this family that can occur in Texas are the Mexican Long-tongued Bat and the Mexican Long-nosed Bat. As is apparent from their name both are found mostly south of the US border in Mexico. The designation as "leaf-nosed bats" comes from the fact that members of this family have an elongated projection on the nose, which bat biologists refer to as a "nose leaf." The purpose of the nose leaf is not completely understood but most experts lean towards it having a role in echolocation. Both these bats are nectar feeders and Agave is an important food source. In fact these bats are important pollinators of the Agave plant. Other types of flowers and fruits also provide food and they likely also consume some insects.

CHAPTER 5

THE BIRDS OF TEXAS

TABLE 2

— THE ORDERS AND FAMILIES OF TEXAS BIRDS —

(in order of appearance)

Class—**Aves** (birds)
Order—**Passeriformes** (perching birds)

Family	**Tyrannidae** (flycatchers)
Family	**Lanidae** (shrikes)
Family	**Corvidae** (jays, crows, ravens)
Family	**Vironidae** (vireos)
Family	**Aluidae** (larks)
Family	**Remizidae** (verdin)
Family	**Paridae** (chickadee family)
Family	**Aegithilidae** (bushtit)
Family	**Certhidae** (creepers)
Family	**Hirunidae** (swallows)
Family	**Bombycillidae** (waxwings)
Family	**Ptilagonatidae** (silky flycatchers)
Family	**Sylvidae** (gnatcatchers)
Family	**Sittidae** (nuthatches)
Family	**Regulidae** (kinglets)
Family	**Troglodytidae** (wrens)
Family	**Turdidae** (thrushes)
Family	**Sturnidae** (mynas & starlings)
Family	**Mimidae** (thrashers)
Family	**Motacillidae** (pipits)
Family	**Paraluidae** (warblers)
Family	**Cardinalidae** (tanagers & grosbeaks)
Family	**Passerilidae** (sparrows)
Family	**Calcariidea** (longspurs)
Family	**Passeridae** (weaver finches)
Family	**Fringilidae** (finches)

Family	**Icteridae** (blackbirds)

Order—**Cuculiformes** (cuckoos)

Family	**Cuculidae**

Order—**Coraciiformes** (kingfishcrs)

Family	**Alcedinidae**

Order—**Piciformes** (woodpeckers)

Family	**Picidae**

Order—**Columbiformes** (doves & pigeons)

Family	**Columbidae**

Order—**Galliformes** (quail & grouse)

Family	**Cracidae** (chachalacas, guans, currasows)
Family	**Phasinidae** (grouse)
Family	**Ondontophorida** (quail)

Order—**Caprimulgiformes** (hummingbirds, swifts & nightjars)

Family	**Trochilidae** (hummingbirds)
Family	**Apodidae** (swifts)
Family	**Caprimulgidae** (nightjars)

Order—**Strigiformes** (owls)

Family	**Tytonidae** (barn owl)
Family	**Strigidae** (typical owls)

Order—**Accipitriformes** (hawks, kites, osprey & eagles)

Family	**Pandionidae** (osprey)
Family	**Accipitridae** (hawks, kites & eagles)

Order—**Falconiformes** (falcons)

Family	**Falconidae** (falcons)

Order—**Ciconiiformes** (storks)

Family	**Ciconiidae**

Order—**Cathartiformes** (vultures)

Family	**Cathartidae**

Order—**Gruiformes** (cranes)

Family	**Gruidae**

Order—**Pelicaniformes** (pelicans, wading birds)

Family	**Pelicanidae** (pelicans)
Family	**Threskiornithidae—**(spoonbill, ibis)
Family	**Ardeidae** (herons, egrets)

Order—**Charadriformes** (gulls, terns, oystercatcher)

Family	**Laridae** (gulls, terns)
Family	**Haematopodidae—**(oystercatcher)

Order—**Gaviiformes** (loons)

Family	**Gaviidae**

Order—**Podicipediformes** (grebes)

Family	**Podicipedidae**

Order—**Anseriformes** (ducks & geese)

Family	**Anatididae**

Class—**Aves** (birds)

Order—**Passeriformes** (perching birds & songbirds)

Family—**Tyrannidae** (flycatchers)

Olive-sided Flycatcher *Contopus cooperi*	**Western Wood Pewee** *Contopus sordidulus*	**Eastern Wood Pewee** *Contopus virens*

Size: Length 7.5 inches.

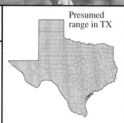
Presumed range in TX

Variation: No variation. No sexual dimorphism and the sexes are alike.

Abundance: Uncommon to rare in Texas.

Migratory status: Seasonal migrant throughout the state. Late April through May and August through September.

Habitat: The summer habitat is coniferous forests of mountains and boreal forests of northern North America.

Breeding: Nest is typically on a branch of a conifer and built of sticks, lichens and rootlets. One clutch per year. 3 to 4 eggs per clutch.

Natural History: These flycatchers are quite acrobatic in the air. They feed in typical flycatcher fashion by sallying forth from a high perch to snatch flying insects. Bees and wasps are reportedly a favorite food. They typically choose to perch on the highest dead snag in a semi-open area where they can survey for flying insect prey. This species avoids deep forest in favor of openings such as bogs, meadows or second growth and may benefit from forest fires or human activities such as logging. Paradoxically, the species has been declining in recent decades. This decline is possibly tied to changes in the winter habitat in tropical America. They are federally listed as Species of Concern by the USF&WS. A few will stop and nest in the mountains of westernmost Texas, but most continue farther north.

Size: About 6 inches.

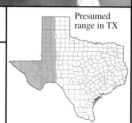
Presumed range in TX

Variation: May be greenish brown or grayish, often pale yellow below.

Abundance: Common in west Texas.

Migratory status: Migrant and summer resident. Most will pass through western Texas in April and May.

Habitat: Favors open and semi-open woodlands for summer habitat. May be seen in all habitats during migration.

Breeding: Breeds from mid May throughout the summer. Nest is built on a horizontal branch high in a tree. Not common as a breeding bird in Texas.

Natural History: This flycatcher is quite common as a migrant in west Texas and few will breed in the region. It is nearly identical to the Eastern Wood Pewee but savvy birders can distinguish them by their voice. Less sophisticated wildlife enthusiasts can rely on range to determine species. Feeds almost exclusively on insects, mainly caught in the air. Hunting method is to sit on an open perch and fly out to catch flying insects on the wing. Studying this bird and its sister species (Eastern Wood Pewee) on their winter habitat is difficult since they winter in the same regions of northern South America. They are mostly silent on wintering ground and both are so similar in appearance that they are impossible to distinguish in the field when not singing. Thus little is known for sure about how they spend the winter.

Size: About 6 inches.

Presumed range in TX

Variation: May be greenish brown or grayish, often pale yellow below.

Abundance: Common in east Texas.

Migratory status: Summer resident. Arrives later than many migrant songbirds, usually in late April or early May.

Habitat: Wood Pewees are forest birds but they favor small openings in the woods or edge areas.

Breeding: Nests are usually built high in trees in a terminal fork. Nest material consists of grasses and lichens. 2 to 4 eggs are laid.

Natural History: Even expert birdwatchers have to resort to listening to the songs of these two identical birds in order to distinguish between them. Range is the most reliable clue for the average observer. These nondescript little brown birds often go unnoticed except for the distinctive call from which they derive their name. Their "pee-a-weee" song is a common summer sound in the woodlands throughout most of US. Like other members of the flycatcher family, they hunt flying insects from high perches, swooping out to catch their food on the wing. They are typically fairly tolerant of humans and can sometimes be closely approached. They are very similar to Eastern Pheobe, but note orange lower bill and pale wing bars on both species of Wood Pewee.

Class—**Aves** (birds)
Order—**Passeriformes** (perching birds & songbirds)
Family—**Tyrannidae** (flycatchers)

Eastern Pheobe *Sayornis pheobe*	Say's Pheobe *Sayornis saya*	Black Pheobe *Sayornis nigricans*
 	 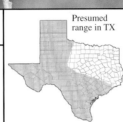	 

Eastern Pheobe
Sayornis pheobe

Size: 7 inches. Wings 10 inches

Presumed range in TX

Variation: No variation among individuals and no sexual dimorphism.

Abundance: Fairly common.

Migratory status: Year-round in eastern Texas, winter in south Texas, and summer only in the panhandle.

Habitat: Woodlands and woods openings. Also in rural yards or parks in wooded regions.

Breeding: Eastern Pheobes are early nesters. Nesting can occur by early March and there will often be a second nesting later in the summer.

Natural History: This species is most easily told from other Flycatchers by its habit of constantly wagging its tail down and up. Its nests are also distinctive, being constructed of mud and lined with mosses. Nests are placed beneath some form of overhang, most often the eaves of buildings. The cup shaped nest is plastered to the surface in the manner of many swallows. These are normally tame little birds that will allow humans to approach to within a few yards before flying off only a short distance. In appearance they are similar to the Wood Pewee but the Eastern Pheobe has a dark bill and lacks wing bars. In Texas this bird is most common in the eastern half of the state and becomes increasingly scarce to the west. It is a fairly common winter bird in the Coastal Plain of Texas but doesn't nest there.

Say's Pheobe
Sayornis saya

Size: 7 to 8 inches.

Presumed range in TX

Variation: Sexes alike. Juvenile has buff colored wing bars.

Abundance: Common in west Texas.

Migratory status: Year-round in west Texas, summer migrant in the Panhandle and winter migrant in south Texas.

Habitat: An arid land species. Inhabits dry grasslands, arid scrub and woodland and the harshest of deserts.

Breeding: 3 or 4 eggs is typical. Nest is usually on a ledge under an overhang of some sort, often an eave of a building. Two broods per year.

Natural History: These birds can be fairly tolerant of people and may place their nest under the eave of an occupied building. Like other Pheobes they will characteristically wag the tail up and down when on a perch. Feeds in typical "flycatcher" fashion by watching for flying insects from a perch and flying out to catch them on the wing. The *Texas Breeding Bird Atlas* reports confirmed nesting in the Chihuahuan Desert, Edwards Plateau and High Plains Ecoregions. Some birds will spend the winter in southeastern Texas in the Western Gulf Coastal Plain and the Southern Texas Plains Ecoregions. Elsewhere in its range in the state it is mostly a seasonal migrant. Its distinctive salmon-colored belly makes this species one of the more easily identified members of the flycatcher clan.

Black Pheobe
Sayornis nigricans

Size: 7 inches. Wings 11 inches

Presumed range in TX

Variation: No sexual dimorphism and no regional variations.

Abundance: Uncommon in Texas.

Migratory status: Mostly a year-round resident. But mainly a winter resident in the lower Rio Grande Valley.

Habitat: In Texas this is an arid land species. But in these dry landscapes it is nearly always found near water.

Breeding: The nest is made of mud and grasses and is sometimes plastered swallow-like against a vertical surface. Usually lays 4 eggs. Rarely more.

Natural History: The Black Pheobe may be regarded as a western, dark form of the Eastern Pheobe that in Texas lives more in deserts rather than forests. The head and breast are nearly black, and the dorsal surfaces are dark, sooty gray. Like other Pheobes it is a constant "tail wagger," and it feeds in typical flycatcher fashion by sallying forth from a perch to snatch flying insect prey in mid-air. Despite having a rather small range in Texas this bird has an enormous range and can be seen from Oregon to Argentina. Throughout most of its enormous range it is mainly a year-round resident. This is a species that may have benefited from the human population explosion, as man-made structures make for readily available nest sites. These are courageous little birds around the nest and will dive bomb potential threats.

Class—**Aves** (birds)
Order—**Passeriformes** (perching birds and songbirds)
Family—**Tyrannidae** (flycatchers)
Genus—***Empidonax***—(empid flycatchers) 9 species in Texas

Acadian Flycatcher
Empidonax virescens

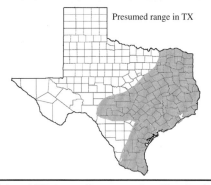

Presumed range in TX

Size: These flycatchers range in size from 5.25 inches (Least Flycatcher) to 6 inches (Gray Flycatcher). Most are about 5.75 inches.

Variation: Nine species of *Empidonax* flycatchers may be seen in Texas. All are so similar in appearance that even expert bird watchers have trouble identifying individual species (except the Gray Flycatcher, which is grayish). Most people must content themselves with calling them all "Empid Flycatchers."

Abundance: Acadian, Willow, Alder, Least, Yellow-bellied are all fairly common but the Acadian is the most common in Texas in summer. Dusky is only seen in western Texas. Hammond's, Cordilleran, and Gray are uncommon to rare.

Migratory Status: Acadian, Willow, and Cordilleran are summer residents and migrants. All others are seasonal migrants the pass through Texas each spring and fall as they migrate from wintering grounds in Latin America to breeding areas well to the north of Texas. Many species may migrate as far north as Alaska.

Habitat: All are woodland or brush loving species. Many, especially the Acadian and Willow Flycatchers, are fond of stream-side habitats, swamps, and marshes. Least Flycatchers prefer regenerative woodlands and edge areas. Yellow-bellied Flycatchers summer in the boreal forests of the far north. Dusky Flycatchers prefer mountains and foothills. Hammond's is also inclined to nest in mountainous regions.

Breeding: The Acadian Flycatcher weaves a flimsy nest of grass on a low branch and lays 2 to 4 eggs. The nest of the Acadian is also somewhat distinctive, with long filaments of grasses hanging down below the nest. Willow Flycatchers build their nest in the fork of a low branch or bush and lay 2 to 4 eggs. Least, Alder, Willow, Hammond's, Gray, and Yellow-bellied all breed well to the north of Texas but a few Cordillerans will breed in the western tip of the state. All usually lay 4 eggs in a nest woven of grasses and fibers and placed in a fork of a tree branch. Alder Flycatcher nests are coarsely woven cups typically placed in low bushes.

Natural History: Some species, like the Acadian Flycatcher, may be less numerous today due to the decline in forested habitats. The Willow Flycatcher on the other hand may be helped by the regeneration of successional forests. Serious birdwatchers find that the most reliable way to identify these small flycatchers is to learn their songs. In fact, Willow and Alder Flycatchers are so similar in appearance that visual identification alone is usually unreliable. To make matters worse, the "empids" also closely resemble the Wood Pewees! Wood Pewees, however, are slightly larger and lack distinctive eye rings.

Willow Flycatcher *Empidonax traillii*	**Alder Flycatcher** *Empidonax alnorum*	**Least Flycatcher** *Empidonax minmus*	**Dusky Flycatcher** *Empidonax oberholseri*
Presumed range in TX	Presumed range in TX	Presumed range in TX	Presumed range in TX
Hammonds Flycatcher *Empidonax hammondi*	**Gray Flycatcher** *Empidonax wrightii*	**Cordilleran Flycatcher** *Empidonax occidentalis*	**Yellow-bellied Flycatcher** *Empidonax flaviventris*
Presumed range in TX	Presumed range in TX	Presumed range in TX	Presumed range in TX

Class—**Aves** (birds)		
Order—**Passeriformes** (perching birds & songbirds)		
Family—**Tyrannidae** (flycatchers)		
Genus—*Myiarchus*—(crested flycatchers) 3 species in Texas		

Great-crested Flycatcher *Myiarchus crinitus*	Ash-throated Flycatcher *Myiarchus cinerascens*	Brown-crested Flycatcher *Myiarchus tyrannulus*

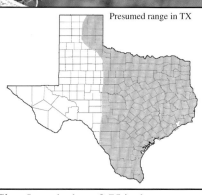Presumed range in TX	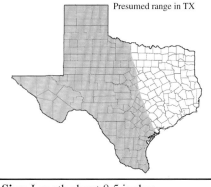Presumed range in TX	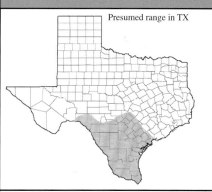Presumed range in TX
Size: Length about 8.75 inches.	**Size:** Length about 8.5 inches.	**Size:** Length about 8.75 inches.

Variation: These three species are quite similar in appearance. Range is often the best clue to identification in the field. Where ranges overlap the Ash-throated has a paler belly and throat compared to the Great-crested. Brown-Crested is almost impossible to distinguish from Ash-throated in the field, except by their songs.

Abundance: Fairly common, especially in the Piney Woods region.	**Abundance:** Common in southern and western Texas, less so in the panhandle.	**Abundance:** Fairly common, especially in the southernmost tip of the state.

Migratory status: All are summer residents in Texas and all winter in tropical regions from Mexico to South America. A few may appear as early as March, but peak arrival is probably in early to mid April. Most are gone by early September.

Habitat: All three can be found in tropical habitats in winter. In summer the Great-crested Flycatcher mainly utilizes the Eastern Temperate Forest ecoregion, but in Texas it ranges westward well into the Great Plains. The Ash-throated uses deserts and desert scrub while the Brown-crested shows a preference for subtropical woodlands and scrub.

Breeding: 5 or 6 eggs are laid in tree hollow, often an old woodpecker hole.	**Breeding:** 4 to 5 eggs in natural cavities or old woodpecker holes.	**Breeding:** 3 to 5 eggs are laid in a natural cavity.

Natural History: In many regards the Ash-throated Flycatcher can be considered to be the western version of the Great-crested and the Brown-crested as the tropical version. All are mainly tropical birds in winter as they will migrate to Mexico or Central America. The Ash-throated ranges as far south as Nicaragua and the Great-crested ranges into northern South America. The range of the Brown-crested goes as far south as Argentina. Where their ranges overlap it is believed that they avoid hybridization by responding only to the calls of their own species. The Ash-throated can live easily in deserts and may never need to drink, obtaining all its moisture requirements from the bodies of its insect prey. These birds often hunt high in the canopy and will hunt insects both on the wing and by foraging for prey in on branches and foliage in the treetops. The Great-crested will also eat fruit. All three species are cavity nesters and all are fond of old woodpecker holes. They depend to some degree on the larger woodpeckers within their breeding range for nest holes. Holes made by Downy Woodpeckers are too small so they need the larger woodpeckers like Red-bellied, Red-headed, Gila Woodpeckers, and the Northern and Gilded Flickers. They will also sometimes use man-made nest boxes.

Class—**Aves** (birds)

Order—**Passeriformes** (perching birds & songbirds)

Family—**Tyrannidae** (flycatchers)

Western Kingbird *Tyrannus vericalis*	**Couch's Kingbird** *Tyrannus couchii*	**Cassin's Kingbird** *Tyrannus vociferans*

Size: Length 8.75 inches.  Presumed range in TX	**Size:** Length 9.5 inches.  Presumed range in TX	**Size:** 9 inches. Wingspan 16 in. 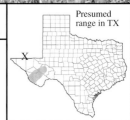 Presumed range in TX
Abundance: Common and widespread throughout western Texas.	**Abundance:** Fairly common within its limited range in the state.	**Abundance:** Uncommon. This bird's range in Texas is rather small.

Variation: The three species on this page can pose a problem for positive identification. Range is always a good clue for field identification. Where ranges overlap note that the Cassin's Kingbird has a grayer breast and a more pronounced white patch below the eye. Couch's Kingbird is larger and has a more pronounced dark patch behind the eye.

Migratory status: Summer resident that winters on the Pacific slope of Central America.	**Migratory status:** Year-round in the lower Rio Grande Valley. Summer resident north to about Corpus Christi.	**Migratory status:** Summer resident in Texas. A short-distance migrant that winters in central and southern Mexico.
Habitat: Prefers open country with some trees present. Savannas, pastures, grasslands, and deserts.	**Habitat:** Favors woodlands and brush, especially in riparian areas or near some body of water.	**Habitat:** In Texas the Cassin's Kingbird inhabits the mountainous areas of the Chihuahuan Desert Ecoregion.
Breeding: Nest is an open cup made from twigs, grasses, rootlets, etc. and lined with finer materials. Usually in a small tree or shrub. Up to 7 eggs.	**Breeding:** Nest is built on a horizontal limb. Materials includes twigs, bark, and frequently Spanish moss. Three to five eggs are laid.	**Breeding:** Breeding has been confirmed in Texas the Guadalupe and Davis Mountains and in riparian habitats along the Rio Grande River.
Natural History: Ranges throughout Texas with the exception of the Piney Woods region where it is replaced by the Eastern Kingbird. Like other flycatchers they are primarily insectivorous but they will also consume fruits and berries such as mulberries. With their lemon yellow bellies contrasted by their gray head, breast, and back these are familiar birds to many Texans. They appear to be a thriving species in Texas and have apparently increased in population since the modern settlement of Texas. Man-made structures such as fences, fence posts, and utility poles and wires are heavily utilized by these birds as they sit and watch for insect prey.	**Natural History:** The Couch's Kingbird was once regarded as a subspecies of the more southerly ranging Tropical Kingbird. South Texas is the only place in the US where this species can be seen regularly. Occasional individuals may wander up the Gulf Coast into Louisiana. They also range southward along the eastern slope of the Sierra Madre Oriental of Mexico into the Yucatan Peninsula. The very similar Tropical Kingbird is increasingly seen in the southern tip of Texas along the lower Rio Grande Valley, The two are so similar in appearance that the only reliable way distinguish them in the field is by learning their calls.	**Natural History:** The three Kingbird species shown on this page are sometimes referred to as the "Yellow-bellied Kingbirds" and the average observer is likely to have to content themselves with that level of identification. Diet is mainly insects caught both on the ground and in the air. Some fruits and berries are also eaten when in season. The bulk of the range for this species is in central Mexico where most birds live year-round. A few birds migrate northward into the US in summer in disjunct populations. Some are known to migrate as far north as eastern Montana in summer. Others migrate into Arizona, New Mexico, California and Colorado.

Class—**Aves** (birds)

Order—**Passeriformes** (perching birds & songbirds)

Family—**Tyrannidae** (flycatchers)

Eastern Kingbird *Tyrannus tyrannus*	**Scissor-tailed Flycatcher** *Tyrannus forficatus*	**Vermilion Flycatcher** *Pyrocephalus rubinus*
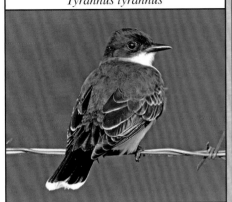		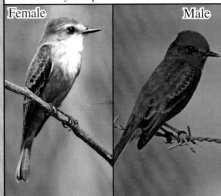 Female / Male

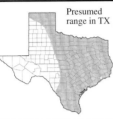 **Size:** Length 8.5 inches.

Abundance: Most common in eastern Texas. Less common to the west.

Presumed range in TX

Variation: No significant variation.

Migratory status: Summer resident that arrives in late March to early May.

Habitat: Prefers open fields and pastures in rural areas. In urban settings it likes open parks and large empty lots. Commonly seen perched on fences.

Breeding: Sturdy nest is built of twigs and grass and is placed on limb near the top of large tree. The average clutch size is 3 to 5 eggs. One clutch per year.

Natural History: The name "Kingbird" is derived from its aggressive defense of territory against other birds, including even large hawks! Hunts flying insects from an open perch, which is frequently a fence or power line. When flying insect prey is spotted they will launch themselves into an attack that often results in an aerial "dogfight" between bird and insect. These are conspicuous birds. Their charcoal gray upper parts contrast strongly with a whitish breast and belly. The bright reddish-orange blaze on the top of the head is usually not visible to the casual observer. Though a common summer resident in Texas, there are many more individuals that will pass through the eastern portions of the state during migration. All will fly south in fall and spend the winter in South America.

 **Size:** Up to 14.5 inches.

Abundance: Fairly common to common in nearly all of Texas.

Presumed range in TX

Variation: Males have longer tails.

Migratory status: Summer resident. Winters in Mexico and Central America.

Habitat: On breeding range the habitat is grassland, pastures, prairies, scrublands, semi-desert and desert. Seen statewide except western tip of the state.

Breeding: Breeds throughout the southern Great Plains region. Nest is fairly low in small trees and bushes. 5 eggs is a typical clutch.

Natural History: The Scissor-tailed Flycatcher is a common summer resident of the southern plains of North America. Most will winter in Mexico and Central America but some will winter in Florida's Everglades. With its long, deeply forked tail this is one of America's most recognizable birds. The length of the tail can vary with both sex and age, with older males having the longest tails. A fairly common to common summer resident from the Big Bend region of Texas eastward to central Louisiana. Summer range extends north to sw Missouri and extreme southern Nebraska. They are known to wander widely and because they are such extravagantly beautiful birds they rarely go unnoticed. Vagrant specimens have been recorded in every state in the southeast and as far north as New Jersey.

 **Size:** 6 inches. Wingspan 10 in.

Variation: A sexually dimorphic bird (unlike most flycatchers).

Presumed range in TX

Abundance: Fairly common.

Migratory status: Year-round resident, summer resident, and winter migrant.

Habitat: Found in a variety of warm climate habitats from deserts to tropical rainforests. In Texas it likes to live in proximity to water (streams, ponds, etc).

Breeding: The brightly colored male performs a breeding display that includes flying high into the air and fluttering downward while singing.

Natural History: This is a warm climate bird that moves northward into Texas in summer. Some birds will winter along the Gulf Coastal Plain and in some regions of south Texas this is a year-round resident species. They feed on insects and catch much of their food on the wing in typical flycatcher fashion. They reportedly eat many honeybees. The bright red colors of the male make this perhaps the most recognizable flycatcher in Texas. Some experts have noted a decline in this species, while still others say they are increasing in range and numbers. Both scenarios could be true as many wildlife populations wax and wane in numbers through the decades. At any rate, the species seems to be secure in most of its range, although habitat loss is always a threat these days.

Class—**Aves** (birds)

Order—**Passeriformes** (perching birds & songbirds)

Family—**Tyrannidae** (flycatchers)	Family—**Lanidae** (shrikes)	Family—**Corvidae** (crows & jays)

Great Kiskadee
Pitangus sulphuratus

Loggerhead Shrike
Lanius ludovicianus

Chihuahuan Raven & Common Raven
Corvus cryptoleucus & Corvus corax

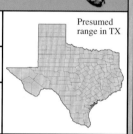

Chihuahuan Raven

Size: 10 inches. Wings 15 inches

Presumed range in TX

Variation: No variation.

Abundance: Fairly common within range.

Size: 9 inches. Wingspan 12 in.

Presumed range in TX

Variation: No variation.

Abundance: Uncommon to rare in Texas.

Size: 19.5 to 24 inches.

Light gray: Chihuahuan only

Dark gray: both species

Variation: Size differences.

Abundance: Both are uncommon to rare.

Migratory status: Year-round resident in southernmost Texas. Appears to be expanding its range northward.

Migratory status: Year-round in most of the state. Mainly just a winter resident in the lower Rio Grande Valley.

Migratory status: Both Raven species are year-round residents in Texas. Some movement may occur in winter.

Habitat: This is a primarily tropical species that has recently expanded its range into Texas. Prime habitat in Texas for this species is riparian woodlands.

Habitat: Open to semi-open habitats are preferred. In Texas this species is utilizes coastal areas, pastures, open fields and edge areas.

Habitat: The Chihuahuan Raven inhabits arid regions in Texas where it is found at lower elevations than the Common Raven, which likes mountains.

Breeding: Builds a large oval-shaped and covered nest with a side opening high in a tree. 2 to 6 eggs may be laid.

Breeding: Shrikes build a bulky nest of sticks in a thick bush or small tree. Lays up to 7 eggs.

Breeding: Nest is large and bulky, sometimes used for years with material added annually. Average about 5 eggs.

Natural History: The Great Kiskadee is mainly a Central and South American species. It has always been found in lowland regions of Mexico and in recent decades has expanded its range northward into southern Texas. They feed on a wide variety of invertebrate prey including flying insects caught on the wing. They also forage in trees and on the ground and have been known to snatch small fish or tadpoles from shallow water in the manner of a kingfisher. They will also eat berries and fruits. This is an extremely common bird in Central and South America. In fact, it is one of the most widespread members of the flycatcher family. And they are becoming more and more common in the southern tip of Texas. Like other Tyrannidae, they are aggressive birds.

Natural History: These fierce little birds are much like a miniature raptor. They hunt mostly insects, but will also attack and kill lizards, mice, small snakes, and birds as large as themselves. Sometimes called "Butcher Bird," they kill with a powerful beak and have the unusual habit of caching food items by impaling the bodies of prey onto a thorn or fence barb. They will form permanent territories which they defend from other shrikes. An endemic North American bird, Loggerhead Shrikes ranges from south-central Canada to southern Mexico. Sadly, this unique species is declining throughout much of the northern portions of its range. Most experts blame modern agricultural practices that create expansive fields of mono-culture crops.

Natural History: Like their relatives the crows, the ravens are intelligent, highly adaptable birds. They are consummate opportunists that will consume a wide variety of plant and animal matter ranging from carrion to human garbage. They are also known for their aerial antics and flight maneuvers and for their playful mischievousness. They are equally at home in remote wilderness or regions of significant human habitation. The Common Raven occurs in Texas in much smaller numbers. The Common Raven is larger than its Chihuahuan cousin but is otherwise nearly impossible to distinguish in the field. The Common Raven can be found in Texas mostly in the Trans-Pecos and Edwards Plateau regions and prefers higher elevation habitats.

Class—**Aves** (birds)

Order—**Passeriformes** (perching birds & songbirds)

Family—**Corvidae** (crows & jays)

American Crow *Corvus brachyrhynchos*	**Fish Crow** *Corvus ossifragus*	**Blue Jay** *Cyanocitta cristata*

American Crow	Fish Crow	Blue Jay
Size: 19 inches. Wings 39 inches Presumed range in TX	**Size:** 17 inches. Wings 33 inches — Presumed range in TX	**Size:** 11 inches. Wingspan 16 in. — Presumed range in TX
Variation: No variation.	**Variation:** No variation.	**Variation:** No variation.
Abundance: Common. 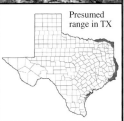	**Abundance:** Rare in Texas.	**Abundance:** Common. 

Migratory status: Year-round resident in most of the state. Mainly a winter resident in the Panhandle.

Migratory status: Year-round resident that may be expanding its range westward along the Red River.

Migratory status: Year-round resident in most of its range in Texas. Winter only in western and southern Texas.

Habitat: Occurs in virtually all habitats except desert areas. Most common where there is a patchwork of woods and open spaces.

Habitat: Mainly a species of the lower coastal plain. Follows major river systems inland. In Texas found along the eastern coast, Sabine and Red Rivers.

Habitat: Nearly statewide from dense woodlands to semi-open farmlands. Also suburban and urban neighborhoods. Woodlands are favored.

Breeding: Crows build a bulky stick nest high in the fork of a tree, usually well hidden by thick foliage. 4 eggs is typical.

Breeding: Large stick nest is placed in a tree crotch. Averages about 4 eggs. A single clutch is produced annually. Often nests in colonies.

Breeding: Builds a stick nest fairly high up on a branch or in a fork. Lays an average of four eggs. Doesn't breed in western Texas.

Natural History: Crows are omnivores that will eat virtually anything, including the young and eggs of other birds. They are among the most intelligent and resourceful of birds. They may be seen in pairs, small groups, or large flocks numbering in the hundreds. Highly adaptable, crows have fared well in human-altered habitats and the species is more common today than prior to European settlement. It is almost certain to remain a common species. As a testament to the crow's intelligence, in rural areas where hunting is commonplace, they are extremely wary of humans; while in protected parks and urban regions they will become quite accepting of the presence of humans. and will raid dumpsters for garbage.

Natural History: Identical to the America Crow but smaller, the Fish Crow occurs throughout America's Coastal Plain. They are often seen in the company of their larger cousin and when seen together the Fish Crow can be distinguished by its smaller size. Expert bird watchers can identify this species by its call, which is higher pitched than that of the American Crow. A southern species that historically was found in coastal areas and lowlands of the lower coastal plain, the Fish Crow has expanded its range northward over the last few decades. Today they range well up into the Mississippi River Valley, appearing as far north as St. Louis. They can be extremely common around estuaries and in coastal areas.

Natural History: The Blue Jay's handsome blue, black, and white feathers and distinctive crest make it one of the most recognizable birds in the state. They mainly eat insects, acorns, and grains, but also eat eggs and young of other songbirds. They will aggressively mob much larger birds like hawks and owls, as well as snakes and house cats. Members of this family are relatively long-lived. The record life span for a wild Blue Jay is 18 years, but a captive specimen was reported to have lived for 26 years. An endemic American bird, Blue Jays are found throughout the eastern half of the United States from about the Rocky Mountains eastward. They also range northward into Canada but well below the Arctic Circle.

Class—**Aves** (birds)
Order—**Passeriformes** (perching birds & songbirds)
Family—**Corvidae** (crows & jays)

Steller's Jay *Cyanocitta stelleri*	**Green Jay** *Cyanocorax yncas*	**Woodhouse's Scrub Jay** *Aphelocoma woodhouseii*

Size: Length 11.5 inches. 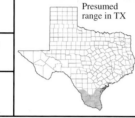 *Presumed range in TX*	**Size:** Length 10.5 inches. *Presumed range in TX*	**Size:** Length 11.5 inches. 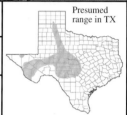 *Presumed range in TX*
Variation: No variation.	**Variation:** No variation.	**Variation:** No variation.
Abundance: Rare in Texas.	**Abundance:** Uncommon.	**Abundance:** Uncommon.

Migratory status: Year-round resident within its very limited range in Texas. Some elevational movement in winter.

Habitat: Coniferous forests and mixed pine-oak woodlands in the western portions of North America. Will also use deciduous woods and riparian habitats.

Breeding: Nest is a bulky cup of twigs, grasses and other matter mixed with mud. Clutch size is usually 4 but may be up to 6. Both parents feed young.

Natural History: This is primarily a montane forest species. It is widespread throughout the Rockies and other mountain ranges in the western United States and Canada. Eats a wide variety of invertebrate prey and occasionally small vertebrates such as mice and lizards. Seeds are widely consumed, especially acorns which are important foods in fall and winter. Berries and fruits are also consumed when available. In parks and picnic areas these birds can become quite tolerant of humans as they learn that campers and picnic goers are a source of easy meals. This species is most common in the Pacific Northwest and the higher elevations of the Rocky Mountains. In Texas they breed only in the Davis and Guadalupe Mountains.

Migratory status: Year-round resident in the southern tip of Texas. Breeds mostly in the Rio Grande valley.

Habitat: A tropical species that ranges from southern Texas to Honduras with disjunct populations in South America. Texas habitat is riparian woodlands.

Breeding: Breeds in riparian woodland and scrub. Three to five eggs is typical. Fledgling birds are tolerated within the parents territory for up to a year.

Natural History: Also frequently called the "Rio Grande Jay" in Texas. Like many of South Texas's iconic bird species this is primarily a tropical bird that ranges northward into the southern tip of Texas. It is one of the species that draws thousands of birdwatchers to the lower Rio Grande Valley each winter. The Green Jay is a regular visitor to the bird feeders that are maintained at state parks, wildlife refuges and visitor centers throughout the lower Rio Grande valley. This makes it an easy species for birders to check off their "life list." Like all members of the Corvidae family the Green Jay is an intelligent and resourceful bird. They have even been observed using sticks to pry off loose bark from trees to get to insect prey.

Migratory status: A year-round resident in Texas. May move short distances in response to harsh weather.

Habitat: Desert grasslands, arid scrub and especially pinyon-pine and juniper woodlands in arid to semi-arid environments.

Breeding: A maximum of five eggs. Nesting in Texas occurs mostly in the Edwards Plateau and in the foothills of the Davis and Guadalupe Mountains.

Natural History: Until recently the Woodhouse's Scrub Jay and the California Scrub Jay were regarded as the same two subspecies of the Western Scrub Jay. Recent taxonomic research has resulted in the splitting of these two disjunct populations into two distinct species. This is a species of the interior southwest with the heart of its range in the Colorado Plateau physiographic province (see Figure 2 on page 4). In Texas this species is probably most common in the Edwards Plateau ecoregion. They may also be locally common in the Big Bend region where there are lots of oak, pine, and cedar, mostly in the foothills of that regions mountain ranges. Insects, small animals, fruits, and seeds are eaten. Acorns are favored.

Class—**Aves** (birds)

Order—**Passeriformes** (perching birds & songbirds)

Family—**Corvidae** (crows & jays)	Family—**Vironidae** (vireos)	
Mexican Jay *Aphelocoma wollweberi*	**White-eyed Vireo** *Vireo griseus*	**Bell's Vireo** *Vireo bellii*

Size: Length 11.5 inches.	**Size:** Total length 5 inches.	**Size:** Length 4.75 inches.
Variation: No variation.	**Variation:** No variation.	**Variation:** No variation in TX.
Abundance: Very rare in TX. 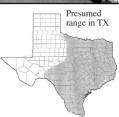 Presumed range in TX	**Abundance:** Fairly common. Presumed range in TX	**Abundance:** Rare in Texas.  Presumed range in TX

Migratory status: Year-round resident. May move attitudinally in response to seasonal weather changes.

Habitat: Semi-arid and arid woodlands of pine, oak, and juniper from desert basins to over 11,000 feet in the mountains of Mexico.

Breeding: Nest is in a tree. Usually near the trunk or in a fork. Up to 6 eggs may be laid.

Natural History: This rare bird is very similar to the Woodhouse's Scrub Jay but is stockier in build. Also note white at base of bill. It occurs in Texas only in the vicinity of Big Bend National Park. Most of its range is south of the US border in Mexico, but they also occur in the mountains of SE Arizona and SW New Mexico. Acorns and the seeds of pines are important winter foods for this species and the will gather and store seeds and nuts. Invertebrates and small vertebrates are also consumed opportunistically. Berries and agave nectar are also listed as food items by Cornell University's ornithology website allaboutbirds.org. These are social birds that often exist in small flocks of related birds numbering from a half dozen to two dozen individuals.

Migratory status: Seasonal migrant in most of eastern half of Texas. Winter resident along the gulf coast.

Habitat: Dense thickets and early successional deciduous woodlands are favored. Also in overgrown fields with small saplings and thickets.

Breeding: Nest is a woven, hanging basket held together with silk from caterpillars or spiders. 3 to 5 eggs.

Natural History: This is the only vireo with a white iris, making identification easy. Nest parasitism by Brown-headed Cowbirds is estimated to be as high as fifty percent, with no young surviving in parasitized nests. Highly insectivorous. Caterpillars are a favorite food item. Will also eat fruit. White-eyed Vireos may be seen year-round in coastal regions. Birds summering farther to north do migrate south in winter, some as far as Central America. Nest parasitism by Brown-headed Cowbirds possess a constant threat and deforestation contributes to the problem. Brown-headed Cowbirds tend to avoid deep woods in favor of more open habitats. Loss of large tracts of woodland makes life easier for the cowbirds and more difficult for the host species.

Migratory status: Summer resident that arrives from mid-March to late April. Flies south in September or October.

Habitat: Successional habitats with dense understory are favored. In dry regions, often found near water or in riparian situations.

Breeding: Successful nesting requires dense understory to hide the nest from Brown-headed Cowbirds. 2 to 4 eggs.

Natural History: In Texas this species appears to be more common along the Rio Grande River in Big Bend National Park. It has apparently declined from historical numbers in the eastern portions of the state (the Texas Breeding Bird Atlas). These birds tend to forage in lower branches and in the dense vegetation of thickets. They feed by gleaning small insects, spiders, etc. from branches and leaves. They will also eat some berries. Both sexes participate in building the nest, which is usually in the fork of a sapling just a few feet off the ground. The population of these birds may have declined in some areas of Texas but they are generally regarded as a species of low concern by monitoring organizations. Brown-headed Cowbirds may be their biggest threat.

Class—**Aves** (birds)
Order—**Passeriformes** (perching birds & songbirds)
Family—**Vironidae** (vireos)

Black-capped Vireo *Vireo atricapilla*	**Gray Vireo** *Vireo vicinior*	**Yellow-throated Vireo** *Vireo flavifrons*

Black-capped Vireo
Vireo atricapilla

Size: 4.5 inches. Wingspan 7 in.

Abundance: Endangered.

Variation: Female has grayer head.

Presumed range in TX

Migratory status: Summer resident that winters on the west coast of Mexico. Arrives in Texas by late March to early April and departs in the fall.

Habitat: Semi-open grasslands with scattered clumps of dense shrubbery and stunted trees are the preferred habitat for this species in Texas. Scrub Oak habitats are also important.

Breeding: Nest is cup shaped and low to the ground in a shrub less than 4 feet from the ground. 3 or 4 eggs are incubated by both sexes.

Natural History: This species was listed as endangered in 1987. The loss of nesting habitat is probably the main reason for this birds decline in Texas. Lack of wildfires that kept trees and shrubs from growing very large coupled with the clearing of land of brush for pastures seems to have been the main reason for the decline. Brown-headed Cowbirds can locate vireo nests much easier when they are not concealed in a thicket and cowbird nest parasitism is a major threat. At Wichita Mountains National Wildlife Refuge in Oklahoma prescribed fire is used to maintain the type of brushy habitat required by this species. In Texas there are no comparable public lands for habitat restoration.

Gray Vireo
Vireo vicinior

Size: 5.5 inches. Wingspan 8 in.

Abundance: Uncommon.

Variation: No variation, sexes alike.

Presumed range in TX

Migratory status: Mainly a summer resident and short distance migrant that winters in the states of Sonora and Baja Sur, Mexico. Year-round in Big Bend.

Habitat: This is a desert species that can be found in all of America's desert regions. In Texas they tend to inhabit lower elevations that other desert dwelling vireos.

Breeding: Nest is a hanging basket attached to stems of a shrub close to the ground. 3 or 4 eggs are laid and incubated by both sexes.

Natural History: The Gray Vireo is a rather plain, drab-colored vireo with a small range in Texas. It spends much of its time in dense vegetation and is thus not a bird that is well known to most Texans. Insects are eaten in summer and some birds will eat fruits in winter. They forage for insects in shrubs low to the ground or on the ground. Springtime males are most conspicuous as they perch in the open and sing their territorial songs. During much of the rest of the year they can be hard to locate. Although they are uncommon they are not regarded as threatened or endangered. But the ongoing destruction of desert habitats across the southwest to create new orchards may be a threat.

Yellow-throated Vireo
Vireo flavifrons

Size: 5.5 inches. Wingspan 9.5 in.

Abundance: Fairly common.

Variation: No variation, sexes alike.

Presumed range in TX

Migratory status: A long-range migrant that winters as far away as northern South America. Returns to North America in April.

Habitat: A woodland bird that will inhabit a wide variety of forest types excluding stands of pure conifers. More common in areas of extensive forest where it prefers edge areas.

Breeding: The nest is a woven basket usually suspended from the fork of a small branch at the mid-story level. Four eggs is typical.

Natural History: The nest is usually located in a branch overhanging a forest opening such as a lane or a stream. Feeds on a wide variety of arthropods with caterpillars being a mainstay. Also eats small amount of berries and seeds in the fall. The biology of this species is not as well understood as with many other vireos, but it is known that it has decreased in numbers in areas of deforestation. As with many small woodland songbirds, the nest of the Yellow-throated Vireo is subject to parasitism by cowbirds. The summer range of this species coincides closely with the Eastern Temperate Forest Level I Ecoregion. The winter range is from southern Mexico to South America.

Class—**Aves** (birds)

Order—**Passeriformes** (perching birds & songbirds)

Family—**Vironidae** (vireos)

Blue-headed Vireo *Vireo solitarius*	**Plumbeous Vireo** *Vireo plumbeus*	**Cassin's Vireo** *Vireo cassinii*

Size: 5.75 inches. Wingspan 9.5 in. **Variation:** Juveniles are drabber. **Abundance:** Fairly common. 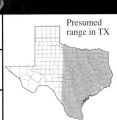 Presumed range in TX	**Size:** 5.5 inches. Wingspan 10 in. **Variation:** No variation. **Abundance:** Fairly common.  Presumed range in TX	**Size:** 5.5 inches. Wingspan 9.5 in. **Variation:** No variation. **Abundance:** Uncommon.  Presumed range in TX
Migratory status: A spring/fall migrant in much of the state and a winter resident along the gulf coast and in south Texas.	**Migratory status:** A spring/fall migrant and rare summer resident in the westernmost Texas. Most pass through but a few nest in the mountains.	**Migratory status:** A spring/fall migrant that passes through west Texas as it travels from wintering grounds in Mexico to the west coast of America.
Habitat: This vireo likes expanses of mature forests, and is also partial to conifers for its summer habitat. It thus summers mostly well to the north of Texas in the boreal forests of Canada.	**Habitat:** In Texas this species uses wooded mountain slopes and riparian habitats. Migrators may be seen almost anywhere in the western tip of the state, but usually associated in areas with trees	**Habitat:** In summer occupies a wide variety of forest habitats from sea level to high in the mountains (at least 8,000 feet). Migrating birds might be seen in almost any habitat.
Breeding: Nest construction is similar to other vireos. A tightly woven cup is suspended from a horizontal fork. Four eggs is typical.	**Breeding:** This is an uncommon breeding in Texas in the mountains of the Big Bend region. 3 to 5 eggs is typical and are incubated by both sexes.	**Breeding:** Does not breed in Texas. Breeds in the Pacific Mountain System from California to British Columbia. Nest is a cup suspended from a branch.
Natural History: Also known as the Solitary Vireo. Blue-headed Vireos breed and rear their young mostly in Canada and in the Appalachian Mountain range. They winter from the lower coastal plain of the southeastern US (including coastal Texas) all the way to Central America. Food is mostly insects, with moths and butterflies and their larva being a major portion of the diet. Most foraging is done in trees well above the forest floor. As is the case with many of America's migrant songbirds, the Blue-headed Vireo is highly dependent upon large tracts of forest. Deforestation can negatively impact local populations.	**Natural History:** The Plumbeous Vireo is very similar to the Blue-headed Vireo and in many respects it can be considered to be the "western" version of that species. The Plumbeous is less colorful, lacking the greenish yellow flanks of the Blue-headed. The three Vireo species on this page were once all regarded as a single species, known as the "Solitary Vireo." These three species divide their respective breeding ranges in North America. The Blue-headed breeds in the Eastern Temperate Forest Ecoregion, The Cassin's breeds mainly in the Pacific Mountains System while the Plumbeous occupies much of the region in between.	**Natural History:** The Cassin's is very similar to the two preceding species, but is not as distinctly marked, being in some respects a "faded" version of the Blue-headed species. Although during migration this species range will overlap that of the Plumbeous Vireo, the Cassin's breeds farther to west along the Pacific Coast from California to British Columbia. These birds feed mainly on insects but spiders and other arthropods may be consumed. In winter they may eat some seeds and fruits. Clear cutting of forests in the Pacific Northwest can negatively impact breeding and deforestation in tropical wintering grounds is also a threat.

Class—**Aves** (birds)

Order—**Passeriformes** (perching birds & songbirds)

Family—**Vironidae** (vireos)

Red-eyed Vireo *Vireo olivaceus*	**Warbling Vireo** *Vireo gilvus*	**Philadelphia Vireo** *Vireo philadelphicus*

Red-eyed Vireo
Vireo olivaceus

Size: 5.25 inches Wingspan 10 in.

Variation: No variation.

Abundance: Common in east.

Presumed range in TX

Migratory status: Both a seasonal migrant and a summer resident.

Habitat: Although a woodland species, the Red-eyed Vireo is very generalized in its habitat requirements. Mature forests, regenerating woodlands and forest fragments are all occupied.

Breeding: 2 to 4 eggs are laid in May. May have two broods per summer with second brood fledging in late August.

Natural History: This is one of the most common summer songbirds in America forests and woodlots, but it is not readily observed due to its habit of staying high in the forest canopy. It is however regularly heard, as it sings incessantly throughout the spring. While on their breeding grounds they are primarily insectivorous feeders, but they do consume some fruits while wintering in the tropics. The population health of the Red-eyed Vireo may be due to its less stringent dependence upon large tracts of forest. This species can subsist happily in small woodlands and regenerative areas. However, in these habitats it is more susceptible to the parasitic nesting of the Brown-headed Cowbird. Winter range is in South America. Red eye color is unique among vireos.

Warbling Vireo
Vireo gilvus

Size: 5 inches. Wingspan 8.5 in.

Variation: No variation.

Abundance: Uncommon.

Presumed range in TX

Migratory status: Passage migrant in most of state. A few summer in Texas.

Habitat: Although this species likes mature trees in its habitat, it avoids dense forest in favor of areas with a mosaic of small woodlands. Riparian woodlands are also utilized.

Breeding: Nesting takes place in mid-summer. Nests are placed high in trees. Four eggs is typical.

Natural History: Perhaps not as common as the Red-eyed Vireo but more widespread. They are persistent singers that are more often heard than seen. They are browner in color and lack the distinctive red iris of the Red-eyed Vireo, They feed by gleaning small insects and other arthropods from canopy foliage. A few seeds and berries are also sometimes eaten. This is one of the most widely distributed members of the North American Vironidae family. Their breeding range extends from coast to coast across the northern two-thirds of the United States as well as much of Canada. By contrast, the winter range is much smaller and restricted to the western half of Mexico and western Central America, from northern Costa Rica northward.

Philadelphia Vireo
Vireo philadelphicus

Size: 5.5 inches. Wingspan 8 in.

Variation: No variation.

Abundance: Uncommon.

Presumed range in TX

Migratory status: Seasonal migrant that passes through en-route to Canada.

Habitat: Philadelphia Vireo can be found in large tracts of forest, but it seems to favor successional woodlands over mature forests. Uses mixed conifer and deciduous woodlands.

Breeding: The breeding range of the Philadelphia Vireo is contained mostly in Canada. Four eggs is typical.

Natural History: The Philadelphia Vireo migrates through the eastern edge of Texas each spring but it does not nest there. They are a somewhat rarely observed bird and are difficult to distinguish from the more common Warbling Vireo. They usually have more yellowish wash below. They are also very similar to the Red-eyed Vireo and their song also closely resembles that species. Their food is mostly caterpillars. As with many other neotropical migrant songbirds that can be seen in eastern Texas, this species is a trans-gulf migrant that makes epic non-stop flights across the Gulf of Mexico during migration. Many other individuals that pass through Texas probably follow the coastline and avoid the perilous journey across 500 miles of open water.

Class—**Aves** (birds)

Order—**Passeriformes** (perching birds & songbirds)

Family—**Vironidae** (vireos)	Family—**Aluidae** (larks)	Family—**Remizidae** (verdin)
Hutton's Vireo *Vireo huttonii*	**Horned Lark** *Eremophila alpestris*	**Verdin** *Auriparus flaviceps*

Size: 5 inches. Wings 8 inches.

Variation: No variation in TX.

Abundance: Uncommon.

Presumed range in TX

Size: 7.5 inches. Wingspan 12 in.

Variation: No variation.

Abundance: Common.

Presumed range in TX

Size: 4.5 inches. Wingspan 6.5 in.

Migratory status: Year-round.

Abundance: Fairly common.

Presumed range in TX

Migratory status: Year-round resident in the mountains of western Texas. Rare summer resident on Edwards Plateau.

Habitat: Woodlands of pinyon pine, juniper and oak in arid foothills of the west Texas mountain ranges, also riparian habitats in desert regions.

Breeding: Nest is a hanging cup built of mosses, grasses, rootlets, and spider webs. Four eggs is typical with a range of three to five.

Natural History: There are several disjunct populations of the Hutton's Vireo. Texas's population is contiguous with the birds of the Sierra Madre Oriental in Mexico. Other populations are on the west coast of North America and in the Sierra Madre Occidental in Mexico. Mexican populations extend all the way to Guatemala in northern Central America. These are small, nondescript birds that are easily confused with other small, greenish-yellow species like the kinglet's and some warblers. Although there is no variation among Texas populations, ornithologists recognize as many as twelve subspecies across the entire range. All subspecies are very similar in appearance.

Migratory status: Year-round in western two-thirds of Texas. Winter resident mostly in eastern one-third of the state.

Habitat: This is a prairie/grassland species. In eastern Texas it is seen mainly in expansive, open fields. Harvested crop fields are the used in winter.

Breeding: Nests on barren ground. Lays 3 to 5 eggs. Breeds in open regions throughout the western two-thirds of the state.

Natural History: This prairie species needs open ground and has probably benefited from human activity in the eastern United States as a result of land clearing and agricultural operations. Closely cropped pastures or tilled lands are primarily used habitats in the eastern US. Except during nesting, these are gregarious birds that are nearly always seen in flocks. They feed on small seeds and tiny arthropods gleaned from what may appear to be nearly barren ground. In winter when insect food is unavailable they eat seeds of weeds and grasses and will take cracked corn around feeders and farm lots. During outbreaks of severe winter weather flocks may move farther south.

Variation: Juveniles lack yellow on head and reddish shoulder patch and are uniformly pale gray.

Habitat: An arid lands species that inhabits brushy desert and arid grassland with woody vegetation such as Mesquite. Also in riparian habitats.

Breeding: Breeding in Texas probably occurs throughout the region of Texas shown on the map above. Nesting season is March to August in Texas.

Natural History: These tiny desert dwellers are active mainly in the morning, especially during the hotter seasons of the year. The feed on insects, fruits and some nectar from flowing shrubs. These birds are endemic to the southwestern portions of North America and range westward to the Baja Peninsula and south well into the central highlands of Mexico. The Verdin is a photo-distinct species in North America. It is the only member of the Remizidae family found in the western hemisphere. Known in the old world by the name "Pendulin Titmice," there are four genera and ten species total. They are probably most closely related to the Chickadees (family Paridae).

Class—**Aves** (birds)

Order—**Passeriformes** (perching birds & songbirds)

Family—**Paridae** (chickadee family)

Carolina Chickadee *Poecile carolinensis*	**Mountain Chickadee** *Poecile gambeli*	**Tufted Titmouse** *Baeolophus bicolor*

Size: 4.75 inches.

Variation: No variation.

Abundance: Very common.

Presumed range in TX

Size: 5.25 inches. Wingspan 8.5 in.

Variation: No variation.

Abundance: Rare in Texas.

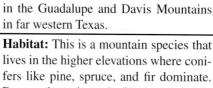
Presumed range in TX

Size: 6 inches. Wingspan 9.75 in.

Variation: No variation.

Abundance: Very common.

Presumed range in TX

Migratory status: A year-round resident in the eastern two-thirds of the state.

Migratory status: A year-round resident in the Guadalupe and Davis Mountains in far western Texas.

Migratory status: A year-round resident. Expanding its range westward in Texas.

Habitat: Carolina Chickadee is primarily a deciduous woodland species but may be found anywhere so long as at least a few trees are present. May be found in urban and rural areas. Shows a preference for edge areas.

Habitat: This is a mountain species that lives in the higher elevations where conifers like pine, spruce, and fir dominate. Ranges throughout the Rocky Mountain west. In Texas found from about 6000 to 7,500 feet in elevation.

Habitat: Small woodlots and successional areas. Favors edge habitats. In both rural and urban habitats. Mainly a woodland species much more common in Texas in the eastern Piney Woods. Increasingly scarce westward in Texas.

Breeding: This species is a cavity nester that will use hollows in limbs, rotted fence posts, etc. or very often, old woodpecker holes. Man-made nest boxes may also be used but natural cavities are preferred. Lays 4 to 6 eggs. Breeds in late winter through spring.

Breeding: A cavity nester that will use knotholes in trees or old woodpecker holes. They will sometimes excavate their own nest hole in soft, rotted snags. The lack of natural cavities can be a limiting factor in their populations. They will use man-made nest boxes.

Breeding: This species is a cavity nester that will utilize natural cavities as well as old woodpecker holes. Nests are lined with fine, soft materials such as grasses, moss, fur, and feathers. May produce two broods per year in Texas. Average of 5 eggs.

Natural History: Among our smallest songbirds, they are a familiar bird at feeders throughout their range. They will become quite acclimated to people and with some patient coaxing they may be induced to land upon an outstretch hand containing sunflower seeds. An acrobatic little bird when searching for insect prey, they can dangle upside down from tiny branches. Their whistling song and their "chick-a-dee-dee-dee" call is distinctive and they can be quite noisy at times. They are hyperactive, tiny birds subject to winter die offs.

Natural History: Females lay up to six eggs which hatch in about two weeks. Two broods per year is not uncommon in southern populations. These are birds of the higher elevations in the Rocky Mountains where cool climates prevail. They are reportedly more common in Texas in the Guadalupe Mountains than in the Davis Mountains farther south (Oberholser 1974). These two mountain ranges represent the southeastern most extension of their range in the US. They will commonly move to lower elevations in winter.

Natural History: Primarily a seed eater in winter, the Tufted Titmouse is one of the first birds to find a new bird feeder. Sunflower seeds are favored, but they also love peanuts. Like Chickadees they are sometimes quite bold around humans servicing feeders. In warm months they forage for small insects and spiders among the foliage of trees. They can sometimes be seen hanging upside down on a small branch or leaf as they search for prey. Their familiar song is a melodic "birdy-birdy-birdy."

Class—**Aves** (birds)

Order—**Passeriformes** (perching birds & songbirds)

Family—**Paridae** (chickadee family)	Family—**Aegithilidae** (bushtit)	Family—**Certhidae** (creepers)
Black-crested Titmouse *Baeolophus atricristatus*	**Bushtit** *Psaltriparus minimus*	**Brown Creeper** *Certhia americana*

Size: 6 inches. Wingspan 9.75 in.

Variation: No variation.

Abundance: Common.

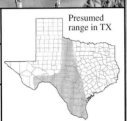
Presumed range in TX

Size: 4.5 inches. Wingspan 6 in.

Variation: See Natural History.

Abundance: Common.

Presumed range in TX

Size: 5.25 inches.

Variation: No variation.

Abundance: Uncommon.

Presumed range in TX

Migratory status: A non-migratory year-round resident.

Migratory status: A non-migratory year-round resident.

Migratory status: Winter resident (Oct. to April) and spring/fall migrant.

Habitat: Brushlands, woodlands and riparian habitats in southern and central Texas. Mexican populations range well into the Sierra Madre Oriental Mts.

Habitat: The Bushtit is a habitat generalist the lives in mountains, foothills, canyons and riparian regions in deserts. Avoids low desert and high mountains.

Habitat: This is a forest species that prefers mature woodlands with large trees for breeding. In winter they are seen in a variety of wooded habitats.

Breeding: Six eggs are typical. Nest is in a natural hollow or old woodpecker hole. Young fledge in less than 3 weeks.

Breeding: The nest is a hanging basket woven from thin grasses, rootlets, etc. and glued together with spider webs.

Breeding: The nest is nearly always built behind a piece of loose bark on the trunk of a large dead tree. 5 or 6 eggs.

Natural History: This species was until recently regarded as a subspecies of the Tufted Titmouse. That premise was supported by the fact that where their respective ranges overlap hybridization frequently occurs. In most respects the Black-crested Titmouse mimics the Tufted Titmouse in natural history and juveniles are nearly identical to the Tufted Titmouse. This bird could be called "the Texas Titmouse." Although it ranges well into northern Mexico its range in the US is mainly restricted to Texas. It can also be found in a small area of south central Oklahoma. One other Titmouse species, the **Juniper Titmouse** (*Baeolophus ridgwayi*) barely ranges into Texas in the Guadalupe Mountains. It is a uniformly drab gray-brown bird but easily recognized as a Titmouse by its prominent crest.

Natural History: Up to seven eggs are laid and both parents will incubate the eggs. The food is mainly insects including many very small insects such as aphids, leaf hoppers, etc. These are hyperactive little birds that seem to never be still, much to the consternation of bird photographers. These are drab-colored birds that are easily overlooked due to the color and small size. They are, however, a gregarious species that often travels in small flocks which tends to make them more conspicuous. And they are fairly common throughout the southwestern United States, the central Rockies, and the west coast. There is some sexual dimorphism and regional color morphs. Males tend to show brown on the head and some birds in southwest Texas have a prominent black mask. The specimen shown above is fairly typical.

Natural History: Brown Creepers feed on small insects, spiders, etc., found in tree-trunk bark crevices. They have the peculiar foraging habit of landing on the trunk at the base of the tree and "creeping" upward, spiraling around the tree as they go. When they reach a certain height, they fly down to the base of another nearby tree and begin again. Generally speaking the Brown Creeper is a bit of a loner, and it is rare to see more than one or two in any one area. This is the only representative of the creeper family (Certhidae) found in North America. Several other species occur in Eurasia and Africa. Population declines in regions where mature forests have been reduced suggests a dependence upon that habitat type. Has probably declined in the eastern US since European settlement.

Class—**Aves** (birds)

Order—**Passeriformes** (perching birds & songbirds)

Family—**Hirunidae** (swallows)

Purple Martin *Progne subis*	**Barn Swallow** *Hirundo rustica*	**Violet Green Swallow** *Tachycineta thalassina*

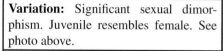

Female   Male

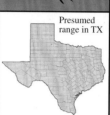

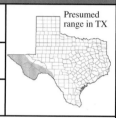

Purple Martin

Size: 8 inches. Wingspan 18 in.

Migratory status: Summer resident.

Abundance: Fairly common.

Presumed range in TX

Variation: Significant sexual dimorphism. Juvenile resembles female. See photo above.

Habitat: Inhabits both rural areas and suburbs. Artificial nest boxes near water in open areas are attractants.

Breeding: Originally nested in natural cavities but today nearly all use artificial nest sites. 3 to 6 eggs is typical but may lay as many as 7 or 8. Purple Martins are colony nesters.

Natural History: Our largest swallow and perhaps the most beloved bird in America. Many people anxiously await the return of Purple Martins each spring to nest boxes erected in their yard. This bird's relationship with humans extends at least as far back as the eighteenth century and today there are at least two national organizations dedicated to Purple Martin enthusiasts. House Sparrows and Starlings sometimes take over "martin houses" unless the landowner is vigilant. Mainly a warm weather species that is dependent upon flying insect prey, Purple Martins are vulnerable to spring cold fronts in the more northern reaches of the summer range. This species is so adapted to nesting in man-made nest boxes that today it is rare to find one nesting in natural cavities.

Barn Swallow

Size: 7 inches. Wingspan 15 in.

Migratory status: Summer resident.

Abundance: Very common.

Presumed range in TX

Variation: Females are paler and less buff colored below. Juveniles resemble adults.

Habitat: Open and semi-open habitats. Most common in agricultural areas but found virtually everywhere in the state.

Breeding: Nest is bowl shaped and made of mud and grasses plastered to roof joists of a barn or eaves of buildings, beneath concrete bridges, etc. Two broods per year is not uncommon.

Natural History: A familiar bird to all who grew up on rural farmsteads. Barn Swallows are common throughout most of North America in summer. Birds that summer in the US winter in Central and South America. European breeders winter in the Mediterranean, Africa, and the Middle East while Asian breeding birds winter throughout southeast Asia to Australia. Thus this is one of the most widespread bird species in the world. Its long association with humans throughout the world has led to the invention of many legends. Barn Swallows nesting in your barn was considered by pioneers as good luck, while destroying a nest in the barn would cause the milk cow to go dry. Flying insects are the main food including pesky flies and even wasps.

Violet Green Swallow

Size: 5.75 inches. Wingspan 13.5 in.

Migratory status: Summer resident.

Abundance: Uncommon.

Presumed range in TX

Variation: Female and juvenile are less greenish above with a dark face. Male (shown above) has white face.

Habitat: This swallow is a western bird that ranges through all types of habitats from Mexico to Alaska.

Breeding: Cavity nester. Nest site is often an old woodpecker hole in trees or in giant cactus. As many as 6 or 7 eggs and usually only a single brood per year. Young fledge at about 3 weeks.

Natural History: Usually seen in flocks, these migratory birds arrive in very early spring in west Texas. They feed almost entirely on the wing on small flying insects. They are widespread throughout the mountains, plateaus, and deserts of the western United States. They are very similar to the following species (Tree Swallow) and in many regards may be considered as the western counterpart of that species. The two species are also similar in appearance with the males of both being brilliantly colored and exhibiting a metallic sheen when seen in bright sunlight. In summer look for this swallow in forested canyons and near high elevation lakes throughout the mountains of the west. During migration they may be seen in a variety of habitats.

Class—**Aves** (birds)

Order—**Passeriformes** (perching birds & songbirds)

Family—**Hirunidae** (swallows)

Tree Swallow *Tachycineta bicolor*	**Northern Rough-winged Swallow** *Stelgidopteryx serripennis*	**Cave Swallow** *Petrochelidon fulva*

Tree Swallow
Tachycineta bicolor

Size: 5.75 inches.

Migratory status: Seasonal migrant and winter resident.

Abundance: Fairly common.

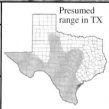
Presumed range in TX

Variation: Female has grayish-brown back. Male (shown above) has metallic blue-green on back.

Habitat: Open and semi-open habitats. Fond of being near water, including small farm ponds and Beaver swamps.

Breeding: A cavity nester, Tree Swallows will use old woodpecker holes or tree hollows. They also use artificial nest boxes and sometimes nest in close proximity to Purple Martins.

Natural History: Tree Swallows are more numerous today than in historical times and are increasing in numbers in the state. Human activities have benefited this species by creating more open lands and also by creating more ponds and lakes throughout the landscape. The proliferation of artificial nest boxes has also helped (they take readily to Bluebird Boxes) and the resurgence of Beaver populations is also credited with helping this species. Flying insects are the primary food items, but they species also eats bayberries during the winter. They are also known to eat snails during the breeding season to obtain calcium for eggshell production. This is a seasonal migrant in most of Texas but some winter along the coast and in the southern tip of the state.

Northern Rough-winged Swallow
Stelgidopteryx serripennis

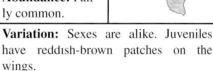

Size: 5.5 inches.

Migratory status: Year-round in south Texas.

Abundance: Fairly common.

Presumed range in TX

Variation: Sexes are alike. Juveniles have reddish-brown patches on the wings.

Habitat: Mainly open and semi-open areas, but can be found in forested regions along rivers or cliffs.

Breeding: Nests in crevices in rock faces, cliffs, etc. Today often uses man-made situations such as road cuts, quarries, etc. Not a colony nester. Lays 4 to 8 eggs.

Natural History: As with other swallows the Rough-winged Swallow feeds by catching flying insects in mid-air. All swallows in America are diurnal hunters whose predatory role is replaced at dusk by the bats. Although this swallow is found from coast to coast across America it is not extremely common anywhere. Unlike the similar Bank Swallow, Rough-winged Swallows are not known to dig their own burrow and availability of nest burrows may be one reason why these swallows tend to be solitary nesters. They will use burrows dug by other species of birds or small mammals as well as natural cavities in cliff faces. They are also known to use man-made structures. In mountainous regions this species is usually associated with river valleys.

Cave Swallow
Petrochelidon fulva

Size: 5.5 inches.

Migratory status: Summer. Year-round in south Texas.

Abundance: Fairly common.

Presumed range in TX

Variation: No sexual dimorphism. Juveniles have pale cheek, throat and forehead.

Habitat: Like most swallows the Cave Swallow favors open and semi-open habitats. Likes to be near water.

Breeding: The name Cave Swallow is derived from the fact that these birds nested historically in caves. Many use caves and sinkholes in Texas for nesting but culverts and bridges are also used.

Natural History: The Cave Swallow has experienced a population boom in the United States over the last century. They were mainly a tropical species found in Mexico, the Caribbean, and South America. Their numbers in the US were likely limited by a lack of suitable caves for nesting. Most experts regard their expansion into Texas to be a direct result of human activities. They now use man-made structures like abandoned buildings, culverts, and beneath bridges for nest sites. They usually nest in colonies. Nests built in sheltered places may be used for several years. Their range in the US is restricted mainly to the state of Texas, where they are now wide-ranging and fairly common birds.

Class—**Aves** (birds)

Order—**Passeriformes** (perching birds & songbirds)

Family—**Hirunidae** (swallows)

Family—**Bombycillidae** (waxwings)

Cliff Swallow *Petrochelidon pyrrhonota*	**Bank Swallow** *Riparia riparia*	**Cedar Waxwing** *Bombycilla cedrorum*

Size: 5.5 inches. Wingspan 13.5 in.

Presumed range in TX

Migratory status: Summer resident.

Abundance: Fairly common.

Variation: Sexes alike.

Habitat: Open areas near large bodies of water are preferred by this species. Historically this species was limited as a breeder to regions with cliff faces.

Breeding: Conical mud nests are plastered beneath sheltered overhangs of concrete structures such as bridges or dams. Four eggs is typical.

Natural History: The Cliff Swallow is primarily a western species that nested historically on cliff faces in the Rocky Mountains. They are more numerous today than even a few decades ago. Man-made structures such as dams and bridges have likely helped this species expand its range. These birds are colony animals that seem to always nest in groups. A source of mud for building nests is required, and therefore there seems to be a preference for nesting near water. Colony size varies from a few dozen to a few hundred nests. In the west where the species is more common and widespread, colonies consisting of several thousand nests are known. Like other swallows, they feed almost entirely upon airborne insects, and they are adept at locating swarms of airborne prey.

Size: 5.25 inches. Wingspan 13 inches.

Presumed range in TX

Migratory status: Summer resident.

Abundance: Uncommon.

Variation: No variation. Sexes alike.

Habitat: Open country. Usually near large rivers. In migration may be seen in a wide variety of habitats but most often observed in valleys, near lakes, etc.

Breeding: Historically nested in high steep banks along major rivers. Nest hole is dug by the parents and may be as much as 2 to 3 feet deep. 4 to 6 eggs.

Natural History: Although widespread across America during migration, this species is rather rare in many regions. Like many swallows, the Bank Swallow nests in large communities. Nest colonies are usually associated with large river systems with exposed cliff faces. Despite being somewhat uncommon in Texas, these birds are found throughout the world; in fact, they are one of the most widespread bird species on earth. The natural nesting habitat has always been riverbanks and bluffs, but today they utilize the banks created by man-made quarries or road cuts through hillsides. During migration Bank Swallows can be seen in the company of other species of migrating swallows. Food is exclusively flying insects caught on the wing. Mostly flies, flying ants, small beetles, and mayflies.

Size: 7 inches. Wings 12 inches.

Presumed range in TX

Migratory status: Winter resident.

Abundance: Fairly common.

Variation: No variation. Sexes alike.

Habitat: Found both in forests and semi-open country including overgrown fields, orchards, etc. May be seen in both rural and urban settings.

Breeding: Builds a nest of grasses. Nest site is typically high on a tree branch. Nesting occurs in June. Lays 3 to 5 eggs. Young fledge in about two weeks.

Natural History: Waxwings are named for the peculiar red-colored waxy feathers on their wings. The name "Cedar" Waxwing comes from their propensity for Eastern Red Cedar trees where they consume large quantities of cedar berries. These birds are highly social and are usually seen in large flocks. They are rarely seen singly or in pairs. They feed mostly on berries and wander relentlessly in search of this favored food item. In summer, insects, mulberries, and serviceberries are important food items. Crabapples and other fruiting trees are also favored. They are highly irregular in occurrence but are frequently seen across the state as they rove around in search of food sources. Large flocks are known to descend on a fruiting bush and consume every berry. They may become intoxicated after feeding on fermented fruits.

Class—**Aves** (birds)

Order—**Passeriformes** (perching birds & songbirds)

Family—**Ptilogonatidae** (silky flycatchers)	Family—**Sylvidae** (gnatcatchers)	

Phainopepla
Phainopepla nitens

Blue-gray Gnatcatcher
Polioptila caerulea

Black-tailed Gnatcatcher
Polioptila melanura

Female

Size: 7.75 inches.	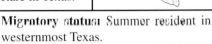 Presumed range in TX
Variation: Female is brown.	
Abundance: Rare in Texas.	

Size: 4.5 inches. Wingspan 6 inches.	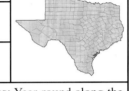 Presumed range in TX
Variation: Male has dark crown.	
Abundance: Fairly common.	

Size: 4.5 inches. Wingspan 5.5 in.	 Presumed range in TX
Variation: No variation in Texas.	
Abundance: Uncommon.	

Migratory status: Summer resident in westernmost Texas.

Migratory status: Year-round along the gulf coast. Summer elsewhere.

Migratory status: Year-round resident in west Texas and southwest Texas.

Habitat: An arid lands species. Most common in the foothills of desert mountain ranges and in riparian areas in deserts.

Habitat: Occupies a wide variety of forested or successional habitats. Most common along wooded streams and bottoms. Prefers deciduous woodlands.

Habitat: An arid land species. Much of its range is in Mexico where it inhabits the Central Highlands and the Sonoran Desert regions.

Breeding: Nests are built in tree forks and contain 2 or 3 eggs. Nest is constructed by the male. Males perform display flights during courtship while carrying nest material in their beak.

Breeding: Nest is a cup-like structure built with lichens and plant fibers glued together with spider web. Nest usually placed at mid-level near the terminus of a branch. 4 to 5 eggs is average.

Breeding: 3 to 5 eggs. Nest is built in shrubs or small trees (Mesquite, acacia, Creasote Bush). In Texas most breeding occurs in the Big Bend region. Also in parts of the South Texas Brush Country.

Natural History: The Phainopepla is the only member of the "Silky Flycatcher" family that can regularly be seen in the United States. Despite their name, they are not closely related to the true flycatchers of the family Tyrannidae. Their closest relative in Texas is probably the Cedar Waxwing. Their favorite food are the berries of the mistletoe plant. Insects and berries of other plant types within their range are also eaten. Phainopeplas inhabit the Chihuahuan, Sonoran, and Mojave Desert regions in the southwestern US. In Texas they are found only in the Big Bend region, where they are uncommon to rare. Like many desert dwelling organisms, the Phainopepla gets its water from its food and has no need to drink.

Natural History: As their name implies, gnatcatchers feed on tiny prey. Any type of small arthropod is a probable food item. They hunt the tips of tree branches and sometimes pick off prey while hovering. Despite their small size, they will chase away larger birds and will mob predators such as hawks, snakes, or house cats. The gnatcatchers are a unique family that is probably most closely related to the wrens. Like many small songbird species the Blue-gray Gnatcatcher is often the victim of nest parasitism by the Brown-headed Cowbird, which lays its eggs in other birds nests. Despite the cowbirds, they seem to be a thriving species and their range has been expanding northward in recent times.

Natural History: This is the southwestern desert counterpart to the Blue-gray Gnatcatcher. It is generally an uncommon species in most of its limited range in Texas, but it can be fairly common in the vicinity of Big Bend National Park. This species is very similar to the Blue-gray Gnatcatcher and the ranges of the two species overlap. The male Black-tailed is recognized by the extensive amount of black on the head. Black-tailed Gnatcatchers are tiny birds that usually stay low to the ground. They feed almost entirely on insects but may eat some fruits. These are hyperactive little birds. When foraging they are constantly in motion and continually flick the tail from side to side. They defend their territory from other birds.

Class—**Aves** (birds)

Order—**Passeriformes** (perching birds & songbirds)

Family—**Sittidae** (nuthatches)

White-breasted Nuthatch	Red-breasted Nuthatch	Brown-headed Nuthatch
Sitta carolinensis	*Sitta canadensis*	*Sitta pusilla*

Size: 5.75 inches. Wingspan 11 in.

Abundance: Fairly common.

Variation: None. Sexes alike.

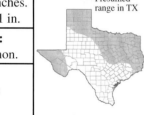
Presumed range in TX

Size: 4.5 inches. Wingspan 8.5 in.

Abundance: Uncommon.

Variation: None. Sexes alike.

Presumed range in TX

Size: 4.5 inches. Wingspan 7.75 in.

Abundance: Uncommon.

Variation: None. Sexes alike.

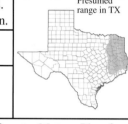
Presumed range in TX

Habitat: This is a bird of deciduous and mixed woodlands. Prefers mature forests but they also occupy re-growth.

Migratory Status: Year-round resident in most of Texas. Winter migrant also.

Breeding: Nests in natural tree cavities or woodpecker holes. Averages 6 eggs per clutch. Only one brood per year is produced and young fledge in late May.

Natural History: Nuthatches are famous for foraging tree trunks in an upside down position. This behavior gives them the opportunity to occupy a different feeding niche from woodpeckers and other bark hunting birds that hunt from an upright position. By creeping down the trunk in an upside-down position, the nuthatches may see tiny prey hidden in crevices visible only from an above perspective and therefore missed by woodpeckers and creepers. This is an example of different species partitioning the same feeding habitat by exhibiting different foraging behavior. In addition to insects they also eat seeds and are regulars at bird feeders. They will cache seeds in bark crevices and they tend to be quite territorial. Pairs will stake out a territory and typically live within that area throughout the year. The only nuthatch that is a full-time inhabitant of deciduous woodlands.

Habitat: Summers in the spruce-fir forests of the north and west. Occupies deciduous woodlands in winter range.

Migratory Status: Winter migrant and winter resident.

Breeding: Cavity nester that excavates their own nest holes in the manner of woodpeckers. Average of 6 eggs. Breeds in boreal forests and mountains.

Natural History: These birds have a tendency to make "irruptive" migrations far to the south in winter every few years and the exact mechanism of their irruptive movements remains something of a mystery. It is believed to be related to cone production in northern coniferous forests where this species usually lives. During the spring and summer the Red-breasted Nuthatch feeds entirely on small arthropods. Seeds are the staple food during winter and Sunflower seeds are a favorite item at bird feeders. They will wedge seeds into bark crevices to hold them fast while using the beak to hammer open the shell in characteristic "nuthatch" fashion. They will glean insects from bark in the same upside down manner as their larger cousin the White-breasted Nuthatch. The Red-breasted Nuthatch seems to avoid using man-made nest boxes. Instead they create their own nest holes.

Habitat: Pine forests. Mature Pine forests with an open understory are the perfect habitat for this southern species.

Migratory Status: Year-round resident in the Piney Woods region of Texas.

Breeding: A cavity nester that will use woodpecker holes, natural knot holes, or man-made nest boxes. 5 eggs is the average clutch size but can be up to 7.

Natural History: This is a species of the pine forests of the southeastern US. Brown-headed Nuthatches benefit from the use of prescribed fire in southern forests. Controlled burns simulate the natural wildfires that created the open understory habitat that was typical of old growth southern pine forests. In fact, the range of this species closely approximates the range of the Longleaf Pine, a tree species that was characteristic of the great southern pine forests that existed prior to European settlement. Many animal species in the southeast are associated with the Longleaf Pine habitat, including the Bachman's Sparrow, another bird species that was indigenous to this once great ecosystem. The Brown-headed Nuthatch has a western counterpart. It is the nearly identical **Pygmy Nuthatch** (*Sitta pygmeae*) which occurs in Texas in the vicinity of the Guadalupe Mountains.

Class—**Aves** (birds)

Order—**Passeriformes** (perching birds & songbirds)

Family -**Regulidae** (kinglets)

Ruby-crowned Kinglet	Golden-crowned Kinglet
Regulus calendula	*Regulus satrapa*

Ruby-crowned Kinglet

Size: 4.25 inches. Wingspan 7.5 inches.

Abundance: Fairly common. During periods of peak migration they can be quite common, especially during fall cold fronts.

Variation: Male has red stripe on head that is most visible when the male is excited. Females lack this red stripe on the crown. Otherwise sexes are very similar. Spring birds and juveniles are grayer above and less yellowish below.

Presumed range in TX

Migratory Status: Winter resident throughout the state. They summer well to the north. A few may spend the winter in the southernmost parts of the state, but will move south if the weather gets to harsh.

Habitat: Summer habitat is undisturbed boreal forest across all of Canada from the Atlantic to the Pacific and well into Alaska. Also summers in the higher elevations of the Rocky Mountains. Winter habitats much more generalized to include deciduous and mixed woodlands as well as swamps and lowlands.

Breeding: Breeds in old growth conifers in the far north. Produces enormous clutches of up to 12 eggs. Nest is built near the tops of spruce trees or fir trees. Nest is constructed of a wide variety of materials including mosses, lichens, blades of grass and conifer needles. Fur, feathers, or animal hair are used to line the nest.

Natural History: This is one of America's smallest songbird species, smaller even than the Chickadee. The bright red blaze on the top of the head of the male is usually not visible unless the feathers of the crown are erected. Males most often display the red feathers on the crown when issuing a challenge to other males, displaying to females, or singing their territorial song. Otherwise their bright red crown feathers will remain hidden from view. In summer they prey on arthropods and their eggs. In winter they will also feed on berries and some seeds. They are hyper-active little birds that forage throughout the canopy as well as along lower branches. Clumps of dead leaves hanging from a tree limb are like magnets to these tiny hunters who will find small spiders, insects, and other diminutive arthropods hiding within the clumps. They are constantly in motion and regularly flick the wings open as they hop quickly from tiny branch to tiny branch at the terminal end of boughs of trees and bushes. Hunts mostly along the tips of smaller branches. Some studies suggest this species may be declining in the eastern United States. Some suggest this decline may be due to logging and forest fragmentation in the breeding range. Birds that winter in Texas are true latitudinal (north-south) migrants. Populations in the living in the Rocky Mountains of the western United States migrate from high elevations to lower elevations (altitude migration). These delightful little birds are not common at bird feeders but they can be lured to feeders with suet, sunflowers, or especially mealworms.

Golden-crowned Kinglet

Size: 4 inches.

Abundance: Fairly common statewide.

Variation: Male has orange crown. Female has yellow.

Presumed range in TX

Migratory Status: A winter resident that usually arrives in October or November.

Habitat: This is a forest species that prefers mature woodlands with large trees for breeding. In winter they are seen in a variety of wooded habitats.

Breeding: Builds its nest in the top of a spruce or fir in northern woodlands. Lays a large clutch of up to 11 eggs and may produce two broods per year.

Natural History: Even smaller than its cousin the Ruby-crowned Kinglet, the Golden-crowned is a hardier bird that can tolerate colder winter weather. However, severe winter conditions can lead to near 100 percent mortality in localized areas. Amazingly, this little carnivore manages to find arthropod prey throughout the winter and does not switch to seeds and berries in cold weather. Hyperactive and always in motion. They often feed by "leaf hawking" (hovering while picking tiny insects from beneath a leaves). In winter they are often seen in small groups or mixed flocks. Although these little birds may be seen throughout the winter in the state, they are probably most common during fall migrations. They can be quite tolerant of human presence.

Class—**Aves** (birds)

Order—**Passeriformes** (perching birds & songbirds)

Family—**Troglodytidae** (wrens)

Cactus Wren *Campylorhynchus brunneicapillus*	**Rock Wren** *Salpinctes obsoletus*	**Canyon Wren** *Caltherpes mexicanus*

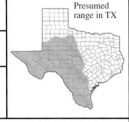

Size: 8.5 inches. Wingspan 11 in. 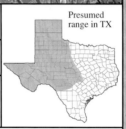 Presumed range in TX	**Size:** 8 inches. Wings 9 inches. Presumed range in TX	**Size:** 5.75 inches. 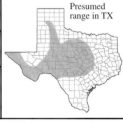 Presumed range in TX
Abundance: Fairly common.	**Abundance:** Fairly common.	**Abundance:** Uncommon.
Variation: No variation in Texas.	**Variation:** No variation in Texas.	**Variation:** Juveniles have fewer spots.

Habitat: Deserts and thorn scrub are the main habitat for this species. In Texas they are also found in the brushlands of the Southern Texas Plains and in the southern Gulf Coastal Plain.	**Habitat:** Deserts, pinyon/juniper woodlands and arid mountains. Usually associates with rocky canyons, boulders, cliffs and rarely talus slopes. Range restricted to the western half of Texas.	**Habitat:** Canyons. Likes steep, rocky arroyos and canyons in the rocky mountain west. Often in the vicinity of streams. Ranges from the Canadian border to southern Mexico.
Migratory Status: Year-round resident.	**Migratory Status:** Year-round resident.	**Migratory Status:** Year-round resident.
Breeding: Nest is usually built in a cactus. In Texas Yucca is also used. 3 or 4 eggs is typical. Multiple broods are the norm.	**Breeding:** Nest is built under a rock overhang or in a rock crevice. 5 or 6 eggs is usual. As many as three broods per year.	**Breeding:** Nests are built within rock crevices. 4 to 6 eggs is usual and they may produce two broods per year. Breeding pairs are monogamous.

Natural History: The name Cactus Wren is appropriate for this species as throughout their range there are always some cactus species. They are fond of nesting in some of the spiniest of cactus but somehow avoid being impaled. The nests are built by the male and are quite large and easily observable in cactus or yuccas. The male will also build extra nests in his territory which he uses for a roost while there are young in the nest. These extra nests may also be used as a roost during cold weather. Many types of insects and arachnids are food items. They also eat cactus fruits, especially the fruits of Prickly Pear. These are the largest members of the wren family in North America and they are usually quite conspicuous as the perch atop cactus and small trees or shrubs. They are often very approachable, especially in parks or around homesteads.

Natural History: This is species is aptly named as it does have an affinity for rocky habitats. The range of the Rock Wren includes nearly all the western US except for the humid Pacific northwest. They range from southern Canada all the way through Mexico and into northern Central America. Although this is a year-round bird in its Texas range, some in the northern parts of their range may move farther to south in very cold winters. In a peculiar behavior this species will gather small stones and pebbles to create a "runway" in front of the nest that is usually situated in a rock crevice. Food is insects and spiders. This is a fairly common bird in western Texas and their populations are probably substantial, but there has been some decline in populations reported. Rock Wrens like to perch conspicuously atop boulders.

Natural History: The Canyon Wren is a rock crevice specialist that will hunt by probing into cracks in vertical cliffs. Their long thin bill, long claws for gripping and somewhat flattened bodies allow them to penetrate deep into narrow cracks where insects, spiders and other invertebrate prey may be hiding. Although their canyon habitats often include flowing streams, they can also be found in extremely dry arroyos in desert regions and they can thrive in areas with no available water. Breeding Bird Surveys report a decline in populations of this species in recent decades. The cause of the decline is not known, but it is in keeping with an overall decline in songbird populations throughout the Americas in the last several decades. In Texas this species is probably most common in the mountains of west Texas and in the Edwards Plateau.

Class—**Aves** (birds)

Order—**Passeriformes** (perching birds & songbirds)

Family—**Troglodytidae** (wrens)

Carolina Wren *Thryothorus ludovicianus*	**Bewick's Wren** *Thryomanes bewickii*	**House Wren** *Troglodytes aedon*

Size: 5.5 inches.  Presumed range in TX	**Size:** 5.25 inches. 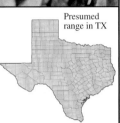 Presumed range in TX	**Size:** 4.75 inches. 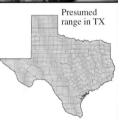 Presumed range in TX
Abundance: Very common.	**Abundance:** Common.	**Abundance:** Common.
Variation: No variation. Sexes are alike.	**Variation:** Several subspecies. See below.	**Variation:** No variation. Sexes are alike.
Habitat: Carolina Wrens are very flexible in habitat choices. They can be seen in remote wilderness or in suburban back yards.	**Habitat:** Brushy thickets and woodlands in semi-arid to arid regions. Especially common in the Edwards Plateau and in south Texas.	**Habitat:** Prefers open and semi-open habitats. These wrens readily associate with humans and are most common in small towns and suburbs.
Migratory Status: A year-round resident in the eastern two thirds of the state.	**Migratory Status:** A year-round resident in the western two thirds of the state.	**Migratory Status:** Winter resident and seasonal migrant (see Natural History).
Breeding: A nest of fine twigs and grass is built in a sheltered place, often provided by man. Eggs number 3 to 6. Females will produce at least two clutches per year.	**Breeding:** As many as 8 eggs may be laid. The nest is usually build in a crevice or under an rock overhang, abandoned building or some other shelter. Will also use man-made nest boxes.	**Breeding:** A cavity nester, the House Wren readily takes to artificial nest boxes. In fact, this species may owe its increase in population to man-made "bird houses." Lays up to 8 eggs.
Natural History: Along with the House Wren, this is one of the most common wrens in the Eastern US. The Carolina Wren adapts well to human-influenced habitats and is well-known for building its nest in an old pair of shoes or in a vase of flowers left on the back porch for a few days. They will become quite tame around yards and porches and frequently endear themselves to their human neighbors. They are voracious consumers of insects, spiders, and caterpillars and help control insect pests around the home. They are also incessant singers whose musical song serves as a dawn alarm for many residents throughout the state. They are most common in the eastern half of the state, especially in the Piney Woods region. In more northern regions they are vulnerable to harsh winters.	**Natural History:** This species is very similar to the Carolina Wren but is more grayish-brown in color (rather than reddish-brown). It also has a noticeably longer tail which it often flicks to the side. Although there are several subspecies recognized, the differences are slight and unapparent to the casual observer. Like other wrens the Bewick's is a voracious consumer of invertebrate prey. When raising a brood of young (up to three per year) these birds will capture copious quantities of insects and spiders. This species range in North America has apparently expanded and contracted over the many decades that ornithologists have been monitoring bird populations in America. Today the Texas Breeding Bird Atlas states "Texas probably has the largest population of Bewick's Wrens in the United States."	**Natural History:** Although mainly a winter resident and seasonal migrant in Texas, some nesting has been recorded in the northeastern panhandle in the last few decades. Although the House Wren may be seen anywhere in Texas, it is probably more common in winter in the southern parts of the state. They are more common today than in historical times, as they favor open and semi-open habitats over dense forests. They also have a strong affinity for human-altered habitats and settlements. They feed on a wide variety of insects, spiders, snails, caterpillars, etc. When feeding large broods of young they catch huge quantities daily. House Wrens range from coast to coast across America and northward into the prairie provinces of Canada. They are known to build several "dummy" nests that are not used.

Class—**Aves** (birds)
Order—**Passeriformes** (perching birds & songbirds)
Family—**Troglodytidae** (wrens)

Winter Wren *Troglodytes hiemalis*	**Sedge Wren** *Cistothorus stellaris*	**Marsh Wren** *Cistothorus palustris*

Winter Wren
Troglodytes hiemalis

Size: 4 inches. Wingspan 5.5.

Abundance: Uncommon.

Variation: No variation in Texas.

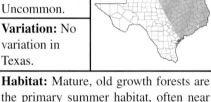
Presumed range in TX

Habitat: Mature, old growth forests are the primary summer habitat, often near a stream or bog. Deciduous and mixed woodlands are utilized in winter, but conifers are preferred.

Migratory Status: Winter resident in the eastern half of the state.

Breeding: Breeds well to the north of Texas, mainly in the boreal forests of Canada. Nest is often constructed in the root wad of an upturned tree. Lays 5 to 9 eggs.

Natural History: Much shyer and more secretive than other wrens, the Winter Wren skulks about under dense bushes and shrubs where it tends to stay close to the ground. This species has likely declined since pre-settlement times due to the destruction of ancient forests. Like other wrens, these birds are strictly carnivorous and feed on a wide variety of small insects, larva, arachnids, amphipoda, etc. As with many other invertivorous birds, they are vulnerable to exceptionally harsh winters. Their stubby, upturned tail makes identification easy, but they are more often heard than seen as they are persistent, loud singers. Winter Wrens are holarctic in distribution, being found in Europe and northern Asia as well as North America.

Sedge Wren
Cistothorus stellaris

Size: 4.25 inches.

Abundance: Uncommon.

Variation: No significant variation in Texas.

Presumed range in TX

Habitat: This is a wetland species that enjoys marshes and wet meadows. Unlike the Marsh Wren it does not occupy cattail marsh but prefers grassy areas. Likes low, wet, grassy meadows.

Migratory Status: Winter resident in the Coastal Plain Province.

Breeding: Nest is built low to the ground, often in a clump of sedges or a small bush. 6 or 7 eggs is typical and some may produce two broods per year. Does not nest in Texas.

Natural History: This is a secretive species that is difficult to observe. Like the Marsh Wren it winters well to the south of its breeding range in northern states and Canada. The natural history of this species is poorly known, but it is known that nesting dates vary considerably from one region of the country to another. Nesting can occur from May to as late as September. Some birds may produce two broods per year in two different regions. The diet is spiders and insects. Sedge Wrens winter in coastal plain of the southeastern United States from the Carolinas all the way to northwestern Mexico. Fall migration begins in September and most birds are usually gone from the northern portions of their range by late October. Spring migration is in April and May.

Marsh Wren
Cistothorus palustris

Size: 5 inches. Wings 6 inches.

Abundance: Uncommon.

Variation: No variation. Sexes alike.

Presumed range in TX

Habitat: Pastures, marshes, and lowland meadows as well as open, grassy edges of wetlands or ponds. Coastal salt marshes are widely used in winter. Lives year-round in Texas coastal areas.

Migratory Status: Year-round on the gulf coast, winter resident elsewhere.

Breeding: Nest is low in grasses or small bush. Nest is built of grasses woven into a ball with an entrance hole in the side. Several unused "decoy" nests are built. Seven eggs is typical.

Natural History: Marsh Wrens are winter residents in much of Texas but can be seen year-round on the gulf coast. They may be seen anywhere in the state where suitable habitat exists during migration periods. These are secretive birds that can be very difficult to observe, even in areas where they are common. They spend most of their time hidden in thick stands of cattails or other vegetation deep in the marsh. Like most wrens, they will sing continuously in the breeding season and most birdwatchers confirm their presence by learning to recognize their song. They will build one or more "decoy" nests that are never used and they are also known to destroy the eggs of other birds that may be nesting in the vicinity of their own nests.

Class—**Aves** (birds)

Order—**Passeriformes** (perching birds & songbirds)

Family—**Turdidae** (thrush family)

Eastern Bluebird *Sialia sialis*	Western Bluebird *Sialia mexicana*	Mountain Bluebird *Sialia currucoides*

Eastern Bluebird
Sialia sialis

Size: 7 inches

Abundance: Fairly common.

Variation: Significant sexual dimorphism. See above.

Presumed range in TX

Habitat: Field edges, woods openings, and open fields, marshes, and pastures. Savanna-like habitats, (i.e. open spaces interspersed with large trees), are a favorite habitat.

Migratory Status: Year-round in east Texas. Winter elsewhere in the state.

Breeding: Bluebirds are cavity nesters that readily take to man-made nest boxes. Two broods per summer is common. 3 to 6 eggs per clutch.

Natural History: The Eastern Bluebird's habit of readily adapting to artificial nest boxes has helped bring them back from alarmingly low numbers decades ago, when rampant logging of eastern forests and competition with European Starlings depleted available nest cavities. They are primarily insect eaters and are vulnerable to exceptionally harsh winters. Harsh winter weather will prompt a mass movement south and prolonged periods of very cold weather can literally wipe out entire populations that are caught too far north. In winter Bluebirds eat many types of berries and will readily eat raisins or peanuts placed in bird feeders. Their popularity among humans has lead to the establishment of The North American Bluebird Society, an organization dedicated to Bluebird conservation.

Western Bluebird
Sialia mexicana

Size: 7 inches.

Abundance: Rare in Texas.

Variation: Female is less colorful, more "washed out."

Presumed range in TX

Habitat: The Western Bluebird is a bird of the southern Rocky Mountains and the US west coast. In Texas this species inhabits the Guadalupe and Davis Mountains.

Migratory Status: Winter migrant and year-round in west Texas mountains.

Breeding: In Texas this species only breeds in the mountains of the Chihuahuan Desert ecoregion. Average clutch size is 5 eggs.

Natural History: This is the western "sister species" of the Eastern Bluebird. They are most common in the mountains of California and the southern Rockies. Their breeding range barely extends into Texas in the west Texas mountains but they are sometimes seen as winter migrants in the Edwards Plateau. Nesting is in hollows and this species relies mainly on woodpeckers for nest sites. Like the eastern species they will also use man-made nest boxes. The main food is insects. They also eat arachnids, mollusks (snails), and terrestrial crustaceans (pillbugs,etc.) In winter they will consume berries and seeds if invertebrate prey is not available. They like semi-open areas with many dead trees and are among the first birds to colonize woodlands ravaged by forest fires or logging.

Mountain Bluebird
Sialia currucoides

Size: 7 inches.

Abundance: Uncommon.

Variation: Female is grayish brown with pale blue wings.

Presumed range in TX

Habitat: Montane forests in the Rocky Mountains are the primary habitat in summer. Winter migrants may follow tree-lined river valleys well out onto the Great Plains.

Migratory Status: Winter resident and rare spring and fall migrant.

Breeding: Mountain Bluebirds nest in tree hollows or sometimes rock crevices. Clutch size is 4 to 8 eggs. Does not breed in Texas.

Natural History: A western species found throughout the mountain west from Mexico to Alaska. In spite of their name, their range sometimes extends well out onto the prairies to the east of the Rockies. They can be seen in Texas in the wide-open plains of the panhandle as well as in the west Texas mountains. In the fall Mountain Bluebirds will gather in flocks numbering from a dozen to over a hundred. They will move to lower elevations for the winter and birds on the eastern slope of the Rocky Mountains may winter in the Great Plains. They also migrate latitudinally and some may winter as far south as central Mexico. Summer foods are a variety of invertebrates but in winter they switch to berries. Juniper berries can be a major source of food in the winter.

Class—**Aves** (birds)

Order—**Passeriformes** (perching birds & songbirds)

Family—**Turdidae** (thrush family)

Townsend's Solitaire *Myadestes townsendi*	Robin *Turdus migratorius*	Clay-colored Thrush *Turdus grayi*
	Male	

Size: 8.5 inches **Abundance:** Uncommon in Texas. **Variation:** Juveniles are heavily spotted. 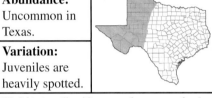Presumed range in TX	**Size:** 10 inches. **Abundance:** Very common in most of Texas. **Variation:** Females are less vividly colored. Presumed range in TX	**Size:** 9 inches **Abundance:** Uncommon in Texas. **Variation:** No variation. Sexes alike. Presumed range in TX
Habitat: Coniferous forests of the western US are the primary habitat. They will also use mixed evergreen/deciduous forests. Moves to lower elevations in winter.	**Habitat:** Virtually all habitats in the state may be utilized. Most common in areas of human disturbance, especially older suburbs. They are fond of hunting earthworms in suburban lawns.	**Habitat:** This is a tropical species that ranges from the southern tip of Texas to northern South America. Inhabits woodlands, shrubby areas and open areas of tropical rainforests.
Migratory Status: Winter resident.	**Migratory Status:** Year-round.	**Migratory Status:** Year-round.
Breeding: The nest is usually on the ground beneath an overhanging bank or under an old stump or root wad. 3 to 5 eggs, 4 is average.	**Breeding:** The 3 to 4 "sky blue" eggs are laid in a nest constructed of mud and grass, often in the crotch of a tree in an urban yard.	**Breeding:** Little is known about nesting in Texas. The nest is a heavy cup of grasses and mud. The 2 to 4 eggs and two broods per year may be produced.
Natural History: Most of the eight species of birds in the *Myadestes* genus occurring in the Americas are found in Mexico and Central America. Townsend's Solitaire is the only member of its genus in the US. Their diet invertivorous in summer and they often hunt flying insects from a perch. Juniper berries are a mainstay of the diet in winter. Subsequently during winter months they will be found in regions where juniper species are common. They occasionally appear well east of the Rocky Mountains in winter, rarely migrating all the way across the Great Plains to central Texas. This species is fond of perching conspicuously atop a dead snag or in the top of pine tree. The name "Solitaire" is appropriate as this species is usually seen singly except during the breeding season.	**Natural History:** Despite the fact that the Robin is a migratory species, individuals are seen in much of Texas year-round. But they are a winter only resident in south Texas. In winter they are sometimes seen in large migratory flocks numbering over 100 birds. Certainly one of the best known of America's bird species, Robins are commonly seen on both urban and rural lawns throughout the America. They may also been seen in remote wilderness areas, especially in the summer when some will nest as far north as the Arctic Circle. Their overall range coincides almost precisely with that of the North American continent. The Latin name *migratorius* is appropriate for this species and its overall range extends from Mexico to the northernmost parts of Alaska. Feeds heavily on earthworms.	**Natural History:** The range of the Clay-colored Thrush is primarily throughout the eastern slope of Mexico, all of the Yucatan, most of Central America and northern Columbia and Venezuela. The southern tip of Texas represents the northernmost extent of their range. The food is mostly invertebrates. In the tropics it is known to follow columns of army ants and pick off insects disturbed by the column. They will also eat fruits. In Texas they are sometimes secretive but in the tropics they can be quite tame and approachable. This tameness my account for it being the national bird of Costa Rica where there are scores of beautiful exotic bird species. Why else would a plain colored species like the Clay-colored Thrush warrant such an honor? Also sometimes called Clay-colored Robin.

Class—**Aves** (birds)		
Order—**Passeriformes** (perching birds & songbirds)		
Family—**Turdidae** (thrush family)		
Veery *Catharus fuscescens*	**Gray-cheeked Thrush** *Catharus minimus*	**Swainson's Thrush** *Catharus ustulatus*

Size: 7 inches. Wingspan 12 in. 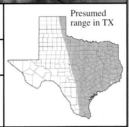 Presumed range in TX	**Size:** 7.25 inches.  Presumed range in TX	**Size:** 7 inches, Wingspan 12. Presumed range in TX
Abundance: Uncommon.	**Abundance:** Uncommon.	**Abundance:** Fairly common.
Variation: From reddish to gray-brown.	**Variation:** No variation. Sexes alike.	**Variation:** Grayish brown to olive-brown.

Habitat: Understory of deciduous woodlands. Most common in second growth forest with thick undergrowth. Rare in urban parks.	**Habitat:** Summer habitats are boreal forests. Winters in South America. May be seen in woodlands of east Texas during migration.	**Habitat:** Moist to wet woodlands and swamps with heavy underbrush and cool, heavily shaded woods. Can be seen in suburbs and parks.
Migratory Status: Spring and fall migrant throughout the eastern two-thirds of the state.	**Migratory Status:** Seasonal migrant in the eastern half of the state. Migrates mostly at night.	**Migratory Status:** Seasonal migrant. Migrates mostly at night but resting birds can be seen during the day.
Breeding: Breeds far to the north of Texas in northern US and in Canada. Nest is hidden in thickets on or near the ground. From 3 to 5 eggs are laid.	**Breeding:** Breeds in remote tundra and taiga in northern Canada and Alaska. Lays 3 to 6 eggs. Nest is constructed in the crotch of a willow or alder bush.	**Breeding:** Builds its moss-lined nest in a coniferous tree in boreal forest well to the north of Texas. Lays 3 to 5 eggs that are blue with brown spots.
Natural History: Although the Veery is widespread during migration, they are hard to observe in much of their range in Texas since most are usually just passing through and they migrate mostly at night. One of the more secretive of the thrushes, they stay mostly in thick undergrowth where they feed on a variety of insects, earthworms, spiders and berries. Bird watchers often confirm this bird's presence by recognizing its distinctive call, which has been described as "hauntingly beautiful." This species has shown a downward population trend in many regions of its range in North America. Factors cited as possibly contributing to this trend are loss of wintering habitat in South America and fragmentation of breeding habitats in North America.	**Natural History:** Secretive and uncommon, the biology of the Gray-cheeked Thrush is poorly known. Its summer habitats are dense spruce forests and willow/alder thickets in the far north. Breeding range extends well into the Arctic Circle and winter range is at least as far south as northern South America. Differentiating between the various thrush species can be challenging. The Gray-cheeked Thrush is easily confused with both the Swainson's Thrush and the Hermit Thrush but can be told by the gray color of the cheek. Another similar thrush, the Bicknell's Thrush (not seen in Texas), is one of America's newest described bird species and was once regarded as being the same species as the Gray Cheeked Thrush. This is our least common thrush species.	**Natural History:** Another secretive, difficult to observe thrush that in migration flies by night and spends its days resting and feeding in heavy undergrowth. As with many of the thrushes, positive identification can be difficult. This species and the Gray-cheeked Thrush are easily confused. The buff-colored cheeks are a good identification character. Like others of its kind the Swainson's Thrush feeds on insects and invertebrates as well as berries. Unlike others of its genus, however, this thrush is known to feed higher in trees (most other thrushes feed mostly on the ground). Spring migration begins in late April and runs through mid-May. Fall migration peaks in September. Like other thrushes this bird is easier heard than seen.

Class—**Aves** (birds)

Order—**Passeriformes** (perching birds & songbirds)

Family—**Turdidae** (thrush family)		Family—**Sturnidae** (mynas)

Hermit Thrush
Catharus guttatus

Size: 7 inches.	
Abundance: Fairly common.	Presumed range in TX
Variation: Varies from reddish brown to gray brown.	

Habitat: Damp woodlands, thickets, and successional areas with heavy undergrowth of bushes and shrubs. Also seen in urban parks where there are a substantial number of trees and shrubs.

Migratory Status: Winter resident from late September to early May.

Breeding: 3 to 5 bluish-green eggs are laid in a nest built just above ground level. Most nesting will occur in the boreal forests of Canada.

Natural History: Any Thrush seen in Texas during the winter is most likely to be this species. They are rather shy but less so than other *Catharus* and they will sometimes visit feeders for suet or raisins. They feed mainly on insects found on the forest floor and beneath leaf mold, but berries are also an important element in the diet, especially in winter. The song of the Hermit Thrush is regarded by many as one of the more beautiful summer sounds in the northern forests. Although secretive, their presence during winter makes them more conspicuous. Unlike most other thrush species, populations of the Hermit Thrush appear stable. As with other thrush species the Hermit Thrush is known for the quality of its song which is often describe as "melancholy." Probably the most common *Catharus*.

Wood Thrush
Hylocichla mustelina

Size: 7 inches.	
Abundance: Uncommon.	Presumed range in TX
Variation: No significant variation and the sexes are alike.	

Habitat: Woodlands. May be found in both mature forests and successional areas. In both it likes thick undergrowth. On wintering grounds uses tropical rainforests.

Migratory Status: Seasonal migrant and summer resident in eastern Texas.

Breeding: Nest is mud, twigs, and grass similar to that of the Robin. Nest may be in understory or at mid-level. Lays 2 to 5 blue-green eggs.

Natural History: The Wood Thrush feeds on insects, spiders, earthworms and other invertebrates found by foraging beneath leaf mold on the forest floor. They will also feed on berries which can be an important food during fall migration. Like many songbirds this species is threatened by the fragmentation of forest habitats throughout North America. Smaller forest tracts make it easier for Cowbirds to find Wood Thrush nests. Consequently nest predation by Cowbirds is increasing and may be one reason for recent population declines. This threat is especially pronounced in the Midwest where so much of the forest habitats have been depleted. The exceptional song of the Wood Thrush is usually described as "flute-like," or "ethereal" and is heard mostly at dawn and dusk.

Starling
Sturnus vulgaris

Size: 8.75 inches.	
Abundance: Very common.	Presumed range in TX
Variation: Juvenile has brownish head and throat.	

Habitat: Urban and suburban areas as well as farms and ranches. Starlings are closely tied to human activity and are rarely seen in true wilderness. They are most common in cities and small towns.

Migratory Status: Year-round resident throughout the state.

Breeding: Nest is made of grass, sticks leaves, etc., stuffed into a cavity. Often uses cracks or holes in man-made structures. Clutch size is typically 5 eggs.

Natural History: The Starling is one of the most familiar birds in America, but ironically it is a non-native species. All the Starlings in America are descendant from a handful of birds released in New York City in the 1890s. Contrary to popular belief, the Starling is not related to the blackbirds. Instead they belong to the same family as the old world mynas. These birds have enjoyed remarkable success since being introduced to North America and they are now found throughout the continent. They represent a real threat to many of our native species, especially those that nest in cavities. Bluebirds in particular have suffered from the loss of nesting sites due to Starlings. In winter they often join grackles and blackbirds in large mixed flocks that can become a messy nuisance in urban and suburban areas.

Class—Aves (birds)

Order—Passeriformes (perching birds & songbirds)

Family—Mimidae (thrasher family)

Gray Catbird *Dumetella carolinensis*	Northern Mockingbird *Mimus polyglottos*	Sage Thrasher *Oreoscoptes montanus*

Size: 8.5 inches. Wingspan 11 in.  Presumed range in TX	**Size:** 10.5 inches. Wingspan 14 in.  Presumed range in TX	**Size:** 8.5 inches. Wingspan 12.5. in  Presumed range in TX
Abundance: Fairly common.	**Abundance:** Common.	**Abundance:** Fairly common.
Variation: No variation. Sexes are alike.	**Variation:** No variation. Sexes are alike.	**Variation:** No variation. Sexes are alike.
Habitat: Edge areas, thickets and overgrown fence rows are this bird's preferred habitat. In urban areas it is often found in older neighborhoods containing landscapes overgrown with large bushes and shrubs.	**Habitat:** Prefers semi-open habitats with some cover in the form of bushes and shrubs. Found in both rural and urban environments. During colder months they are usually found in the vicinity of berry producing plants.	**Habitat:** Sagebrush plains and deserts. In summer resides largely in the Great Basin Desert region. In winter moves south to America's other desert regions, including the Chihuahuan Desert of Texas. Usually around sagebrush.
Migratory Status: Winter resident on the gulf coast, summer resident in northeast Texas, migrant in central Texas.	**Migratory Status:** Year-round resident throughout most of Texas. Some may migrate short distances in response to cold.	**Migratory Status:** Mostly a winter resident in west Texas. Seasonal migrant in the panhandle.
Breeding: The loosely constructed nest is made of sticks, vines, and leaves placed in dense bushes. Three to four eggs is common.	**Breeding:** The nest is made of sticks and is usually in a thick bush or small tree. 3 to 4 eggs are laid and more than one nesting per season is usual.	**Breeding:** Nests are built in a dense shrub. The nest opening often faces east to catch the warming rays of the morning sun. 4 or 5 eggs are laid.
Natural History: The Gray Catbird is much more secretive than its relative the Mockingbird. Food includes all manner of insects, spiders, larva and berries. Feeds both in the trees and on the ground. When feeding on the ground will use the bill to flip over dead leaves. Named for their call which sounds remarkably like a meowing cat, these shy birds are often heard but unseen as they "meow" from beneath a dense shrub. Like their cousins the Mockingbirds, Gray Catbirds have a large repertoire of songs and they are accomplished mimics of other bird species. They winter along the lower coastal plain of the US, Florida, the Caribbean, Mexico, and Central America.	**Natural History:** The name "Mocking Bird" is derived from this birds habit of mimicking the calls of other birds. And they have a huge repertoire of songs. They are known to mimic the calls of everything from warblers to blue jays and even large hawks. New songs are learned throughout their life and the number of different songs recorded by this species is up to 150. They feed largely on insects, but in the winter will switch to berries and fruits. Mockingbirds have a reputation among rural folk as a useful bird that will chase away other pesky birds such as blackbirds and other species that can be garden pests. They will aggressively defend food sources.	**Natural History:** The various species of Sagebrush that are the dominant plants in much of the American west make up a special ecosystem that has many signature animal species. The Sage Thrasher is one of those signature species. Although they may be found in a variety of arid landscapes in winter and during migration, they breed mainly in regions dominated by sagebrush plants. They feed mostly on the ground and spend more time walking than flying. In breeding season males will sit atop the highest available perch and sing for extended periods. They are the smallest of the thrashers and are the only representative of the *Oreoscoptes* genus.

Class—**Aves** (birds)

Order—**Passeriformes** (perching birds & songbirds)

Family—**Mimidae** (thrasher family)

Brown Thrasher	Long-billed Thrasher	Curve-billed Thrasher
Toxostoma rufum	*Toxostoma longirostre*	*Toxostoma curvirostre*

Size: 11.5 inches. Wingspan 13 in.  Presumed range in TX

Abundance: Fairly common.

Variation: No variation. Sexes are alike.

Size: 11.5 inches. Wingspan 12 in. 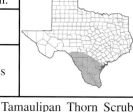 Presumed range in TX

Abundance: Uncommon.

Variation: No variation. Sexes are alike.

Size: 11 inches. Wingspan 13.5.  Presumed range in TX

Abundance: Fairly common.

Variation: No variation in Texas.

Habitat: Edges of woods, thickets, fence rows, overgrown fields and successional areas. Suburban lawns that have adequate cover in the form of bushes and shrubs may also be used. Avoids deep woods.

Migratory Status: Year-round in east Texas. Winter resident elsewhere in Texas.

Breeding: Builds a stick nest in the heart of a dense shrub, usually within a few feet of the ground. Lays two to five eggs in late spring.

Natural History: During warm weather the Brown Thrasher feeds on insects and small invertebrates of all types. It uses its long bill to overturn leaves and debris beneath trees and shrubs and also actively hunts in the grass of urban lawns. In winter they will eat berries and sometimes come to feeders for raisins or suet. During the breeding season males perch atop bushes or small trees and serenade all within earshot with their song. Though the Brown Thrasher lacks the repertoire of its cousin the Mockingbird, it does possess one of the most varied song collections of any bird in America. They are seen year-round in the Piney Woods region of Texas where they are a breeder. They are winter residents or winter migrants in central and south Texas.

Habitat: The Tamaulipan Thorn Scrub of southern Texas is the habitat of this species in the US. Much of its range is south of the border in northeastern Mexico. Dense brush and riparian thickets are the primary habitat.

Migratory Status: Year-round resident in the lower Rio Grande Valley.

Breeding: Nest is always in a densely packed bush or thorny shrub and is a bulky cup of twigs lined with grasses or moss. 2 to 5 eggs are laid.

Natural History: Nearly identical to the Brown Thrasher but has a slightly longer bill and a grayer face. This species replaces the Brown Thrasher as a breeding bird in the southern tip of Texas. But the two occur together in the winter when Brown Thrashers summering farther to the north migrate southward. Highly insectivorous but they also eat spiders and some berries and fruit. They forage on the ground, using the bill to flip leaves and organic detritus to search for prey. The biggest threat to this species in its US range is loss of habitat. Most of the Tamaulipan Thorn Scrub in the lower Rio Grande Valley has been converted to agriculture. Ironically, fire suppression by humans has allowed shrub growth into grasslands and added replacement habitat.

Habitat: Semi-open scrub, brushlands, desert and semi-desert areas. Texas level III ecoregions inhabited are primarily Chihuahuan Desert, High Plains, Edwards Plateau, South Texas Brushlands, and Western Gulf Coastal Plain.

Migratory Status: A non-migratory year-round resident.

Breeding: The nest is usually built in a shrub, cacti or small tree fairly close to the ground. 3 to 5 eggs are laid and two broods per year may be produced.

Natural History: The food of the Curve-billed Thrasher is mainly arthropods including large numbers of insects and arachnids. They will also eat some plant material in the form of seeds and berries. They have also been known to steal dog food from porches and patios. Most foraging is done on the ground and this species spends more time on the ground than in bushes or trees. They move through their habitat using their beak to flip leaves and debris in search of prey. Like other Mimidae, these birds are fierce defenders of the their nesting territory and will chase off other birds that wander to close to the nest. Although still a fairly common bird in Texas, the species has experienced a population decline in the last few decades.

Class—**Aves** (birds)

Order—**Passeriformes** (perching birds & songbirds)

Family—**Mimidae** (thrasher family)	Family—**Motacillidae** (pipits)	
Crissal Thrasher *Toxostoma crissale*	**American Pipit** *Anthus rubescens*	**Sprague's Pipit** *Anthus spragueii*

Crissal Thrasher	**American Pipit**	**Sprague's Pipit**
Size: 11.5 inches. Wingspan 12.5 in.  Presumed range in TX	**Size:** 6.5 inches. Wingspan 10.5 in.  Presumed range in TX	**Size:** 6.5 inches. Wingspan 10 in.  Presumed range in TX
Abundance: Uncommon.	**Abundance:** Uncommon.	**Abundance:** Uncommon.
Variation: No variation in Texas.	**Variation:** Seasonal plumage changes.	**Variation:** No significant variation.
Habitat: In Texas this species is restricted to the Chihuahuan Desert Ecoregion where it favors dense thickets of thorny brush and cactus.	**Habitat:** In migration and in winter the American Pipit is usually seen in expansive open areas such as harvested crop lands or mud flats.	**Habitat:** Grasslands. Summers are spent in native mixed grass prairies in North Dakota, Montana and southern Canada. Winters in southern plains.
Migratory Status: Year-round. Some altitudinal migration in mountains.	**Migratory Status:** Winter resident and seasonal migrant.	**Migratory Status:** A winter resident in Texas.
Breeding: Breeds from early spring through late summer. Two or three eggs are laid in a nest built of twigs and placed in a dense shrub.	**Breeding:** Breeds in tundra areas and southward into the higher altitudes of the Rocky Mountains. Lays 3 to 7 eggs in a nest on the ground.	**Breeding:** Nest is the ground and is a domed structure made of grasses. Three to six eggs are laid, Does not nest in Texas.
Natural History: As is the case with other thrashers in the American west, the Crissal Thrasher is a decidedly terrestrial bird that is nearly always seen on the ground. When hard pressed they may take to the wing and fly a short distance, but they normally evade threats by running along the ground. In appearance these birds are similar to the Curved-billed Thrasher, but Crissal's Thrasher may be recognized by the cinnamon color under the tail. Most of this bird's range is in the northern deserts an arid highland regions in Mexico. In addition to being found in the Chihuahuan Desert of Texas they also range across the Sonoran and Mojave deserts. They range in the US from west Texas across southern New Mexico, southern Arizona and into southern California. Their populations are stable but the conversion of desert to agriculture may be a threat.	**Natural History:** The American Pipit is a hardy species that nests in America's coldest climates. They move south in the winter where they are easily overlooked. Their brown winter plumage is highly cryptic, especially where they usually reside in expansive, open fields or mud flats. During migration and in winter they may be seen in the company of flocks of Horned Larks or rarely with Lapland Longspurs (another winter migrant from the far north). Characteristically wags its tail up and down. Despite being widespread (their range includes all of North America), they are relatively unknown birds to many. The specimen shown is in spring breeding plumage. Fall and winter birds are browner and have heavy brown streaks on the breast. Sometimes go by the name "Water Pipit," but that name belongs to the similar Eurasian species.	**Natural History:** Few animals are more reliant on natural prairies than the Sprague's Pipit. Nesting occurs almost entirely in natural prairie and overgrazed pastures, croplands and non-native grasslands are avoided. Native, natural prairie is today increasingly rare in North America and populations of this species has declined by as much as 80 percent in the last half century. Limited cattle grazing that mimics the impact of historical bison herds can be beneficial to this and other prairie species. Limited cattle grazing and periodic fires can control the growth of shrubs and trees on the prairie. Conversely, too much grazing is detrimental. Wildlife managers today implement controlled burns on native grasslands to emulate the historical conditions that maintained America's native grassland habitats while controlling non-native plants.

Class—**Aves** (birds)

Order—**Passeriformes** (perching birds & songbirds)

Family—**Parulidae** (warblers)

Blue-winged Warbler	Golden-winged Warbler	Tennessee Warbler
Vermivora cyanoptera	*Vermivora chrysoptera*	*Leiothlypis peregrina*

Female

Spring

Fall

Size: 4.75 inches.

Abundance: Fairly common.

Migratory Status: Seasonal migrant.

Presumed range in TX

Size: 4.75 inches.

Abundance: Rare.

Migratory Status: Seasonal migrant.

Presumed range in TX

Size: 4.75 inches.

Abundance: Fairly common.

Migratory Status: Seasonal migrant.

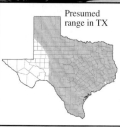
Presumed range in TX

Variation: Hybrids with Golden-winged produces 3 different variants.

Variation: Female (shown above) lacks the black throat patch of the male.

Variation: Females and fall plumages more greenish overall.

Habitat: Overgrown weed fields with ample brushy undergrowth and early successional woodlands constitute this bird's primary habitat. Least common in areas of intensive agriculture.

Habitat: Second growth woodlands and overgrown fields. Summer range is in the boreal forest of Canada and in the higher elevations of the Appalachian Mountains.

Habitat: Summer habitat is the boreal forest of Canada. Winter habitat in Central America is semi-open forest and forest edges. In migration may be seen anywhere in eastern Texas.

Breeding: Nest is near the ground in or under a low bush often at the edge of a woodland/field interface. From 4 to 6 eggs are laid in May.

Breeding: Nests on or near the ground at the base of a bush, hidden in thick grass and weeds. Nest is a cryptic bowl of dead leaves and grass. 4 to 5 eggs.

Breeding: Nest is on the ground at the base of a tree or among upturned roots. Nest is usually well hidden. Clutch size ranges from 3 to 8.

Natural History: A shrub land specialist, the Blue-winged Warbler experienced an upswing in populations as a result of deforestation by pioneering Europeans settlers of eastern North America. In recent years there has been a decline in their numbers in the northeastern US as forests have begun recovering from the rampant logging of the last century. In North America they are most common in the Appalachian Plateau Province and rare in the agricultural regions of the Interior Lowlands Province. In Texas they are a seasonal migrant. These birds sometimes hybridize with the similar Golden-winged Warbler and produce at least three additional forms of difficult to identify hybrid birds. Populations of this species have declined in recent years due to loss of habitat.

Natural History: This species is a rare migrant in Texas during migration. But actual sightings of this bird may be difficult as they are increasingly rare. They are a highly sought species with the state's birdwatchers. Loss of winter habitat and nest parasitism by the Brown-headed Cowbird are possible reasons for a recent population decline. But hybridization with Blue-winged Warblers, which are now expanding their range northward, may be the main reason for the increasing rarity of the Golden-winged Warbler. They winter in a variety of forest habitats in Mexico, Central America and northern South America from sea level to 7,000 feet. Like many other warblers, some individuals of his species will make the perilous journey across the Gulf of Mexico in the spring.

Natural History: The numbers of this species passing through the state each spring and fall fluctuates depending upon the previous year's abundance of its primary summer food, the Spruce Budworm. In the northern forests of Canada in good budworm years, this is one of the most common bird species. In years of diminished budworm populations, the population of these birds also crashes. This relationship provides a valuable insight into the intricate interdependencies of unrelated organisms. This is an inconspicuous bird as it feeds high in trees and migrates later in the spring after trees are fully leaved. Thus it is difficult to detect despite being common. The name comes from the fact that the first scientifically collected specimen was from Tennessee. Usually seen April/May and Sept./Oct.

Class—**Aves** (birds)

Order—**Passeriformes** (perching birds & songbirds)

Family—**Parulidae** (warblers)

Orange-crowned Warbler *Leiothlypis celata*	**Nashville Warbler** *Leiothlypis ruficapilla*	**Virginia's Warbler** *Leiothlypis virginiae*

Orange-crowned Warbler
Leiothlypis celata

Size: To 5.5 inches.

Abundance: Fairly common.

Migratory Status: Seasonal migrant.

Presumed range in TX

Variation: Female slightly duller. Varies regionally.

Habitat: Summers in northern woodlands (Canada and Rocky Mts.) where it prefers habitats with significant understory. Also found in old weedy fields, brier thickets, etc., during migration.

Breeding: Breeds in northern Canada and as far north as Alaska and well into the Arctic Circle. Western subspecies breeds along west coast. Lays 4 to 5 eggs.

Natural History: Like most warblers, this species is highly insectivorous, but in winter it also eats some fruit and is known to feed at the sap wells created by sapsucker woodpeckers. Feeds deliberately in the lower branches of trees and in bushes. These can be very common birds on their northern breeding grounds, but they are mainly seen only during migration in Texas. A few winter along the gulf coast in Texas. Their range coincides with the North American Continent. They sometimes linger well north of their summer range and have been seen very rarely in northern states in winter. Orange streak on crown from which it derives its name is not typically visible in the field. Winters across the southeastern US from the Carolinas to coastal Louisiana, and south to northernmost Central America.

Nashville Warbler
Leiothlypis ruficapilla

Size: To 4.75 inches.

Abundance: Fairly common.

Migratory Status: Seasonal migrant.

Presumed range in TX

Variation: Two subspecies are recognized but there is no variation in Texas.

Habitat: Summer habitat includes tamarack bogs and boreal forests. Prefers second growth and open woodlands with shrubby undergrowth. Avoids the deep woods.

Breeding: Nests on the ground under bushes or in hummocks of grasses or sphagnum moss. Clutch size ranges from 3 to 6. Does not breed in Texas.

Natural History: This warbler species has benefited from human alterations to the American landscape (they prefer logged-over, second growth habitats). However, some human alterations have also had a very negative effect. As with many other migrant songbirds, they are vulnerable to towers, power lines, and antennas. No one knows exactly how many birds are killed during migration each year by flying into these obstacles, but some estimate the number to be in the millions. Insects are eaten almost exclusively by this warbler. Summers in northern US and Canada, winters in Mexico. Ornithologists recognize two distinct subspecies in North America. One migrates through the Rocky Mountain west; the other subspecies stays east of the Great Plains. Most birds seen in Texas will be the eastern subspecies.

Virginia's Warbler
Leiothlypis virginiae

Size: 4.75 inches.

Abundance: Uncommon.

Migratory Status: Summer resident.

Presumed range in TX

Variation: Male has chestnut-colored patch on top of head.

Habitat: Summer resident birds in Texas use wooded canyons and riparian woods in foothills and mountains. Migrants may be seen in a variety of habitats throughout the Big Bend region.

Breeding: Nest is on the ground, an unusual nesting strategy for a warbler. Nest is often sheltered by a rock or clump of grass. 3 to 5 eggs.

Natural History: The Virginia Warbler is very similar to the Nashville Warbler and they are "sister species," with the Nashville Warbler occurring in the eastern US and the Virginia's Warbler occupying the drier mountains of the west. Food is typical for a warbler and consists of a variety of arthropod prey, including many caterpillars. They will also consume nectar. This is a an uncommon and declining species. Nest parasitism by Brown-headed Cowbirds is a threat. Climate change may also pose an additional threat as the western half of North America faces increasing drought conditions that may eliminate much of the riparian habitat preferred by this species. These are inconspicuous little birds that are easily overlooked. They are most obvious during breeding when they sing.

Class—**Aves** (birds)

Order—**Passeriformes** (perching birds & songbirds)

Family—**Parulidae** (warblers)

Lucy's Warbler *Leiothlypis luciae*	**Black-and-white Warbler** *Mniotilta varia*	**Northern Parula** *Setophaga americana*

Size: 4.5 inches. Wingspan 7 in.	 Presumed range in TX	**Size:** 5.5 inches. Wingspan 8.25 in.	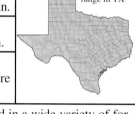 Presumed range in TX	**Size:** 4.5 inches. Winspan 7 inches.	 Presumed range in TX
Abundance: Rare in Texas.		**Abundance:** Fairly common.		**Abundance:** Fairly common.	
Variation: Male has red patch on crown.		**Variation:** Female has more white on face.		**Variation:** Female is less vividly colored.	

Habitat: This is a desert species. They favor riparian habitats in desert areas. In Texas they occur in the western portion of the Rio Grande Valley. Most are summer residents but a few are year-round in parts of the Rio Grand valley.	**Habitat:** Found in a wide variety of forest types, but mature and second growth deciduous forests are the primary habitat. Mixed conifer-hardwood forests are also used. Likes woodlands with dense understory.	**Habitat:** Habitat is forest. Mostly bottomland woods or swamps or along streams and rivers. In Texas this species is seen mostly in the eastern part of the state, especially in the Piney Woods region where it breeds and summers.
Migratory Status: Mostly a summer resident. A few may be year-round.	**Migratory Status:** Seasonal migrant and summer resident.	**Migratory Status:** Summer resident and seasonal migrant.
Breeding: This is one of the few warblers that nests in natural cavities. Rock crevices and old woodpecker holes are the main nesting sites. From three to seven eggs are laid.	**Breeding:** Nest is constructed of dry leaves, dead grasses, and the bark of grapevines. Placed in a depression on the ground at the base of tree or stump. Lays 3 to 5 eggs.	**Breeding:** Nests high in trees. Sycamores, Bald cypress, and Hemlocks are reported as favorite nest trees. In the deep south nests are often built in Spanish moss. 4 or 5 eggs.
Natural History: The Lucy's Warbler is an uncommon to rare bird in Texas. They occur only along a narrow strip of the upper Rio Grande River Valley in the Big Bend region. Where they do occur, however, they may sometimes be common since they tend to congregate in suitable habitat within the region. A very similar species, the **Colima Warbler** *Leiothlypis crissalis* can be found breeding in parts of west Texas in summer. It is primarily a Mexican bird but a few move north into the Chisos Mountains every year. It is a very rare bird in Texas. The cinnamon-colored crown of the male is not typically visible except when excited (such as when defending territory from other birds), or when singing.	**Natural History:** Feeds by plucking tiny creatures from tree bark and branches. Its feeding habits are more similar to that of woodpeckers, nuthatches, and creepers than to most warblers. This species is dependent upon deciduous and mixed conifer forests, and it can be sensitive to deforestation. But overall it does not appear to have been significantly impacted throughout its wider range. While this species can be seen throughout the state during migration, it nests in Texas mostly in the Piney Woods region of the state where ample woodlands are found. Like many warblers it spends much of its time in the canopy which makes it difficult to observe. When seen, its black and white color is distinctive.	**Natural History:** The Northern Parula feeds by gleaning tiny arthropods from tree branches. They tend to feed and spend much time in the middle an upper story of the forest. This habit coupled with their small size make them difficult to observe. These handsome little warblers are most common in deep forests and are least common in the northeast. They are one of the smallest warblers, but are strikingly colored, especially the males. They are early spring migrators arriving as early as March. They winter from south Florida to Central America. The **Tropical Parula** is a nearly identical species that is found in the southernmost tip of Texas. It ranges along the lower Rio Grande Valley and in the southern part of the Gulf Coastal Plain.

Class—**Aves** (birds)

Order—**Passeriformes** (perching birds & songbirds)

Family—**Parulidae** (warblers)

Yellow Warbler	Chestnut-sided Warbler	Magnolia Warbler
Setophaga petechia	*Setophaga pensylvanica*	*Setophaga magnolia*

 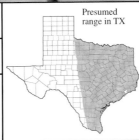

Size: 5 inches. Wings 8 inches.

Abundance: Common.

Variation: Male has reddish streaks on breast and sides

Presumed range in TX

Habitat: Thickets of willow or buttonbush in wet lowlands are the classic habitat for this species. Mesic upland woods may also be used. Riparian habitats are favored in desert regions.

Migratory Status: Passage migrant though out the state.

Breeding: Nest is built in the upright fork of a sapling and averages four or five eggs. Nest is a cup-like structure made mostly from grasses.

Natural History: This is one of North America's most wide ranging of the warblers. The summer breeding range encompasses the entire northern two thirds of North America, from the Atlantic to the Pacific and extends as far north as the Arctic Circle. They can be seen as migrants statewide in Texas. Spring migrants pass through in early April to early May. Fall migration is early. In fact this is one of the earliest fall migrators, leaving breeding areas in mid July. Bolstered by the young of the year, fall birds are more numerous. Feeds on a variety of insects and arthropods and uses a variety of foraging techniques including gleaning of leaves and branches, flying from perch to seize airborne prey, and picking insects from leaves and branches while hovering

Size: 5.5 inches.

Abundance: Common.

Variation: Colors more subdued on female.

Presumed range in TX

Habitat: A bird of successional areas and shrubby second growth. Forest edges, early regenerative timber harvest areas and forest clearings are favored for nesting.

Migratory Status: Seasonal migrant through out eastern Texas.

Breeding: Nests fairly low to the ground in thick cover of dense sapling growth. 3 or 4 eggs are laid in late spring or early summer.

Natural History: This is one of the few warbler species that has benefited from deforestation. They are probably more common now than they were in the days prior to the European settlement of America. Despite their overall increase in population, they are negatively impacted by modern agricultural practices. The clearing of fence rows and overgrown field corners and conversion of successional habitats into cropland eliminates their preferred habitat. They are thus absent from most regions of intensive agriculture. As with many other migrant warbler species that travel through the state, the Chestnut-sided warbler breeds mostly far to the north in Canada or New England. Can be seen in Texas mainly in the Piney Woods region during spring migration.

Size: 5 inches.

Abundance: Common.

Variation: Colors more subdued on female.

Presumed range in TX

Habitat: Summer habitat for most is in spruce forests in Canada. In Texas it can be seen statewide in wooded areas during migration. Winters in Mexico, Central America and Caribbean.

Migratory Status: Seasonal migrant. Seen in Texas mostly in spring.

Breeding: Nests in evergreen trees. 4 eggs laid. Breeds in the far north across Canada, New England, and in the northern Appalachians.

Natural History: Feeds on insects (including large numbers of caterpillars) that are caught near the ends of branches in dense conifer trees. Known to feed on the Spruce Budworm and may enjoy greater survival of offspring during years of budworm outbreaks. This is an abundant species that appears to be stable in population numbers. Leaves Central American wintering grounds in February and passes through Texas from April to early May. They are fairly common migrants throughout the eastern half of the state in spring. Fall migration begins in September and may last into October. Fall migration routes generally more easterly than spring, thus they are usually observed in Texas during spring migration. The longevity record is just under nine years.

Class—**Aves** (birds)

Order—**Passeriformes** (perching birds & songbirds)

Family—**Parulidae** (warblers)

Audubon's Yellow-rumped Warbler *Setophaga coronata*	**Myrtle Yellow-rumped Warbler** *Setophaga coronata*	**Black-throated Gray Warbler** *Setophaga nigrescens*

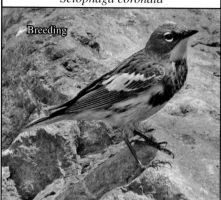
Breeding

Breeding

Size: 5.5 inches.

Abundance: Common. Maybe the most common warbler in the US.

Variation: Two forms, "Myrtle" and "Audubon's" (see photos above). Seasonal plumage variations (see small photo lower right).

Presumed range in TX

Winter

Size: 5 inches

Abundance: Uncommon to rare in Texas

Variation: Female has white throat, male's throat is black.

Presumed range in TX

Habitat: Outside its breeding range this warbler is a habitat generalist. It can be seen virtually anywhere in the state during spring or fall migrations. Summer habitat is boreal forests of the north and montane forests in the west.

Habitat: Inhabits dry western forests. Pine forests, pine-oak forests, and pinyon juniper forests.

Migratory Status: Mainly a winter resident in Texas. But in the panhandle it is more likely to be seen as a seasonal migrant.

Migratory Status: Seasonal migrant through the western end of Texas.

Breeding: Breeds in the boreal forest of Canada and Alaska. Nest is built on the branch of a conifer. Clutch size is usually 4 or 5 eggs. One clutch per year. Like many warbler species they are vulnerable to nest parasitism by cowbirds.

Breeding: Nest is in a tree on the fork of a branch. May produce two broods per year of 3 to 5 eggs.

Natural History: There are two morphologically distinct forms of this common warbler, one in the eastern US and one in the western US. Both forms can be seen in Texas. The form seen in east Texas is called the "Myrtle Warbler." The form seen in west Texas is call "Audubon's Warbler." Both forms also exhibit seasonal plumage changes, with winter birds and juveniles resembling females. Decades ago the two color morphs of Yellow-rumped Warbler in the United States were considered to be two distinct species. That taxonomy was changed when it was discovered that where the ranges of the two overlap hybrids frequently occurred. More recent studies utilizing molecular analysis suggests that the original designation of two separate species may have been correct after all. It is expected that the two forms will once again be divided into distinct species sometime soon. In summer these birds feed mainly on insects, but if bad weather necessitates they are capable of surviving on berries during the winter. Unlike most warblers that will winter in the tropics, Yellow-rumped warblers are hardy birds and in mild winters they can be seen as far north as southern IL, IN and OH in the Midwest and NJ on the east coast. This ability to overwinter in northerly regions is the result of their ability to feed on and digest berries. Populations of this bird seem fairly stable and it is probably in less jeopardy than many other warblers. Their striking yellow, black and white breeding colors are replaced in winter by a much more subdued pattern (see photos above). In all plumages males tend to be more brightly colored. Yellow-rumped Warblers can be seen throughout most of Texas all winter. Except perhaps in the northern panhandle region where they are mostly seasonal migrants.

Natural History: Although this species is hard to observe in Texas they are actually fairly common farther to the west. They often migrate with other western warblers like the Hermit Warbler and the Townsend's Warbler. They will move through the branches methodically searching for insect food. Many warblers present identification problems for birdwatchers, but the Black-throated Gray is usually easy to identify. They are strikingly colored birds with distinct black and white markings and a small bright yellow spot in front of the eye. While this is a rare bird in Texas, they are fairly common farther to the west and in the Rocky Mountains in summer. They spend the winter in Mexico. These warblers sometimes wander east and in the summer months they may be seen almost anywhere in Texas on rare occasions.

Class—**Aves** (birds)

Order—**Passeriformes** (perching birds & songbirds)

Family—**Parulidae** (warblers)

Golden-cheeked Warbler *Setophaga chrysoparia*	**Black-throated Green Warbler** *Setophaga virens*	**Townsend's Warbler** *Setophaga townsendi*

Male

Male

Female

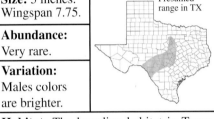

Size: 5 inches. Wingspan 7.75.

Abundance: Very rare.

Variation: Males colors are brighter.

Presumed range in TX

Size: 4.5 inches. Wingspan 7.75 in.

Abundance: Fairly common.

Variation: Female lacks black on throat.

Presumed range in TX

Size: 5 inches. Wingspan 8 in.

Abundance: Uncommon.

Variation: Male colors are brighter.

Presumed range in TX

Habitat: The breeding habitat in Texas coincides with the range of the Ashe Juniper. In winter they inhabit the central highlands region of Mexico and southward into Nicaragua.

Habitat: This warbler requires significant tracts of unbroken forests. Except for migration, it is an inhabitant of conifer and mixed conifer/deciduous forests, especially those containing hemlock.

Habitat: Summer and winter habitats are forests in mountainous regions. Uses mature old growth forests mainly. In migration will use all types of habitats including vegetated areas in deserts.

Migratory Status: Summer resident.

Migratory Status: Seasonal migrant.

Migratory Status: Seasonal migrant.

Breeding: An early breeder that returns from wintering grounds as early as mid March. Nest may occur by the first week of April and continue into June. Three to five eggs is usual.

Breeding: Does not breed in Texas. Most nesting occurs in Canada, the northern Great Lakes and in the Appalachian Mountains. Lays 4 eggs in nest usually built in a conifer.

Breeding: Nesting takes place in the Pacific Northwest. Males arrive on the breeding habitat before females. Nest is usually in a large conifer tree. Three to seven eggs are reported.

Natural History: The Golden-cheeked Warbler breeds only in Texas. In this regard it is unique among all the birds that may be seen in the Lone Star State. It is also an endangered species. That fact coupled with its rarity and stunning colors make it a favorite among birders. But it is a challenging species to find as most of its breeding range is contained on private lands. Habitat loss on both the breeding grounds in Texas and in it wintering grounds in Latin America are a threat. The nesting habitat in Texas of mature juniper/oak woodlands can take decades to recover once disturbed, and logging on the winter range in Latin America has reduced habitat there. Nest parasitism by Brown-headed Cowbirds is also a problem. Caterpillars are a favorite food along with other insects.

Natural History: Like others of its kind, this small, handsome warbler faces many threats. Red Squirrels are reportedly an important nest predator in the boreal forests of Canada and New England. In places nesting threats may come from other birds like the Blue Jay and from common and widespread Woodland Rat Snakes. Sharp-shinned Hawks are always a threat to the adults, while Brown-headed Cowbirds parasitize the nest. Human activities such as forest fragmentation threaten populations as a whole. Add to that the impact of Woolly Adelgid insects on hemlock trees and you have an uncertain future for this and many other warbler species. Like many warblers, they spend most of their time high in the treetops and they can thus be difficult to observe.

Natural History: The Townsend's Warbler favors the moist forests of the Pacific Northwest for its summer breeding grounds. But during migration it may be seen foraging in low desert shrubs like Creosote Bush. They will also frequent lawns and parks in small towns throughout their migratory route which often crosses expansive deserts. During migration they are especially attracted to small oasis-type habitats where there are water features present. During migration they can be conspicuous but on their breeding grounds in the Pacific Northwest they typically stay high in the tops of very tall trees. The food in summer is mostly insects. Food during winter in the tropics includes nectar, berries, and "honeydew" produced by scale insects.

Class—**Aves** (birds)

Order—**Passeriformes** (perching birds & songbirds)

Family—**Parulidae** (warblers)

Blackburnian Warbler *Setophaga fusca*	Yellow-throated Warbler *Setophaga dominica*	Grace's Warbler *Setophaga graciae*

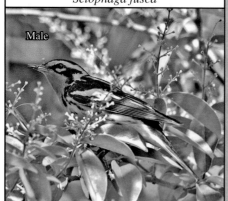
Male

Size: 4.5 inches. Wingspan 8.5 in.

Abundance: Fairly common.

Migratory Status: Seasonal migrant.

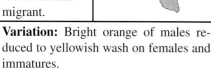
Presumed range in TX

Size: 5.25 inches.

Abundance: Fairly common.

Migratory Status: Year-round in Texas.

Presumed range in TX

Size: 5 inches. Wingspan 8.

Abundance: Rare in Texas.

Migratory Status: Summer resident.

Presumed range in TX

Variation: Bright orange of males reduced to yellowish wash on females and immatures.

Variation: Sexes are similar and there is no significant variation between adults and juveniles.

Variation: Female has gray rather than black crown but otherwise the sexes are very similar. Juveniles are browner.

Habitat: Summers mostly in mature coniferous and mixed forests. Migration habitat is highly variable. Birds that breed in the Appalachians favor groves of Eastern Hemlock.

Habitat: Found mostly along wooded stream corridors. Also uses bottomland forest and mature woodlands with open understory. Known to often associate with Sycamore trees.

Habitat: Mountain pine forests (especially Ponderosa Pine). In Texas this species is found in high elevation forests in the Guadalupe and Davis Mountains.

Breeding: Does not nest in Texas. Elsewhere nest is usually in a conifer and well concealed amid foliage. Average of 4 to 5 eggs.

Breeding: Nest is placed high in a tree, often a Sycamore. Nest is made of grasses and spider web and lined with soft materials. Four eggs is typical.

Breeding: Little is known about the breeding behavior of this species since it nests high in tall trees in high elevation mountains. Three eggs is typical.

Natural History: The beautiful blaze orange coloration on the head, throat, and breast of the Blackburnian Warbler is unmistakable. They are probably fairly common during migration. However, this is a difficult species to observe due to the fact that it is primarily a treetop dweller. Thus few people who are not trained to look for them will see them. They feed mostly on caterpillars. Blackburnian Warblers seen in Texas are merely passing through en route to boreal forests far to the north. Some will nest in the southern Appalachians as far south as northern Georgia, but those that pass through Texas are on their way to more northerly regions in Canada. Forest fragmentation on wintering grounds in South America may poses a threat.

Natural History: This warbler species can be seen all summer in eastern Texas's Piney Woods region. They can be seen in winter along the Western Gulf Coastal Plain and are seasonal migrants throughout the southern and eastern portions of the state. This is another "treetop" species that spends most of its time high in the canopy. It feeds on diminutive arthropods gleaned in a very deliberate fashion from branches, bark, leaves, and petioles. This species retreated from the northern portions of its breeding range several decades ago, but is now showing a resurgence back into those areas. The cause of this population fluctuation is unknown but possibly relates to habitat alterations by man and a subsequent recovery of those habitats. Often nests in clumps of Spanish Moss.

Natural History: This species ranges as far south as Guatamala, Belize, Honduras and Nicaragua. It is a year-round resident of the tropics but some birds range northward in summer into the southwestern United States. Throughout its range it inhabits montane forests where it usually stays high in the treetops. This appears to be a species in decline and some estimates report declines of up to 50 percent over the last several decades. A loss of mature trees to logging is likely at least partly responsible. They are also apparently vulnerable to nest parasitism by cowbirds. Fire suppression and other forest management practices that favor the growth of younger trees also plays a role, especially in the mountains of the southwestern United States.

Class—**Aves** (birds)

Order—**Passeriformes** (perching birds & songbirds)

Family—**Parulidae** (warblers)

Pine Warbler *Setophaga pinus*	**Prairie Warbler** *Setophaga discolor*	**Palm Warbler** *Setophaga palmarum*
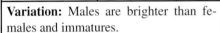		

Pine Warbler	Prairie Warbler	Palm Warbler
Size: 5.5 inches. Wingspan 8.75 in. **Abundance:** Common. **Migratory Status:** Year-round resident.	**Size:** 4.25 inches. **Abundance:** Fairly common. **Migratory Status:** Summer resident.	**Size:** 5.5 inches. Wingspan 8 in. **Abundance:** Fairly common. **Migratory Status:** Winter resident on gulf. 
Variation: Males are brighter than females and immatures.	**Variation:** Sexes very similar but female colors more subdued.	**Variation:** Exhibits seasonal variation. Shown above is breeding plumage.
Habitat: Pine forests are the primary habitat, but they are also seen in deciduous and mixed woodlands, especially during migration. In Texas they are most common in the Piney Woods.	**Habitat:** Semi-open habitats. Old, overgrown fields, shrubby successional areas, second growth woodlands and cedar glades. Very rare to absent in intensive agricultural areas.	**Habitat:** Summer habitat consists of bogs and woods openings in boreal forests. Transient in a variety of habitats during migration. Winter habitat is open woodlands, mangroves, and thickets.
Breeding: Builds its nest high in pine trees. This is one of the earliest nesting warblers, with 3 or 4 eggs laid as early as mid-April. Breeding range is limited to regions where pines occur.	**Breeding:** Breeds in the eastern part of the state. An average of four eggs (3 to 5) are laid May to June. In Texas this species breeds exclusively in the South Central Plains Level III Ecoregion.	**Breeding:** Nests of moss on the ground in a northern bog, usually at the base of a conifer tree. Clutch size is 4 or 5. Many nest in remote wilderness. Does not nest in Texas.
Natural History: As its name implies, this species seems to be always found in association with pine trees. This is the only warbler whose range is contained entirely within the United States and Canada. It is also the only one of its kind to regularly change its diet from insects to seeds in the winter. Thus it is one of the few warblers that can be seen at bird feeders. These birds can reach high densities in winter in the southern pine forests, when resident populations are supplemented by northern migrants. Pine Warblers are much more tolerant of cold weather than other warblers, perhaps because they are able to switch from insects to seeds as a food source. In Texas this species breeds exclusively in the South Central Plains Level III Ecoregion (a.k.a. "Piney Woods").	**Natural History:** Insects, spiders, slugs, and other soft-bodied arthropods are listed as food items. Feeds from the ground all the way up to tree-tops, but mainly gleans lower bushes and shrubs. Tail-bobbing is a common behavior in this species. The Prairie Warbler winters farther north than many warbler species. While some fly as far as the Yucatan Peninsula, others stay in the northern Caribbean or in Florida. They can be fairly common in the Florida Everglades during winter. Despite having benefited from clearing of forests the last century, there are unexplained declines in some populations in recent years. Males show fidelity to breeding areas and may return year after year. Seen in south Texas as a spring/fall migrant. Summers in the "Piney Woods."	**Natural History:** This species nests in the boreal forests of Canada and winters along the southeastern US coast and throughout the Caribbean. Unlike most warblers that spend most of their time high in the canopy, the Palm Warbler is a decidedly terrestrial species that hunts primarily on the ground or in low shrubs. It is one of the most northerly wintering of the warblers and most winter in Florida (thus the name Palm Warbler). The winter range also includes much of the Texas gulf coast. Their summer habitats are very far to the north, well into northern Canada. Food is mainly insects, mostly caught on the ground. Includes grasshoppers, beetles, lepidopterans, flies and bee larva. Some berries and nectar may be consumed in winter.

Class—**Aves** (birds)

Order—**Passeriformes** (perching birds & songbirds)

Family—**Parulidae** (warblers)

Bay-breasted Warbler	Cerulean Warbler	American Redstart
Setophaga castanea	*Setophaga cerulea*	*Setophaga ruticilla*

Size: 5.5 inches. Wingspan 9.

Abundance: Fairly common.

Migratory Status: Seasonal migrant.

Presumed range in TX

Size: 4.25 inches.

Abundance: Uncommon.

Migratory Status: Seasonal migrant.

Presumed range in TX

Size: 5 inches. Wingspan 7.75 in.

Abundance: Uncommon.

Migratory Status: Summer resident.

Presumed range in TX

Variation: See photos above. Female resembles fall male.

Variation: Female is bluish green with faded gray streaks.

Variation: Significant sexual dimorphism. See photos above.

Habitat: Summer habitat is spruce/fir woodlands of Canada. During migration it is found in a variety of habitats. Winter habitats are tropical forests of Central and South America.

Habitat: Summer habitat is primarily deciduous forests. Both bottomland forest and moist upland woods. Requires mature forests with predominance of larger trees.

Habitat: Prefers deciduous woodlands over conifers. More common in second growth areas and riparian thickets. Larger woodlands are preferred over small woodlots.

Breeding: Nests in dense conifer trees on a horizontal limb. Nest is cup shaped and made of woven twigs, pine needles and grasses. Average clutch size is 5 or 6 eggs.

Breeding: Nest is a tight cup woven around forked branches in the mid to upper canopy level. Average clutch size is 3 or 4 to as many as 5. Breeding habitat includes thick understory.

Breeding: The nest is woven of thin fibers of grass or bark strips and placed in the crotch of an upright branch or trunk. Usually 4 eggs. Has declined as a breeding bird in Texas.

Natural History: This long distance migrant is not commonly seen by residents of Texas as they pass through rather quickly. They migrate later than most other warblers and don't usually appear in Texas until mid May. Their primary food in summer is the Spruce Budworm caterpillar and their populations may rise and fall with the availability of this insect. In winter they will eat fruit. These birds are less common today than decades ago. Populations have declined possibly due to spraying of Canadian forests to control spruce budworms. Ironically, the best controller of destructive insect pests may be insect eating birds like the Bay-breasted Warbler and its kin. They winter from southern Central America to northwestern South America.

Natural History: The Cerulean Warbler hunts high in the canopy, gleaning tiny invertebrates from small branches and leaves. Searches both upper and lower surface of leaves for food. Like many species dependent upon forests, this warbler experienced significant population declines following the European settlement of America. Today many states list it as a threatened species. Protection of large tracts of deciduous woodlands is probably the best conservation action that can be taken to help the species. Unfortunately, not enough of this type conservation takes place in America. Winters in the Andes Mountains. In spring migration, it flies across the gulf to the southeastern US coast, often stopping to rest and feed on barrier islands before moving north.

Natural History: The striking bright orange-on-black colors of the male flash like neon in the heavily shaded forests where this species makes its home. The female's yellow and black colors are only slightly less evident. They are active little birds that display their bright colors by regularly spreading their tail feathers and drooping their wings. They hunt tiny insects among the foliage and often catch flying insects in mid-air. This species is much more common in forested regions and it may be absent from expansive agricultural regions. Small numbers may winter in coastal Louisiana, the lower Rio Grande valley an the everglades region of south Florida. Most winter from NW Mexico to northern South America. Clearing of tropical forests is a threat.

Class—**Aves** (birds)

Order— **Passeriformes** (perching birds & songbirds)

Family—**Parulidae** (warblers)

Hooded Warbler *Setophaga citrina*	**Wilson's Warbler** *Cardellina pusilla*	**Canada Warbler** *Cardellina canadensis*

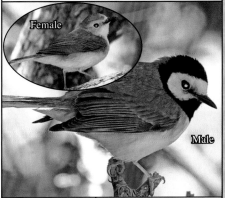

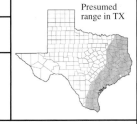

Hooded Warbler	**Wilson's Warbler**	**Canada Warbler**
Size: 5 inches.	**Size:** 4.75 inches.	**Size:** 5.5 inches.
Abundance: Uncommon.	**Abundance:** Fairly common.	**Abundance:** Uncommon.
Variation: Black "hood" is reduced in females.	**Variation:** Black "cap" more prominent in males.	**Variation:** Females have less black on breast and throat.
Habitat: A forest species. Most common in heavily forested regions but may be found anywhere that there is significant woodlands. Texas breeding habitat is large woodland tracts in the Piney Woods region.	**Habitat:** Summer breeding habitat is in the boreal forests of Canada, Pacific Northwest, northern Rockies, and Alaska. Winter habitat is tropical forests. May be seen almost anywhere in Texas during annual migration.	**Habitat:** Favors moist northern forests with thick understory shrubs. Known to associate with conifers on breeding grounds. Summers in northern forests in Canada and in the higher elevations of the Appalachian Mountains.
Migratory Status: Summer resident in Piney Woods, migrant in coastal plain.	**Migratory Status:** Seasonal passage migrant. Spring migration is in April.	**Migratory Status:** Seasonal passage migrant
Breeding: Cup-shaped nest of grasses, bark, and dead leaves is woven into two or more upright limbs of a small bush near the ground. Nest sites are usually associated with dense shrubs. 4 eggs.	**Breeding:** Nest is usually on the ground. Uniquely, the nest of this warbler is usually placed in a small depression. In some regions they nest above ground. From 2 to 7 eggs may be laid.	**Breeding:** Nest is on the ground and hidden amid dense vegetation or beneath the root wad of a fallen tree. In Canada nest is often placed amid carpet of moss. Four or five eggs is typical.
Natural History: Like many small, woodland birds the Hooded Warbler is more likely to be heard than seen. On their breeding grounds in the eastern US they require large tracts of woodlands and they have declined in areas where intensive agriculture or development has resulted in the loss of this habitat. This handsome little warbler is a good example of why the protection of extensive tracts of forest can be so important in the conservation of neotropical migrant songbirds. With the largest eyes of any warbler, this species is adapted to a life spent in heavy shade. Unlike most warblers that tend to be treetop dwellers, this species often feeds on the ground or in low shrubs. Spring migrants arrive in late March and April.	**Natural History:** They migrate later in spring than most other warblers and they can be seen into the month of May. Spring migration through Texas begins in early April. Fall migration starts in September. They are more numerous in the Rocky Mountain states and the Pacific states than they are in the eastern United States. However, some studies indicate that they are declining in the west. In western regions they are fond of stream-side habitats and some biologists blame the loss of riparian habitat for decline in western populations. They range as far north as the Arctic Ocean in summer and as far south as Panama in winter. The common name honors early naturalist and ornithologist Alexander Wilson.	**Natural History:** A few will nest in parts of the Midwestern US or in the Appalachians but most (over 80 percent) will nest in Canada. Although they do migrate through eastern Texas they do so mostly at night and pass through quickly en route to breeding grounds farther to the north. The Canada Warbler has been in decline for several decades. Loss of breeding habitat in North America as well as degradation of wintering habitat in South America is probably to blame. Unlike many warblers that fly across the Gulf of Mexico, this species migrates along the coast of Texas in April. Fall migration begins in August. Future threats include the Woolly Adelgid, and alien insect that is decimating hemlock forests in the north.

Class—**Aves** (birds)

Order—**Passeriformes** (perching birds & songbirds)

Family—**Parulidae** (warblers)

Prothonotary Warbler *Protonotaria citrea*	**Worm-eating Warbler** *Helmitheros vermivorus*	**Swainson's Warbler** *Limnothlypis swainsonii*

Size: 5.5 inches. Wingspan 8.75 in.

Abundance: Fairly common.

Variation: Female's colors are less vivid.

Presumed range in TX

Size: 5 inches. Wingspan 8.5 in.

Abundance: Rare in Texas.

Variation: No variation. Sexes are alike.

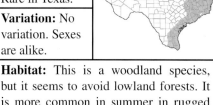
Presumed range in TX

Size: 5.5 inches. Wingspan 9 in.

Abundance: Rare in Texas.

Variation: No variation and sexes are alike.

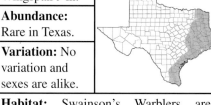
Presumed range in TX

Habitat: Prothonotary Warblers always nest near water. They are most common in swamps and marshes but can also be seen along lake shores, riparian areas, and in the vicinity of small ponds. Most common in the southern tip of the state.

Migratory Status: Summer resident in the Piney Woods region of Texas.

Breeding: Unlike other warblers that build a nest, the Prothonotary Warbler nests in tree cavities. They will also use artificial nest boxes. Lays 4 or 5 eggs.

Natural History: The dredging and draining of swamplands throughout the eastern United States significantly reduced breeding habitat for this warbler in the first half of the twentieth century. Loss of wetlands in the US has stabilized somewhat in the last few decades, but the species now faces threats from habitat loss on its wintering grounds in northern South America. In some areas of its range it has recently benefited from the placement of artificial nest boxes. Feeds on aquatic insects, snails and tiny crustaceans. In winter they will also eat fruits and nectar. In Texas this species breeds mostly in the South Central Plains Level III Ecoregion (i.e. "the Piney Woods"). A few probably breed farther to the west where suitable wetland habitats exist.

Habitat: This is a woodland species, but it seems to avoid lowland forests. It is more common in summer in rugged regions with steep slopes. It may occur in a wide variety of habitats during migration.

Migratory Status: Mostly a migrant but a few summer in eastern Texas.

Breeding: Nests are built on the ground in deep woods and are often hidden beneath overhanging vegetation. 4 to 5 eggs is typical.

Natural History: This is a species that specializes in feeding amid low bushes, searching the dead leaf clusters and low hanging foliage for insects, spiders, and primarily, caterpillars. Like many of America's neo-tropical migrant songbirds, the Worm-eating warbler is highly dependent upon deciduous forests for breeding habitat. They need large tracts of woodland. They winter in Mexico, Central America and the West Indies. Despite their name, earthworms are not an important item in their diet. Caterpillars, spiders and insects are primary foods. Migrants can be seen in Texas throughout the Gulf Coastal Plain and South Central Plains Level III Ecoregions. Some will breed and summer in the South Central Plains but their breeding populations have declined in Texas.

Habitat: Swainson's Warblers are known to associate with stands of giant cane in the southern US. In the Appalachians they frequent Rhododendren thickets. Winter habitat is tropical forest.

Migratory Status: Migrant and summer resident.

Breeding: The nest is built on the ground and is made of dead leaves, rendering difficult to locate. Lays 3 to 4 eggs. Breeds in eastern Texas.

Natural History: Very few Americans ever see this rare and secretive warbler. It has a reputation for being a difficult species to locate and even seasoned birdwatchers may go their entire lives and not see this species. It is very similar in appearance to the Worm-eating Warbler, but the Swainson's Warbler is primarily a ground dweller and the Worm-eating Warbler is more of a low bush species. In thick cover it moves mouse-like quietly along on the ground, foraging for food among the leaf litter. Although it ranges across much of the southeastern US in summer, it is nowhere common. Breeding in Texas is in the Piney Woods region of eastern Texas. Wintering grounds are most of Caribbean, Cuba, and the Yucatan Peninsula.

Class—**Aves** (birds)

Order—**Passeriformes** (perching birds & songbirds)

Family—**Parulidae** (warblers)

Ovenbird *Seiurus aurocapilla*	Louisiana Waterthrush *Parkesia motacilla*	Northern Waterthrush *Parkesia novaboracensis*

Size: 5.5 inches. Wingspan 9.5 in.  *Presumed range in TX*	**Size:** 6 inches. Wingspan 9.5 in. 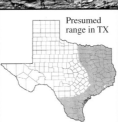 *Presumed range in TX*	**Size:** 6 inches. Wingspan 10 in.  *Presumed range in TX*
Abundance: Fairly common.	**Abundance:** Uncommon.	**Abundance:** Uncommon.
Variation: Females, fall birds more greenish.	**Variation:** No variation and sexes are alike.	**Variation:** No variation and sexes are alike.

Habitat: Mature, contiguous forests. Seems to prefer upland woods. A substrate of abundant leaf litter is an important element to this bird's habitat. Probably absent from many areas of its former range in America where forests no longer exist.	**Habitat:** Louisiana Waterthrush uses forested streams as the preferred habitat. In migration they may also be seen along the edges of swamps or small woodland ponds. More inclined to use streams and flowing waters. Restricted to the forested eastern half of Texas.	**Habitat:** Northern Waterthrush is more inclined to use stillwater environments rather than flowing waters. Bogs are a favored habitat in the summer breeding range. In migration they are often seen around the edge of woodland ponds or swamps.
Migratory Status: Seasonal migrant.	**Migratory Status:** Summer resident.	**Migratory Status:** Seasonal migrant.
Breeding: Nests is on the ground and is constructed of leaves and grass. Nest is unique in that it has a domed roof with an opening in front. 3 to 6 eggs.	**Breeding:** Nesting can occur as early as April in Texas. 4 to 6 eggs are laid in a nest placed in tree roots along a the banks of a stream.	**Breeding:** Breeds from northern Great Lakes and New England all the way to the Arctic Circle in Alaska. Nest is on the ground and well hidden.
Natural History: This large warbler is a ground dweller and is usually observed on the ground or in low foliage. Food is a wide variety of insects and arthropods taken mostly on the ground among the leaf litter. The song of the Ovenbird is distinctive and has been variously described as "emphatic" and "effervescent." Often two nearby birds will sing at once, with their overlapping songs sounding like a single bird. This species has experienced a decline in the last few decades. Forest fragmentation and Brown-headed Cowbird nest parasitism may be to blame. The name "Ovenbird" is derived from the fact that the nest is shaped rather like the old fashioned brick ovens that had a domed roof and opened to the front. Winters in Florida and tropical Americas.	**Natural History:** This species is famous for its incessant "tail bobbing" behavior. The entire rear half of the body constantly wags up and down when foraging in stream side habitats. Requires ecologically healthy stream habitats and this species may be a barometer of overall stream health. Although current populations appear stable, stream degradation in its breeding range has probably reduced its numbers from historical times. Distinguishing between this species and the nearly identical Northern Waterthrush can be very difficult. During migration both species can be seen in Texas. Only the Louisiana Waterthrush will be seen in Texas in the summer. The northern species summers in the far northern portion of North America.	**Natural History:** The Northern Waterthrush is so similar to the Louisiana Waterthrush that most casual observers will not be able to tell them apart. Of the two, the Northern is slightly smaller and has a narrower "eyebrow." The Northern Waterthrush just passes through Texas while the Louisiana Waterthrush breeds in eastern part of the state. Northern breeds in bogs and beaver ponds in boreal forests of Canada and Alaska. Both species associate with wetland habitats and in migration both can be seen in woodland habitats. Northern Waterthrush feeds in wet, soggy places and will wade in shallow water. It uses its bill to flip dead leaves and often feeds on the top of half submerged logs. Like the Louisiana Waterthrush, this species "tail bobs."

Class—**Aves** (birds)

Order—**Passeriformes** (perching birds & songbirds)

Family—**Parulidae** (warblers)

Kentucky Warbler	Common Yellowthroat	Mourning Warbler
Geothlypis formosa	*Geothlypis trichas*	*Geothlypis philadelphia*

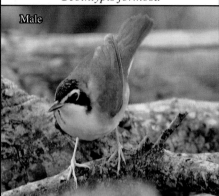
Male

Male

Size: 5 inches.

Abundance: Fairly common.

Variation: Female has reduced black mask.

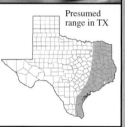
Presumed range in TX

Size: 5 inches.

Abundance: Common.

Variation: Female lacks the prominent black mask.

Presumed range in TX

Size: 5.5 inches.

Abundance: Uncommon.

Variation: Female has less contrasting head color.

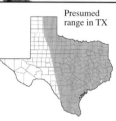
Presumed range in TX

Habitat: Throughout its summer range the Kentucky Warbler enjoys deciduous bottomland forests and wooded riparian habitats. Within this macro-habitat it requires a micro-habitat of dense undergrowth.

Habitat: Likes thick vegetation in wetland areas. Cattails and sedges in marshes and swamp edges are especially favored. Avoids deep woods but may be seen around edges of woods, especially near streams.

Habitat: The Mourning Warbler's summer/breeding habitat is mostly in the boreal forests and bogs of Canada. In migration they are most likely to be seen in dense regenerative woodlands. Usually seen on or near the ground.

Migratory Status: Summer resident and seasonal migrant.

Migratory Status: Summer resident and seasonal migrant.

Migratory Status: Seasonal migrant in early May and late September.

Breeding: A ground nester. The nest is constructed of dead leaves and grasses and is usually well hidden. Four to five eggs are laid by mid-May.

Breeding: The nest is woven from wetland grasses among cattails or sedges. Four to six eggs are laid in late May or early June. Cowbird parasitism occurs.

Breeding: Nests on the ground in dense vegetation or a clump of grass. Lays an average four eggs. Does not breed in Texas.

Natural History: Kentucky Warblers are a fairly abundant and widespread bird in suitable habitats throughout the southeastern United States. In Texas they breed mainly in the Piney Woods region in the easternmost portion of the state. They can also be seen during migration in the Gulf Coastal Plain. They are most common in the southernmost portion of the state. Like other small warblers they are easily overlooked. The Cornell Laboratory of Ornithology (birds online) website reports that this species appears to be in decline. Destruction of mature tropical forests may be to blame. It is also possible that fragmentation of large forests tracts in North America could be a threat. A handsome warbler, it feeds low to the ground on a wide variety of invertebrates.

Natural History: The Common Yellowthroat is one of the more abundant warblers in America and their summer range includes most of North America south of the Arctic. They do tend to avoid the desert southwest and dry southern plains. But they may occur in both regions in riparian habitats along rivers and streams. They feed low to the ground on almost any type of tiny invertebrate. Their behavior when foraging is rather "wren-like" as they negotiate dense stands of cattails, reeds, and tall grasses. They tend to stick to heavy cover and when flushed make short flights into deep cover. Nearly all of Texas's Common Yellowthroats move south in the fall, but a few linger in Gulf Coastal Plain the southern part of the state throughout the winter.

Natural History: This warbler likes second growth areas with lush undergrowth. It prefers these conditions both in its summer breeding grounds in boreal forests as well as its wintering grounds in tropical forests. Thus it is one of the few neotropical migrant warblers that has actually benefited from man's insatiable appetite for wood products. They are not easily observed as they are a secretive bird that "skulks" in dense thickets. Unlike many neotropical migrant songbirds that make long distance flights across the Gulf of Mexico, this warbler follows the coastline north though Mexico, Texas and Louisiana before flying inland up the and dispersing across northern regions. Most of its breeding range is in Canada and in the Great Lakes region.

Class—**Aves** (birds)

Order—**Passeriformes** (perching birds & songbirds)

| Family—**Parulidae** (warblers) | | Family—**Cardinalidae** (tanagers & grosbeaks) |

MacGillivray's Warbler
Geothlypis tolmiei

Size: 5.25 inches.

Abundance: Uncommon.

Variation: Hood of female is much lighter.

Presumed range in TX

Habitat: Requires dense understory and thickets. Frequently uses regenerative woodlands created by past forest fires or logging. Summer habitat is boreal forests. In winter uses a variety of dense, shrubby habitats.

Migratory Status: Seasonal migrant. Migrates mostly at night.

Breeding: Nest is low to the ground in a dense shrub or conifer sapling. Four eggs is typical but can be as many as six.

Natural History: Very similar to the Mourning Warbler and is the western counterpart of that species. They forage in low shrubs and saplings and mostly stay near the ground. Insects are probably the main food. They are apparently fairly more common than sightings would indicate because they are secretive and inhabit dense thickets. Forests that are naturally regenerated following fires provide good breeding habitat for this species. However, timber plantations featuring a single tree species planted after clear cutting are not used. On the other hand, environmentally conscientious logging operations that mimic the action of low intensity forest fires may benefit this species. The American Bird Conservancy website lists this as a declining species.

Painted Redstart
Myioborus pictus

Size: 5.75 inches.

Abundance: Rare in Texas.

Variation: Juvenile lacks red on breast.

Presumed range in TX

Habitat: The summer habitat is wooded canyons of the "sky island" mountain ranges in North America's desert southwest. Usually likes canyons with permanent water but will also use heavily vegetated slopes near water.

Migratory Status: Summer resident in the Chisos and Davis Mountain ranges.

Breeding: Nest is built on the ground. Nest location is under a shelter place on a steep slope on the side of a canyon. Three to seven eggs are laid.

Natural History: When foraging the Painted Redstart consistently spreads its tail feathers and opens and closes it wings. In so doing, it exposes the bright white colors on the wings and tail. This "color flashing" behavior is believed to be a way of flushing insect prey from their hiding places. Although they share the name "redstart" they are not closely related to the American Redstart (*Setophaga ruticilla*) on page 104. Rather, they belong to a group of mainly tropical birds found in Central and South America. Their genus (*Myioborus*) contains a dozen species, most of which are South American. The Painted Redstart is the only member of the genus that ranges into the United States. They are most common in the US in southeastern Arizona in summer.

Hepatic Tanager
Piranga flava

Male

Size: 12.5 inches.

Abundance: Rare in Texas.

Variation: Male is reddish, female yellowish.

Presumed range in TX

Habitat: Summer habitat in the US is in mountain ranges in the arid southwest. They are most common in the desert mountain ranges Arizona and New Mexico but also occur in the mountains of westernmost Texas.

Migratory Status: Summer resident. Arrives in Texas in mid April.

Breeding: Nests in trees in pinyon-juniper and pine-oak woodlands at mid to higher elevations (5,000 to 8,000 feet). As many as six eggs, average of four.

Natural History: Mainly a tropical species, the Hepatic Tanager ranges northward into the southwestern US in summer. In the fall they retreat back to their wintering grounds in Mexico where they inhabit a variety of forested environments. In Texas they can be seen in the "sky island" habitats of the Davis, Chisos and Guadalupe Mountain ranges. They may be vulnerable to droughts and their continued presence in Texas may be threatened by climate change if current trends towards warmer and drier conditions in the southwestern US continue into the future. The food is mainly insects. Young are raised on a diet of insects and invertebrates. Fruits and berries are also eaten by the adults especially in the tropical regions of their range.

Class—**Aves** (birds)

Order—**Passeriformes** (perching birds & songbirds)

Family—**Cardinalidae** (tanagers & grosbeaks)

Scarlet Tanager *Piranga olivacea*	**Summer Tanager** *Piranga rubra*

 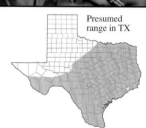

Size: 6.5 inches.

Abundance: Fairly common during migration.

Migratory Status: A seasonal migrant that flies across the Gulf of Mexico and begins to arrive in Texas in early April.

Presumed range in TX

Variation: Sexual and ontogenetic plumage variations. Juvenile males resemble females for the first year of their lives. See photos above.

Habitat: The summer habitat for the Scarlet Tanager closely coincides with the Eastern Temperate Forest Level I ecoregion. It prefers large tracts of unbroken woodlands.

Breeding: The thin, saucer-like nest of the Scarlet Tanager is placed on the fork of an outer branch. Four eggs is typical. Only one brood is produced.

Natural History: The Scarlet Tanager is one of the most strikingly colored birds in America. Unfortunately, this specie's dependence upon larger tracts of forested land means that its future is uncertain. Forest fragmentation leads to vulnerability to cowbird nest parasitism. Throughout much of the Midwest, where deforestation and fragmentation of forests has been rampant, this species is in decline. In the Midwestern portion of its summer range it is becoming uncommon except where large tracts of deciduous woodlands remain. Food in summer is mostly insects, including wasps and hornets, a habit that makes them a valuable bird to have around the rural homestead. Add to that their gaudy black and red plumage and you have a bird that all Americans should strive to protect. They winter from Panama to northwestern South America. The spring migration northward begins in March. They cover long distances quickly and are on their breeding grounds in northern US by mid to late May.

Size: 6.75 inches.

Abundance: Fairly common in eastern Texas.

Migratory Status: A summer resident that flies across the Gulf of Mexico and begins to arrive in Texas in early April.

Presumed range in TX

Variation: Sexual and ontogenetic dimorphism. See photos above. The mottled yellow-green and bright red of the juvenile male entering its second year can be seen in early spring.

Habitat: Like their Scarlet Tanager cousins, Summer Tanagers are primarily birds of the eastern forests. However, this species does range much farther to west.

Breeding: The rather flimsy nest is on a terminal fork of a branch that is usually low over an opening such as a creek bed. The typical clutch size is 3 to 4.

Natural History: Summer Tanagers feed on a variety of woodland insects and larva, but they also eat some berries and fruits. One of their primary food items, however, is bees and wasps, a fact that makes them an attractive species to have around the rural homestead. Immature males resemble females their first summer. By the following spring they begin transformation into the bright red plumage of the adult male. During this transformation they are one of the most colorful birds in eastern woodlands (see photos above). Breeding bird surveys in recent years have detected a slight decline in populations of this species. Landscape changes in their wintering grounds may be the reason. They will winter from southern Mexico to northern South America. Like many migratory songbirds they often migrate at night. In Texas this species is most common in the forests of the South Central Plains Level III Ecoregion (i.e. the Piney Woods). But they can also be seen in more westerly regions of the state.

Class—**Aves** (birds)

Order—**Passeriformes** (perching birds & songbirds)

Family—**Cardinalidae** (tanagers & grosbeaks)

Western Tanager *Piranga ludoviciana*	**Northern Cardinal** *Cardinalis cardinalis*	**Pyrrhuloxia** *Cardinalis sinuatus*

Size: 7.25 inches.

Abundance: Uncommon.

Variation: Sexually dimorphic. See photos.

Presumed range in TX

Size: 8.75 inches.

Abundance: Common.

Variation: Sexually dimorphic. See photos.

Presumed range in TX

Size: 8.75 inches.

Abundance: Common.

Variation: Male has red on face and belly.

Presumed range in TX

Habitat: During migration can occur in almost any habitat, including deserts. The primary summer habitats are montane forests and boreal forests where conifers like spruce, fir, and pine are dominant.

Migratory Status: Mainly a seasonal migrant. A few breed at high elevations in the west Texas mountains.

Breeding: Nest is a rather flimsy platform of sticks placed in the fork of a horizontal limb. 3 to 4 eggs.

Natural History: Often regarded as the western counterpart to the Scarlet Tanager, this species ranges throughout the Rocky Mountain region. It ranges farther north than any other Tanager, going as far as the southern tip of the Northwest Territory. Most Western Tanagers seen in Texas will be passage migrants but a few will nest and spend the summer in the higher mountains of the Trans-Pecos region. Some may be seen in the High Plains region as well but they apparently don't breed there. Spring arrival in Texas is in early to mid April and most will leave in October. They spend the winter months in Mexico and throughout Central America. Food is a variety of invertebrates including bees and wasps. They may also consume nectar.

Habitat: From undisturbed natural areas to suburbs, the Northern Cardinal favors edge areas with shrubs and brush. Avoids areas of extensive forests in favor of successional habitats. Fond of rural lawns with trees and shrubby.

Migratory Status: Year-round resident that breeds nearly statewide. Very rare in the western tip of the state.

Breeding: Nest is usually in a thick shrub or bush. About 4 eggs on average. Two broods per year.

Natural History: Conspicuous and highly recognizable, the Northern Cardinal enjoys the distinction of being the state bird for a total of seven states. They are mainly seed and berry/fruit eaters, but they will eat insects and feed insects to the young. They are common birds at feeders throughout their range, especially during winter, and they are equally abundant in rural and urban regions. In the last century they have expanded their range farther to the north into the Great Lakes region and New England. Today they are seen throughout much of the United States east of the Rockies. The southern extent of their range is northern Central America. More common in eastern Texas. Throughout their range they are often known by the name "Redbird."

Habitat: This is an arid land species that ranges throughout both the Chihuahuan and Sonoran Deserts but also lives in mesquite scrub, arid brushlands, and dry savanna habitats. Their range extends southward well into Mexico.

Migratory Status: A year-round resident Some seasonal movement may occur in response to exceptional cold.

Breeding: Nest is in a bush or tree. Nest is constructed by the female. Three or four eggs are laid.

Natural History: The Pyrrhuloxia enjoys more arid habitats than its eastern cousin the Cardinal. Where the ranges of the two overlap the Pyrrhuloxia occupies drier habitats. They are found in the US in Texas, New Mexico and in Arizona. In Texas they are most common in the southern tip of the state. They also range throughout northern Mexico except for the higher elevations of the Sierra Madre Occidental. The food of this species includes a wide variety of seeds as well as berries and fruits. Insects are also an important dietary item especially for the young. Like its cousin the Northern Cardinal this species will come to bird feeders where sunflower seeds are offered. In spite of some slight declines in population this species appears to be thriving.

Class—**Aves** (birds)

Order—**Passeriformes** (perching birds & songbirds)

Family—**Cardinalidae** (tanagers & grosbeaks)

Rose-breasted Grosbeak *Pheucticus ludovicianus*	**Black-headed Grosbeak** *Pheucticus melanocephalus*	**Blue Grosbeak** *Passerina caerulea*

Size: 8 inches.

Abundance: Fairly common.

Variation: Sexually dimorphic. See photos above.

Presumed range in TX

Habitat: A forest species primarily, but enjoys edge areas and regenerative woodlands with thick shrubby cover. May be fairly common in suburbs with adequate cover in the form of bushes.

Migratory Status: Seasonal passage migrant. Passes through Texas in April/May and in September to November.

Breeding: 3 to 5 eggs are laid in a nest of twigs, grass, and plant fibers. Nesting begins in late May. May rarely produce two broods per year.

Natural History: Many Rose-breasted Grosbeaks seen in Texas are passage migrants that nest farther to the north. But nesting is widespread in the northern third of the state where they will reside throughout the summer. A few will nest in central Texas as well. In southern Texas they merely pass through the state in spring and again in the fall enroute to wintering habitats in Central and South America. Food in summer about 50/50 insects and plant material such as seeds, fruits, flowers, and buds. During migration they are readily attracted to bird feeders where sunflower seeds are a favorite food. Birdwatchers throughout the state enthusiastically await the return of migrant songbirds each spring, and the Rose-breasted Grosbeak is a favorite.

Size: 8.25 inches.

Abundance: Uncommon.

Variation: Sexually dimorphic. See photos above.

Presumed range in TX

Habitat: Primary habitat is montane woodlands of the Rocky Mountain west. Riparian woodlands of Oak, Cottonwood and willow as well as in mountain pine forests.

Migratory Status: Summer resident in the mountains of the Trans-Pecos region. Migrant through desert areas.

Breeding: Three or four eggs are laid. Nesting in Texas is in mountainous areas from about 4,000 to 8,000 feet elevation. Breeds in westernmost Texas.

Natural History: Black-headed Grosbeaks arrive in west Texas in April and breeding/nesting occurs from May through June. Southward migration may begin as early as August and last into late October. Occurs in Texas as a breeding bird only in the Trans-Pecos area, but migrants and strays may appear farther to the east in the Edwards Plateau and throughout the panhandle. They winter throughout most of central and southern Mexico as far south as the Isthmus of Tehuantepec. Climate change may impact the distribution of this species (and many others) in the desert regions of North America. The current trend has the southwest becoming drier. If that continues, many bird species may shift their summer ranges to less hostile environments.

Size: 6.75 inches.

Abundance: Fairly common.

Variation: Female and juvenile are reddish brown.

Presumed range in TX

Habitat: On summer range the Blue Grosbeak enjoys overgrown fields dominated by forbs and saplings. Also uses fence rows, thickets, brambles, etc. Winters in Mexico and Central America.

Migratory Status: A summer resident that arrives from its winter range in April and May.

Breeding: Nest is a tightly woven cup placed in a low bush or tangle of vines, brush. About 4 eggs. Double brooding is known in the southern part of range.

Natural History: In Texas this bird is more common in the eastern portion of the state and in the Edwards Plateau and Trans-Pecos. It is least common in central Texas. Recent breeding bird surveys suggest that this species is expanding its range northward in North America and they may soon become more common in northern regions. During summer they feed mostly on crickets, grasshoppers and other insects, but eat mostly seeds in the early spring and fall. They will often visit bird feeders at these times. Waste grain may also be a food source in fall. The summer range of the Blue Grosbeak stretches from coast to coast across the southern US. The bright blue color of the male is in sharp contrast to the reddish-brown color of the female.

Class—**Aves** (birds)

Order—**Passeriformes** (perching birds & songbirds)

Family—**Cardinalidae** (tanagers & grosbeaks)

Indigo Bunting *Passerina cyanea*	**Lazuli Bunting** *Passerina amoena*	**Varied Bunting** *Passerina versicolor*

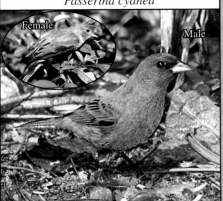

Size: 5 inches.	**Size:** 5.5 inches.	**Size:** 5.5 inches.
Abundance: Fairly common.	**Abundance:** Rare in Texas.	**Abundance:** Uncommon.
Variation: Sexually dimorphic. See photos above.	**Variation:** Sexual and seasonal variations. See Natural History.	**Variation:** Sexually dimorphic. See Natural History below.

Presumed range in TX

Habitat: Edge areas, fence rows, rural roadsides with substantial brushy/weedy cover. Overgrown fields with tall weeds or early successional woodlands are favorite habitats.

Migratory Status: Summer resident.

Breeding: Two broods are common. Lays 2 to 4 eggs in a nest of woven grasses that is usually placed in thick cover only a few feet above the ground.

Natural History: Indigo Buntings are common in summer throughout the eastern half of America. Probably more so today than in historical times when forests dominated much of the habitats in the eastern US. The neon blue color of the male makes it one of the most striking of North American birds. These birds are found throughout the eastern United States in summer, generally ranging from the short grass plains eastward to the Atlantic and as far north as southern Canada. They are most common in the southeastern US. Their annual migration may encompass up to 2500 miles and many make the long flight across the Gulf of Mexico. Large flocks appear along the gulf coast in early April. Seeds and berries are the primary food but insects are eaten during the breeding season. They will come to bird feeders.

Habitat: Can be seen in summer throughout the Rocky Mountain west as far north as southern British Columbia. It favors brushy areas from the shortgrass prairies west to the Pacific.

Migratory Status: Seasonal migrant.

Breeding: Breeds in riparian woodlands. Nest is low to the ground and in a dense bush. Does not regularly breed in Texas. Three to four eggs.

Natural History: Lazuli Bunting feed in the understory of woodlands and in thickets. Many insects are eaten and they also eat berries and seeds. They pass through western Texas on their spring migration in late April through mid May. The fall migration begins very early, with some individuals heading south by late July. At this time they are beginning to undergo their annual molt and they will pause their migration for over a month to complete the molt. They then continue moving south to their winter range in western Mexico. Female Lazuli Buntings are much less strikingly colored, being brownish with a bluish on the tail and wings. Juvenile and non-breeding males are also duller but still handsome with a buff-colored breast and a pale bluish wash on the wings and face. These beautiful birds can be lured to feeders with millet seed.

Habitat: In Texas uses areas of thorny brush and riparian thickets. Probably more common in foothills and in foothill canyons but may also occur in lower desert basins.

Migratory Status: Summer resident.

Breeding: Nest is usually low to the ground in a dense shrub or tangle of vines. Three or four eggs is typical. Eggs hatch in two weeks.

Natural History: The nesting behavior of the Varied Bunting seems to coincide with the summer monsoon season. Thus it leaves the US later than many migrants, sticking around into early fall. Its winter range is in Mexico and northern Central America (Guatemala). These birds exhibit both sexual and seasonal dimorphism. In the female, the red and purple colors of the male are replaced by a uniformly tan color. In non-breeding males, the red colors are replaced by brown. When seen in shadows or from a distance the dark purple of the breeding male can appear black. This is one of the least known of Texas's songbird species. They tend to stick to heavy cover and rarely come to backyard bird feeders. To see this bird usually requires a concerted effort and they are high on the list of birds pursued by avid bird watchers.

Class—**Aves** (birds)

Order—**Passeriformes** (perching birds & songbirds)

Family—**Cardinalidae** (tanagers & grosbeaks)

Family—**Thraupidade** (tanagers)

Painted Bunting	**Dickcissel**	**Morelet's Seedeater**
Passerina ciris	*Spiza americana*	*Sporophila morelleti*

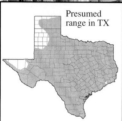
Female

Female — Male

Female — Male

Size: 5.5 inches.

Presumed range in TX

Abundance: Fairly common.

Variation: Sexual dimorphism. See above.

Size: 6.25 inches.

Presumed range in TX

Abundance: Fairly common.

Variation: Female lacks black bib. See above.

Size: 4.5 inches.

Presumed range in TX

Abundance: Rare in Texas.

Variation: Female and juvenile brownish.

Habitat: Likes semi-open habitats. Successional areas, overgrown fence rows bordering open fields, rural roadsides and weedy fields are used in summer throughout most of Texas.

Habitat: Fallow lands with weeds, saplings, and grasses. Weedy fields in open areas are the preferred habitat. Original range was probably natural prairie regions.

Habitat: Likes open and semi-open habitats with abundant tall grasses, weeds, and saplings. In Texas found only in the southernmost tip of the state in the lower Rio Grande Valley.

Migratory Status: Summer resident that arrives as early as March. Most will be gone from state by mid-October.

Migratory Status: Summer resident. Some birds appear as early as mid-March but most arrive in April.

Migratory Status: Year-round resident but populations in Texas have declined significantly from historical records.

Breeding: Nest is usually built low to the ground in a bush. Grasses are tightly woven and attached to stems. Three to four eggs.

Breeding: Breeds across much of Texas. Produces only one brood per year. Nest is in a shrub low to ground. 4 eggs is usually but may be as many as 6.

Breeding: Breeding in Texas occurs from April to July. Nest may be in a small tree or bush or sometimes built in tall weeds. Three or four eggs laid.

Natural History: The plumage of the male Painted Bunting is one the most colorful of any North American bird and they are a favorite of American birdwatchers. Males don't acquire their characteristic coloration until their second spring. Juvenile males resemble females. There are two different populations of Painted Buntings that nest and summer in the US. The eastern population is disjunct from the larger populations that occupy regions west of the Mississippi River. The Cornell University website "Birds of North America" state that this is a species in decline. But that assessment refers mainly to the populations in the eastern US. In Texas the species seems to be faring well. Loss of habitat is probably the main threat.

Natural History: The bulk of the Dickcissel's summer range is in the central Great Plains, including much of Texas. Originally nested in natural prairies but today has expanded its range eastward into suitable habitats created by deforestation and subsequent conversion of woodlands to cropland and pasture. They are also known to wander well outside their core range and are sometimes seen as fare east as the Atlantic coast. Flocks numbering in the thousands have been recorded during migration. Eats seeds almost exclusively during migration and on winter range. During breeding is more omnivorous, consuming insects. An open country bird, the Dickcissel is uncommon in Texas in the more heavily forested regions and is absent from desert regions.

Natural History: Sometimes called the White-collared Seedeater and formerly placed in the sparrow family (Emberzidae). The name "Morelet's" Seedeater honors early french naturalist Pierre Morelet, who collected zoological specimens in Mexico, Central America and the Caribbean. This species' population has ebbed and flowed in Texas in recent decades. Prior to the 1950s the species was fairly common in the lower Rio Grande Valley but then declined to nearly zero. In the last twenty years there seems to have been something of a resurgence of the species into its historical range in the state, but it remains quite rare in Texas today. The cause of this fluctuation is unknown. It is quite common farther south in Mexico and throughout Central America all the way to Panama.

Class—**Aves** (birds)

Order—**Passeriformes** (perching birds & songbirds)

Family—**Passeriledae** (sparrows)

Eastern Towhee	Spotted Towhee
Pipilo erythrophthalmus	*Pipilo maculatus*

Male

Male

Female

Female

Size: 8 inches. Wingspan 10.5 in.

Abundance: Fairly common.

Variation: Sexually dimorphic. See photos above.

Migratory Status: A winter resident throughout the eastern one-third of Texas.

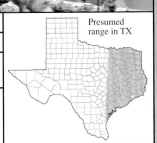
Presumed range in TX

Size: 8 inches. Wingspan 10.5 in.

Abundance: Fairly common.

Variation: Sexually dimorphic. See photos above.

Migratory Status: Mostly a winter resident. A few summer in the west Texas mountains.

Presumed range in TX

Habitat: Successional woodlands, overgrown fields/fence rows, edges of stream courses and woodlots where vines, briers, weeds and saplings are predominate.

Habitat: Successional woodlands, overgrown fields, riparian habitats in desert areas, wooded canyons, forested mountain slopes and shrubby habitats.

Breeding: Nests are well hidden and low to the ground or even on the ground. Usually 4 eggs. Does not nest in Texas.

Breeding: The only nesting in Texas occurs in the mountains of the Trans-Pecos region (Chisos, Davis and Guadalupe Mts.)

Natural History: Towhees are our largest member of the sparrow family. The Eastern Towhee is sometimes called "Rufous-sided Towhee." The widespread range of the Eastern Towhee corresponds closely to the Eastern Temperate Forest ecoregion, but they normally do not occur in dense populations. Most bird feeders in rural areas of the eastern US will have a pair for the winter, but rarely more than two pairs. Spends most of its time on the ground or in low bushes and thickets. Food is mostly seeds and in winter and insects in summer. Berries and fruits like crabapple are also consumed in fall and winter. Historical publications suggest this species may be expanding its range farther to north.

Natural History: The Spotted Towhee was once regarded as a subspecies of the Eastern Towhee and the two are very similar in most regards. The Spotted Towhee is recognized from the Eastern species by the presence of white spotting in the back and wings. Where the ranges of the two species overlap hybridization sometimes occurs. Winter migrants from the northern portions of their range begin to arrive in Texas in late October and most will leave the state in May. Those that inhabit the mountains of west Texas will stay year-round and breed in the state. Feeds on the ground with a characteristic thrusting backwards of both feet to throw away leaf litter and detritus and reveal prey organisms hiding below.

Class—**Aves** (birds)
Order—**Passeriformes** (perching birds & songbirds)
Family—**Passeriledae** (sparrows)

Canyon Towhee *Melozone fusca*	Green-tailed Towhee *Pipilo chlorurus*	Olive Sparrow *Arremonops rufivirgatus*

Size: 9 inches. Wings 11.5 in. 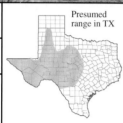	**Size:** 7.25 inches. 	**Size:** 6.25 inches. 
Abundance: Fairly common.	**Abundance:** Fairly common.	**Abundance:** Uncommon.
Variation: Juveniles have faint streaks.	**Variation:** Reddish crown is duller on female.	**Variation:** No variation. Sexes alike.

Presumed range in TX (maps shown for each species)

Habitat: In Texas inhabits the Chihuahuan Desert, Edwards Plateau and parts of the High Plains and Southwestern Tablelands Level III Ecoregions.	**Habitat:** Mountains and canyons of the western US. Inhabits brushy, lower slopes, open montane forests and areas with sagebrush and thick cover.	**Habitat:** In Texas this species is found in the Southern Texas Plains and the Western Gulf Coastal Plain in "Thornscrub Habitats."
Migratory Status: Year-round resident.	**Migratory Status:** Winter resident.	**Migratory Status:** Year-round resident.
Breeding: Bulky nest made from twigs and grass is tucked deep with a bush or cactus. Average number of eggs is three but can be as high as six. Nesting season in Texas is April through September.	**Breeding:** Nest is constructed of twigs and grass and built in a low bush or on the ground. Three or four eggs are laid. May produce two broods per year. Does not nest in Texas.	**Breeding:** Nest is well hidden in a dense bush, cacti, or on the ground. The nest is domed and two to five eggs are laid. Breeding occurs from late March through September in Texas.
Natural History: Western Texas represents the northern and eastern edge of this species' range in the North America. They are also found throughout southern New Mexico, Arizona and southward throughout north central Mexico. Some research has suggested that the Chihuahuan Desert populations of this species may be distinct from those found in the Sonoran desert farther to west. Like other Towhees, these birds feed mostly on the ground seeking prey beneath the leaf litter. These are decidedly arid land birds, and they are the most desert adapted of the Texas Towhees. They time their breeding cycle to coincide with spring and late summer rains when insects and other invertebrate prey is most available. In winter they will feed heavily on seeds of grasses and forbs as well as on berries, including Poison Oak berries.	**Natural History:** This is a bird of the western US that summers in the Rocky Mountains and winters in desert regions. All towhees are ground-feeding birds that scratch around in the leaf litter using both feet to toss detritus backward as they search for the many types of invertebrate prey that lives in the litter. The Green-tailed Towhee forages mostly beneath thick cover and they can be a hard species to see. Their reddish crown is most apparent when they are excited or defending territory against another bird. A hundred percent of the population summers in the western United States. About half will winter in the desert regions of the southwestern US and the other half in Mexico. Populations of this bird appear stable but climate change may affect their summer range if serious drought conditions continue in the Western US.	**Natural History:** Living only the southernmost portion of the state, these sparrows are unknown to many Texans. Even those who live within their range may fail to notice them, as they are rather drab in color and somewhat secretive in habits. They stay close to or on the ground and skulk around beneath dense cover in the thorn scrub thickets that characterize the "South Texas Brush Country." Mainly a Latin American species, the bulk of their range is along both coasts of Mexico and in the Yucatan Peninsula, with populations existing as far south as Panama. They are frequently the victim of nest parasitism by cowbirds and clearing of brush can enhance the impact on the population by making it easier for cowbirds to find the nest. These birds forage mostly on the ground and often use both feet to overturn leaves and detritus for prey.

Class—**Aves** (birds)

Order—**Passeriformes** (perching birds & songbirds)

Family—**Passeridae** (sparrows)

Cassin's Sparrow *Peucaea cassinii*	**Bachman's Sparrow** *Peucaea aestivalis*	**Rufous-crowned Sparrow** *Aimophila ruficeps*

Size: 6 inches.

Abundance: Fairly common.

Variation: No variation among adults. Young have streaks.

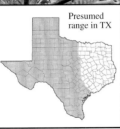
Presumed range in TX

Habitat: Inhabits a variety of desert habitats in the southwestern US and Mexico and in the higher elevations of the Shortgrass Prairies.

Migratory Status: Year-round resident.

Breeding: Breeding begins in March. Nest is constructed on the ground usually beneath a clump of grass. Four or five eggs are incubated for eleven days.

Natural History: Birds in the northern portions of their range in Texas will move south in winter. They may also move in response to drought and rainfall, moving from dry regions to areas that have enjoyed recent precipitation. Along the Rio Grande Valley and in the Southern Texas Plains and the southern half of the Western Gulf Coastal Plain they can be seen year-round. These are rather drab colored grayish-brown sparrows that are easily confused with many other types of sparrows. They are somewhat shy and secretive and although fairly common can be difficult to find. American Breeding Bird Survey populations are stable or slightly declining. Another similar sparrow, **Botteri's Sparrow** (*Peucaea botterii*) is a very rare summer resident in the southernmost portion of the Western Gulf Coastal Plain in Texas. It is regarded as a Threatened Species in Texas.

Size: 6 inches.

Abundance: Rare.

Variation: No significant variation among adult birds.

Presumed range in TX

Habitat: The Bachman's Sparrow is endemic to the southern pine forests. It is most numerous in habitats where fire keeps down dense undergrowth.

Migratory Status: Year-round resident.

Breeding: Nest is on the ground. Woven from grasses and concealed at the base of a shrub or clump of grass. About 5 eggs. Two broods is common.

Natural History: The range of the Bachman's Sparrow in Texas coincides closely with the South Central Plains ecoregion. The Bachman's Sparrow is one of the less well-known bird species to most Texans. They live deep in the pine forests and tend to be rather shy and secretive and they thus are easily overlooked. This species is often found sympatrically with the Red-cockaded Woodpecker. The favorite habitat is long-leaf pine/wiregrass woodlands. Almost none of this habitat remains in a virgin state in America, but state and federal forest agencies today manage many thousand of acres to help regenerate this unique and important habitat throughout. Bachman's Sparrow is a threatened species in Texas. It may be found the "Piney Woods" region of Texas and another local name for the species is "Piney Woods" Sparrow. Logging of pine forest is a threat.

Size: 6 inches.

Abundance: Uncommon.

Variation: No variation among adults. Young have streaks.

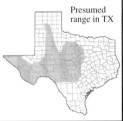
Presumed range in TX

Habitat: Dry, rocky hillsides with scattered shrubs in arid and semi-arid country are where you can find this unusual sparrow.

Migratory Status: Year-round resident.

Breeding: Nesting occurs from early April to late July. Nest is on the ground and hidden beneath a clump of grass or bush. Two to five eggs are laid.

Natural History: These sparrows spend most of their time on the ground and when the do fly it is usually for a short distance. They are very local in habits and tend to stay within their home territory. Monogamous, mated pairs may stay together year-round. The range of this species in Texas includes parts of the High Plains, Central Great Plains, Southwest Tablelands, and Cross Timbers ecoregions but they are probably most common in the Chihuahuan Desert and the Edwards Plateau. The *Texas Breeding Bird Atlas* in a report from the 2003 breeding bird survey indicates a significant decline in this species in the state. In addition to the range in Texas their total range includes parts of western Oklahoma, much of New Mexico, Arizona and California. It is also a widespread species in Mexico. Fire suppression has resulted in a decrease of habitat in some areas.

Class—**Aves** (birds)

Order—**Passeriformes** (perching birds & songbirds)

Family—**Passerilidae** (sparrows)

American Tree Sparrow *Spizelloides arborea*	Chipping Sparrow *Spizella passerina*	Clay-colored Sparrow *Spizella pallida*

Size: 6.25 inches.	**Size:** 5.5 inches. Wingspan 8.5 in.	**Size:** 5.5 inches. Wingspan 7.5 in.
Abundance: Uncommon.	**Abundance:** Common	**Abundance:** Fairly common.
Variation: Seasonal plumage changes.	**Variation:** No variation among adults.	**Variation:** Non-breeding birds are paler.

 Presumed range in TX

 Presumed range in TX

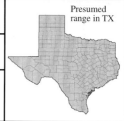 Presumed range in TX

Habitat: In winter they use overgrown fields, edge areas and brushy patches with weeds and grasses. Tallgrass Prairies are a favorite refuge. Summer habitat is typically open tundra and taiga.	**Habitat:** Edge areas and woods openings. Thrives in human-altered habitats including farmsteads, suburban yards and parks. Can be fairly common in urban and suburban neighborhoods.	**Habitat:** This is an open country species that prefers grasslands. Often uses abandoned fields taken over by weeds, grass, and brush. Might be seen in a wide variety of habitats in migration.
Migratory Status: Winter migrant.	**Migratory Status:** Winter resident.	**Migratory Status:** Seasonal migrant.
Breeding: Nest is on the ground. 4 to 6 eggs. These hardy sparrows will nest as far north as the Arctic Circle and well above the tree line.	**Breeding:** Breeds earlier than most other sparrows. Nests may be complete and eggs can being laid as early as mid-April. Nest is quite flimsy.	**Breeding:** Typically nest is close to the ground in grassy or brushy environments. 4 eggs is typical. Breeding is well to the north of Texas.
Natural History: The American Tree Sparrow is a northern species that is only seen in Texas in winter when heavy snow cover in the northern regions pushes migrating flocks southward. Like most sparrows, seeds are the staple food in winter. Seeds are also eaten in summer months but insects are more important, especially when rearing young. Seeds of a wide variety of grasses and weeds are consumed and this species is regularly seen at bird feeders in northern states. Despite its name this species can be found in summer on treeless, arctic tundra. Winter migrants begin to arrive in the northern US by late October and may reach Northern Texas by November. Degree of southerly movement can be dictated by weather conditions. Until recently this species was in the genus *Spizella* with other similar sparrows.	**Natural History:** Chipping Sparrows move to the deep south in winter. Nesting has been widely recorded in the state but most Chipping Sparrows in Texas move northward in the spring. They adapt well to the human disturbance of natural habitats and they are undoubtedly more common today than prior to the European settlement of America. They can be quite common in areas of intensive agriculture and also in urban/suburban environments. In fact, this is one of the most common sparrows in much of America and they will often forage in lawns. They can also be a common bird at feeders. They feed mostly on the seeds of grasses and forbs, and do most of their foraging on the ground. Insects are eaten during the breeding season and are fed to the young. This species is most common in Texas during winter when migrants increase the population.	**Natural History:** The core range for this species is in the Great Plains region. Range expansion eastward into the Great Lakes region apparently began in the 1920s. It is still an uncommon to rare bird in the east but it may be increasing in numbers. In its core range in the Great Plains ecosystem this species continues to maintain healthy population numbers in spite of the fact that this is one of the most damaged of all America's natural habitats. It is still one of the more common birds in the northern plains of Canada and North Dakota in summer. Winter range is mostly in Mexico and Texas is in the heart of their migratory route so they can be seasonally common. A few may winter in western or southern Texas. A drab bird that lacks prominent features. In fall plumage they are difficult to distinguish from the Chipping Sparrow.

Class—**Aves** (birds)

Order—**Passeriformes** (perching birds & songbirds)

Family—**Passerilidae** (sparrows)

Brewer's Sparrow *Spizella breweri*	**Field Sparrow** *Spizella pusilla*	**Black-chinned Sparrow** *Spizella atrogularis*

Brewer's Sparrow

Size: 5.5 inches. Wingspan 7.5 in.

Abundance: Fairly common.

Variation: No variation among adults.

Presumed range in TX

Habitat: An arid land species that summers in the sagebrush deserts of the inter-mountain west. Winter habitat is often in desert grasslands or other desert habitats, especially sagebrush habitats.

Migratory Status: Seasonal migrant and winter resident.

Breeding: Nests in sagebrush desert. Nest is usually in a Big Sagebrush bush. Nest is built out of twigs of sagebrush. Two to five eggs are produced.

Natural History: Some wildlife species are so tied to a particular plant community that they are referred to as "habitat obligates." The Brewer's Sparrow is a classic example of a habitat obligate. In the case of the Brewer's Sparrow that plant community is sagebrush. Throughout the high plateaus, arid foothills and deserts of the west various species of sagebrush are the dominant plant species. A handful of bird species are nearly completely dependent upon sagebrush, including the Brewer's Sparrow. As with many other habitats in America, the "Sagebrush Sea" is under assault. Threats are invasive species, improper grazing, development, intense wildfires, and climate change. In Texas Brewer's Sparrow is a migrant in the Panhandle and a winter resident in the Trans-Pecos regions.

Field Sparrow

Size: 5.75 inches.

Abundance: Fairly common.

Variation: Immature has dark streaks.

Presumed range in TX

Habitat: Open and semi-open areas with good cover in the form of weeds and taller grasses. Also shrubby, early regenerative woodland areas. Old overgrown fence rows are also favored.

Migratory Status: Mostly a winter resident. A few stay year-round.

Breeding: Nest is on the ground usually at the base of a clump of grass or in a low bush. Two broods per year is common. Two to five eggs.

Natural History: Another species that has adapted well to man-made changes in natural landscapes, the Field Sparrow is probably more numerous today than in historical times. Unlike many sparrows, however, the Field Sparrow is a "country" sparrow that prefers rural regions over towns and suburbs. Although they are seen year-round in parts of Texas, most move farther north in the spring. Food is mostly grass seeds. Insects are also eaten, especially during the breeding season. Very similar to the American Tree Sparrow, but has all pink bill instead of dark upper mandible. Although still a common species the Field Sparrow has experienced population declines in recent years. Perhaps due to habitat changes in much of its range. Its aversion to towns and suburbs may be one reason it seems less common.

Black-chinned Sparrow

Size: 5.75 inches.

Abundance: Rare in Texas.

Variation: Female lacks black on chin.

Presumed range in TX

Habitat: In Texas this species inhabits brushy hillsides and foothills of the mountain ranges in the Chihuahuan Desert Level III Ecoregion. In winter they may be seen in desert scrub.

Migratory Status: Mostly a winter resident.

Breeding: Very rare breeder in Texas in the Guadalupe Mountains. Possible breeder in the Chisos and Davis Mountains. Lays two to five eggs.

Natural History: This is a rare bird in Texas. It can be seen in winter in the Trans-Pecos region where it inhabits the regions mountain ranges. The rugged and harsh environments inhabited by the Black-chinned Sparrow, coupled with its scarcity in Texas make it a species that is unfamiliar to most Texans. This is a rather nondescript species. The female (shown above) is uniformly gray except for its brownish wings. The male is slightly more distinguishable with a black patch on the chin which gives the species its common name. The Black-chinned Sparrow is most common in west Texas in the winter, but a few will stay though the summer in the mountains of west Texas. This is a species that has declined in many areas and it does not fare well where the land is extensively grazed by cattle.

Class—**Aves** (birds)

Order—**Passeriformes** (perching birds & songbirds)

Family—**Passerilidae** (sparrows)

Vesper Sparrow *Pooecetes gramineus*	**Lark Sparrow** *Chondestes grammacus*	**Black-throated Sparrow** *Amphispiza bilineata*

Vesper Sparrow — **Size:** 6.25 inches. **Abundance:** Fairly common. **Variation:** No variation among adults.

Presumed range in TX

Lark Sparrow — **Size:** 6.25 inches. **Abundance:** Fairly common. **Variation:** No variation among adults.

Presumed range in TX

Black-throated Sparrow — **Size:** 5.5 inches. Wingspan 7.75 in. **Abundance:** Common. **Variation:** Juvenile lacks black throat.

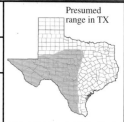
Presumed range in TX

Habitat: This is a bird of open country. Its natural habitats are grasslands and today it also uses agricultural fields. Prefers dry areas and upland fields over wet meadows or marshes.

Habitat: The Lark Sparrow is restricted to open habitats and is most common in dry grasslands of the southwestern US. It favors open field/brushy ecotones and dry uplands.

Habitat: An arid land species that inhabits deserts and dry mountains. Canyons, arroyos, and scrubby brushlands in arid regions of southwestern North America. Favors dry shrubland habitats.

Migratory Status: Winter resident. Migrant in the panhandle.

Migratory Status: Year-round in southern Texas, summer resident everywhere.

Migratory Status: Year-round resident in Texas portion of its range.

Breeding: Nest is on the ground in open fields, sometimes concealed by grass tussock. 3 to 5 eggs. May produce two broods per year. Does not breed in Texas.

Breeding: Nest is usually on the ground but may be in a low bush. Three to six eggs is typical. They are known to sometimes use the abandoned nest of another bird.

Breeding: Nest is built low in a desert shrub or cactus. Nest is positioned in shade away from the afternoon sun. Two to five eggs are laid and there may be two broods per year.

Natural History: The Vesper Sparrow is much more common in the western region of North America, but they do range into the eastern US. They are declining in the eastern portions of their range which includes much of the Midwest and great lakes region. They winter across North America south of about thirty-five degrees latitude. Some winter in Mexico as well. In some places this species may nest in crop fields and pastures, especially in the Great Plains. By contrast, it is uncommon, rare, or absent the more heavily wooded regions of North America. Their range includes nearly the entire conterminous United States, but they are by far more common in the Great Plains Level I Ecoregion. The northward migration out of Texas begins in early April.

Natural History: Although they do range into the eastern United States their core range is west of the Mississippi River and they are a common sparrow species in the western part of the country. Males are reported to perform a courtship "dance" that resembles that of a turkey's strutting behavior. The Lark Sparrow's facial pattern of vivid black and white stripes with chestnut cheek patch is distinctive. As with most sparrows, seeds are the primary food in winter. During warmer months both seeds and insects are eaten. Grasshoppers are reported to be a major food item in summer. These birds can be seen year-round in most of Texas, but those in the northernmost part of the state are short-distance migrants that move farther to the south in winter.

Natural History: The Black-throated Sparrow inhabits all four of America's Desert regions (Chihuahua, Sonora, Mojave, and Great Basin deserts). They also range widely across the arid regions of Mexico, including all of the Baja Peninsula and the Central Plateau. In Texas they are most common in the Chihuahuan Desert, Edwards Plateau and Southern Texas Plains Level III Ecoregions. Although they migrate in some parts of their range (Great Basin Desert and Mojave Desert), in Texas they are non-migratory. Plants common within their Texas habitat includes octillo, yucca, juniper, mesquite, acacia, and Creosote Bush. With their bright white facial lines enhanced by a large black throat patch and dark gray head color, they are easily recognized.

Class—**Aves** (birds)

Order—**Passeriformes** (perching birds & songbirds)

Family—**Passerilidae** (sparrows)

Sagebrush Sparrow *Artemisiospiza nevadensis*	Lark Bunting *Calamospiza melanocorys*	Savannah Sparrow *Passerculus sandwichensis*

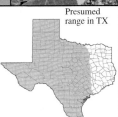

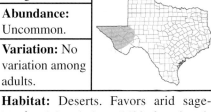

Size: 6 inches. Wings 8.25 in.	**Size:** 7 inches. Wings 10.5 in.	**Size:** 5.5 inches.
Abundance: Uncommon.	**Abundance:** Fairly common.	**Abundance:** Common.
Variation: No variation among adults.	**Variation:** Sexual and seasonal dimorphism.	**Variation:** Various shades of brown.

Presumed range in TX

Habitat: Deserts. Favors arid sagebrush plains below 5500 feet in elevation. Also uses Creosote Bush/Saltbush/cactus dominated desert, mesquite scrub and shrub covered desert foothills.

Habitat: The Lark Bunting is a classic "grassland obligate species." Its summer range in North America is contained entirely on the prairies and grasslands of the Great Plains and the short grass prairies of the inter-mountain plateaus.

Habitat: This is a grass loving species that is common in prairies and plateaus in the west. They are also common in the eastern United States but their habitat is always in open areas. Fields, pastures, reclaimed strip mines, etc.

Migratory Status: Winter resident in far west Texas.

Migratory Status: Mainly a winter resident, but some breed in the panhandle.

Migratory Status: Mainly a winter resident in Texas.

Breeding: Nest is usually in a shrub or clump of grasses. They typically produce more than one brood of up to four eggs.

Breeding: Males engage in an in-flight breeding display that involves flying upward and then setting the wings and gliding downward while singing loudly.

Breeding: Nests on the ground beneath overhanging vegetation. 4 to 5 eggs is typical. Nesting in the east is mostly in glaciated regions of the Midwest.

Natural History: The taxonomy of the Sagebrush Sparrow has been revised and re-revised on several occasions. Today two distinct but similar species are recognized that were once both considered to be the same species known as the "Sage Sparrow." In 2013 the westernmost population native to California was designated a distinct species and is today known as the Bell's Sparrow. All other populations in the US (including those in Texas) are now called Sagebrush Sparrow. The summer range of this species is in the sagebrush dominated Great Basin Desert. Winters in the Great Basin are harsh, and the Sagebrush Sparrows migrate a relatively short distance to the milder climates of the Sonora and Chihuahuan deserts in the southwest US and northern Mexico.

Natural History: The plumage of the breeding male Lark Bunting makes it perhaps the most easily recognized sparrow in America. By contrast, the non-breeding males resemble the mottled brown color of the females, which is easily confused with a wide variety of sparrow species! Birds seen in Texas during the winter will resemble the female shown above. In an unusual nesting tactic these birds will nest in loose colonies. Some males may have multiple breeding partners and others may not breed at all but will still help feed and rear the young birds. Nesting is on the ground and a maximum of five eggs may be laid. Two broods per year is not uncommon. Most nesting takes place in the northern great plains but some will nest in the Texas Panhandle.

Natural History: This is one of the most widespread songbirds in America. The range of the Savannah Sparrow includes the entire North American continent and parts of the northern Caribbean. As with many wide-ranging species there are several regional color morphs. The overall pattern is the same but the shades of brown can vary from brown to reddish-brown to chocolate. Texas birds will resemble the specimen shown in the photo above. The name comes from the Georgia town of Savannah (where the first specimen was described) rather than from the habitat type. As with many grassland animals the Savannah Sparrow has experienced population declines in areas of intensive agriculture or urbanization. Delaying cutting of hayfields benefits the species.

Class—**Aves** (birds)
Order—**Passeriformes** (perching birds & songbirds)
Family—**Passerilidae** (sparrows)

Grasshopper Sparrow *Ammodramus savannarum*	**Henslow's Sparrow** *Centronyx henslowii*	**LeConte's Sparrow** *Ammospiza leconteii*

Size: 5 inches. **Abundance:** Fairly common. **Variation:** No variation among adults. Sexes alike.  Presumed range in TX	**Size:** 5 inches. **Abundance:** Rare. **Variation:** Females and immatures are browner. 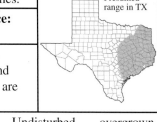 Presumed range in TX	**Size:** 5 inches. **Abundance:** Rare. **Variation:** No variation among adults. Sexes alike. 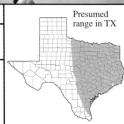 Presumed range in TX
Habitat: A grassland species, the Grasshopper sparrow likes short and mid-grass prairie. In the eastern regions of its range it uses heavily grazed pastures and hayfields.	**Habitat:** Undisturbed, overgrown grassy/weedy fields in open areas. Unmowed hayfields and re-claimed strip mines are used today. Original habitat is Tallgrass Prairie.	**Habitat:** Winter habitat is wet meadows, damp hayfields and marshy areas as well as grassy, upland fields. Summer habitat is the prairie regions of Canada. Shows an affinity for wetlands.
Migratory Status: Year-round.	**Migratory Status:** Winter resident.	**Migratory Status:** Winter resident.
Breeding: Nest is on the ground and well hidden beneath overhanging grass. Two broods per summer is usual with 4 to 5 eggs per clutch.	**Breeding:** Nest is on the ground in thick grass and well concealed. 2 to 5 eggs are laid in May. Double-broods are known. Young fledge at only 10 days.	**Breeding:** 4 to 5 eggs are laid in a nest woven from grass and placed in a clump of grass. Nests widely across south central Canada and Great Lakes region.
Natural History: Its name is derived from the sound of its song which mimics the buzzing sound made by some types of orthopteran insects. Throughout its range (which includes most of the US east of the Rocky Mountains) it is a rather inconspicuous bird. Though fairly common in the state it is unfamiliar to most Texans. It is a somewhat secretive bird except when breeding, spending much time on the ground hidden among grasses. Feeds entirely on the ground. Food is mostly grasshoppers and other insects in summer. In winter eats both insects and seeds, especially tiny grass seeds. Although it has been experiencing a population decline for several years, it is not yet regarded as a threatened species. Most breeding in Texas occurs in the High Plains and Southwestern Tablelands Level III Ecoregions (i.e. the Panhandle).	**Natural History:** Henslow's Sparrow is nowhere a common species and its relative scarcity and secretive nature make it one of the least familiar birds in the state. This is a species in decline throughout its range. Not surprising since the tallgrass prairies that once provided ample nesting habitat are all but gone. Insects, especially grasshoppers and crickets, are important food items in the summer. In winter eats mostly seeds, especially small grass seeds. Snakes are reported to be a major predator on nests, along with a variety of carnivorous mammals. Breeds sparingly across much of the Midwest but can be seen in Texas only in the winter and only in the eastern third of the state. Modern agricultural practices that have converted grasslands to croplands are the biggest threat to the species. Efforts to restore patches of grassland will help.	**Natural History:** This is a small and secretive sparrow that eludes attempts to study it closely. Little is known about many aspects of its biology. For instance only a small number of nests have ever been found. Usually remains hidden from view in dense grasses, and when flushed flies only a short distance before diving back into cover. Food items listed include small grass seeds and arthropods. There is even less information available regarding the habits of birds that winter in Texas. This is a species that has experienced a precipitous population decline. Loss of grassland habitat on the breeding grounds has been the main driver in this population decline. Although populations appear stable now, some believe climate change may pose a real threat to future habitat. Their secretive habits make it difficult to assess populations.

Class—**Aves** (birds)

Order—**Passeriformes** (perching birds & songbirds)

Family—**Passerilidae** (sparrows)

Nelson's Sparrow *Ammospiza nelsoni*	Seaside Sparrow *Ammospiza maritima*	Fox Sparrow *Artemisiospiza iliaca*

Size: 5 inches. **Abundance:** Uncommon. **Variation:** No variation among adults. Sexes alike.  Presumed range in TX	**Size:** 6 inches. **Abundance:** Uncommon. **Variation:** Several geographical color morphs. See below.  Presumed range in TX	**Size:** 7 inches. **Abundance:** Fairly common. **Variation:** Variable. Photo above is typical for Texas. 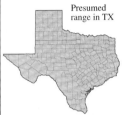 Presumed range in TX

Habitat: Primary habitat is marshes, both fresh (in summer) and brackish and salt marshes in winter. Summer habitat is mostly in Canada. Winters in saltmarsh along the southeastern coast.

Habitat: Lives in salt and brackish water marshes along the eastern coastline of North America. Ranges from southern New England to Mexico. Range is restricted to coastal regions.

Habitat: The Fox Sparrow is a lover of dense cover and thickets. Thick weeds and shrubs bordering woodlands or thickets. A mixture of brier, saplings, weeds, regenerating timberlands, etc.

Migratory Status: Winter resident in marshes along the Gulf Coast.

Migratory Status: Year-round resident in marshes along the Gulf Coast.

Migratory Status: Winter resident in most of Texas. Migrant in panhandle.

Breeding: Nest is a cup-like structure placed amid and supported by upright grass stems. 3 to 5 eggs is typical. Does not breed in Texas.

Breeding: Nest is a cup woven from blades of dried grass. Coarse grass stems make up the outer nest with finer grasses used as liner. 2 to 5 eggs.

Breeding: Nests are low to the ground or even on the ground. Breeding is in the boreal forests of Canada and in the northern Rockies. Usually 4 eggs.

Natural History: Nelson's Sparrow winters along the southeastern coastline of the US from the Chesapeake Bay to Texas. Most spend the summer in the Canadian plains or along the southern shore of Hudson Bay. In migration it may use grassy fields. This species requires large tracts of undisturbed marshland or grassland habitat and both habitats have experienced significant alteration or outright destruction. Subsequently, loss of grassland habitat in central Canada and loss of coastal marshes poses a significant threat to this species. Few Texans will ever see this sparrow unless a concerted effort is made by visiting coast marshes in winter. Until recently this species was considered conspecific with the Salt Marsh Sparrow (*A. caudacutus*) which ranges along the Atlantic coastline.

Natural History: Several subspecies of the Seaside Sparrow are recognized. Two of those subspecies are now probably extinct. Another, the Cape Sable Seaside Sparrow of the Everglades region is endangered. There is some argument regarding the subspecies status but at least two subspecies occur in Texas. The coastlines of North America have been subjected to two centuries of man-made alterations. Harvesting of salt grass hay, draining projects aimed at creating cattle pasture or filling marshes for development have had major impacts. Ditching to drain marshes as part of mosquito control is another serious threat, along with the widespread spraying of insecticides to kill mosquitoes. Future threats may be loss of marshes to coastal erosion as climate change brings sea level rise and more frequent storms.

Natural History: The Fox Sparrow is widespread across the North American Continent, summering in the far north (Canada, Alaska, and the northern Rockies) and wintering across much of the southern United States. Several distinct subspecies are recognized. The "Red" subspecies (*iliaca*) is the form seen in the eastern US and most Texas specimens will resemble the photo above. Western birds tend to be darker. They feed on a variety of insects and other arthropods in summer and subsist mainly on seeds in winter. They can be an occasional to regular visitor at bird feeders during winter, especially during periods of snowy weather. Unlike many other sparrows, the Fox Sparrow is never seen in large flocks and it is rare to have more than one or two at a time visiting feeders.

Class—**Aves** (birds)

Order—**Passeriformes** (perching birds & songbirds)

Family—**Passerilidae** (sparrows)

Song Sparrow *Melospiza melodia*	Lincoln's Sparrow *Melospiza lincolnii*	Swamp Sparrow *Melospiza georgiana*

Size: 6.5 inches. Wingspan 8.25 in.

Presumed range in TX

Abundance: Common.

Variation: Variable regional color morphs.

Habitat: Overgrown fields, dense underbrush, and rank weeds are the preferred habitat of the Song Sparrow throughout their range. They are especially common in edge habitats.

Migratory Status: Winter resident throughout the state.

Breeding: Nests are built low to the ground in weeds or shrubs. Four eggs is typical. Breeds far to the north. Does not breed in Texas.

Natural History: Both the common and scientific names of the Song Sparrow are references to its distinct and melodic song. Primarily seed eaters, these sparrows migrate in response to heavy snow cover, and they are common at bird feeders throughout the southern United States each winter. Sharp-shinned and Cooper's Hawks are major predators of adults, and the young and eggs are vulnerable to a variety of snake predators. However, they remain a thriving species. There are dozens of subspecies nationwide with light and dark color morphs. Most Texas specimens resemble the photo above. One of the earliest and most comprehensive studies of bird biology was conducted on this species. The range of the Song Sparrow includes the conterminous United States and most of Canada.

Size: 5.5 inches. Wingspan 7.25 in.

Presumed range in TX

Abundance: Fairly common.

Variation: No variation among adults.

Habitat: Summer habitat is boreal regions of Canada and northern Rockies where it occupies damp woodlands with dense brush such as willow. Spruce bogs and wetlands are favored.

Migratory Status: Winter resident in most of the state. Migrant in panhandle.

Breeding: Nests on the ground amid sedges or at the base of willow in boreal wetlands. Lays 3 to 5 eggs. Does not breed in Texas.

Natural History: Lincoln's Sparrows are more common west of the Mississippi and they are rather rare in much of the eastern US. In Texas they are a fairly common to common bird. This a somewhat shy and secretive bird and it tends to stick to heavy cover. When excited they will raise the feathers on the back of the head giving them a "crested" look. Due to their secretive habits the biology of these sparrows is not well understood. They feed on insects in summer and seeds in winter. Unlike many sparrows they rarely visit feeders except during periods of harsh winter weather. In appearance they are very similar to the Song Sparrow, but the Lincoln's Sparrow has finer streaking. This bird was not named after the famous US president, but rather named by J. J. Audubon after a friend and colleague.

Size: 5.75 inches. Wingspan 7.25 in.

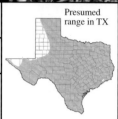
Presumed range in TX

Abundance: Common.

Variation: Regional subspecies variation.

Habitat: Summers in wetlands. Swamps, marshes (including salt marsh in coastal regions) and wet meadows. More diverse habitats may be used in winter, including upland fields.

Migratory Status: Winter resident in most of Texas. Migrant in panhandle.

Breeding: Nest is made of grasses and placed in cattails, grasses or low bush. Three to six eggs, four is average. Does not nest in Texas.

Natural History: Secretive and elusive, the Swamp Sparrow is less familiar to Texas residents than most of its kin. They will visit feeders during the winter, but they are rarely a commonly seen bird at feeders. These birds are highly dependent upon wetlands for breeding, and they may be negatively impacted by loss of wetland habitat. At this time, however, populations appear stable. Grassy fields are also heavily used and can be an important winter refuge. Although they can be quite common in summer habitats and in the bayous of the deep south in winter, they do not flock and are nearly always seen singly. There are three distinct subspecies of Swamp Sparrow recognized by professional orinithologists. The differences are slight and most lay persons will not be able to distinguish them.

Class—**Aves** (birds)

Order—**Passeriformes** (perching birds & songbirds)

Family—**Passerilidae** (sparrows)

White-throated Sparrow *Zonotrichia albicollis*	**White-crowned Sparrow** *Zonotrichia leucophrys*	**Harris's Sparrow** *Zonotrichia querula*
	Juvenile 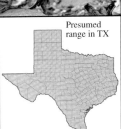Adult	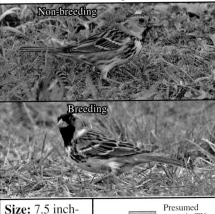Non-breeding 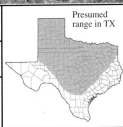Breeding

Size: 6.75 inches. **Abundance:** Common. **Variation:** Variable. See Natural History.	**Size:** 7 inches. Wingspan 9.5 in. **Abundance:** Common. **Variation:** See below for ontogenetic variation	**Size:** 7.5 inches. **Abundance:** Fairly common. **Variation:** See below for seasonal variation.
Presumed range in TX	Presumed range in TX	Presumed range in TX

Habitat: Brushy thickets, fence rows, weedy fields, edge areas, and regenerative woodlands. Both in upland and lowland areas. Can be seen in both rural and urban areas but always in the vicinity of bushes, shrubs, or tall weeds

Habitat: May be seen in any area where there are weeds, grasses, or brush in sufficient amount to provide good cover for roosting and escape from predators Woodland edges and overgrown fence rows are best.

Habitat: In Texas this sparrow likes edge areas where woodlots meet fields or pastures. Overgrown fence rows and fallow fields with tall weeds are a favorite habitat. Will come to backyard feeders where there is some cover.

Migratory Status: Winter resident in most of Texas. Migrant in panhandle.

Migratory Status: Winter resident throughout Texas.

Migratory Status: Winter resident in central Texas.

Breeding: Breeds in a broad band across Canada and the northeastern US, as well as MI, WI, and MN. Nest is on the ground in open areas, forest edges, etc. Four eggs is typical.

Breeding: Breeds in boreal regions, tundra, and mountain meadows. Nest is in a low bush with about 4 eggs. Breeds very far to the north in northern Canada and Alaska.

Breeding: Breeds exclusively in northern Canada. Nesting occurs at the boreal forests/tundra interface. Nest is on the ground beneath a small shrub such as an alder or a stunted spruce.

Natural History: There are two color morphs of this species. One has a bright white eyebrow and one has a tan eyebrow. Juveniles always have tan eyebrows and a faintly streaked breast. As these birds are ground foragers, snow cover is one of the most important conditions that influence migratory patterns. Feeds mostly on insects in summer and switches to seeds in winter. Berries are also heavily consumed when in season. When feeding uses both feet with a backwards thrusting motion to clear away leaf litter. They are well represented at bird feeders in winter. A short-distance migrator, this species winters mostly within the southern United States. This is one of the south's more common sparrows in winter

Natural History: Juveniles of this species have chestnut crown instead of white. Age-related differences in color, pattern or other morphological characters are what is known in biology as "ontogenetic variation." White-crowned Sparrows produce multiple broods (as many as four per season in some western populations). Most will have at least two broods annually. Some summer well into the Arctic Tundra and make annual migrations of over 4000 miles up and down the continent. Eats insects and seeds in summer, mostly seeds in winter. Forages on the ground near cover. Less common than the White-Throated Sparrow, but still a familiar bird at winter feeders. This is one of our most highly studied songbirds.

Natural History: The black around the bill is reduced on non-breeding birds and the facial color changes from gray to brownish. Juvenile has very little black on head and throat. The breeding range of this species is so remote that human influences on the local environment are minimal. On the wintering ground in the southern plains, however, habitat alteration can be significant. The Audubon Society web page "Guide to North American Birds" states that this species population appears to be stable at present. However, their assessment of the impact of climate change is a dire one, with an estimate of a 100 percent loss of breeding habitat in the event of a three degree Celsius increase in global temperatures.

Class—**Aves** (birds)

Order—**Passeriformes** (perching birds & songbirds)

Family—**Passerilidae** (sparrows)	Family—**Calcariidae** (longspurs)

Dark-eyed Junco
Junco hyemalis

Slate-colored

White-winged

Pink-sided

Oregon

Lapland Longspur
Calcarius lapponicus

Winter plumage

Size: 6.25 inches. Wingspan 9.25 inches.

Abundance: Common in winter throughout Texas.

Migratory Status: Winter resident in Texas.

Variation: Several different regional color morphs exist and six of these can be seen in Texas. The four pictured above are the Slate-colored, White-winged, Pink-sided, and Oregon morphs. In addition to these four the Gray-headed and Red-backed morphs may also be seen in parts of the state.

Presumed range in TX

Habitat: Occupies a wide variety of habitats in winter, but is most fond of semi-open areas such as woods openings or edges of woods. Summer habitat is boreal forests of the far north and montane forests in the higher elevations in mountains.

Breeding: Nest is on the ground, often concealed in a clump of ferns. Four eggs is usual. Compact nest is made of dead leaves and grasses with finer grasses as an inside liner. Most nesting occurs well to the north of Texas, but some breeding has been recorded in the higher elevations of the Guadalupe Mountains. Some populations may produce two broods in a summer.

Natural History: Juncos are a familiar winter bird at feeders throughout America. They arrive with the colder weather fronts and are often associated with snowstorms. In fact a common nickname in much of America is "Snowbird." Northern migrants arrive in Texas in late fall (earliest arrival is September but most won't be see in Texas until December). Most will leave the state by mid April but a few may linger into May. Those that summer in the southern United States do so only at the highest elevations in the Appalachian Mountains (above 3,500 feet). The combined summer, winter, and migratory ranges of the Dark-eyed Junco includes nearly all of the North American continent except Florida. Most of the Dark-eyed Juncos seen in the eastern US will be the "Slate-colored Junco." The various other color morphs are seen mostly in the western US. Similarly, most individuals in eastern Texas are the Slate-colored morph with other color morphs being seen in west Texas.

Size: 6.25 inches.

Abundance: Uncommon.

Migratory Status: Winter resident.

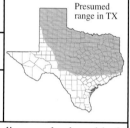
Presumed range in TX

Variation: Breeding male has black throat. Non-breeding similar to female.

Habitat: Winter migrants use very open areas with nearly bare ground. Large acreage harvested crop fields are the primary habitat for wintering flocks.

Breeding: Nests on the ground in a shallow depression on the Arctic Tundra. In places it may be the only nesting songbird. Females begin nesting almost immediately after arriving on the breeding grounds.

Natural History: This hardy bird breeds and summers in Arctic Tundra and is circumpolar in its distribution. Eggs (3 to 7) are not laid until early June. Southward migration begins in early fall. It is very common on its breeding grounds where it is sometimes the only songbird present. In winter they move far to the south, but are not very abundant east of the Mississippi River. Birds seen in Texas are in winter plumage. Lapland Longspur can be seen across most of Texas in winter, but they are most common in winter in the central Great Plains region and in mild winters may not be seen in southern Texas at all. They often flock with Horned Larks and American Pipits. Birds seen in Texas will be in winter plumage.

Class—**Aves** (birds)
Order—**Passeriformes** (perching birds & songbirds)
Family- **Calcaridae** (longspurs)

Smith's Longspur *Calcarius pictus*	Chestnut-collared Longspur *Calcarius ornatus*	Thick-billed Longspur *Rhynchophanes mccownii*

Size: 6 inches.

Abundance: Rare in Texas.

Variation: Seasonal and sexual plumage variations.

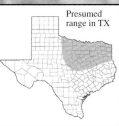
Presumed range in TX

Size: 6 inches.

Abundance: Uncommon.

Variation: Seasonal and sexual plumage variations.

Presumed range in TX

Size: 6 inches.

Abundance: Uncommon

Variation: Sexual and ontogenetic plumage variations.

Presumed range in TX

Habitat: In winter the Smith's Longspur seeks out open areas with short grasses. In migration they use similar habitats including closely grazed pastures or crop stubble.

Habitat: This grassland species prefers the short-grass prairie and desert grassland. In Texas they winter in the Warm Deserts and the South Central Semi-Arid Prairies Level II Ecoregions.

Habitat: Like other longspurs this is a grassland specialist. They inhabit Short-grass Prairie in the northern Rocky Mountain states of MT, WY, and CO as well as SK and AB provinces in Canada.

Migratory Status: Winter resident.

Migratory Status: Winter resident.

Migratory Status: Winter resident.

Breeding: This species nests in the high arctic tundra from the shores of Hudson Bay to the Arctic Ocean coast of Alaska. The nest is on the ground under a small shrub, often on a raised tussock. Up to six eggs may be laid.

Breeding: Nest is on the ground in a shallow depression lined with grasses. Nest is usually near an object like a grass tussock or even a cowpie. Three to five eggs are laid and there may be more than one brood per season.

Breeding: Females scrape out a small dish beneath a grass tussock or small shrub on the open prairie. The nest is lined with grasses and two to six eggs are laid. This species prefers to nest in drier regions than other longspurs.

Natural History: Breeding males are brightly colored with black and white facial markings and a clean, buffy colored breast and belly. Non-breeding males and females are streaked with various shades of light and dark brown in a "sparrow-like" pattern. The Longspurs in general are not well-known birds among the non-birding, non naturalist community. Even many professional wildlife biologists and birders have never seen these species, since most are rather uncommon birds with a restricted range in North America. In summer they inhabit remote, unpopulated regions and in winter plumage they are nondescript birds that tend to avoid urban regions.

Natural History: After wintering in the southwestern US the Chestnut-collared Longspur migrates to the northern Great Plains to nest and summer in shortgrass prairies. During migration they use heavily grazed pastures and harvested crop fields and reportedly have an affinity for Prairie Dog towns. The breeding males are handsomely patterned with a large chestnut "collar," black and white facial markings, a cream-colored throat and a black belly. Females and winter males are much more subdued in color with females being rather drab mottled brown with faint brown streaks on the breast. Non-breeding males are a "faded, washed-out version" of the breeding plumage. Most birds seen in Texas will be in winter plumage.

Natural History: Females and juveniles exhibit a "sparrow-like" plumage of streaked and mottled brown. As with so many other North American grassland species, this species has declined significantly from historical times, but the remaining population today seems to be stable. However, the conversion of grassland to cropland remains a real threat to this and many other grassland species. In fact, the grassland adapted birds are the most threatened bird group in America. Their winter range in Texas is in the Warm Deserts and the South Central Semi-Arid Prairies Level II Ecoregions. These ecoregions are used as winter range by many grassland birds including many of North America's grassland adapted sparrow species.

Class—**Aves** (birds)

Order—**Passeriformes** (perching birds & songbirds)

Family—**Passeridae** (weaver finches)	Family—**Fringillidae** (finches)	

House Sparrow
Passer domesticus

Red Crossbill
Loxia curvirostra

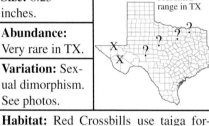

House Finch
Haemorhous mexicanus

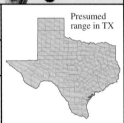

Size: 6.25 inches.

Abundance: Very common.

Variation: Sexual dimorphism. See photos.

Presumed range in TX

Size: 6.25 inches.

Abundance: Very rare in TX.

Variation: Sexual dimorphism. See photos.

Presumed range in TX

Size: 6 inches. Wings 9.25 in.

Abundance: Common.

Variation: Sexual dimorphism. See photos.

Presumed range in TX

Habitat: The House Sparrow's name comes from its affinity for human habitations. These are mostly urban birds but do occur in rural areas near farms.

Habitat: Red Crossbills use taiga forests in Canada as their summer habitat. Western populations exist in the conifer forests of high elevation in the Rockies.

Habitat: As implied by the name, House Finches are usually associated with human habitation, but they can be found both in cities and rural areas.

Migratory Status: A non-migratory year-round resident throughout Texas.

Migratory Status: Rare winter migrant and very rare resident in high mountains

Migratory Status: Year-round resident throughout the state.

Breeding: Builds a bulky nests of grass, feathers, paper strips, etc. placed in hollows. 5 to 6 eggs on average.

Breeding: Nest is made of twigs and lined with lichens, grass, or conifer needles. 3 eggs are usual.

Breeding: Nest of grasses is usually placed in dense evergreen shrub, cedar, or conifer tree. Lays 3 to 5 eggs.

Natural History: A European immigrant, the House Sparrow was released into the United States about 150 years ago. They have spread across the continent and they are now perhaps the most familiar bird species in America. Originally native to Eurasia, they have effectively colonized much of the world. They roost communally in dense vegetation. Roosting sites are often in yards or foundation plantings next to houses. They are common scavengers around outdoor restaurants and fast food parking lots. They are often considered to be a nuisance bird, but their tame demeanor endears them to many. Despite being extremely common in urban areas, they are quite rare in wilderness. These highly successful birds may nest up to four times in a season. Despite their common name, House "Sparrow," they are not closely related to sparrows. They are in the Weaver Finch family.

Natural History: This is surely the most unusual songbird species in Texas. The unique scissor-like beak of the crossbills is an adaptation for feeding on the seeds of conifers. The curved, crossed beak is used to pry open cones enough to allow the tongue to scoop out the seed. Seeds of pine, hemlock, spruce, and fir are the primary foods, but a variety of other seeds are also eaten and they will visit feeders for sunflower seeds. Their foraging habits are nomadic and flocks wander searching for cone bearing trees. They are prone to nomadic "irruptions." During an irruption year they sometimes move as far south as northern and western Texas. In most winters they will not be seen in Texas at all, (except for a few individuals that have been confirmed breeding in the higher elevations of the west Texas mountains). Some experts now believe this bird may consist of several identical species!

Natural History: House Finches have extended their range into the eastern United States over the last few decades. Originally native to the southwestern United States, the first House Finches appeared in the Midwest in the 1960s and began to become widespread in the '80s. Today they are found throughout the United States including all of the states east of the Mississippi River. Primarily a seed eater, these birds can be very common at urban feeders. Weed seeds, fruit, buds and flowers are also reported to be eaten. Birds seen at feeders sometimes exhibit signs of a disease (mycoplasmal conjuctivitis) that causes swelling of the eyes with occasional blindness or death. Similar to and easily confused with the less common Purple Finch, which has a larger head and lacks dark streaking on the belly of the males. Purple Finch male also has deeper purple on the head.

Class—**Aves** (birds)

Order—**Passeriformes** (perching birds & songbirds)

Family—**Fringillidae** (finches)

Purple Finch *Haemorhous purpureus*	**American Goldfinch** *Spinus tristis*	**Lesser Goldfinch** *Spinus psaltria*

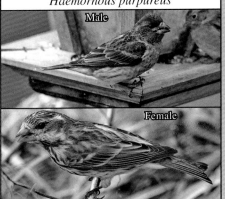
Male

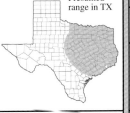
Female

Summer male | Winter male

Male | Female

Size: 6 inches.

Abundance: Uncommon.

Variation: Sexual dimorphism. See photos above.

Presumed range in TX

Size: 5 inches.

Abundance: Common.

Variation: Female and juvenile resemble winter male.

Presumed range in TX

Size: 4.5 inches.

Abundance: Fairly common.

Variation: Variable. Sexual and regional variation.

Presumed range in TX

Habitat: Summer habitat is moist coniferous forests. In winter they are seen in almost all habitats across the eastern half of the United States.

Migratory Status: Winter resident.

Breeding: Nest of twigs, roots and grasses is built in a fork on the outer portion of a branch of a conifer. 3 to 6 six eggs per clutch. 2 broods per year. Does not nest in Texas.

Natural History: The Purple Finch seems to a be declining species in the eastern United States. Competition with the House Finch may be to blame. Although Purple Finches are seen in Texas every winter, they may be sporadic in occurrence. Some will move well south in some years; all the way to the gulf coast in years of poor cone production. Seeds are the major food item, including seeds of trees (elm, maples, ash) and seeds of fruits. Buds are also eaten. Insects are also consumed. As with most other seed eaters, the Purple Finch will frequent bird feeders in winter. It may be fairly common at feeders one year, but rare or absent the next. Most likely to be seen at feeders during or following snowstorms. Easily confused with the House Finch, but is larger headed and has a heavier bill.

Habitat: Edge areas and successional habitats, fence rows, overgrown fields and floodplains in open and semi-open areas.

Migratory Status: Winter resident.

Breeding: 4 to 6 uniformly white eggs are laid. Nest is a tightly woven cup of grasses usually wrapped around a triad of upright branches. Does not nest in Texas.

Natural History: This well-known species is widespread across North America. The transition of the male Goldfinch into its strikingly yellow breeding plumage in spring is a profound example of a condition that is common in many male birds in which they acquire bright colors during the breeding season. The Goldfinch is a common visitor to bird feeders and is especially attracted to thistle seeds. Unlike many other species that eat seeds in winter and insects in summer, the Goldfinch is mainly a seed eater. Weed seeds, grass seeds, and especially seeds from forbs like thistles, sunflowers, and coneflowers are consumed. This species is apparently immune to parasitism by the Brown-headed Cowbird, as young cowbirds cannot develop on a diet that contains no insects.

Habitat: Overgrown fields with tall weeds are a favorite habitat along with forest openings and second growth thickets. Riparian habitats in deserts.

Migratory Status: Year-round resident.

Breeding: Riparian habitats are favored for nesting. Nest is near the terminus of a tree branch and is a tight cup with three to six eggs. Nesting occurs from mid-March through June.

Natural History: Males of the Lesser Goldfinch vary regionally and sometimes within the same population. All are yellow below. Some males have a black cap with greenish yellow back, some have black cap reduced to black forehead, some are uniformly black dorsally with black head and face. Females and juveniles have olive backs with dull yellow belows and reduced or no black on head. All have some black and white in wings. Feeds mostly on seeds, especially small weed seeds. At feeders favors thistle seeds. Also eats some small insects. Not as widespread as the American Goldfinch but can be locally common in Texas. There is some evidence that the population of this species has declined in Texas. The current range extends all the way to southern South America.

Class—**Aves** (birds)

Order—**Passeriformes** (perching birds & songbirds)

Family—**Fringillidae** (finches)

Family—**Icteridae** (blackbirds)

Pine Siskin *Spinus pinus*	**Yellow-breasted Chat** *Icteria virens*	**Bobolink** *Dolichonyx oryzivorus*

Male

Female

Male

Size: 5 inches. Wings 9 inches.

Presumed range in TX

Abundance: Uncommon.

Variation: Males have a yellowish wash.

Size: 7 inches. Wingspan 9.75 in.

Presumed range in TX

Abundance: Fairly common.

Variation: No variation and sexes are alike.

Size: 7 to 8 inches.

Presumed range in TX

Abundance: Rare in Texas.

Variation: Sexually dimorphic.

Habitat: Pine Siskins prefer coniferous woodlands but in winter they are often seen in mixed or even pure hardwood forests. A winter only species in Texas where it inhabits a variety of habitats.

Migratory Status: Winter migrant.

Breeding: Nest is woven of grasses, twigs, rootlets, etc. and lined with mosses or fur. Three to four eggs is typical. May nest in loose colonies. Does not nest in Texas.

Natural History: The Pine Siskin is a coniferous forest species, though it is also found in mixed deciduous/coniferous woodlands and in pure deciduous woods during winter irruptions. It is mostly a bird of the far north and the Rocky Mountains. They sometimes range as far south as the gulf coast in winter. In Texas they are most common in the northern part of the state, but they are nomadic in the winter and their erratic movement means they may be common in one area and rare in another. Likewise they may be present in an area one year and absent the next. Feeds on seeds of coniferous trees, grass seeds and weed seeds and will regularly visit feeders in winter and where thistle seeds are favored. Insects are also eaten during breeding. They are often seen in the company of Goldfinches.

Habitat: This bird likes overgrown fields, second growth areas and early successional regenerating woodlands. It avoids the deep woods. More common in the Piney Woods of eastern Texas.

Migratory Status: Summer resident.

Breeding: Nests low to the ground in brier thickets or a dense shrub such as a multiflora rose. Nest is cup-like. Lays 2 to 5 eggs. Most nesting in Texas is in the eastern part of the state.

Natural History: The Yellow-breasted Chat was originally regarded as a type of warbler but are now considered to be in the blackbird family. They are not easily observed due to their secretive nature and preference for dense vegetation. In Texas they are a seasonal migrant in the panhandle and in southern Texas and a summer resident elsewhere in the state. Foods are a wide variety of arthropods with a preference for crickets, grasshoppers, caterpillars and spiders. They are also known to eat some fruits and berries. These birds are probably more numerous today than prior to deforestation. They are a widespread species with two distinct populations, one in the eastern US and one in the Rocky Mountain West. The two groups are separated by the Great Plains.

Habitat: Bobolinks are open country birds and they are usually seen in pastures and hayfields. Their original habitats were tallgrass prairies, which no longer exist in any significant amount.

Migratory Status: Seasonal migrant.

Breeding: Females breed with a number of males and a clutch of 5 eggs may have several fathers. Nest is woven of grasses and placed on the ground. Does not nest in Texas.

Natural History: Bobolinks are one of the greatest migrators of any songbird seen in America. They will nest in the northern US and Canada and winter in southern South America in the open grasslands of the Pampas region of Uruguay and Argentina. Thats a round trip of nearly 20,000 miles! In Texas this is a rare species that is seen only in the eastern edge of the state and then only briefly during migration. This is a species that has experienced significant population declines in the last half century as its summer breeding habitat in the Tallgrass Prairies of North America have disappeared under the plow. Food items include seeds, grains and many invertebrates during breeding. Many people are surprised to learn that these handsome birds are in the blackbird family.

Class—**Aves** (birds)

Order—**Passeriformes** (perching birds & songbirds)

Family—**Icteridae** (blackbirds)

Eastern Meadowlark *Sturnella magna*	Western Meadowlark *Sturnella neglecta*	Yellow-headed Blackbird *Xanthocephalus xanthocephalus*
		Male Female

Size: 9.5 inches. Wingspan 14 in. **Abundance:** Common. **Variation:** No variation and sexes are alike.	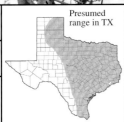 Presumed range in TX	**Size:** 9.5 inches. Wingspan 14.5 in. **Abundance:** Common. **Variation:** No variation and sexes are alike.	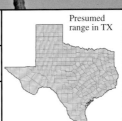 Presumed range in TX	**Size:** 9.5 inches. Wingspan 15 in. **Abundance:** See photos above. **Variation:** Sexual and seasonal variation.	Presumed range in TX

Habitat: Open, treeless pastures and fields that are kept closely grazed or mowed. They like short grasses and avoid overgrown areas. In winter they are often seen in harvested croplands or emerging wheat fields.	**Habitat:** Open, treeless pastures and fields that are kept closely grazed or mowed. They like short grasses and avoid overgrown areas. Favors open regions with short grasses even more than the Eastern Meadowlark.	**Habitat:** A marsh specialist. Throughout their range in the western US they are common around "prairie potholes" lake-shores, marshes, beaver ponds and creeks where cattails and sedges dominate.
Migratory Status: Year-round resident.	**Migratory Status:** Year-round resident.	**Migratory Status:** Winter resident.
Breeding: Nest is on the ground and well hidden beneath overhanging grasses or under the edge of a grass tussock. 3 to 5 eggs.	**Breeding:** Nest is on the ground. Woven from grass stems and may be open or domed, with or without tunnel-like entrance. Lays 5 or 6 eggs.	**Breeding:** A cup-like nest is woven around several upright stalks of cattail or sedge. Averages 3 to 5 eggs and produces only one clutch per season.
Natural History: As might be expected of a bird that loves open spaces, the Eastern Meadowlark is least common in forested regions of the state. Even in the heavily wooded regions however, this bird can be found in areas of open habitat. They feed mostly on insects in warmer months, with grasshoppers and crickets being a dietary mainstay in the summer. During winter they will eat seeds and grain. They tend to occur in small flocks during the winter, but pair off and scatter in the breeding season. This species is fond of perching on fence wires and posts. The following species (Western Meadowlark) is nearly identical. Expert birders rely on listening to the birds songs to make a positive identification. In Texas the range overlaps that of the western species, but they do not interbreed.	**Natural History:** In appearance (and most other respects) the Western Meadowlark is very similar to the eastern species. Visually, the yellow on the throat of the Western extends farther beneath the lower jaw (malar). One might reasonably wonder how two so similar species can co-exist without interbreeding. The answer is likely in the fact that their songs are decidedly different. Thus breeders respond only to the songs of their own species. In Texas the breeding range is in the western half of the state, but they will migrate into eastern Texas during winter months. Most reside in the Great Plains region. A third Meadowlark Species (the Chihuahuan Meadowlark *S. liliana*) has recently been described. Its range range includes the Chihuahuan Desert Level III Ecoregion in western Texas.	**Natural History:** Feeds heavily on aquatic insects during the breeding season and feeds them to the young exclusively. In fall and winter switches to weed seeds and grains. When engaged in territorial displays and singing the males are quite conspicuous. Females are more discreet and sometimes difficult to observe. Adult males migrate separately from females and juveniles. They are seemingly less tolerant of cold than most other blackbirds as they will arrive on northern breeding grounds later and depart earlier than other blackbirds. Winters in the southwestern United States and most of Mexico. Greatest abundance in summer is in the Dakotas. In Texas this is mostly a winter resident and a seasonal migrant, but there are records of rare breeding in the state in the panhandle region.

Class—**Aves** (birds)

Order—**Passeriformes** (perching birds & songbirds)

Family—**Icteridae** (blackbirds)

Red-winged Blackbird	Rusty Blackbird	Brewer's Blackbird
Agelaius phoeniceus	*Euphagus carolinus*	*Euphagus cyanocephalus*

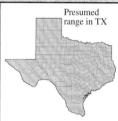

Size: 9 inches.	**Size:** 9 inches.	**Size:** 9.5 inches.
Abundance: Common.	**Abundance:** Rare.	**Abundance:** Fairly common.
Variation: Sexually dimorphic. See photos above	**Variation:** Seasonal and sexual variation. See photos above.	**Variation:** Sexually dimorphic. See photos above.

Presumed range in TX

Habitat: The Red-wing Blackbirds favorite breeding habitat is marsh or wet meadows. They are also found along roadside ditches and the edges of ponds in open areas.

Habitat: Wintering Rusty Blackbirds favor wetland habitats. Floodplain forests, edges of swamps and woods bordering marshes make up the bulk of this birds winter habitat in Texas.

Habitat: Favors open country. It is often seen in harvested or plowed agricultural fields, pastures, etc. It may also frequent feedlots where it feeds on waste grain.

Migratory Status: Year-round resident throughout the state.

Migratory Status: Winter resident in Texas.

Migratory Status: Winter resident in Texas.

Breeding: The nest of the Red-winged Blackbird is a woven basket usually suspended from two or three cattail blades and is most often positioned over water. Two to four eggs are laid. Young are fed enormous quantities of insects.

Breeding: Breeding occurs far to the north (as far as the arctic). Nest is built in trees and bushes near permenant water. An average of four eggs (as many as six) are laid in a bulky nest of twigs, lichens and grass.

Breeding: As many as 8 eggs may be laid, but 5 or 6 is probably average. Often nests in loose colonies of twenty or more pairs. Nest is constructed in a tree and four to five eggs is common. There may be as many as seven eggs.

Natural History: In winter Red-winged Blackbirds often join large mixed flocks that can include several species of blackbirds. All together the blackbirds are probably the most numerous birds in America in winter. Males sing conspicuously in spring. Like the other blackbirds on this page, the Red-winged has benefited from human alterations to America's natural habitats, thriving in open land and agricultural areas. Food is almost entirely insects and the along with other members of the blackbird family (Icteridae) this species plays an important role in insect control. The bright red and yellow "epaulets" on the wing of the male are greatly reduced in winter, but some color is still visible on the wing.

Natural History: In the last few years Rusty Blackbirds have garnered the attention of birdwatchers and conservationists concerned about an apparently significant decline in the population of this species. The loss of wet woodlands to agriculture throughout much of their wintering grounds in the southern US may be partly to blame. Unlike many blackbirds that regularly intermingle with other species, the Rusty Blackbird seems to remain mostly segregated from the large winter flocks of grackles, cowbirds, Starlings and Red-wingeds. These birds summer far to the north and are seen in Texas only in winter. Food is insects, seeds, grains, etc. Summer range is wetland areas in the boreal forests of Canada and Alaska.

Natural History: The Brewer's Blackbird is a western species that historically inhabited the Great Plains and Rocky Mountain Regions all the way to the Pacific Ocean. With the clearing of land brought on by human activities, the Brewer's Blackbird began to invade the Eastern Temperate Forest Level I Ecoregion in the early 1900s. Although they are still uncommon east of the Mississippi River compared to our other blackbirds, birdwatchers report sporadic sightings in the east. Feeds mostly on grains and seeds of grasses or weeds in winter. Summer diet is largely insects, including prodiguous numbers of grasshoppers. These are common birds in western North America.

Class—**Aves** (birds)

Order—**Passeriformes** (perching birds & songbirds)

Family—**Icteridae** (blackbirds)

Common Grackle *Quiscalus quiscula*	Boat-tailed Grackle *Quiscalus major*	Great-tailed Grackle *Quiscalus mexicanus*
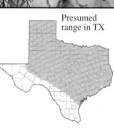	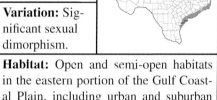	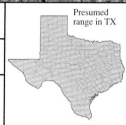

Size: 12.5 inches.	Presumed range in TX	**Size:** 16 inches. Wingspan 17 to 23.	Presumed range in TX	**Size:** 18 inches. Wingspan 19 to 23.	Presumed range in TX
Abundance: Very common.		**Abundance:** Uncommon.		**Abundance:** Common.	
Variation: Female is less vividly colored.		**Variation:** Significant sexual dimorphism.		**Variation:** Female is brown with dark wing.	

Habitat: Grackles favor agricultural areas and open fields/croplands. They are also common in urban areas where they inhabit lawns, parks, etc. In winter roosts in large flocks in small woodlots.

Habitat: Open and semi-open habitats in the eastern portion of the Gulf Coastal Plain, including urban and suburban areas. Common on lawns, in parks and shopping mall parking lots.

Habitat: This species is most common in regions where the habitat has been modified by humans. In urban areas they frequent lawns and parks. In rural areas farms, ranches and homesteads.

Migratory Status: Year-round resident.

Migratory Status: Year-round resident.

Migratory Status: Year-round resident.

Breeding: Grackles often nest in groups that may consist of a dozen or more pairs. The nest is built in the upper branches of medium-size trees and several nests can be in the same tree, or in adjacent trees.

Breeding: Often nests near water. Peak nesting period in Texas is in May but can be anytime from April through June. Nests in loose colonies. Two broods per year is common. 4 eggs is typical.

Breeding: Builds a large, bulky nest of grasses, small twigs, and bark strips. Nest is in a tree and usually placed in an upright fork. They may nest in colonies. Favors small woodlots near open areas for nesting. Up to 5 eggs.

Natural History: Grackles are known for forming large flocks during the winter that will roost communally and can number in the thousands. When these large congregations move into a town or neighborhood they can become a messy nuisance, but their reputation for spreading disease is exaggerated. Throughout most of the year they are busy consuming millions of insect pests. The number of insects consumed by all the blackbird species is staggering. In harsh winter weather they may descend on backyard bird feeders in large flocks that overwhelm the regular residents, creating consternation among backyard birdwatchers. The two color morphs known as "bronze" and "purple" reflect the color of the iridescence of the plumage.

Natural History: The Boat-tailed Grackle owes its name to its long, deeply V-shaped tail. This species has a strong affinity to human habitation and it can be quite common in the vicinity of fast food restaurants, dumpsters, and parking lots in urban and suburban regions. Human refuse has become an important part of its diet. In wilder, more natural habitats it feeds on insects and some small vertebrates such as small frogs, lizards or crabs. Although they are not widespread in Texas, they are fairly common in areas of human habitation along the coasts and near estuaries. They are very similar to the Common Grackle and at times the two species may be seen in close proximity. The Boat-tailed is larger and has a longer, V-shaped tail.

Natural History: The Great Tailed Grackle has been increasing in population and expanding its range for several decades. Originally it was mainly a Latin American species that range northward as far as southern Texas. Now they can be seen in summer as far north as Nebraska and Iowa. Northern populations may retreat southward in harsh winter weather. In Texas they are found statewide but they are probably least common as a breeding bird in the Piney Woods and the Edwards Plateau. They also tend to avoid the drier regions of the Chihuahuan Desert in west Texas but they do occur in that region where water is present. In addition to insects they will prey on small vertebrates like frogs or even small fish. Grains, seeds, berries and fruits are also eaten.

Class—**Aves** (birds)

Order—**Passeriformes** (perching birds & songbirds)

Family—**Icteridae** (blackbirds)

Bronzed Cowbird	**Brown-headed Cowbird**	**Scott's Oriole**
Molothrus aeneus	*Molothrus ater*	*Icterus parisorum*

 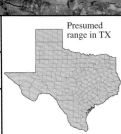

Size: 8.5 inches.

Abundance: Uncommon.

Variation: Female is duller and less glossy.

Presumed range in TX

Size: 7.5 to 8 inches.

Abundance: Common.

Variation: Sexually dimorphic. See photos.

Presumed range in TX

Size: 9 inches. Wingspan 12.5.

Abundance: Fairly common.

Variation: Sexually dimorphic. See below.

Presumed range in TX

Habitat: Natural habitats are native prairie and coastal marshes but today uses agricultural fields and has benefited from the activity of farming in south Texas.

Habitat: Open fields and agricultural areas primarily, but can also be common in towns and suburbs. Inhabits edge areas and woods openings but avoids deep forest.

Habitat: This species ranges throughout most of the Chihuahuan Desert and Edwards Plateau. They can be seen in canyons and juniper/pinyon woodlands. Most common along the Rio Grande.

Migratory Status: Summer resident mostly. A few winter in southern Texas.

Migratory Status: Mostly a year-round resident. Summer only in panhandle.

Migratory Status: Summer resident that arrives in early April to mid May.

Breeding: Female cowbirds lay their eggs in the nest of other bird species, a unique nesting strategy known as "brood parasitism" (see below). As many as 40 eggs may be laid in dozens of songbird nests.

Breeding: Female cowbirds lay their eggs in the nest of other bird species, a unique nesting strategy known as "brood parasitism" (see below). As many as 40 eggs may be laid in dozens of songbird nests.

Breeding: Spring males arrive in Texas before the females and establish a breeding territory. Females arrive within a few days. Nest is built in a tree or yucca. The average clutch size is three eggs and there may be two broods.

Natural History: Both the Bronze Cowbirds and the Brown-headed Cowbird employ a unique breeding strategy in that the adults play no role in rearing their young. Instead the female lays an egg in another species' nest and the adoptive parents rear the young cowbird, usually to the detriment of host bird's own offspring. Originally a Mexican and Central American species, the Bronze Cowbird moved into southern Texas in the 1950s and just a few years later became established in coastal Louisiana. Along with the more common Brown-headed Cowbird they pose a real threat to many songbird species within their range. Over two hundred songbird species have been recorded as having the nest parasitized by cowbird eggs.

Natural History: The disappearance of extensive forest tracts has allowed the Brown-headed Cowbird to parasitize many more woodland songbirds than was possible prior to settlement. As a result, this species has increased in numbers and now poses a real threat to many smaller songbird species, especially the warblers. In winter Cowbirds will join with mixed flocks of other blackbird species. They can become an unwelcome nuisance at backyard bird feeders during harsh weather. Some concerned bird lovers keep pellet guns handy for the specific purpose of dispatching Brown-headed Cowbirds that appear at their feeders. While controversial this radical means of controlling an out of control species is welcomed by some.

Natural History: All the Orioles exhibit sexual dimorphism. In the Scott's Oriole the female has the black on the throat and breast much reduced and replaced by dusky olive on the head and back. Juvenile males resemble females. The food of this oriole is insects, berries, fruits and nectar and they will visit feeders for fruits like oranges or nectar. This is one of the few birds that will eat the Monarch Butterfly. Somehow they select only those with less amounts of milkweed toxins. They have an affinity for yucca plants and will forage and nest withing the blade like foliage. They are a short distance migrant. Their wintering grounds are in the highlands of south-central Mexico and on the southern Baja Peninsula.

Class—**Aves** (birds)

Order—**Passeriformes** (perching birds & songbirds)

Family—**Icteridae** (blackbirds)

Baltimore Oriole *Icterus galbula*	**Orchard Oriole** *Icterus spurius*

Size: 7.25 inches. Wingspan 11.5 inches.

Abundance: Fairly common in the eastern half of the state.

Migratory Status: A seasonal migrant. Migrants from the tropics begin to arrive in Texas by the first week of April and continue through the second week of May. Fall migration is mostly in September. Winters in Central and South America.

Variation: Significant sexual and age-related dimorphism (see photos above). Immature male less vividly colored.

Habitat: Savanna-like habitats are preferred. Pastures with scattered large trees, parks and lawns in urban areas, or farms and ranches in rural areas. During migration may be seen in a variety of habitats.

Breeding: The nest is an easily recognizable "hanging basket" woven from grasses and suspended from a tree limb. 4 to 6 eggs is typical. Favors elm trees for nesting.

Natural History: These handsome orange and black birds are a favorite with backyard birdwatchers. They will come to nectar feeders and fruits such as oranges, and they relish grape jelly. In addition to nectar and fruit they feed heavily on insects. In some areas of their range they have adapted well to human activities. Small town neighborhoods and city parks are among their habitats today. Although they are fond of semi-open habitats and avoid dense forests, they do like the presence of some mature trees in their habitat. Thus, they may decline from areas where intensive agriculture reduces the presence of small woodland patches and large trees.

Size: 7.25 inches. Wingspan 9.5 inches.

Abundance: Fairly common statewide.

Migratory Status: Summer resident that breeds in most of the state. Returns in early April through mid-May. Departs from breeding range early as late July but most leave in September. Winters from southern Mexico to northern South America.

Variation: Significant sexual and ontogenetic plumage variation. Immature males resemble female (see photos).

Habitat: This species shows a preference for semi-open habitats and narrow strips of woodland bordering rivers and streams. Their name comes from the fact that they are fond of orchards and they will often nest in fruit trees.

Breeding: The nest is a rounded basket woven from grasses and suspended from a forked tree branch. Four eggs is typical, but can be as many as six.

Natural History: Like the larger Baltimore Oriole, Orchard Orioles will eat fruit. They also feed on a wide variety of arthropods gleaned from tree branches and leaves, as well as from weedy fields. Immature males resemble females but have a large black throat patch. These birds are somewhat gregarious and they often occur in flocks on tropical wintering grounds. They are also known to nest in small colonies where ideal habitat exists. Spraying for insects in orchards can be dangerous for these insect and fruit eaters as it can be for other bird species, many of which are highly susceptible to insecticides.

Class—**Aves** (birds)

Order—**Passeriformes** (perching birds & songbirds)

Family—**Icteridae** (blackbirds)

Hooded Oriole *Icterus cucullatus*	**Bullock's Oriole** *Icterus bullockii*	**Altamira Oriole** *Icterus gularis*

Size: 8 inches.

Abundance: Fairly common.

Variation: Female is greenish yellow with grayish wings.

Habitat: An arid land species that prefers open areas with scattered trees. Seems to have an affinity for palm trees and is attracted to towns with planted palms. In Texas it was once common along the lower Rio Grande River.

Migratory Status: Summer resident. Arrives in mid March. Leaves in Sept.

Breeding: Nest is a hanging basket built in a tree. Three to five eggs are laid. Nesting is in May and June in Texas.

Natural History: As with other oriole species a mix of insects and fruits are eaten. They are easily attracted to backyard feeders with oranges sliced in half. This species has expanded its range farther north in recent decades. But conversely it has become less common in the lower Rio Grande Valley which has always been its stronghold in Texas. Cowbirds and changing agricultural practices (switching from orchards to cotton) are blamed for this decline. The **Audubon's Oriole** (*Icterus graduacauda*) is a very similar species native to Mexico that can sometimes be seen along the lower Rio Grande Valley in extreme southern Texas. It differs from the Hooded Oriole in having an all black head.

Size: 9 inches.

Abundance: Fairly common.

Variation: Female has orange head and gray back.

Habitat: Mesquite woodlands are the favored habitat of the Bullock's Oriole in Texas. They also use riparian woodlands and in urban areas can be common in parks or suburbs with scattered large trees.

Migratory Status: Summer resident that arrives in March and April.

Breeding: Nesting occurs as early as April and as late as July. Nest is a complex, hanging pouch woven from grasses that can take weeks to build.

Natural History: This oriole is widespread in the state but is probably most common in Texas in the panhandle region. Food is typical of orioles and consists of a variety of arthropod prey, including bees and wasps which have had the stinger removed by the oriole. A variety of berries and fruits are also eaten and they will take nectar from flowers. On rare occasion small vertebrates like baby lizards may become food. In the northern plains they have been known to hybridize with the Baltimore Oriole. Juvenile males and females lack black on the head and females are dusky olive above rather than black. Juvenile males take up to eighteen months to gain their adult plumage. This is one of the most common Oriole species in Texas.

Size: 10 inches.

Abundance: Uncommon.

Variation: Sexes similar. Juveniles have olive backs.

Habitat: A tropical species that ranges as far south as Nicaragua. Throughout its range in Latin America it occupies a wide range of habitats. In Texas it is found only in the lower Rio Grande Valley where it favors wooded areas.

Migratory Status: A non-migratory year round resident of southernmost Texas.

Breeding: The large, finely woven, basket-like nest is suspended from a branch high in a tree. Nesting occurs from March to July. Lays 2 to 6 eggs.

Natural History: This is a tropical and sub-tropical species whose range barely enters the US in the southern tip of Texas. It is our largest oriole. Their populations in Texas have fluctuated between being fairly common and expanding northward to experiencing declines. This bird is very similar to the Hooded Oriole, but the Altamira Oriole is larger, is deeper orange overall (including an orange upper wing bar as opposed to white on the Hooded) and has a thicker bill. Food is typical of orioles. Includes insects, nectar from flowers and fruits. Their elaborate nests are usually built in trees overhanging open area such as a creek or sometimes a lawn. On rare occasions nests may be built hanging from a power line!

Class—**Aves** (birds)

Order—**Cuculiformes** (cuckoos)

Family—**Cuculidae**

Yellow-billed Cuckoo *Coccyzus americanus*	**Black-billed Cuckoo** *Coccyzus erythropthalmus*	**Groove-billed Ani** *Crotophaga sulcirostris*

Size: 12 inches. Wingspan 18. 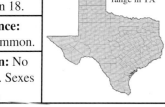 Presumed range in TX	**Size:** 12 inches. Wings 17.5 in.  Presumed range in TX	**Size:** 13.5 inches.  Presumed range in TX
Abundance: Fairly common.	**Abundance:** Uncommon.	**Abundance:** Fairly common.
Variation: No variation. Sexes are alike.	**Variation:** No variation. Sexes are alike.	**Variation:** No variation. Sexes alike.
Habitat: Open woodlands, edge areas, regenerative woodlands near open fields, overgrown fence rows, etc. Uses similar habitats on winter range.	**Habitat:** Successional areas, thickets, and mature woodlands with some open areas. Shows a preference for being near water (riparian areas, lakes, etc.).	**Habitat:** The habitat in Texas is in the Southern Texas Plains (i.e. South Texas Brush Country) and in the southern tip of the Western Gulf Coastal Plain
Migratory Status: Summer resident.	**Migratory Status:** Seasonal migrant.	**Migratory Status:** Year-round resident.
Breeding: Breeds from early June through summer in the northern US. Nesting in Texas occurs from May to July. Nest is flimsy and placed in thick vegetation. 2 to 4 eggs. Hatchlings grow rapidly and fledge in 3 weeks.	**Breeding:** Breeds in the northern US and southern Canada. Nest is built in a shrub or tree usually within 10 feet of the ground. Clutch size averages 2 to 4 eggs. More eggs may be laid when caterpillars are more abundant.	**Breeding:** The most unusual aspect of this birds breeding biology is the fact that it is a communal breeder. Several females will lay eggs in a single nest and they are incubated by all members of the colony.
Natural History: The Yellow-billed Cuckoo is one of the latest arriving of America's neotropical migrant songbirds. They often go by the nickname "Rain-crow" and folklore states that they call right before a rain. Although much more common than the Black-billed Cuckoo, Yellow-billed Cuckoos are not abundant birds today. Like our other cuckoo, their numbers have diminished significantly in modern times. Caterpillars are an important food and widespread pesticide use is likely the major contributing factor in their decline. Loss of habitat is also certainly a factor in their decline. These are secretive birds that are heard more often than seen. Their call is quite distinctive and is heard most frequently during the "dog days" of mid to late summer. More common in the eastern half of the state.	**Natural History:** Although once common, the Black-billed Cuckoo has declined in abundance over the past several decades. Widespread use of pesticides may be to blame. Caterpillars are a primary food and pesticide depleted caterpillar numbers results in a scarce food source for the birds. Ironically, large flocks of these handsome birds once acted as a natural control of caterpillars and historical observers reported seeing flocks of Black-billed Cuckoos descend on a tree full of caterpillars and eat every caterpillar on the tree! Today it is rare to see more than one or two of these birds at a time. Cicadas are another important insect food, and in years of cicada outbreaks cuckoos (and many other birds species) will produce larger clutches and successfully rear more young.	**Natural History:** These are remarkably social birds. In addition to their communal egg incubation strategy, some of the non-breeding juveniles from a previous brood may help feed the young. Despite the communal nesting, they form monogamous pair bonds that persist from one breeding season to the next. Local groups will frequently forage together in small flocks. These are mainly tropical birds and their range extends southward all the way to northern South America. South Texas represents the northernmost extension of their range. Some of these northern birds may move a short distance in winter to escape severe cold fronts. Their diet is variable but includes mostly arthropods, fruits, and seeds. Their large, odd shaped bill and long tail are distinctive.

Class—**Aves** (birds)

Order—**Cuculiformes** (cuckoos)	Order—**Coraciiformes** (kingfishers)
Family—**Cuculidae**	Family—**Alcedinidae**

Greater Roadrunner
Geococcyx californianus

Size: 23 inches.	
Abundance: Fairly common.	 Presumed range in TX
Variation: No sexual variation. Juvenile less glossy.	

Habitat: The main habitat is desert and desert grasslands. Mesquite woodlands, oak savannah and brushlands are also widely used. Some open ground is a requirement. Most common in west Texas. Rarest in the Piney Woods region.

Migratory Status: Year-round resident.

Breeding: Nest is usually constructed off the ground in a small tree, bush, or cactus. The nest is made of sticks and twigs and is quite large (over a foot in diameter). Clutch size varies from two to six, rarely more.

Natural History: Roadrunners are voracious predators that consume almost any species of animal they can swallow. Snakes (including venomous) and lizards are a large portion of the food but birds and small mammals are also chased down and eaten. They can run up to 26 mph. They are such rapacious hunters, in fact, that more than one biologist has noted their uncanny similarity to the prehistoric "Raptor" dinosaurs. Some biologists have remarked that if they grew to six feet tall there would be no surviving humans within their range! An exaggeration perhaps, but also a testament to their predatory prowess. This species began a range expansion to the north and east in the late nineteenth century and is still a thriving species today.

Belted Kingfisher
Megaceryle alcyon

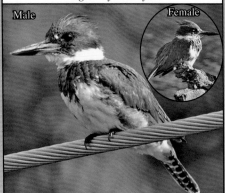

Size: 13 inches.	
Abundance: Fairly common.	 Presumed range in TX
Variation: Slight sexual variation. See photos above.	

Habitat: Kingfishers require clear waters to feed and they haunt creeks, rivers, lakes, swamps and farm ponds. They are found statewide in Texas but they summer mostly in the north central and eastern parts of the state.

Migratory Status: Year-round resident.

Breeding: The nest is in a hole dug by the birds in a dirt bank. Both sexes participate in digging the burrow. Five to eight eggs are laid. Breeding occurs from April to July and there may be two broods per summer.

Natural History: The Belted Kingfisher is one of the most widely distributed birds in North America. In fact, they range throughout the continent from Alaska and northern Canada south to Panama. Although widespread (they may be seen in any county throughout the state) they are widely dispersed. The presence of suitable nesting habitat in the form of vertical earthen cliffs may be a limiting factor in their abundance. Human activities such as digging of quarries and road cuts through hills and mountains may have helped this species in modern times by providing the requisite vertical banks for nest sites. Small fish are the primary food item. They are known for diving headfirst into the water to catch fish near the surface.

Green Kingfisher
Chloroceryle americana

Size: 8.5 inches	
Abundance: Uncommon.	 Presumed range in TX
Variation: Female lacks broad rust-colored band on breast.	

Habitat: An aquatic dependent species that likes still, clear freshwater environments within the Edwards Plateau and the South Texas Brush country. They are widespread south of the US throughout Mexico, Central and South America.

Migratory Status: Year-round resident.

Breeding: Breeding in Texas takes place from early spring through early summer. Nest is a burrow dug in an earthen bank. Burrow entrance is often concealed by overhanging vegetation. Five eggs is typical.

Natural History: Most of the food is small fishes that are caught by plunging into the water, usually from a perch on an nearby limb. In addition to fish they also eat aquatic insects and crustaceans. The **Ringed Kingfisher** (*Megaceryle torquata*) is another kingfisher species that occurs rarely in extreme southern Texas. It is a very large bird, twice the size of the Belted Kingfisher. The Ringed Kingfisher began expanding its range northward out of Mexico several decades ago and the first record of breeding in Texas was in 1970. It is a tropical species that is widespread throughout South America as well as in Central America and Mexico. At this time it is still a rare species in Texas, found only in the extreme southern tip of the state.

Class—**Aves** (birds)

Order—**Piciformes** (woodpeckers)

Family—**Picidae**

Red-headed Woodpecker *Melanerpes erythrocephalus*	**Acorn Woodpecker** *Melanerpes formicivorus*	**Golden-fronted Woodpecker** *Melanerpes aurifrons*

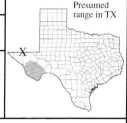

Size: 9.25 inches.	**Size:** 9 inches.	**Size:** 9.5 inches
Abundance: Uncommon.	**Abundance:** Uncommon.	**Abundance:** Fairly common.
Variation: Juveniles have gray-brown heads and brown wings.	**Variation:** Red and white patches on head converge on male.	**Variation:** Male has red patch on crown, lacking on female.
Presumed range in TX	Presumed range in TX	Presumed range in TX

Habitat: Savanna-like habitats with widely spaced, large trees are the preferred habitat of the Red-headed Woodpecker. They seem to show a preference for areas near lakes or rivers.

Migratory Status: Year-round resident.

Breeding: Nest hole is usually in a dead tree but it is also fond of using utility poles. 5 eggs is typical and some may produce two broods per summer.

Natural History: Once regarded as very common, this handsome woodpecker has declined significantly in the last century. It eats large amounts of acorns and other mast, especially in fall and winter, and may move about in fall and winter in search of areas with good mast crops. Insects are regularly eaten in warmer months and some may be caught on the wing, but they also commonly forage on the ground. They may be found throughout the eastern half of the state in summer but populations in the north may migrate south in winter. They seem to be relatively uncommon and overall this species has experienced a nationwide population decline. The Red-headed Woodpecker was apparently well known to many native Americans, and was a war symbol of the Cherokee.

Habitat: In the US oak and pine/oak woodlands. In California, desert mountain ranges. Also in eastern Arizona and western New Mexico and in the mountains of the Big Bend region of Texas.

Migratory Status: Year-round resident.

Breeding: Cavity nester. Young are fed by the parents and by other members of the colony. Up to 17 eggs from several females have been recorded in a nest.

Natural History: Acorn woodpeckers are colony animals. They live together in small bands of over a dozen individuals and the females lay their eggs in a communal nest and share incubation duties. These woodpeckers are famous for the way they cache acorns for the winter. They will select a tree to be used for acorn storage and excavate small round holes the diameter of an acorn. Acorns are then gathered and placed in the hole. Selected "granary" trees are easily recognized and may contain thousands of holes stuffed with acorns. These birds are very common in California's Sierra Nevada Mountains and in the Pacific coastal ranges of California and Oregon. They are also common from northern Mexico to northern Central America. They are quite active and noisy in the mornings and are easily located.

Habitat: Arid and semi-arid habitats with open and semi-open mesquite woodlands. Probably most common as a breeding bird in the Southern Texas Plains and Edwards Plateau.

Migratory Status: Year-round resident.

Breeding: Cavity nester. Mature Mesquite trees are a favorite nest site but any type of dead or living tree may be used. Four or five eggs is usual.

Natural History: This is the southern Great Plains counterpart of the common and well-known Red-bellied Woodpecker that inhabits the Eastern Temperate Forest Level I Ecoregion. The two species are very similar and where their ranges overlap in southwestern Oklahoma they sometimes hybridize. In addition to a wide variety of insects and other arthropods they also eat nuts like acorns and pecans, the fruits of the prickly pear cactus, persimmons, a variety of berries and grains such as corn. Texas and Oklahoma represent the northernmost extension of this birds range, which extends southward all the way to Nicaragua. Although the species can be found in a wide variety of habitats in Texas it seems to favor old growth Mesquite and often chooses mature Mesquite as a nest site.

Class—**Aves** (birds)		
Order—**Piciformes** (woodpeckers)		
Family—**Picidae**		

Red-bellied Woodpecker *Melanerpes carolinus*	**Yellow-bellied Sapsucker** *Sphyrapicus varius*	**Red-naped Sapsucker** *Sphyrapicus nuchalis*

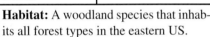

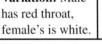
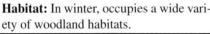

Size: 9.5 inches Wings 16 inches. **Abundance:** Common. **Variation:** Female has gray crown.	Presumed range in TX	**Size:** 8.5 inches. Wings 16 inches. **Abundance:** Fairly common. **Variation:** Male has red throat, female's is white.	Presumed range in TX	**Size:** 8.5 inches. Wings 16 inches. **Abundance:** Uncommon. **Variation:** Female has less red on nape and throat	Presumed range in TX

Habitat: A woodland species that inhabits all forest types in the eastern US.	**Habitat:** In winter, occupies a wide variety of woodland habitats.	**Habitat:** In Texas, uses oak/pine forests in mountains and riparian habitats.
Migratory Status: Year-round resident.	**Migratory Status:** Winter resident.	**Migratory Status:** Winter resident.
Breeding: Nests in holes excavated by the adults. Uses dead trees or sometimes old telephone poles. 4 to 5 eggs are laid in mid April to early June	**Breeding:** Nest is an excavated hole in dead tree or a living tree with heart rot. Clutch size ranges from 2 to 7 eggs. Does not breed in Texas.	**Breeding:** Nesting occurs in the Rocky Mountains north of Texas. Aspens are a favorite nest tree. The male excavates the nest hole. Three to seven eggs.

Natural History: Feeds on all types of tree dwelling arthropods as well as seeds, nuts, fruit and berries. Widespread and common throughout the eastern half of the US, generally east of the Rocky Mountains. These woodpeckers are known to take over the nest holes of the endangered Red-cockaded Woodpecker where their ranges overlap in the southern United States. Conversely, the introduced Starling sometimes takes over the nest hole of the Red-bellied Woodpecker. Due to its fairly large size and its tendency to be quite vocal year-round, the Red-bellied Woodpecker is a fairly conspicuous bird in both rural and urban areas throughout their range. Because both males and females have a significant amount of red on the head they are often misidentified as the much rarer Red-headed Woodpecker. Like other woodpeckers they will come to bird feeders for suet or sunflower seeds.

Natural History: The Sapsuckers are unique among woodpeckers in that they create feeding opportunities by drilling small holes into the bark of trees. These holes, called "sap wells" fill with sap which the sapsucker then drinks. Sapsuckers regularly visit the "sap wells" to maintain them and defend them from other sapsuckers. They create these sap wells in many types of trees, but maples and birches are the favorite tree species due to the high sugar content of their sap. Many other birds species benefit from the sapsuckers activities, especially the Ruby-throated Hummingbird which will also drink sap from the woodpeckers holes. The sap also attracts insects which in turn feed many species of insectivorous birds. In addition, the nest holes excavated by the sapsucker may be used other birds, flying squirrels, etc. Though widespread across Texas in winter they are not a common bird anywhere in the state.

Natural History: The western version of the very similar to the Yellow-bellied Sapsucker. In fact, until a few decades ago the two were regarded as the same species. In most regards the natural history of the Red-naped Sapsucker mirrors that of its eastern cousin. One important difference is the type of trees available for creating sap wells. The Red-naped uses willow, birch, alder and several other western tree species. In spite of the fact that some favorite "sap well" trees may wind up with thousands of small holes through the bark there doesn't appear to be any negative effects to the tree. The sap wells of all sapsuckers are a food source by other species of birds, insects and even mammals like nectar consuming bats. The many insects attracted to the sap are themselves a food source for other insects, spiders, birds, and small mammals. Meanwhile, abandoned nest holes are used by many other species.

Class—**Aves** (birds)

Order—**Piciformes** (woodpeckers)

Family -**Picidae**

Ladder-backed Woodpecker *Dryobates scalaris*	**Downy Woodpecker** *Picoides pubescens*	**Hairy Woodpecker** *Picoides villosus*

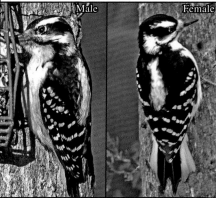

Size: 7.25 inches.	**Size:** 6.5 inches. Wingspan 12.	**Size:** To 10 inches.
Abundance: Fairly common.	**Abundance:** Common.	**Abundance:** Uncommon.
Variation: Female lacks red on nape.	**Variation:** Female lacks red spot on head.	**Variation:** Male has red spot on nape.

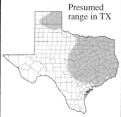 Presumed range in TX

 Presumed range in TX

Habitat: Arid and semi-arid regions. Habitats range from desert to Mesquite woodlands, thorn scrub and riparian woodlands with deciduous trees.

Habitat: Occupies a wide variety of woodland habitats throughout its range in the state. Use riparian woodlands in grassland habitats.

Habitat: A forest species that likes woodlands with large, mature trees. They are more common in Texas in the Piney Woods region.

Migratory Status: Year-round resident.

Migratory Status: Year-round resident.

Migratory Status: Year-round resident.

Breeding: The nest hole is excavated in dead tree limbs or trunks, wooden fence posts or yuccas. In the Sonora Desert it will use Saguaro cactus.

Breeding: Nests is usually excavated in a snag or a dead limb, often in a living tree. Eggs range from 3 to as many as 8. Eggs hatch in 12 days.

Breeding: Nest hole may be in dead snags or living trees with heart rot. Large dead branches of living trees may also be used. Four eggs is typical.

Natural History: The name Ladder-backed Woodpecker comes from the pattern of rows of white lines on the black back. This basic color pattern is common among several species of woodpeckers in the *Picoides* genus. The range of the Ladder-backed Woodpecker includes all of Mexico and most of the desert southwest. They occur in the Chihuahua, Sonora and Mojave deserts as well as in the southern Great Plains. In many respects this woodpecker is the western desert counterpart of the next species on this page (Downy Woodpecker). The collective ranges of the two species essentially covers the entire North American continent south of the Arctic Circle. Where ranges of the two species meet hybridization may rarely occur. In Texas "Ladder-backs" are probably most common in the Edwards Plateau Level III Ecoregion (a.k.a. "Texas Hill Country").

Natural History: Ranging across all of North America except the far north and the desert southwest, the Downy is one of the most widespread woodpeckers in America and is the most common. These appealing little woodpeckers are well known and frequent visitors to bird feeders where they eat suet and seeds. Arthropods are the most important food item making up as much as 75 percent of the diet. Fruit and sap is also eaten. Like other woodpeckers, the Downy's abandoned nest holes in dead limbs and trunks may be utilized by a wide array of other species as a home and shelter. Many small cavity nesting birds may use old woodpecker holes, and mice, lizards, snakes, tree frogs, spiders, and insects can often be found using old nests. The Downy Woodpecker is very similar to the Hairy Woodpecker but is smaller and has a thinner beak. It is also much more common.

Natural History: The woodpeckers are a prime example of the wildlife biologist's mantra "there is life in dead trees." When a tree dies in a forest it is immediately invaded by a myriad of life forms from fungi to wood boring insects. These life forms attract larger species which prey upon them and as in the case with the woodpeckers utilize them for denning. Wherever possible landowners are encouraged to leave dead trees standing. Even a fallen log becomes a mini-ecosystem. The range of the Hairy Woodpecker closely coincides with that of the smaller Downy Woodpecker. The two are often confused, but the Hairy is a much larger bird and has a heavier, longer bill. Hairy Woodpeckers vary somewhat geographically in both size and coloration. Western specimens have fewer white spots on the wings. Specimens shown above are typical for the eastern United States.

Class—**Aves** (birds)

Order—**Piciformes** (woodpeckers)

Family—**Picidae**

Red-cockaded Woodpecker *Picoides borealis*	**Northern Flicker** *Colaptes auratus*	**Pileated Woodpecker** *Dryocopus pileatus*

Size: 8.5 inches.	**Size:** 12.5 inches.	**Size:** 16.5 inches.
Abundance: Rare.	**Abundance:** Fairly common.	**Abundance:** Uncommon.
Variation: Female lacks red "cockade."	**Variation:** Male has black "mustache."	**Variation:** Sexual dimorphism. See above

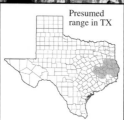

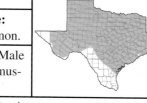

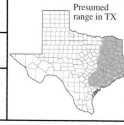

Presumed range in TX

Habitat: Old growth pine forests and mature pine savannas.

Migratory Status: Year-round resident.

Breeding: Nest is excavated into the trunk of a mature, living pine tree, usually infected with heartwood fungus.

Natural History: Very similar to the two preceding species but much rarer. The name comes from the presence of a tiny red spot on each side of the nape of the male (often very hard to see in the field). This woodpecker is an endemic of the southern pine forests and pine savannas that were once common across the southeast. It is a specialist of the habitat known as "Longleaf Pine/Wiregrass Habitat." As much as ninety percent of this habitat is now gone from the southeast (nearly 100 percent of the virgin Longleaf Pines are gone). As a result the Red-cockaded Woodpecker is today listed as a federally endangered animal. Attempts to restore mature Longleaf Pine/ Wiregrass habitats are being undertaken by both state and federal forest management agencies in the southeast and the Red-cockaded Woodpecker has begun to recover. Nesting colonies are closely monitored and protected. State and federal agencies mark nest trees with a ring of white paint around the trunk.

Habitat: Semi-open areas and open lands with at least a few large trees.

Migratory Status: Winter mainly.

Breeding: Nest is usually excavated in a fairly large diameter dead tree. Also uses natural hollows. 6 to 8 eggs.

Natural History: In addition to feeding on insects (mainly ants) usually caught on the ground, the Flicker also eats berries and in winter, grains. Two distinct color morphs occur in North America. The "Yellow-shafted Flicker" is native to the eastern US. In the Rocky Mountain west the "Red-shafted Flicker" occurs. The two are distinguished by the dominant color on the underside of the wing, which is visible only in flight. Most birds seen in Texas are the Yellow-shafted morphs. The Red-shafted morph can be seen in the northern panhandle. The Northern Flicker (like many other woodpeckers) is regarded as a "keystone" species that is important to the ecosystem by providing excavations used by other species for shelter and nesting. Thus recent unexplained declines in the population of this species is a cause for concern. In Texas the Northern Flicker is mostly a winter resident but the populations in the northeastern portion of the state are year-round residents.

Habitat: A forest species, the Pileated Woodpecker prefers mature woodlands.

Migratory Status: Uncommon.

Breeding: Nest is a hollow cavity excavated into the trunk of a tree. Nests are usually fairly high up. 4 eggs.

Natural History: By far America's largest woodpecker, Pileated Woodpeckers play an important role in the mature forest ecosystem. Their large nest cavities are utilized as a refuge by many other woodland species including small owls, Wood Ducks, bluebirds and squirrels. In the boreal forests of Canada the Pine Marten is reported to use their holes. Using their powerful, chisel-like beaks to break apart dead snags and logs they also help accelerate decomposition of large dead trees. In addition to mast and fruit such as wild cherries, they eat insects, mainly Carpenter Ants and wood boring beetle larva. In Texas they occur mainly in the South Central Plains ecoregion where ample forests exist. Successional forest are used but they do need some mature trees and especially large, dead trees and fallen logs. They are also seen in semi-open areas where large tracts of woods occur nearby. Floodplain forests and expansive swamps are a favorite habitat.

Class—**Aves** (birds)

Order—**Columbiformes** (doves & pigeons)

Family—**Columbidae**

Rock Pigeon *Columba livia*	**Band-tailed Pigeon** *Patagioenas fasciata*	**Eurasian Collared Dove** *Streptopelia decaocto*

Rock Pigeon

Size: 13 inches.

Abundance: Very common.

Variation: Highly variable. See Natural History below.

Presumed range in TX

Habitat: Farms and ranches in rural areas. Parks, vacant buildings and streets in urban environments.

Migratory Status: Year-round resident.

Breeding: Nests on man-made ledges and beneath overhangs in cities. Bridges and barns are used in rural areas. Multiple nesting with 2 eggs per clutch.

Natural History: Although the Rock Pigeon is about the same overall length as the Mourning Dove and Collared Dove, the pigeon is a much stockier, heavier bird that weighs over twice as much as the Mourning Dove. Despite the fact that this familiar bird ranges from coast to coast across North America, the Rock Pigeon is not a native species. It was introduced into North America by the earliest European settlers in the 1600s. Pigeons followed the first settlers into the west, colonizing towns and settlements and living in close proximity to rural farms and livestock. Today they are one of the most familiar urban birds in America and are also common around farms and ranches. Young pigeons known as "Squab" are eaten in many places throughout the world. Rock Pigeons are incredibly variable and can exhibit almost any color or pattern. Specimen above is typical wild morph.

Band-tailed Pigeon

Size: 14 inches.

Abundance: Rare in Texas.

Variation: Juvenile lacks white marking on back of neck.

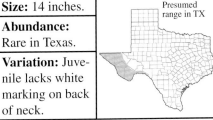
Presumed range in TX

Habitat: In Texas Band-tailed Pigeons inhabit high elevation mountain forests in the Chihuahuan Desert Ecoregion.

Migratory Status: Year-round resident.

Breeding: Apparently can breed throughout the summer. A bulky stick nest is placed on a limb near the trunk of a tree. Only one or two eggs.

Natural History: Although rare in Texas these birds are common in much of the western US and Rocky Mountain states. They can be quite common in the coastal regions of northern California in the temperate rainforests. The west coast population is distinct from the birds that inhabit Texas and the arid southwestern US. There are other populations living in Baja Sur, Mexico, Nicaragua, Panama and in South America. They are strict vegetarian that will eat berries and fruits as well as nuts such as pine nuts and especially acorns. Acorns are the most important food item. They resemble the Rock Pigeon and the two species are closely related. But the Band-tailed Pigeon is a bird of wilderness. Although they can be seen in parks and in the vicinity of suburbs built into forested areas, they avoid the large cities that are inhabited by the Rock Pigeon. This is a long-lived species that may survive over twenty years.

Eurasian Collared Dove

Size: 13 inches.

Abundance: Fairly common.

Variation: No variation in adults. Sexes are alike.

Presumed range in TX

Habitat: Open lands. Agricultural areas and small towns are favored over wilderness or forests.

Migratory Status: Year-round resident.

Breeding: Usually nests in trees or bushes near human habitation. Lays 2 eggs per clutch but can nest several times per year.

Natural History: This bird is a newcomer to the US. Originally native to Eurasia, the Collared Dove has colonized much of the United States since its release in the Bahamas in the 1970s. Since then they have rapidly expanded their range north and west. Breeding in Texas was recorded in the late 1980s. They soon colonized the entire state of Texas and continue to spread farther north. In food habits and other aspects of its biology the Collared Dove is similar to the Mourning Dove. Young Collared Doves disperse widely and this species continues to increase across North America. Cold weather does not seem to be a limiting factor but food availability may limit range expansion. How far this species will extend its range in North America is still unknown. As with all other members of the Columbidae family, young birds are fed a semi-liquid "crop milk" regurgitated from the adults crop.

Class—**Aves** (birds)
Order—**Columbiformes** (doves & pigeons)
Family—**Columbidae**

White-winged Dove *Zenaida asiatica*	**Mourning Dove** *Zenaida macroura*	**Inca Dove** *Columbina inca*

Size: 11.5 inches. **Abundance:** Common. **Variation:** No variation among adults. 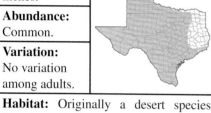	**Size:** 12 inches. Wingspan 18 in. **Abundance:** Very common. **Variation:** No variation among adults. 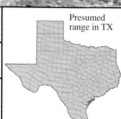	**Size:** 8.25 inches. **Abundance:** Fairly common. **Variation:** No variation among adults. 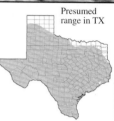

Habitat: Originally a desert species found mostly in the Rio Grande valley. But in recent decades it has expanded its range northward and adapted to urban and suburban areas.

Habitat: Can be found in virtually all habits in the state except wetlands and expansive forests. Agricultural areas and open lands with short grass or areas of bare ground are the favored habitat.

Habitat: Inca Doves are habitat generalists. They show a preference for human disturbed habitats. Farms, ranches, and parks in urban areas. Open ground is a requirement. Avoids forests.

Migratory Status: Year-round in the Big Bend area. Summer elsewhere.

Migratory Status: Year-round resident throughout the state.

Migratory Status: Year-round resident in most of the state.

Breeding: Nest is usually in a dense tree or tall shrub in a thicket. Often in a riparian habitat. One or two eggs with two broods per year,

Breeding: Builds a flimsy nest of small sticks in sapling or low branch usually from 6 to 15 feet above ground. Two eggs is usual with multiple broods per year.

Breeding: Nesting is usually near human habitation. May build more than one nest before laying two eggs. Several broods per year is common.

Natural History: The White-winged Dove is a thriving species that appears to be expanding its range. Wandering individuals have been seen hundreds of miles outside their range in recent years. Its stronghold in Texas has always been in the lower Rio Grande valley but loss of riparian thickets to agriculture has negatively impacted populations there. They are most common in Texas today in the brush country of the South Texas Plains and the southern part of the Western Gulf Coastal Plain. Their range has expanded in the last few decades and they can now be found nearly statewide with the exception of the South Central Plains (Piney Woods) ecoregion. Seeds, grains, berries, and the fruits of cacti are important food items. In the Sonora Desert they show a preference for the seeds and fruit of the Saguaro Cactus.

Natural History: Although these birds are found year-round in Texas their numbers swell each fall with migrants from farther to the north. Mourning Doves are regarded as a game species throughout much of the United States including Texas. The U.S. Fish and Wildlife Service estimates that as many as 20 million are killed each fall across America during dove season. While that seems an appallingly high number, the Mourning Dove is actually one of the most numerous bird species in America and the total population is estimated at around 350 million birds! Seeds are the chief food item. They will eat everything from the tiniest grass seeds to every type of seed crop produced by man, including corn, wheat, sorghum, millet, and sunflower as well as peanuts and soybeans.

Natural History: Historically the Inca Dove was primarily a Latin American species whose range barely extended in the US along the border with Mexico. But in recent years this and other southwestern dove species are thriving and expanding their ranges farther to north. Human activities resulting in more open ground and available foods from waste grains from modern agricultural may be the most important factor fueling the explosion of these a dove species in America. Climate change may also be playing a role, especially for the Inca Dove that does not like extremely cold weather. Inca Doves are common throughout Mexico and Central America and the southern limit of their range is in Panama. Feeding by Inca Doves is almost entirely by picking up seeds and grain on the ground.

Class—**Aves** (birds)

Order—**Columbiformes** (doves & pigeons)

Family—**Columbidae**

Order—**Galliformes** (quail & grouse)

Family—**Cracidae** (chachalacas)

Common Ground Dove *Columbina passerina*	**White-tipped Dove** *Leptotila verreauxi*	**Plain Chachalaca** *Ortalis vetula*

Size: 6.5 inches. Wingspan 10.5 in.

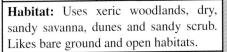
Presumed range in TX

Abundance: Fairly common,

Variation: No variation among adults.

Habitat: Uses xeric woodlands, dry, sandy savanna, dunes and sandy scrub. Likes bare ground and open habitats.

Migratory Status: Year-round resident.

Breeding: Nest is a slightly concave platform woven of grasses and twigs and placed in a low bush. Sometimes nests on the ground. Two eggs is typical.

Natural History: This is the smallest member of the Columbidae family. Unlike other doves this species is not seen in large flocks but rather in mated pairs. These small doves are fairly common in Texas but they may have declined in the southeast where they were once quite common. The cause of this decline is unknown. Most members of the genus *Columbina* are tropical birds and this was once the most northerly ranging species of the genus. Today that distinction probably belongs to the Inca Dove that has expanded it range as far north as Colorado. Ground Doves occur across the southern US from the Carolinas to southern California. They range southward through Mexico and Central America into northern South America and they are well distributed throughout the Caribbean. Their diet includes a wide variety of seeds and berries as well as some insects. In flight they show bright reddish brown wings.

Size: 11.5 inches.

Presumed range in TX

Abundance: Uncommon.

Variation: No variation among adults.

Habitat: Texas habitat is woodlands and thickets along the lower Rio Grande River valley. Mostly in parks and refuges.

Migratory Status: Year-round resident.

Breeding: Breeds as early as February but may breed anytime throughout the summer. Two eggs are laid in a flimsy nest in a tree or thick bush.

Natural History: This species is still fairly common in protected state parks and national wildlife refuges in the lower Rio Grande valley. Despite loss of much of its natural habitat of riparian woodlands and brush lands to agriculture, it has adapted to using orchards and even suburban neighborhoods. Like most other members of the Columbidae family they feed mostly on the ground. Walking around and picking up seeds, grains, berries and sometimes eating fruits of wild plums, hackberry, prickly pear, and mesquite. In orchards they will eat oranges and grapefruits and their seeds. This is one of the most widespread doves in the western hemisphere. Its range includes both coasts of Mexico and much of Central America and it is even more widespread in South America. The White-winged Dove is the only US representative of the genus *Leptotila*, which has a total of eleven dove species in the neotropics.

Size: 22 inches. Wings 26 inches.

Presumed range in TX

Abundance: Uncommon.

Variation: No variation among adults.

Habitat: The south Texas brush country is this birds habitat in the US. South of the border it lives in many habitats.

Migratory Status: Year-round resident.

Breeding: Builds a nest in a tree or bush (unusual for a member of the Galliformes family). Breeds from spring through summer. Two to four eggs.

Natural History: One of four species of Chachalaca and the only one that ranges into the US. The others are found in Mexico and Central America. The range of the Plain Chachalaca is mostly contain in that geographic region as well. Chachalacas are primarily tree dwellers, an unusual characteristic for a grouse. These are uncommon birds in Texas generally, but they can be seen with regularity in the parks and refuges in the lower Rio Grande valley. This region is well known to birders as a place to view many bird species that cannot be seen elsewhere in the United States and bird watchers travel here in large numbers to view unusual bird species. In this regard the Plain Chachalaca and his neotropical avian kin are an important element in the economy of that portion of the state. Chachalaca's are legal to hunt in parts of Texas. While they very rarely hunted in Texas, they are a food item in many other regions.

Class—**Aves** (birds)

Order—**Galliformes** (quail & grouse)

Family—**Phasinidae** (grouse)

Ring-necked Pheasant *Phasianus colchicus*	**Greater Prairie Chicken** *Tympanuchus cupido*	**Lesser Prairie Chicken** *Tympanuchus pallidicinctus*

Male

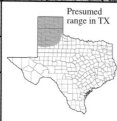
Female

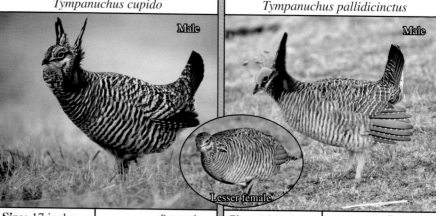
Male

Lesser female

Male

Size: To 35 inches.

Abundance: Uncommon.

Variation: Sexual dimorphism. See above.

Presumed range in TX

Size: 17 inches. Wingspan 28 in.

Abundance: Very rare in TX.

Variation: Sexually dimorphic. See below.

Presumed range in TX

Size: 16 inches. Wingspan 25 in.

Abundance: Rare in Texas.

Variation: Sexually dimorphic. See below.

Presumed range in TX

Habitat: Prefers a mosaic of crop lands interlaced with cover such as wetlands, grassy patches, overgrown fence rows, pastures, and marshes.

Migratory Status: Year-round resident.

Breeding: Nests on the ground in thick cover such as tall grasses, cattails, etc. Lays up to 15 eggs. Rarely, two females will use the same nest.

Natural History: Ring-necked Pheasants are an alien species from Asia that were introduced into America in the late 1800s. The species has thrived in the Great Plains region where adequate natural habitats still exist. It was once a common bird in the Midwest region, but began to decline as more land was cleared for row crops. Despite conservation efforts recovery to the numbers seen prior to modern agriculture has not occurred. More recent conservation efforts aimed at restoring patches of natural grasslands should help this and many other wildlife species. This is a popular game bird throughout its range in America and sportsmen's organizations such as "Pheasants Forever" are actively involved in raising money for habitat conservation and restoration. Permanent, self-sustaining populations of Ring-necked Pheasant in Texas exist only in the Panhandle region.

Habitat: A grassland species. Most inhabit the Great Plains Ecoregion. The single Texas population is in the Western Gulf Coastal Plain Ecoregion.

Migratory Status: Year-round resident.

Breeding: Nest is a shallow scrap on the ground. Nesting in northern Great Plains populations occurs early May. Twelve eggs is average, with a maximum of 17.

Natural History: Females are slightly smaller than males and they lack the bright orange throat patch and yellow "eyebrow." Males have longer pinnae feathers. Although the Greater Prairie Chicken is widespread in the northern Great Plains the population that once lived in the Western Gulf Coastal Plain of Texas and Louisiana has been largely wiped out. Overhunting and conversion of habitat to agriculture were the main factors causing the decline. Known as the subspecies *attwateri* (Attwater's Prairie Chicken), this endangered subspecies exists today only on the Attwater Prairie Chicken National Wildlife Refuge in Colorado County and on private land in Goliad County. The population is maintained by a captive breeding program that releases about 300 birds a year. Non-native fire ants have reduced insect prey vital to the survival of the young.

Habitat: A shortgrass prairie specialist. Endemic to arid grassland habitats dominated by Little Bluestem, Sand Bluestem and Sand Sagebrush.

Migratory Status: Year-round resident.

Breeding: Nest is a scrape on the ground beneath a tuft of grass or a small shrub. Nesting is in areas with heavier cover or taller grasses. Up to 12 eggs.

Natural History: Females are slightly smaller than males and they lack the brightly orange throat patch and yellow "eyebrow." Males have longer pinnae feathers. Although the Lesser Prairie Chicken outnumbers the Greater Prairie Chicken in Texas, it is still a rare and declining bird. They have recently been proposed for listing as a federally endangered species. Overhunting for many decades coupled with the loss of habitat to cropland and overgrazing are the main culprits in the decline. More recently, the profusion of oil wells throughout the southern plains has impacted reproduction. Female Lesser Prairie Chickens will not nest within several hundred yards of any vertical structure over six feet tall. Oil wells, telephone poles, windmills, and planted trees render much habitat unsuitable for nesting and thus further fragment an already fractured population.

Class—**Aves** (birds)

Order—**Galliformes** (quail & grouse)

Family—**Phasinidae** (grouse)	Family—**Ondontophoridae** (quail)

Wild Turkey
Meleagris gallopavo

Male Rio Grande

Female Rio Grande

Male Merriam's

Male Eastern

Montezuma Quail
Cyrtonyx montezumae

Size: 8.75 inches

Abundance: Rare in Texas.

Migratory Status: Year-round resident.

Presumed range in TX

Variation: Male has black and white on head and white spots on black body. On female the same areas are brown.

Habitat: Oak/juniper/pine woodlands with interspersed grassy areas in desert mountain ranges. Texas range is restricted to western part of the state.

Breeding: Nest is on the ground beneath a clump of grass that serves as a roof for the nest. Lays as many as 14 eggs but 10 or 12 is average. When confronted with a threat, the baby quail will grasp detritus in their feet and hide beneath by rolling onto their back.

Size: To 47 inches. Eastern subspecies is largest.

Abundance: Fairly common.

Migratory Status: Year-round resident.

Variation: There are five subspecies of Wild Turkey in the US. Three subspecies occur in Texas. The Eastern Wild Turkey can be found in eastern Texas. The Rio Grande Wild Turkey is widespread in central and southern Texas and spottily distributed in western Texas. A few Merriam's Turkeys inhabit the west Texas mountains.

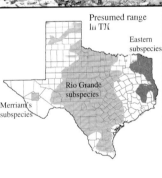

Presumed range in TX

Eastern subspecies

Rio Grande subspecies

Merriam's subspecies

Habitat: Inhabits all major habitats in the state except for urban areas. The eastern subspecies will use expansive forests but they are most common in mixture of woodlands and farms. The Rio Grande subspecies also uses large woodlands as well as riparian corridors in open prairie as well as using habitats dominated by brushlands.

Breeding: Nests on the ground in thick cover such as thickets, honeysuckle, Multiflora Rose, or tall grasses. Lays up to 14 eggs.

Natural History: The courtship of the male Wild Turkey includes a "strutting" display that involves spreading the tail feathers, drooping the wings and producing a low frequency "drumming" sound. When attempting to attract females in the spring breeding season males become quite vocal and regularly emit a loud "gobble" that can be heard for a mile. The saga of the disappearance and resurgence of the Wild Turkey in America is one of wildlife managements greatest success stories. In pioneer days turkeys were abundant in Texas but by the early 1900s the eastern subspecies had disappeared from the state and the Rio Grande population was greatly reduced. Re-stocking efforts aided by sportsmen groups like the National Wild Turkey Federation has been highly successful and Wild Turkeys are now found in suitable habitats throughout the state.

Natural History: The bulk of the range of the Montezuma's Quail is in the mountains and high plateaus of Mexico. Their range extends into the US in several mountain ranges in the desert southwest from west Texas through southern New Mexico and into southern Arizona. They are a rare species in Texas. These are secretive little quail that prefer to hunker down and remain motionless when approached, only flushing when the threat is very close. This behavior coupled with their preferred habitat of mountain woodlands and meadows with dense grasses make them a hard species to observe. In protected enclaves such as Davis Mountains State Park they are occasionally observable from blinds placed near water sources.

Class—**Aves** (birds)

Order—**Galliformes** (quail & grouse)

Family—**Ondontophoridae** (quail)

Northern Bobwhite *Colinus virginianus*	**Gambel's Quail** *Callipepla gambelii*	**Scaled Quail** *Callipepla squamata*

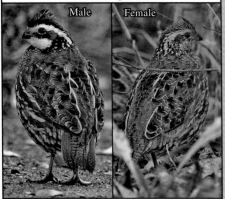
Male · Female
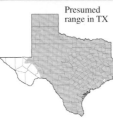

Male · Female

Size: 10 inches. | Presumed range in TX

Abundance: Fairly common.

Variation: Sexually dimorphic. See photos above.

Size: 10 inches. | Presumed range in TX

Abundance: Uncommon in Texas.

Variation: Female lacks black face and brown cap on head.

Size: 10 inches. | Presumed range in TX

Abundance: Common.

Variation: No significant variation and sexes are alike.

Habitat: Small woodlands, edge areas and overgrown fields bordering agricultural land are the favorite habitats generally. In southern and western Texas they are also fairly common in grasslands and brushlands.

Habitat: Gambel's is a desert quail. They occur in creosote flats, cactus and thorn bush desert basins and in the lower foothills of desert mountain ranges and in Riparian habitats in desert basins. Endemic to all desert regions.

Habitat: Inhabits short grass prairies in the panhandle and desert grasslands and desert scrub in the Chihuahuan Desert. Also common in the Tamaulipan Thorn Scrub habitats of the South Texas Plains. The most common quail in west Texas.

Migratory Status: Year-round resident.

Migratory Status: Year-round resident.

Migratory Status: Year-round resident.

Breeding: Ground nester. Clutch size averages about 15 eggs but nest failure due to predation is high. Multiple nestings are not uncommon.

Breeding: Males call from conspicuous perches in the desert when breeding. Nest is on the ground in the shade of a shrub or grass tussock. Up to 15 eggs.

Breeding: Nests are on the ground and concealed within a clump of cactus or yucca or beneath a dense shrub. Seven to fourteen eggs are laid.

Natural History: Bobwhite have always been an important game bird in the United States. In recent decades, however, the species has experienced significant population declines, especially in the northern portions of its range. Some blame a resurgence in predators for the decline. But the real culprit is modern agricultural practices that have eliminated fence rows and created expansive crop fields with no ground cover. This is the main factor contributing to the decline of the Bobwhite. Through fall and winter they will stick together in family groups known as a "covey." Mortality can be high and survivors from more than one covey (flock) will often join together as winter wanes. In spring adults pair off for breeding with the resultant offspring and their parents producing the next fall's covey.

Natural History: This is a true desert species and it inhabits all of the desert regions of the southwestern US. But it is less common in the Chihuahan Desert than the Scaled Quail. It is probably most common in the Sonora Desert in southern Arizona and northwestern Mexico. The characteristic feather plume protruding from the forehead is shared by both sexes and is unique among Texas quail. In the desert cities of Phoenix and Tucson in Arizona these birds are quite common in suburbs will forage in lawns, especially if a water source or seed feeder is available. Like other quail species they travel in small groups (coveys) for most of the year but in spring they are more likely to occur in pairs. At night they seek a roost off the ground in trees, shrubs or cactus. Droughts affect population densities.

Natural History: The range of the Scaled Quail overlaps that of both the Northern Bobwhite to the east and the Gambel's Quail to the west. Hybridization with the Gambel's Quail has been observed in some areas of the Scaled Quail's range but it is unknown if hybrids occur in Texas. Rainfall amounts are one of the factors determining distribution for this species. Wetter regions tend to have thicker vegetation and less open spaces. The Scaled Quail thrives in regions where rainfall is less than 27 inches per year or drier. These birds can be fairly conspicuous at times as they sometimes sit on the limbs of scantily leafed desert shrubs and trees several feet off the ground. Moderate grazing can improve habitat as they like shorter grasses, however overgrazing destroys habitat.

Class—**Aves** (birds)

Order—**Psittaciformes** (parrots)

Family—**Psittacidae**

Monk Parakeet *Myiopsitta monachus*	**Budgerigar** *Melopsittacus undulatus*	**Green Parakeet** *Psittacara holochlorus*

Size 11.5 inches. **Abundance:** Uncommon. **Migratory Status:** Non-migratory, year-round resident.  Presumed range in TX	**Size:** 7 inches. **Abundance:** Uncommon. **Migratory Status:** Non-migratory, year-round resident. 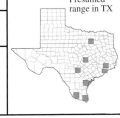 Presumed range in TX	**Size:** 13 inches. **Abundance:** Rare in Texas. **Migratory Status:** Non-migratory, year-round resident.  Presumed range in TX
Variation: No significant variation among adults	**Variation:** Selective breeding by man has produced many color variants.	**Variation:** No significant variation among adults.
Habitat: Native to South America where it uses forests and savannas. In the US has adapted well to urban parks and isolated populations can be found as far north as Chicago and New England.	**Habitat:** Native to Australia. In Texas restricted mainly to urban environments. Not known to thrive in wild environments. May possibly be seen anywhere in the state in towns an cities.	**Habitat.** In its native habitats, the Green Parakeet prefers semi-open woodlands and scrub/brushlands. Although found in tropical regions, it prefers deciduous forest over rainforest.
Breeding: Nest is built of sticks and is large and bulky. 4 to 6 eggs.	**Breeding:** A cavity nester but may use man-made nest boxes. Up to 12 eggs.	**Breeding:** Lays up to 4 eggs in tree cavities or on cliff faces.
Natural History: Although this is an uncommon species in Texas, it is the most common member of the Psittacidae family in the state. A native of South America and a popular bird in the pet industry, it has become widely established in several cities in the state. Its native habitat is South American grasslands, but in Texas it is mainly an urban species and it has adapted quite well to living with humans. There are established colonies in San Antonio, Austin, Dallas, Houston, Corpus Christi, and Brownsville. It no doubt occurs in isolated populations other regions of the state as well. Unlike most Psittacidae which nest in hollows, the Monk Parakeet is famous for its enormous stick nests that are often built on power poles. Nests are communal structures used by several birds. They can cause problems for electrical transmissions.	**Natural History:** The Budgerigar (a.k.a. "Budgie") is probably the best known "pet parakeet" in the world. Native to Australia, they have been widely sold in pet stores around the globe for many decades. Captive breeders have developed a wide variety of colors and patterns in this iconic parakeet. The photo above is an example of the wild color morph. Escaped pet birds may be seen almost anywhere and breeding populations frequently become established in warmer regions of North America. However, these little parakeets are vulnerable to freezing weather and exceptionally cold weather fronts can devastate wild populations. In their native Australia these birds travel in huge flocks and sometimes are a nuisance to grain farmers. But their huge flocks numbering hundreds of thousands are also a quintessentially Australian phenomena.	**Natural History:** While rare in Texas generally, this species can be fairly common in a few local hot spots in the lower Rio Grande Valley. It may also be seen in several urban centers in the state. Urban birds are almost certainly escaped pets (or their descendents) and it is much rarer outside the lower Rio Grande Valley. The native range is from northern Central America to northern Mexico, with Mexican populations coming to within 150 south of the Rio Grande Valley. Whether Texas populations are wild birds that have moved north from Mexico or reproducing birds from captive origins is unclear. But there is an argument for natural range expansion as there has been significant habitat alterations and habitat losses in northern Mexico. The name Green Parakeet is appropriate, as these are solidly green-colored birds.

Class—**Aves** (birds)

Order—**Psittaciformes** (parrots)

Family—**Psittacidae**

Red-crowned Parrot *Amazona viridigenalis*	**Red-lored Parrot** *Amazona autumnalis*	**Yellow-headed Parrot** *Amazona oratrix*

Red-crowned Parrot
Amazona viridigenalis

Size 12 inches.

Abundance: Generally rare.

Migratory Status: Non-migratory, year-round resident.

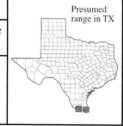
Presumed range in TX

Variation: No significant variation among adults.

Habitat: These are forest birds. In Texas they use urban parks, tree-lined neighborhoods and riparian woodlands.

Breeding: Cavity nester. Uses old woodpecker holes or natural cavities. Two to five eggs are laid.

Natural History: The native range is a relatively small area of northeastern Mexico where there has been a catastrophic loss of forest habitat. This parrot is today quite rare except for local populations that exist in areas well outside its native range. Breeding populations which have originated from escaped or released caged birds are now found in southern California, Hawaii, Florida. The birds of the lower Rio Grande Valley in Texas may have come from birds that wandered north from Mexico. Red-crowned Parrots mate for life. They are gregarious birds that love to flock and will roost together in flocks. For many years this species was exploited for the pet bird industry and it is now an endangered species in its native habitat in Mexico. US populations are also considered endangered. Food is nuts, seeds and fruits. Official mascot of the city of Brownsville.

Red-lored Parrot
Amazona autumnalis

Size: 14 inches.

Abundance: Rare in Texas.

Migratory Status: Non-migratory, year-round resident.

Presumed range in TX

Variation: No significant variation among adults.

Habitat: Lowland forests from northern Mexico to northern South America. Generally below 2,000 feet elevation.

Breeding: Cavity nester. Uses old woodpecker holes or natural cavities. Three or four eggs is typical.

Natural History: In spite of many sightings in the lower Rio Grande Valley, this parrot is not included in the Texas Breeding Bird Atlas. Feral birds are sometimes seen with flocks of other parrot species, especially the similar looking Red-crowned Parrot. It can be distinguished from the Red-crowned by the amount of red present on the head. In the Red-lored, the red is present only on the forehead and between the eye and beak (the lores). Also, the top of the head is bluish gray. In the Red-crowned the red color extends from the lores and up over the crown of the head. Populations of this parrot have declined significantly in some parts of its range. Collecting for the captive bird trade is blamed for this decline. Many inclined to purchase a pet parrot are unaware of the impact of poaching on parrot species. In spite of captive breeding programs poaching remains a problem.

Yellow-headed Parrot
Amazona oratrix

Size: 14 inches.

Abundance: Rare in Texas.

Migratory Status: Non-migratory, year-round resident.

Presumed range in TX

Variation: Adults from Central American regions have less yellow on head.

Habitat: Semi-open habitats in tropical lowlands are the primary habitat. Tamaulipas to northern Honduras.

Breeding: Nests in tree hollows. Pairs mate for life and two or three eggs is the typical clutch size.

Natural History: Endangered in its native habitats. Overcollecting for the pet trade is apparently the main reason for this species' decline. The popularity of parrots as pets has been a major threat to the survival of many psittacine birds, including all three of the species shown on this page. The practice of captive breeding offers one solution to this conservation problem, but illegal trade in wild caught birds continues. The release or accidental escape of pet birds is one reason for the appearance of parrots as aliens throughout the world, but intentional release of birds may be even more of a problem. Captive parrots require a lot of attention. Neglected birds can become problematic. They can be noisy and aggressive toward humans. Additionally, they are long-lived birds that can be difficult to re-home. The solution for frustrated owners is often simply to let them go.

Class—**Aves** (birds)

Order—**Caprimulgiformes** (humingbirds, swifts & nightjars)

Family—**Trochilidae** (hummingbirds)

Ruby-throated Hummingbird *Archilochus colubris*	**Black-chinned Hummingbird** *Archilochus alexandri*	**Buff-bellied Hummingbird** *Amazilia yucatanensis*

Male

Female

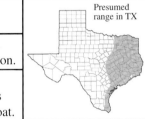

Male / Female

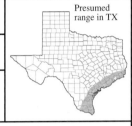

Size: 3.75 inches.

Abundance: Fairly common.

Variation: Female lacks ruby-red throat.

Presumed range in TX

Size: 3.75 inches.

Abundance: Fairly common.

Variation: Female lacks purple throat.

Presumed range in TX

Size: 4.25 inches.

Abundance: Rare in Texas.

Variation: No variation among adults.

Presumed range in TX

Habitat: Woodlands. Both deciduous and mixed forests are utilized. Edge areas and open fields are used for feeding.

Habitat: Open and semi-open country in arid and semi-arid habitats. Avoids true desert but will use riparian habitats.

Habitat: In Texas it is most common in thickets, brush, and woodland in the Western Gulf Coastal Plain ecoregion.

Migratory Status: Summer resident.

Migratory Status: Summer resident

Migratory Status: Winter migrant.

Breeding: Nest is a tiny cup of fine plant fibers and lichens glued together with spider webs. Two eggs is typical.

Breeding: Tiny nest is usually built near the end of a horizontal branch. Only two eggs.

Breeding: Breeding has been observed in the extreme southern tip of Texas but only very rarely. Two eggs are laid.

Natural History: The tiny hummingbirds are ounce for ounce one of the world's greatest travelers. Many fly across the Gulf of Mexico each year during migration. Considering that they weigh barely more than 0.1 of an ounce that is a remarkable feat of endurance! The range of the Ruby-throated Hummingbird includes all of the Eastern Deciduous Forest Level 1 Ecoregion, as well as portions of the Boreal Forest and Great Plains Ecoregions. Nectar is the major food item for hummingbirds and they show a preference for red, tubular flowers. They possess a highly specialized beak and tongue for reaching nectar deep within flowers. They will also eat some small, flying insects caught on the wing, and are known to pluck tiny invertebrates from foliage or small spiders from their webs. These birds will readily use artificial nectar feeders containing a mix of 1 part sugar to 4 parts water. This is the most commonly seen hummingbird in east Texas.

Natural History: Closely related to the Ruby-throated Hummingbird and can be regarded as its western counterpart. Its range includes most of Mexico and virtually all of the southwestern US as well as much of the Rocky Mountains. Like all hummingbirds they have are remarkably rapid metabolism. They can consume three times their body weight in nectar daily and their heart rate is as much as 480 beats per minute! They also are capable of slowing their metabolism at night or during cool environmental conditions to save energy. In a condition known as "torpor" they can drop their body temperature by up to 50 degrees Fahrenheit and slow their heartbeat and breathing. In this condition they are in a state similar to hibernation but it usually lasts only a few hours. Like others of their kind, they feed on flower nectar while hovering. They will also eat tiny insects, most of which are flying insects caught on the wing. Males perform flight displays.

Natural History: In a reverse behavior of most hummingbirds, this bird moves northward following the breeding season and sometimes winters along the Western Gulf Coastal Plain of Texas and Louisiana. The range of this species follows the gulf coastal plain of Mexico southward to the Yucatan Peninsula, where it can be found farther inland throughout the peninsula. The name comes from the unusual buff color of the breast and belly. That characteristic along with a red bill, reddish tail, and green throat helps make identification easier. Like other hummingbirds the colors can be difficult to discern in low light or heavy shade. Even in bright sunlight hummingbird colors tend to be dependent upon the angle of view. Bright colors often associated with the males (especially on the throat) can appear to be black until the light hits at the correct angle to reveal the true colors. This is the only hummingbird in Texas with a green throat in males.

Class—**Aves** (birds)

Order—**Caprimulgiformes** (humingbirds, swifts & nightjars)

Family—**Trochilidae** (hummingbirds)

Blue-throated Mountain Gem *Lampornis clemencia*	**Lucifer Hummingbird** *Calothorax lucifer*	**Broad-tailed Hummingbird** *Selasphorus platycercus*

Size: 5 inches.

Abundance: Rare in Texas.

Variation: Male has blue gorget. Female is gray.

Size: 4.25 inches.

Abundance: Rare in Texas.

Variation: Female lacks bright purple gorget of male.

Size: 4 inches.

Abundance: Uncommon.

Variation: Male has pink throat, female is gray.

Habitat: Habitat in Texas is in shaded canyons in the desert mountain ranges in the Chihuahuan Desert of west Texas (Davis, Chisos, and Guadalupe Mountains).

Habitat: This is a desert-adapted species but more in mountains than in low desert basins. Uses canyons and arid, cactus, and shrub-studded slopes of desert mountain ranges.

Habitat: Inhabits desert mountain ranges in west Texas where it can be seen in forests and meadows. Ranges as high as 10,000 feet in the Rocky Mountains.

Migratory Status: Summer resident.

Migratory Status: Summer resident.

Migratory Status: Summer resident.

Breeding: Most breeding is in Mexico. Only one or two eggs are laid but there may be more than one brood per year.

Breeding: Two eggs are laid and incubated by the female only. Nest site is frequently in a cactus.

Breeding: Breeds in higher elevations in the mountains. Nest is built low to ground. Two eggs on average.

Natural History: Formerly known as the Blue-throated Hummingbird. It was an appropriate name as the gorget (throat patch) of this species is bright blue (when seen in good light). This is a primarily Mexican bird that ranges throughout the Sierra Madre. Found both in Sierra Madre Oriental (east) and Sierra Madre Occidental (west). Some move northward in spring to nest and summer in Chihuahuan Desert Mountain ranges from west Texas to southeastern Arizona. This is the largest hummingbird that nests in the US. They prefer cooler climates than many hummingbirds and thus always found in mountain ranges. In Mexico this species ranges as high as 12,000 feet in elevation. They will come to nectar feeders where their large size ensures they will dominate other, smaller hummingbird species.

Natural History: A species of the Central Mexican Plateau that barely enters the US in the mountains of west Texas and a few Chihuahuan Desert mountain ranges in southwest New Mexico and southeastern Arizona. Food typical for a hummingbird is nectar and tiny insects. The flowers of the Agave are a favorite food. Like other hummers it will sometimes raid spider webs to steal small insects from the web. The gorget (throat patch) of the male is exceptionally large and characteristically flares out on each side of the throat. The decurved bill is rather long for such a small hummingbird they have a rather long, narrow tail when perched. The males tail is forked but this feature is visible only when the male is displaying to the female. This is one of several hummingbird species indigenous to the Chihuahuan Desert and Mexican Plateau.

Natural History: The Broad-tailed Hummingbird winters in the high mountains of Mexico and summers in the high mountains of the western US. Many will merely pass through western Texas in route to summer breeding grounds as far north as the mountains of Idaho and Wyoming. A few will nest and spend the summer in the west Texas mountain ranges. Nights in their high mountain valley habitats can be quite cold and necessitate entering torpor overnight. In some areas where hummingbird feeders are in place year-round (such as state parks or nature preserves), a few hummingbirds may linger throughout the winter. The widespread use of hummingbird feeders not only entertains wildlife enthusiasts but also makes life a bit easier for hummingbirds, who today face remarkable adversities in a modern world.

Class—**Aves** (birds)

Order—**Caprimulgiformes** (humingbirds, swifts & nightjars)

Family—**Trochilidae** (hummingbirds)	Family—**Apodidae** (swifts)	
Rufous Hummingbird *Selasphorus rufus*	**Chimney Swift** *Chaetura pelagica*	**White-throated Swift** *Aeronautes saxatalis*

Size: 3.75 inches. Wingspan 4.5 in.

Abundance: Fairly common.

Variation: Female has a green back.

Presumed range in TX

Size: 5.5 inches. Wingspan 14 in.

Abundance: Fairly common.

Variation: No variation. Sexes are alike.

Presumed range in TX

Size: 6.5 inches. Wingspan 15 in.

Abundance: Fairly common.

Variation: No variation. Sexes are alike.

Presumed range in TX

Habitat: Winter range in southern Mexico is montane forests. Summer range in the Pacific Northwest is meadows and forest openings. Migrants are seen in a wide variety of habitats.

Migratory Status: Seasonal migrant.

Breeding: Courting males perform a typical hummingbird flight display of aerial acrobatics. Two eggs is typical.

Natural History: Although the summer range of this species is in the western US, these birds are known to wander widely and a few are seen in the eastern US virtually every year. Some will even spend the winter along the gulf coast. They are the most northerly ranging of the hummingbirds and breed as far north as the southern Yukon and southeastern Alaska! Because it travels so far and passes through such a wide range of habitats and climates this species may be highly vulnerable to climate change. As it travels across the continent from north to south it must time its movements to coincide with the blooming of nectar-producing food plants and the emergence of small insect prey. A changing climate can affect the timing of these annual occurrences. For a bird that has the enormously high energy requirements of a hummingbird, a mistimed migration could be fatal.

Habitat: Mainly seen in open and semi-open country and in urban/suburban areas. Historically Texas range was restricted to the eastern part of the state. They moved west in recent decades.

Migratory Status: Summer resident.

Breeding: Nest is a flimsy cup plastered to the inside of a chimney. Two to five eggs are laid.

Natural History: This is a species that has benefited from human population expansion. Historically, the Chimney Swift nested mainly in hollow trees. These birds require a vertical surface within a sheltered place for nesting. When people began to build houses and large structures like schools, churches, and factories equipped with chimneys, their populations exploded. Today they are perhaps less common than a few decades ago when most dwellings and other buildings had chimneys. Some nesting in natural hollows still occurs. Swifts have long, narrow, pointed wings that allow for extreme maneuverability and these birds feed entirely on the wing. Small flying insects are their prey. During migration they are sometimes seen in large flocks that can contain over 1,000 birds. Today the greatest population densities occur in the vicinity of urban centers.

Habitat: Virtually all habitats in the western half of the US are withing the range of the White-throated Swift. They are most common in canyons and mountainous areas with steep cliffs.

Migratory Status: Year-round resident.

Breeding: Nest is usually deep in a rock crevice on a steep cliff face, or in man-made structures. Four to five eggs is usual.

Natural History: While there are year-round populations in western Texas, there are also seasonal migrants and winter residents present in parts of the state. Their summer range extends northward to southern British Columbia and their year-round range goes south to Nicaragua. Looking like a "cigar with wings" the swifts are extremely fast and agile fliers. They are able to make rapid twists and turns in pursuit of small flying insect prey. In their favorite habitat of canyons and cliff faces updrafts of air sweep flying insects into their domain. They have even been known to engage in aerial foraging in the updrafts created by weather fronts and approaching storms. Saliva is used to glue a half-moon shaped nest of small twigs to rock inside of a vertical crack in a cliff face. Nesting sites may be used by repeated generations of birds. These swifts can live for at least ten years.

Class—**Aves** (birds)

Order—**Caprimulgiformes** (humingbirds, swifts & nightjars)

Family—**Caprimulgidae** (nightjars)

Common Nighthawk *Chordeiles minor*	Lesser Nighthawk *Chordeiles acutipennis*	Common Pauraque *Nyctidromus albicollis*

Size: 9.5 inches. Wingspan 24 in.  Presumed range in TX	**Size:** 9 inches. Wingspan 22 in.  Presumed range in TX	**Size:** 11.5 inches.  Presumed range in TX
Abundance: Fairly common.	**Abundance:** Fairly common.	**Abundance:** Uncommon.
Variation: No variation and sexes are alike.	**Variation:** No variation and sexes are alike.	**Variation:** Male has white spots, females are buff.
Habitat: Open and semi-open areas. Can be common around cities and towns but also in rural areas.	**Habitat:** In summer, inhabits desert areas with scrubby brush and cacti, rocky arroyos, lava flows, and gravel substrate.	**Habitat:** A tropical species whose range extends into extreme south Texas. Habitat there is riparian thickets, woods.
Migratory Status: Summer resident.	**Migratory Status:** Summer resident.	**Migratory Status:** Year-round resident.
Breeding: No nest is constructed and 2 eggs are laid on bare gravel. Many nests are on flat, gravel-covered rooftops. Eggs are heavily mottled with gray	**Breeding:** No nest is constructed and the eggs are laid directly on the ground. The 2 speckled eggs are cryptic. Nest may be in full sun or partial shade.	**Breeding:** Two eggs are laid on bare ground. In Texas nesting is in late spring or early summer. Nesting is in semi-open woods or brushy areas.

Natural History: Nighthawks often go by the nickname "Bullbat." They can be quite common in urban areas in summer but they are also seen in open and semi-open rural areas. Like other nightjars, the Common Nighthawk feeds on the wing, catching moths and other flying insects. But unlike the others this bird is active both at night and at dawn and dusk, or sometimes on cloudy days. Around towns and cities they chase airborne insects attracted to streetlights at night. This is one of the great travelers of the bird world, wintering in South America. Their summer range includes nearly all of North America south of the Arctic. Nighthawks are usually seen in flight, but they will occasionally be spotted resting atop a fence post in open country or sitting on the ground in gravel areas. They often migrate in large flocks, sometimes numbering over 1000 birds. They have experienced a precipitous population decline in recent years.

Natural History: The cryptic nature of the plumage of the nightjars is well illustrated on the specimen shown above. These birds fly low and slow over the desert at dawn, dusk, and into the night. They feed on flying insects including some very large moths and beetles that are scooped into the enormous gape of their jaws. Days are spent roosting on limbs or on the ground. When roosting on a limb they sit horizontally aligned with the limb, which helps them to blend in. Even when roosting on the ground they are remarkably well camouflaged. These birds can be seen in the most remote and hostile desert regions of North America or they may be seen catching insects around streetlights of large towns and cities. They have even been known to roost and nest on flat rooftops in urban areas. They will open their huge mouths to cool themselves in the desert heat and they can endure cold snaps by entering into a state of torpor.

Natural History: This is one of the most common nightjars in tropical America and is found throughout most of South America as well as Central America and the lowlands of Mexico. In forests and thick brush they will use roadways as flight lanes. They can be seen sitting on the edge of rural roads in south Texas where their eye-shine is easy to see in the headlights of a passing vehicle. Flies mostly at dusk and dawn and spends the day quietly roosting, sometimes in plain sight but nearly invisible with its camouflaged plumage. This species has declined in areas where the land has been cleared for agriculture, but it is still a fairly common bird where adequate habitat still exists. This is mainly a species of coastal plains and interior lowlands. Its range in South America is quite extensive and it is found throughout most of the continent north of Argentina and east of the Andes Mountains.

Class—**Aves** (birds)

Order—**Caprimulgiformes** (humingbirds, swifts & nightjars)

Family– **Caprimulgidae** (nightjars)

Common Poorwill *Phalaenoptilus nuttallii*	**Chuck-wills-widow** *Antrostomus carolinensis*	**Whip-poor-will** *Antrostomus vociferus*

Size: 7.75 inches.	**Size:** 12 inches. Wingspan 26 in.	**Size:** 9.75 inches.
Abundance: Uncommon.	**Abundance:** Fairly common.	**Abundance:** Uncommon.
Variation: No variation and sexes are alike.	**Variation:** No significant variation, sexes alike.	**Variation:** No variation, sexes alike.

Presumed range in TX

Habitat: Inhabits arid regions of the western US. Occurs in desert and arid grasslands but also in dry forests in mountainous areas.

Migratory Status: Summer resident and seasonal migrant.

Breeding: Eggs are laid directly on the ground in a shallow scrape. Female always lays two eggs. Two broods per year are common. Young birds are fed by regurgitation.

Natural History: This is the smallest member of the Caprimulgidae family. Unlike many other nightjars, the range of this species is contained entirely in North America. Its summer range is in the western US and southwestern Canada. Birds that summer in the US and Canada winter in northwestern Mexico (including the Baja Peninsula). Feeds less by catching insects in flight than other nightjars. Rather, it often hunts by leaping upward from a perch to snatch passing insects in flight. Like other nightjars it forages mostly at dawn and dusk and on moonlight nights. Days are spent roosting quietly and relying on cryptic plumage to keep it hidden. The common name comes from the two-noted call "poor-will." These are rarely seen birds but they are probably more common than sightings would indicate.

Habitat: A forest species that summers in all types of forests in the southeastern US. Both pure deciduous and mixed hardwood/pine forests are used.

Migratory Status: Summer resident and seasonal migrant.

Breeding: Nests on the ground usually in woodlands with an open understory. No nest is constructed. Eggs are deposited on leaf litter or in pine forest on a bed of pine needles. 2 eggs are laid.

Natural History: Chuck-wills-widow in summer is a forest bird that breeds mainly in the Eastern Temperate Forest Level I Ecoregion of North America (see Figure 4 on page 8). Its breeding range in Texas extends westward into the southern portions of the Great Plains Level I Ecoregion where there are sufficient woodland habitats. In winter they retreat to Mexico, the Caribbean, Central America, and northern South America. Some will stay in the US in the southernmost tip of Texas. Although they favor woodlands they like to hunt in open areas such as clearings or along the edge of the woods where it borders an open field or marsh. This is the largest member of the Caprimulgidae family and it is easily confused with the Whip-poor-will. But even novice birders can recognize the difference in their calls.

Habitat: A forest species that hunts along forest edge, power-line cuts through wooded area. Upland xeric woods are favored over lowlands.

Migratory Status: Seasonal migrant and winter resident along the coast.

Breeding: Nests on the ground amid leaf litter. No nest is built and the eggs (usually 2) are laid on the ground. Nest is usually in open understory woodland. Eggs are white with brown speckles.

Natural History: Few animals exhibit a more cryptic color and pattern than this species. When resting on the forest floor during the day they are nearly invisible. This is an uncommon species that is absent from deforested regions of the state. Very similar to the Chuck-wills-widow, which is smaller (9.75 inches) and browner than the Whip-poor-will. The two are easily differentiated by their songs, usually described as *whip-prrr-weel* for the Whip-poor-will and as *chuk-wills wee-dow* for the Chuck-will's-widow. Both calls are usually repeated rapidly and at times incessantly. Equipped with a very large mouth for feeding on moths and other large flying insects, both species are nocturnal and catch most of their food in mid-air. Both have experienced unexplained declines over the last decade.

Class—**Aves** (birds)

Order—**Strigiformes** (owls)

Family—**Tytonidae** (barn owls)	Family—**Strigidae** (typical owls)	
Barn Owl *Tyto alba*	**Long-eared Owl** *Asio otus*	**Short-eared Owl** *Asio flammeus*

Barn Owl

Size: 16 inches.

Abundance: Uncommon.

Variation: Females have more buff on breast, sides.

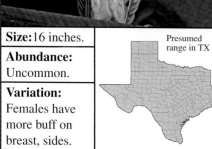
Presumed range in TX

Habitat: Prefers open and semi-open habitats. Short grass pastures are a favorite hunting ground. Probably more common around farms and small towns

Migratory Status: Year-round non-migratory resident statewide.

Breeding: Nested in hollows in trees or in caves historically. Now uses old buildings or barns. Up to 11 eggs.

Natural History: The Barn Owl is one of the most widespread owl species in the world, being found throughout most of North America south of Canada, all of Central and South America, most of Europe and sub-Saharan Africa, parts of southern Asia, and all of Australia. Recent taxonomic investigations suggest there may be several distinct species worldwide. In spite of its wide range, they are usually not common anywhere. Small rodents are the primary prey, especially mice and voles. When feeding a large brood of young a pair of Barn Owls may catch over two dozen mice in a single night. Like other owls their hearing is so acute they can catch mice unseen beneath leaves by homing in rustling sounds. Ironically, man's attempts to control rodents with poisoned baits may be in part responsible for the demise of rodent eating species like the Barn Owl.

Long-eared Owl

Size: 15 inches.

Abundance: Uncommon.

Variation: Female is darker, more rusty facial disk, larger.

Presumed range in TX

Habitat: Prefers open and semi-open woodlands and riparian habitats in open regions. Breeds and summers in boreal regions and mountains.

Migratory Status: Mostly a winter migrant, less commonly a winter resident.

Breeding: Nests in trees in abandoned stick nests built by hawks, crows or other large bird species. 5 or 6 eggs.

Natural History: Although this rare owl could possibly be seen anywhere in the state in winter, most sightings are in the western portions of the state. They are more common in Texas in the northwestern portion of the state. Elsewhere in Texas they are most likely to be seen in harsh winters when deep snows farther to north force them to move south. They are secretive birds that hide by day in dense junipers or pines. Their name comes from the well-developed feather tufts on the head which are erected when resting. These "ear tufts" are folded against the head and not visible on owls in flight. Long-eared Owls during winter can sometimes be seen in small flocks that roost in close proximity to each other. They show a definite preference for conifers for their daytime roosts. Their food is almost exclusively small mammals, mostly voles and mice of the *Peromyscus* genus.

Short-eared Owl

Size: 15 inches.

Abundance: Uncommon.

Variation: Females tend to be slightly darker.

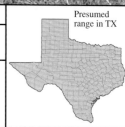
Presumed range in TX

Habitat: These are open country birds and the primary habitat is prairie, marsh, and tundra. In forested regions they haunt fields, pastures, and meadows.

Migratory Status: Winter migrant and rare winter resident.

Breeding: Nest is on the ground. A slight depression is scraped out by the owl and lined with grasses. 5 or 6 eggs.

Natural History: Although they have been documented statewide, these owls are most likely to be seen in the panhandle region. They may move much farther south (all the way into northern Mexico) during extreme winter weather. They are most likely to be seen in open regions. Unlike most owls they roost on the ground, usually in open fields with tall grasses. The food is mostly small rodents. Voles are the most significant item in their diet. Rodent prey is located mostly by sound while flying low and slow over open, grassy fields. Most hunting is done at night or dusk and dawn, but these owls are more diurnal than most and may hunt during the day. The erectile feathers on the face that form the "ears" are not usually visible unless the owl is agitated or defensive. They appear to be in decline in much of America and are an endangered species in some states.

Class—**Aves** (birds)

Order—**Strigiformes** (owls)

Family—**Strigidae** (typical owls)

Flammulated Owl *Psiloscops flammeolus*	**Western Screech Owl** *Megascops kennicottii*	**Eastern Screech Owl** *Megascops asio*

Flammulated Owl
Psiloscops flammeolus

Size: 6.75 inches.

Abundance: Rare in Texas.

Variation: Gray and reddish morphs.

Presumed range in TX

Habitat: Xeric woodlands in the Rocky Mountain range. Prefers large trees in its habitat, especially Ponderosa Pine and other large conifers.

Migratory Status: Seasonal migrant.

Breeding: A cavity nester. Mostly uses old woodpecker holes but will use any natural cavity.

Natural History: When discussing the importance of individual species in the local ecology, biologists often use the term "keystone species." That term refers to a species that is integral to the health of an ecosystem and one in which other species occurring within the ecosystem are dependent. Nearly all the owl species that appear in this book will use natural cavities in trees for nesting. In many cases, these natural cavities are provided by some type of woodpecker species. Small woodpeckers make small cavities for smaller owls like the Flammulated Owl. Large Woodpeckers like the Flickers and the Pileated create larger cavities for larger owls like the Barred or Barn owls. Thus the woodpeckers are a keystone species that makes life easier for many other species that might otherwise have difficulty finding suitable nesting sites. The diet of the Flammulated Owl is mostly insects caught high up in large trees.

Western Screech Owl
Megascops kennicottii

Size: 8.5 inches. Wings 20 inches.

Abundance: Rare in Texas.

Variation: Brown and gray color morphs.

Presumed range in TX

Habitat: A forest species mainly found in mountain forests and in riparian woodlands in desert areas. Also can be found in urban parks with large trees.

Migratory Status: Year-round resident.

Breeding: Nests in natural cavities and old woodpecker holes. The same cavity may be used year after year. 2 to 7 eggs.

Natural History: The two screech owls found in Texas are very similar and were once regarded as being the same species. Unlike the Eastern Screech Owl the vocalizations of the western species does not include the classic "screeching" sound produced by the Eastern Screech Owl. Indeed the difference in vocalization is one of the factors supporting the separation into two species of these two very similar owls. Western Screech Owls are widespread across the western US from southeastern Alaska southward well into Mexico (west of the Sierra Madre Oriental). They are found generally below 7000 feet. In Texas they are uncommon and restricted in range to the Chihuahuan Desert and the Edwards Plateau. In Texas's desert regions they occur in wooded regions of lower mountain slopes and in tree-lined arroyos, canyons, and along streams. Their range slightly overlaps that of the Eastern Screech Owl in the hill country.

Eastern Screech Owl
Megascops asio

Red morph

Gray morph

Size: 8.5 inches.

Abundance: Fairly common.

Variation: Red and gray color morphs.

Presumed range in TX

Habitat: All types of habitats within the state may be used, including suburban areas and in the vicinity of farms. Favors edge areas, fence rows, etc.

Migratory Status: Year-round resident.

Breeding: Nest is in tree hollows and old woodpecker holes. 4 to 6 eggs are laid and young fledge in June.

Natural History: The eerie call of the Eastern Screech Owl is often described as "haunting and tremulous." Despite being at times vocal birds, these small owls often go unnoticed. They may even live in suburban yards and small towns, especially if older, large trees with hollow limbs and trunks are present. They feed on insects such as crickets and grasshoppers and on a wide variety of small vertebrate prey including mice, voles, and songbirds that are plucked from their roosts at night. These wide-ranging birds are found throughout the eastern United States as from the Atlantic to the Rocky Mountains and from southern Canada to Florida and Mexico. Birds in the northern portions of their range can be negatively impacted by severe winters. There are two common color morphs of the Eastern Screech Owl. Red morphs dominate in much of the eastern US. In Texas, most are the gray morph.

Class—**Aves** (birds)
Order—**Strigiformes** (owls)
Family—**Strigidae** (typical owls)

Ferruginous Pygmy Owl *Glacidium brasilianum*	**Elf Owl** *Micrathene whitneyi*	**Burrowing Owl** *Athene cunicularia*

Size: 6.75 inches.	 Presumed range in TX	**Size:** 5.75 inches.	 Presumed range in TX	**Size:** 9.5 inches. Wingspan 21 in.	 Presumed range in TX
Abundance: Rare in Texas.		**Abundance:** Uncommon.		**Abundance:** Uncommon.	
Variation: Males tend to be darker.		**Variation:** Grayish and rufous morphs.		**Variation:** Young have buff-colored breast and belly.	

Habitat: Texas habitat includes both mesquite woodlands and Rio Grande riparian forests, the latter of which have largely been destroyed for agriculture.	**Habitat:** Deserts and thorn forests are listed as habitat in the US. In Texas it has also been found in riparian woodlands in the lower Rio Grande valley	**Habitat:** Open country. In Texas they are found mainly throughout the Great Plains and in the Western Gulf Coastal Plain.
Migratory Status: Year-round resident.	**Migratory Status:** Summer resident.	**Migratory Status:** Year-round resident.
Breeding: Cavity nester. Loss of woodland habitat has created a shortage of nesting cavities in Texas. Three or four eggs is usual but can be up to five.	**Breeding:** Nests in natural cavities and in old woodpecker holes. Elf Owls arrive on the breeding grounds in west Texas as early as March. Usually 3 eggs.	**Breeding:** Nest is in an old Armadillo or Prairie Dog burrow. In some instances they may use a man-made structure or dig their own burrow. 4 to 6 eggs.

Natural History: This species is widespread throughout Latin America from northern Mexico south to Argentina. It was once much more common in southern Texas prior to the clearing of forests in the Rio Grande Valley for agriculture and development. Today it is a threatened species in Texas. It is more diurnal than many other owls and can sometimes be seen in the open in daylight. In spite of their small size, they are fierce little birds. They will eat large amounts of invertebrates including large insects and scorpions but they are known to take prey as large as quail and cotton rats, the latter of which is a formidable prey. Many species of songbirds are also on the menu for this owl, including some species that are much larger than the predator. They are most active dawn and dusk. Hunting tactics are to ambush prey with a quick dash from a perch.

Natural History: The Elf Owl is not only the smallest owl in America, it is also the world's smallest raptor. These strictly nocturnal hunters prey mostly in insects and other small arthropod prey. West Texas birds are a short distance migrants that winter in Mexico. Most birds that summer in the lower Rio Grande Valley also move into Mexico in the winter, but there may be a few that stay in the valley year-round. These tiny nocturnal birds would easily go unnoticed but for their characteristic vocalizations that resemble the sound of a yipping puppy. They will tolerate human activity enough so that they may nest in a suburban yard and will use man-made nest boxes. In the Sonora Desert the giant Saguaro Cactus is a favorite nesting site, usually in an old Gilded Flicker or Gila Woodpecker nest. Their home range during nesting season may only include a few acres.

Natural History: Burrowing Owls are found throughout the western US and there are disjunct populations in Florida and the Caribbean. In addition, they are widespread in Central and South America. The food of the Burrowing Owl includes almost any animal small enough to be killed and swallowed. Insects and other invertebrates are a major part of the diet but lizards, small snakes, frogs, rodents, and a few birds are also eaten. They hunt both day and night and are probably the most diurnal of all the owls. In the Great Plains region they often associate with Prairie Dog towns where they appropriate empty Prairie Dog burrows. They are usually more active at dawn and dusk in hot, desert regions. They often perch conspicuously on dead snags, atop tall cacti, or on fence posts. Burrowing Owls have long legs and can run fast enough to catch some prey on the ground.

Class—**Aves** (birds)

Order—**Strigiformes** (owls)

Family—**Strigidae** (typical owls)

Barred Owl *Strix varia*	**Great Horned Owl** *Bubo virginianus*

Fledgling

On nest

Size: 21 inches. Wingspan 42 inches.

Abundance: Fairly common.

Variation: No sexual variation. Three subspecies are known in America with a fourth in central Mexico, two subspecies occur in Texas.

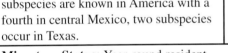
Presumed range in TX

Migratory Status: Year-round resident.

Habitat: Woodlands primarily. Especially in bottomlands, swampy areas, and riparian corridors, but also upland woods.

Breeding: Nest is usually in tree cavities but they are known to nest in open tree crotches or old hawk nests. Usually 2 (rarely 3 or 4) eggs are laid.

Natural History: The Barred Owl ranges throughout the eastern half of the United States from the eastern edge of the great plains eastward. In Texas they are most common in the Piney Woods region. The eight-noted call of the Barred Owl is described as "Hoo-hoo, hoo-hoo, hoo-hoo, hooaahh." In addition, the species is capable of a wide array of hoots, screeches, and coarse whistles. Small vertebrates are the main prey, especially rodents like voles, mice, and flying squirrels. Birds, lizards, small snakes, and amphibians are also eaten. In the eastern United States the range of the Barred Owl closely coincides with that of the Red-shouldered Hawk and the two predators are often regarded as ecological counterparts occupying the same niche at different times. The western counterpart of the Barred Owl, the **Spotted Owl** (*Strix occidentalis*) is a rare western owl found in Texas only in the Guadalupe Mountains and possibly also in the Davis Mountains.

Size: 23 inches. Wingspan 44 inches.

Abundance: Fairly common.

Variation: Males are slightly smaller and have a larger white patch on throat. There are ten subspecies in North America and two occur in Texas.

Presumed range in TX

Migratory Status: Year-round resident.

Habitat: Woodlands, semi-open and open habitats are all utilized, but most common in mosaic of upland woods and fields.

Breeding: One of the earliest nesting birds in America. Horned Owls may be sitting on eggs by late January. Nest is often an old hawk nest. 2 eggs is usual.

Natural History: This widespread species occurs throughout the Americas from Alaska to southern South America. In the US, specimens from the western portions of the country are much paler than those seen in the east. There are two subspecies in Texas. The Eastern subspecies is found in the east half of the state and the Pale form in the west. In the eastern United States, Red Cedars and other evergreen trees are a favorite roosting site. The Great Horned Owl is the ecological counterpart of the Red-tailed Hawk, hunting much the same prey in the same regions; with the hawk hunting by day and the owl at night. These powerful predators eat a wide variety of small animals. Rabbits are a favorite food item. They are also known to eat larger mammals like muskrats, groundhogs, and even skunks or rarely, domestic cats! They can be a problem at times for those who raise chickens and leave them out in the open at night. But they also consume many rodents.

Class—**Aves** (birds)

Order—**Accipitriformes** (hawks, kites, osprey & eagles)

Family—**Pandionidae** (osprey)

Family—**Accipitridae** (hawks, kites, eagles)

Osprey *Pandion haliaetus*	**Swallow-tailed Kite** *Elanoides forficatus*	**White-tailed Kite** *Elanus leucurus*

Size: 30 inches.

Abundance: Fairly common.

Variation: Females are slightly larger than males.

Presumed range in TX

Size: 22 inches.

Abundance: Rare in Texas.

Variation: No variation except juveniles have shorter tails.

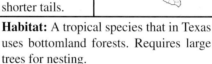
Presumed range in TX

Size: 15 inches.

Abundance: Uncommon.

Variation: Juvenile has mottled wings.

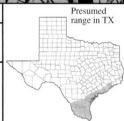
Presumed range in TX

Habitat: Typically seen along coastlines and in the vicinity of large lakes and rivers inland. Always near water.

Habitat: A tropical species that in Texas uses bottomland forests. Requires large trees for nesting.

Habitat: Open country. Likes grasslands, pastures, and coastal marshes. Also uses savanna-like habitats.

Migratory Status: Winter resident along the Coastal Plain and seasonal migrant elsewhere in the state.

Migratory Status: Summer resident in the extreme southeastern corner of Texas.

Migratory Status: Year-round resident in south Texas in the coastal plain and the lower Rio Grande valley.

Breeding: Bulky stick nest is often built on man-made structures like bridges and power line towers. 2 to 4 eggs.

Breeding: The nest is built of sticks and Spanish Moss and is usually near the crown of a very tall Pine tree. Two eggs.

Breeding: Nest is made of twigs and grass and placed in a tree. Four eggs is usual.

Natural History: Subsists mainly on fish and no other raptor is as specialized for piscivorous lifestyle. Hunting tactics consist of a steep dive that ends with the Osprey plunging feet first into the water, allowing them to catch fish up three feet below the surface. Most fish caught in fresh water are non-game species, thus they have little to no impact on sport fisheries. Like the Bald Eagle, Osprey populations in the mid-United States plummeted dramatically in the first half of the twentieth century. The same types of conservation efforts that restored the Bald Eagle (including re-introduction programs), have brought Osprey numbers back to respectable levels. Once regarded as an endangered species, the Osprey has recovered enough to have recently been delisted. Most states now boasts healthy populations of nesting Ospreys and they continue to increase across the country.

Natural History: Among the many unique and beautiful birds of Texas, the Swallow-tailed Kite stands out for its striking black-and-white color, long, forked tail, and gracefulness in flight. Add to that a delicate, almost fragile appearance and you have a bird that never fails to elicit appreciation from both avid birdwatchers and typical residents lucky enough to see it. Almost never seen perched, the Swallow-tailed Kite is seemingly always aloft. Its graceful command of invisible air currents gives the impression of effortlessness in flight. It feeds mostly on the wing and will pluck prey from treetops or out of the air. It usually then eats while in flight. In addition to insects, will eat lizards, frogs, small snakes, and nestling birds. These birds formerly ranged much farther north in summer and they once could be seen throughout most of the Piney Woods region of Texas.

Natural History: Another primarily tropical kite that ranges into southern Texas and is also a very rare resident in the Everglades region of Florida. They are also a fairly common bird along the western coastline of America as far north as southern Washington. The bulk of the range is in Mexico, Central America, and down into South America. When not breeding these birds are quite gregarious and will roost communally. Hunts by soaring and hovering as well as from a perch. In food preference this kite is a small mammal specialist and it feeds almost entirely on small mammals. This is a rather rare situation for a predator. Since every meal must first be hunted down and killed, most predators are consummate opportunists and will take a wide variety of prey species. Like other kites, this bird has a graceful countenance in the air. The name "kite" is appropriate for these birds.

Class—**Aves** (birds)

Order—**Accipitriformes** (hawks, kites, osprey & eagles)

Family—**Accipitridae** (hawks, kites, eagles)

Mississippi Kite *Ictinia mississippiensis*	**Bald Eagle** *Haliaeetus leucocephalus*	**Golden Eagle** *Aquila chrysaetos*

Mississippi Kite

Ictinia mississippiensis

Size: 14 inches.

Abundance: Fairly common.

Variation: Juveniles are streaked with brown on the breast.

Presumed range in TX

Habitat: In Texas, the Mississippi Kite mostly frequents forests along major rivers, open woodlands, and savanna-like habitats in prairies regions.

Migratory Status: Summer resident and seasonal migrant.

Breeding: In Texas most breeding is in the panhandle and in west-central Texas. Some breeding occurs in northeast Texas and in the coastal plain. Two eggs.

Natural History: With their small beaks and feet, the Mississippi Kite appears somewhat delicate looking compared to other raptors. In flight they are one of the most graceful. The several species that make up the raptor group known as kites are mainly tropical birds. The Mississippi Kite is the most northerly ranging of the kites, and they can rarely be seen as far north as Iowa and Kansas. Long distance migrants, they begin to arrive in the southern US by early May and leave for South America by mid-September. These are gregarious birds that may nest communally, and in some parts of their range it is not uncommon to see several nests in close proximity or see groups of birds soaring together. They feed on insects and small vertebrates. Flying insects are taken on the wing and lizards may be plucked from tree limbs.

Bald Eagle

Haliaeetus leucocephalus

Juvenile / Adult

Size: 31 inches.

Abundance: Uncommon.

Variation: Juvenile has brown head and tail for first few years.

Presumed range in TX

Habitat: Like Ospreys, Bald Eagles are usually associated with water. Large rivers, lakes, wet prairies, and marshes. In dry regions follows river valleys.

Migratory Status: Winter resident mostly. Year-round in southeast Texas.

Breeding: Extremely bulky stick nest is re-used and gets larger each year. Nest is located in large trees or power poles, Usually only 2 eggs per clutch.

Natural History: Bald Eagles were highly endangered just a few decades ago. Stringent protection, banning of the pesticide DDT, and a widespread education campaign has led to a remarkable recovery. They first began to recover as a breeding species in most of the country in the 1980s following years of strict protection and banning of DDT. Bald Eagles feed largely on fish and carrion but are also capable hunters. Some birds specialize in hunting migratory waterfowl in winter, picking off birds wounded by hunters. Bald Eagles wander widely in the winter and may be seen virtually anywhere in the state, but they are nowhere numerous. Most nesting in Texas is in the southeastern part of the state around large rivers, lakes, or expansive wetlands. The National emblem of the United States of America since 1782.

Golden Eagle

Aquila chrysaetos

Size: 30 inches.

Abundance: Rare in Texas.

Variation: Female is about 20 percent larger. Juveniles have white in tail.

Presumed range in TX

Habitat: Rugged mountains, deserts, and open plains of the western US and rugged regions of Canadian tundra. May occur at very high elevations.

Migratory Status: Year-round resident and winter migrant.

Breeding: A large stick nest up to 6 feet across is usually built on the face of a steep cliff in a remote area. Usually lays 2 eggs.

Natural History: Although Golden Eagles wander widely and may be seen almost anywhere in the state in winter, they are rare east of the Panhandle and the Trans-Pecos regions. While slightly smaller than the Bald Eagle, Golden Eagles are the most fearsome hunting bird in America. Ground squirrels and other small mammals make up the bulk of their prey, with larger species like jackrabbits and the young of wild sheep, goats, and Pronghorn also taken. They are sometimes persecuted by sheep ranchers in western North America, who blame them for killing young lambs in the spring. Indigenous to the entire northern hemisphere, in America the Golden Eagle is found mostly in the west. Like many large raptors they are capable of significant seasonal movements. Ancient Mongolian falconers trained them to hunt wolves!

Class—**Aves** (birds)

Order—**Accipitriformes** (hawks, kites, osprey & eagles)

Family—**Accipitridae** (hawks, kites, eagles)

Northern Harrier *Circus cyaneus*	**Sharp-shinned Hawk** *Accipiter striatus*	**Cooper's Hawk** *Accipiter cooperii*

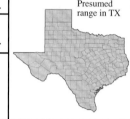

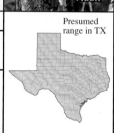

Size: 18 inches.

Abundance: Fairly common.

Variation: Male is slate gray. Female is brown.

Presumed range in TX

Habitat: Open country. Pastures, marshes, agricultural fields, wet prairies, and grasslands. Will hunt harvested croplands in winter and during migration. Coastal marshes are a favorite winter habitat.

Migratory Status: Winter resident.

Breeding: This is one of the few hawks that nests on the ground The nest is usually placed in thick grasses and is built from grasses and weed stems. Lays 4 to 6 eggs with as many as 9 recorded.

Natural History: The range of the Northern Harrier is holarctic and includes Europe and northern Asia as well as North America. Unlike most diurnal raptors that hunt entirely by sight, the Northern Harrier mimics the technique used by owls and hunts largely by sound. A special "parabola" of feathers surround the face and direct sound waves to the ears. It hunts by flying low to the ground with a slow, buoyant flight that resembles a giant butterfly. Food is mostly small mammals and birds but reptiles and amphibians are also listed as food items. Roosting and nesting on the ground and hunting as much by sound as by sight, the Northern Harrier is unique among America's diurnal raptors.

Size: To 13 inches.

Abundance: Fairly common.

Variation: Females are larger. Juveniles are streaked brown.

Presumed range in TX

Habitat: Forests and thickets. Uses edge areas and second growth woodlands and riparian woods in open country and deserts. May be found in both rural and urban areas where vegetative cover is present.

Migratory Status: Winter resident.

Breeding: Conifers are a favored locale for placing the nest. Breeds in montane forests in the west, boreal forests in the far north, and in dense deciduous forests in the east. Lays as many as 8 eggs, with 5 to 6 being the average.

Natural History: A relentless hunter of small songbirds, the Sharp-shinned Hawk is sometimes seen raiding backyard bird feeders, and they are known to pluck baby songbirds from nests. These small raptors are capable of rapid, twisting flight while pursuing their small songbird prey through woodlands and thickets. They are more common during migration when birds that have summered farther north move through the state. Although many birds are winter residents in the state, others are migrants that wander widely as the make their way farther south. The Sharp-shinned Hawk is a widely distributed species that ranges across all of North America south of the arctic region and southward all the way to southern Central America.

Size: To 19 inches.

Abundance: Fairly common.

Variation: Females are larger. Juveniles are streaked brown.

Presumed range in TX

Habitat: Woodlands, regenerative areas, and edge habitats are favored. Uses riparian woods in open country and in deserts. Can be seen in prairie habitats during migration. Can also be seen in tree-lined urban yards and city parks.

Migratory Status: Year-round resident.

Breeding: Stick nest is built high in tree and eggs are laid in April or May. Nest is often in a pine tree and in a fork nestled against the trunk. The nest is large and bulky and built mainly by the male. Clutch size averages 4 to 6.

Natural History: Feeds almost exclusively on birds and is known to haunt backyard bird feeders. Cooper's Hawks are fierce hunters that will fearlessly attack birds as large or larger than themselves, including grouse, waterfowl, and domestic chickens. Although quite widespread and fairly common, they are not as observable as the *Buteo* hawks since they tend to stay in wooded areas and thickets with heavier cover than their bulkier cousins. These birds are fast fliers and capable of great maneuverability, an adaptation to hunting in forest and thickets. They have adapted well to human activities and they sometimes exist in urban areas, especially in parks and heavily wooded neighborhoods.

Class—**Aves** (birds)

Order—**Accipitriformes** (hawks, kites, osprey & eagles)

Family—**Accipitridae** (hawks, kites, eagles)

Harris's Hawk *Parabuteo unicinctus*	**Red-shouldered Hawk** *Buteo lineatus*	**Broad-winged Hawk** *Buteo platypterus*

Adult   Juvenile

Size: 20 inches.

Abundance: Uncommon.

Variation: No significant variation among adults.

Presumed range in TX

Size: 17 inches.

Abundance: Fairly common.

Variation: Sexes alike. Juveniles streaked brown.

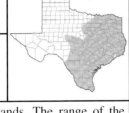
Presumed range in TX

Size: 15 inches.

Abundance: Uncommon.

Variation: Light and dark morphs. Light morph above.

Presumed range in TX

Habitat: In the US inhabits arid and semi-arid country. In Texas, found in southern Texas, the Edwards Plateau, the southern High Plains and parts of the Chihuahuan Desert.

Habitat: Woodlands. The range of the Red-shouldered Hawk encompasses the entire Eastern Temperate Forest Level I Ecoregion and wooded portions of the southern Great Plains Ecoregion.

Habitat: Favors large tracts of unbroken deciduous woodlands in upland areas as summer habitat. Winters in forested regions from southern Mexico to South America.

Migratory Status: Year-round resident.

Migratory Status: Year-round resident.

Migratory Status: Seasonal migrant.

Breeding: Uniquely among raptors, a family unit may include two males and one female.

Breeding: Bulky stick nest is in the fork of a tree about 20 to 40 feet high and often near water. 2 to 4 eggs in April.

Breeding: Stick nest is in a tree crotch, usually in deep woods. Lays 2 to 3 eggs on average. Rare nester in east Texas.

Natural History: In Texas, this raptor is more common in the Southern Texas Plains and in the southern portion of the Western Gulf Coastal Plain. Their overall range includes much of northern Mexico and parts of South America. These are the most social of American raptors and they are frequently seen in small groups that will hunt cooperatively. They are powerful birds with strong talons and a fearsome attitude when hunting. They will pursue prey on foot through thick cover. When hunting cooperatively, one bird will pursue prey on foot while another that is perched nearby will swoop in when the prey breaks cover. Small and medium-size mammals are their main prey, especially ground squirrels and rabbits. They become quite tame in captivity and this trait along with their fierce hunting behavior has made them a favorite with falconers.

Natural History: The Red-shouldered Hawk is the daytime counterpart of the Barred Owl, and the two species often occur in the same territory. They are vocal birds. Their call, described as "kee-ah, kee-ah, kee-ah" is rapidly repeated about a dozen times. They can be fairly tame if unmolested and their raucous calling will not go unnoticed when the nest is nearby. They feed on a wide variety of small vertebrates but mostly eat reptiles, amphibians, and rodents. The range of the Red-shouldered Hawk coincides closely with the level 1 ecoregion known as the Eastern Temperate Forest. However, a disjunct population (subspecies *elegans*) is found on the west coast of North America in the Mediterranean California Ecoregion. In Texas this hawk is most common in portions of the state that are heavily forested, i.e. South Central Plains and East Central Texas Plains Level III Ecoregions.

Natural History: A decidedly woodland raptor whose breeding range in North America closely mirrors the Eastern Temperate Forests Level I Ecoregion. In Texas they are seen as migrants throughout the eastern one-third of the state and as a summer resident and nesting bird in the South Central Plains Level III Ecoregion. They are less conspicuous than most hawks except during the migration when they band together in large flocks known as "kettles." Extremely large flocks that may contain 1000 birds are seen during fall migrations. The Western Gulf Coastal Plain of Texas is one of the best places to witness these huge migratory flocks. Southward moving flocks coalesce as they follow the coast along the Gulf of Mexico. Food includes insects, but consists mostly of small vertebrates like rodents as well as a large amount of reptile and amphibian prey.

Class—**Aves** (birds)

Order—**Accipitriformes** (hawks, kites, osprey & eagles)

Family—**Accipitridae** (hawks, kites, eagles)

Swainson's Hawk *Buteo swainsoni*	**Zone-tailed Hawk** *Buteo albonotatus*	**Rough-legged Hawk** *Buteo lagopus*

Dark juvenile · Typical adult

 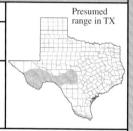

Size: 19 inches.	**Size:** 20 inches.	**Size:** 21 inches.
Abundance: Fairly common.	**Abundance:** Rare in Texas.	**Abundance:** Uncommon.
Variation: Light and dark morphs. See Natural History below.	**Variation:** Juvenile is chocolate brown with streaked breast.	**Variation:** Light and dark morphs. Sexes alike.

Presumed range in TX (×3)

Habitat: An open country species. Characteristic of the Great Plains and deserts of the western US. Mainly a prairie species but summers as far north as Alaska. Winters in the grasslands of the Pampas region of Argentina.

Migratory Status: Summer resident.

Breeding: Nest is built in a tree with the male doing most of the work. Often chooses a solitary tree in an otherwise treeless grassland. As many as five eggs are laid, with three being an average.

Natural History: About ninety percent of the Swainson's Hawks seen in Texas will resemble the photo above. Dark morph birds are rather rare. These hawks form large "kettles" in fall migration that can number in the thousands. Insects, especially grasshoppers, are an important food item for these grassland hawks. They will sometimes land and walk around on the ground catching grasshoppers. Small to medium-size mammals like rodents and rabbits are also important, especially when raising their young. Snakes are also a food item. On its wintering grounds in Argentina it apparently feeds heavily on dragonflies. Most spring migrants arrive in April and May. Weeks long fall migration begins in August.

Habitat: Mainly a Latin American species found throughout most of Mexico and Central America all the way to South America. Birds that summer in the US use riparian woodlands in deserts and foothill canyons in mountains.

Migratory Status: Summer resident.

Breeding: Nest may be high in a large tree or on a cliff face. Most nesting in Texas appears to be in the Davis and Chisos Mountains in the Big Bend region.

Natural History: The Zone-tailed Hawk is a threatened species in Texas. It is a rare breeder in the arid western part of the state and a very rare winter resident in the lower Rio Grande river valley. They arrive in Texas in early spring and leave the state by early October. Birds that summer in Texas are short-distance migrants that winter in southern Mexico. The food of the Zone-tailed Hawk is almost any type of small vertebrate animal. In flight they resemble the Turkey Vulture. A closer look, however, will reveal the broad white band in the tail of the adult birds and a series of narrow white bands in the tail of the juvenile. They are sometimes seen soaring in the company of vultures which may help fool prey animals.

Habitat: Summer habitat is Arctic Tundra. In winter they move southward into the northern half of the US. A few will winter in the Panhandle region. In harsh winters they may move farther south, some as far as northern Mexico.

Migratory Status: Winter migrant.

Breeding: Nests well to north in Arctic or subarctic regions of tundra and taiga. Clutch size (3 to 7) is prey dependent. In years of abundant lemming populations they will raise more young.

Natural History: The Rough-legged Hawk is an arctic species that moves south in winter. Their migrations are sporadic depending upon weather, snow cover, and prey availability, but they can be in winter in the Panhandle. They prey primarily on small mammals and lemmings are an important food on the breeding grounds. In winter they take mice, voles, and shrews mostly. Hunts by soaring and hovering over open country. They can face into the wind and remain in a stationary hover for over a minute. While these are fairly large hawks, they have small feet and small beaks, and are thus unable to take the larger prey taken by hawks like the Red-tailed Hawk. Their name comes from the presence of feathers on the leg.

Class—**Aves** (birds)
Order—**Accipitriformes** (hawks, kites, osprey & eagles)
Family—**Accipitridae** (hawks, eagles, kites)
Red-tailed Hawk– *Buteo jamaicensis*

Typical adult showing red tail

Light morph

Dark morph

Juvenile eating Gray Squirrel

Typical adult

Presumed range in TX

Size: 19 to 22 inches.

Abundance: Common throughout the state. Perhaps slightly more common in the eastern and central parts of the state.

Migratory Status: Year-round resident. Numbers are supplemented in winter with migrants from farther north.

Variation: Highly variable. Can vary from nearly solid dark brown to very pale (almost white). Most adult birds are like the typical adult specimens pictured above. Light and dark morphs are mostly western birds and winter migrants. Females are about 20 percent larger than males. Juveniles have brownish tails with dark crossbars. Some experts recognize as many as 16 subspecies throughout North America.

Habitat: Found in virtually all habitats within the state. Likes open and semi-open areas and is least common in continuous forest, although they do occur there. Favors a mosaic of woodlands, farmland, fencerows, overgrown fields, etc.

Breeding: In the eastern US the large stick nest is built high in trees. In mountainous areas may build on cliff faces. Nest is usually situated in place that is remote from human activities. Lays 2 to 4 eggs. Young fledge at six weeks.

Natural History: This is the most common and widespread large *Buteo* hawk in America. Their range includes all of North America south of the Arctic and much of the Caribbean and Central America. The Red-tailed Hawk is generally regarded as the daytime counterpart of the Great Horned Owl, hunting by day many of the same species in the same habitats utilized by the owl at night. "Red-tails" prey mostly on rodents (mice, voles, and ground squirrels). But much larger prey like rabbits may also be taken on occasion. In some areas, ground dwelling birds like pheasants and quail are taken, and they have been known to attack large flocks of blackbirds. In summer they also take large snakes such as the Woodland Rat Snake (*Pantherophis*). Large examples of these snakes (which are strong constrictors) have been known to turn the tables and end up killing a hungry hawk. During winter these large hawks sometimes resort to eating carrion and can regularly be seen feeding on road kills. In much of the eastern US the Red-tailed Hawk is often known by the nickname "Chicken Hawk," a name given in the mistaken belief that they prey on chickens. Although they may certainly catch a few chickens occasionally, their main food is rats, mice, and other rodents, making them an overall useful species to man. Their habit of perching conspicuously in dead trees, snags, and power poles along highways makes them one of the more easily observed of America's hawk species. Historically, the Red-tailed Hawk and other raptors were regarded as varmints, and for many decades they were shot on sight by uninformed individuals. By the 1950s many birds of prey were becoming scarce in America. Since the amendment of the migratory bird treaty act in the early 1970s providing federal protection to all of America's raptor species, Red-tailed Hawks have become common once again.

Class—**Aves** (birds)

Order—**Accipitriformes** (hawks, kites, osprey & eagles)

Family—**Accipitridae** (hawks, eagles, kites)

Order—**Falconiformes** (falcons)

Family—**Falconidae**

Ferruginous Hawk *Buteo regalis*	**White-tailed Hawk** *Geranoaetus albicaudatus*	**Crested Caracara** *Caracara plancus*

Size: 23 inches.

Abundance: Uncommon.

Variation: A rare morph is a dark reddish brown.

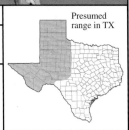
Presumed range in TX

Habitat: This is a western species that ranges throughout the Rocky Mountain states and the western Great Plains. It favors open country. Mountain plateaus, prairies, and deserts.

Migratory Status: Winter resident.

Breeding: Nest may be built in a tree or on a cliff face. They sometimes nest on the ground atop a steep hill or rock outcrop in open country. Two to four eggs is average but can be up to eight.

Natural History: The Ferruginous Hawk has the distinction of being the largest *Buteo* hawk in America. They are powerful hunters capable of taking prey the size of a jackrabbit. They are mainly ground squirrel specialists and they haunt Prairie Dog towns and ground squirrel colonies throughout the west. On occasion they will hunt from the ground, stalking and chasing prairie dogs on foot. Bird watchers eager to see this hawk know that Prairie Dog towns are one of the best places to look for this species. Like other birds of prey, they will feed on road kill carcasses of both small animals like jackrabbits and larger animals like deer or Pronghorn. These may be important food sources in the northern portions of their range winter.

Size: 20 inches.

Abundance: Uncommon.

Variation: Light and dark morphs. Juveniles are dark.

Presumed range in TX

Habitat: This is a tropical species whose range extends north into the Western Gulf Coastal Plain of Texas where it favors coastal prairies and natural grasslands.

Migratory Status: Year-round resident.

Breeding: Nest is usually in a bush or low tree only a few feet above the ground. Shows a preference for nesting near water. Two or three eggs are laid and there is only one brood per year.

Natural History: Many raptor species will hunt the leading edge of wildfires to pick off fleeing animals. The White-tailed Hawk is known for this behavior. Although this is a common and widespread raptor in Latin America they occupy only a small area in the US in the Western Gulf Coastal Plain of Texas. Small mammals such as rodents are the main prey, but they also take the young of larger species like jackrabbits. Reptiles, amphibians, birds, crabs, crayfish, and insects are also in their diet. They are monogamous birds that show fidelity to both their mate and their nest site, which may be used for many years. In choosing their nest site in brushy, semi-open habitat, they may avoid competition with Caracaras and Red-tailed Hawks, both common in their range.

Size: 23 inches.

Abundance: Fairly common.

Variation: Juveniles have buff-colored throat.

Presumed range in TX

Habitat: Texas habitat is in the open and semi-open brushlands, savannas, and prairies of south Texas. Elsewhere in their range throughout Latin America they inhabit a wide variety of habitats.

Migratory Status: Year-round resident.

Breeding: Nest is made of sticks, grasses, forbs, etc. and placed in the top of a tree. Most nests are relatively low (less than 15 feet). Nests may be re-used and be quite bulky. 2 to 4 eggs.

Natural History: In appearance, the Caracara looks like a hybrid between a vulture and an eagle. In habits they are also bimodal, feeding both on carrion and hunting down small animals ranging from insects to small mammals and snakes. Extreme opportunists, they will eat virtually any type of small animal they can catch and kill. They will also raid the nest of other birds and steal the eggs (or the fledglings) and they have even been known to scratch open turtle nests for eggs. This is strictly a warm climate species. They range from south Texas through Mexico and Central America as well as much of South America. In North America they are restricted to semi-tropical environments. In Texas they often go by the name "Mexican Buzzard."

Class—**Aves** (birds)

Order—**Falconiformes** (falcons)

Family—**Falconidae**

American Kestrel *Falco sparverius*	Merlin *Falco columbarius*	Aplomado Falcon *Falco femoralis*
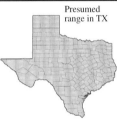	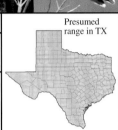	

American Kestrel
Falco sparverius

Size: 9 inches.

Abundance: Common.

Variation: Sexual dimorphism. See photos.

Habitat: Throughout its range, the Kestrel is seen in open country. Least common in forested regions but may occur there in open areas.

Migratory Status: Year-round resident.

Breeding: Usually nests in tree cavities or old woodpecker holes within trees situated in open fields. May also nest in man-made structures. 4 to 5 eggs.

Natural History: While the Kestrel is a fairly common bird in open regions throughout America, there has been some decline in populations in the eastern United States in recent years. But they remain America's most common falcon species. Though they are sometimes called "Sparrow Hawk," these are true falcons. The Kestrel is widespread throughout North and Central America and as many as seventeen subspecies are recognized. They are often seen perched on power lines and poles along roadways in rural farmlands throughout the country, but they are uncommon in the heavily forested regions. Insects are the major food in summer (especially grasshoppers). In winter they eat small mammals and rarely, small birds. Hunts both from a perch and by hovering over open fields. Availability of suitable nest cavities may limit distribution in places.

Merlin
Falco columbarius

Size: 11 inches.

Abundance: Uncommon.

Variation: Male has blue-gray back; female, immatures brown.

Habitat: Habitat is open regions. In Texas it is most common in coastal marshes and dunes in winter. Also seen in grassland and desert.

Migratory Status: Winter resident.

Breeding: Breeds far to the north in Canada, Alaska, and parts of the north-central Rockies and plains. Uses old crow or hawk nests as well as cliffs.

Natural History: The Merlin is seen in Texas mainly in winter (or as an occasional wandering bird). These small falcons are only slightly larger than the Kestrel and they are easily confused with that species. The facial markings of the Merlin are less distinct than the Kestrels, and they appear somewhat stockier in build. Summering mostly far to the north and wintering along coastlines, their migration routes are mostly in the western United States or along the Atlantic coast. Like most falcons however, these birds are prone to wander widely. Although they may occur almost anywhere in the state they are most common in coastal regions and in expansive marsh, prairies, or pastures. Food is mostly small birds, especially shorebirds. In urban areas they may focus on common species like house sparrows. Insects are also food items.

Aplomado Falcon
Falco femoralis

Size: 16 inches.

Abundance: Very rare in TX.

Variation: Adult has solid white throat, striped on juvenile.

Habitat: Like most falcons, Aplomado Falcons favor open areas or savanna habitats where their speed in flight can be most effectively used to catch prey.

Migratory Status: Year-round resident.

Breeding: Uses nests built by other large birds like crows, ravens, or hawks. Two to four eggs per clutch and only one clutch per year.

Natural History: Now an Endangered Species in Texas, Aplomado Falcons were once fairly common along the Rio Grande River and in the Big Bend region of the state. Experts still debate the reasons for their demise, but human-induced changes to the land were undoubtedly a factor. Several decades, worth of efforts to re-introduce these handsome falcons to their historic range in the state have enjoyed some success. While this is a rare bird in the US, they are much more common south of the Rio Grande and can be seen throughout Latin America all the way down to the southern tip of South America. These fast-flying falcons take birds from the air and lizards and small mammals on the ground. Large insects are also a part of the their diet. They usually occur in pairs with the two birds sometimes hunting cooperatively.

Presumed range in TX

Class—**Aves** (birds)

Order—**Falconiformes** (falcons)
Family—**Falconidae**

Order—**Ciconiiformes** (storks)
Family—**Ciconiidac**

Peregrine Falcon *Falco peregrinus*	Prairie Falcon *Falco mexicanus*	Wood Stork *Mycteria americana*

Peregrine Falcon
Falco peregrinus

Size: 16 inches.

Abundance: Rare.

Variation: Adult has white breast. Juvenile's is mottled.

Presumed range in TX

Habitat: Prefers cliffs in remote wilderness areas but has adapted to living among skyscrapers in many cities.

Migratory Status: Rare summer resident in west Texas mountains, winter resident along the coast and migrant elsewhere in state.

Breeding: Nests on ledges of cliff faces and on man-made structures like skyscrapers and bridges. Four eggs is typical, sometimes up to six.

Natural History: Falcons are fast flying birds and the Peregrine is among the fastest. Hunts pigeons, waterfowl, grouse, etc. Hunting technique usually involves soaring high above and diving in on birds in flight, or diving towards resting birds and panicking them into flight. Once airborne, no other bird can match the Peregrine's speed. Diving Peregrines may reach speeds approaching 200 mph, making them perhaps the fastest animal on earth. In eastern US this species has been re-introduced after being extirpated as a breeding bird many decades ago. The name "peregrine" means "wanderer," and these birds may be seen almost anywhere in the state, albeit quite rarely. Historically, this falcon went by the name "Duck Hawk." An appropriate name since waterfowl are among its favorite prey.

Prairie Falcon
Falco mexicanus

Size: 16 inches.

Abundance: Uncommon.

Variation: Juveniles have heavy streaking on the breast.

Presumed range in TX

Habitat: Prairies, deserts, inter-mountain plateaus with sagebrush steppe, alpine regions and tundra.

Migratory Status: A few live year-round in the Trans-Pecos region of western Texas. Most are winter residents and wandering migrants.

Breeding: Nests in crevices and rock platforms on sheer cliff faces. On rare occasions may use an abandoned hawk nest. About four or five eggs, rarely six.

Natural History: In Texas the Prairie Falcon is a rare resident of the western prairies and deserts where there are steep escarpments or cliffs and canyons. They wander well to the east and may rarely be seen in central regions of the state. They hunt both from a high perch atop a rock promontory or by soaring. They will also fly close to the ground at high speed and suddenly appear in close proximity to surprised prey. When prey is spotted from soaring altitude they dive at high speed and they can out-fly most any avian prey. In addition to birds they will eat small mammals like ground squirrels. In winter when ground squirrels are scarce, they switch to eating mostly birds. Their biggest enemy may be the Great Horned Owl, against which the diurnal falcons have no defense in the dark of night.

Wood Stork
Mycteria americana

Size: 40 inches.

Abundance: Rare in Texas.

Variation: Juveniles have downy feathers on head and neck.

Presumed range in TX

Habitat: Mostly freshwater swamps but also in marine estuaries. May be seen in any aquatic habitat.

Migratory Status: A seasonal migrant that is seen in Texas mostly in late summer or fall. Birds that come to Texas are engaged in post-breeding dispersal.

Breeding: Bulky stick nest is built in trees such as cypress or oaks, usually over water or on islands. Clutch size can be as many as 5 eggs.

Natural History: This is North America's only stork species. In addition to Texas and much of the southeast, they can also be found on both coasts of Mexico, throughout the Yucatan Peninsula, and across the Caribbean. They also occur in South America. Migrants occur rarely along the coast of Texas. These huge wading birds feed on all types of aquatic vertebrates which they usually capture by feel. Feeding storks swish their thick bills back and forth in the shallow waters of drying pools and snap the beak shut on anything touched. Fish are the main prey but all types of vertebrates have been recorded in the diet, as well as invertebrates such as crustaceans and insects. Adults have an all black head and black bill with wrinkled skin on the head and neck. They resemble large, long beaked vultures.

Class—**Aves** (birds)

Order— **Cathartiformes** (vultures)	Order—**Gruiformes** (cranes)
Family—**Cathartidae**	Family—**Gruidae**

Turkey Vulture *Cathartes aura*	Black Vulture *Coragyps atratus*	Whooping Crane *Grus americana*

Size: 26 inches.	Presumed range in TX	**Size:** 25 inches.	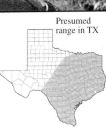Presumed range in TX	**Size:** 59 inches.	Presumed range in TX
Abundance: Common.		**Abundance:** Common.		**Abundance:** Very rare.	
Variation: Skin on face is pinkish gray on immature birds.		**Variation:** Old birds have lighter gray heads with more wrinkles.		**Variation:** Juveniles have rusty blotches, rusty heads.	

Habitat: Seen in all habitats throughout the state. Less common in urban areas and expansive swamps.

Habitat: Found in a wide variety of habitats throughout the state. Can be very common around cattle ranches.

Habitat: In migration, uses marshes or harvested agricultural fields. Winters on the marshes of the gulf coast of Texas.

Migratory Status: Year-round with some short distance migration in winter.

Migratory Status: Year-round resident and winter migrant/ winter resident.

Migratory Status: Winter resident at Aransas National Wildlife Refuge.

Breeding: Nests in large tree hollows or on the ground in hollow logs. May nest on cliff ledges. Lays two eggs.

Breeding: No nest is built and the two eggs are laid on a bare surface. The nest site is often in a derelict building.

Breeding: Breeds in shallow marshes. Texas population breeds in Woods Buffalo National Park in Canada.

Natural History: The absence of feathers on the head and neck of vultures is an adaptation for feeding on carrion. Vultures may stick the head deep inside a rotting carcass and feathers would become matted with filth. The bare skin on the neck and face, on the other hand, is constantly exposed to the sterilizing effects of sunlight. Turkey Vultures are one of the few birds with a well developed sense of smell, and food is often located by detecting the odor of rotting flesh. Sight is also important and they become quite familiar with the landscape of their territory. They are quick to notice a fresh carcass on a roadway within their territory and they have benefited from a near constant supply of road-killed animals. Newly mowed fields and other disturbed areas within their range are closely scanned for small animal victims. Highly social, they roost communally, sometimes with Black Vultures.

Natural History: America's vultures are named for the color of the skin on the face. Turkey Vultures have reddish skin (like a turkey); Black Vultures have dark gray or black facial skin. Black Vultures also have shorter tails and lesser wing span, giving them a much "stubbier" look than the Turkey Vulture. Vultures were once regarded as a threat to livestock by spreading disease. In fact, the powerful digestive juices of the gut of vultures destroys bacteria. They may actually help control diseases. Both the Turkey Vulture and the Black Vulture have the unappealing habit of defecating on the legs and feet as a way of disinfecting the feet (which can become quite nasty when the birds feed on rotted carcasses). Black Vultures lack the well developed sense of smell of Turkey Vultures, but they do have keen eyesight. Although smaller than the Turkey Vulture, they are more aggressive and often out compete their larger cousin.

Natural History: Standing five feet tall, with a wingspan of seven feet and a weight of fifteen pounds, the Whooping Crane is one of the largest bird species in America. In 1941 the population of Whooping Cranes migrating to the Texas gulf coast was down to only 15 birds. The population that migrates to the gulf coast of Texas today consists of about 500 birds. An addition 100 or so migrate through the eastern US and winter in the southeastern Gulf Coastal Plain or Florida. While still highly endangered the Whooping Crane is slowly recovering. Few species have enjoyed a more robust effort by humans to salvage them from extinction. Captive breeding programs and re-introductions have included such intensive efforts as the use of ultralight aircraft to lead young birds on their first migratory flights. Aransas National Wildlife Refuge and the marshes, estuaries, and tidal flats nearby are the winter sanctuary for this species.

Class—**Aves** (birds)

Order—**Gruiformes** (cranes)
Family—**Gruidae**

Sandhill Crane
Antigone canadensis

Size: 42 inches.

Abundance: Fairly common.

Variation: Juveniles lack the red crown and white cheek.

Presumed range in TX

Habitat: Open lands, farm fields, mudflats, marshes, and shallow water areas. In migration uses harvested crop fields. Summer habitat in the far north includes wetlands throughout most of Canada as well as into the tundra regions of Canada and Alaska.

Migratory Status: Winter resident.

Breeding: Typically lays 2 eggs on a platform nest built of vegetation. There are non-migratory breeding populations in parts of the southern United States, but it does not breed in Texas.

Natural History: Populations were seriously depleted by the beginning of the twentieth century, but the species has recovered dramatically in the last few decades. The largest populations are seen west of the Mississippi River and number tens of thousands. Eastern populations have been slower to recover but are now reasonably healthy. Several states including Texas now treat them as a game species and have regulated hunting seasons. As much as 70 percent of the world population gathers along a fifty-mile stretch Platte River Valley in Nebraska in mid-March during migration. If a tornado followed the Platte River for a few miles at that time of year, it could devastate the population.

Order—**Pelicaniformes** (waders & pelicans)
Family—**Pelacanidae** (pelicans)

Brown Pelican
Pelacanus occidentalis

Size: 51 inches.

Abundance: Fairly common.

Variation: No significant variation among adults.

Presumed range in TX

Habitat: Coastlines. Beaches, estuaries, islands, marshes, mangroves, and all other shallow marine habitats. Rarely strays too far from the coast either inland or out to sea. Range in Texas is restricted to the Western Gulf Coastal Plain Level III Ecoregion.

Migratory Status: Year-round resident.

Breeding: Nest is a stick platform placed in the top of a small tree or bush. Mangroves are a favorite nest site. Sometimes nest on the ground. Usually lays 3 eggs.

Natural History: The Brown Pelican is a marine species that is closely tied to coastal regions and rarely seen more than a few miles inland. Groups of Brown Pelicans flying in formation is a common sight along America's coastlines. They make spectacular head-first plunges into the sea to capture fish near the surface. As with the other pelican species, they have an expandable pouch on the lower bill that is capable of "vacuuming" large quantities of water into the mouth, pulling in with it nearby fishes. Pelicans are awkward and ungainly on land but in flight they are quite graceful. Brown Pelicans are renowned for their ability to skim the surface just inches above the water, sometimes disappearing in troughs between the waves.

White Pelican
Pelacanus erythrorhynchos

Size: 62 inches.

Abundance: Uncommon.

Variation: No significant variation among adults.

Presumed range in TX

Habitat: Mostly freshwater swamps but also in marine estuaries. In Texas they may be seen in any aquatic habitat that affords expansive open water. Rivers and large lakes are the primary winter habitat, but they can also be common in coastal marshes.

Migratory Status: Winter resident.

Breeding: Nests in colonies in protected areas such as islands on large lakes. Most nesting occurs on large lakes and marshes in the northern plains. A few breed along the gulf coast. Lays 2 eggs.

Natural History: Most commonly seen in Texas along coastlines and in estuaries, salt marshes, and inland lakes. They are mostly winter residents in Texas but a few birds may linger throughout the summer. Unlike their cousin the Brown Pelican, which feeds by plunging into the water, White Pelicans feed in a more placid manner. Flocks of feeding White Pelicans corral fish by swimming in a coordinated group and dipping the head beneath the surface in perfect unison. The appearance of a feeding flock is that of a perfectly choreographed ballet. Competition between baby White Pelicans in the nest is fierce, and the strongest nestling often kills its sibling. May be seen statewide in suitable habitats during migration.

Class—**Aves** (birds)

Order—**Pelicaniformes** (waders & pelicans)

Family-**Threskiornithidae**—(spoonbill, ibis)

White Ibis *Eudocimus albus*	White-faced Ibis *Plegadis chihi*	Roseate Spoonbill *Platalea ajaja*

Size: 25 inches.		**Size:** 25 inches.		**Size:** 25 inches.	
Abundance: Fairly common.	Presumed range in TX	**Abundance:** Uncommon.	Presumed range in TX	**Abundance:** Uncommon.	Presumed range in TX
Variation: Adults are alike. Ontogenetic variation.		**Variation:** Juvenile lacks white lines on face.		**Variation:** Juvenile birds are much paler. Adults alike.	

White Ibis	White-faced Ibis	Roseate Spoonbill
Habitat: Fresh and saltwater marshes, estuaries, swamps, flooded fields, pastures, and rice fields. Almost any shallow water habitat may be used.	**Habitat:** Shallow water wetlands are where this species is most common. They will use flooded agricultural fields, roadside ditches, marshes and swamps.	**Habitat:** Found in all types of shallow aquatic habitats in the state. Swamps, marshes (fresh and salt), shallow lakes, mangroves, canals, etc.
Migratory Status: Year-round resident on the coast. Migrant inland.	**Migratory Status:** Year-round resident on the coast. Migrant throughout Texas.	**Migratory Status:** Year-round resident along the gulf coast of Texas.
Breeding: Nest is in a low tree or bush. Often nests in colonies, including rookeries with herons or egrets. 2 to 5 eggs.	**Breeding:** Nest is placed in low trees or bushes or sometimes in reeds or sedges above water. Three to five eggs.	**Breeding:** Breeds colonially. Nest is built in trees or shrubs over water or on an island. 3 to 4 eggs is average.
Natural History: Feeds by tactile sense with the decurved bill but also hunts by sight. Crustaceans are the main prey, especially fiddler crabs, but many types of aquatic organisms are eaten. These birds can be seen both in wilderness and in the midst of urban sprawl. They are usually associated with water (marshes, swamps, canals, estuaries, etc.) but they are also commonly seen in suburban lawns and around retention ponds within shopping malls or apartment complexes. Like many other wading birds, White Ibis are colony birds that roost and nest in large groups. While this species has adapted admirably to mankind's changes to ecosystems, it is much less numerous than it once was, and loss of freshwater wetland habitats throughout its range poses a real threat to its ability to maintain a healthy population. Prolonged droughts can negatively impact this species.	**Natural History:** Food items are mainly invertebrates, especially worms, crustaceans, and aquatic insects. Much food is caught by probing in the mud. Some small vertebrates are eaten as well, including fish and frogs. Migrants in arid or semi-arid regions will be attracted to any body of water. Many birds that summer in the western US will winter in Mexico. But along the gulf coast of Texas they are year-round residents. In fact, Texas boasts a greater abundance of these birds than most other states. Although these birds have actually expanded their range in the US in the last few decades, their overall population is in decline. Draining of wetlands for agriculture and widespread use of pesticides are often cited as possible reasons for the decline. They are also negatively impacted by drought and climate change may pose a threat. Regarded as a Threatened Species in Texas.	**Natural History:** Feeds by feel. The unique "spoon" shaped bill is swept back and forth through the water in a semi-open position and snaps shut when aquatic organisms are touched. Small fish, crayfish, crabs, and insects are known food items. Spoonbill populations are today recovering from a very low ebb at the beginning of the twentieth century. They are still not as numerous as they were historically, and given the pressures being exerted on natural environments by a large and still growing human population, this species will likely never again be as common as it was prior to the European invasion of America. These beautiful birds can be viewed up close on their breeding rookery at the Houston Audubon Society's bird sanctuary at High Island, Texas. This wonderful sanctuary hosts scores of species and is known worldwide for its birdwatching opportunities.

Class—**Aves** (birds)

Order—**Pelicaniformes** (waders & pelicans)

Family-**Ardeidae**—(herons, egrets)

American Bittern *Botaurus lentiginosus*	Least Bittern *Ixobrychus exilis*	Great Blue Heron *Ardea herodias*

Female

Male

Size: 26 inches.

Abundance: Uncommon.

Variation: No significant variation and sexes are alike.

Presumed range in TX

Habitat: Large freshwater marshes are used in summer, coastal marshlands in winter.

Migratory Status: Winter resident. Migrant only in the panhandle.

Breeding: Nest is in dense emergent vegetation of the marsh and is well hidden. 3 to 5 eggs is typical. Does not breed in Texas.

Natural History: The biology of this species is not well known. Presumably, they may be seen anywhere in suitable habitats in the state in migration, and they will winter along the Texas coast. But few visitors will ever see one, as they are usually quite secretive and remain hidden among thick stands of cattails or sedges. Hunts by stealth and may remain motionless for long periods of time. The eyes of this heron are situated with a downward slant, better facilitating the bird's ability to see into the water. When startled they will throw the head back and point the beak straight up. The streaked brown pattern of the neck and breast is remarkably cryptic amid vertical stalks of marsh grasses and sedges, and an individual in "frozen" posture becomes almost invisible. Like most herons, an opportunistic feeder. Eats fish, amphibians, crayfish, small mammals, and some insects.

Size: 13 inches.

Abundance: Uncommon.

Variation: Sexually dimorphic. See photos above.

Presumed range in TX

Habitat: Favors marshes with dense growths of tall grasses and sedges. Uses both fresh and brackish marshes.

Migratory Status: Summer resident in east Texas and year-round on the coast.

Breeding: Nest is a well concealed platform built amid dense growth of cattails or other sedges/grasses. Up to six eggs are laid.

Natural History: This smallest of American herons is also a secretive bird that often stays hidden in dense marsh grasses and sedges. When alarmed they point their bill skyward and freeze, mimicking the vertical vegetation of their habitat. These small herons move with ease through thick stands of marsh vegetation. When flushed they fly only a short distance just above the vegetation before dropping back down. Despite their seemingly weak flying abilities, some will migrate great distances from wintering areas in Mexico and the Caribbean to summer breeding grounds that may be as far north as northern Minnesota. They have very long toes for grasping stems of grass and sedge. Feeds on small fish, insects, crayfish, and amphibians. This species has declined significantly over the last century. In some areas of its summer range it is now threatened.

Size: 47 inches.

Abundance: Common.

Variation: No significant variation among adults in Texas.

Presumed range in TX

Habitat: Along rivers and streams, swamps, marshes, ponds, and wet meadows and floodplains.

Migratory Status: Year-round resident and seasonal migrant.

Breeding: Nests in colonies. Nest is a platform of sticks in tree or bush above water. Nest is a bulky platform of sticks. 3 to 4 eggs is typical.

Natural History: The largest heron in North America, the Great Blue Heron will eat almost anything it can swallow. Fish and frogs are major foods, but it also eats snakes (including the young of the venomous Cottonmouth), salamanders, small mammals, and even small turtles. Birds are sometimes eaten, including other, smaller heron species. All food items are swallowed whole. Large prey is killed by stabbing repeatedly with the beak or by bashing against a hard object. Smaller prey is often swallowed alive. Hunts both day and night and reportedly has good night vision. Great Blue Herons are found throughout most of the United States and much of Canada, including in riparian habitats in desert regions. Sexes are alike but juveniles will have streaked breast and neck and are duskier overall than adults. Populations in Texas increased in winter by northern migrants.

Class—**Aves** (birds)

Order—**Pelicaniformes** (waders & pelicans)

Family-**Ardeidae**—(herons, egrets)

Great Egret *Ardea alba*	**Snowy Egret** *Egretta thula*	**Little Blue Heron** *Egretta caerulea*

Great Egret
Ardea alba

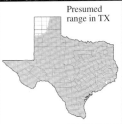

Size: 39 inches.

Abundance: Common.

Variation: Breeding adults acquire large feather plumes.

Presumed range in TX

Habitat: Along major streams, lakes, swamps, and marshes. Also wet meadows, low lying areas, and open fields.

Migratory Status: Year-round resident (gulf coast), summer resident (east Texas), winter resident (Rio Grande valley).

Breeding: Nests in colonies, often with other wading bird species. Nest is a platform of sticks in tree or bush above water. Lays 3 or 4 eggs.

Natural History: This heron species (along with the Snowy Egret and several other herons) was nearly hunted to extinction during the last half of the nineteenth century. The long, wispy feathers of breeding birds (known as "plumes") were once used to adorn the hats of fashionable ladies. The plumes are most pronounced during the breeding season. Thus the catastrophic impact of the plume hunters was magnified as hunters killed birds at their nesting colonies. Killing of parent birds doomed nestlings as well. Efforts to save this and other plume bird species led to some of America's earliest laws to protect wildlife. Today this species is still a symbol of conservation efforts and is the logo of the National Audubon Society. It is also known by the names Common Egret or Great White Egret. Individuals wander far to the north in late summer.

Snowy Egret
Egretta thula

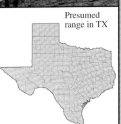

Size: 24 inches.

Abundance: Common.

Variation: Breeding adults acquire large feather plumes.

Presumed range in TX

Habitat: In the vicinity of streams, lakes, swamps, and marshes. Also low lying area, roadside ditches, etc.

Migratory Status: Year-round resident (gulf coast), summer resident (east Texas), wandering migrant elsewhere.

Breeding: Like other herons they will nest in colonies with different heron species. Nest is made of sticks and twigs. 3 to 5 eggs is average.

Natural History: As with several other heron species, the Snowy Egret during breeding season sports long "plume" feathers on the back. The plumes of the Snowy Egret were once highly valued and their value exceeded that of gold on an ounce for ounce basis. As with other plume bird species, the Snowy Egret was nearly wiped out by the feather trade of the late 1800s. Today the species has recovered to healthy numbers but remains under threat due to its dependence upon coastal wetlands. This species feeds on smaller prey such as worms, insects, crustaceans, amphibians, and small fish. It is an active feeder that often chases prey through the shallows rather than using the stealth method employed by its larger cousins. It also often feeds by swishing its feet in the mud to disturb benthic organisms. Similar to the Great Egret but smaller.

Little Blue Heron
Egretta caerulea

Size: 24 inches.

Abundance: Fairly common.

Variation: Significant ontogenetic plumage variation.

Presumed range in TX

Habitat: Wetlands. Inhabits swamps, marshes, lake shores, etc. May be seen in roadside ditches and small ponds.

Migratory Status: Year-round on the Texas gulf coast. Summer resident throughout most of eastern Texas.

Breeding: Builds a stick nest platform in bushes and low trees in wetlands. Lays 2 to 5 eggs. Breeding in Texas is in the eastern half of the state.

Natural History: Even within the heart of its range along the lower coastal plains of the southeastern US, the Little Blue Heron is generally less common than other heron species. In places, however, it can be common. The dark plumage of adults and its rather secretive nature make it one of the least observable of our herons. Like most herons, it is an opportunistic feeder that eats almost anything it can swallow. Food is mostly frogs, fish, crustaceans, and insects. It is a daytime hunter that hunts by stalking slowly through wetland habitats. First-year birds are solid white, transforming to blue at one year of age. The transitional plumage of the juvenile is unique, and produces for a brief time a white bird with blue splotches. Blue increases throughout the molt, ending in a solid blue adult. See photos above.

Class—**Aves** (birds)

Order—**Pelicaniformes** (waders & pelicans)

Family-**Ardeidae**—(herons, egrets)

Tricolored Heron *Egretta tricolor*	**Reddish Egret** *Egretta rufescens*	**Cattle Egret** *Bubulcus ibis*

White morph
Typical

Tricolored Heron	Reddish Egret	Cattle Egret
Size: 26 inches. 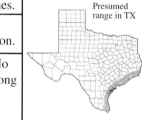 Presumed range in TX	**Size:** 30 inches.  Presumed range in TX	**Size:** 19 inches.  Presumed range in TX
Abundance: Fairly common.	**Abundance:** Uncommon.	**Abundance:** Common.
Variation: No variation among adults. Sexes alike.	**Variation:** Two distinct color morphs. See photos above.	**Variation:** Breeding male has orange highlights.

Habitat: Shows a distinct preference for estuaries and salt and brackish marshes in coastal regions, but it may use freshwater habitats as well.

Habitat: More tied to salt water than any other American heron. Mainly restricts itself to coastal lagoons, shallow bays, and salt marsh.

Habitat: Unlike other herons, these birds are less tied to aquatic situations and are usually seen in open pastures and fields in association with cattle.

Migratory Status: Year-round resident.

Migratory Status: Year-round resident.

Migratory Status: Year-round resident.

Breeding: Will nest in colonies with other heron species. Nest is a flimsy platform of sticks built above water. 3 to 4 eggs is usual. Maximum of 5 eggs.

Breeding: Nest is built of sticks and often placed in a fork of a mangrove over water. Three or four eggs is typical but could be as many as seven.

Breeding: Stick nest built in trees or bushes. Nests are usually over water. Nests in large colonies. 3 or 4 eggs is average.

Natural History: Although it is found throughout the Caribbean and in southern Mexico and Central America, the range of the Tricolored Heron in the US is restricted to the lower coastal plain from Texas to the Florida Peninsula. Its food consists mostly of small fishes. The Tricolored Heron is less likely to be seen in large flocks than many other herons, and they are usually seen singly or in pairs. At one time this was a very common bird along America's gulf coast. But there is some evidence that this species is now declining in its range in North America. No definitive explanation for the decline is known. Loss of habitat and contamination by chemicals in the food chain are possible explanations. Its status elsewhere in its range is not known. Its range in Texas is restricted to coastal regions. This species is also commonly called "Louisiana Heron."

Natural History: This is the least common heron species in America. In Texas it is regarded as a Threatened Species. The Reddish Egret is widespread along America's southern coastlines and can be found from Florida to southern California. But in the US it is nowhere a common species. This is strictly a coastal species and although some rare wanderers have been recorded well inland in the US, it is very rare to see this bird away from saltwater habitats. As with many other of its relatives, the Reddish Egret was hard hit by plume hunters in the late 1800s and the species was all but wiped out in many areas of its range. An all-white color morph (see inset photo above) is rather rare in the US, but occurs much more commonly in other regions such as in the Caribbean, Mexico, and Central America. Will flare its wings in an umbrella to shade the water when searching for fish.

Natural History: The Cattle Egret is one of our most interesting heron species. Originally native to Africa, Cattle Egrets began an inexplicable range expansion in the early 1800s. They first migrated across the Atlantic to South America and then appeared in North America around 1950. The species continues to expand its range and is today an uncommon summer migrant as far north as the Great Lakes. Their name is derived from their habit of associating with cattle herds in pastures. Before expanding their range out of Africa, they associated with herds of Cape Buffalo, Hippopotamus, and wild ungulates. They feed mostly on insects that are disturbed by the large grazers they follow through pastures and grasslands. Develops orange highlights on throat and crown during breeding (see photo above). Year-round on the coast and summer resident elsewhere in the state.

Class—**Aves** (birds)

Order—**Pelicaniformes** (waders & pelicans)

Family—**Ardeidae**—(herons, egrets)

Green Heron *Butorides virescens*	**Yellow-crowned Night Heron** *Nyctanassa violacea*	**Black-crowned Night Heron** *Nycticorax nycticorax*

Size: 19 inches.

Abundance: Common.

Variation: Juvenile birds are browner, have streaked throat.

Presumed range in TX

Habitat: Usually seen in the vicinity of water. Swamps, marshes, ditches, streams, lakes, and small ponds.

Migratory Status: Year-round on the coast. Summer in east Texas, winter in SW Texas, migrant in the Panhandle.

Breeding: Usually nests singly rather than in colonies. Nest is a stick platform in a tree fork. Lays 3 to 5 eggs.

Natural History: In many areas the Green Heron often goes by the name "Shy-poke." This is one of our most familiar herons and its range encompasses all of the eastern United States as well as the west coast. It also ranges southward throughout Central America. When flushed, it nearly always emits a loud "squawking" alarm call. Feeds mostly in shallow water and often feeds from a perch on a floating log or a limb just above the waters surface. Hunts by stealth and may remain frozen for long periods as it watches and waits for prey. Fish is the primary food item with small frogs probably being the next most common prey. Amazingly, this species has been reported to catch insects and worms to use as bait for luring in fish. While the Green Heron is one of our most common wading birds, it is dependent upon wetlands and loss of wetland habitats is a threat.

Size: 25 inches.

Abundance: Uncommon.

Variation: Juveniles are brown with white streaks.

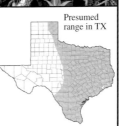
Presumed range in TX

Habitat: Swamps and marshes mostly, but may be seen in most aquatic habitats. Favors heavier cover than many herons.

Migratory Status: Summer resident. Most birds that spend the summer in Texas will winter on the Mexican coast.

Breeding: Flimsy stick nest is fairly high in tree, usually over water. Three to five eggs. Breeds throughout east Texas.

Natural History: These birds are often active at night, hence the name "night heron." Food is mostly crustaceans. Crabs are important foods in coastal regions, while crayfish are eaten in freshwater areas. A classical ambush predator, the Yellow-crowned Night Heron does most foraging from a stationery position, sitting like a statue and waiting for prey to wander into striking range. They will also stalk slowly and methodically with very slow, deliberate movements that are largely undetectable to prey. Diet may be supplemented with fish and invertebrates, but this heron is mainly a crustacean specialist. Has recovered nicely from low numbers decades ago and now seems to be expanding its range farther to the north. Today they range well into the Midwest in summer with a few isolated breeding colonies as far north as Minnesota and Pennsylvania.

Size: 25 inches.

Abundance: Uncommon.

Variation: Juveniles are heavily streaked brown and white.

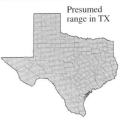
Presumed range in TX

Habitat: Utilizes all types of aquatic habitats in the state, with fresh and saltwater marshes being most widely used.

Migratory Status: Summer resident in most of state. Year-round in south Texas and on coast. Mainly winter in west Texas.

Breeding: Nests in large colonies that are often situated on an island. Three or four eggs per nest. Breeds in Texas.

Natural History: Although the Black-crowned Night Heron may be locally common near breeding colonies, it is not a commonly seen bird. Surprisingly, this is a widespread species that is found not only in much of the US, but in fact throughout most of the world. They can be found on every continent except Australia and Antarctica. As its name implies, this species is often active at night. The food is primarily fish. However, the list of known foods is quite long and includes insects, leeches, earthworms, crustaceans, gastropods, amphibians, snakes, small turtles, small mammals, and even birds! Prefers to feed in shallow water along the margins of weedy ponds, marshes, and swamps. This species has been widely studied as an apex predator that can accumulate toxins and it may be considered a barometer of environmental contamination.

Class—**Aves** (birds)

Order—**Suliformes** (cormorants, frigatebird & anhinga)

Family—**Phalacrocoracidae**—(cormorants)		Family-**Anhingidae**—(anhinga)

Double-crested Cormorant
Nannopterum auritum

Size: 33 inches.

Abundance: Common.

Variation: Young browner with whitish throat, breast.

Presumed range in TX

Habitat: Lakes, rivers, estuaries, marshes and swamplands. Uses both freshwater and saltwater habitats. Tends to favor saltwater habitats in winter, moving inland to freshwaters in summer.

Migratory Status: Winter resident.

Breeding: Large colonies nest on islands. Bulky nest of sticks. 2 to 4 eggs.

Natural History: Cormorants are rarely seen far from water. They are thoroughly aquatic birds that have webbed feet and frequently submerge and swim underwater in search of fish. Their exclusive diet of fish and their uncanny aquatic abilities have caused these birds to come into conflict with man. Occurring in large flocks, they will concentrate in areas where food is most readily available. Under natural conditions they catch a wide variety of fish species and thus do not impact significantly upon fisheries. However, around fish farms or hatcheries they can become quite a nuisance. Nearly wiped out by the pesticide DDT a half century ago, they have made an incredible comeback. In some regions they have come to be seen as an ecological problem by crowding out other colonial nesting bird species and impacting negatively on fish stocks. Winter resident in eastern two-thirds of Texas and migrant elsewhere.

Neotropic Cormorant
Nannopterum brasilianum

Size: 25 inches.

Abundance: Fairly common.

Variation: Juveniles are browner, lack white facial lines.

Presumed range in TX

Habitat: The habitat for this species in Texas is coastal marshes, estuaries, inter coastal waterways, bays, and to a lesser extent on inland lakes. They prefer sheltered inlets with shallow waters.

Migratory Status: Year-round resident.

Breeding: Nests in colonies, often with other wading birds. Up to six eggs.

Natural History: As implied by the name, this is mainly a neotropical species whose range extends northward into the coastal regions of Texas. This is actually one of the most wide ranging of the cormorants and can be found all the way to Tierra del Fuego on the southern tip of South America. Although the bulk of their range in Texas is along the coast, they have been documented well inland on lakes and reservoirs. The population of this species in Texas has fluctuated over the last century, but today they are apparently increasing their range. Most breeding in Texas occurs along the coast. Like all cormorants, the primary food is fish. Cormorants are excellent swimmers and are able to swim and catch fish underwater. Shrimp, frogs, and insects are also listed as food items. Feathers will become waterlogged after prolonged underwater swimming. Fishing forays are followed by drying feathers with outstretched wings.

Anhinga
Anhinga anhinga

Male

Female

Size: 35 inches.

Abundance: Uncommon.

Variation: Sexually dimorphic. See photos above.

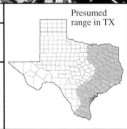

Presumed range in TX

Habitat: Totally aquatic and always seen near water except when in flight migration. Most types of freshwater habitats are used, with slow moving rivers being a favorite habitat.

Migratory Status: Summer resident.

Breeding: Stick nest is always built over water. Clutch size is 3 to 5 eggs.

Natural History: The local nickname "Snakebird" comes from the way this bird sometimes swims with the body beneath the water and just the head and long, snake-like neck sticking above the surface. They are also known by the nickname "Water Turkey," a reference to their vague resemblance to a turkey. The feathers of the Anhinga are not waterproof as is the case with some aquatic birds such as ducks. As a result, immediately after emerging from the water the water-logged feathers render them flightless. After emerging from a swim they can be seen perched in the sun with the wings spread, attempting to dry their feathers. Their swimming ability is remarkable and they are quite adept at catching fish while underwater. The long, stiletto-like bill, coupled with the long neck, which can be withdrawn and then plunged forward with blinding speed, creates a great "spear-fishing" technique for capturing fishes.

Class—**Aves** (birds)

Order—**Suliformes** (cormorants, frigatebirds & anhinga)

Family—**Frigatidae**—(frigatebird)	Family—**Sulidae**—(gannets & boobys)	

Magnificent Frigatebird
Fregata magnificens

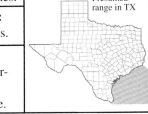

| | | ### Northern Gannet | | ### Masked Booby |

Northern Gannet
Morus bassanus

Masked Booby
Sula dactylatra

Size: 40 inches.

Abundance: Rare in Texas.

Variation: Sexual dimorphism. See photos above.

Presumed range in TX

Size: 37 inches.

Abundance: Rare in Texas.

Variation: Juveniles are gray-black with white spots.

Presumed range in TX

Size: 32 inches.

Abundance: Very rare in TX.

Variation: Juvenile has brown head and neck.

Presumed range in TX

Habitat: Mainly a tropical species that uses warm, shallow water habitats. Common near islands, mangroves, lagoons, etc. Also uses pelagic waters. Common along shorelines in the tropics.

Habitat: Closely tied to the sea, Northern Gannets ply the waters of the continental shelf. They come to land only to breed on cliffs or remote islands. Breeding occurs far to the north.

Habitat: Masked Boobys traverse the warm tropical seas of the world. They are fairly common throughout the Caribbean and on rare occasions wander up to the southern tip of Texas.

Migratory Status: Summer migrant.

Migratory Status: Winter migrant.

Migratory Status: Summer migrant.

Breeding: Breeds on mangrove islands. Nest is built on the leeward side of island. Lays a single egg.

Breeding: Breeding colonies are usually situated on a cliff. Lays a single egg. Does not breed in Texas.

Breeding: Nest is on the ground on bare islands. Sometimes uses man made structures. Only one or two eggs.

Natural History: This is a tropical bird that ranges northward along the southern US coastlines in summer. Although they may be seen anywhere along the gulf coast in summer they are an uncommon to rare migrant in Texas. These birds are rarely seen perched. They are masters of the air and can soar almost indefinitely without flapping their wings. They feed mainly on small fish and squid plucked from the surface. They will also follow shrimp and fishing boats to scavenge whatever is discarded. In tropical regions they follow small fishing boats for fish guts. They are well-known for stealing food from other sea-going birds such as gulls, terns, Pelicans, etc., and this habit has earned them the nickname of "Man-of-War Bird," a reference to the pirate ships of old. Morphologically their body is mostly wings. Their small feet are used only for perching and they never walk.

Natural History: Though mainly a marine species, the Northern Gannet sometimes shows up far inland. These birds are native to both sides of the North Atlantic, and are found from France to Norway on the European side of the Atlantic. In North America they summer in maritime provinces of Canada and winter along the coast as far south as Florida and Texas. They are rather rare and are usually only seen in marine environments. Although they may range many miles out into the ocean, they are not a true pelagic (open ocean) bird. They feed by diving from height of up to 120 feet and may reach speeds of over 100 mph in a dive. Their plunging dive can penetrate up to seventy feet below the surface. A variety of marine organisms may be eaten opportunistically but the main food is fish and squid. Among the most common fish eaten are mackerel and herring.

Natural History: This is a very rare bird in Texas waters but occasional individuals may stray north in summer. They are most likely to be seen offshore from the southern end of Padre Island. They always stay out over open water and rarely use estuaries or inter coastal areas. With their streamlined shape they are very similar in appearance to the preceding species (Northern Gannet) but are distinguished by their black "mask" on the face around the bill. Both the Masked Booby and the Northern Gannet engage in spectacular "plunge dives" into schools of fish. While they may hunt singly, they have excellent vision and they can see other birds miles away on the open sea and will congregate wherever there are other birds feeding. Within a short time hundreds of birds will gather above large schools of prey fishes. Somehow they manage to avoid collisions.

Class—**Aves** (birds)

Order—**Gruiiformes** (rails & cranes)

Family—**Rallidae** (rails)

Purple Gallinule *Porphyrio martinica*	**Common Gallinule** *Gallinula galeata*	**American Coot** *Fulica americana*

Purple Gallinule	Common Gallinule	American Coot
Size: 13 inches.	**Size:** 14 inches.	**Size:** 15 inches.
Abundance: Uncommon.	**Abundance:** Fairly common.	**Abundance:** Common.
Variation: Juvenile is olive green. Adults are alike.	**Variation:** Juvenile is paler gray without red bill and forehead.	**Variation:** Juvenile paler gray with yellowish beak.

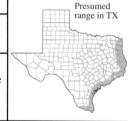 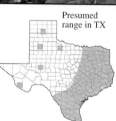 

Presumed range in TX

Habitat: Favors freshwater marshes. Also uses edges of lakes or sometimes rice fields in coastal regions. Requires ample floating aquatic vegetation.

Habitat: Freshwater wetlands such as marshes and swamps and lake shores with abundant vegetation. Most common in the Western Gulf Coastal Plain.

Habitat: Rivers, lakes, large ponds, marshes, and swamps. Virtually all permanent aquatic habitats in the state are used.

Migratory Status: Summer resident in the Piney Woods and along the coast.

Migratory Status: Year-round along the coast. Summer resident elsewhere.

Migratory Status: Year-round resident throughout the state in aquatic habitats.

Breeding: Nest is usually over water and often a platform built on floating vegetation. Clutch size varies but can be at least as high as 6 eggs.

Breeding: Nest is a platform of vegetation slightly above the water line and usually well concealed. Nests throughout the state. As many as ten eggs.

Breeding: Breeds widely throughout the US in summer including in most of Texas. Nest is a platform built amid emergent vegetation. About six eggs.

Natural History: Neon blue and purple plumage with a bright red cere and long yellow legs make this an almost gaudy bird. Although definitely tropical in appearance and mostly restricted in range to the deep south, this species is known for rare individual birds that have wandered far to the north. There is one record of nesting in southern Ohio! By contrast, the species ranges as far south as South America. Summer birds can be seen northward into the Carolinas, southern Georgia, and southern Alabama, but these birds retreat southward into peninsula Florida and coastal regions of Mexico in winter, swelling the ranks of those that live there year-round. They will forage atop floating vegetation such as water lilies or hyacinths. Adults feed mostly on plant material but they will eat aquatic insects and insects are fed to the young.

Natural History: Sometimes known as the Common Moorhen, but that name is properly reserved for a very similar bird that lives in Europe. Although these birds may be seen in suitable habitat throughout they rather secretive. In the deep south and in Florida they can be quite common and usually more observable than they are in more northerly portions of their range. They feed largely on seeds of aquatic plants but also eat animal matter, most predominately snails and insects. Although similar to the American Coot in size and appearance, the Common Gallinule is rarely seen in the open and prefers to stay close to heavy cover. Additionally, they don't form large flocks as do American Coots. However, they can be quite tame and approachable within the heart of their range in Florida and the lower Coastal Plain.

Natural History: During migration and in winter, American Coots gather in large flocks on open water and behave more like ducks than rails. During the breeding season they act more like rails and live among cattails and reeds in freshwater marshes. But they are not as elusive as the rails and are usually easily observed even in summer. They are considered a game species, but rarely hunted as most waterfowl hunters regard them as a "trash" species. They sometimes go by the nickname "Mud Hen." Although the feet are not webbed as with ducks and geese, their long toes are equipped with lateral lobes which flare out when swimming and create an ample surface for pushing against the water. They feed both on land (on grasses) and in the water (aquatic plants, algae, and aquatic invertebrates, small fish, and small amphibians).

Class—**Aves** (birds)

Order—**Gruiformes** (rails & cranes)

Family—**Rallidae** (rails)

King Rail	Virginia Rail	Clapper Rail
Rallus elegans	*Rallus limicola*	*Rallus crepitans*

King Rail	Virginia Rail	Clapper Rail
Size: 16 inches.  Presumed range in TX	**Size:** 9.5 inches. 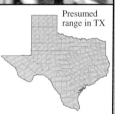 Presumed range in TX	**Size:** 14.5 inches  Presumed range in TX
Abundance: Uncommon.	**Abundance:** Uncommon.	**Abundance:** Fairly common.
Variation: No variation among adults.	**Variation:** No variation among adults.	**Variation:** No variation among adults.
Migratory Status: Year-round resident in coastal areas. Summer elsewhere.	**Migratory Status:** Winter resident on the coast, migrates throughout the state.	**Migratory Status:** Year-round non-migratory resident in coastal regions.
Habitat: Marshes. Found throughout the coastal areas of Texas and in swamps and marshes in the eastern edge of Texas.	**Habitat:** Primarily a marsh dweller. In migration may visit ponds, swamps, or wet meadows. Uses fresh, brackish, and salt marshes in Florida.	**Habitat:** An obligate of salt marsh that ranges along America's coastlines from Massachusetts to northern Mexico. Found in salt marsh along states coast.
Breeding: Builds a loosely woven cup from marsh vegetation. Breeds sporadically in suitable habitat in the Piney Woods region.	**Breeding:** Builds a nest platform of aquatic vegetation a few inches above water level. Nest is usually well hidden among vegetation. Lays 8 or 9 eggs.	**Breeding:** Nest is built in the marsh amid emergent vegetation. Some nests may be inundated by high tides. Clutch size can range from 4 to 16 eggs.
Natural History: Rails are well adapted to life in the marsh. They move with ease through thick grasses and rarely fly except when migrating. They can run quite fast through the grass and rarely offer more than a glimpse. They can also swim and dive beneath the surface, using the wings to swim underwater. Despite the fact that rails are listed as a game bird by most state wildlife agencies, almost no-one hunts them, due probably to their scarcity and secretiveness. They feed mostly on aquatic insects and their larva, spiders, and other invertebrates. Some plant material is also eaten. The species has declined from its historical breeding range in the central United States and is today quite rare except in the lower coastal plain from Texas to the Carolinas. Probably most common in Texas along the coast.	**Natural History:** The Virginia Rail is more common than the larger King Rail, but this is not a common bird in the state and this fact coupled with its secretive nature means that it is a species that remains unfamiliar to most Texans. Historically, this species was much more common in America, but today very little of the wetland habitats that once occurred in the eastern United States remain. As a result, this species along with its larger cousin the King Rail are both species being monitored by many state wildlife agencies in their former breeding range in the Midwest. Birds that winter along the coast breed well to the north of Texas in prairie marshes and wetland areas across the western US and as far north as southern Canada. In migration will fly across most regions of the state. A few may stop and rest in suitable habitat here and there.	**Natural History:** Despite the fact that The Clapper Rail is listed as a game bird in many states, almost no-one hunts them, due probably to their secretiveness and the difficulty of accessing their habitats within expansive salt marshes. Rail hunters must pole through the marsh at high tide to flush birds for gunning. Few people not actively seeking this secretive bird will ever see one as they typically remain hidden in thick marsh grasses. At low tide they can sometimes be glimpsed as they emerge onto bare mud flats. They can, however, easily be heard calling within the marsh. They feed mostly on aquatic insects and their larva, spiders, and other invertebrates. Some plant material is also eaten. In the northern portions of their range along the Atlantic coast they may be migratory, but Texas birds are sedentary.

Class—**Aves** (birds)

Order—**Gruiformes** (rails & cranes)

Family—**Rallidae** (rails)

Sora *Porzana carolina*	**Black Rail** *Laterallus jamaicensis*	**Yellow Rail** *Coturnicops noveboracensis*

Size: 9 inches.

Abundance: Fairly common.

Variation: No variation among adults.

Presumed range in TX

Size: 6 inches.

Abundance: Rare.

Variation: No variation among adults.

Presumed range in TX

Size: 7.25 inches.

Abundance: Rare.

Variation: No variation among adults.

Presumed range in TX

Migratory Status: Winter resident in south and seasonal migrant statewide.

Habitat: Primarily a marsh dweller. Favors heavily vegetated wetlands. Winter habitat includes coastal marshes. Summers on inland marshes.

Breeding: Builds a nest platform of aquatic vegetation a few inches above water level. Nest is well hidden in dense upright plants. Does not breed in Texas. Lays 8 to 11 eggs.

Natural History: The Sora is one of the more observable of America's rails. Still, it is fairly secretive, especially during fall migration. They are usually observable on both breeding and wintering grounds, but catching a glimpse of this species can be difficult. They are vocal birds, however, and their whinnying call can be heard for a long distance. They feed on a variety of aquatic invertebrates but also eat seeds of aquatic plants, particularly wild rice. Soras have exceptionally long toes, an adaptation that allows for walking across floating vegetation. Although the Sora is one of the most common and widespread rail species in America, their dependence upon wetlands renders them vulnerable. America's wetlands remain under a constant assault from land developers and agricultural interests.

Migratory Status: Some are year-round residents, others are winter only.

Habitat: In summer uses shallow fresh-water marshes, wet meadows, and some man-made wetlands. Salt marshes above high tide are winter habitat.

Breeding: In Texas this species breeds only in a few areas of high coastal marsh. Some migrate to inland marshes to breed. Nest is woven of grasses with a side opening. Six eggs are laid.

Natural History: Of all the birds in Texas this little rail may be the most difficult to see. Not only is it quite rare (a Threatened Species in Texas), but it is also a secretive and mainly nocturnal species. Its habitat is thick marsh grasses where it rarely emerges into the open. Add to that its dark coloration that hides it well in the shadow of tall marsh grasses coupled with its small size (no bigger than a sparrow), and you have a species that is remarkably difficult to observe. It comes as no surprise that this is a difficult species to study and there is much to be learned about its natural history. Many wildlife agencies around the country do engage in research aimed at understanding this rare species and more information is becoming available. However, it remains one of the least understood birds in Texas.

Migratory Status: Winter resident along the central and upper gulf coast.

Habitat: In summer uses shallow fresh-water marshes or wet meadows. Salt and brackish marshes and rice fields are winter habitat.

Breeding: Nest is a covered cup made of sedges and above high water mark. Nest is well hidden in dense stands of emergent vegetation. Nesting occurs mostly in Canada and northern US.

Natural History: In every aspect of its natural history this species is difficult to study. Like the Black Rail it is rare, secretive, and inhabits densely vegetated marshes where it rarely emerges into the open. Birdwatchers have learned to visit rice fields during fall harvest to see birds flushed from the field of densely packed rice plants. After spending the winter in the coastal plain from Texas to the Carolinas, Yellow Rails fly north into Canada to breed. They migrate at night and are almost never seen during migration. Known food items include seeds of marsh plants and many types of aquatic invertebrates. When approached, they will run through the marsh grasses with ease and almost never fly. Populations of this bird have crashed in the last century, possibly due to loss of habitat.

Class—**Aves** (birds)

Order—**Charadriiformes** (shorebirds)

Family—**Charadriidae** (plovers)

Black-bellied Plover *Pluvialis squatarola*	**Golden Plover** *Pluvialis dominica*	**Wilson's Plover** *Anarhynchus wilsonia*
	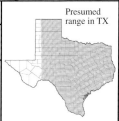	

Size: 11.5 inches.

Abundance: Fairly common.

Variation: Seasonal plumage variations (see above).

Presumed range in TX

Migratory Status: Winter resident.

Habitat: Beaches are the preferred winter habitat. Inland migrants will use shorelines, mudflats, and bare fields.

Breeding: Nest is a shallow cup scraped into the Arctic tundra and lined with lichens. 4 eggs are laid.

Natural History: Black-bellied Plovers occur in both the new and old worlds and in fact they are one of the most widespread shorebirds in the world. North American birds winter along both coastlines from just south of Canada to South America, including the Caribbean. Summers are spent within the Arctic Circle of Alaska and Canada. During migration they are seen mostly along America's coastlines and in the great plains region. Unlike many shorebirds, the Black-bellied Plover exhibits nocturnal tendencies and will often feed at night. Food items are marine worms and small clams and mussels plucked from the mud at low tide. On the breeding grounds in the far north they will eat insects, small freshwater crustaceans and berries. Climate change may be a threat if tundra nesting habitat undergoes transformation. Migrants stop off at wetlands and flooded fields across America to rest and fed.

Size: 10.5 inches.

Abundance: Uncommon.

Variation: Seasonal plumage variations (see above).

Presumed range in TX

Migratory Status: Seasonal migrant.

Habitat: Beaches are the preferred winter habitat. Inland migrants will use shorelines, mudflats, and bare fields.

Breeding: Nest is a scrape on tundra soil. 4 eggs are laid and young are highly precocial, able to walk immediately.

Natural History: Like the similar Black-bellied Plover, the American Golden Plover is a long distance traveler that nests in the Arctic and spends its winters in southeastern South America. Its epic migrations sometimes include extensive flights over vast expanses of open ocean. Many migrate through inland regions and they are known for their propensity to appear almost anywhere during migrations. Food items include some plant material (berries, seeds, foliage) as well as a wide variety of invertebrate prey. Like many shorebirds, the American Golden Plover was hunted relentlessly during the days of "market hunting" throughout the 1800s. Tens to perhaps hundreds of thousands were killed annually. Today they are still legally hunted hunted in some South American countries. Habitat loss remains an ever present threat as is climate change. Migrants are observed east of the Rocky Mountains.

Size: 8 inches.

Abundance: Uncommon.

Variation: Non-breeders are drabber, lack black band on breast.

Presumed range in TX

Migratory Status: Summer resident.

Habitat: Beaches mainly. Also mud flats in tidal areas and coastal lagoons. Ranges well down into South America.

Breeding: Nests all along Florida's coastline on dunes and sandy islands. 3 eggs are laid in a shallow scrap.

Natural History: Differing from all other American plovers, the Wilson's Plover does not travel inland. Instead this plover stays close to the sea. They can be seen on the Texas coast in spring and summer. Winters are spent in the Caribbean or northern South America. Fiddler crabs are reported to be a favorite food item along with other crustaceans and insects, worms, and other benthic invertebrates. Large, hard-shelled prey like fiddler crabs are reduced to manageable swallowing size by removing the legs and large claw, then swallowing the body. The name "Wilson's Plover" honors early American naturalist Alexander Wilson. Wilson was a contemporary of John James Audubon and is regarded by many as the father of North American Ornithology. No less than five bird species in America today bear his name. Loss of habitat from beach development is a significant threat to this species.

Class—**Aves** (birds)

Order—**Charadriiformes** (shorebirds)

Family—**Charadriidae** (plovers)

Snowy Plover *Anarhynchus nivosus*	Piping Plover *Anarhynchus melodus*	Semipalmated Plover *Charadrius semipalmatus*

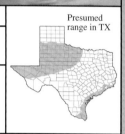

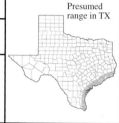

Snowy Plover	Piping Plover	Semipalmated Plover
Size: 6.25 inches.	**Size:** 7.5 inches.	**Size:** 7.25 inches.
Abundance: Rare.	**Abundance:** Threatened.	**Abundance:** Fairly common.
Variation: Seasonal plumage variation. Winter birds are paler,	**Variation:** Seasonal plumage variations. Winter birds are paler.	**Variation:** Seasonal plumage variations. See photos above.

Presumed range in TX

Migratory Status: Winter resident on the coast. Summer in western Texas.

Migratory Status: Winter resident along the coast.

Migratory Status: Winter resident on the coast. Migrant in much of the state.

Habitat: Sandy beaches and dunes are the primary habitat in winter. Inland populations use alkaline lake shores.

Habitat: Summer habitat is the Great Plains and coastal areas of the northeast. In winter uses southern beaches.

Habitat: Winter habitat is along coastlines. Summer habitat is open tundra. Migrants favor mud flats and shorelines.

Breeding: Breeding in Texas occurs. Shallow scrap is lined with shells, 3 to 6 eggs is usual.

Breeding: Nest is a scrape on sand or gravel, often near a clump of grass in an elevated place on the beach. 4 eggs.

Breeding: Nests on the ground, usually near water. Nesting grounds are in northern Canada and Alaska. 4 eggs.

Natural History: Snowy Plovers can be found in two distinct populations in America, an eastern and western population. Both are imperiled by loss of habitat due to development of beach and dune areas along the coast. Western populations in California are regarded as federally threatened. Among the eastern population some states regard them as a Threatened Species, and birds that nest on the coast of Mississippi and Alabama are considered Endangered. Some will migrate inland to breed on alkaline lakes of the west (including in Texas), where human intrusion has less impact than for those that breed on coastal beaches. Their pale color and small size helps nesting birds to blend in with their surroundings. When foraging on open beaches they are more observable, but overall these little plovers are usually overlooked by most beach goers.

Natural History: The Piping Plover is a rare species that breeds primarily on sandy beaches along America's Atlantic coastline and in the Northern Great Plains. The eastern population is endangered. Widespread coastal development and near complete utilization of beaches by man has made successful nesting on beach habitats very problematic for the Piping Plover. In recent years, conservation efforts which attempt to mitigate human interference may the only hope for the species. Closing of beaches to human activity where nesting occurs along with erecting predator exclusion fences around nests are two conservation actions that are regularly taken by conservation teams up and down America's Atlantic coast. Recent political trends aimed at decimating environmental regulations may spell doom for this and many other species facing similar threats across America.

Natural History: Most Semipalmated Plovers migrate along the coasts of North America, but a few travel overland and they are regularly seen in inland areas. Most sightings will likely be along the gulf coast or lake shores or alkaline lakes as they tend to favor shorelines and other open spaces. The food of the Semipalmated Plover is mostly invertebrate animals plucked from the mud. They hunt these "benthic" organisms along the edges of marshes, lakes, seashores, etc. Aquatic food items include insect larva (especially fly larva), polychaete worms, crustaceans, and small bivalves. On dry land these plovers will eat spiders, flies, and beetles. Most foraging is done along waters edge or in very shallow water or on exposed mudflats. Baby plovers are highly precocial and young Semipalmated Plovers are able to feed themselves immediately.

Class—**Aves** (birds)

Order—**Charadriiformes** (shorebirds)

Family—**Charadriidae** (plovers)

Family—**Haematopidae** (oystercatcher)

Killdeer *Charadrius vociferus*	**Mountain Plover** *Anarhynchus montanus*	**American Oystercatcher** *Haematopus palliatus*
Young		

Size: 10.5 inches.	**Size:** 9 inches.	**Size:** 17 inches.
Abundance: Common.	**Abundance:** Rare.	**Abundance:** Uncommon.
Variation: No variation among adults. Sexes are alike.	**Variation:** No variation among adults. Sexes are alike.	**Variation:** Seasonal plumage variations. See photos above.

Presumed range in TX

Migratory Status: Year-round resident.

Migratory Status: Summer and winter.

Migratory Status: Year-round.

Habitat: Open lands. Mudflats, agricultural fields, lake shores, sandbars, heavily grazed pastures, and even gravel parking lots.

Habitat: On short grass prairies this bird uses prairie dog towns and other places where there is a good amount of exposed earth.

Habitat: Lives on the coast. Uses barrier islands, intercoastal areas, shorelines, and beaches. Especially likes jetties and rocky shorelines.

Breeding: Lays 4 eggs directly on the ground. Nest is often in gravelly or sandy situations in wide-open spaces. Young are very precocial and they will run about within hours of hatching.

Breeding: Breeds in the short grass prairies. Nest is a shallow scrape on bare soil. Nesting is preceded by a flight display of the male. Three or four eggs is typical. Young are precocious.

Breeding: Nest is a scrape on bare sand, gravel, or shell. Most nesting is in or behind dunes backing the beach. Empty barrier Islands with dunes are a favorite nesting site. Lays 3 eggs.

Natural History: Although the Killdeer is found state-wide, they are much more common in areas where open habitats are more widespread. This is a species that has likely benefited significantly from human alterations of natural habitats. The creation of open spaces where there was once grassland or forest has resulted in a habitat boom the Killdeer. They are found all over North America south of the Arctic Circle. They were once hunted for food and their populations suffered a serious decline in the days of "market hunting." They feed on the ground and earthworms are a major food source along with grasshoppers, beetles, and snails. A few seeds are also consumed. Baby Killdeer are highly precocious and can walk immediately after hatching. Least common in the hot, arid desert areas of western Texas.

Natural History: Hundreds of years ago this was a common breeding species on the short-grass plains of North America. They began to decline almost immediately with advent of agriculture on the Great Plains. Much of the population of this species wintered in California's central valley where agriculture effectively eliminated its winter habitat. It is estimated that the population has declined by 80 percent in the last half century. Oddly, neither the state of Texas or the U.S. Fish and Wildlife Service have listed it as threatened or endangered. The name "Mountain" Plover is a misnomer, as this is a grassland species and not found in mountains. In Texas a few breed in the Panhandle and in the Trans-Pecos regions. More birds are found in the state in winter. Winter habitats are mostly in south Texas.

Natural History: The common name Oystercatcher aptly describes the feeding habits of this unusual species. The laterally flattened bill is adapted for prying open the shells of mollusks like oysters and mussels. The technique involves stalking through shallows in search of mollusks with shells open and quickly inserting the blade-like bill into the open bivalve. It then stabs with the bill until the abducter muscle is severed allowing the shell to be pried open and the contents extracted. This species is completely dependent upon beaches and coastal dunes as habitat. Human encroachment and coastal development have ravaged these habitats for decades and today this is one of America's most threatened natural habitats. In the year 2000, a population census revealed the entire population of only 10,000 birds.

Class—**Aves** (birds)

Order—**Charadriiformes** (shorebirds)

Family—**Recurvirostridae** (stilts and avocet)

Family—**Scolapacidae** (sandpipers)

American Avocet *Recurvirostra americana*	Black-necked Stilt *Himantopus mexicanus*	Wilson's Phalarope *Phalaropus tricolor*

Male

Female

Size: 18 inches.

Presumed range in TX

Abundance: Uncommon.

Variation: Breeding birds are brighter in color.

Migratory Status: Winter and breeder on the coast. Breeder in the Panhandle.

Habitat: Marshes, shallow lakes, and wetlands. Especially fond of saline wetlands and alkaline lakes of the west.

Breeding: Nests on the ground in a shallow scrape lined with grass. Nest may be on sand or mud. Four eggs.

Natural History: With its dramatic coloration, long legs and long, upturned bill this is one of the most striking birds in America. Even those with little interest in birds will not fail to notice the American Avocet. Feeds by sweeping the upturned bill back forth through the water. Feeds mostly on small aquatic insects (especially midges) and eats both adult insects and their aquatic larva. They also feed on brine shrimp and brine flies in saline wetlands and alkaline lakes in the Great Basin region of the western US. Along the coastal marshes where they spend the winter, amphipods and marine worms are important foods. Their breeding habitat is mostly in the prairies and inter-mountain basins of the western United States, where they utilize marshes and wetlands. Some will nest in the coastal regions of south Texas. May be seen as a migrant statewide.

Size: 14 inches.

Presumed range in TX

Abundance: Uncommon.

Variation: No variation among adults. Sexes are alike.

Migratory Status: Winter resident and breeder on coast. Breeder in west Texas.

Habitat: Marshes and flooded fields, especially flooded pastures or grassy roadside ditches filled with rainwater.

Breeding: Nests in or adjacent to wetlands in clumps of vegetation. 4 eggs. In west Texas nests on lakes and playas.

Natural History: Common names for birds are usually descriptive. None more so than this species with its black neck and long, stilt-like legs. With their exceptionally long legs, Black-necked Stilts can feed in fairly deep waters. They thus take advantage of foods not available to many of the shorter-legged shorebirds that may share their habitat. Their food is mostly aquatic invertebrates, but a few small fishes are also taken. They winter along southern coastlines of North America and in Mexico and Central America, where many are residents that will breed on these wintering grounds. But some move inland to breed and summer on marshlands in the western United States. Breeding in Texas is on the coast or in the western end of the state. They may be seen in shallow water habitats throughout the state during migratory periods.

Size: 10 inches.

Presumed range in TX

Abundance: Fairly common.

Migratory Status: Seasonal migrant throughout the state.

Variation: Sexual, seasonal, and ontogenetic variations. See photos above.

Habitat: Uses marshes on breeding range; shallow water habitats along lake shores, ponds, etc. in migration.

Breeding: Breeds on inland marshes and wetlands in the west-central US and Canada. Always lays 4 eggs.

Natural History: Phalaropes are known for the unique role reversal of the sexes. In these birds, the female is the most vividly colored while the male has drab plumage. Even more unusual, it is the male that incubates the eggs in the nest. These birds are salt lake specialists and during migration they congregate in large flocks around alkaline and highly saline lakes of the interior of North America. The winter habitat is similar saline lakes in the Andes Mountains of South America. Birds seen in Texas are migrators. The slightly smaller (8 inch) **Red-necked Phalarope** (*P. lobatus*) is a related species that can also be seen in Atlantic and Pacific waters off the coast and in rare occasions inland in the western US. These birds are migrants moving between northern breeding grounds and wintering areas in tropical seas. They are very rarely seen in western Texas.

Class—**Aves** (birds)

Order—**Charadriiformes** (shorebirds)

Family—**Scolopacidae** (sandpipers)

Greater Yellowlegs *Tringa melanoleuca*	**Lesser Yellowlegs** *Tringa flavipes*	**Solitary Sandpiper** *Tringa solitaria*

Size: 14 inches.

Abundance: Fairly common.

Variation: Speckles less prominent in winter and young.

 *Presumed range in TX*

Size: 10.5 inches.

Abundance: Fairly common.

Variation: Speckles less prominent in winter and young

Presumed range in TX

Size: 8.5 inches.

Abundance: Fairly common.

Variation: Winter plumage has reduced light speckles.

 *Presumed range in TX*

Migratory status: Both species will winter along the coast and may be seen state-wide in suitable habitats during migration.

Migratory status: Winter resident along coast, seasonal migrant statewide.

Habitat: Both species are seen in a wide variety of wetland habitats during migration. In winter both species use freshwater and saltwater habitats in coastal Texas.

Habitat: Uses variety of wetland habitats. Sometimes seen on beaches.

Breeding: Greater Yellowlegs breeds in northern bogs, Lesser Yellowlegs in drier, more upland habitats. Both species nest on the ground and 3 to 4 eggs is the typical clutch size for both.

Breeding: Lays three to five eggs. Nests in trees, an unusual trait for a sandpiper. Uses old nest of other birds.

Natural History: These two related species are sometimes seen together. When seen together they are easily recognized by size. When not found in mixed flocks they are best identified by the shape of the bill. The Greater Yellowlegs bill is longer and ever so slightly upturned at the tip. The Greater Yellowlegs is the least social of the two, and although it is seen in small flocks it can also be seen singly. Both species were once heavily hunted and during the days of market hunting both species experienced steep population declines. Hunting still occurs in some areas of their migratory range, especially in the Caribbean. Both spend the summer in the boreal regions of Canada and Alaska and winter from the Gulf Coast of the southeastern United States southward into South America. Food items for the Greater include both aquatic and terrestrial invertebrates as well as some small aquatic vertebrates like small frogs or fish. Lesser Yellowlegs food items are mainly invertebrates, both aquatic and terrestrial, but some small fish are also eaten. Both feed mostly by wading in shallows, but the Lesser is a more active feeder, wading rapidly and picking food from both the surface and the water column. It will also feed in this manner in terrestrial habitats such as grassy shorelines or meadow areas. Greater Yellowlegs feeds both diurnally and at night, when it employs a sweeping motion of the bill back and forth through the water, apparently catching food by feel. The major threat to both species today is probably loss of habitat, both on wintering grounds in South America (loss of wetlands) and on summer range in North America, i.e logging in boreal forests (Greater), and loss of wetlands in Alaska (Lesser).

Natural History: As implied by their name, Solitary Sandpipers are nearly always seen alone during migration. In this respect they differ markedly from most other members of their family. They also differ in their nesting habits, as they are the only North American member of the Scolapacidae family that nests in trees. When feeding it wades in shallows and plucks its food from the surface or beneath the water. Food is mostly invertebrates, both aquatic and terrestrial. Insects make up the bulk of the terrestrial foods. They also take aquatic insects and their larva, small crustaceans, snails and some vertebrate prey such as small minnows or tadpoles. Due to their solitary habits and the fact that they breed in trees in remote boreal forests, little is known about their population status, but it appears to be stable.

Class—**Aves** (birds)

Order—**Charadriiformes** (shorebirds)

Family—**Scolopacidae** (sandpipers)

Willet *Tringa semipalmata*	**Ruddy Turnstone** *Arenaria interpres*	**Spotted Sandpiper** *Actitis macularius*
	 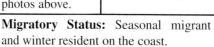	

Size: 15 inches.	**Size:** 9.5 inches.	**Size:** 7.5 inches.
Abundance: Fairly common.	**Abundance:** Fairly common.	**Abundance:** Fairly common.
Variation: Winter plumage lacks brown speckling, is uniformly gray.	**Variation:** Seasonal plumage variations. See photos above.	**Variation:** Winter birds lack the dark spots on the breast.

Presumed range in TX

Migratory Status: Seasonal migrant and winter resident on the coast.

Migratory Status: Seasonal migrant and winter resident on the coast.

Migratory Status: Seasonal migrant statewide and winter resident on coast.

Habitat: Uses variety of wetland habitats in migration. Common on Texas beaches in summer.

Habitat: Winters on sandy beaches along the gulf coast. Also uses lake shores and mud flats in inter-tidal areas.

Habitat: In migration uses edges of ponds, lake shores, stream courses and river bars. Coastal marshes in winter.

Breeding: Lays 4 eggs in nest on the ground. Nests on the edge of wetlands in the northern plain.

Breeding: Breeds in the arctic tundra and coastlines from Siberia and Alaska across Canada to Greenland.

Breeding: Nests on the ground in grassy situations. Lays 2 to 4 eggs. Does not nest in Texas.

Natural History: The Willet is a true "shorebird" that is quite familiar to those who frequent America's seashores. Both coasts of America are home to Willets during the winter, and some will nest in coastal marshes. Others fly into the interior of North America and nest as far north as the central Canadian prairie. Many that winter on Texas coast are among those that nest in northern prairies. It is these migrants that can be seen in freshwater habitats. Crustaceans, mollusks, insects, small fish, and polycheate worms are listed as food items. Feeds both day and night. In the 1800s they were hunted for food and for their eggs, which were also eaten, resulting in a significant decrease in populations. Today these are fairly common shorebirds whose population appears stable at an estimate of about a quarter of a million birds. They are known to live at least ten years.

Natural History: Most Ruddy Turnstones travel up and down America's coastlines during migration, but a few migrate through inland regions of the continent, including across Texas. This is one of the most northerly ranging birds in America, traveling to the northernmost extreme of the continent to breed each summer. Its name comes from its habit of using its beak to overturn pebbles and stones on beaches in search of small invertebrate prey. It also feeds on ocean carrion found on beaches. On the breeding grounds the primary food source is mosquitoes and other dipeteran insects. The unusual genus (*Arenaria*) contains only two species and their position in the phylogeny of the shorebirds is unclear. Some will winter as far south as Brazil, but a fair number will spend the winter along the Texas coastline and a few may linger into the summer.

Natural History: Unlike most sandpipers that exhibit strong flocking tendencies, the Spotted Sandpiper is always seen singly or in very small groups. This is one of the most widespread sandpipers in America and one of the few that nests in the lower forty-eight. The distinctly spotted breast along with a habit of constantly bobbing up and down makes the Spotted Sandpiper one of the most recognizable members of the Scolapacidae family. Feeds on a wide variety of aquatic and terrestrial invertebrates, especially dipteran (fly) larva. Also eats significant quantities of mayflies, crickets, grasshoppers, caterpillars, beetles, and mollusks, crustaceans, and worms. Many will winter well into the tropics, some as far as South America. Others will spend the winter in the southern US, including the coast of Texas and in aquatic habitats in southern Texas.

Class—**Aves** (birds)
Order—**Charadriiformes** (shorebirds)
Family— **Scolopacidae** (sandpipers)

Upland Sandpiper *Bartramia longicauda*	**Whimbrel** *Numenius phaeopus*	**Long-billed Curlew** *Numenius americanus*

Size: 12 inches.	**Size:** 17.5 inches.	**Size:** 23 inches.
Abundance: Uncommon.	**Abundance:** Uncommon.	**Abundance:** Uncommon.
Variation: Fall and juvenile plumages paler than breeding.	**Variation:** Juveniles have a slightly darker head and neck.	**Variation:** No sexual dimorphism, juveniles resemble adults.

Presumed range in TX

Migratory Status: Seasonal migrant that may be seen in open habitats.

Migratory Status: Winter resident on the coast that migrates through Texas.

Migratory Status: Winter resident on the coast that migrates through Texas.

Habitat: An obligate of grasslands and prairies. Migrants will also use pastures and fields.

Habitat: Winter habitat in Texas is mostly coastlines. Will also use mudflats and lakeshores.

Habitat: Breeding habitat is the short grass and mixed grass prairies of the western great plains region.

Breeding: Nest is a shallow scrape on the ground lined with grass. 4 eggs.

Breeding: Breeds in the far north. Typically 4 eggs in nest on ground.

Breeding: Nest is a shallow bowl or scrape. 4 eggs is usual.

Natural History: The bulk of the Upland Sandpiper's summer range is in the northern Great Plains. A few summer very sparsely east of the Mississippi River into the Midwestern US. Unlike most other members of the sandpiper family, the Upland Sandpiper avoids coastal areas in favor of prairies and grasslands well into the interior of the continent. Historically, these birds were much more numerous. Market hunting in the late nineteenth century saw countless numbers of dead Upland Sandpipers shipped by rail from their nesting grounds on the northern plains to markets in the east. At the same time, they were being hunted mercilessly on their winter habitats in the Pampas of South America. Even more devastating to their populations was the conversion of the native American prairie to cropland. Amazingly, the species survives. They are an uncommon to migrant throughout the state.

Natural History: The likelihood of seeing this species in migration is not great, but those who do see it will have no trouble recognizing it. Its large size and long, down-curved bill is quite distinctive. On wintering grounds they feed mostly on crabs and the long, crescent shaped bill is thought to be an adaptation for penetrating the burrows of Fiddler Crabs in marine inter-tidal zones. On arctic breeding grounds insects are the major food but some berries are also eaten. Most of these birds migrate along the coastlines of America, but a few travel inland. Most inland migration is through the western Great Plains but some migrate through the Mississippi flyway or down the Atlantic coast. Summering and nesting in the Arctic of Alaska and Canada and wintering in South America, this species has been known to make non-stop migratory flights lasting several days and covering over 3,000 miles!

Natural History: Historically, these birds were fairly common along the Atlantic coast of America in migration periods. Today they are extremely rare along the east coast and most remaining birds are in the Pacific Coast Flyway and the Prairie Flyway populations. All nesting occurs in the northern great plains and the inter-mountain west. The name "Long-billed" Curlew is appropriate as this birds bill is so long as to appear to be a liability. In fact, it is a specialized tool used to remove crustaceans from their burrows. In Texas this species can be seen in winter and spring along the coast. Birds that spend the winter along the coast are joined by migrants from farther south in the spring, and spring on the coast of Texas is the best bet for seeing them in the state. Their habitat preferences are salt marsh mudflats and exposed tidal areas where they can use their specialized bill to probe for benthic organisms.

Class—**Aves** (birds)
Order—**Charadriiformes** (shorebirds)
Family—**Scolopacidae** (sandpipers)

Marbled Godwit *Limosa fedoa*	**Hudsonian Godwit** *Limosa haemastica*	**Red Knot** *Calidris canutus*
		Summer

Size: 18 inches. 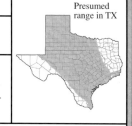Presumed range in TX **Abundance:** Uncommon. **Migratory Status:** Seasonal migrant and winter resident.	**Size:** 15.5 inches. Presumed range in TX **Abundance:** Uncommon. **Migratory Status:** Spring migrant only from mid April to late May.	**Size:** 10.5 inches. Presumed range in TX **Abundance:** Rare in Texas. **Migratory Status:** Seasonal migrant and winter resident.
Variation: Breeding birds show distinct barring on belly.	**Variation:** Winter plumage is gray. Summer birds have reddish breasts.	**Variation:** Winter birds are drab gray brown with off-white breast and belly.
Habitat: Summer habitat is in the Great Plains. In Texas uses coastal areas. Marshes, intertidal mud flats, etc.	**Habitat:** Winter habitat is coastal areas in southern South America. Summer habitat is Arctic tundra.	**Habitat:** Summer habitat is arctic tundra. Winter and migration habitat is inter-tidal areas and beaches/coastlines.
Breeding: Breeds in the northern plains of Canada, Dakotas, Montana. Nest is on the ground. 4 eggs.	**Breeding:** Nests north of the treeline in Arctic tundra. Nest is in a dry spot in "Muskeg" bogs or wet Arctic meadows.	**Breeding:** Does not nest in Texas. Nests on tundra all the way to the Arctic Ocean. 4 eggs is typical.
Natural History: Although this species is a fairly common migrant and breeding bird on the prairies of America's Great Plains region, it is an uncommon species in Texas. Worms, bivalves, crustaceans, and insects are major food items. Oddly for a shorebird, plant tubers are also included in its diet. Like many of its kin this species was decimated by overhunting during the late 1800s and it has never fully recovered. Loss of native prairie to agriculture has probably retarded recovery and remains as a major threat to the species. Although it is similar in appearance to the Whimbrel and Long-billed Curlew, it can easily be differentiated from those two large shorebirds by its bill, which is slightly upturned rather than curved downward. It can also be confused with the Upland Sandpiper, which has a much shorter bill. The similar Hudsonian Godwit has gray winter plumage.	**Natural History:** These long-distance migrants are only seen in Texas in the spring when some will stop briefly in coastal mudflats and marshes. They are not seen in the fall because they typically make non-stop flights from northern Canada back to South America! They are one of the greatest travelers in the animal world, flying from southern South America to the arctic and back each year. These annual migrations can cover over 10,000 miles. Their return flight from Canada to South America is usually over open ocean and may involve a non-stop flight of several thousand miles. Their long bill is inserted deep into the mud for invertebrate prey. The tip of the bill is flexible enough to allow them to probe around for worms deep in the mud. They also eat crustaceans. mollusks, and many insects. Uncontrolled hunting in the last century negatively impacted populations.	**Natural History:** This is North America's largest member of the *Calidris* genus. Like many other Sandpiper species, the Red Knot is a remarkable traveler, with some covering nearly ten thousand miles in a round trip journey from southern South America to the Arctic and back each year. Some birds may fly non-stop for thousands of miles across great expanses of ocean, mountains and deserts. Nesting is on the most northerly land masses in North America including northern Greenland and Canada's Arctic Archipelago. During the North American winter, some will be enjoying summer in the southern hemisphere as far south as Terra del Fuego on the southern tip of South America. Along the way, these world travelers will sometimes stop for a brief rest somewhere along the coasts of eastern North America. They are typically seen in coastal Texas in winter.

Class—**Aves** (birds)
Order—**Charadriiformes** (shorebirds)
Family—**Scolopacidae** (sandpipers)
The "Peep" Sandpipers Genus—*Calidris* (5 species in Texas pictured below)

Least Sandpiper *Calidris minutilla*	**White-rumped Sandpiper** *Calidris fuscicollis*	**Semipalmated Sandpiper** *Calidris pusilla*

Baird's Sandpiper *Calidris bairdii*	**Western Sandpiper** *Calidris mauri*	Combined range of the "peep" Sandpipers in TX
	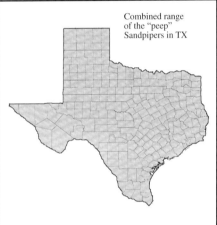	

Size: Least Sandpiper 6 inches. Semipalmated Sandpiper 6.25 inches; Western Sandpiper 6.5 inches. White-rumped and Baird's Sandpipers both reach 7.5 inches.

Abundance: All are fairly common. Least Sandpiper, Western Sandpiper and the Semipalmated are probably the most commonly seen of the "Peep" sandpipers.

Migratory Status: Semipalmated Sandpiper, Baird's Sandpiper and White-rumped Sandpiper are seasonal migrants in Texas. Western Sandpiper and Least are both migrants and winter residents.

Variation: All five of these species exhibit seasonal plumage changes. All are comparably paler in winter than in summer.

Habitat: The name "Mudpiper" would be a more appropriate name for these birds as they favor mud flats and flooded fields over sandy beaches. All can be seen along the coastlines but many migrate through the interior of North America.

Breeding: All "peep" sandpipers nest on the ground in the barren arctic tundra. 4 eggs is typical.

Natural History: These five species are all similar in their natural history and are confusingly alike in appearance. While serious birders and professional ornithologists take pride in being able to correctly identify any species, most casual observers are satisfied with calling these homogeneous birds simply "peeps." Food habits and feeding methods are also similar in these sandpipers, with mud dwelling benthic invertebrates making up the bulk of the diet in winter and during migration. Aquatic insect larva and some terrestrial insects are eaten on the breeding grounds. The hordes of mosquitoes for which the arctic tundra is famous in summer make up a high protein smorgasbord for both the adult birds and the newly hatched young. All the sandpipers are known for their epic migrations. Some species travel non-stop for a thousand miles or more over open ocean. Flights lasting as long as five days have been reported. Quite a feat of endurance for birds that can weigh as little as 0.75 to 1.5 ounces! Recent population declines have been reported for the Least Sandpiper and the Semipalmated Sandpiper. By contrast, the Western Sandpiper is one of the most abundant shorebirds in America with a total population estimate of 3.5 million birds. Least Sandpiper, Western Sandpiper, and Baird's Sandpiper can be seen statewide, White-rumped and Semipalmated Sandpiper are seen mostly in the eastern half of the state.

Class—**Aves** (birds)

Order—**Charadriiformes** (shorebirds)

Family—**Scolopacidae** (sandpipers)

Stilt Sandpiper *Calidris himantopus*	**Sanderling** *Calidris alba*	**Dunlin** *Calidris alpina*

 Summer

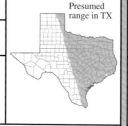 Winter

 Summer

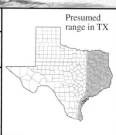 Winter

Size: 8.5 inches.

Abundance: Uncommon.

Migratory Status: Seasonal migrant and winter resident.

Presumed range in TX

Size: 8 inches.

Abundance: Fairly common.

Migratory Status: Seasonal migrant and winter resident.

Presumed range in TX

Size: 8.5 inches.

Abundance: Fairly common.

Migratory Status: Winter resident and seasonal migrant.

Presumed range in TX

Variation: Winter birds are much paler, more grayish.

Variation: Significant seasonal variation (see photos above).

Variation: Significant seasonal plumage changes (see photos above).

Habitat: Ponds, marshes, flooded fields, and lake shorelines. Uses salt marsh and brackish marshes in winter.

Habitat: Shorelines. In winter lives on the beach. During migration, frequents lake shores and river bars.

Habitat: During migration, uses flooded agricultural fields, mud flats, and seasonally flooded lowland pastures.

Breeding: Nests in lowland areas near the Arctic Ocean. Lays 4 eggs.

Breeding: Nests on arctic tundra on bare ground. Lays 4 eggs.

Breeding: Another high arctic breeder. Lays 4 eggs on ground in open tundra.

Natural History: The Stilt Sandpiper gets its name from its long legs. The long legs are an adaptation that allow it to feed in deeper water than most other *Calidris* sandpipers. Its body shape and habit of feeding in deeper water rather than on mud flats is unusual for its genus and mimics the yellowlegs sandpipers (genus *Tringa*). The migratory routes for this sandpiper are mainly west of the Mississippi River, but many will use the Atlantic coastal flyway. They nest along the northernmost coast of North America and will spend the winter in the interior of the South American continent. As with many other sandpiper species, the Stilt Sandpiper shows a remarkable fidelity to the nest site. After migrating thousands of miles from South America, they often return to the same exact spot on the arctic coastline to lay their eggs. A few may winter on the lower gulf coast of Texas.

Natural History: Unlike most members of the sandpiper family, which are more likely to be found on mudflats, the Sanderling is commonly found on seashores. Except during migration or when breeding, these birds inhabit sandy beaches throughout the Americas. Any person who has been to the seashore has probably been amused by watching this species running back and forth in front of the waves. On beaches it feeds by running just in front of oncoming wave and chasing right behind receding wave, picking up tiny marine crustaceans, bivalves, and polychaetes. On the breeding ground it will eat both terrestrial and aquatic invertebrates and insects. Most Sanderlings migrate along the coastlines of America or through the great plains. Some can be seen in inland areas, however, especially along the shores of the great lakes. They are common on Texas beaches in winter.

Natural History: The Dunlin winters along both coasts of North America where it haunts estuaries and intertidal regions. A few may be seen in winter along northern Atlantic coastlines but most move farther south. In southern Louisiana and gulf coastal Texas it often uses rice fields in winter. Various clams, insects, worms, and amphipods are picked from the mud or plucked from vegetation with its moderately long, probing bill. Like other shorebird species it is usually seen in flocks, sometimes numbering in the thousands or even tens of thousands. In the early 1800s, market hunters killed these birds in enormous numbers. Using cannon-like shotguns known as "punt guns" that were loaded with bird shot, a single blast could kill scores of shorebirds in a closely packed flock. Todays threats include pesticides and other contaminants and loss of wintering habitat.

Class—**Aves** (birds)
Order—**Charadriiformes** (shorebirds)
Family—**Scolopacidae** (sandpipers)

Pectoral Sandpiper *Calidris melanotos*	**Buff-breasted Sandpiper** *Calidris subruficollis*	**Wilson's Snipe** *Gallinago delicata*

Pectoral Sandpiper
Calidris melanotos

Size: 8.5 inches.

Abundance: Fairly common.

Migratory Status: Spring/fall migrant. Arrives as early as late March

Presumed range in TX

Variation: Male breeding plumage is darker brown and more vivid.

Habitat: Migrants use wet meadows, flooded fields, marshes and lake or pond shorelines, as well as mud flats.

Breeding: Nests on the ground in the arctic coastal plain. Nest is a shallow depression lined with grass. 4 eggs.

Natural History: Breeding males of this species perform displays in which they erect the feathers of the breast, droop the wings, raise the tail feathers, and emit soft "hooting" sounds. They are the only member of the sandpiper family that vocalizes in this manner. They also perform flight displays above the heads of grounded females. These birds are remarkable travelers that breed in the high arctic and winter in the "Pampas" region of southern South America. Some individuals will cross the Arctic Ocean to breed in Siberia, then migrate back to South America, a round-trip journey of over 18,000 miles each year! The food is mostly small mud-dwelling invertebrates. In Texas this species is most likely to be seen during migration in flooded crop fields in agricultural regions or open areas where receding waters leave mud flats.

Buff-breasted Sandpiper
Calidris subruficollis

Size: 7.5 inches.

Abundance: Rare.

Migratory Status: Migrant. April/ May and August/ September.

Presumed range in TX

Variation: Juvenile birds are similar to adults but tend to be paler on the breast.

Habitat: Favors dry habitats. Likes short grass fields, prairies, pastures, golf courses, sod farms, etc.

Breeding: Nest is a shallow scrape on the tundra. Lays 3 to 4 eggs. Has elaborate courtship behavior.

Natural History: Males perform breeding displays that consist of spreading wings and leaping and fluttering. These displays usually occur in a confined area (known as a Lek). They are one of the few sandpipers that exhibit this behavior. These birds are great travelers. They winter in the pampas region of southern South America and fly to the shores of the Arctic Ocean for breeding in the spring. Most transit through the US in the great plains region, but in fall a few will move southward through the eastern half of the country. Their tame behavior and unusual tendency to return to a wounded flock member made them easy targets for market hunting in the late 1800s. This, coupled with the destruction of the native American prairies devastated this species and they have never fully recovered. Today they are one of our rarest sandpipers.

Wilson's Snipe
Gallinago delicata

Size: 10.5 inches.

Abundance: Fairly common.

Migratory Status: Winter resident and spring/fall migrant.

Presumed range in TX

Variation: No sexual or seasonal plumage differences.

Habitat: Mudflats, flooded grassy fields, marshes, river bars, ditches, temporary pools and grassy pond banks.

Breeding: Nesting takes place well to north of Texas. Lays 4 eggs in nest on a hummock within marsh or swamp.

Natural History: As with other members of the sandpiper family, the beak of the Wilson's Snipe contains sensory pits near the tip which helps to locate invertebrate prey hidden in the mud. It also shares the Woodcock's rearward positioned eyes for watching behind and above while feeding. This is another highly camouflaged species that is nearly invisible when immobile. It is one of the most common and widespread members of the sandpiper family that often relies on its cryptic coloration when approached. Sitting quietly until nearly trod upon, it will burst from the grass with a twisting, erratic flight while emitting a raspy call. Like the Woodcock, the Wilson's Snipe is regarded as a game bird, but few people hunt them. Their populations have been negatively impacted by loss of wetland habitats. Fairly common but easily overlooked.

Class—**Aves** (birds)

Order—**Charadriiformes** (shorebirds)

Family—**Scolopacidae** (sandpipers)

Short-billed Dowitcher *Limnodromus griseus*	**Long-billed Dowitcher** *Limnodromus scolopaceus*	**Woodcock** *Scolopax minor*

Size: 11 inches.

Abundance: Fairly common.

Migratory Status: Winter resident and migrant.

Presumed range in TX

Variation: See photos above.

Habitat: In inland migrations Short-billed Dowitchers use mud flats and lake shores. They also use coastal habitats.

Breeding: Breeds in bog and muskeg habitats of northern Canada and Alaska. Nest is on the ground. Lays four eggs.

Natural History: This is a long-distance migrant that winters from the gulf coast to northern South America. In spring they fly all the way to the arctic circle where the boreal forest begins to transit into tundra. Here among the stunted remnants of northern forests they breed, nest, and rear their young before flying south in early fall. Dowitchers feed by probing the mud with their exceptionally long bill. When feeding they insert and withdraw the bill rapidly in a "sewing machine" motion. Distinguishing between the Short-billed and Long-billed Dowitchers is difficult. First of all, bill length is not a factor in making an identification because the bill length varies between male and female of both species, resulting in significant overlap of bill lengths. In breeding plumage the Short-billed has more pronounced dark barring on the flanks. In winter plumage they are even more similar. See photos of both above.

Size: 11.5 inches.

Abundance: Fairly common.

Migratory Status: Winter resident across southern and western Texas.

Presumed range in TX

Variation: See photos above.

Habitat: Lakes, marshes, ponds, and flooded fields inland. Will also use coastal marshes (both salt and brackish).

Breeding: Nests in the arctic slope of Alaska and Siberia. Nest is built in marsh grasses. Four eggs are typical.

Natural History: Nearly identical to the Short-billed Dowitcher. Distinguishing between the two in the field is difficult even for experts. In spite of the name, the length of the bill is not a good identification characteristic. The Long-billed is slightly larger at 11.5 inches. It migrates earlier in the spring and later in the fall than the Short-billed. It also is more likely to be seen in inland habitats during migration while the Short-billed favors stopping in coastal areas. Like many shorebirds, both species of Dowitcher were heavily hunted during the days of market hunting. At that time, it was not known that the two similar Dowitchers constituted two distinct species. The existence of two species was not finally confirmed until 1950. Although both species have recovered from the lows experienced during the great slaughter of shorebirds in the late1800s, their populations are still well below historical numbers.

Size: 11 inches.

Abundance: Uncommon.

Migratory Status: Mainly a winter resident. A few may be year-round.

Presumed range in TX

Variation: Females are larger.

Habitat: Swamps, regenerative woodlands, thickets, and weedy fields in bottomlands or uplands with moist soils.

Breeding: Nest is on the ground and not concealed. Lays 4 eggs as early as late February.

Natural History: The Woodcock is unique among American sandpipers in that it is strictly an inland species. It is also the only member of its family that breeds widely throughout the Eastern Temperate Forest Level I Ecoregion. Woodcock are known for their elaborate courtship flights that consist of an upward twisting corkscrew accompanied by a twittering call. The long beak is used to probe moist soils for invertebrates. Among its unique features are a flexible upper bill that aids in extracting the favorite food, earthworms, and eyes which are situated far back on the head, allowing for backward vision while feeding. One of the most remarkably cryptic of the sandpipers, Woodcocks are nearly impossible to detect when motionless on the forest floor. Although their nests are often in the open, brooding Woodcock will remain motionless even when closely approached, as their cryptic colors render them invisible.

Class—**Aves** (birds)

Order—**Charadriiformes** (shorebirds)

Family—**Laridae** (gulls & terns)

Laughing Gull *Leucophaeus atricilla*	**Bonapartes Gull** *Chroicocephalus philadelphia*	**Ringed-billed Gull** *Larus delawarensis*

 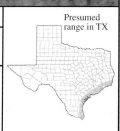

Laughing Gull	Bonapartes Gull	Ringed-billed Gull
Size: 16.5 inches.	**Size:** 13.5 inches.	**Size:** 17.5 inches.
Abundance: Common.	**Abundance:** Fairly common.	**Abundance:** Very common.
Migratory Status: Year-round non-migratory resident.	**Migratory Status:** Winter resident and migrant.	**Migratory Status:** Mostly a winter resident in Texas.

Presumed range in TX

Variation: Seasonal plumage variations (see photos above).

Habitat: These are primarily coastal birds that sometimes wander inland.

Breeding: Nests in colonies along the Atlantic and Gulf Coasts. Nests are built on the ground in salt marshes or islands. 3 eggs is typical.

Natural History: Although they are commonly seen in a variety of habitats as much as 60 miles inland, they are quite rare in the interior of the continent. These gulls are much more tied to the coasts and are quite common and familiar along both the Atlantic and Gulf coasts. Following breeding, some birds may follow major river systems well into the continent and a few make it into the interior of the continent. Likewise some will migrate northward along the Atlantic Coast as far as New England in summer. Like many gulls they exhibit seasonal plumage changes as well as age related (ontogenetic) plumage changes. For instance, it takes three years for the Laughing Gull to obtain the characteristic black hood worn in summer plumage. These are apparently long-lived birds with a longevity record of nineteen years.

Variation: Summer plumage has all black head (not usually seen in Texas).

Habitat: Frequents large rivers and larger lakes but also coastal habitats.

Breeding: The only gull that nests in trees, using conifers bordering remote lakes in Canada and Alaska. Typically lays 3 eggs.

Natural History: Many people tend to lump all gull species together and refer to them all as "seagulls." Most species, however, including the Bonaparte's Gull, are often inland birds during the breeding season. Like other gulls, many Bonaparte's Gulls will spend the winter along America's coastlines and sometimes far out to sea. Small to moderately large flocks can be seen on inland rivers and lakes throughout the winter. In Texas they may also be seen around harbors, coastal bays and beaches. One of our smaller gulls, they feed mostly on small fish such as shad and shiners, but like other gulls they are highly opportunistic feeders and will eat a wide variety of insects and other invertebrates. Unlike other gull species however, they are not typically seen around towns or dumps. They are widespread in winter and can be seen on inland lakes.

Variation: Juveniles are brownish gray and have greenish legs and bill.

Habitat: Uses both coastal and inland aquatic habitats. Lakes, rivers, shores.

Breeding: Nests in inland areas well to the north in Canada and northern US. Nest is on the ground on sandbars or rocky beaches. Lays 2 to 4 eggs.

Natural History: The Ring-billed Gull is one of the most common and widespread gull species in America. Most population estimates put their number in the millions, and they may be increasing. This is the gull commonly seen around inland lakes in summer and along coastal beaches in winter. They are also seen in urban parking lots or hanging around fast food restaurants ready to swoop in and grab a dropped french fry. They can be common in garbage dumps and may be seen foraging with starlings and other urban birds around dumpsters. These are highly gregarious birds that travel in flocks and nest in colonies. Food is almost anything, from carrion to insects, fish, rodents, earthworms, and human refuse. In Texas they are most common in winter, but some may linger and be seen into summer.

Class—**Aves** (birds)

Order—**Charadriiformes** (shorebirds)

Family—**Laridae** (gulls & terns)

Herring Gull *Larus argentatus*	**Franklin's Gull** *Leucophaeus pipixcan*	**Black Tern** *Chlidonias niger*

Size: 25 inches.

Abundance: Uncommon.

Migratory Status: Mostly a winter resident in Texas.

Presumed range in TX

Size: 14.5 inches.

Abundance: Uncommon.

Migratory Status: Seasonal migrant. April/May and Oct./Nov.

Presumed range in TX

Size: 9.75 inches.

Abundance: Fairly common.

Migratory Status: Seasonal migrant and summer resident.

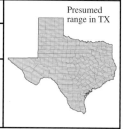
Presumed range in TX

Variation: Highly variable as juvenile. Younger birds are dark brownish gray with dark eyes and get lighter with age. Males are larger than females.

Variation: Seasonal plumage variation. In winter birds (and juveniles) the black hood is replaced by white with large gray smudge behind the eye.

Variation: In winter and in juvenile birds the dramatic black color of the breast and belly is replaced by white. Transitional birds are blotched.

Habitat: Coastlines, offshore islands, barrier islands, beaches, and shorelines in general. Both salt and freshwater.

Habitat: Migrants use lakes, rivers, marshes, flooded fields and pastures. Almost always seen in flocks.

Habitat: Habitat in is shallow, freshwater marshes, salt marshes and tidal mud flats.

Breeding: Nest is on the ground in a bowl shaped scrape lined with vegetation. 2 or 3 eggs are laid.

Breeding: Breeds in marshes in the great plains of Canada and north central US. Lays 2 to 4 eggs.

Breeding: Nesting is in marshes in the northern US and Canada. Nest may be a scrape or floating platform. 2 to 3 eggs.

Natural History: Like the smaller Ring-billed Gull, the Herring Gull is an opportunistic feeder that will eat almost anything, including human garbage. This fact may account in part for their population rebound in recent decades. Like other gull species, they are gregarious and they often nest in large colonies. Only about 50 percent of the young gulls hatched each year reach adulthood, but the species seems to be thriving. Their numbers were drastically reduced during the 1800s but they have recovered completely and may be more numerous now than in historic times. The presence of man-made garbage dumps that serve as a smorgasbord for these birds may explain their recent population expansion. They are widespread in their distribution and are common on both of America's coastlines.

Natural History: Adults in breeding plumage have a faint pinkish blush on the breast and belly feathers. These breeding birds pass through the state in spring and early summer, and re-appear during southward migration in the fall. Fall birds don't have the pinkish blush on the breast and may also lack the black hood. They mature slowly and it takes three years to achieve the mature adult plumage shown in the photo above. Franklin's Gull is an opportunistic feeder that will eat both plant and animal matter. Most foods are invertebrates (insects, worms, crustaceans, etc.). While most people think of gulls as birds of the coastlines (i.e. "Seagulls"), the Franklin's is an inland species for much of the year. They do spend the winter along the Pacific coast of South America.

Natural History: Winters along coastlines from Central America to northern South America. There is a European subspecies that winters in Africa. Like most terns these birds are highly social and usually seen in flocks. Unlike other terns, however, they feed heavily on insects, especially in summer. This is the only inland tern seen in Texas that has a dark breast and belly. Although the number of Black Terns today is estimated to be in the hundreds of thousands, this figure is paltry compared to the size of the population that existed before modern agricultural practices destroyed much of their breeding habitat. These birds are mainly a seasonal migrant in Texas but some will be seen in the state through the summer. They will nest far to the north in northern plains states, the Great Lakes, and Canada.

Class—**Aves** (birds)

Order—**Charadriiformes** (shorebirds)

Family—**Laridae** (gulls & terns)

Least Tern *Sterna antillarum*	Common Tern *Sterna hirundo*	Forster's Tern *Sterna forsteri*

Size: 9 inches.

Abundance: Fairly common.

Migratory Status: Summer on the coast. Migrant elsewhere.

Presumed range in TX

Variation: No variation in Texas. Birds that nest on coasts may be a distinct subspecies from inland nesters.

Habitat: Beaches and dunes are the main habitat, both in summer and winter. Also uses islands on inland rivers. May frequent inland lakes in summer.

Breeding: Nest is a scrape on sand with 2 to 3 eggs. May nest near other shorebird species.

Natural History: The Least Tern is, as its name implies, our smallest tern species. They are widespread in distribution along America's coastlines and a distinct population also nests inland on major rivers in the middle of the continent. All Least Terns winter along southern coastlines and some as far south as the Caribbean and Central America. In the 1800s these birds were killed and skinned to adorn womens hats. This bird's habitat (sandy beaches and dunes) is also highly valued real estate for humans. Thus coastal development is a major threat to the species today. Until recently, inland nesting populations were federally endangered. Some local coastal populations remain seriously threatened. The food is mostly small fishes, usually caught in shallow waters. They will also eat crustaceans and insects.

Size: 15 inches.

Abundance: Uncommon.

Migratory Status: Seasonal migrant and rare winter resident.

Presumed range in TX

Variation: First year and winter birds have white foreheads and black bill. White on forehead reduced on second year.

Habitat: Migrating birds usually associate with major rivers and large lakes. Islands and dunes are frequently used. Also seen on Florida beaches in winter.

Breeding: Nests mostly in Canada and along the northern Atlantic coastline. Lays 2 or 3 eggs.

Natural History: The Common Tern is well known to conservationists. They are symbolic of the fight to save many of America's bird species from wanton slaughter. From the early European settlement of North America to the late 1800s, unregulated over-hunting of America's wildlife nearly wiped out many species. Millions of herons, egrets, waterfowl, and shorebirds were killed for food and for the millinery trade. At the same time, America's large mammal species also suffered dramatic population declines. Today many wildlife species, including terns, have recovered dramatically, but tern populations are still below historical numbers nationwide. Common Tern nesting colonies situated in coastal areas are in many states now afforded strict protections.

Size: 14 inches.

Abundance: Fairly common.

Migratory Status: Winter resident and seasonal migrant.

Presumed range in TX

Variation: Exhibits both seasonal and age-related plumage variations (see photos above).

Habitat: Marshes. Both fresh and salt. Also beaches and coastlines. May also use inland rivers and lakes in in winter.

Breeding: Breeds mostly on inland marshes in the center of the continent. 1 to 4 eggs in nest of matted vegetation.

Natural History: Forster's Terns can be seen statewide in Texas, usually frequenting the states major river systems and large impoundments or natural lakes. They are also common on beaches. They are sometimes seen in the company of gulls and other tern species, especially in winter along the coastlines of Texas where gulls and terns can both be common. These medium-size terns feed almost exclusively on small fish that are captured by diving from above. When "fishing" they fly back and forth over water with the bill pointed downward, and plunge headlong into the water. They are graceful fliers that sometimes hover when schools of fish are located. Although they may be seen almost anywhere in the state during migration, they are most common along the gulf coast in winter.

Class—**Aves** (birds)

Order—**Charadriiformes** (shorebirds)

Family—**Laridae** (gulls & terns)

Royal Tern *Thalasseus maximus*	Sandwich Tern *Thalasseus sandvicensis*	Caspian Tern *Hydroprogne caspia*

Royal Tern
Thalasseus maximus

Size: 20 inches.

Abundance: Fairly common.

Migratory Status: Year-round resident on the gulf coast.

Presumed range in TX

Variation: Forehead turns white in winter and black crest has white speckling. In summer both are solid black.

Habitat: A coastal species that can be seen on gulf beaches of the state. May move a short way up rivers, creeks.

Breeding: Breeds in large colonies on barrier islands or remote beaches and dunes. Usually lays a single egg.

Natural History: This is one of the more commonly seen large terns on Texas beaches. It is surpassed in size only by the very similar appearing Caspian Tern, from which the Royal Tern can be differentiated by its bright orange bill (more reddish in the Caspian Tern). Most food is caught by "plunge diving" from heights of up to 30 feet. Fish and shrimp are two of the main foods consumed. Most foraging is done in shallow waters and often in bays or estuaries and tidal areas. Never feeds in fresh water but may travel long distances up and down the coast when feeding. Very large flocks will gather when schools of prey are located. Often these flocks will include pelicans, gulls, and other tern species. Threats include entanglement in fishing line and nets and ingesting of baited hooks or even artificial lures. Lives over twenty-five years.

Sandwich Tern
Thalasseus sandvicensis

Size: 15 inches.

Abundance: Uncommon.

Migratory Status: Year-round resident on the gulf coast.

Presumed range in TX

Variation: Forehead turns white in winter and black crest has white speckling. In summer both are solid black.

Habitat: A coastal species that frequents beaches, boat docks and pilings. Rarely more than a mile from shore.

Breeding: Most nesting is on barrier islands. Nest is a shallow scrape. Colony nester. 1 or 2 eggs is typical.

Natural History: This is one of the most recognizable of our tern species. Its black bill with a bright yellow tip is unique among Texas terns. Found throughout the Gulf of Mexico coastline and ranges as far north as the Delmarva Peninsula in summer. Can also be found throughout the gulf coast and the Caribbean as well as coastal areas of Central and South America. They are an uncommon breeding bird, but several breeding colonies are known to exist in the state. Most breeding colonies in the US are along the western gulf coastal region from Louisiana through Texas. Declined significantly during millinery trade. Severe storms that can destroy ephemeral barrier island breeding sites are a modern threat. The most pressing human threat may be the robbing of eggs from the nest by people in the Caribbean and South America.

Caspian Tern
Hydroprogne caspia

Size: 21 inches.

Abundance: Uncommon.

Migratory Status: Winter on the coast, migrant elsewhere.

Presumed range in TX

Variation: In winter birds the black cap becomes mottled with white. Juveniles are similar to winter adults.

Habitat: Mainly coastal birds in winter, they use rivers, large lakes, and marshes in migration.

Breeding: North American populations nest on large bodies of water in the interior of the continent. 1 to 3 eggs.

Natural History: The worlds largest tern and also the most widespread. Found all over the world, the Caspian Tern breeds on every continent except Antarctica. Despite its wide range it is not as common in North America as many other terns. Feeds almost entirely on fish. Feeds by hovering and diving. When diving, often submerges completely. Food is mostly fish. This is the only large tern regularly seen inland. Nesting occurs on the Great Lakes and on large lakes in Canada. They are found along the southern coastlines and in winter tend to stay along the coasts. In Texas they are seen throughout the gulf coast in winter and as migrant they may be seen in the eastern half of the state. Nesting has been recorded in the northeast on eastern Lake Ontario and northern Lake Champlain. These large terns are known to live up to twenty-six years.

Class—**Aves** (birds)

Order—**Charadriiformes** (shorebirds)	Order—**Gaviiformes** (loons)	Order—**Podicipediformes** (grebes)
Family—**Haematopus** (gulls & terns)	Family—**Gaviidae**	Family—**Podicipedidae**
American Oystercatcher *Haematopus palliatus*	**Common Loon** *Gavia immer*	**Least Grebe** *Tachybaptus dominicus*

Summer

Winter

Size: 17 inches.  Presumed range in TX	**Size:** 32 inches.  Presumed range in TX	**Size:** 9.5 inches.  Presumed range in TX
Abundance: Uncommon.	**Abundance:** Uncommon.	**Abundance:** Uncommon.
Migratory Status: A year-round resident along the coast.	**Migratory Status:** Winter resident on the gulf coast.	**Migratory Status:** Year-round in south Texas. Summer in east Texas.

Variation: On young chicks the bill is not fully developed until about 6 weeks.

Habitat: Habitat is beaches and dunes primarily. Barrier Islands are a favorite habitat. Winter habitat includes mud flats and salt marshes.

Breeding: Nest is a scrape on bare sand, gravel or shell. Lays 3 eggs. Most nests in Texas are on the southern coast.

Natural History: The common name Oystercatcher aptly describes the feeding habits of this unusual species. The laterally flattened bill is adapted for prying open the shells of mollusks like oysters and mussels. The technique involves stalking through shallows in search of mollusks with shells open and quickly inserting the blade-like bill into the open bivalve. It then stabs with the bill until the abducter muscle is severed, allowing the shell to be pried open and the contents extracted. This species is completely dependent upon beaches and coastal dunes as habitat. Human encroachment and coastal development have ravaged these habitats for decades and today this is one of America's most threatened natural habitats. In the year 2000, a population census revealed the entire population of American Oystercatchers to be only around 10,000 birds.

Variation: Exhibits significant seasonal plumage changes. See photos above.

Habitat: Highly aquatic. In inland areas the Common Loon lives on lakes but in Texas they are usually seen along the coasts in winter.

Breeding: Nests is built on small islands in northern lakes. Usually lays 2 eggs. Chicks often ride on adult's back.

Natural History: On lakes and marshes in the far north, the call of the Common Loon echoes through the wilderness. The sound is so distinctive and unique that it has inspired many poetic depictions. "Haunting," "ethereal," and "lonely" are words that are often used in conjunction with describing its yodeling cry that can carry for a great distance. They call both day and night on the breeding grounds in the northern half of the continent, but they are rarely heard calling on their winter range. Remarkable swimmers, they dive beneath the surface and propel themselves through the water with their powerful webbed feet. Fish are the main food item. Their legs are positioned so far back as to be almost useless on land. In Texas they are winter residents along the coast. Migrants may be seen statewide on rivers and lakes.

Variation: Adults are dark gray, juveniles are lighter, more brownish.

Habitat: Heavily vegetated wetlands, ponds and lakes. River swamps and brackish water marshes are also used and will sometimes use small ponds.

Breeding: The floating nest is of aquatic plants and anchored to standing vegetation. 3 to 5 eggs.

Natural History: A neotropical species that ranges northward into south Texas. They are common in wetlands throughout much of Latin America but are less common within their Texas range. This species can be difficult to observe due to its small size and tendency to stay hidden among emergent aquatic plants. While they are mainly restricted to south Texas they may rarely move north in summer into some areas in the eastern part of the state. Baby Least Grebes are quite precocious and can swim almost immediately after hatching. They will soon follow their mother around while foraging but tend to return to the nest for resting for the first couple of weeks of their lives. They are also known to ride on their mothers' backs at times in the manner of other grebes and loons. Sometimes hides by submerging with just the bill exposed for breathing,

Class—**Aves** (birds)

Order—**Podicipediformes** (grebes)

Family—**Podicipedidae**

Pied-billed Grebe *Podilymbus podiceps*	**Horned Grebe** *Podiceps auritus*	**Eared Grebe** *Podiceps nigricollis*

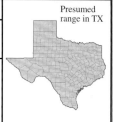

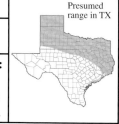

Size: 13 inches.

Abundance: Uncommon.

Migratory Status: Winter on the coast, migrant elsewhere.

Presumed range in TX

Variation: Winter birds are grayer and lack the prominent dark ring on bill.

Habitat: Completely aquatic, the Pied-billed Grebe uses everything from large lakes to small farm ponds. Also open water areas of swamps and marshes.

Breeding: Nests on floating platform of aquatic vegetation among emergent plants in marsh. Four to eight eggs are laid.

Natural History: This little grebe evades potential threats by submerging and they sometimes swim with just the head sticking out the water. They feed on a wide variety of small fish and other aquatic vertebrates as well as crustaceans and insects. This is probably the most widespread and common grebe in North America and they range from coast to coast. They may be seen year-round in Texas but their numbers increase in winter with migrants from farther north. They can be seen all winter across the southern half of the US, but tend to concentrate along the gulf coast in winter. Their summer range extends well into Canada. These little grebes are almost never seen in flight as they escape threats by diving and swimming. When threatened, they can swim for long distances underwater.

Size: 14 inches.

Abundance: Uncommon.

Migratory Status: A winter resident in east Texas. Rare migrant elsewhere.

Presumed range in TX

Variation: Winter plumage (shown) is usually seen in Texas.

Habitat: In winter this species uses the larger lakes as well as large marshes with open water. Also coastal/intercoastal areas. Not usually on ponds.

Breeding: Nests on floating platform among emergent vegetation. Nesting is far to the north of Texas, mostly in Canada. 5 to 7 eggs.

Natural History: As is the case with other grebes (and loons), their adaptations for an aquatic lifestyle include the legs being positioned far back on the body. The legs can also be flared outward to a remarkable degree to facilitate underwater swimming maneuvers. As a result of this adaptation, these birds are very clumsy on land and walk with difficulty. Breeding birds (not usually seen in Texas) are handsomely marked with chestnut neck and flanks and golden brown head stripe that flares out to form "horns." The specimen shown above is in winter plumage and is typical of fall migrants and winter residents. Food is small fish, crustaceans, insects, etc. Their summer range is in Canada and Alaska, but their winter range includes both coastal and inland regions of the eastern third of the state.

Size: 12.5 inches.

Abundance: Fairly common.

Migratory Status: Winter resident in Texas. Migrant only in Panhandle.

Presumed range in TX

Variation: Significant seasonal plumage variation (see photos above).

Habitat: While wintering in Texas they are most common in shallow coastal habitats (marshes, bays, estuaries). Will also use large lakes in inland areas.

Breeding: Nesting is in shallow lakes and ponds throughout the Rocky Mountain west from northern AZ and NM well into northwestern Canada. Up to 8 eggs.

Natural History: After wintering in the southwestern US, Mexico, and northern Central America the Eared Grebe moves to breeding areas in the central and northern Rockies for the summer. In the fall they migrate to saline lakes and fatten up on brine shrimp and brine flies. Utah's Great Salt Lake and California's Mono Lake are two of the main areas for this annual feast. This species is known to biologists for the remarkable physiological changes it undergoes throughout the year. When feasting at brine lakes in the fall their breast muscles that are used in flight decrease to the point where they become flightless. This change makes room for a significant increase in their digestive organs needed to accommodate the massive food intake. The process is then reversed before fall migration.

Class—**Aves** (birds)
Order—**Podicipediformes** (grebes)
Family—**Podicipedidae**

Western Grebe *Aechmophorus occidentalis*	**Clark's Grebe** *Aechmophorus clarkii*

Winter

Summer

Size: 25 inches.	**Size:** 25 inches.
Abundance: Uncommon to rare in Texas.	**Abundance:** Very rare winter resident and migrant in western Texas.
Variation: No sexual dimorphism and very little seasonal plumage change. Non-breeding birds characteristic black and white plumage is less sharply defined.	**Variation:** No sexual dimorphism and very little seasonal plumage change. Non-breeding birds' characteristic black and white plumage is less sharply defined.

Presumed range in TX

Presumed range in TX

Migratory Status: Winter resident in the Trans-Pecos region and a rare migrant west of the Trans-Pecos and Panhandle.	**Migratory Status:** Winter resident in the Trans-Pecos region and migrant in the Panhandle.
Habitat: Freshwater lakes and marshes with open water areas are the main habitat. In the fall and winter they are also seen in salt and brackish water habitats along the west coast. Their range in North America is generally from the Great Plains westward to the Pacific coast, except for the desert regions of Arizona an New Mexico.	**Habitat:** Summer habitat is on large lakes and marshes throughout the Rocky Mountain west and in the northwestern Great Plains. In winter most move to the Pacific Coast where they inhabit bays, estuaries, and coastal marshes. A few will winter in western Texas, especially on Balmorhea Reservoir in the Trans-Pecos region.
Breeding: The nest is built in shallow water amid cattails or reeds near the edge of open water. Nest is platform of vegetation that rises above the high water mark. Two or three eggs are laid. Baby grebes will ride on the mother's back.	**Breeding:** The nest is built in shallow water amid cattails or reeds near the edge of open water. Nest is platform of vegetation that rises above the high water mark. Two or three eggs are laid. Baby grebes will ride on the mother's back.
Natural History: Both the Western and Clark's Grebes are famous for their elaborate, perfectly synchronized mating rituals. The mating ritual includes paired grebes running side-by-side across the top of the water and "dancing" face-to -face while holding aquatic plants in the bill. Most Grebe species migrate at night and the Western Grebe is no exception. Their food is mostly fish but they will eat almost any type of small aquatic vertebrate as well as some invertebrate prey.	**Natural History:** Very similar to the Western Grebe, and in fact until 1985 the two were considered conspecific. The ranges of the two species overlap considerably throughout the western US. Distinguishing between the two species requires looking closely at the head. On the Western Grebe the black cap extends below the eye on the side of the face. On the Clark's Grebe the white on the extends above the eye. Clark's has a bright yellow bill, Western's is greenish-yellow.

Class—**Aves** (birds)

Order—**Anseriformes** (waterfowl)

Family—**Anatidae** (ducks, geese & swans)

Snow Goose	Canada Goose	Greater White-fronted Goose
Chen caerulescens	*Branta canadensis*	*Anser albifrons*

Size: 30 inches.

Abundance: Common.

Migratory Status: Winter migrant.

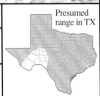
Presumed range in TX

Variation: Two distinct color phases occur (see above). Juveniles are gray.

Habitat: During migration through the the central US these geese are mostly seen in very large agricultural crop fields. Summer habitat is Arctic Tundra.

Breeding: Nests only in the high Arctic Tundra of Canada and Alaska.

Natural History: Snow Goose populations have exploded in the last few decades, probably as a result of having so much habitat and food available throughout migration routes and on wintering grounds. The grain fields of Midwestern and southern United States provides more than an adequate food source. Mid-continent populations are expanding their migration routes eastward from their historical range west of the Mississippi River. Today they can be found east of the Mississippi every winter and they are sometimes seen as far east as the Appalachian Plateau. There is also an east coast population that winters along the Atlantic coast from New Jersey to the Carolinas. Snow Geese usually occur in huge flocks numbering thousands of birds. Tens of thousands may congregate on refuges. The **Ross's Goose** (*C. rossii*) is a is a smaller version of the Snow Goose that may rarely be seen in the company of regular Snow Geese.

Size: 36 to 45 inches.

Abundance: Fairly common.

Migratory Status: Winter migrant.

Presumed range in TX

Variation: Subspecies vary significantly in size with light and dark morphs.

Habitat: Habitat includes all types of aquatic situations, from urban parks to remote and inaccessible marshes, swamps or beaver ponds.

Breeding: Nests above the water line but near water. 4 to 8 eggs is typical.

Natural History: This is the most recognized wild goose in America, due in large part to the fact that tame and semi-tame populations are found in parks and on rivers, ponds, and lakes in both urban and rural regions. Resident Canada Geese are numerous, but their numbers are swelled dramatically during winter, as birds from farther north visit the lower 48 for either a brief stopover or a months long stay. The characteristic "V formation" of Canada Geese in flight is a familiar sight and their musical, honking call is to many a symbol of wild America. They are heavily hunted throughout America both for sport and for food. They are long-lived birds and have been known to survive over forty years. There are several races of Canada Goose and they vary in size and in the shade of darkness in color. An identical dwarf species of goose called the **Cackling Goose** (*B. hutchinsii*) is the size of a Mallard. It sometimes occurs within flocks of Canada Geese.

Size: 28 inches.

Abundance: Fairly common.

Migratory Status: Winter migrant.

Presumed range in TX

Variation: Juveniles lack white on the face and black on belly.

Habitat: When migrating they will use large agricultural fields for feeding and roost on open water or bays in large lakes.

Breeding: Breeds in the Arctic Coastal Plain. Average clutch size is 4 or 5.

Natural History: Although they may migrate throughout much of the state, White-fronted Geese are found in their greatest numbers in the eastern half of the state. While they are holarctic in distribution, they are not as common in North America as the Canada Goose or Snow Goose. Most of the North American populations of these geese use the Mississippi and Central Flyways, but a smaller population occurs in the Pacific Flyway. Oddly, they are rarely seen in the Atlantic Flyway. Mississippi Flyway birds will usually winter along the gulf coast from Louisiana and Texas to northeastern Mexico. Central flyway birds are seen throughout the state but are rare in the Panhandle and Trans-Pecos regions. During migration small flocks may be seen traveling with larger flocks of Canada or Snow Geese, but they tend to segregate themselves when resting or feeding. Like the Snow Goose, they appear to be expanding their migration routes eastward.

Class—**Aves** (birds)

Order—**Anseriformes** (waterfowl)

Family—**Anatidae** (ducks, geese & swans)

Black-bellied Duck *Dendrocygna autumnalis*	**Fulvous Duck** *Dendrocygna bicolor*	**Ruddy Duck** *Oxyura jamaicensis*
		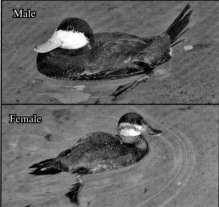

Size: 21 inches.

Abundance: Fairly common.

Migratory Status: Resident and migrant in south Texas.

Presumed range in TX

Variation: Juveniles have dark bills and are uniformly plumage.

Habitat: Wetlands of many types are used including freshwater swamps and marshes, natural lakes, salt and brackish water marshes, and coastal estuaries.

Breeding: Will use natural cavities in trees or sometimes nest on the ground. Breeds from spring to late summer. Clutch size averages about a dozen.

Natural History: This tropical and semi-tropical duck has expanded its range in the last century and it appears to be a thriving species. They seem to be moving farther north into eastern Texas and can also now be found in much of Louisiana and throughout the Florida peninsula. Black-bellied Ducks are fond of perching in trees and in fact the species is sometimes referred to as the "Black-bellied Tree Duck." They are also called Black-bellied Whistling Ducks, a reference to their call. The Black-bellied Duck is a new world species and is restricted in distribution to the Americas. They can be found from the southern US to Argentina. These ducks are mainly vegetarians and they feed mostly at night. Shallow water habitats are the main habitats used for feeding but they also feed on land.

Size: 19 inches.

Abundance: Fairly common.

Migratory Status: Mainly a summer resident. A few winter in south TX.

Presumed range in TX

Variation: Juveniles are less vividly colored than adults.

Habitat: Tends to favor coastal areas where the main habitat is marshlands. In regions where rice is grown, rice fields are an important habitat.

Breeding: The nest is usually constructed on mats of floating vegetation. 12 to 14 eggs is common. Precocial young can swim and dive immediately.

Natural History: Fulvous Ducks have expanded their breeding range in recent decades. They regularly wander north of the area shown on the map above and may expand their breeding range northward in the future. Their current migratory and breeding range in the US includes most of the gulf coast region. Rare wanderers have been recorded well to the north along the Atlantic coastline. They feed on plant material in shallow water habitats and in the western gulf (Louisiana and Texas) rice fields are a favorite foraging area. They range from the gulf coast of the US to South America and can also be found in Hawaii, east Africa, and parts of Asia. They sometimes roost in trees which accounts for their other common name, "Fulvous Tree Duck." Like the preceding species, their call is a whistle.

Size: 15 inches.

Abundance: Fairly common.

Migratory Status: Winter resident in most of the state.

Presumed range in TX

Variation: Sexually dimorphic. See photos above.

Habitat: Marshes, ponds, lakes, and to a lesser extent rivers. This is a true "Prairie Pothole" species and most summer in the northern plains.

Breeding: Nest is usually built in cattails or other aquatic vegetation. Nearly 90 percent of nesting occurs in the northern plains. 7 or 8 eggs is average.

Natural History: Ruddy Ducks are primarily western birds that range generally from the Great Plains to the west coast. Winter range includes most of the eastern US. A few may linger into summer on both the lower and upper Rio Grande. The larva of aquatic insects of the order Diptera (flies, mosquitoes, midges) are a primary food. Although these are small ducks, their eggs are quite large and are in fact the largest eggs (relative to body size) of any North American duck. Populations of ducks of all species including the Ruddy Duck are today well below historical numbers. But this species seems to be expanding its breeding range eastward into the Great Lakes region. About eighty percent of the population winters along the coasts, including the entire coast of Texas.

Class—**Aves** (birds)

Order—**Anseriformes** (waterfowl)

Family—**Anatidae** (ducks, geese & swans)

Cinnamon Teal *Spatula cyanoptera*	**Blue-winged Teal** *Spatula discors*	**Shoveler** *Spatula clypeata*

Cinnamon Teal
Spatula cyanoptera

Size: 16 inches.

Abundance: Common.

Migratory Status: Winter resident and seasonal migrant.

Presumed range in TX

Variation: Significant sexual dimorphism (see photos above).

Habitat: Large marshes in the western half of the state. Mainly a freshwater bird but will winter in brackish marshes.

Breeding: Nest is on the ground and well hidden in grasses or sedges. Like other ducks, they use down from their breast to line the nest. Up to 16 eggs.

Natural History: Most of America's duck species range throughout the continent. The Cinnamon Teal, however, is found only in the western half of North America. A distinct and separate population can be found in southern South America. Food items are a wide variety of aquatic plants and their seeds and many types of small aquatic invertebrates. They have a rather large bill which they will use to sieve tiny organism from the water in a manner similar to their relative the Shoveler. They are also closely related to the Blue-winged Teal and have been known to hybridize with that species. All three species on this page (Cinnamon Teal, Blue-winged Teal, and Shoveler) were until recently regarded as members of the genus *Anas* (a.k.a. "puddle ducks"). Most Cinnamon Teal winter in Mexico and they are found country-wide there in winter.

Blue-winged Teal
Spatula discors

Size: 15.5 inches.

Abundance: Common.

Migratory Status: Mostly a fall through spring resident.

Presumed range in TX

Variation: Significant sexual dimorphism (see photos above).

Habitat: Marshes, beaver ponds, bays, and other shallow water habitats. Uses mostly freshwater wetlands.

Breeding: Nest is concealed in dense vegetation near water but above high water line. Lays 6 to 12 eggs. Breeds mostly to the north of Texas.

Natural History: The food of this species is mostly plant material including algae and aquatic greenery. Many seeds and grains are also eaten, especially in winter when they converge on rice fields and other flooded agricultural areas in America's lower coastal plain. Breeding females will consume large amounts of invertebrates during the breeding season. These ducks are early fall migrators and one of the last to migrate back north in the spring. A few will linger well into late spring or even early summer. Many will winter as far south as South America, but substantial numbers can be seen along the lower coastal plain of North America all winter, including all of coastal Texas. Most breed and spend the summer on the central prairies of the US and Canada and some will nest as far north as Alaska. A few will nest in the Panhandle region.

Shoveler
Spatula clypeata

Size: 19 inches.

Abundance: Common.

Migratory Status: Winter resident statewide in Texas.

Presumed range in TX

Variation: Significant sexual dimorphism (see photos above).

Habitat: Prefers shallow habitats. Swamps, marshes, flooded fields, bays. Uses mostly freshwater habitats.

Breeding: Breeds in northern and western United States (including Alaska) and in Canada. Averages 10 to 12 eggs.

Natural History: The Shoveler's name is derived from the unique shape of its bill, which is a highly effective sieve for straining tiny organisms from water. They are often observed swimming along with the bill held under water or skimming the surface. Like several of America's duck species, the Shoveler is holarctic in distribution and breeds in Europe and Asia as well as North America. Eurasian birds winter southward to north Africa and the Pacific region. All ground nesting birds are vulnerable to mammalian predators and the Shoveler is no exception. Red Foxes and Mink are significant predators on the nesting females, while skunks are a major threat to the eggs. Shovelers nest in North America's "Prairie Pothole" region and during years of drought modern farming practices reduce cover for nesting ducks, increasing nest predation.

Class—**Aves** (birds)

Order—**Anseriformes** (waterfowl)

Family—**Anatidae** (ducks, geese & swans)

Gadwall *Mareca strepera*	American Widgeon *Mareca americana*	Mallard *Anas platyrhynchos*

Size: 20 inches.

Abundance: Common.

Migratory Status: Winter resident statewide in Texas.

Presumed range in TX

Variation: Significant sexual dimorphism (see photos above).

Habitat: Marshes and potholes of the great plains in summer. Uses all aquatic habitats in winter.

Breeding: Nests among thick vegetation near water, often on islands in marshes or lakes. Lays 7 to 12 eggs.

Natural History: Gadwalls breed and summer largely in the great plains region. In winter they are seen all across the southern half of America, with the greatest numbers wintering along the western gulf coast coastal plain of Texas and Louisiana. Populations of this duck can fluctuate significantly depending upon water levels in the prairies of Canada and the north-central US. Droughts and poor agricultural practices that eliminate habitat can cause populations to plummet. Conversely, good rainfall and good wildlife conservation practices by farmers have shown to be a real boon to this and many other duck species that depend on the marshes and potholes on the great plains for nesting habitat. Adult Gadwalls feed mostly on plant material. Ducklings rely heavily upon high protein invertebrates for growth and development.

Size: 19 inches.

Abundance: Fairly common.

Migratory Status: Winter resident statewide in Texas.

Presumed range in TX

Variation: Significant sexual dimorphism (see photos above).

Habitat: Winter range includes all types of aquatic habitats in the state (swamps, marshes, lakes, ponds, etc.).

Breeding: Nests near shallow freshwater wetlands and potholes mostly in the North American prairie. 3 to 12 eggs.

Natural History: The American Wigeon also goes by the name "Baldpate," a reference to the white crown of the male. This duck has a very similar old world counterpart, the Eurasian Wigeon, which ranges throughout much of Europe and Asia. American birds feed mostly on plant material, but females when breeding opt for a higher protein diet of invertebrates. One of the more northerly ranging members of the "puddle duck" group, some individuals will summer as far north as the Arctic coastal plain of Alaska. These ducks may be seen in Texas from November through March, but peak numbers occur in mid-winter. Some merely pass through the state headed to tropical regions, but many will stay throughout the winter. As with other puddle ducks, this species is susceptible to population declines during droughts.

Size: 23 inches.

Abundance: Common.

Migratory Status: Winter resident statewide in Texas.

Presumed range in TX

Variation: Significant sexual dimorphism (see photos above).

Habitat: Found in aquatic situations everywhere, from deserts to tundra to southern swamplands, ponds, lakes, etc.

Breeding: Nests on the ground in close proximity to water. Lays up to 13 eggs and will re-nest if nest is destroyed.

Natural History: By far the most familiar duck in America. The Mallard has been widely domesticated but it is also the most common wild duck in the United States. Many parks and public lakes around the country have semi-wild populations that are non-migratory. Highly adaptable, this is the most successful duck species in America, perhaps in the world. It is the source of all breeds of domestic duck except the Muscovey and they are thus an important food source for humans. They are also a highly regarded game bird and they are hunted throughout North America. They range throughout the northern half of the globe and their range in the western hemisphere closely coincides with the North American continent. Sometimes hybridizes with the Mexican Duck where their ranges overlap in Texas.

Class—**Aves** (birds)

Order—**Anseriformes** (waterfowl)

Family—**Anatidae** (ducks, geese & swans)

Mexican Duck *Anas diazi*	Mottled Duck *Anas fulvigula*	Pintail *Anas acuta*
		 Male Female

Size: 23 inches.

Abundance: Uncommon.

Migratory Status: Year-round resident in Texas.

Presumed range in TX

Variation: Sexes are alike. Similar to a very dark female Mallard.

Habitat: Mainly freshwater habitats including marshes, ponds, lakes, and slow moving rivers.

Breeding: Nest is on the ground and often some distance from open water. Up to 9 babies are led to the water by the mother.

Natural History: Until recently, the Mexican Duck was regarded as a subspecies of the ubiquitous Mallard. Some experts still consider that to be the correct taxonomic designation. Either way, this duck could be reasonably regarded as the Mexican equivalent of the North American Mallard. About 90 percent of its range is in Mexico, and its habits and natural history resembles that of the Mallard. Its range in Texas generally follows the Rio Grande River, but it also includes much of the Trans-Pecos region. In appearance it resembles a very dark female Mallard. It is also quite similar to the Mottled Duck and is known to hybridize with both those species. The easiest way to distinguish between the Mexican Duck and the Mottled Duck is by range. Female Mallards are not as dark.

Size: 22 inches.

Abundance: Fairly common.

Migratory Status: Year-round resident of coastal Texas.

Presumed range in TX

Variation: Sexual differences are weak. Female has black blotches on bill.

Habitat: Marshes and wet prairies are the primary habitat. Uses man-made wastewater treatment wetlands.

Breeding: Nests near water but often in overgrown fields or cattle pastures. Clutch size is 8 to 12 eggs typically. Breeds in Texas

Natural History: Mottled Ducks are closely related to both the Mallard and the Mexican Duck. The Mottled Duck is totally adapted to life in the deep south and along with the Mexican Duck is the only "puddle duck" species that does not migrate. Unlike most ducks, these birds are not seen in large flocks and are usually seen in pairs or in a family group consisting of the female and her brood. It also shows a definite preference for fresh water over saltwater habitats, although it may be found near the coast in freshwater situations. In Florida, this species is threatened by hybridization with captive reared Mallards that have been released or escaped. Continued development and subsequent loss of wetland habitat is also a threat. In appearance this species is very similar to the female Mallard.

Size: 25 inches.

Abundance: Fairly common.

Migratory Status: Winter resident throughout Texas.

Presumed range in TX

Variation: Significant sexual dimorphism. See photos above.

Habitat: Open country. Uses large wet prairies, salt marshes, estuaries, and bays. Summers on prairie potholes.

Breeding: Breeds in marshes, potholes, and tundra in the northern and western portions of the continent. 3 to 12 eggs. Does not breed in Texas.

Natural History: Northern Pintail populations are in decline. Modern agricultural practices on the great plains of the US and Canada are the greatest threat. They are also highly susceptible to droughts in the prairie regions, which limit breeding habitat. Food is mostly plant material but some aquatic invertebrates are also eaten. On wintering grounds, waste grain from farming operations has become an important food source. In recent decades the species has benefited from a number of conservation efforts by state and federal agencies as well as private organizations, most notably Ducks Unlimited, an organization funded by duck hunters. Conservation efforts that have recently benefited the species are reduced hunter harvest and changing agricultural practices in the prairie pothole region.

Class—**Aves** (birds)

Order—**Anseriformes** (waterfowl)

Family—**Anatidae** (ducks, geese & swans)

Green-winged Teal *Anas crecca*	**Wood Duck** *Aix sponsa*	**Redhead** *Aythya americana*

Green-winged Teal
Anas crecca

Size: 14 inches.

Abundance: Fairly common.

Migratory Status: Winter resident throughout Texas.

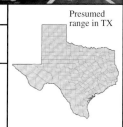 Presumed range in TX

Variation: Significant sexual variation. See photos above.

Habitat: Winter range includes all types of aquatic habitats in the state (swamps, marshes, lakes, ponds, etc.). Uses both fresh and brackish marshes.

Breeding: Nest is in dense vegetation in wetland habitats of the far north. 6 to 9 eggs are laid as early as May.

Natural History: This is the smallest of America's "puddle ducks," and also one of the more common. They range throughout the northern hemisphere, with a distinct subspecies being found in Eurasia. They are fast and agile fliers and flocks of Green-winged Teal move back and forth across the southern half of the continent all winter in response to weather patterns. Populations of this duck appear stable and may even be increasing. About 90 percent of the population breeds in Canada and Alaska where they favor river deltas and boreal wetlands over the typical "pothole" habitats used by many puddle ducks. Their remote nesting habitats are largely undisturbed by man, which may account in part for this species' abundance. As with many species, the increasing daylight hours of spring triggers migration and breeding instincts.

Wood Duck
Aix sponsa

Size: 18.5 inches.

Abundance: Common.

Migratory Status: Resident and seasonal migrant.

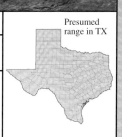 Presumed range in TX

Variation: Significant sexual dimorphism (see photos above).

Habitat: Beaver ponds, swamps, flooded woodlands, and farm ponds are among the favorite habitats. Even small creeks are frequently used.

Breeding: Nests in tree hollows and takes readily to artificial nest boxes. Lays about 8 to 12 eggs typically.

Natural History: Male Wood Ducks are one of the most brilliantly colored birds in America. The bulk of the Wood Duck population in America occurs in the forested eastern half of the country. Populations plummeted during the latter half of the nineteenth century as America's forests were felled and swamplands drained. Populations began to recover by the 1950s and today the species is thriving. Wood Ducks are widely hunted and make up a significant number of ducks killed by hunters annually. Although they are a small duck, they are considered by many as highly palatable. Although Wood Ducks are year-round residents in east Texas, their numbers are swelled each winter by birds that summered farther to the north and moved south in winter. Some birds seen in Texas in winter may have been hatched in Canada.

Redhead
Aythya americana

Size: 19 inches.

Abundance: Fairly common.

Migratory Status: Winter migrant/resident in Texas.

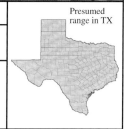 Presumed range in TX

Variation: Significant sexual variation. See photos above.

Habitat: Primarily a marshland species that alternates between prairie potholes and gulf coastal marshes. In migration they will use a variety of habitats.

Breeding: Breeds almost entirely in the "prairie pothole" region. Females often lay their eggs in other ducks' nests.

Natural History: An entirely North American species, the Redhead is mostly a vegetarian and feeds heavily on tubers and aquatic vegetation. Most Redhead's congregate in winter on the western gulf coast of Louisiana, Texas and northwest Mexico. In fact hundreds of thousands will concentrate in this region each winter. Here they feed mostly on the roots of Shoal grass. They will also eat some animal matter, mostly aquatic invertebrates. Redheads are easily decoyed and during the days of market hunting their populations suffered dramatic declines. Recovery in the last few decades has been significant and in a good year the population may reach a million birds. Reproductive success is often tied to weather conditions in the "Prairie Pothole" region of the Great Plains. Drought years result in poor production.

Class—**Aves** (birds)

Order—**Anseriformes** (waterfowl)

Family—**Anatidae** (ducks, geese & swans)

Canvasback *Aythya valisineria*	Lesser Scaup *Aythya affinis*	Ring-necked Duck *Aythya collaris*
 Male 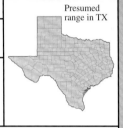 Female	 Male 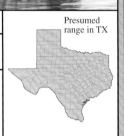 Female	 Male  Female

Size: 21 inches.

Abundance: Uncommon.

Migratory Status: Winter resident throughout most of state.

Presumed range in TX

Variation: Significant sexual variation. See photos above.

Habitat: Primarily a marshland species that alternates between prairie potholes in summer and gulf coastal marshes in winter. In migration uses lakes and marshes for resting and feeding.

Breeding: The large nest is built from grasses and hidden vegetation. Clutch size averages around 7 or 8.

Natural History: One of the most adept divers of the "Diving Ducks," Canvasbacks have been known to dive to a depth of 30 feet. Feeds mostly on plant material including roots and rhizomes, but will also eat mud-dwelling invertebrates. Strictly a North American species and one of the least common duck species in America. They are vulnerable to droughts, habitat loss (mostly from agriculture), and water pollution that can impact the abundance of aquatic food plants. The Canvasback population is closely monitored by the U.S. Fish and Wildlife Service and in years of low numbers hunting of this species may be banned. Even in years when hunting is allowed, the bag limits are typically very low. The species name (*valisineria*) is also the genus name for Water Celery, one its favorite foods.

Size: 16.5 inches.

Abundance: Fairly common.

Migratory Status: Winter resident throughout most of Texas.

Presumed range in TX

Variation: Sexually dimorphic. See photos above.

Habitat: Likes larger bodies of water and deeper water than many other ducks. Regularly uses large lakes and rivers in the state as well as flooded river bottoms.

Breeding: 8 to 10 eggs is typical. Nests in west-central US, Canada and in Alaska.

Natural History: These ducks are the most widespread and common of the "diving ducks." Diving ducks are capable of diving deeper and prefer deeper waters than the "puddle ducks." They are also more clumsy on land and need a running start on the water to get airborne. They thus favor larger lakes and rivers over small ponds and swamplands. They are known for forming large flocks in open water (called "rafts"). These rafts sometimes number in the thousands. A slightly larger version of the Lesser Scaup, known as the **Greater Scaup** (*Athya marila*) can also be seen in the northeastern part of the state in winter. The Greater Scaup, however, is a rare species in Texas. Both species like open water. The Greater Scaup tends to favor coastal areas and salt or brackish marshes in winter.

Size: 17 inches.

Abundance: Uncommon.

Migratory Status: Mainly a winter resident.

Presumed range in TX

Variation: Sexually dimorphic. See photos above

Habitat: Open water habitats including shallow bays and flooded river bottoms. Also uses open marshes and large rivers and lakes, where it tends to use mostly shallow-water areas.

Breeding: Nests in subarctic regions of Canada and the northern Rockies in the United States. Lays 6 to 14 eggs.

Natural History: Closely related to and very similar in appearance to the scaups, the Ring-necked Duck should be called the Ring-billed duck. Although there is a brownish ring around the neck of the male, it is only visible when the bird is in the hand. The broad white ring near the tip of the bill and the narrow white ring at the base of the bill are both readily discernible on birds in the field. Unlike its relatives the Scaups, which will feed on crustaceans, insects, and other aquatic invertebrates, the diet of the Ring-necked Duck is mostly vegetarian. Also unlike the Scaups, Ring-billed Ducks favor small lakes, ponds and swamps over large rivers and lakes. The Ring-necked Duck is an endemic North American species, but like most waterfowl it is prone to wander off the continent.

Class—**Aves** (birds)

Order—**Anseriformes** (waterfowl)

Family—**Anatidae** (ducks, geese & swans)

Bufflehead *Bucephala albeola*	**Common Goldeneye** *Bucephala clangula*	**Surf Scoter** *Melanitta perspicillata*

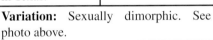

Size: 13.5 inches.

Presumed range in TX

Abundance: Fairly common.

Migratory Status: Winter resident/migrant in Texas.

Variation: Sexually dimorphic. See photo above.

Habitat: Most winter in saltwater habitats on the coast but a few overwinter on inland lakes and rivers. In summer they use boreal forests and parklands in Canada.

Breeding: Cavity nester. Nest is often an old woodpecker hole. Clutch size ranges from a few to over a dozen eggs.

Natural History: America's smallest of the diving ducks, the Bufflehead is one of the few duck species that will remain with the same mate year after year. Breeding pairs usually return to the same pond or marsh to breed each year as well. With the exception of some seeds, these ducks are mostly carnivorous, feeding on aquatic insects, crustaceans, and mollusks. Unlike the puddle ducks which often feed on the surface, the Bufflehead finds all its food by diving. Although they are often seen on deep water lakes, they feed in the shallows along the banks or in the backs of bays. Although rarely seen in large flocks, this is one of the few duck species that has actually increased in numbers in the last few decades. Due to their carnivorous feeding habits, they are not highly regarded as a food species.

Size: 18.5 inches.

Presumed range in TX

Abundance: Uncommon.

Migratory Status: Winter resident/winter migrant in Texas.

Variation: Significant sexual variation. See photos above. Juvenile like female.

Habitat: In winter this species uses large lakes and rivers inland. They are also fairly common in winter in coastal regions. In summer they are a bird of the boreal forests.

Breeding: Cavity nester that will use artificial nest boxes. May nest over a mile from water. 7 to 12 eggs.

Natural History: As with other diving ducks, the Common Goldeneye is an excellent swimmer that feeds by diving beneath the surface. They propel through the water using only the feet, with the wings held tight against the body. They are mostly carnivorous but they do eat some plant material in the form of tubers and seeds. Aquatic invertebrates are the main food and include (in order of importance) crustaceans, insects, and mollusks. Fish constitute only a small portion of the diet. Male Common Goldeneyes engage in a complex courtship display to attract females or reinforce the pair bond. These ducks are holearctic in distribution, breeding in boreal forests throughout the northern hemisphere. Although widely hunted, they are not regarded as a very palatable duck for eating.

Size: 20 inches.

Presumed range in TX

Abundance: Rare in Texas.

Migratory Status: Winter migrant on northeast gulf coast.

Variation: Significant sexual variation. See photos above.

Habitat: In winter the Surf Scoter uses coastlines. As implied by their name, they are often seen just offshore in ocean surf. In summer they move inland to lakes and rivers.

Breeding: Nests on the ground in northern Canada and Alaska. Nest is in the vicinity of water but on land.

Natural History: Feeds mostly on mollusks (i.e. clams, mussels, marine snails) gleaned from the bottom by diving in relatively shallow water in the surf zone. They also will eat crabs and various marine invertebrates (worms and sea squirts), as well as some small fish. Aquatic vegetation is consumed to a lesser extent. Young eat insects. This species is a northern duck that is fairly common along the northern portions of both coasts of North America. Their summer range is in the far north, where the boreal forests begin to give way to Arctic Tundra. In winter they move to the coasts and sometimes range as far south as the gulf coast. In Texas they are a rare visitor to the extreme northeastern section of the gulf coast. Winter storms can sometimes cause them to appear on inland lakes in winter.

Class—**Aves** (birds)

Order—**Anseriformes** (waterfowl)

Family—**Anatidae** (ducks, geese & swans)

Common Merganser *Mergus merganser*	**Red-breasted Merganser** *Mergus serrator*	**Hooded Merganser** *Lophodytes cucullatus*
 Breeding male  Non-breeding male	 Male  Female	 Male  Female

Size: 25 inches. **Abundance:** Uncommon. **Migratory Status:** Winter resident and winter migrant.	**Size:** 23 inches. **Abundance:** Fairly common. **Migratory Status:** Winter migrant and coastal resident.	**Size:** 18 inches. **Abundance:** Fairly common. **Migratory Status:** Winter resident and migrant in Texas.
Habitat: In winter uses large lakes and rivers. Small creeks are used in summer. Uses coastal bays in winter in some areas but avoids the Texas coast.	**Habitat:** Uses larger lakes and rivers during migration. Boreal wetlands in summer. Most spend the winter along America's coastline.	**Habitat:** In winter uses swamps, shallow bays of lakes, and river floodplains. Less likely to be seen in saltwater habitats. Often seen in small ponds.
Variation: Exhibits sexual dimorphism in breeding plumage (see photos above). Winter plumages are similar in both sexes.	**Variation:** Significant plumage variations between the sexes during the breeding season. Winter males and juveniles resemble females.	**Variation:** Significant sexual variation (see photos above). Does not exhibit seasonal plumage changes seen in the other two merganser species.
Breeding: Nests in tree cavities or sometimes in root crevices on the ground. 10 or 12 eggs is average.	**Breeding:** Nests on the ground. Nest is well hidden beneath overhanging vegetation or in cavities. 5 to 24 eggs.	**Breeding:** Cavity nester. Most nest in the great lakes region. Does not nest in Texas. Lays 12 eggs maximum.
Natural History: Most Common Mergansers seen in Texas will be in non-breeding plumage. A bird of northern climates and cold waters, the Common Merganser spends the summer on lakes in the boreal forests of Canada, Alaska and in the cold water streams of the Rocky Mountains. They are also found throughout Eurasia. Fish is the primary food for this species. Their bill is serrated for holding slippery prey and they are excellent divers and underwater swimmers. They are proficient fishermen and can dive to a depth of tens of yards and have been known to stay submerged up to two minutes. They do eat many invertebrates as well and will use their bill to probe in mud or gravel for aquatic insects, mollusks, crustaceans, and worms. Usually seen in small flocks but may congregate in winter.	**Natural History:** During winter these birds show a preference for coastal regions where they use estuaries and saltwater bays and salt/brackish water marshes. Like its larger relative the Common Merganser, the Red-breasted has a holarctic distribution and is found in Europe and Asia as well as North America. In summer this species ranges even farther north than its larger cousin, being found as far north as the Arctic Ocean and southern Greenland. Food is mostly small fish that are grasped with the serrated bill. Also eats aquatic invertebrates and amphibians. Feeds both in shallow water and in deep water up to at least 25 feet deep. Flocks may feed cooperatively, with all the birds diving together to corral schools of minnows. Has been observed chasing minnows cooperatively with some heron species.	**Natural History:** Unlike our other two merganser ducks, both of which are holarctic in distribution, the Hooded Merganser is strictly a North American duck. Another odd distributional trait is the fact that these birds are rare in the great plains region, where many North American duck species are most common. They have a more diverse diet than the larger mergansers, feeding less on fish and more on aquatic invertebrates that are located by means of well developed underwater vision capability. Winter waterfowl surveys indicate that over 50 percent of the population winters in the Mississippi flyway. Most likely to be seen in Texas in December, January, and February, but records exist for both spring and fall. While still a fairly common species, they are less numerous than prior to European settlement.

CHAPTER 6

THE CROCODILIANS OF TEXAS

TABLE 3

— THE ORDERS AND FAMILIES OF TEXAS CROCODILIANS —

Class—**Eusuchia**
Order—**Crocodylia** (crocodilians)

Family	**Alligatoridae** (alligators & caimans)

Class—**Eusuchia**
Order—**Crocodylia** (crocodilians)
Family—**Alligatoridae** (alligators & caimans)

American Alligator
Alligator mississippiensis

Male

Female on nest

Hatchling

Presumed range in TX

Size: Females are usually under 8 feet. Record for male is 19 feet, 2 inches.

Abundance: Fairly common in the southeastern part of the state and all along the lower gulf coastal plain. Becoming increasingly common in areas farther to the west and north.

Variation: Young are vividly marked with yellow and black bars on sides and tail. Bright colors tend to fade with age. Old adults can be quite dark. Adult males are larger than adult females.

Habitat: Inhabits all freshwater habitats in the state (marshes, lakes, rivers, canals, reservoirs, and even roadside ditches). Most common in parks and preserves, in the Western Gulf Coastal Plain Level II Ecoregion, and in the southwestern portion of the South Central Plains Level II Ecoregion.

Breeding: Female constructs a dome nest from palm fronds, leaves, and other organic detritus. Up to 50 eggs may be laid. Female often guards the nest until the young hatch in about three months. Baby Alligators are about eight to nine inches in length. They grow at the rate of about a foot a year for the first few years of life.

Natural History: No other animal in the state conjures images of "the deep south" more than the American Alligator. By the 1950s they had been nearly exterminated in much of their range. With the passage of the Endangered Species Act in 1973 they were afforded full protection and began to make a remarkable comeback. In 1985 the species was delisted from the endangered species list. Today, they are once again a common animal and are now treated as a game species by many state wildlife agencies including Texas Parks and Wildlife. As a game animal they are protected, but can be harvested in accordance with state wildlife regulations. Controlled harvest through hunting, coupled with "nuisance Alligator" control programs, keeps their numbers in check and helps protect the state's human inhabitants from these potentially dangerous crocodilians. Most attacks on humans are the result of Alligators having been fed by humans. A fed Alligator not only loses any natural fear of humans, but worse, comes to associate people with food. That can be a deadly combination in such a large and powerful wild animal.

CHAPTER 7

THE TURTLES OF TEXAS

TABLE 3

— THE ORDERS AND FAMILIES OF TEXAS TURTLES —

Class—**Chelonia** (turtles)
Order—**Cryptodira** (straight necked turtles)

Family	**Chelydridae** (snapping turtles)
Family	**Kinosternidae** (mud & musk turtles)
Family	**Emydidae** (sliders & box turtles)
Family	**Trionychidae** (softshell turtles)
Family	**Testudinidae** (tortoises)
Family	**Cheloniidae** (sea turtles)
Family	**Dermatochelyidae** (leatherback)

Class—**Chelonia** (turtles)
Order—**Cryptodira** (straightneck turtles)
Family—**Chelydridae** (snapping turtles)

Common Snapping Turtle	**Alligator Snapping Turtle**
Chelydra serpentina	*Macrochelys temminckii*

Size: Maximum length 20 inches. Record weight 86 pounds.

Variation: No variation occurs in Texas specimens. Specimens found on the Florida peninsula differ slightly.

Abundance: Very common. Found nearly statewide in Texas.

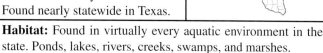
Presumed range in TX

Size: Maximum length 31 inches. Record weight 251 lbs.

Variation: No species variation in Texas. Males attain a larger size than females. All really large specimens are males.

Abundance: Rare in Texas and declining throughout its range.

Presumed range in TX

Habitat: Found in virtually every aquatic environment in the state. Ponds, lakes, rivers, creeks, swamps, and marshes.

Habitat: Large rivers and their impoundments. Also oxbow lakes and small tributaries near their confluence with rivers.

Breeding: Eggs are deposited in underground chambers excavated by the female turtle. A typical clutch contains 25 to 50 eggs. Hatchlings are about the size of a quarter.

Breeding: Adult females leave the water to lay up to 50 eggs in an underground chamber dug by the turtle. The leathery shelled eggs hatch in three or four months.

Natural History: These common turtles can be found in any aquatic habitat in the state, including tiny farm ponds or tributaries narrow enough for a person to step across. They even can exist in waters that are heavily polluted with sewage and industrial effluents. They will feed on some plant material but are mainly carnivorous and will eat virtually anything they can swallow. Fish, frogs, tadpoles, small mammals, baby ducks, crayfish, and carrion are all listed as food items. Hatchling turtles often must travel long distances to find a home in a pond or creek, and adults occasionally embark on long overland treks, presumably in search of a more productive habitat after depleting the food source in a small pond or creek. These long hikes overland usually occur in the spring. The ferociousness of a captured snapping turtle is legendary and their sharp, powerful jaws can inflict a serious wound. When cornered on land they will turn to face an enemy and extend the long neck in a lunging strike that is lighting fast and so energetic that it may cause the entire turtle to move forward several inches. By contrast, when under water they almost never bite. The ambient temperature of the eggs during development determines the sex of the hatchlings. Cooler temperature produces males, warmer females.

Natural History: Alligator Snapping Turtles are the most completely aquatic of any American freshwater turtle. In fact, they never leave the water except for egg-laying excursions by the female. Unlike most aquatic turtles, they do not bask and rarely show more than the tip of the snout when coming up to breath. They spend most of their time "bottom walking" or lying in ambush in the muck or mud. They possess a specialized structure on the tongue that resembles a worm and can be wriggled to effectively lure fish into striking distance. They also eat other turtles, carrion, crayfish, and in fact probably any type of animal matter that can be swallowed. Mussels are reportedly an important food item, the hard shell being no match for the powerful jaws of these huge turtles. The longevity of this turtle in the wild is unknown, but some specimens have been in captivity for over seventy years, suggesting a long life-span. These unique turtles have declined significantly throughout their range. They are regarded as a Threatened Species in Texas and are thus legally protected. The adults have no real natural enemies other than man, but the nests are heavily preyed upon by raccoons, skunks, foxes, and coyotes. Baby turtles also have many enemies, including large predatory fishes, but soon outgrow most threats.

Class—**Chelonia** (turtles)

Order—**Cryptodira** (straightneck turtles)

Family—**Kinosternidae** (mud & musk turtles)

Genus—*Kinosternon* (mud turtles) 3 species in Texas

Eastern Mud Turtle *Kinosternon subrubrum*	**Mexican Mud Turtle** *Kinosternon hirtipes*

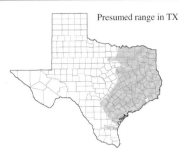 Presumed range in TX

 Presumed range in TX

Mexican Mud Turtle

Size: Average 5 to 6 inches.

Abundance: Rare in Texas.

Variation: Young have lateral keels.

Yellow Mud Turtle
Kinosternon flavescens

 Presumed range in TX

Size: 3.5 to 4.5 inches.

Abundance: Fairly common.

Variation: There are three species of Mud Turtles in Texas but all are very similar in appearance and will closely resemble the Eastern Mud Turtle shown above. The sexes are alike except males have a slightly concave plastron.

Size: Average 4 to 5 inches.

Abundance: Fairly common.

Variation: Males are slightly larger.

Habitat: Mud Turtles are highly aquatic turtles that inhabit almost any type of aquatic habitat. Although they are mostly freshwater turtles, the Eastern Mud Turtle may be found in brackish water marshes along the coast or in brackish estuary swamps. The Yellow Mud Turtle can be found in man-made ponds built for watering livestock as well as streams and marshes. Because it inhabits arid regions it must sometimes travel overland if its habitat dries out. The Mexican Mud Turtle lives in permanent waters. It is mainly a Mexican species and it is found in Texas only in a single drainage system in the Big Bend region, which also constitutes its entire range in the United States.

Breeding: Eastern Mud Turtles reach sexual maturity at about 5 to 7 years of age. Breeding is in the spring and eggs are laid throughout the summer. Females lay up to at least 8 eggs but smaller clutches of 4 to 6 are more common. In a few cases, they may lay more than once in a season, but repeat clutches typically contain fewer eggs. Eggs are laid underground in a nest excavated by the female in friable soil, frequently sand or sandy loam. Reproduction in the Yellow Mud Turtle is very similar to that described for the Eastern Mud Turtle. Little is known about reproduction in the Mexican Mud Turtle but it is presumably similar to the Eastern and Yellow Mud Turtles.

Natural History: The Mexican Mud Turtle often goes by the name Rough-legged or Rough-footed Mud Turtle or sometimes Mexican Rough-footed Mud Turtle. It and the Yellow Mud Turtle are both monotypic species. The Eastern Mud Turtle is a wide ranging species that has a total of three subspecies. The subspecies of Eastern Mud Turtle found in Texas is subspecies *hippocrepis*. It is commonly known as the Mississippi Mud Turtle and its range in the US is basically from the Mississippi River westward, into and throughout eastern Texas. Farther to the west, it is replaced by the Yellow Mud Turtle, but apparently the two do occur sympatrically in a few areas of Texas. The Mexican Mud Turtle is very rare in Texas and only occurs in a few areas in the Big Bend region. It is regarded as a Threatened Species by the Texas Parks and Wildlife Department. All mud turtles are omnivorous opportunistic feeders that will eat almost anything edible. Young mud turtles and smaller individuals eat many types of insects. Older more mature specimens eat crayfish, small fish, snails, and small amphibians and amphibian larva. They are also carrion eaters and sometimes benefit from living around boat docks where fish heads and fish entrails may be regularly available. All age groups consume a variety of aquatic plant material including algae. The three species of mud turtle found in Texas are all very similar in appearance and in natural history, except for the ecological regions they inhabit. The eastern species is a denizen of the Eastern Temperate Forests; the Yellow Mud Turtle lives mainly in the Great Plains and parts of the North American Deserts. Meanwhile the Mexican species is found mainly in the highlands of central Mexico and barely ranges into the US in western Texas. The Kinosternidae family is widespread in Mexico and Central America and there are at least two dozen species, most of which are found in Latin America. It is thus believed that this unique family of turtles likely evolved in that region and a few species spread northward into North America.

Class—**Chelonia** (turtles)
Order—**Cryptodira** (straightneck turtles)
Family—**Kinosternidae** (mud & musk turtles)
Genus—*Sternotherus* (musk turtles)

Common Musk Turtle *Sternotherus odoratus*	**Razor-backed Musk Turtle** *Sternotherus carinatus*

Size: About 4 inches in carapace length as an adult. Record 5.9 inches.	 Presumed range in TX	**Size:** About 4 to 5 inches in carapace length as an adult. Record is just under 7 inches.	 Presumed range in TX
Abundance: Common.		**Abundance:** Fairly common.	
Variation: In some regions females are larger than males, but it is not known if that type of sexual dimophism applies in Texas.		**Variation:** No subspecies are recognized and there appears to be little variation in adult specimens. Males have longer tails.	

Habitat: Primarily a stream dweller, but can be found in a variety of aquatic habitats including swamps, oxbows, lakes, marshes, etc. They reach their highest densities in waters with abundant aquatic vegetation.	**Habitat:** Highly aquatic. Inhabits swamps and slow moving rivers and streams. Prefers habitats with little to no current and mud bottom. Waters with abundant aquatic vegetation will be preferred habitats.
Breeding: Female lays 2 to 5 eggs under leaf litter or sometimes merely on top of the ground. Eggs hatch into tiny turtles that are barely an inch in length.	**Breeding:** Females reach sexual maturity at 4 to 5 years of age. Eggs are laid in spring with probably 4 to 5 per clutch. There may be two clutches per year.
Natural History: Nocturnal and crepuscular and completely aquatic in habits. Unlike most aquatic turtles in America, the Musk Turtle rarely basks, but when it does it may climb several feet up into branches that overhang the water. When disturbed while basking they will launch themselves clumsily into the safety of the water. Since they seldom leave the water, the carapace is often covered with a thick growth of algae. Their name comes from the presence of musk producing glands that emit an unpleasant odor when the turtles are handled. This musk also accounts for their other common name "Stinkpot." The Common Musk Turtle is widespread throughout the eastern US, being found from the gulf coast north to the great lakes, but they are absent from most of the higher elevations of the Appalachian Plateau. They occur throughout the eastern half of Texas where they are one of the most common turtles. They are an omnivorous species that feeds on a variety of aquatic plant and animal matter. Mollusks (snails, mussels) are listed as a food item. Undoubtedly also takes carrion opportunistically. Feeds by "bottom walking" under water. Like many turtle species, the Eastern Musk Turtle is a long-lived species and one captive zoo specimen lived for 55 years.	**Natural History:** The name Razor-backed Mud Turtle comes form the raised vertebral scutes on the top of the carapace. The possible function of this feature is not known. It may have something to do with heat absorption of basking turtles or possibly it is a defense against certain predators like herons, who might find its rough edged shell difficult swallow. That herons will eat small turtles and swallow them whole is a known fact. Other potential predators of adult turtles include large predatory fishes, alligators, and larger turtles like the Common Snapping Turtle and Alligator Snapping Turtle. Baby musk turtles are the most vulnerable of course, and are eaten by many predators. Their biggest enemy may be man as these turtles are regularly caught on hook and line by fishermen using worms or cut bait. They are closely related to the Common Musk Turtle and the two share much of their range distribution in Texas. Their food is mainly animal matter and includes insects, snails, small bivalves, crustaceans, amphibians, and aquatic plants. Carrion is also consumed and like many other carnivorous aquatic turtles in Texas they likely benefit from the discarded portions of fish cleaned around boat docks. The longevity record for this species is nearly 22 years, but they likely can survive longer.

Class—**Chelonia** (turtles)

Order—**Cryptodira** (straightneck turtles)

Family—**Emydidae** (aquatic & box turtles)

Genus—*Graptemys* (map turtles) 5 species in Texas

Texas Map Turtle *Graptemys versa*	**Sabine Map Turtle** *Graptemys sabinensis*

Presumed range in TX

Size: Female to 8.5 inches. Male to 4.5.

Abundance: Fairly common.

Variation: Females are a third larger. Male have longer claws on the front feet.

Size: Female to 8.5 inches. Male to 5.5 inches.

Abundance: Fairly common.

Variation: Females grow up to a third larger than males. Males have longer claws on the front feet.

False Map Turtle *Graptemys pseudogeographica*	**Ouachita Map Turtle** *Graptemys ouachitensis*

 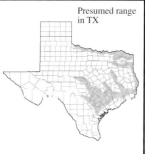  

Presumed range in TX

Size: Female to 11 inches. Males are smaller.

Abundance: Fairly common in rivers in eastern Texas.

Variation: Male is smaller, only about 6 inches and have longer claws on the front feet.

Size: Female to 9.5 inches.

Abundance: Fairly common in the Red River.

Variation: Male smaller, to 5.5 inches and has longer claws on the front feet.

Habitat: These are river turtles primarily. Some may also occur in smaller creeks or in river swamps and river oxbows and natural lakes. They also live in man-made impoundments of their endemic river systems. Rarely found in ponds and they do not disperse by making overland treks. They disperse by moving up and down stream channels.

Breeding: Most species produce and average of about a dozen eggs per clutch. Two or three clutches per year is probable.

Natural History: The map turtles are a diverse group of aquatic turtles consisting of 14 species, 5 of which can be found in Texas. All except one species are indigenous to rivers that drain into the Gulf of Mexico. They reach their greatest diversity in the rivers of the central and western gulf coast drainages and several species are restricted to a single river system. They are characterized by the presence of a pronounced dorsal "keel" on the top of the back and a serrated posterior margin to the carapace. They are locally known by the nickname "Sawbacks." Females are as much as twice the size of males. Males have elongated claws on the front feet. Several species are adapted for feeding on freshwater mollusks. The name "Map" Turtle comes from the presence of light lines on the head, neck, and legs that resemble the lines on a topographic map. Most Texas species are fairly common in larger rivers of the state. All are wary and will retreat into the water when approached. The Cagle's Map Turtle (not pictured) is probably the least common and is restricted in range to the San Antonio River system.

Cagle's Map Turtle
Graptemys caglei

Size: Female to 8.5 inches. Male to 5 inches.

Abundance: Uncommon. Restricted range.

Variation: Male has longer claws on front feet.

Presumed range in TX

Class—**Chelonia** (turtles)		
Order—**Cryptodira** (straightneck turtles)		
Family—**Emydidae** (aquatic & box turtles)		
Genus—*Pseudemys* (cooters)		

River Cooter *Pseudemys concinna*	**Rio Grande Cooter** *Pseudemys gorzugi*	**Texas River Cooter** *Pseudemys texana*

Size: To 14.75 inches.

Abundance: Common in the Piney Woods of the eastern part of the state.

Presumed range in TX

Size: To 14.75 inches.

Abundance: Fairly common within range. Restricted to the Rio Grande Valley.

Presumed range in TX

Size: To 12.5 inches.

Abundance: Common in several central Texas rivers systems.

Presumed range in TX

Variation: There is little variation among adults in these species. Young turtles are more vividly marked and older turtles tend to have their carapace markings reduced or obscured. Males have exceptionally longer claws on the front toes and are usually somewhat smaller than females.

Habitat: The cooter turtles are all highly aquatic in habits. And collectively the three species shown above inhabit just about every type of freshwater aquatic habitat found in the state. Rivers, springs, and spring runs are a primary habitat for all these turtles, along with lakes, canals, swamps, marshes, and even man-made cattle tanks and small farm ponds.

Breeding: Female cooters are believed to reach sexual maturity at about five or six years of age (with a carapace length of about 9 inches). Gravid females leave the water and travel overland to suitable nesting localities which may be very near the waters edge or hundreds of yards away from a river bank or lake shore. A flask-shaped cavity is excavated by the female's hind feet and an average of about 20 eggs are laid. Multiple nestings may occur. Females will use water stored in the cloaca to soften the ground when digging a nest in which to lay her eggs. The young turtles hatch in about 3 months (less if weather is exceptionally warm, longer if exceptionally cool). As with many egg laying reptiles, chelonians, and crocodilians, ambient temparature in the nest determines the sex of the offspring. Predation on nests by mammalian predators like Raccoons, Virginia Opossum, and skunks can be very high. Babies are about the size of a half dollar coin and are highly vulnerable to all types of land and aquatic predators as well as many birds.

Natural History: All three of the species shown on this page are rather similar in appearance and in their natural history. The exact taxonomy of the *Pseudemys* genus has been a nightmare for herpetologists for decades. The above three species were all once regarded as subspecies of the **River Cooter** (P. *concinna*) and some herpetologists still consider that to be the more accurate representation of their taxonomy. Still others will insist that they are all just slightly different geographic populations of the same wide ranging species. That argument is bolstered by the fact that interbreeding between the species is apparently not uncommon where the ranges of different species of *Pseudemys* meet. Utilization of DNA analysis is adding to the scientific understanding of these turtles, but has still not completely resolved the controversy regarding their phylogeny and proper taxonomy. Lifespan for these turtles is probably about 20 to 25 years. Historically, cooter turtles were hunted for food by native Americans and they are probably still consumed by some people living in Texas. Of the three *Pseudemys* species found in Texas the River Cooter and the Texas Cooter are the most common. River Cooters are wide ranging and found throughout much of the American south. In Texas they inhabit the drainages of the lower Red River, the Trinity River, and the Sabine River. The Texas Cooter is a Texas endemic, found in several major river systems in the state (i.e. the Colorado, Brazos, Guadalupe, and San Antonio watersheds). Meanwhile the Rio Grande Cooter is restricted to the Rio Grande drainage and is probably the least common of the three Texas *Pseudemys* species. It is regarded by the IUCN as "Near Threatened," but it is not listed as threatened or endangered by Texas Parks and Wildlife. Like other aquatic Emydidae turtles, the cooters can store large amounts of water in the cloaca which can aid in long overland treks from one pond or cattle tank to another water source. If caught and handled they will void this extra water. Voiding the stored water may threaten their survival in arid areas or during droughts. These turtles are also sometimes called "sliders," but that name should be reserved for the *Trachemys* genus on the next page.

Class—**Chelonia** (turtles)

Order—**Cryptodira** (straightneck turtles)

Family—**Emydidae** (aquatic & box turtles)

Pond (Red-eared) Slider *Trachemys scripta*	Big Bend Slider *Trachemys gaigeae*	Southern Painted Turtle *Chrysemys dorsalis*

Size: Average carapace length is 6 to 8 inches. Record 12 inches.  Presumed range in TX	**Size:** Averages about 8 inches. Maximum 11. Presumed range in TX	**Size:** Averages about 4 to 5 inches. Maximum 8.1 inches.  Presumed range in TX
Abundance: Common.	**Abundance:** Uncommon. Listed as vulnerable by IUCN.	**Abundance:** Uncommon in Texas.
Variation: Babies have green carapace with yellow markings.	**Variation:** Males are smaller. Females have a higher domed carapace.	**Variation:** Males are slightly smaller with longer tails and longer front claws.
Habitat: Most common in large bodies of water but can be found in any aquatic habitat in the state except for very small streams.	**Habitat:** The upper Rio Grande River. In Texas found only in the Big Bend region. Inhabits the Rio Grande River, and adjacent sloughs.	**Habitat:** Avoids fast-flowing streams in favor of still or slow moving waters. Common in swamps, marshes, ponds, and lakes throughout its range.
Breeding: Females leave the safety of the water and crawl hundreds of yards to upland areas to deposit their eggs in an underground nest chamber dug with the hind legs. Large females may lay 20 eggs, younger females lay fewer.	**Breeding:** Very little is known about the breeding habits of this species. Reproduction is presumably similar to the Red-eared Slider. Turtles of the United States and Canada by Ernst, Lovich, and Barbour reports 6 to 11 eggs.	**Breeding:** Females lay 10 to 15 eggs within a flask-shaped underground nest chamber dug with the turtle's hind legs. Egg laying occurs from late May to early July. Eggs hatch in about 10 weeks. Hatchlings are the size of a quarter.
Natural History: Highly aquatic but sometimes seen far from water. Omnivorous. Eats a variety of water plants as well as mollusks, minnows, dead fish, aquatic insects, crustaceans, etc. Young are more carnivorous, while mature turtles will consume more plants. Old specimens tend to darken with age and very old specimens may have a black carapace. These are hardy turtles that will emerge from the mud to bask on logs on warm, sunny days throughout the winter. There are three subspecies of this turtle. The **Red-eared Slider** (*T. s. elegans*) is the subspecies found in Texas. They were once sold as pets and they have been widely introduced all across the US. Today they may be seen almost any aquatic habitat anywhere in the country.	**Natural History:** Also often called the Mexican Plateau Slider. This species' range in the US is apparently contained entirely in the upper reaches of the Rio Grande River and nearby water sources such as river sloughs or cattle tanks within the Rio Grande Valley. It is known to occur as far upstream as central New Mexico in the Rio Grande Valley. It is a similar species to the Red-eared Slider and was originally regarded as a subspecies of that turtle. Its natural history has been little studied, but presumably it is similar to that of the Red-eared Slider. This is one of the few species in the genus *Trachemys* that does not have a subspecies. Most of the other 19 species have several subspecies. Most members of the genus are found in Latin America.	**Natural History:** The Painted Turtles of the *Chrysemys* genus are among the most common and widespread of the Emydidae turtles in America. Like other aquatic members of their family, they spend a great deal of time basking on floating logs and they are quick to slide into the water if approached too closely. These are omnivorous turtles that eat a very wide array of plant and animal foods as well as carrion. Although an aquatic turtle, they may be seen well away from water sources, especially in the spring. In Texas the Southern Painted Turtle has a rather restricted range but they are widespread throughout much of the southeastern US. Until recently they were considered to be a subspecies of the more northerly ranging Eastern Painted Turtle (*C. picta*).

Class—**Chelonia** (turtles)

Order—**Cryptodira** (straightneck turtles)

Family—**Emydidae** (aquatic & box turtles)

Chicken Turtle *Deirochelys reticularia*	**Diamondback Terrapin** *Malaclemys terrapin*	**Ornate Box Turtle** *Terrapene ornate*

Size: Average carapace length 6 inches. Record 10 inches.

Presumed range in TX

Abundance: Western subspecies is rare in TX.

Variation: There are three subspecies of this turtle. All three subspecies are very similar in appearance. The subspecies occurring in Texas is the Western Chicken Turtle (*D. r. miaria*).

Habitat: Primarily aquatic. Uses a variety of freshwater habitats with abundant aquatic vegetation. Favors lentic waters over flowing streams.

Breeding: Clutch size varies from 5 to a dozen eggs. Two clutches per year is not uncommon. Females reach sexual maturity at around 5 or 6 years old.

Natural History: There seems to be some disagreement as to whether the name "Chicken" turtle is a reference to this species exceedingly long neck or whether it is a reference to the taste of its flesh. During dry seasons or droughts when wetlands dry up, these turtles commonly bury themselves beneath pine straw or leaf mold and enter a period of torpor. Crayfish are a major food item for this species. Large aquatic insects and their larva are also prey items. Although they are widespread throughout the southern US, Chicken Turtles don't seem to be as plentiful as the larger Emydidae turtles. That apparent scarcity may be a reflection of their wariness. They will abandon basking and dive into the water if approached.

Size: Average 6 to 9 inches for female. Male to 5 inches.

Presumed range in TX

Abundance: Uncommon and declining.

Variation: There are seven subspecies but only one occurs in Texas. The Texas subspecies is *littoralis*, the Texas Diamondback Terrapin. Females are larger and have wider heads.

Habitat: Diamondback Terrapins are coastal specialists. They inhabit salt marshes, intercoastal waterways, and estuaries all along the Texas coastline

Breeding: Eggs are laid in sandy soils above the high tide line. Clutch size ranges from 4 to 18. As with many turtles, soil temperature determines sex.

Natural History: Diamondback Terrapins have declined significantly throughout their range. They have recovered somewhat from the days of market hunting when they were harvested for food in astronomical numbers, but they are much less common today than just a few decades ago. They are probably most common today in undisturbed salt marsh and uninhabited barrier islands. These turtles are adapted to living in both fresh water and salt water, but their main habitat is salt and brackish water marshes. Salt marsh snails are one their main foods, along with crabs, mussels, marine worms, and some plant material. They possess enlarged and thickened labial regions which is an adaptation for crushing hard shelled prey.

Size: Max 6.5 inches. Averages 4 to 5 inches total length.

Presumed range in TX

Abundance: Fairly common, nearly statewide.

Variation: Male has concave plastron (females is flat) and red eye. Amount of yellow spotting in head is variable as is the prominence of light markings on the carapace.

Habitat: Prefers more xeric conditions than the Eastern Box Turtle. Inhabits remnant prairie and desert out west and dry woodlands in eastern Texas.

Breeding: Lays up to 6 eggs in mid-summer. Eggs hatch in fall. Babies are tiny replicas of the adult, but lack the ability to close the plastron.

Natural History: This turtle could be regarded as a western, dry-land version of the Eastern Box Turtle. They range throughout the great plains and well into the desert southwest. They are more carnivorous than their eastern cousins, but they do consume some vegetable matter. Insects, snails, and earthworms are probably the main food items. Some small vertebrate prey may be consumed and they are known to scavenge for carrion as well. Populations in the Sonoran and Chihuahuan Deserts were once regarded as a distinct subspecies. For unknown reasons, the Ornate Box Turtle spends more time in hibernation than the Eastern Box Turtle. In habits and habitats, the box turtles are intermediate between the aquatic and land turtles.

Class—**Chelonia** (turtles)

Order—**Cryptodira** (straightneck turtles)

Family—**Emydidae** (aquatic & box turtles)		Family—**Testudinidae** (tortoises)
Three-toed Box Turtle *Terrapene triungus*	**Eastern Box Turtle** *Terrapene carolinensis*	**Texas Tortoise** *Gopherus berlandieri*

Size: Average 4 to 6 inches. The record length is just under 8 inches.

Abundance: Historically, these were very common turtle in Texas but they have declined significantly in recent decades.

Variation: Three-toed may have a horn-colored carapace, or may show faint light spots or radiating lines. The color and pattern on the head and legs is also variable. Eastern is highly variable in color and pattern and no two are exactly alike.

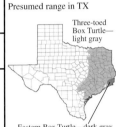

Presumed range in TX

Three-toed Box Turtle— light gray

Eastern Box Turtle—dark gray

Size: 6 to 8 inches. Record 9.

Abundance: Threatened.

Variation: Males have a concave plastron and elongated gular scute.

Presumed range in TX

Habitat: Occupies a wide variety of habitats from open fields and pastures to deep woods. Can be found in both upland areas and lowlands, but is most common in damp woods, edge areas near creeks and streams, and wooded bottomlands.

Habitat: In Texas inhabits arid and semi-arid scrub habitats with sandy soils. Sea level to 2,700 feet in Mexico.

Breeding: Breeding takes place in late April and May with egg deposition in late June or early July. Up to 6 eggs may be laid but 2 or 3 is more common. Females may dig the nest by day or night. Young hatch in late fall and some may overwinter in their underground nest chamber before emerging the following spring. Newly hatched baby Box Turtles do not possess the hinged plastron and are thus unable to tightly close themselves within their shell.

Breeding: Breeds in summer. Egg deposition probably occurs twice a year, in the early summer and early fall. As few as one or as many as five eggs may be laid but two or three is probably typical. Babies are about 2 inches in length.

Natural History: These familiar turtles often go by the name "Terrapin." They are primarily diurnal and are most active in the morning and the late afternoon. They sometimes burrow into the mud during hot weather, and overwinter by burrowing themselves into loose soil or deep leaf litter. The hibernation burrow is quite shallow, only a few inches deep. Studies have shown that they are tolerant of some freezing, a trait that enables survival of such a shallow hibernator. Still, hibernation is a significant source of mortality among adults. Their diet is omnivorous and they consume berries, fruits and mushrooms as well as a wide variety of insect prey and other invertebrates. Earthworms and snails are a favorite animal food and blackberries and mulberries are among the favorite plant foods. Box Turtles are known for their longevity and reports of their living up to a century are common but difficult to verify. Some researchers report a lifespan of 80 years, some say over 100, while others say 30 to 40 years is probably the average in the wild. When threatened they will retract the head and feet into the shell, which can then close tightly by means of hinges on the front and back of the plastron. The muscles that close the shell are remarkably strong and efforts to pry open the shell of a frightened Box Turtle are futile. They are tough little turtles that can sometimes survive serious injury such as the shell being cracked open by a glancing blow from an automobile tire. Turtles with badly deformed but completely healed shells are sometimes found. In regions where wildfires are common, many are seen with shells that are completely scarred by fire. There is some concern among conservationists that commercial collecting of these turtles for foreign pet markets may be threat to their long-term survival. Habitat degradation and automobiles are probably much more imminent threats. Burgeoning human populations continue to destroy natural habitats and countless numbers of Box Turtles die on Texas roadways every summer.

Natural History: The Texas Tortoise is one of only four species of tortoise found in the US. All are found in warmer climates. The Texas Tortoise is the smallest member of the tortoise family in the US. It also is the only one that does not regularly dig an extensive burrow for refuge. Although they may occasionally dig a burrow if the substrate is friable, they are more likely to use abandoned mammal burrows or natural cavities such as a rock shelf. They do create shallow depressions (known as pallets) in the shade beneath shrubs or cacti. There may be several of the pallets within the tortoises home range. These are diurnal animals that are most active in mid-morning and late afternoon during the spring and fall. Their activity periods decrease when temperatures are least favorable (i.e. colder winter months and during hottest summer months). Strictly vegetarian, they feed on cactus (especially *Opuntia*) and a variety of grasses and forbs.

Class—**Chelonia** (turtles)

Order—**Cryptodira** (straightneck turtles)

Family—**Trionychidae** (softshell turtles)

Smooth Softshell Turtle	Spiny Softshell Turtle
Apalone mutica	*Apalone spinifera*

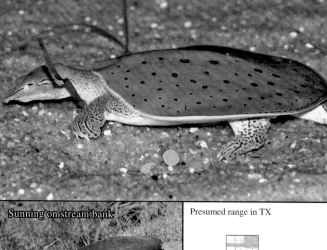

Close-up of head showing tubular snout

Presumed range in TX

Sunning on stream bank

Presumed range in TX

Size: 12 to 14 inches.

Size: Maximum of 18 inches.

Abundance: Uncommon in Texas.

Abundance: Fairly common.

Variation: There are two subspecies found in the US. The Midland Smooth Softshell (subspecies *mutica*) occurs in Texas. Females attain a much larger size than males.

Variation: There are 6 subspecies in America (some say 5) and 4 of them occur in Texas. The differences in subspecies are insignificant to the lay observer. Females are larger.

Habitat: Essentially an inhabitant of streams, both large rivers and small creeks. Flowing water is a requirement for this species, but it is found in large river impoundments.

Habitat: Occurs in both large and small streams and in impoundments. May also be found in farm ponds in some areas. Shows a preference for habitats with sandy substrates.

Breeding: Eggs are laid in excavated chambers on exposed sandbars in late spring or early summer. About a dozen eggs is typical.

Breeding: A dozen or more eggs are laid between May and August (most in June or July). Nests are often on sandbars of creeks or rivers.

Natural History: The Smooth Softshell is found mostly in flowing streams with fine gravel or sand bottoms. They are capable of great speed in the water and will actively forage for fish and other small aquatic animals. They are also ambush predators that burrow into the soft substrate of streams and extend their long necks with blinding speed to grab passing fish. Insects are also an important food item, along with various small aquatic animals and some plant material such as seeds and berries. Because of their permeable skin and requirement of clear streams and rivers these turtles may be under significant threat from water pollution. Damming of major rivers can also impede their natural movements and dispersal. Siltation from agricultural runoff alters preferred stream substrates of sand or fine gravel All species of softshell turtles have elongated, snorkel-like snouts which they will use to breathe when buried in sand or mud at the waters edge.

Natural History: Crayfish, fish, and insects are the primary food items, but dead fish and other carrion can be an important food item, especially in lakes where fishing is common. Spiny Softshells are active from spring through fall. They hunt both by ambush and by active pursuit. When immobile they can remain under water or several hours. Because of the soft, permeable shells and skin, softshells are more susceptible to dehydration than other turtle species and thus they seldom stray far from water. These turtles are harvested as food in many parts of their range, and much of this harvest is to date unregulated. Some believe this practice may pose a long-term threat to the species. A greater threat is water pollution and the widespread degradation of streams. Like all softshell turtles the Spiny has a long and flexible neck, which makes handling these turtles without being bitten difficult. Wild adults may bite savagely if handled.

Class—**Chelonia** (turtles)

Order—**Cryptodira** (straightneck turtles)

Families—**Cheloniidae & Dermochelyidae** (sea turtles)

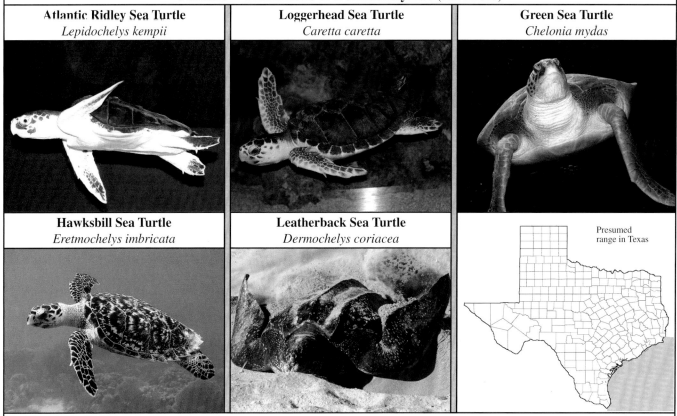

Atlantic Ridley Sea Turtle
Lepidochelys kempii

Loggerhead Sea Turtle
Caretta caretta

Green Sea Turtle
Chelonia mydas

Hawksbill Sea Turtle
Eretmochelys imbricata

Leatherback Sea Turtle
Dermochelys coriacea

Presumed range in Texas

Size: Atlantic Ridley is Texas's smallest sea turtle with a maximum carapace length of about 30 inches and a record weight of 110 pounds. The Hawksbill reaches 45 inches and 280 pounds. Next is the Loggerhead Sea Turtle at about four feet in length and nearly 500 pounds (claims of over 800 pounds exist). The Green Sea Turtle is 60 inches and maximum of 835 pounds. The Leatherback is the world's largest living turtle at 8 feet in length and 1,500 pounds.

Abundance: Green Turtle and Loggerhead are fairly common. Others are rare or very rare in Texas waters.

Variation: All exhibit some sexual size-related dimorphism. In Loggerhead, Leatherback and Atlantic Ridley males are smaller. In Green Sea Turtles males have a longer carapace. In the Hawksbill the sexes are alike.

Habitat: Warm seas. These turtles are found in tropical oceans around the globe. Some wander north into temperate waters in summer (most notably the Leatherback).

Breeding: All must come ashore to nest and lay their eggs on sandy beaches above the high tide mark. Nesting by Leatherbacks and Hawksbills in Texas was been recorded only very rarely. Green Turtles are the most common nesting species in Texas, followed by the Loggerhead and Atlantic Ridley. All sea turtle nests are subjected to predation by a variety of egg-robbing mammals such as raccoons. Hatchlings run a gauntlet of predators between the nest and the sea, and are then subject to predation by all manner of creatures once in the ocean. Surviving to maturity is a real long shot for a baby sea turtle. Add to that the widespread robbing of eggs for food by humans, the confusion created by artificial lights in developed areas, the hazards of fishing nets, hooks, and pollution and the outlook for the long-term survival of the worlds sea turtle population looks grim.

Natural History: In all sea turtles the legs and feet are modified into flippers. They are extremely well adapted morphologically and physiologically for a life in the ocean. Except for females coming ashore to nest once every few years, these turtles live their entire lives at sea. Jellyfish are an important food item, especially for the Leatherback. The presence of plastic bags in the ocean today is a real hazard for sea turtles who mistake the bags for jellyfish and eat them. Crustaceans, fish, sponges, and shellfish are also food items of most species. Green Turtles are mainly vegetarian and feed on Eelgrasses. Leatherbacks apparently have the ability to maintain body temperature through metabolic activity even when in cold northern waters. The sea turtles were once an important food source for humans and the Green Turtle's name is derived from the color of its fat. Human exploitation along with beach development has seriously impacted on these turtles. Heroic efforts to protect nesting beaches and outlaw exploitation have helped in the effort to conserve these species, but like the ocean ecosystem itself, the future of the world's sea turtles remains in doubt. The Leatherback is quite different from other sea turtles in many respects, but most notably in the fact that it has a leathery shell. It is the sole species of the family Dermochelyidae. All others are in the family Cheloniidae.

CHAPTER 8

THE REPTILES OF TEXAS

TABLE 5

— THE ORDERS AND FAMILIES OF TEXAS REPTILES —

Class—**Reptilia** (reptiles)

Order—**Squamata** (snakes and lizards)
Suborder—**Lacertilia** (lizards)

Family	**Crotaphytidae** (collared lizards)
Family	**Iguanidae** (iguanas)
Family	**Phrynosomatidae** (spiny lizards)
Family	**Polychrotidae** (anoles)
Family	**Scincidae** (skinks)
Family	**Teiidae** (whiptail lizards)
Family	**Anguidae** (glass & alligater lizards)
Family	**Eublepharidae** (banded geckos)
Family	**Gekkonidae** (old world geckos)

Suborder—**Serpentes** (snakes)

Family	**Leptotyphlopidae** (blind snakes)
Family	**Colubridae** (harmless egg laying snakes)
Family	**Dipsadidae** (small rear-fanged snakes)
Family	**Natricidae** (harmless live-bearing snakes)
Family	**Elapidae** (coral snakes & cobras)
Family	**Viperidae** (vipers)

THE REPTILES OF TEXAS

PART 1: LIZARDS

Class—**Reptilia** (reptiles)

Order—**Squamata** (lizards & snakes)

Family—**Crotaphytidae** (collared & leopard lizards)

Eastern Collared Lizard *Crotaphytus collaris*	**Reticulate Collared Lizard** *Crotaphytus reticulatus*	**Long-nosed Leopard Lizard** *Gambelia wislizenii*

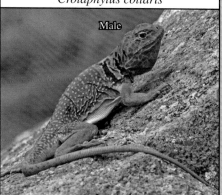
Male

Size: 8 to 14 inches.

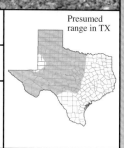
Presumed range in TX

Abundance: Uncommon.

Variation: Sexual and age-related dimorphism (see photos).

Size: 8 to 16 inches.

Presumed range in TX

Abundance: Rare.

Variation: Sexual and age-related dimorphism (see below.).

Size: Record 15.5 inches.

Presumed range in TX

Abundance: Rare in Texas.

Variation: Females are larger. Juveniles have reddish spots.

Habitat: Arid and semi-arid regions. Including pinyon/juniper woodlands and xeric upland deciduous woodlands. Also in desert and semi-desert scrub. Favors areas with large boulders.

Habitat: Mostly inhabits the Southern Texas Plains Level II Ecoregion where it favors sandy or gravelly substrates. Found among rocky outcrops or escarpments, but also in non-rocky areas.

Habitat: This is a desert species. It inhabits all of America's deserts. In Texas it is restricted in distribution to the Chihuahuan Desert and the southern tip of the High Plains Level II Ecoregions.

Breeding: Lays about a dozen eggs on average but may lay up to 22. Two clutches per year has been reported. Eggs are often laid under a rock.

Breeding: Up to 11 eggs are laid in a nest dug into soil or sometimes a pile of sticks in a woodrat nest. Hatchlings are about 3.5 inches long.

Breeding: Breeding females develop orange to red spots on the sides,. Average clutch is 7 or 8 eggs with a maximum of 11. Only one clutch per year.

Natural History: The bright colors are more intense when breeding, especially in the males. Gravid females also become more colorful. These large lizards are notoriously carnivorous and any terrestrial arthropod is a potential victim. But they also prey on small vertebrates, mostly small snakes and other lizards and they are not above cannibalizing the juveniles of their own species.

Female

Juvenile

Natural History: A large and highly predatory lizard that feeds on many types of insects and arthropods as well as small vertebrates including other lizards and small snakes. They are quite athletic and can run with great speed. They are also good leapers and have been known to snatch butterflies from the air. They also eat some plant material, especially the fruits of the Prickly Pear. Their greatest enemy is the Roadrunner, a reptile eating specialist that is a major predator of all types of lizards in Texas. These are typically solitary and territorial lizards except when breeding. They are a heat loving species and in the morning hours can often be observed sunning in the open, usually perched on a large rock or boulder. Their range extends southward across the Rio Grande into the Mexican states of Tamaulipas, Coahuila, and Nueva Leon.

Natural History: Like their cousins the Collared Lizards the Leopard Lizard is a fierce hunter of other lizards and they will attack individuals that are nearly as large as themselves. They are fast and athletic and can chase down other lizards. Unlike the Collared Lizards who love rocky places, the Leopard Lizard lives in flat desert basins and open desert foothills. In addition to other lizards it will prey on small snakes and a variety of arthropods and even some plant material in the form of berries. These are diurnal animals that live in some of the hottest places in America. Although they are a hot climate species that enjoys warming in the sun on desert mornings, they will seek shade beneath a cactus or shrub during the middle of the day. In much of their range they are probably most common in Creosote Bush dominated regions.

Class—**Reptilia** (reptiles)
Order—**Squamata** (lizards & snakes)
Family—**Phrynosomatidae** (spiny, horned & earless lizards)
Genus—*Holbrookia & Cophosaurus* (earless lizards)

Greater Earless Lizard
Cophosaurus texanus

Size: Maximum of 7.25 inches.

Abundance: Fairly common.

Variation: Color varies to match the substrate. There are two subspecies, both found in Texas. The difference in the subspecies is very slight. Males are slightly larger than females.

Presumed range in TX

Lesser Earless Lizard
Holbrookia maculata

Size: Maximum of 5.1 inches.

Abundance: Declining in Texas.

Variation: There are three subspecies in Texas. The Common Lesser Earless is found in the Panhandle, the Chihuahuan Earless in the Big Bend, and the Prairie Earless in central Texas.

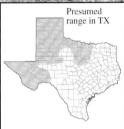

Presumed range in TX

Plateau Spot-tailed Earless Lizard
Holbrookia lacerata

Size: Maximum of 6 inches.

Abundance: Declining in Texas.

Variation: There are two subspecies, the Northern (subspecies *lacerta*) and the Southern (subspecies *subcaudatus*). They are nearly identical but the northern subspecies has dark spots on the side fused into rows.

Presumed range in TX

Keeled Earless Lizard
Holbrookia propinqua

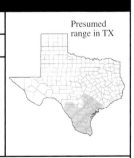

Size: To 5.5 inches.

Abundance: Fairly common.

Variation: The Texas population is currently regarded as a subspecies called the Northern Keeled Earless Lizard (subspecies *propinqua*). Some suggest it may be a distinct species different from Mexican populations.

Presumed range in TX

Habitat: Greater Earless Lizards are semi-arid to arid land animals. The Common Lesser Earless Lizard is mainly an animal of the Great Plains Level I Ecoregion, but one subspecies is adapted to the Chihuahuan Desert Ecoregion. In Texas it is probably most common in the Panhandle in areas of sandy or gravelly soils. The Spot-tailed Earless Lizard can be found in Texas in the Edwards Plateau and in parts of southern Texas. Keeled Earless Lizards inhabit sandy areas and barrier islands in south Texas.

Breeding: Earless Lizards lay 4 to 6 eggs per clutch and some may produce two clutches per year.

Natural History: Insects are the main food item and beetles are a primary prey among the insects. The Greater Earless and the Common Earless Lizards are the most common members of the group, but the Common is threatened in the Panhandle region by loss of habitat, mainly to agricultural activities. The Spot-tailed Earless Lizard is in decline and has disappeared from many areas of its former range. Some experts blame insecticides and widespread use of herbicides for the decline. The southernmost population of this lizard in south Texas has become very rare. Some experts consider the southern population to be a distinct species, while others regard it as merely a subspecies. The Keeled Earless Lizard is still fairly common in suitable habitat but has experienced declines in recent decades. Development and habitat loss are the major issues for this species.

Class—**Reptilia** (reptiles)

Order—**Squamata** (lizards & snakes)

Family—**Phrynosomatidae** (spiny, horned & earless lizards)

Texas Horned Lizard *Phrynosoma cornutum*	**Greater Short Horned Lizard** *Phrynosoma hernandesi*	**Round-tailed Horned Lizard** *Phrynosoma modestum*

Size: Record length 7.1 inches. Averages about 4 inches. 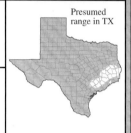 Presumed range in TX	**Size:** Record length 6.8 inches. Averages about 4 inches.  Presumed range in TX	**Size:** Averages about 3.5 inches. Record length 4.1 inches.  Presumed range in TX
Abundance: Once common. Now a threatened species.	**Abundance:** Rare in Texas. Only in west Texas mountains	**Abundance:** Fairly common in west Texas. Uncommon elsewhere.
Variation: Young have proportionately smaller "horns." No variation in adults.	**Variation:** Females are larger but no other variation among adults in Texas.	**Variation:** Color varies to match substrate. Gray, brown, orange or reddish.
Habitat: Widespread in Texas in open habitats. Deserts, brushlands, scrub, and arid and semi-arid grasslands. Prefers rocky or sandy soils and requires open spaces for sunning.	**Habitat:** In Texas inhabits arid mountain ranges where it can occur in sparse grass meadows, foothills, pine/juniper woodlands, and high mountains. Has been observed as high as 10,000 feet.	**Habitat:** Rocky or pebbly soils seemed to be preferred. Arid grasslands and open woodlands. Has been recorded as high as 7000 feet. Probably most common in Texas in the Trans-Pecos region.
Breeding: Lays up to two dozen eggs (maximum of 50).	**Breeding:** Viviparous. Gives birth to an average of 12 to 20 young in summer	**Breeding:** Female lays up to a dozen eggs. Hatchlings are tiny, 0.75 of an inch.
Natural History: Also called "Horny Toad" or "Horned Toad." Both are misnomers as they are not toads but lizards. Despite their fierce appearance these are docile lizards that cannot be induced to bite even when handled and they have long been a favorite "pet lizard" for many youngsters, although they are very difficult to keep alive in captivity. Ants are the favorite food item and they are sometimes seen perched atop anthills. They love the sun and heat and are one of the few animals that are active during mid afternoon on summer days in Texas. They have a tendency to bask in the warmth of paved roadways and they are killed in huge numbers in Texas each year by automobiles. They are preyed upon by dozens of predators but their worst natural enemy is probably the Roadrunner. Their cryptic coloration is their main defense.	**Natural History:** The Greater Short-horned Lizard has the smallest "horns" of any horned lizard species. These are montane lizards of the western US. They range throughout much of the Rocky Mountain west well to the north of Texas, all the way to Canada border in Montana, and barely extending into Alberta and Saskatchewan. The few mountain ranges in western Texas represent the southernmost limit of distribution in the US. They can also be found in northern Mexico. Because they often live in high elevation habitats they are more cold tolerant than other *Phrynosoma* species. Foods are a variety of insects but ants and beetles appear to be the main items in their diet. Some experts believe there may be several different species of Short-horned Lizards yet to be described within this wide ranging species.	**Natural History:** Although still fairly common locally within its broad range, this species appears to be declining and may be extirpated from some areas of its range. This species is well camouflaged and nearly impossible to detect until it moves. They have been observed to tuck in their legs and hunch up their back in a very convincing attempt to mimic a pebble. When all else fails to protect them from a predator they may resort to squirting blood from the eye, a defense mechanism shared with at least two other horned lizard species including the Texas Horned Lizard. Some research has shown this defense to be particularly elicited by an attack by canid predators (Middendorf and Sherbrook 1992). In spite of this rather off-putting display, these little lizards are quite docile and can be handled freely without any attempt to bite.

Class—**Reptilia** (reptiles)

Order—**Squamata** (lizards & snakes)

Family—**Phrynosomatidae** (spiny, horned & earless lizards)

Genus—*Sceloporus* (spiny lizards)

Texas Spiny Lizard *Sceloporus olivaceus*	**Prairie Fence Lizard** *Sceloporus consobrinus*	**Southwestern Fence Lizard** *Sceloporus cowlesi*

Size: Can reach a maximum of 11.75 inches.	Presumed range in TX	**Size:** Averages 4 to 5 inches. Maximum 7.25.	Presumed range in TX	**Size:** Averages 3.5 to 4.5 inches. Maximum 7.	Presumed range in TX
Abundance: Common in habitats with trees throughout east-central Texas.		**Abundance:** Probably the most common *Sceloporus* lizard in Texas.		**Abundance:** Common in Chihuhuan Desert in the western end of the state.	

Variation: Males have blue ventrolateral blotches and more pronounced dorso-lateral light lines.

Variation: Males have blue patches on the throat and belly. Females are slightly larger. Lateral stripes are variable.

Variation: Blue belly patches are greatly reduced or absent on females. Juveniles resemble females.

Habitat: Woodlands. Oak savanna, forests and riparian woodlands in grasslands or semi desert regions.

Habitat: Prairies, savannas, and open or semi-open woodlands. Rocky outcrops, eastern populations inhabit forests.

Habitat: Desert grasslands, open woodlands, mountain forests, and open parks in desert mountain ranges.

Breeding: Larger females may lay two dozen or more eggs per clutch and they can produce multiple clutches per year.

Breeding: Five or six eggs per clutch is average. Two clutches per year is common. Eggs hatch in mid summer.

Breeding: Breeding is similar to the previous two species with up to 10 eggs laid in early summer.

Natural History: This is a large lizard that is highly predatory on insects. Its preferred hunting method is to perch head down on a tree trunk a few feet off the ground and watch the surrounding area for any insect movement. When prey is spotted it will dash down the tree and across the ground to seize it prey. Its coloration is highly cryptic when on a tree trunk and it has the ability to alter its color and pattern to match the bark of the tree on which it is perched. Unlike many of the state's native reptiles the Texas Spiny Lizard seems to be thriving an possibly expanding its range in the state. They adapt well to urban areas and can be found in city parks and suburbs. They appear to outcompete their smaller relative (the Prairie Fence Lizard) where the ranges of the two overlap.

Natural History: This species is very similar to the Eastern Fence Lizard and was once regarded as a subspecies of that lizard species. Indeed, some populations of the Prairie Fence Lizard live in woodlands and act very much like their eastern counterparts from the deciduous forests of the eastern US. The Mississippi River is now regarded as the dividing line between the two similar species. Prey for this species in any type of small arthropod. Grasshoppers, crickets, spiders, beetles, and ants are all important food items but are by no means the only arthropods eaten. Like most predatory lizards the Prairie Fence Lizard is a true opportunistic feeder that will eat almost anything small enough to be swallowed whole. Lizard eating snakes like kingsnakes, milksnakes, and Patch-nosed snakes are major enemies.

Natural History: This is the desert counterpart of the Prairie Fence Lizard and was once regarded as a subspecies of that species. Like most *Sceloporus* it is frequently seen basking on rocks, logs, tree trunks. Favorite basking areas offer a quick escape into thick grass or rocks and they show a high fidelity to these favored spots. Food items and enemies are similar to the other *Sceloporus* lizards on this page with lizard eating snakes and raptors being major enemies. Their biggest enemy is probably the Greater Roadrunner. The coloration on these lizards typically matches the substrate within their environment. Lizards from areas of white sands will be very pale while those from other areas may be gray or brown. These common lizards are easily observed basking in the open in morning hours.

Class—**Reptilia** (reptiles)

Order—**Squamata** (lizards & snakes)

Family—**Phrynosomatidae** (spiny, horned & earless lizards)

Genus—*Sceloporus* (spiny lizards)

Twin-spotted Spiny Lizard *Sceloporus bimaculosus*	Crevice Spiny Lizard *Sceloporus poinsetti*	Blue Spiny Lizard *Sceloporus cyanogenys*

 Presumed range in TX    Presumed range in TX    Presumed range in TX

Size: Can reach a maximum of 13 inches.

Size: Can reach a maximum of 11.5 inches.

Size: Maximum of 14.5 inches. Average 10 to 11.

Abundance: Uncommon to rare in Texas. Restricted to part of Trans Pecos.

Abundance: Fairly common within its limited range in the state.

Abundance: Uncommon in Texas. More widespread in Mexico, especially Tamaulipas.

Variation: Female lacks blue blotches on throat and belly. Also has smaller black patch at shoulder. Juveniles have a more distinct pattern.

Variation: Blue patches on throat and belly are less distinct on females. Ground color may vary from very dark gray to light smoky gray or brownish.

Variation: Juveniles lack blue coloration or have it greatly reduced. Amount of blue is variable in adults and is usually most pronounced on the tail.

Habitat: The Chihuahuan Desert. Arroyos and canyons, rock piles, and often in the vicinity of woodrat nests.

Habitat: Rocky places. Canyons and arroyos, cliff faces, and hillsides with rocky outcrops and lava flows.

Habitat: In the Southern Texas Plains Ecoregion this lizard is found on rocks or on man-made concrete structures.

Breeding: An average of about 8 to 10 eggs but can be twice that. Two clutches per year may occur.

Breeding: This is a live-bearing lizard. An average of 10 young (up to two dozen) are born in late spring.

Breeding: Live bearer. Little is known about reproduction in this species. Presumably similar to the Crevice Spiny.

Natural History: These large *Sceloporus* really live up to the name "Spiny" lizard as their scales are enlarged, terminate sharply and protrude noticeably out from the body. They associate with drainages and show arboreal tendencies, climbing into mesquite trees and bushes. They are active above ground from early spring to late fall. Brumation occurs from December through March typically. Their name comes from their pattern of two rows of dark spots along the dorsum, which may be pronounced or faded and barely discernible. Food is a wide variety of insects and arthropods but ants are a major food source. Coachwhip snakes and Patch-nosed snakes are their major predators as are raptorial birds and the ferocious reptile hunter the Greater Roadrunner.

Natural History: Like the preceding species this lizard exhibits a true "Spiny" appearance. This is another large *Sceloporus* that can reach nearly a foot in length, though most are smaller. In Texas this species is found in the Trans-Pecos region and in the western edge of the Hill Country. As implied by their name, they love the crevices of horizontal layered rocks. Within these cracks they retreat from daytime predators and sleep at night. They are vulnerable at night to nocturnal lizard eating snakes who fit easily into their cracks. In Texas they are found in the Chihuahuan Desert and Edwards Plateau Ecoregions. Insects, spiders, and centipedes are known prey items and mature adults also eat the flower blossoms of herbaceous plants.

Natural History: This species can be considered as a larger and more colorful version of the Crevice Spiny Lizard. In habits and habitat preferences it mirrors that species. Although limited in distribution in Texas it is widespread in northeastern Mexico. This is a mainly insectivorous species that feeds on grasshoppers, crickets, beetles and even wasps. They have also been known to eat other, smaller lizard species. Although not every specimen exhibits bright blue colors, the most colorful versions of this lizard are striking animals. Various shades of blue or blue-green are exhibited dorsally with reddish-brown colors around the jaws and front legs. All this demarcated by a broad, distinct black collar around the shoulders that is bordered by a narrower white band.

Class—**Reptilia** (reptiles)
Order—**Squamata** (lizards & snakes)
Family—**Phrynosomatidae** (spiny, horned & earless lizards)
Genus—*Sceloporus* (spiny lizards)

Canyon Lizard *Sceloporus merriami*	Graphic Spiny Lizard *Sceloporus grammicus*	Dunes Sagebrush Lizard *Sceloporus arinicolus*

Size: Average 4 to 5 inches. Record 6.25 inches.	 Presumed range in TX	**Size:** 4 to 5 inches. Maximum 8.7 inches.	 Presumed range in TX	**Size:** 4 to 5 inches. Maximum 6 inches.	 Presumed range in TX
Abundance: Fairly common within their rather limited range in Texas.		**Abundance:** Rare in Texas. Barely ranges into southern Texas.		**Abundance:** A rare species found in Texas only in the Monahans Sand Dunes area.	

Variation: Variable. Varies from pale with very light spots to dark brown with very darks spots. Three subspecies in Texas and four more in Mexico.	**Variation:** Very little variation in this species. Males are slightly more boldly marked with dark, wavy lines dorsally and sometimes a greenish sheen.	**Variation:** Males are slightly larger as adults and have blue patches on the belly. Breeding females have orange or yellow on the lower sides.
Habitat: Boulder piles and rocky outcroppings of canyons and arroyos. Also steep canyon walls and dilapidated concrete structures.	**Habitat:** Mesquite scrub. In South Texas Plains this lizard can be seen on trunks of Mesquite or other small trees. Most of its range is in Mexico.	**Habitat:** Adapted to a special habitat known as "Sand Dune/Shinnery Oak" that exists in a small area in west Texas and adjacent SE New Mexico.
Breeding: Lays small clutches of 4 or 5 eggs in early spring and again in late summer.	**Breeding:** Little is known about reproduction in this species. Presumably similar to other viviparous *Sceloporus*.	**Breeding:** Females are reported to lay three to six eggs and can produce two clutches per year.
Natural History: Shown above is the Merriam's Canyon Lizard (*S. m. merriami*). The specimen shown is a pale individual whose ground color matches the color of the rocks within its habitat. Cryptic colors and patterns that match the organisms habitat is a common phenomenon among lizards and snakes in southwestern North America. Specimens of this lizard from other areas tend to be much darker and have pronounced dark spots dorsally. Canyon Lizards hunt by ambush. Clinging to a near vertical surface, they watch for insect prey and capture with a quick, darting motion. The range of this lizard in Texas is restricted to the Chihuahuan Desert Level III Ecoregion. Within this limited region they can be common.	**Natural History:** This species also goes by the name "Mesquite" Spiny Lizard, a reference to its preferred habitat in the mesquite dominated scrub lands of northeastern Mexico. While they are widespread in Mexico their range barely enters Texas in the lower Rio Grande Valley. The *Sceloporus* genus of lizards has undergone extensive and repeated revisions throughout the history of the science of herpetology (the study of reptiles an amphibians). The *Sceloporus* genus is widespread and contains many distinct populations that closely resemble each other. Thus lizard experts find them exasperatingly confusing to classify. Adding to the problem is the fact that some populations show significant local morphological variations.	**Natural History:** The tendency of North American *Sceloporus* lizards to exhibit colors and patterns to match their habitat is well known. The Dunes Sagebrush Lizard is one of the most definitive examples of this type of cryptic adaptation. The range of this species in Texas is mainly in the Monahans Sandhills State Park in western Texas. As with any species that has such a restricted range and specialized habitat, the Dunes Sagebrush Lizard is highly vulnerable to changes in its habitat. The Center for Biological Diversity, citing threats from oil and gas exploration and ranching interests has petitioned for protection for this species under the Endangered Species Act. But at this time protections have not yet been granted

Class—**Reptilia** (reptiles)

Order—**Squamata** (lizards & snakes)

Family—**Phrynosomatidae** (spiny, horned & earless lizards)

Genus—*Sceloporus* (spiny lizards)

Rosebelly Lizard *Sceloporus marmoratus*	**Eastern Side-blotched Lizard** *Uta stejnegeri*	**Ornate Tree Lizard** *Urosaurus ornatus*
		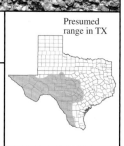

Rosebelly Lizard
Sceloporus marmoratus

Size: 3 to 4 inches. Maximum 5.5 inches.

Presumed range in TX

Abundance: A common species that can be seen in urban parks and wilderness.

Variation: Females are slightly smaller and have reduced or absent color patches on the lower sides and belly.

Habitat: An arid land lizard that typically associates with trees such as large Mesquite or large cacti.

Breeding: Females lay 2 to 6 eggs that hatch into tiny replicas of the adult in about two and half months.

Natural History: The more colorful examples of this *Sceloporus* species are delicately beautiful. Breeding males have contrasting light and dark stripes on the back and a rose-colored patch on the lower sides that is sometimes edged in pale blue. There is usually a black blotch that borders the rose belly patch anteriorly and posteriorly. Primarily a insect eater. Smaller insects are the main prey. Like most small lizard species and all *Sceloporus* lizards this species is capable of a defensive mechanism known as autotomy, the voluntary breaking off of the tail to escape a predator. When the lizard's tail breaks it will wriggle and squirm for several seconds which tends to focus the predators attention while the lizard makes its escape. They then have the ability to regenerate much of the lost tail.

Eastern Side-blotched Lizard
Uta stejnegeri

Size: 3.5 to 4.5 inches. Maximum of 5.5.

Presumed range in TX

Abundance: Uncommon, but fairly common in some localities in west Texas.

Variation: Variable. Some exhibit colorful blue flecking while others are plainly mottled browns or grays.

Habitat: Inhabits arid and semi-arid regions where it is found in a variety of habitats.

Breeding: Two to five eggs per clutch. Will produce multiple clutches. Egg laying begins in early spring.

Natural History: Hunts in a fashion typical of most lizards in the Phrynosomatidae family, which is to sit and wait for prey to come into view and then make a quick predatory dash. Prey items are all manner of small arthropods including ants, beetles, flies, grasshoppers, termites, spiders, and even scorpions. Until recently, there was one wide ranging species of Side-blotched Lizard found throughout the western half of North America. There were seven subspecies recognized, one of which was the Eastern Side-blotched Lizard (subspecies *stejnegeri*). More recent research has resulted in the elevation of the Eastern Side-blotched to full species status, although most text sources still treat it as a subspecies. Strangely, the speed of these lizards has been shown to correlate with throat coloration!

Ornate Tree Lizard
Urosaurus ornatus

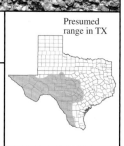

Size: Maximum length of 5.4 inches.

Presumed range in TX

Abundance: Common in the Chihuahuan Desert and Edwards Plateau Ecoregions.

Variation: Varying shades of gray, dark individuals may an obscured dorsal pattern. Female lacks blue belly patches.

Habitat: Arid environments. Found in rocky canyons, cliff faces, and tree trunks in open woodlands and savanna.

Breeding: Egg layer that may lay over a dozen eggs or as few as two. Capable of more than one clutch per year.

Natural History: In areas where they are found this is one of the most observable lizards. They are commonly seen on cliff faces or on the trunks of trees. They occur in riparian areas in the desert and in open woodlands in the Edwards Plateau. Small insects, spiders and other arthropods are their food. They will sometimes sit in the open on a rock or a tree trunk, especially in the morning hours. Although they are well camouflaged when on a tree trunk they will often reveal themselves as they make short dashes in pursuit of small insects. Population densities can be quite high in localized ideal habitat and under these conditions there is always a great deal of territorial activity between nearby lizards. They are easy to find under these circumstances as they chase intruders that wander into their territory.

Class—**Reptilia** (reptiles)
Order—**Squamata** (lizards & snakes)
Family—**Polychrotidae** (anole lizards)

Green (Carolina) Anole *Anolis carolinensis*	Brown Anole *Anolis sagrei*

Green phase

Brown phase

Size: Maximum length 9 inches. Average length 4 to 5 inches. The tail can be as much as two-thirds of the total length.

Presumed range in TX

Size: Maximum length 9 inches. Average 4 to 5.

Presumed range in TX

Abundance: Common. Probably most common in the Western Gulf Coastal Plain ecoregion.

Abundance: Rare in Texas

Variation: Changes color from bright green to brown. Green in foliage, brown when on bark. Also brown when cold.

Variation: Males have ridge on the top of the back.

Habitat: Mainly woodlands and woodland edges. Also overgrown fields, swamps, suburban landscape plantings, virtually anywhere there is vegetation. They require humid climates and moist environments.

Habitat: More terrestrial than the Carolina Anole and less likely to be seen more than a few feet off the ground.

Breeding: Lays only one or two eggs in late spring or early summer. Eggs hatch in 1 to 2 months. Mating may continue throughout the summer and eggs may be laid several times continuously all through the summer.

Breeding: The female lays a single egg about every two weeks all summer long. Eggs hatch in about a month.

Natural History: The Green Anole often goes by name "Chameleon" but that name is properly reserved for old world lizards of the family Chamaeleonidae. It is also commonly called the Carolina Anole, an appropriate name since its species name is *carolinensis*. Like the true chameleons, this lizard does have the ability to change its colors and to a degree is able to match its background. When on bark or soil it is usually brown, changing to green when amid bushes and other vegetation. When cold, the color is also brown, but will change to green when the lizard is exposed to the warming rays of the sun. These little lizards are active diurnal foragers and can be seen leaping from branch to branch in low bushes as the search for tiny insect prey. Like many insect eaters they are highly vulnerable to insecticides. Ironically, the lizards may do a better job of controlling the insects. Male Green Anoles possess a flap of skin on the throat known as a "Dewlap." On breeding males the dewlap becomes bright red and it is expanded to advertise the males presence to nearby females or to warn away other lizards intruding into its territory.

Natural History: Introduced. Native to the Caribbean, these Anoles first appeared in Florida a century ago, but in the last 40 years they have become very common and widespread throughout the US gulf coastal region. They are an invasive, introduced species and there is evidence that they are out competing the native Green Anole. Where they occur together the Green Anole tends to stay higher in vegetation. Unlike the native Green Anole, the Brown Anole does not change color from brown to green, but remains consistently brown.

Class—**Reptilia** (reptiles)
Order—**Squamata** (lizards & snakes)
Family—**Scincidae** (skinks)

Coal Skink	Prairie Skink	Four-lined Skink
Plestiodon anthracinus	*Plestiodon septentrionalis*	*Plestiodon tetrogrammus*

Size: To 7 inches.	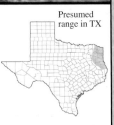 Presumed range in TX	**Size:** To 8 inches	Presumed range in TX	**Size:** To 7 inches	 Presumed range in TX
Abundance: Uncommon.		**Abundance:** Uncommon.		**Abundance:** Uncommon.	
Variation: Young are darker and have blue or black tails.		**Variation:** Young are darker and have blue tails.		**Variation:** Sexual, ontogenetic, and subspecies variation. See below.	

Habitat: Coal Skinks inhabit the forest floor in damp woodlands. They are frequently found near creeks.	**Habitat:** Mainly a grassland species. Also in woodlands. Sandy soils that facilitate burrowing are preferred.	**Habitat:** Mainly an arid land species. Lives in dry grasslands, thorn scrub and woodlands in desert mountain ranges.
Breeding: From 6 to 12 eggs are laid under rocks, logs or other sheltering structures. Females will remain with and guard the eggs until hatching. Babies are less than 2 inches in length.	**Breeding:** Mating occurs in spring and an average of about dozen eggs are laid in moist soils usually beneath a rock or log. Eggs hatch in about two months. Apparently only one clutch annually.	**Breeding:** Clutch sizes range from 3 to 12. Eggs are laid in the spring and hatch in mid summer. Babies are tiny, barely over two inches long. As with many skink species, the female guards eggs.
Natural History: Termites, ant larva and pupae, and earthworms are listed as known food items. Probably feeds on a wide variety of small insects and other tiny invertebrates encountered in the leaf litter on the forest floor. As with all skinks found in Texas, they are diurnal. They shelter at night beneath logs, stones, or loose bark on dead snags, stumps, etc. The range of this species in Texas is restricted to part of the South Central Plains Level III Ecoregion (i.e. Piney Woods). Throughout their range they seem to not be equally distributed but rather occur in disjunct populations here and there. There seems to be a paucity of locality records for this species in Texas, but it could potentially occur anywhere within the South Central Plains Ecoregion. The range map above shows the area where it is most likely to occur, but it may not be an accurate representation of the range of this species in the state.	**Natural History:** Prairie Skinks range through much central US from Texas into southern Manitoba, Canada. There are two disjunct populations and there seems to be some disagreement among herpetologists regarding the status of the northern and southern populations (known as the Northern and Southern Prairie Skinks.) Some regard the two populations as subspecies while others consider them to be two distinct species. They are treated here as subspecies. The subspecies in Texas is *obtusirostris*. These small skinks are apparently not very common overall, although they may be more common than records would indicate as they are secretive and difficult to observe. They likely have small home ranges and spent much of their time hiding beneath rocks or logs. These skinks seem to favor mesic habitats and are usually found in the vicinity of streams. They are known to enter water to escape and enemy.	**Natural History:** Sexes are similar but males have orange on the throat. Juveniles are black with blue tails. There are two subspecies in Texas. The Short-lined Four-lined Skink (subspecies *brevilineatus*) is found in the southern tip of Texas while the Long-lined Four-lined Skink (subspecies *tetragrammus*) occupies the rest of the species' range in the state. These are secretive lizards except when sunning in the mornings or actively foraging in morning and early evening. They are diurnal in habits and spend the night hiding beneath rocks or in crevices. Although they inhabit arid regions they prefer a micro-habitat that is relatively moist. This they find along streams or in wooded mountain canyons where there is an abundance of moisture retaining leaf litter. Spiders and a wide variety of small insect species are listed are food items. The lizards themselves are prey for many other predators but lizard eating snakes are the main threat.

Class—**Reptilia** (reptiles)

Order—**Squamata** (lizards & snakes)

Family—**Scincidae** (skinks)

Five-lined Skink *Plestiodon fasciatus*	Broad-headed Skink *Plestiodon laticeps*

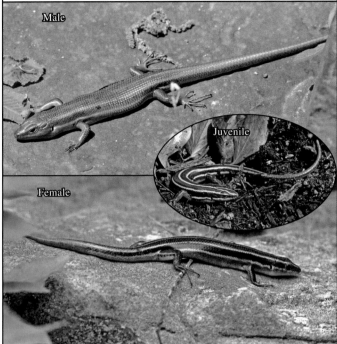

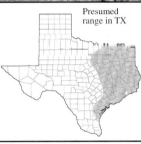

Size: 5 to 7 inches.	**Size:** Maximum of 13 inches.
Abundance: Very common.	**Abundance:** Fairly common.
Variation: Young are brightly colored with distinct pale yellow stripes and blue tails. Females resemble young but tail is steel color. Males are brown with reddish cheek patches. See photos.	**Variation:** Young have blue tails and yellow stripes and resemble Five-lined Skinks. Adult females have indistinct lines, males are brown with bright red cheeks.

Presumed range in TX

Habitat: Most common in damp woodlands but also found in swamps and in drier upland areas. Patches of sunlit areas for basking is important. Woodland opening and edge areas.	**Habitat:** Mesic woodlands, swamps, wetland areas and also dry upland woods with moist micro-habitat. Requires some open areas for sunning.
Breeding: Eggs (6 to 12) are laid in May or early June in rotted logs, stumps, sawdust, mulch or other moisture retaining material. Female remains with eggs until hatching.	**Breeding:** Females will vigorously defend their eggs that are usually laid on the ground in a hollowed out depression beneath sheltering log or inside a hollow stump.
Natural History: The young of this species are strikingly colored with bright blue tails and they sometimes are mistaken by lay persons as being another species going by the name "Blue-tailed Skink." These common and well-known lizards are fond of sunning on decks, porches, sidewalks, and patios of homes in rural areas. They can often be found in suburban environments as well, particularly older neighborhoods with abundant large trees and shrubbery. They feed on a wide variety of insects, spiders, and arthropods and they are a useful species in controlling invertebrate pests around the home. Unfortunately they are highly vulnerable to insecticides. Ironically, spraying for insect pests outside the home kills some of the best natural insect controllers in the animal kingdom. Like the male Broad-headed Skink, breeder male Five-lined Skinks develop bright red cheeks. In appearance nearly identical to the Broad-headed Skink but smaller and less bulky.	**Natural History:** These very large skinks are quite arboreal and often den in tree hollows many feet above the ground. These arboreal dens are used only during summer and hibernation takes place underground. In much of the southeast they are known as "Scorpion Lizards" and some believe the myth that they are dangerously venomous. Although they will bite if handled, they are totally harmless to humans. This is the largest skink species in the southeast and the largest individuals can barely exceed a foot in length. Insects are the main food but they will also eat small mammals such as baby mice. Breeding males develop bright red, grotesquely swollen cheeks, i.e. the Broad-headed name. The range in Texas encompasses the entire South Central Plains Ecoregion but extends west into the East Central Texas Plains and Blackland Prairies and south into Western Gulf Coastal Plain. Larger overall and has broader head than the Five-Lined Skink.

Class—**Reptilia** (reptiles)

Order—**Squamata** (lizards & snakes)

Family—**Scincidae** (skinks)

Great Plains Skink *Plestiodon obsoletus*	**Many-lined Skink** *Plestiodon multivirgatus*	**Ground Skink** *Scincella lateralis*

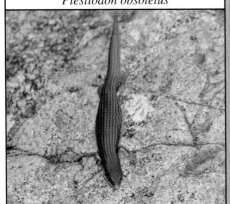  

Size: Average about 8 or 9 inches. To 13.75.

Presumed range in TX

Abundance: Fairly common. Secretive and more common than sightings would indicate.

Variation: Significant age-related variation. Young are solid black with blue tails. Color of adults also variable from gray to dark brown to tan.

Habitat: A grassland species. Micro-habitats are rocky areas, especially flat rocks that offer cover and shelter from the elements.

Breeding: Females lay up to 25 eggs (usually about half that amount) in moist soils or moisture retaining humus.

Natural History: With a record length that is three-quarters of an inch longer than the Broad-headed Skink, this is the largest skink species found in Texas. They are large enough to feed on baby mice, but the main food is insects like grasshoppers, crickets, and beetles. As with other skink species the breeding males develop swollen heads. Like most other lizards in Texas (and all skinks) the tail is easily broken off if the lizard is grabbed or restrained by the tail. Lizard tails will regenerate slowly, but the re-grown tail is never as long as the original, Most older lizard will have lost their tail in a close encounter at some time in their lives. An original, unbroken tail may be twice the length of the head and body on most skinks.

Size: Average about 6 inches. Maximum 8.

Presumed range in TX

Abundance: Rare. Occurs in disjunct and erratically distributed localities in west Texas.

Variation: Variable. In fact another name for this species is Variable Skink. Most have black and white lines running down the back. Some are solid brown.

Habitat: Inhabits arid or semi-arid grasslands and desert where it occupies more mesic habitats. Rocky situations and mountain canyons.

Breeding: Oviparous. Females lays up to a dozen eggs in moist situations. Female stays with eggs until hatching.

Natural History: There are two subspecies of this rare skink. The subspecies native to Texas is *epipleurotus*, commonly called the Variable Skink due to the fact that its color and pattern is highly variable. Many examples of this skink have alternating light and dark longitudinal lines on the back. Other specimens may be uniformly dark brown or tan with black outlined scales. Some may be intermediate between the lined form and the unlined form. In addition to occurring in disjunct localities throughout its limited range, it is also a secretive animal that spends much of its time hidden beneath rocks or within the labyrinth of crevices in talus piles. During warmer weather they are active in mornings and early evenings mainly.

Size: Average 3 to 4 inches. Maximum 5.75 inches.

Presumed range in TX

Abundance: Fairly common to common in wooded habitats in eastern half of the state.

Variation: Color may vary from reddish brown to golden brown or chocolate brown. Color often has a metallic quality. Some have small dark flecks.

Habitat: Dry upland woods and pine woodlands. Micro-habitat consists of leaf litter and detritus on the forest floor where more mesic conditions exist.

Breeding: Small clutches of 3 to 5 eggs is typical. May lay twice per year. Newly hatched young are tiny!

Natural History: These tiny ground dwellers dive quickly beneath leaf litter when approached and they are easily overlooked. Often, their presence is revealed by the rustling sound made as they forage through the dry leaves. Despite being rarely observed, they can be quite common in many areas. Foods are tiny insects and other small invertebrates living among the leaf litter on the forest floor. They also go by the name "Little Brown Skink." They are widespread throughout the southeastern half of America and are most common in the deep south. They are among the smallest native lizards found in Texas. The best way to observe these common but cryptic lizards is to listen for their rustling sounds in the leaf litter.

Class—**Reptilia** (reptiles)

Order—**Squamata** (lizards & snakes)

Family—**Teidae** (whiptail & tegu lizards)

Genus—*Aspidoscelis* (whiptails)

Size: Most are from 6 to 10 inches as adults. Maximum length achieved by several species can be up to 12.5 inches.

Abundance: Generally, these are common lizards and their active, diurnal habits make them among the more commonly observed lizards in Texas. Some varieties are widespread and very common (Six-lined Racerunner—*Aspidoscelis sexlineatus* and Common Spotted Whiptail—*Aspidoscelis gularis*). A few are uncommon or rare and have limited distribution in the state. But all residents of Texas most likely have at least one species of whiptail lizard in the area.

Variation: A highly variable genus with as many as ten species in Texas. All exhibit a dorsal pattern of contrasting light and dark markings that are variously striped, spotted, checkered or often a combination of stripes and spots or checkered markings.

Habitat: The only universal requirement for these lizards is access to sunshine. They avoid thick woodlands and are most common in grasslands, deserts, semi-open and open slopes of mountains and rugged plateaus.

Breeding: The *Aspidoscelis* genus is famous among biologists because in some species there are no males and reproduction is accomplished by parthenogenesis (the development of unfertilized eggs into embryos). Several species found in Texas are unisexual species. It is believed that in most cases these Unisexual species arose from the hybridization of two similar species where their ranges overlap. There is confirmed evidence that some Unisexual *Aspidoscelis* species are capable of sexual reproduction as well, further complicating the understanding of the phylogeny and taxonomy of this fascinating genus of lizards and calling into question long standing definitions of exactly what constitutes a biological species.

Natural History: The *Aspidoscelis* lizards are a common and diverse genus in the southwestern United States. These speedy lizards can reach a speed of up to 20 mph. They are active at higher temperatures than many reptiles and they will spend the first few minutes of the day basking in the sun to raise their body temperature. At night they retreat to an underground burrow dug into loose soil. Food is mainly insects and other invertebrates but larger individuals may include small vertebrates in the diet. Identifying this group of lizards is a challenge even for trained herpetologists and species/subspecies classifications of the genus is constantly undergoing changes as more data is accumulated. In areas where more than one species occur together the average observer will likely have to content themselves with identifying them simply as "Whiptail Lizard."

Marbled Whiptail
Aspidoscelis marmorata

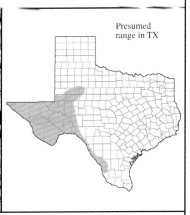

Presumed range in TX

Desert Grassland Whiptail
Aspidoscelis uniparens

Presumed range in TX

Order—**Squamata** (lizards & snakes)

Family—**Teidae** (whiptail & tegu lizards)

Genus—*Aspidoscelis* (whiptails)

Six-lined Racerunner—*Aspidoscelis sexlineatus*

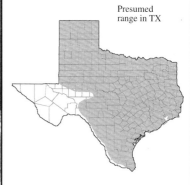

Presumed range in TX

Common (Texas) Spotted Whiptail—*Aspidoscelis gularis*

Presumed range in TX

Little Striped Whiptail *Aspidoscelis inornata*	**Laredo Striped Whiptail** *Aspidoscelis laredoensis*	**Plateau Spotted Whiptail** *Aspidoscelis scalaris*
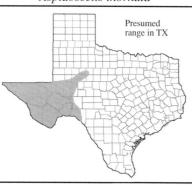Presumed range in TX	Presumed range in TX	Presumed range in TX
Common Checkered Whiptail *Aspidoscelis tessalata*	**New Mexico Checkered Whiptail** *Aspidoscelis neomexicanus*	**Chihuahuan Spotted Whiptail** *Aspidoscelis exsanguis*
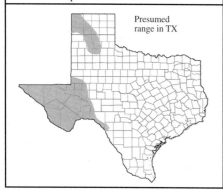Presumed range in TX	Presumed range in TX	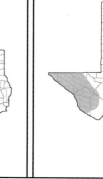Presumed range in TX

Class—**Reptilia** (reptiles)
Order—**Squamata** (lizards & snakes)
Family—**Anguidae** (glass & alligator lizards)

Texas Alligator Lizard *Gerrohonotus infernalis*	**Slender Glass Lizard** *Ophisaurus attenuatus*

Size: Record length 20 inches. Average about 12 to 14 inches.

Abundance: Generally regarded as uncommon.

Variation: Ground color varies from tan to dark brown. Young are more vividly marked with darker colors and reddish head.

Presumed range in TX

Size: Maximum total length of 46.5 inches.

Abundance: Uncommon to rare, spottily distributed.

Variation: Young lizards are tan above with dark brown sides. Old adults often have a "salt and pepper" appearance.

Presumed range in TX

Habitat: Regions where rocks are predominant. Canyons, rocky hillsides and desert mountains. Usually in the vicinity of permanent streams. In Texas it is found in the Edwards Plateau and Chihuahuan Desert Level III Ecoregions.

Habitat: Favors sandy, friable soils in open or semi-open habitats. Old fields, sandy woodlands, pine/wiregrass uplands. Avoids wetlands. The range shows the general distribution in Texas, but it is absent from many the areas shown.

Breeding: Females guard the eggs throughout incubation and will fight to defend them. Clutch sizes can be as many as two dozen or as few as five or six eggs.

Breeding: Lays up to 20 eggs often in a clump of grass. Female stays with eggs during incubation, which lasts up to two months.

Natural History: This lizard's name comes from their superficial resemblance to an alligator. These are unique lizards in several respects. They have a type of armored exterior created by thick, non-overlapping scales. They also have a fold of skin along the side of the body known as a "dorso-lateral fold." This fold is also present on other species having armored scales such as the legless lizards. The immobility of the armored scales inhibits the ability to expand the thoracic cavity. The dorso-lateral fold allows for thoracic expansion which in necessary for breathing. These lizard also sometimes when alarmed exhibit a threat display that consists of a wide gaping of the jaws. Finally, they possess a prehensile tail which is unusual in North American Lizards. This feature may have evolved as an adaptation for an arboreal lifestyle. Indeed this lizard does like to climb into low bushes and trees.

Natural History: The only lizard in Texas without external limbs. Some species of legless lizards possess the skeletal features of the pelvic and pectoral girdles, which are associated with anchoring and supporting limbs in vertebrate animals. As such, this group of reptiles provides an excellent example of an intermediate stage in the evolution of snakes from lizard-like ancestors. These lizards are often confused with snakes due to their lack of limbs. They are easily recognized as lizards, however, by the presences of ear openings and eyelids. When grasped these lizards will thrash about wildly and break off their tail. The apparent fragility of these lizards and the shiny appearance of their skin has led to the common name "glass lizard." The highly specialized escape mechanism of breaking off the tail is shared with many other lizard species, as is the rare ability to regenerate a new tail.

Class—**Reptilia** (reptiles)

Order—**Squamata** (lizards & snakes)

Family—**Eublepharidae** (banded geckos)

Texas Banded Gecko	**Reticulated Gecko**
Coleonyx brevis	*Coleonyx reticulatus*

Size: Average about four inches. Maximum just under five inches.

Abundance: Fairly common.

Variation: This is a variable species. Some color morphs are banded with clean light bands while others have small spots within the light bands.

Presumed range in TX

Habitat: Mainly a species of the Chihuahuan Desert Ecoregion but also ranges into the southern part of the Edwards Plateau and South Central Plains Ecoregions.

Breeding: Females produce two clutches of eggs per year and nearly always lay two eggs at a time.

Natural History: As is true with the habits of most geckos, the Texas Banded Gecko is a nocturnal animal. By day they hide under rocks, in crevices or other sheltered places. This family of geckos (Eublepharidae) also go by the name "Eyelidded Geckos," an appropriate moniker since unlike some geckos from the old world that lack eyelids, the Eublepharidae geckos do possess movable eyelids. These tiny lizards feed on a wide variety of small insects (especially termites and ants). They will also eat larva and some small arachnids. In fact, any tiny arthropod small enough to be swallowed is potential prey. In the hot environments of the desert, most animals lead a nocturnal existence. These geckos prowl slowly about in the darkness when their food is also active. When prey is spotted, they will attack and grasp the prey in the mouth. Small items are crushed in the jaws. Larger prey items are disabled by repeatedly bashing them against the ground. In spite of their name, some specimens may appear more mottled than banded.

Size: Averages four to five inches. Maximum 6.75 inches.

Abundance: Rare.

Variation: Juvenile specimens exhibit a banded pattern similar to the Texas Banded Gecko. With age the bands fade and are replaced by a pattern of spots.

Presumed range in TX

Habitat: Cliff faces, rocky canyons, and boulder-strewn hillsides and desert. The range of this in species in Texas appears to be contained within the southern tip of the Big Bend region.

Breeding: Females produce two clutches of eggs per year and nearly always lay two eggs at a time.

Natural History: This species is large for a gecko. Like other geckos, it is a nocturnal animal. It is apparently more active on rainy nights. Unlike many other geckos the examples shown on this page lack the special adhesive toe pads that allow for climbing with ease on vertical surfaces. Geckos that have that special adhesive toe pad adaptation are famous for being able to walk upside down across a ceiling. But the Eublepharidae family of geckos (represented on this page) lack that ability and are thus largely confined to a terrestrial existence. These Eublepharidae geckos are native species in Texas, unlike many of the species shown on the following page that have been introduced. The Eublepharidae are a rather small family of geckos with just over two dozen species currently known. Seven species occur in the western hemisphere. Four species occur in the southwestern US from California to Texas, but only the two shown on this page range into the state of Texas.

Class—**Reptilia** (reptiles)

Order—**Squamata** (lizards & snakes)

Family—**Gekkonidae** (true geckos)

Rough-tailed Gecko *Cyrtopodion scabrum*	Mediterranean Gecko *Hemidactylus turcicus*	Common House Gecko *Hemidactylus frenatus*

Size: 3 to 4.625 inches.  Presumed range in TX	**Size:** 4 to 5 inches. 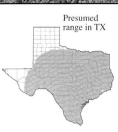 Presumed range in TX	**Size:** 4 to 5.5 inches.  Presumed range in TX
Abundance: Rare. Very limited distribution in Texas. Found only in the Galveston area.	**Abundance:** Fairly common. The most widespread introduced gecko in Texas.	**Abundance:** Apparently pretty rare in Texas generally, but can be fairly common around Houston.
Variation: There is no significant variation and juveniles are miniature replicas of the adult.	**Variation:** Ground color varies, may be tan, pinkish, or yellowish. Juveniles are miniature replicas of the adult.	**Variation:** Ground color varies from gray to tan. Males are larger than females.
Habitat: Native habitat is desert areas where it associates with rocky habitats. Also found in the vicinity of human altered habitats (i.e. around buildings).	**Habitat:** Apparently can survive in temperate climates throughout North America. Relies on urban and suburban areas where it associates with structures.	**Habitat:** A native of the Indo-Pacific region that today has colonies throughout the world. The name House Gecko is appropriate. Houses are its habitat.
Breeding: Egg layer. Apparently produces on one or two eggs per clutch. However, multiple clutches per year are typical.	**Breeding:** A fairly prolific species, female Mediterranean Geckos will lay multiple clutches of two eggs at a time from spring through fall.	**Breeding:** Two eggs are always laid. The eggs are hard shelled rather than leathery like most reptile eggs. This feature allows them to resist dessication.
Natural History: A non-native introduced gecko. Native range is in the middle east from northwest Africa to Pakistan and maybe northern India. This species has also been introduced into scattered localities in Arizona, southern Nevada and southeastern California. The Galveston, Texas introduction may have occurred through stowaways on ocean going cargo ships. Other introductions are likely from escaped or released captives from the exotic pet industry. In Texas this species can be seen on the walls of many structures around the Galveston docks, which lends credence to the theory that they arrived in Texas aboard container ships from the middle east. In their native range they are also commonly seen on the walls of houses and buildings.	**Natural History:** Native to the Mediterranean region of southern Europe and northern Africa. This species has become extremely widespread across the southern United States and is today found from the Atlantic coast of Georgia to northwestern Mexico, including nearly all the eastern half of Texas. In an odd twist for a "wild" animal, the Mediterranean Gecko seems unable to exist in true wilderness. Rather, they thrive in areas of human habitation where they live on (or sometimes in) peoples homes, structures, and buildings in parks, around old industrial buildings, etc. On the range map shown above this species exists mainly in towns and cities and is unlikely to be encountered in rural regions or wilderness outside of towns, cities and metropolitan regions.	**Natural History:** Even more of a human-adapted species than the Mediterranean Gecko. This lizard today has colonies on every continent except Antarctica. The exotic pet industry is responsible for much of this lizard's invasive tendencies, but the shipping industry has also contributed greatly to spreading it around the world. All non-native species can pose a threat to local ecosystems and the geckos are no exception. This species is probably the worst when it comes to out-competing native species, and in fact is known to prey on many of the smaller native lizards. All the geckos on this page possess sticky toe pads and lack eyelids. These are the "true geckos." Fortunately for Texas's native lizards, this species is not widespread in Texas today.

THE REPTILES OF TEXAS

PART 2: SNAKES

Class—**Reptilia** (reptiles)
Order—**Squamata** (lizards & snakes)
Family—**Leptotyphlopidae** (thread snakes)

Plains Thread Snake

Plains Thread Snake
Rena dulcis

Size: Maximum length of about 10 inches.

Abundance: Rarely seen but possibly not a very rare snake.

Presumed range in TX

Variation: Three subspecies are found in Texas. Differences are imperceptible.

Habitat: Sandy or friable soils in arid and semi-arid plains.

Breeding: Egg layer. Hatchlings are tiny, thread-like, and 3 inches long.

Natural History: All three species of blind snakes in the genus *Rena* are very similar in appearance. Experts use a magnifying glass to closely examine the scales on the head to distinguish between species. To some degree, locality can be used to distinguish the different species. But this method is unreliable if the snake is observed in an area where the ranges of two species overlap. These small, shiny, uniformly reddish brown serpents have short, blunt heads that are the same diameter as the body and they are easily mistaken for an earthworm. Close examination will reveal the presence of scales and a dark spot on each side of the head that are the eyes.

New Mexico Thread Snake
Rena dissecta

Size: Maximum of 11.5 inches.

Abundance: Unknown. Possibly not a rare snake.

Presumed range in TX

Variation: No variation. Some experts treat it as a subspecies of *R. dulcis*.

Habitat: Arid, sandy grasslands and deserts where there is some moisture.

Breeding: Egg layer. Hatchlings are tiny, thread-like, and 2.5 inches long.

Natural History: All the snakes on this page have subterminal mouths that are tucked under the snout and so small that the only food available to them are the smallest of soil organisms. Termites and ants are reportedly the main prey. The three species of thread snakes found in Texas are for all practical purposes identical. Thus a single photo is provided to depict all three species. Professional herpetologists use a magnifying glass to examine the arrangement of the scales on the head to determine the correct species ID. Unlike other "typical" snake species, all thread snakes have scales that are the same size on the back and the belly. They also have blunt tails and vestigial eyes covered by scales.

Western Thread Snake
Rena humilis

Size: Maximum of 13.5 inches.

Abundance: Unknown. Possibly not a rare snake.

Presumed range in TX

Variation: Two subspecies are recognized but only one occurs in Texas.

Habitat: Desert grassland and rocky canyons. Hides under stones.

Breeding: Egg layer. Hatchlings are tiny, thread-like, and 3.5 inches long.

Natural History: The thread snakes are often mistaken for some type of an earthworm. It is difficult to determine which end of the snake is the head, since the head and tail are the same size and the eyes are hidden beneath a scale, appearing as two tiny dark spots. With a maximum length of 13.5 inches, this is largest of the thread snakes found in Texas. The average person not intentionally looking for a thread snake will likely never see one. To find this snake requires looking under flat rocks and other cover in canyons vegetated hillsides. They are often more common in the vicinity of water, such as a rocky canyon with a small creek. All thread snakes are uniformly colored.

Class—**Reptilia** (reptiles)
Order—**Squamata** (lizards & snakes)
Family—**Colubridae** (harmless egg-laying snakes)
Genus—**Tantilla** (crowned snakes)

Flat-headed Snake
Tantilla gracilis

Size: Maximum of 12.125 inches.

Abundance: Common. The most widespread member of the *Tantilla* group in Texas.

Variation: No significant variation occurs in snakes of this species in Texas.

Presumed range in TX

Plains Black-headed Snake
Tantilla nigriceps

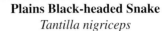

Size: Maximum of 16 inches.

Abundance: There is little data on the abundance of this snake in Texas, but is likely fairly common.

Variation: No significant variation occurs in snakes of this species in Texas.

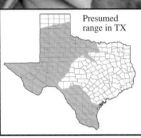
Presumed range in TX

Smith's Black-headed Snake
Tantilla hobartsmithi

Abundance: Rare in Texas.

Variation: Juveniles are more vividly colored.

Presumed range in TX

Trans-Pecos Black-headed Snake
Tantilla cucullata

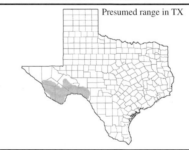
Presumed range in TX

Size: Maximum of 9.125 inches.

Abundance: Fairly common.

Variation: This species is not pictured but it is very similar to other Black-headed Snakes in Texas. Juveniles have greenish or blue tails.

Mexican Black-headed Snake
Tantilla atriceps

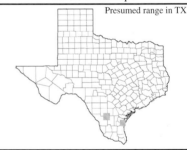
Presumed range in TX

Size: Maximum of 12.25 inches.

Abundance: Very limited range.

Variation: This species is not pictured but it is very similar to other Black-headed Snakes in Texas. Juveniles more distinctly marked.

Habitat: The collective ranges of the *Tantilla* snakes in Texas includes all the state's ecoregions. Most species seem to prefer friable soil types and abundant ground cover in the form of flat stones under which they hide.

Breeding: All *Tantilla* are egg layers and most produce small clutches of only two or three eggs. Clutches of only a single egg are common in some species. Baby snakes are 3 to 3.5 inches in length.

Natural History: The *Tantilla* snakes are a widespread group of tiny serpents that are found mostly in Latin America. There are at least a dozen species found across the southern half of the US with an additional fifty (or more) species ranging throughout Latin America south to Argentina. They produce a mild venom and possess grooved teeth in the rear of the upper jaw which are used to introduce the venom into their tiny invertebrate prey. The venom is not toxic enough to pose a threat to a human, and even it were their tiny mouths and minuscule teeth make it impossible to bite a human. Add to that the fact that their venom glands are so small that no appreciable amount of venom could be injected anyway and you have a venomous snake that is completely harmless to man. The main difference between species is the pattern produced by the black pigment present on the head.

Class—**Reptilia** (reptiles)

Order—**Squamata** (lizards & snakes)

Family—**Colubridae** (harmless egg-laying snakes)

Scarlet Snake *Cemophora coccinea*	Glossy Snake *Arizona elegans*	Central American Indigo Snake *Drymarchon melanurus*

Size: 24 to 30 inches for a large adult.	 Presumed range in TX	**Size:** 3 feet on average. Record is 55.5 inches.	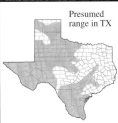 Presumed range in TX	**Size:** Averages 6 feet. Record 8 feet, 4 inches.	 Presumed range in TX
Abundance: This is an uncommon to rare snake in most of its range.		**Abundance:** Fairly common in good habitat throughout its range in Texas.		**Abundance:** Uncommon to rare. Populations harmed by habitat loss and droughts.	

Variation: There are 3 subspecies and 2 occur in Texas. Differences between subspecies are very slight and both subspecies resemble the photo above. | **Variation:** There are at least 8 subspecies and 3 are found in Texas. All three resemble the specimen above but some may be more brownish or grayish. | **Variation:** There is very little variation in this species. But the color on the chin and throat can vary from reddish to orange-brown.

Habitat: In Texas this species is found in part of South Central Plains and in the southern portion of the Western Gulf Coastal Plains Level III Ecoregions. | **Habitat:** This is an arid to semi arid land species that favors friable soils that allow for burrowing. Will utilize flat rocks for shelter where soils are harder. | **Habitat:** The Indigo Snake is a resident of the thorn brush communities of the Southern Texas Plains and the southern tip of the Western Gulf Coastal Plain.

Breeding: Probably breeds in early spring. Lays from 2 to 9 eggs in late June or early July. Eggs hatch in late August or early September. | **Breeding:** Lays 10 to 20 eggs in moist situations. The tiny baby snakes hatch in the summer and are just under 10 inches in total length. | **Breeding:** Probably lays about a dozen eggs. Baby Indigo Snakes can be over two feet in length. Large enough to swallow a grown mouse or fence lizard.

Natural History: The range of the two subspecies that occur in Texas is disjunct. But both subspecies prefer habitats with loose, sandy soils that facilitate burrowing. They are probably most common in dry, upland woods but they can occur in overgrown fields and successional habitats. The main food of adult Scarlet Snakes are reptile eggs and the newly hatched young of reptiles. In captivity they will also eat baby mice and small mammals are probably part of the diet of wild specimens as well. Young Scarlet Snakes probably feed on insects and other small invertebrate prey since they are two small to swallow most vertebrates. Their color and pattern causes them to often be confused with the venomous Coral Snake. | **Natural History:** This snake is regularly encountered, which suggests if must be a fairly common species since it is a secretive and mainly nocturnal animal. During the day Glossy Snakes are usually hidden in small mammal burrows or beneath rocks or organic detritus. These snakes feed mainly on lizards and small rodents, which they kill by constriction. There are a total of eight recognized subspecies of this wide ranging snake and three of them can be found in Texas. All three Texas subspecies exhibit the same "glossy" appearance due to the smoothness of their scales. All are patterned with many dark saddles down the middle of the back with smaller, similarly colored circular blotches on the sides. | **Natural History:** One of the largest snakes in Texas and perhaps the greatest enemy of the Western Diamondback Rattlesnake. Young and juvenile rattlers are a favorite food. Other snakes are also regular items on the menu for this species. In addition they eat lizards, baby turtles, and small mammals. These are diurnally active snakes that prowl the south Texas brush-lands mainly in the morning hours. They have smooth, shiny, blue-black scales and they are an impressive and handsome snake. Wild individuals may sometimes bite savagely if captured and their strong jaws and large teeth can inflict a painful (but venomless) bite. In captivity they tame easily and were once a popular animal in the pet trade.

Class—**Reptilia** (reptiles)
Order—**Squamata** (lizards & snakes)
Family—**Colubridae** (harmless egg-laying snakes)
Racers—*Coluber constrictor* (5 subspecies in Texas)

Southern Black Racer	Buttermilk Racer
subspecies—*priapus*	subspecies—*anthicus*

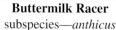

Size: The maximum length for this subspecies is just under 5.5 feet. Most are around 4 feet long.

Presumed range in TX

Variation: Juveniles exhibit a saddled pattern.

Abundance: This is a common snake throughout its very limited range in Texas.

Size: The record length is 70 inches. Most adults are around four feet in length.

Presumed range in TX

Variation: Juveniles exhibit a saddled pattern. See inset above.

Abundance: Common within its limited range in the state. Restricted to the "Piney Woods."

Tan Racer	Eastern Yellow-bellied Racer	Mexican Racer
subspecies—*ethridgei*	subspecies—*flaviventris*	subspecies—*oaxaca*

Size: Maximum of nearly 6 feet.

Presumed range in TX

Variation: Juveniles exhibit a saddled pattern.

Abundance: Common.

Size: Record length 70 inches.

Presumed range in TX

Variation: Juveniles exhibit a saddled pattern.

Abundance: Very common.

Size: Maximum of about 40 inches.

Presumed range in TX

Variation: Juveniles exhibit a saddled pattern.

Abundance: Fairly common.

Habitat: The racers are habitat generalists that can utilize nearly all the habitat types found within their respective ranges in Texas. The only habitat in which they are not found is in permanent wetlands.

Breeding: About a dozen (from 5 to 20) eggs are laid in rotted logs, humus, or other moisture retentive medium. Eggs are laid in early summer and hatch in about two months. Racers reproduce annually.

Natural History: Racers are strictly diurnal. In very hot weather they tend to be active mostly in the mornings or late afternoon. These are active snakes that prowl around in search of a wide variety of prey that ranges from grasshoppers to baby rabbits. Many lizards, frogs, and other snakes (especially garter snakes) are regularly eaten by the adults. They will also feed on fish trapped in small pools during droughts. They are apparently intelligent, curious snakes that will follow livestock and other large animals in hopes of capturing insects and other prey that may be disturbed by the larger animals passing. This is probably how they gained the reputation as aggressive snakes that will chase a human. Their name "Racer" is appropriate as they can reach a blazing 12 to 15 mph. These snakes are habitat generalists that will eat almost anything. They are among the most widespread and successful snakes in America.

Class —**Reptilia** (reptiles)

Order—**Squamata** (lizards & snakes)

Family—**Colubridae** (harmless egg-laying snakes)

Speckled Racer *Drymobius margaritiferus*	**Coachwhip**—*Masticophis flagellum* (2 subspecies in Texas)

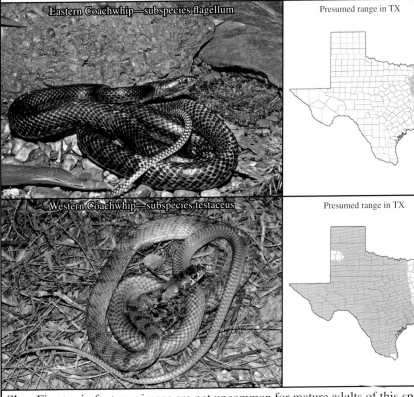

Eastern Coachwhip—subspecies flagellum

Presumed range in TX

Western Coachwhip—subspecies testaceus

Presumed range in TX

Presumed range in TX

Size: Record length 50 inches.

Abundance: Rare in Texas.

Variation: No significant variation in adults.

Habitat: Restricted to riparian woodlands in two counties along the lower Rio Grande River.

Breeding: Apparently can breed at any time of the year. 2 to 8 eggs are laid.

Natural History: This is Mexican and Central American species whose range barely enters the US in the lower Rio Grande Valley of Texas. The ground color is black with a bright blue green spot on each scale, making for a strikingly beautiful snake. Most racers are indiscriminate feeders that may prey on a wide variety of small animals and insects, but the main food of the Speckled Racer appears to be anuran amphibians (frogs and toads). Some researchers report anurans to make up nearly 90 percent of their diet in tropical regions. These snakes are rather rare in Texas as the natural habitats of the lower Rio Grande Valley have been radically altered by modern agricultural practices. They do manage to hang on in protected enclaves such as national wildlife refuges, state parks and private sanctuaries. It is still a common species in suitable habitat in Latin America however and the only threatened populations are those in Texas.

Size: Five to six foot specimens are not uncommon for mature adults of this species. The record length is 8.5 feet.

Abundance: Coachwhips are fairly common in some regions of the state and uncommon in others.

Variation: Two subspecies (see photos above). The eastern subspecies is the most variable of the two. Most specimens of the eastern subspecies resemble the photo above, but this is some variation in how far back on the body the dark pigment prevails. In some specimens it may include the entire snake except for the tail. The Western subspecies is usually tan or yellowish throughout its entire length but it sometimes has narrow, dark bands on the back. Some specimens from the Chihuahuan Desert Ecoregion are reddish rather than tan or yellow. Juveniles show a pattern of dark bands or blotches.

Habitat: Xeric and semi-xeric habitats in upland areas seems to be the preferred habitat. Most common in open woods, overgrown fields and scrub.

Breeding: Female will deposit up to two dozen eggs in moist places.

Natural History: The Coachwhip is one of the longest snake species in Texas, surpassed by only the Texas Indigo Snake and the Bullsnake, both of which are heavier bodied snakes. Most Coachwhips are about six feet when grown. Like their relatives the racers, coachwhips are agile snakes and although mainly terrestrial they are excellent climbers and they will not hesitate to dash up into bushes and small trees when hard pressed by a pursuing predator. They hunt mainly by sight and are active during the day, retreating beneath cover at night. Any animal small enough to be swallowed can be prey and their diet includes many other reptiles including smaller snake species like the garter snakes. Like their relatives the racers, these snakes are fierce fighters when captured. In many respects they are a larger, even faster and a more vicious version of the Racer.

Class—**Reptilia** (reptiles)
Order—**Squamata** (lizards & snakes)
Family—**Colubridae** (harmless egg-laying snakes)

Schott's Whipsnake *Masticophis schotti*	**Striped Whipsnake** *Masticophis taeniatus*	**Long-nosed Snake** *Rhinocheilus lecontei*
	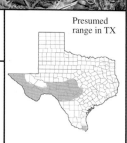	

Schott's Whipsnake

Size: Record length 66 inches.

Abundance: Fairly common. Also found in northeast Mexico.

Presumed range in TX

Variation: There are two subspecies in Texas. Shown above is the *schotti* subspecies.

Habitat: Found in the Mesquite and Thorn Brush country of south Texas, often in the vicinity of permanent water.

Breeding: Little is known about reproduction in this species. Up to a dozen eggs are laid.

Natural History: In Texas this snake is found mostly in the Southern Texas Plains Level III Ecoregion. The two subspecies are very similar in appearance, but the *ruthveni* subspecies is less strikingly patterned and lacks the thin, light stripes of the *schotti* subspecies shown above. This is an alert, active species that is capable of rapid locomotion when frightened or threatened. They appear to have good eyesight that is attuned to movement and they actively forage during daylight hours. They prey mainly on lizards. Spiny lizards (*Sceloporus* genus) and Whiptail lizards (*Aspidoscelis* genus) are the main prey items but larger specimens will also eat small mammals. In addition, almost any type of small vertebrate and large insects like grasshoppers and caterpillars may be consumed. Some experts place this species in the genus *Coluber*.

Striped Whipsnake

Size: Usually about 4 feet. Record 5 feet.

Abundance: Fairly common in the Edwards Plateau and Chihuahuan Desert.

Presumed range in TX

Variation: There are two subspecies. The Central Texas Whipsnake (subspecies *girardi*) is more common in Texas.

Habitat: An arid land species found in the Chihuahuan Desert and in the Edwards Plateau. Usually near water.

Breeding: Little is known about reproduction in this species. Up to 15 eggs are laid. Hatchlings are 14 inches long.

Natural History: This is another fast moving, highly active species that prowls by day in search of almost any type of small vertebrate prey as well as large insects. The main food (nearly 90 percent) is lizards (mostly Spiny Lizards). Small snakes are also eaten and in the case of the large adult snakes small mammals may be consumed. Like other similar snakes like racers and coachwhips, the whipsnakes are diurnally active and shelter at night beneath flat rocks, crevices, or animal burrows. In hot weather they are most active in the morning hours. In cool weather they may be active throughout the day. Some experts now place this species in the same genus as the Racers (genus *Coluber*), but that designation has not been universally accepted within the herpetological community. That the two groups are related however is not in dispute.

Long-nosed Snake

Size: Average about 2.5 feet. Record 41 inches.

Abundance: Fairly common and widespread in the western half of Texas.

Presumed range in TX

Variation: Some variation in the amount of red or black present and in the amount of light speckling.

Habitat: Desert and semi-desert, arid grasslands, dry savanna, rocky canyons and mesquite woodlands.

Breeding: 10 or fewer eggs are laid. May produce two clutches per year. Hatchlings are less than 10 inches long.

Natural History: This species has a tendency for fossorial (burrowing) habits. As such it thrives in areas with sandy or loose gravel soils. The pointed and somewhat upturned snout likely aid this snake in burrowing. These snakes are strong constrictors. Over 50 percent of their diet is lizards but small snakes and reptile eggs have also been confirmed in their diet. Small mammals are frequently consumed. Most lizard prey is probably captured at night when lizards are sleeping in rock crevices or burrowed into sandy substrates. Because of the presence of red, black, and yellow colors on this snake it is sometimes confused with the venomous Coral Snake. But the ranges of the two species do not overlap. Some experts recognize two subspecies. The subspecies found in Texas would be *tessellatus*, the Texas Long-nosed Snake.

Class—**Reptilia** (reptiles)

Order—**Squamata** (lizards & snakes)

Family—**Colubridae** (harmless egg-laying snakes)

Variable (Western) Groundsnake *Sonora semiannulata*	**Trans-Pecos Rat Snake** *Bogertophis subocularis*	**Baird's Rat Snake** *Pantherophis baiirdi*

Size: To 19 inches.

Presumed range in TX

Abundance: Fairly common.

Variation: Highly variable. See examples above.

Habitat: Inhabits a wide variety of upland habitats within its range. Apparently rare or absent in mesic situations.

Breeding: Clutches are small. As few as one and a maximum of six eggs are laid from spring throughout summer.

Natural History: The name Variable Ground Snake is a very appropriate moniker for this snake. It can be uniformly colored, striped, blotched or banded. Ground colors range from tan, gray, brown, or orange. Almost any combination of color and pattern can occur in snakes within the same population. These are small snakes with tiny mouths. Thus the food of the Variable Ground Snake is entirely invertebrates. Grubs, caterpillars, crickets, grasshoppers, centipedes, spiders, and scorpions are known foods. One source (the Missouri Department of Conservation website) lists Black Widow Spiders as being a food item!

Size: Averages about 4.5 feet. Record 5.5 feet.

Presumed range in TX

Abundance: This is an uncommon to rare snake in Texas.

Variation: Ground color varies from tan or yellowish to grayish. Some specimens have the dark dorsal markings greatly reduced.

Habitat: A desert species. In Texas this species is endemic to the Chihuahuan Desert Ecoregion. Also widespread in the Mexican state of Chihuahua.

Breeding: As few as three or as many as a dozen eggs are laid. 13 inch hatchlings emerge in 6 to 8 weeks.

Natural History: That this is a strictly nocturnal species is revealed by the rather large and somewhat bulging eyes. These snakes are highly desired by reptile enthusiasts who keep snakes as pets. The Trans-Pecos Rat Snake is only one of several snake species native to the Trans-Pecos region of Texas that are valued by snake keepers. Historically, the region was well known among snake collectors and was heavily hunted by a method known as nighttime "road cruising." Today the pet industry relies on captive bred snakes, a practice that has had a positive conservation impact by making it more economically feasible to purchase a captive hatched snake than to travel to the region and "road cruise" for many hours in search of a snake that will likely not be encountered.

Size: Averages about 4 feet. Record 5 feet 2 inches.

Presumed range in TX

Abundance: This is an uncommon to rare snake in Texas.

Variation: Ground color varies from tan to gray-brown or light brown. Some are tinged with orange or yellowish. Dark lateral stripes vary in intensity.

Habitat: Wooded river canyons and adjacent forested ridges. Also in the rugged desert mountain ranges up to 10,000 feet in elevation.

Breeding: As many as two dozen eggs may be laid but usually much less. Hatchlings are lighter than adults.

Natural History: Like the preceding species, this snake has always been highly prized by snake collectors. Today they are widely bred in captivity taking much pressure off the wild population. These are rare snakes. They feed mainly on rodents but also eat lizards, frogs, and bats. Bird eggs and nestling birds are important foods during nesting season. Small caves and deep cracks in rock faces used as a daytime refuge for this mainly nocturnal species. In caves it may hunt for roosting bats. Juvenile snakes are patterned with a series of dark blotches on the back similar to the young of the related Texas Rat Snake. In addition to its range in Texas, this species also ranges southward into the northern portion of the Mexican state of Chihuahua.

Class—**Reptilia** (reptiles)

Order—**Squamata** (lizards & snakes)

Family—**Colubridae** (harmless egg-laying snakes)

Western (Texas) Rat Snake *Pantherophis obsoleta*	**Great Plains Rat Snake** *Pantherophis emoryi*	**Slowinski's Corn Snake** *Pantherophis slowinskii*

Size: Average 5 to 6 feet as adults. Record 7 feet 4 inches.  Presumed range in TX	**Size:** Average about three and half to four feet. Record six feet  Presumed range in TX	**Size:** Average about three and half to four feet. Record 59 inches.  Presumed range in TX
Abundance: Common in the eastern half of Texas.	**Abundance:** Uncommon to fairly common in some areas.	**Abundance:** Fairly common but restricted range in Texas.
Variation: Most show a blotched pattern on the back, but in some individuals this pattern is obscured by an overall dark coloration. The color between the dorsal blotches may be yellowish, brownish, or reddish. Young are light gray with charcoal blotches.	**Variation:** Dark blotches on the back vary from nearly black to grayish, brown, or dark olive. Very old individuals may darken and have an obscured pattern. Hatchling snakes are very brightly colored with dark blotches on a pale gray background.	**Variation:** Most specimens from the Texas portion of this snake's range are grayish or brownish and closely resemble the Great Plains Rat Snake but with reddish instead of gray or brown blotches. Some individuals from the "Piney Woods" region show more reddish.
Habitat: Mainly a woodland snake. They are least common in areas of intensive agriculture or urbanized areas, but they can persists in urban regions if there is some cover and large trees.	**Habitat:** True to its name, this species is found in the southern portion of the Great Plains Ecoregion. It also occurs in the Chihuahuan Desert Ecoregion in Texas.	**Habitat:** Occupies a variety of woodland habitats from mature forest to second growth woodlands. Like other rat snakes it is attracted to old barns where rodent prey is abundant.
Breeding: An egg layer that breeds in the spring and lays up to twenty eggs. Eggs are laid in old woodpecker holes or hollow limbs or on the ground in rotted stumps, beneath logs, or anywhere moist enough to prevent dessication.	**Breeding:** Breeds in the spring and will lay as many as two dozen eggs. Eggs hatch in about two months, Hatchlings are about 10 inches in length and are miniature replicas of the adult. Little is known about the diet of the young.	**Breeding:** There is little information available about reproduction in this species. Presumably it would be similar to that of the closely related Great Plains Rat Snake and the Corn Snake of the east. Both can lay up to two dozen eggs.
Natural History: This is the most arboreal snake species in Texas. Excellent climbers, they can ascend straight up a tree trunk using only the bark to gain a purchase with their belly scales. They often choose a den site in old woodpecker holes or tree hollows. They will climb to great heights in search of bird nests. In addition to baby birds and eggs they will also eat rodents, squirrels, and other small mammals. They are fond of hunting rodents in barns and derelict buildings in rural regions.	**Natural History:** Adult Great Plains Rat Snakes prey on a variety of small vertebrates but eat mainly rodents like mice and voles, and birds and bird eggs are also eaten. They will eat bats which they hunt in caves and rock crevices in cliffs and rock faces. There is evidence that this species has declined in the peripheral areas of its range. The status of Texas populations is not known for sure but appears to be stable. These are harmless and useful snakes that are important controllers of rodent pests.	**Natural History:** For many years this species was regarded as an intergrade between the Great Plains Rat Snake of the western plains and the Corn Snake of the southeastern US. It was later considered to be a subspecies of the Great Plains Rat Snake and then finally elevated to species status as the Slowinski's Rat Snake. There is still some disagreement among experts regarding its true taxonomy. The name *slowinskii* honors a professional herpetologist who died from the bite of a venomous snake.

Class—**Reptilia** (reptiles)

Order—**Squamata** (lizards & snakes)

Family—**Colubridae** (harmless egg-laying snakes)

Bullsnake/Gopher Snake *Pituophis catenifer*		Louisiana Pine Snake *Pituophis ruthveni*
Bullsnake—subspecies *sayi*	**Sonoran Gopher Snake**—subspecies *affinis*	

Size: Record 8 feet, 9 inches.

Presumed range in TX

Abundance: Common. One of the most common large snakes in Texas.

Variation: No significant variation among Texas specimens.

Habitat: Prairies are the primary habitat. Prefers dry, loose soils that allow easier burrowing. Avoids mesic soils.

Breeding: The eggs are quite large and baby Bullsnakes are up to a foot in length at hatching. Clutch size can be up to two dozen but is usually about half that amount.

Natural History: Also goes by the name "Gopher Snake," an appropriate name since they are apparently a major predator of the Pocket Gophers. In addition to gophers and ground squirrels, the Bullsnake will eat any type of warm blooded prey that is small enough to be swallowed, which can include animals the size of tree squirrels and young rabbits. Small rodents probably make up the bulk of its diet but birds and their eggs are also eaten and this species will sometimes climb trees in search of bird nests. When cornered these snakes will hiss loudly and strike repeatedly. An unofficial record length of 9 feet 8 inches was measured at Reptile Gardens in South Dakota on a dead snake from Texas. Dead snakes can be stretched but care was taken not to stretch the snake and get an accurate measurement.

Size: Record 7 feet, 8 inches.

Presumed range in TX

Abundance: Common. The most common large snake in its range.

Variation: No significant variation among Texas specimens.

Habitat: A desert species that also adapts to human-altered habitats such as irrigated farmlands and orchards.

Breeding: The eggs are quite large and baby Sonoran Gopher Snakes are up to a foot in length at hatching. Clutch size can be up to two dozen but is usually about half that amount.

Natural History: This species is essentially a desert-adapted version of the Bullsnake, and is regarded by experts as a subspecies of that snake. The color of the Sonoran Gopher Snake tends to be more orange as opposed to yellow on the Bullsnake and the dorsal blotches toward the tail are much darker. The most diagnostic difference between the two snakes is in the shape of a single scale on the rostral (nose). This subtle difference is apparent only to professional herpetologists who examine specimens closely. Given that it is such a large snake its ability to exist in some of the harshest environments in America is impressive. The presence of desert-adapted prey species such as Kangaroo Rats and other rodents provide an abundant food source as well as refuge in the underground burrows of those species.

Size: Record 5 feet, 8.25 inches.

Presumed range in TX

Abundance: Very rare. This is one of the rarest snake species in America.

Variation: No significant variation among Texas specimens.

Habitat: Dry upland woods in the South Central Plains Level III Ecoregion. Especially Longleaf Pine forests.

Breeding: There is little information available on reproduction of this species in the wild. Presumably breeding is similar to the Bullsnake and the Sonoran Gopher Snake.

Natural History: This rare snake is listed as federally endangered by the U.S. Fish and Wildlife Service. It is listed as Threatened by Texas Parks and Wildlife. The primary habitat of this species is mature Longleaf Pine/Wiregrass habitats within the South Central Plains Level III Ecoregion of eastern Texas and west-central Louisiana. Virtually all the mature, old growth Longleaf Pine were cut for timber many decades ago. Although efforts to restore this habitat type are underway in some places by the US Forest Service, it can take up to two hundred years to restore an "old growth" Longleaf Pine forest. Thus the species that depend on this type of habitat (like the Louisiana Pine Snake, Red-cockaded Woodpecker, Bachman's Sparrow, etc.) face serious threats to their survival.

Class—**Reptilia** (reptiles)

Order—**Squamata** (lizards & snakes)

Family—**Colubridae** (harmless egg-laying snakes)

Speckled Kingsnake *Lampropeltis holbrooki*	**Desert Kingsnake** *Lampropeltis splendida*	**Gray-banded Kingsnake** *Lampropeltis alterna*

Size: Average about 4 feet. Maximum 6 feet 2 inches. Presumed range in TX	**Size:** Average about 4 feet. Record length 5 feet. Presumed range in TX	**Size:** Average about 3 feet. Record length is just over 57 inches. Presumed range in TX
Abundance: A fairly common to common snake.	**Abundance:** A fairly common to common snake.	**Abundance:** Uncommon to rare except a few places in west Texas.
Variation: Varies in the size and color of the light "speckles," which may be yellow, off-white or pale blue-green.	**Variation:** Some variation in amount of light speckling on the dorsal scales. Some may be solid black dorsally.	**Variation:** This snake highly variable in color and pattern. See Natural History section below for descriptions.
Habitat: Mature woodlands, successional areas, weedy fields and edge habitats. They are absent from areas where large amounts of land has been converted to row crops and intensively urbanized regions.	**Habitat:** In Texas this species is found in the Chihuahuan Desert, Southern Texas Plains and the southernmost portion of the Western Gulf Coastal Plain ecoregions. Often associates with streams in arid and semiarid habitats.	**Habitat:** In Texas this species is endemic to the Chihuahuan Desert Level III Ecoregion. It inhabits most of that regions mountain ranges and can also be found in riparian habitats in the region's river valleys.
Breeding: An annual breeder that lays 8 to 12 eggs in early summer. Eggs are laid in moisture retaining medium, often inside rotted stumps or logs. Eggs hatch in about 60 days.	**Breeding:** An annual breeder that lays 8 to 12 eggs in early summer. Eggs are laid in moisture retaining medium, often inside rotted stumps or logs. Eggs hatch in about 60 days.	**Breeding:** Up to a dozen eggs may be laid about a month after breeding, which occurs soon after emerging from brumation in the spring. Hatchlings are about 10 inches in length.
Natural History: Kingsnakes are best known for their habit of killing and eating other snakes, including venomous species. These powerful constrictors are immune to the venom of pit vipers and will kill and eat any snake that is small enough to be swallowed whole. They also eat rodents, birds, lizards, and baby turtles. They are mainly terrestrial in habits but have been found inside of standing dead trees several feet off the ground. They may be active both day and night but are mostly crepuscular and during hotter months tend to become more nocturnal. Kingsnakes are favorite captive pet of many reptile enthusiasts in America.	**Natural History:** The Desert Kingsnake is closely related to the Speckled Kingsnake. In fact, the two were once regarded as being the same species (but different subspecies). Some still question whether the two are in fact separate species or a single species with two subspecies. In many ways the Desert Kingsnake is the arid land counterpart of the Speckled Kingsnake. Other snakes are an important part of this snake's diet (including venomous ones) along with many lizards and small mammals like mice. They are active both at night and in the morning hours, but during hot summer weather conditions they will be mostly nocturnal.	**Natural History:** The different color morphs that occur in this snake are so different from each other that for many years herpetologists regarded each color morph as a separate species! In addition to the form shown above, they can also be dark gray with red bands edged in black, light gray with red bands edged in black, gray with red bands edged in black and separated by black rings. Solid gray specimens are known as are snakes with longitudinal dark stripes! The relative scarcity of this species coupled with its handsome color morphs has made it popular favorite among reptile keepers. It feeds mostly on lizards but also eats small rodents.

Class—**Reptilia** (reptiles)

Order—**Squamata** (lizards & snakes)

Family—**Colubridae** (harmless egg laying snakes)

Yellow-bellied (Prairie) Kingsnake	Western Milksnake	Tamaulipan (Mexican) Milksnake
Lampropeltis calligaster	*Lampropeltis gentilis*	*Lampropeltis annulata*

Size: Averages 3.5 feet. Record 58 inches.

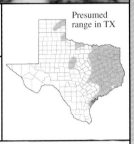
Presumed range in TX

Abundance: Fairly common but rarely encountered above ground.

Size: Averages 30 inches. Record 41 inches.

Presumed range in TX

Abundance: Generally an uncommon species throughout its range.

Size: A small snake reaching about 30 inches.

Presumed range in TX

Abundance: Generally an uncommon species throughout its range.

Variation: Three subspecies are found in the US. But only one of those occurs in Texas. The subspecies that is found in Texas is known as the Prairie Kingsnake (subspecies *calligaster*).

Variation: The taxonomy of the North American Milksnake complex has been the subject of much disagreement and revision among professional herpetologists for many decades. Traditionally, the North American Milksnake complex consisted of as many as 25 subspecies. Some of those subspecies have been elevated to full species status in recent years. Many others are now regarded as regional color morphs.

Habitat: Prefers open fields overgrown with weeds, brush and briers, but can also be found in woodlands and woodland edges.

Habitat: Eastern Texas populations inhabit woodlands mainly. The west Texas populations inhabit grasslands, stream courses and desert mountains.

Habitat: Found throughout the Mesquite/thorn brush country of the South Texas Plains as well as the southern portion of the Western Gulf Coastal Plain.

Breeding: Females produce about a dozen eggs that are laid in an underground nest chamber in early summer.

Breeding: Clutch sizes vary from as few as 6 to as many as 17. Eggs are laid in early summer and hatch in the fall.

Breeding: Breeds in early spring. Four to eight eggs is average but as many as a dozen may be laid.

Natural History: This is a subterranean species that is only rarely seen above ground, usually in early spring. It feeds mostly on small mammals which it hunts in their underground burrows. They also eat bird eggs and nestlings, but they are a threat only to those that nest on or near the ground. Lizards and other snakes are occasionally eaten as well, but are not an important a part of the diet. Despite the fact that this is a fairly common snake within its range in eastern Texas, they are rarely observed due to their burrowing habits. They are most commonly observed in early spring during periods of heavy rainfall, when the ground becomes saturated and many underground rodent burrows fill with water.

Natural History: There is quite a bit of geographical variation in this species. Snakes from the Great Plains ecoregion are usually less vividly colored and may appear "faded" when compared to specimens from the eastern part of Texas where the red bands are vividly colored a bright, fire engine red. The juvenile snakes of this species are always brightly colored. Some experts still retain the old taxonomic status for this species and consider populations in the eastern half of the state as being a distinct subspecies known as the Louisiana Milk Snake (subspecies *amaura*). Likewise, the population that inhabits the Big Bend region is sometimes regarded as another subspecies *celaenops* (the New Mexico Milk Snake).

Natural History: Milksnakes are easily confused with the venomous Texas Coral Snake that is found across the southern half of the state. To distinguish between these snakes, note the arrangement of the brightly colored rings on the body and use this handy poem: "red touches yellow, kill a fellow; red touches black, venom lack." This distinction is applicable to both the Western Milksnake and the Tamaulipan Milksnake. This species is also sometimes called the Mexican Milk Snake, which may be a more appropriate name since it also occurs in the states of Neuvo Leon and Coahuila as well as in Tamaulipas. These snakes, like most milksnakes, are primarily nocturnal and crepuscular in habits.

Class—**Reptilia** (reptiles)

Order—**Squamata** (lizards & snakes)

Family—**Colubridae** (harmless egg-laying snakes)

Rough Green Snake *Opheodrys aestivus*	**Smooth Green Snake** *Opheodrys vernalis*	**Texas Lyre Snake** *Trimorphodon vilkinsonii*

Size: Record 3 feet 11 inches.

Abundance: Probably fairly common and may be expanding its range west.

Presumed range in TX

Size: Record 31 inches.

Abundance: Very rare in Texas. Only two isolated populations in the Coastal Plain.

Presumed range in TX

Size: Record 41 inches.

Abundance: Rarely encountered but fairly common within its limited range in Texas.

Presumed range in TX

Variation: This species is typically remarkably uniform in appearance. A very rare blue morph can occur with an abnormality omitting yellow pigments.

Variation: Throughout its rather large range across the northern US from New England to the Dakotas this species is uniform in appearance.

Variation: This species is fairly uniform in color and pattern throughout its range in the southwestern United States. Juveniles are more brightly colored.

Habitat: Open fields, pastures, and edges of woods and fields. Often common in wetlands where there are low bushes and shrubs overhanging water. Most common near water (stream courses, lake shores, marshes, etc).

Habitat: Open fields, pastures, meadows, and edges of lakes, ponds or marshes. Generally a snake of open habitats, but may be found in open woods. In Texas restricted to two locations in the northern Gulf Coastal Plain.

Habitat: A desert species that inhabits the foothills and mountains at least to 5,500 feet. Usually associates with rocky habitats, i.e. talus slopes, rocky canyons, and rock outcrops. Occasionally occurs in upland desert.

Breeding: 3 to 12 eggs are laid in late spring or early summer. The babies are slender, miniature replicas of the adult.

Breeding: Clutch size is relatively small and may be as few as three or four eggs or as high as a dozen.

Breeding: Probably lays about a dozen eggs beneath flat rocks or in rock crevices or some other form of cover.

Natural History: Rough Green Snakes live in dense bushes and shrubs where their bright green color renders them invisible. Arthropods of many varieties are their prey. Food includes spiders, caterpillars, crickets, and grasshoppers to name a few of their favorites. These snakes are sometimes called "grass snakes" in reference to their bright green coloration. There is a widespread belief that they have become extremely rare and endangered. While in much of their range their populations are stable, they are certainly vulnerable to habitat destruction wrought by modern agricultural practices as well as the widespread use of insecticides. In Texas they are most common near water.

Natural History: Like the similar Rough Green Snake the Smooth Green Snake often goes by the common name "Grass Snake" or "Green Grass Snake." These small snakes eat a variety of invertebrate prey including slugs, spiders, millipedes, crickets, grasshoppers and caterpillars. This diet makes them exceptionally vulnerable to insecticides and widespread applications of chemicals on agricultural fields may pose a serious threat to this handsome little snake. Unlike the larger Rough Green Snake that climbs into bushes and small trees, the Smooth Green Snake tends to stay close to the ground. The Smooth Green snake has smooth scales; the Rough Green has rough (keeled) scales.

Natural History: Although this is a rear-fanged and technically venomous species, its venom seems to be toxic to lizards but significantly less toxic to mammals or birds. In addition to lizards it also feeds on bats in caves and occasionally on birds. Bats and birds are killed by constriction, while lizards are largely subdued by the venom. Uniquely among Texas's non-pit viper snakes, the Lyre Snake has elliptical pupils. When threatened these snake will raise the forepart of the body and rapidly vibrate the end of the tail, giving a pretty good imitation of a rattlesnake. These are nocturnal snakes that are not often encountered by people. Many records are specimens seen on roads at night.

Class—**Reptilia** (reptiles)
Order—**Squamata** (lizards & snakes)
Family—**Colubridae** (harmless egg-laying snakes)

Big Bend Patch-nosed Snake *Salvadora deserticola*	**Eastern Patch-nosed Snake** *Salvadora grahamiae*	**Western Hook-nosed Snake** *Gyalopian canum*

Size: Record length 45 inches.	 Presumed range in TX	**Size:** Record length 47 inches.	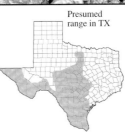 Presumed range in TX	**Size:** Averages 10 inches. Record 15.	 Presumed range in TX
Abundance: Fairly common within its limited range in Texas.		**Abundance:** Fairly common within its limited range in Texas.		**Abundance:** Fairly common but not frequently observed.	

Variation: South Texas specimens may have wider dark stripes and can vaguely resemble garter snakes.

Habitat: This is a desert species. It inhabits flat desert basins, desert mountain foothills and mesas. Favors rocky canyons.

Breeding: Clutches of 5, 6, and 12 eggs have been reported. Little is known about where eggs are laid.

Natural History: Patch-nosed Snakes are diurnal and active throughout the day in mild weather. During hot weather they restrict their activity to morning and late afternoon. Known food items include lizards, small snakes, reptile eggs, and small mammals. These are alert and agile snakes that can catch fast moving lizards. The name "Patch-nosed" comes from the unusually large rostral scale that curls up and over the snout. This species was until recently regarded as a subspecies of the Western Patch-nosed Snake (*Salvadora hexalepis*). It was recently elevated to full species status although many reference materials still refer to it as a subspecies of *S. hexalepis*. The *Salvadora* genus are all very similar and they remain confusing to sort out, even for expert herpetologists.

Variation: Overall ground color hue can be yellowish, tan or pastel orange. The dark striping is consistent.

Habitat: Inhabits middle and higher elevations in the desert mountain ranges of west Texas. Most common between 4,000 and 6,000 feet elevation.

Breeding: Nature Serve Explorer website reports "5 to 10 eggs in spring or early summer, hatching in August."

Natural History: The two patch-nosed snakes shown on this page are very similar in appearance, food preferences, and lifestyle. But the Eastern tends to be more a species of mountain slopes and tends to avoid the low desert basins. Both species can often be found in close proximity to one other, however. There are two subspecies of the Eastern Patch-nosed snake recognized, but only one (subspecies *grahamiae*) known as the Mountain Patch-nosed Snake, occurs in Texas. As a diurnally active species this snake is vulnerable to predation by hawks, but they may also be preyed upon by larger diurnal snakes like the Coachwhip which is a notorious killer of other small snake species. The biggest enemy of these snakes today, however, is probably the automobile. Multi-lane highways can be an impassible barrier.

Variation: Generally some shade of brown. May be tan or yellowish or with a pinkish hue. Gray-brown is typical.

Habitat: Found throughout the Chihuahuan Desert Ecoregion and through the Edwards Plateau into the southern Great Plains in the southern Panhandle.

Breeding: Little is known about reproduction in this species. Up to 5 eggs have been reported.

Natural History: Mainly a desert species but also found in semi-arid grasslands and plateaus. Nocturnal and crepuscular in habits it is thought to feed mainly on spiders, centipedes, and scorpions. When captured this species often exhibits a unique defensive mechanism known as "anal popping," which produces an audible popping sound from the cloaca. This behavior is so unique it may actually confuse and deter some predation attempts. The hooked snout is thought to be an adaptation for a burrowing lifestyle and this species spends much of its time hidden. This species is often called the "Chihuahuan" Hook-nosed Snake, an appropriate name since its range closely coincides with that of the Chihuahuan Desert region. It can be found well down into north-central Mexico.

Class—**Reptilia** (reptiles)

Order—**Squamata** (lizards & snakes)

Family—**Colubridae** (harmless snakes)	Family—**Dipsadidae** (rear-fanged snakes)	

Tamaulipan Hook-nosed Snake
Ficimia streckeri

Ring-necked Snake
Diadophis punctatus

Chihuahuan Nightsnake
Hypsiglena jani

Size: Averages 11 inches. Record 19.

Presumed range in TX

Abundance: Rarely seen but likely fairly common in suitable habitat.

Variation: Ground color may be brown, olive of grayish brown.

Habitat: Endemic to the Southern Texas Plains thorn bush habitats and the lower Rio Grande River Valley in Texas.

Breeding: No information is available on breeding in this species, but it is a known egg layer.

Natural History: Like the Western Hook-nosed Snake this species has a distinctive upturned snout which forms a hook. This feature is believed to aid the snake in burrowing. The name Tamaulipan Hook-nosed comes from the fact that most of this species range is in the Mexican state of Tamaulipas. It is also sometimes called the Mexican Hook-nosed Snake, also appropriate as its range includes parts of several other Mexican states. Finally, the name Eastern Hook-nosed Snake has also been applied since it is the most easterly ranging of the Hook-nosed snakes. The variety of common names can be confusing and provides a good example the importance of scientific names. Food is small invertebrates including spiders and centipeds. Like the similar Western Hook-nosed Snake, this species is known to produce a popping sound from the cloaca when agitated or threatened.

Size: Average about 14 inches. Record 2 ft.

Presumed range in TX

Abundance: Common. In some regions maybe the most common snake.

Variation: A variable species with 12 subspecies nationwide. Three in Texas.

Habitat: A woodland species that lives in rotted logs, stumps, and beneath rocks and leaf litter on the forest floor.

Breeding: Lays up to a dozen eggs, in rotted logs or other moisture retaining places. Young are about 5 inches long.

Natural History: Ringneck snakes are often uncovered by humans beneath boards, stones, leaves, or other debris. The distinctive yellow or cream-colored collar around the neck readily identifies them, and even those unfamiliar with reptiles have no trouble recognizing this species. There are three similar subspecies found in Texas. All except the Regal Ring Snake of the Trans-Pecos region exhibit the characteristic ring around the neck. They feed mostly on soft-bodied insects and other invertebrates. Earthworms are a favorite food. When threatened they will often hold aloft the tightly curled tip of the underside of their bright yellow tail. This defense mechanism is probably designed to direct an attackers attention away from the vulnerable head to the less vulnerable tail. Despite having enlarged rear-fangs for inducing mild venom into prey, they are harmless to man.

Size: Average about 14 inches. Record 2 ft.

Presumed range in TX

Abundance: Fairly common but secretive and rarely observed.

Variation: Ground color varies from gray to brown or tan.

Habitat: Widely distributed in arid and semi-arid regions of Texas and including most of the western half of the state.

Breeding: Lays four to six eggs in the spring. Young hatch about two months later.

Natural History: The Nightsnakes are represented by seven species that range from the southwestern US all the way to Costa Rica. All are small, secretive, and nocturnal. They are most commonly observed hiding beneath flat stones in rocky habitats. Although this is a venomous species, its venom seems to affect mainly reptiles and may not be toxic to mammals. Besides that, they are such small snakes with such tiny mouths that there is virtually no chance of them using their rear fangs to successfully envenomate a human. Their food seems to be lizards and small snakes mostly as adults, although it is likely that invertebrates are also eaten by the young. Some sources also list amphibians and small mice as food items. There are several species of Night Snakes in the US and collectively they range over much of the western half of the country from Canada to Mexico.

Class—**Reptilia** (reptiles)

Order—**Squamata** (lizards & snakes)

Family—**Dipsadidae** (rear-fanged snakes)

Western Worm Snake *Carphophis vermis*	**Black-striped Snake** *Coniophanes imperialis*	**Cat-eyed Snake** *Leptodeira septentrionalis*

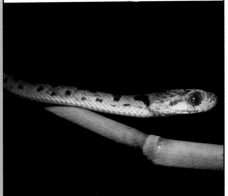

Size: Record length 13.4 inches.

Presumed range in TX

Abundance: Rare. Found only in the extreme NE corner of Texas

Variation: There is no significant variation and young resemble adults.

Habitat: Found in a variety of habitats, but mostly in woodlands. Like other small terrestrial snakes its micro-habitat is beneath the leaf litter, logs, rocks, etc.

Breeding: From 1 to 12 eggs are laid in late June or July and hatch in 2 or 3 months. Hatchlings are only about 3 inches in length.

Natural History: A confirmed burrower that lives under leaf litter, logs, rocks and even man made debris such as old boards, discarded shingles, etc. Feeds on tiny soft-bodied invertebrates such as insect larva, termites, and earthworms. The aptly named worm snakes do in fact resemble earthworms. Their tiny, conical head and smooth glossy scales help to facilitate burrowing through tiny tunnels created by earthworms, termites or insect larva. These snakes are often turned up in back yards by people gardening, raking leaves, or doing other types of yard work. Worm Snakes possess tiny grooved teeth in the rear of the jaw that serve to introduce a mild venom into the bodies of prey. These tiny teeth are too small to penetrate human skin and these snakes are thus completely harmless to man.

Size: Averages about 14 inches. Record 20 inches.

Presumed range in TX

Abundance: Rare in Texas. Only in the extreme lower Rio Grande Valley.

Variation: Stripes vary from black to brown or tan.

Habitat: A Mexican and Central American species that ranges northward into extreme south Texas. Tropical scrub forests is its primary habitat in Texas.

Breeding: Up to 10 eggs are laid in loose soils with some moisture. Eggs hatch in about six weeks. Hatchlings are about 6.5 inches in total length.

Natural History: The Black-striped Snake inhabits lowland areas throughout eastern Mexico and Central America. Its range barely extends into Texas near the mouth of the Rio Grande. Although very limited in distribution they can apparently still be found in the state. In Belize they often go by the nickname "Road Guarder," an apparent reference to the fact that they are usually observed crossing roads. In habits they are nocturnal and crepuscular and usually spend the day hiding beneath flat objects. Although they are technically a rear-fanged venomous species, their venom is not known to have any effect on humans. Clinical Toxinology Resources website states the following: "Bites by this species are not expected to cause medically significant effects and the only risk, probably small, is infection."

Size: Averages about 24 inches. Max 38 inches.

Presumed range in TX

Abundance: Rare in Texas. Regarded as a threatened species in Texas.

Variation: No significant variation among adults or juveniles.

Habitat: In Texas this species inhabits tropical scrub and tropical deciduous woodlands in the extreme southern tip of the state.

Breeding: Up to a dozen eggs are produced annually. Eggs hatch in about 3 months. Young snakes are about nine inches in length.

Natural History: The name Cat-eyed Snake comes from the elliptical shape to the pupil of this snakes eyes. This is technically a venomous species in possession of enlarged teeth in the rear of the jaw for inducing venom into prey. But the venom is quite mild and they are regarded as harmless to man. Rare bites have caused moderate localized swelling and pain and occasionally some bruising and discoloration, but nothing more serious. Cat-eyed Snakes feed mostly on frogs and lizards. Mainly a Mexican species they range southward as far as the state of Veracruz. Their presence in south Texas is threatened by agriculture and urban development which has significantly reduced their habitat in the state. Only the presence of a few small refuges and parks scattered throughout the area prevents their extirpation.

Class—**Reptilia** (reptiles)
Order—**Squamata** (snakes & lizards)
Family—**Dipsadidae** (rear-fanged snakes)

Eastern Hog-nosed Snake
Heterodon platirhinos

Black morph • Hatchling

Hooding

Yellow-spotted morph

Playing dead

Orange-spotted morph

Size: Averages about 2.5 feet. Maximum 45 inches.

Abundance: Generally uncommon. It may be fairly common, however, in regions of dry, sandy, upland woods in the eastern third of Texas.

Habitat: Eastern Hog-nosed Snakes are most common in habitats with sandy soils which facilitate easy burrowing. They tend to be more common in sandy creek bottoms and river valleys or sandy upland prairies. But they can be found in upland woods and fields with less friable soils. The presence of healthy populations of toads may be the most important factor in determining the distribution and abundance of this species. Although they are widespread in the eastern US, they are only locally abundant and may be absent from some areas of their range.

Breeding: Eastern Hog-nosed snakes breed in early spring and lay up to two dozen eggs. Nests are probably in an underground chamber in sandy soil. Young snakes are about 8 inches in length and always have a spotted pattern. Babies are grayish brown with well defined dark gray or black blotches (see inset photo above).

Variation: Highly variable (see photos). Individuals range from solid black to uniform olive green. Others may be variously spotted or blotched with dark saddles on a yellowish or orange background. Often one color morph will be dominant in a given area. The young always exhibit a spotted pattern.

Natural History: The Eastern Hog-nosed Snake is famous for the elaborate performance it puts on when threatened. First, they will spread the neck like a cobra (hence the nickname "Spreading Adder"), and with the mouth wide open they will strike repeatedly. They always intentionally miss with the strike and never bite even when picked up and handled. The initial "cobra display" is always accompanied by loud hissing. When their complicated bluff fails to deter the threat, they will roll onto their backs, stick out their tongue and give a convincing impression of being dead. They do have one behavioral trait that betrays their antics however. If rolled onto their belly while they are feigning death, they will immediately flip over onto their backs once again! Their primary food is frogs and toads. They possess enlarged teeth in the back of the upper jaw that are used to puncture the bodies of toads that have gulped air and inflated themselves in an attempt to become to large to be swallowed. The saliva of these snakes is mildly toxic, but is not considered to be a threat to humans. The food is almost entirely toads and frogs, making them one of the more specialized feeders among Texas snakes. Salamanders are reported to have been found in the stomachs of a few individuals as well. Mice are also sometimes listed as prey items. Anecdotal evidence suggests they may be declining. Their habit of feeding on toads and frogs almost exclusively may make them vulnerable to insecticides, as frog and toads are primarily insect eaters and poisoning through secondary ingestion is a possibility.

Presumed range in TX

Class—**Reptilia** (reptiles)

Order—**Squamata** (lizards & snakes)

Family—**Dipsadidae** (rear-fanged snakes)

Mexican Hog-nosed Snake *Heterodon kennerlyi*	**Plains Hog-nosed Snake** *Heterodon nasicus*	**Dusty Hog-nosed Snake** *Heterodon gloydi*

Size: To about 25 inches.	Presumed range in TX	**Size:** To about 25 inches.	Presumed range in TX	**Size:** Maximum length 25 inches.	Presumed range in TX
Abundance: Rare.		**Abundance:** Fairly common.		**Abundance:** Very rare.	
Variation: Blotches may be brown, tan or gray-brown.		**Variation:** Blotches may be brown, tan or gray-brown.		**Variation:** Color of the dark blotches varies from brown to black.	

Habitat: Inhabits the south Texas brushlands and the Chihuahuan Desert Ecoregion. Most commonly found along river valleys and steam courses.	**Habitat:** Widespread throughout the Great Plains Ecoregion. In Texas most of its range is in the Panhandle region where it lives in prairies.	**Habitat:** Dry, sandy grassland regions. The remaining populations of this rare species are disjunct and widely scattered from Missouri to Texas.

Breeding: Egg layer. Clutch sizes are probably about a dozen with mature females but may be twice that amount. Incubation periods vary from two to three months. Hatchlings are only about five inches in length.

Natural History: Until relatively recently these three species were regarded as subspecies of *Heterodon nasicus* (the Plains Hog-nosed Snake). Some herpetologists still insist that the subspecies designation for the three similar species is warranted. Despite these types of disagreements, all biologists do agree that taxonomy (the scientific naming of families, genus, species, and subspecies of organisms) should reflect their phylogeny (evolutionary history and relationships to each other). With the advent of DNA analysis technologies, new information is brought to light regarding the taxonomic classification of organisms. But there remains some disagreement in the scientific community regarding how much weight should be placed on these molecular studies. As it now stands, the three very similar species shown above are accepted as individual species by the Reptile Database (www.reptile database.org.) That website is usually this authors final arbiter for taxonomic classification of reptiles. All the hog-nosed snakes favor alluvial soils that are loose and friable. Such soil types are prime habitat for toads which are the primary prey of most Hog-nosed snakes. This group of three hog-nosed snakes are less specialized in their feeding habits than is the Eastern Hog-nosed Snake (preceding page, which is a toad and frog eating specialist.) Mexican Hog-nosed Snakes feed mainly on lizards and small mammals like mice. The Western Hog-nosed feeds on frogs and toads as well as the eggs of turtles and some small mammals like baby mice. Of the three species shown above the Dusky Hog-nosed Snake is the rarest. It occurs in widely scattered, isolated populations from southeastern Missouri through eastern Oklahoma and portions of eastern Texas. It is likely that the widely scattered remaining populations of this snake are remnants of a once wide ranging distribution across the eastern edge of the Great Plains. Whether the shrinking populations are the result of recent human activities that have altered its natural habitats or the result of a natural sequence of environmental events is unknown. But it is apparent that the species was once much more widespread. The three species of Hog-nosed Snakes shown above are less inclined to elaborate death-feigning displays than is the Eastern Hog-nosed Snake. Rather these "western species" of Hog-nosed Snakes will typically limit their display to flattening the head and neck and hissing loudly when threatened or handled by humans.

Class—**Reptilia** (reptiles)

Order—**Squamata** (lizards & snakes)

Family—**Dipsadidae** (rear-fanged snakes)	Family—**Natricidae** (harmless live-bearing snakes)	

Mud Snake
Farenciaa abcura

Rough Earth Snake
Virginia striatula

Smooth Earth Snake
Virginia valeriae

Size: 6 feet 9.5 inches.

Presumed range in TX

Abundance: Rarely observed but probably fairly common in suitable habitat.

Size: Maximum of 12.75 inches.

Presumed range in TX

Abundance: Common in the Piney Woods, less common in the western part of range in Texas.

Size: Maximum of 15.5 inches.

Presumed range in TX

Abundance: An uncommon species in Texas, but can be quite common in more eastern regions.

Variation: Two subspecies are recognized but only the western subspecies (*reinwardtii*) occurs in Texas.

Variation: Varies from brown to reddish or grayish brown. Young are miniature replicas of the adults.

Variation: There are three subspecies nationwide but only one in Texas. The color is always some shade of brown.

Habitat: This is a snake of swamps, marshes, and wetland areas. In Texas they are found only in the eastern part of the state.

Habitat: Found in almost any wooded habitat with moist soil and abundant cover in the form of leaf litter. Avoids very dry soil conditions.

Habitat: Smooth Earth Snakes are basically a forest species but they can also be found in open fields near forests and around forest edges.

Breeding: Lays very large clutches of eggs (the record is over 100). Eggs are place in hollows of floating logs or stumps above the water line.

Breeding: Moderately sized litters of 4 to 9 young reported in the book Amphibians and Reptiles of Arkansas. Breeds in spring, gives birth in summer.

Breeding: These snakes are live bearers that give birth to from four to twelve young. Young snakes are easily mistaken for an earthworm.

Natural History: Few people who are not actively seeking this species will ever see one. Living among the tangled mass of vegetation and plant roots in the muck of swamps and marshes, they prey primarily on several species of aquatic salamanders along with frogs and fish. They specialize in feeding on a number of large, totally aquatic salamanders (i.e. sirens and amphiumas). The tail of this snake terminates in a stiff, sharp spine that is erroneously believed to be able to sting. Some also believe these snakes to be the mythical "hoop snake," that according to legend can take its tail into its mouth forming a hoop and then roll down hills. This fable also sometimes includes the myth that the spine on the tail is used as a deadly stinger, but in reality the spine is quite harmless.

Natural History: This tiny snake seems to thrive in both wilderness and rural yards and even suburban areas. It is frequently encountered by people doing yard work (raking leaves or mulching landscapes). It and the very similar Smooth Earth Snake are told apart by the presence of keeled scales on the back of the Rough Earth Snake. Both snakes have characteristically conical shaped heads, which are probably an adaptation for a burrowing lifestyle. The food is mainly earthworms but a variety of invertebrate prey has been documented including gastropods, grubs, and rarely small vertebrates such as tiny frogs and baby lizards. While they are found in upland areas they favor moist conditions, but they seem to avoid swamps and permanent wetlands.

Natural History: The Earth Snakes are tiny, docile snakes that could not manage to bite a human even if they were so inclined, which they are not. Their food consists of small insects, snails, and mostly, earthworms. These are secretive little serpents that sometimes emerge to prowl about on the surface after summer rains. Otherwise they are easily overlooked except by herpetologists who know where to find them beneath logs, stones or amid accumulated humus on the forest floor. As with other small snakes that burrow beneath detritus on the floor of woodlands, these little snakes are occasionally turned up by rural residents as they rake mulch from flower beds in the spring. Young snakes resemble the adults and measure about three to three and half inches in length.

Class—**Reptilia** (reptiles)

Order—**Squamata** (lizards & snakes)

Family—**Natricidae** (harmless live-bearing snakes)

Glossy Swamp Snake *Liodytes rigida*	Graham's Crayfish Snake *Regina grahamii*	Lined Snake *Tropidoclonion lineatum*

Size: About 2 feet. Record 33 inches.	 Presumed range in TX	**Size:** Average 2 feet. Record 47 inches.	 Presumed range in TX	**Size:** Average 18 inches. Record 22 inches.	 Presumed range in TX
Abundance: Rare but maybe more common than records would indicate.		**Abundance:** Uncommon and discontinuously distributed in Texas.		**Abundance:** Apparently common in some areas but discontinuously distributed in TX.	

Glossy Swamp Snake	Graham's Crayfish Snake	Lined Snake
Variation: Brown to very dark brown. Sometimes with two dark vertebral stripes down the back on lighter colored specimens.	**Variation:** Usually some shade of brown, sometimes tinged with yellowish or olive. May be dark brown. Baby snakes are identical to adults.	**Variation:** Ground color varies from brown to olive to grayish. Dark spots bordering pale dorsal stripe vary in prominence.
Habitat: Aquatic. Found in waters with abundant vegetation. Swamps, marshes, canals, ditches, sphagnum bogs, ponds, and sometimes in rice fields.	**Habitat:** Aquatic. Prefers lentic waters. Found in lakes, swamps and backwaters, marshes, and streams with low flow rates.	**Habitat:** Native to prairie regions. Dixon and Wehler in *Texas Snakes a Field Guide* report it as common in some Texas cities.
Breeding: Live-bearer. Litter size ranges from 6 to 14 young (from *Amphibians and Reptiles of Louisiana* by Boundy and Carr).	**Breeding:** Live-bearer. Breeds in the spring (April and May) and gives birth to about a dozen (as many as 20) young in late summer.	**Breeding:** Live-born young number 5 to 10. Babies are quite small, usually only about 4 inches in length. Breeds in late summer and births a year later.
Natural History: The Glossy Swamp Snake ranges throughout the lowlands of the coastal plain from the Carolinas to Texas. There are three subspecies, one of which (the Gulf Glossy Swamp Snake-*L.r. sinicola*) is found in Texas. This is a rather secretive species Thus its natural history is not well known. They seem to be quite aquatic in habits and live among dense aquatic vegetation. There are records of them being found away from water and they will leave their secretive hideouts amid aquatic vegetation on rainy nights and have been captured crossing roadways at night during periods of heavy rains. Crayfish are reportedly the main food item but sirens, frogs, fish, and aquatic invertebrates are also listed as food.	**Natural History:** Widespread in the central and southern plains. Also in much of the Mississippi Valley and in the western Gulf Coastal Plain. But their range today is fragmented with many small pockets of disjunct populations and they are not found in some regions where their absence is not easily explained. Probably they were once more continuously distributed and have retreated from many areas due to alterations to or total loss of suitable local habitats. Their food is ectothermic vertebrates including fish and frogs, but mainly they prey on soft bodied crayfish. They are very similar in many respects to the Glossy Swamp Snake, from which they may be distinguished by the lack of black spots on the belly.	**Natural History:** This species has a long gestation period than can be as much as a year. Like many species indigenous to the prairie, the Lined Snake may have historically been a much more common animal in the Great Plains. Today they are most common in places like where ample prairie habitat remains. The range in Texas consists of several disjunct populations. Many small snakes relish earthworms, but the Lined Snake apparently eats them almost exclusively. In appearance, the Lined Snake closely resembles the garter and ribbon snakes of the genus *Thamnophis,* but its exact relationship to those snakes in unknown. The behavior of curling the end of the tail when threatened is reminiscent of the Ringneck Snakes.

Class—**Reptilia** (reptiles)

Order—**Squamata** (lizards & snakes)

Family—**Natricidae** (harmless live-bearing snakes)

Brown (Dekay's) Snake *Storeria dekayi*	**Red-bellied Snake** *Storeria occipitomaculata*	**Black-necked Garter Snake** *Thamnophis cyrtopsis*

Size: Average 12 inches, record 19. 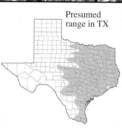 Presumed range in TX	**Size:** Average 10 to 12 inches, record 16. 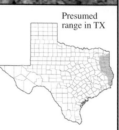 Presumed range in TX	**Size:** Average about 30 inches, record 42 inches.  Presumed range in TX
Abundance: Common throughout the eastern half of the state.	**Abundance:** Fairly common in the eastern part of the Piney Woods Region.	**Abundance:** Fairly common in areas where permanent water occurs.

Variation: There is very little variation in this species in Texas. Specimens from the Coastal Plain were once considered a separate subspecies.

Variation: There are three subspecies recognized. The subspecies found in Texas is *S. o. obscura*, the Florida Red-bellied Snake.

Variation: Chihuahuan Desert populations belong to the subspecies *cyrtopsis* and Edwards Plateau populations to the subspecies *ocellatus*.

Habitat: Woodlands, grassy fields, and wetlands. Found even in urban areas, especially vacant lots littered with old boards or scrap tin.

Habitat: Mostly found in wooded areas, in both lowland and uplands. They can also be found in fields around the edges of woods. Prefers moist environs.

Habitat: An arid land species that associates with permanent water sources in canyons, in the vicinity of springs and along stream courses.

Breeding: Gives birth to 5 to 20 young (rarely more, as many as 40). Baby snakes are about 3 inches long with the girth of a matchstick.

Breeding: Live-bearer. Litters number from 5 to 15. Newborn babies are only about three inches in length an no bigger around than a matchstick.

Breeding: Live-bearer. Up to two dozen young may be produced by large, mature females. As few as 3 or 4 in young, smaller females.

Natural History: This diminutive snake is often found in vacant lots of large cities and towns, where it hides beneath boards, trash, even small pieces of cardboard. It feeds primarily on earthworms and slugs, but also reportedly eats insects, amphibians eggs, and tiny fishes. Brown Snakes are known to hibernate communally, an odd behavior for a tiny snake that should have no trouble finding adequate crevices in which to spend the colder months. These snakes are sometimes called "Dekay's Snake," in honor of an early American naturalist. These little snakes make interesting pets and will readily eat earthworms in captivity. They are mainly woodland snakes but the range in Texas invades the Great Plains along river valleys.

Natural History: Redbelly Snakes usually remain hidden by day beneath rocks, logs, etc., and emerge at night to hunt insects and small soft-bodied invertebrates such as earthworms, slugs, beetle larva, isopods, etc. These snakes sometimes exhibit a peculiar behavior when threatened. If voiding of feces and musk fails to discourage a handler, they will curl their upper lip in an strange expression of apparent ferocity. It is a purely fallacious display, however, as their tiny teeth could never penetrate human skin. Although these little snakes are widespread across much of the eastern US, they are less common than many other small snake species. The name comes from their bright red, orange, or pink-colored belly.

Natural History: The range of the Black-necked Garter Snake includes much of the southwestern US and nearly the entire country of Mexico west of the Gulf Coastal Plain. Within its range in the arid southwestern US, it is usually associated with permanent water sources such as streams and springs. They may be seen basking or actively foraging along the stream bank. In these habitats they hunt frogs and their larva (tadpoles). Fish are also eaten and both fishes and tadpoles are especially targeted when trapped in drying pools. Like most Garter Snakes the Black-necked is an opportunistic predator and food items probably vary seasonally and may include insects and other invertebrate prey. They are active both day and night.

Class—**Reptilia** (reptiles)

Order—**Squamata** (lizards & snakes)

Family— **Natricidae** (harmless live-bearing snakes)

Common Garter Snake *Thamnophis sirtalis*	**Checkered Garter Snake** *Thamnophis marcianus*

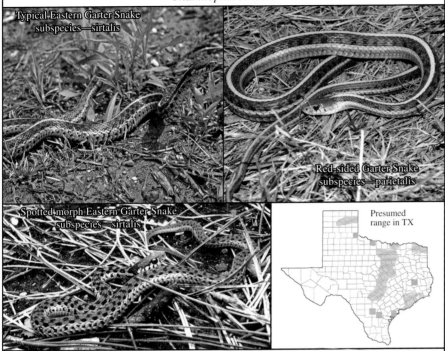

Typical Eastern Garter Snake subspecies—sirtalis

Red-sided Garter Snake subspecies—parietalis

Spotted morph Eastern Garter Snake subspecies—sirtalis

Presumed range in TX

Presumed range in TX

Size: Record 43 inches.

Abundance: Common. The most common and widespread Garter Snake in Texas.

Size: Average 2 feet. Maximum of 51 inches (Eastern Garter Snake subspecies).

Abundance: This species is uncommon in Texas.

Variation: There are 9 subspecies of this widespread snake in the United States. Three subspecies are found in Texas. The Eastern Garter Snake (subspecies *sirtalis*) occurs in extreme NE Texas and portions of the Western Gulf Coastal Plain. The Red-sided Garter Snake is a Great Plains subspecies that barely enters the state along the Red River in Grayson and Cook Counties. Finally, the Texas Garter Snake (subspecies *annectens*) can be found in a narrow band through central Texas with isolated populations in the northern Panhandle.

Variation: There is very little variation in this species. Young resemble adults.

Habitat: This is mainly an arid land Garter Snake species. In Texas they occupy the Warm Deserts, South Central Semi-Arid Prairies, Tamaulipas-Texas Semi-Arid Plains, and the southern Western Gulf Coastal Plain Level II Ecoregions (Figure 7 on page 8).

Habitat: A habitat generalist that favors pastures, fields, and rural yards. They can be seen almost anywhere, including vacant lots in urban areas. Populations in semi-arid regions often associate with river valleys or stream courses.

Breeding: Litter size varies with age and size of the female. May be as few as a half dozen or as many as 3 dozen.

Breeding: Garter Snakes are live-bearers that give birth to enormous litters of up to 60 babies (average 20 to 30). Baby Eastern Garter Snakes are usually born in late summer or very early fall and are about 7 or 8 inches in length.

Natural History: Garter snakes are non-specialized feeders that will eat insects, earthworms, frogs, toads, salamanders, fish and rarely small mammals such as baby mice or voles. Their name is derived from their resemblance to the old fashioned "garters" that were used to hold up men's socks. The name has been widely familiarized to "Garden Snake" in many places. Still appropriate, as they are often encountered in people's gardens. They are a ubiquitous species that may be found in both wilderness or urban regions. They are most common in successional areas and edge habitats and are often found near streams or edges of wetlands. They can also be quite common in suburban areas where they will live among landscape plantings in peoples yards. This is one of America's best known snakes. Even people who are unfamiliar with snakes typically recognize the Garter Snake as a harmless and useful species. If captured these snakes will expel feces and vile smelling musk in an attempt to make themselves as unpalatable as possible to a potential predator. They may bite also, and larger snakes can break the skin causing small lacerations or punctures, but the overall effect of their bite is not a significant injury.

Natural History: The Checkered Garter Snake avoids the higher elevations of desert mountain ranges and is adapted to dry environments in deserts and plains. But like most members of its genus, it often associates with permanent water sources along rivers and streams. Like most Garter Snake species this is an unspecialized feeder that will eat almost any type of small vertebrate prey as well as a wide variety of invertebrates. The overall range of the Checkered Garter Snake includes much of the Texas and eastern New Mexico and it also ranges well down into northern Mexico at least as far south as Zacatecas. This species is often referred to as the "Marcy's Garter Snake."

Class—**Reptilia** (reptiles)

Order—**Squamata** (lizards & snakes)

Family—**Natricidae** (harmless live-bearing snakes)

Plains Garter Snake *Thamnophis radix*	Western Ribbon Snake *Thamnophis proximus*

Subspecies *proximus*
Orange-striped Ribbon Snake

Subspecies *orarius*
Gulf Coast Ribbon Snake

Size: Averages 15 to 28 inches.

Presumed range in TX

Abundance: Rare in Texas. Found only in the northern Panhandle.

Variation: Mid-dorsal stripe varies from yellow-orange to bright orange.

Habitat: A Great Plains species that in its limited range in Texas is usually found near water.

Breeding: Live-born young can number over two dozen, but usually fewer.

Natural History: A prairie species whose range barely extends into Texas in the northernmost portion of the Panhandle. Very widespread across the Great Plains region from Oklahoma to the prairie provinces of Canada. This species is well adapted to the cold environments of the northern plains and they are among the earliest snakes to emerge in the spring. Prey species are typical of the Garter Snake/Ribbon Snake clan; i.e. frogs, toads, insects and earthworms. Some experts recognize an eastern subspecies (*T. r. radix*) ranging from Indiana across Illinois and into eastern Iowa; and a western subspecies (*T. r. haydeni*) throughout the rest of the range in the Great Plains region. The differences between the two are very slight and today most experts consider the two subspecies to be conspecific with no subspecies. They are very similar to other Garter Snakes but the mid-dorsal stripe of the Plains Garter Snake tends to be more orange in color.

Size: Most are about 20 to 30 inches. as adults. The record length is 39 inches.

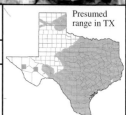
Presumed range in TX

Abundance: Fairly common.

Variation: There are 4 subspecies in Texas. Shown above are the Orange-striped Ribbon Snake (subspecies *proximus*) and the Gulf Coast Ribbon Snake (subspecies *orarius*)

Habitat: Lives mostly in semi-aquatic habitats, i.e. wet meadows, swamps, marshes, and edges of streams and lakes. Also damp, weedy fields in bottomlands.

Breeding: Live bearing. Gives birth to between 10 and 20 young. Births usually occur in August. Newborn snakes are 8 to 10 inches in length and very slender, no bigger around than a matchstick.

Natural History: Ribbon Snakes are extremely elongated, slender-bodied snakes and they have exceptionally long tails. They are very similar in appearance to the Garter snakes and in many respects they are a slimmer, elongated version of the Garter Snakes. They are alert and fast moving snakes that are diurnally active. They hunt by actively foraging rather than utilizing the "ambush" method used by many snake species. They are keenly attuned to movement and catch much of their food by "flushing" it from cover as they move through their environment. Ribbon Snakes are more semi-aquatic in habits than their cousins the Garter Snakes and they are usually found in the vicinity of permanent water and they frequently enter water to pursue fish or tadpoles. The Red-striped Ribbon Snake (subspecies *diabolicus*) is the most adapted to arid landscapes and in fact it sometimes goes by the name "Arid Land Ribbon Snake." But even this subspecies is closely tied to water and inhabits canyons and stream courses within its dry environments. Frogs, toads, fish, and lizards are listed as some of this snake's prey. During certain times of the year tadpoles and the recently transformed young of frogs and toads are a primary food item. During periods of drought these snakes will gorge on small fishes trapped in drying pools. Insects and earthworms are also important in the diet. There are four subspecies of the Western Ribbon Snake and all four can be found in Texas. The most widespread is the Orange-striped Ribbon Snake (*T. p. proximus*), found in the Southeast US Plains and the eastern half of the South Central Semi-Arid Prairies Level II Ecoregions (see Figure 7 on page 8). The Gulf Coast Ribbon Snake (subspecies *orarius*) ranges throughout the Texas-Louisiana Coastal Plain Level II Ecoregion. The Arid Land Ribbon Snake (subspecies *diabolicus*) is a snake of the Tamaulipas-Texas Semi-Arid Plains Level II Ecoregion while the Red-striped Ribbon Snake subspecies (*T. p. rubrilineatus*) inhabits mostly the Level III Ecoregion known as the Edwards Plateau (i.e. "the Texas Hill Country"). See maps on pages 9 and 10 (Figures 7 and 8).

Class—**Reptilia** (reptiles)
Order—**Squamata** (lizards & snakes)
Family—**Natricidae** (harmless live-bearing snakes)

Salt Marsh Water Snake *Nerodia clarkii*	**Plain-bellied Water Snake** *Nerodia erythrogaster*

Adult Yellow-bellied morph · Juvenile

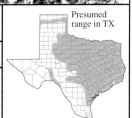

Presumed range in TX

Size: Maximum of 3 feet.

Abundance: Fairly common in salt and brackish marshes.

Variation: No significant variation in Texas.

Habitat: Unique among American snakes in that it lives exclusively in salt/brackish water marshes and estuaries.

Breeding: A live-bearer that produces as many as 22 young per litter. Babies are about 7 to 9 inches in length. Nothing is known about the food of young.

Natural History: The Salt Marsh Water Snake is the only North American Water Snake known to thrive in saltwater habitats. They are mainly nocturnal in summer but can be diurnally active in spring and fall. They are not well known to the average Texan as there are few people who venture into their habitats in coastal marshes. During periods of heavy rainfall (and especially during hurricanes or tropical storms) they may move out of the marshes and onto nearby roadways. There are three subspecies of this snake but only one, the Gulf Saltmarsh Water Snake (*N. c. clarkii*) occurs in Texas. This is the most colorful of the three subspecies and it is often deeply reddish. This subspecies is known to hybridize with the Southern Water Snake where their ranges meet. It feeds on crabs, shrimp, and small fish stranded in tidal pools at low tide.

Size: Average length is three to four feet. The record length is 5 feet 4 inches.

Abundance: Fairly common.

Variation: Until recently, there were 4 subspecies of this variable water snake. Today all are regarded as a single species with various geographical variations.

Habitat: Although this snake is primarily aquatic, it is less tied to water than most water snakes and they will often wander far from permanent water. They may be found in creeks, lakes, ponds, swamps, and marshes. They also occur in seasonal marshes and wet meadows and they may be found in dry habitats on occasions. They will move long distances overland as they travel from one aquatic habitat to another (such as moving from one small pond or wetland to another).

Breeding: These are among the more prolific of the water snakes and large females will produce litters numbering over forty babies. Breeding takes place in early spring and birthing occurs in late summer Baby snakes are distinctly blotched and are 9 to 10 inches in length.

Natural History: These snakes feed primarily on aquatic and semi-aquatic vertebrates such as frogs, toads, salamanders and fish. They are active both day and night in the spring but are more nocturnal or crepuscular during hot weather. Like many other water snakes, they are fierce fighters if caught and will bite and smear the attacker with foul smelling feces and a pungent musk. As with most water snake species, the female grows considerably larger than the male. They will wander far from water and may even be seen in the driest of habitats atop wooded ridges at higher elevations not usually associated with water snakes. Some experts now lump all four subspecies the Plain-bellied Water Snake into one highly variable species. There are two distinct pattern morphs of this snake in Texas. Each was once regarded as a distinct subspecies. The morph known as the Yellow-bellied Water Snake is shown above on the left. The other morph was called the Blotched Water Snake and that population is characterized by the retention of juvenile characteristics into adulthood. The "Blotched" Water Snake morph thus resembles the photo of the juvenile snake on the above right. The "Yellow-bellied" morph is found in the South Central Plains Level III Ecoregion. Throughout the rest of the species' range in Texas, most specimens will resemble the photo on the right above, although the dorsal blotches may vary significantly in their color and boldness. Some specimens will have dorsal blotches that are brown, some may be nearly black and some may be reddish brown in color. In some cases, the dark dorsal blotches may be obscured by an overall dark coloration dorsally. This is especially true in old adults.

Class—**Reptilia** (reptiles)

Order—**Squamata** (lizards & snakes)

Family—**Natricidae** (harmless live-bearing snakes)

Diamondback Water Snake	Southern Water Snake
Nerodia rhombifer	*Nerodia fasciata*

Subspecies confluens
Broad-banded Water Snake

Subspecies pictiventris
Florida Water Snake

Size: Average 4 ft. Record 64 inches.

Presumed range in TX

Abundance: Fairly common, especially in eastern Texas.

Variation: The dorsal pattern is more evident on young snakes and freshly molted specimens. Females are larger.

Habitat: Diamondback Water Snakes frequent most aquatic habitats within their range except for small ponds and smaller streams. They show a definite preference for large swamps and marshes, lakes, and reservoirs.

Breeding: Produces very large litters of up to 30 or 40 babies in late summer. Babies are 8 to 10 inches long.

Natural History: The water snakes have a reputation among herpetologists for their pugnacious attitudes and none is more deserving of that reputation than the Diamondback Water Snake. When captured they will thrash wildly and bite savagely and repeatedly. The bite, though harmless, can be painful. Larger individuals can produce numerous punctures and lacerations which will bleed profusely due to an anti-coagulant present in the saliva. These snakes attain an impressive size and can be very heavy bodied. A large female may have a girth the size of a man's wrist. Like all water snakes they are mainly nocturnal during hot summer months. In the early spring they can be very obvious as they bask on logs, beaver lodges, and branches.

Size: The Broad-banded subspecies averages barely three feet and reaches a maximum of 45 inches. The introduced Florida subspecies can get much larger, reaching 5 feet.

Presumed range in TX

Abundance: Broad-banded subspecies is fairly common.

Variation: There are three subspecies of Southern Water Snake and two can be found in Texas, although only one (the Broad-banded Water Snake) is native to the state.

Habitat: Southern Water Snakes live in swamps, marshes. sloughs, lakes, and flooded ditches. They can be found in virtually any aquatic habitat in the eastern third of the state except marine environments, but they prefer still, quiet waters over flowing streams. They may inhabit sluggish, slow moving creeks.

Breeding: The native Broad-banded subspecies breeds in early spring and gives birth in late summer to one or two dozen young. The introduced Florida subspecies breeds in early spring and gives birth in late summer to one or two dozen young. Very large females of the Florida subspecies can give birth to up to 60 young.

Natural History: There are three subspecies of this water snake in the southern United States and two occur in Texas. The Broad-banded Water Snake (*N.f.confluens*) is found in the eastern third of the state while the Florida Water Snake (*N.f.pictiventris*) has been introduced into the lower Rio Grande River Valley. According to the book *Texas Snakes, A Field Guide* by Dixon and Werler, this snake was apparently initially introduced into the state by a commercial animal dealer in the Brownsville area. The food of both subspecies is mostly frogs and fish, but they also eat salamanders, crayfish, and tadpoles. They are active hunters that search for prey in shallow waters where fish and tadpoles can be more easily pursued. They are active both day and night but mostly nocturnal in hot weather. Like all water snakes, they are fond of basking atop floating vegetation, drift, or tree limbs overhanging water and they are especially conspicuous in the early spring. The common name of the species (Southern Water Snake) comes from the fact that all subspecies are basically southern snakes. Only the Broad-banded species is naturally occurring in the state of Texas. Although found in the Coastal Plain of Texas, the Southern Water Snake cannot survive in the salt marsh habitats used by the Salt Marsh Water Snake and thus restricts its activity to freshwater habitats. The more brightly colored individuals of the Broad-banded subspecies are handsome snakes. Many specimens are bright yellow with dark reddish brown or dark brown bands. The newborn young are especially vibrant in color. By contrast, the introduced Florida subspecies of the lower Rio Grande Valley is usually much drabber in appearance (see photos above).

Class—**Reptilia** (reptiles)

Order—**Squamata** (lizards & snakes)

Family—**Natricidae** (harmless live-bearing snakes)

Mississippi Green Water Snake *Nerodia cyclopion*	**Brazos Water Snake** *Nerodia harteri*	**Concho Water Snake** *Nerodia paucimaculata*

Mississippi Green Water Snake — *Nerodia cyclopion*

Size: 3 to 3.5 feet. Record 50 inches.

Abundance: Uncommon to rare in Texas. Range restricted to SE coast.

Presumed range in TX

Variation: Little variation exists in this snake in Texas. Young specimens tend to be lighter in color.

Habitat: These snakes are totally aquatic and inhabit large bodies of water. Large lakes, oxbows, rivers, and the mouths of larger creeks.

Breeding: The 15 to 20 young are born in late summer and are about 6 to 8 inches long at birth,

Natural History: Primarily nocturnal in habits. In the spring it may be seen sunning by day atop drift, beaver lodges, or branches overhanging water. Mississippi Green Water Snakes feed mainly on fish but they may also eat frogs and salamanders. They are much more piscivorous than most other water snakes and show a definite preference for large bodies of water. Unlike many other water snakes that sometimes wander far overland, the Mississippi Green rarely ventures far from water. The name Mississippi "Green" Water Snake is somewhat misleading. Although many specimens have and olive or greenish hue, some may be more brownish or even reddish brown. Old adults can be quite dark dorsally and as with most water snakes the young are more vividly colored.

Brazos Water Snake — *Nerodia harteri*

Size: Average about 30 inches. Record 41.5.

Abundance: May be fairly common within its very restricted range but generally rare.

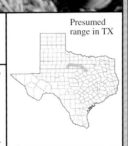
Presumed range in TX

Variation: Very little variation. Brown to grayish brown with brownish blotches and rarely a dark dorsal stripe.

Habitat: Endemic to the Brazos River where it inhabits rocky riffle areas. Found only along about 182 miles of stream (Dixon and Werler).

Breeding: Females give birth to up to 23 young. (Source: Brazos River Authority www.brazos.org.)

Natural History: This is one of the few snake species that is endemic to the state of Texas. Because it has such a limited range it is regarded as a threatened species by the Texas Parks and Wildlife Department. This species was formerly regarded as being conspecific with the Concho Water Snake (next account) and both species are unique among the water snakes in their habitat preferences. They are the only North American Water Snakes that seem to prefer riffle areas in flowing streams. Rocky substrates and rocky shorelines are also characteristic of this species habitat along the Brazos River and a few of its tributaries. The food of this species is apparently mostly fish but amphibians are also reported as food items. This species has one of the smallest known ranges of any North American snake species.

Concho Water Snake — *Nerodia paucimaculata*

Size: Average about 20 inches. Record 25.5.

Abundance: May be fairly common within its very restricted range but generally rare.

Presumed range in TX

Variation: There is little variation in this species. Ground color may vary slightly from pale brown to gray-brown.

Habitat: A denizen of the upper Colorado River and the Concho River. Primary habitat is riffle areas with rocky substrates.

Breeding: Average litter size is probably about a dozen. Baby snakes are born in late summer.

Natural History: Like most water snakes, the Concho Water Snake is primarily a nocturnal snake during hot summer months, but they may be active diurnally in spring and fall. Like the preceding species this snake has a very limited range and it was once regarded as a federally threatened species. In a controversial decision it was delisted by the U.S. Fish and Wildlife Service in 2011. The current population status of both the Concho and Brazos Water Snakes is being studied, but both species have experienced significant population declines from a historical perspective. Moreover, both have been extirpated from much of their historical range along their native rivers. Given the very limited distribution of these two species and their reliance on a specific habitat niche, protection would seem warranted.

Class—**Reptilia** (reptiles)

Order—**Squamata** (lizards & snakes)

Family—**Elapidae** (cobra)	Family—**Viperidae** (vipers)—subfamily—**Crotalinae** (pit vipers)	
Texas Coral Snake *Micrurus tener*	**Eastern Copperhead** *Agkistrodon contortrix*	**Broad-banded Copperhead** *Agkistrodon laticinctus*

Size: Average about 2.5 feet. Record 47.75 inches.

Abundance: Fairly common in southeastern Texas.

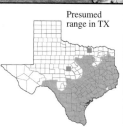
Presumed range in TX

Variation: No significant variation in Texas specimens.

Habitat: Woodlands with abundant amount of organic woodland detritus (leaf litter, pine needles, etc.)

Breeding: Clutches of up to a dozen eggs are laid in early to mid summer. Babies are about 6 inches in length. This is the only venomous egg-laying snake in Texas.

Natural History: The coral snakes are America's only representatives of the Elapidae family, which includes such famously dangerous snakes as the cobras, mambas, and Australian Death Adder. There are over seventy species of coral snakes in tropical America ranging from Mexico to southern South America. The Texas Coral is one of three coral snakes found in the US and is the only species found in Texas. They feed mostly on other snakes and lizards. They can be common in some areas and sometimes appear in yards or gardens. The venom of the coral snakes is a powerful neurotoxin that kills by blocking nerve impulses to vital organs. Death is usually by suffocation due to paralysis of the diaphragm. Considered on a drop for drop basis, they have the most toxic venom of any North American serpent.

Size: Average 2.5 to 3 feet. The record is 58 inches.

Abundance: Can be quite common in portions of eastern Texas.

Presumed range in TX

Variation: Varying shades of brown, tan, or reddish brown.

Habitat: A woodland species mainly. Often found in edge areas or in successional woodlands.

Breeding: From 4 to 12 young are born in late August through September. The resources required to produce a litter are considerable. Thus many copperheads produce litters only ever other year.

Natural History: Like most pit vipers copperheads are primarily nocturnal, especially during hotter months. In early spring and fall they may be seen abroad during the day. Young snakes eat some invertebrates and small vertebrates such as young frogs, lizards, and small snakes. Larger snakes prey on small mammals (mice and voles), and the young of ground nesting birds. Insects are also taken, especially cicadas and during years when the Periodic Cicada emerges by the millions they will stuff themselves with these high protein, high fat insects. In areas of undisturbed habitat these can be common snakes but they are secretive and discreet. They account for more snakebites than any other venomous snake in the US, mainly because they are common throughout the highly populated eastern US.

Size: Average about 2.5 feet. The record is 37.25 inches.

Abundance: Fairly common, especially in central Texas.

Presumed range in TX

Variation: Snakes from the Big Bend have light centers in the dark bands.

Habitat: Woodlands, wooded stream courses, and forested areas from the Edwards Plateau to the Big Bend region.

Breeding: Broad-banded Copperheads typically produce small litters of only 3 or 4 young, but as many as 10 have been recorded. The babies of this species are larger than babies of the eastern species.

Natural History: This species was once regarded as being two subspecies of the Eastern Copperhead, one called the Broad-banded Copperhead (subspecies *laticinctus*) and another known as the Trans-Pecos Copperheard (subspecies *pictigaster*). Some experts still consider that to be an accurate representation of the relationships of North American Copperhead populations. Where the ranges of the two copperheads found in Texas meet hybrid individuals are not uncommon. The presence of what is mainly a woodland species in the arid regions of western Texas is thought to be the result of changes in the climate of Texas within the last 15,000 years. Until that time (known as the Pliestocene epoch), west Texas was a much cooler and wetter climate suitable for deciduous woodland.

Class—**Reptilia** (reptiles)

Order—**Squamata** (lizards & snakes)

Family—**Viperidae** (vipers)—subfamily—**Crotalinae** (pit vipers)

Northern Cottonmouth *Agkistrodon piscivorus*	**Pygmy Rattlesnake** *Sistrurus miliarius*	**Western Massasauga** *Sistrurus tergeminus*
	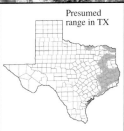	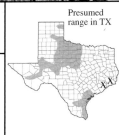

Size: Average 3 feet. Record 5feet, 2 inches.	**Size:** About 18 inches. Maximum 25 inches.	**Size:** Averages 18 inches. Record 34.75.
Abundance: Fairly common especially in southeastern Texas.	**Abundance:** Uncommon to rare in Texas. Found only in eastern Texas.	**Abundance:** Uncommon to rare and discontinuously distributed in Texas.

Presumed range in TX

Variation: Adults vary from uniform brown to nearly black. Freshly molted specimens show a pattern of dark bands on an olive or grayish background.	**Variation:** Ground color varies from grayish brown to pale brown. Sometimes with a reddish or purplish tint. Juveniles resemble adults.	**Variation:** Ground color varies from very pale gray to dark gray. Two subspecies occur in Texas, the Western (*tergiminus*) and Desert (*edwardsi*).
Habitat: Wetlands primarily. A highly aquatic species, the cottonmouth inhabits mostly swamps and marshes, but they can also be found at times in creeks, lakes, or ponds.	**Habitat:** In Texas this snake is found mainly in the South Central Plains (Ecoregion, but also occurs in the eastern portion the Gulf Coastal Plain. It favors woodlands bordering wetlands.	**Habitat:** Western subspecies is native to the Great Plains Level I Ecoregion in northern Texas. Desert grasslands and Shortgrass Prairies are used by the Desert subspecies in west and south Texas.
Breeding: Produces 3 to 12 babies in late August or early September. Unlike the copperhead, female cottonmouths may reproduce annually.	**Breeding:** Breeds in the fall with young being born the following summer in July or August. The tiny babies can coil on a coin the size of a dime.	**Breeding:** Breeds in spring with young born in late summer or fall. Average of about 6 young per litter with a maximum of 11.
Natural History: The name "Cottonmouth" is derived from the habit these snakes have of gaping open the mouth when threatened. The inside of the mouth is white, hence the name. Cottonmouths attain a large size and have powerful venom that is capable of killing a human. Frogs, fish, salamanders, and small mammals are prey. Young Cottonmouths have a strongly banded pattern and and resembles their cousin the Copperhead, and like the Copperhead young Cottonmouths have a bright yellow tail tip used to lure prey. In Texas the range of these water loving snakes invades the arid western regions along major rivers, including the Colorado and Brazos Rivers.	**Natural History:** These tiny rattlesnakes are both secretive and cryptic and are thus easily overlooked. Though they can be found in dry, upland woods they show a preference for areas near water, swamps, marshes, and especially near springs and seeps. They are mainly nocturnal in warm weather but may move about diurnally in spring and fall. Food items include frogs, lizards, and mice as well as some invertebrates. Their tiny rattle is audible for a distance of only a few feet. They are quick to strike if molested and although they possess a virulent venom, their small venom glands probably do not hold enough volume to kill a healthy adult human.	**Natural History:** The Western Massasauga is an uncommon to rare snake throughout its rather discontinuous range across the southern Great Plains from Missouri to western and southern Texas. It can be locally fairly common, especially in the southern coastal plain and south Texas brush country. The Desert subspecies (*edwardsi*) is the smaller of the two subspecies found in Texas and reaches a maximum length of only 21 inches (from *Texas Snakes, A Field Guide* by Dixon and Werler). Food items listed include rodents, lizards, frogs, and small snakes. No sources reviewed listed invertebrates as food items, but they are possibly eaten by young snakes.

Class—**Reptilia** (reptiles)

Order—**Squamata** (lizards & snakes)

Family -**Viperidae** (vipers)—subfamily—**Crotalinae** (pit vipers)

Timber (Canebrake) Rattlesnake *Crotalus horridus*	Western Diamondback Rattlesnake *Crotalus atrox*	Prairie Rattlesnake *Crotalus viridis*

Size: Average about 4 feet. Record 6 feet 2 inches.  Presumed range in TX	**Size:** Averages about 4 feet. Record length is 7 feet 4 inches. 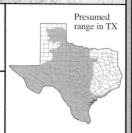 Presumed range in TX	**Size:** Averages about 3 feet. Record is just under 5 feet. 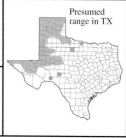 Presumed range in TX
Abundance: Uncommon to rare in most of its range in TX.	**Abundance:** Fairly common. Most common in south Texas.	**Abundance:** May be fairly common in parts of Panhandle.
Variation: Ground color may be brownish, pinkish, or yellowish.	**Variation:** Varies from brownish to light smoky gray to dark gray.	**Variation:** Usually greenish or olive. Occasionally more brownish or tan.
Habitat: As their name implies, Timber Rattlesnakes are forest animals. They inhabit both mature forests and second growth woodlands. Both upland forests and bottomland woods are utilized.	**Habitat:** Most habitats in the western two thirds of Texas are utilized. It tends to avoid densely forested areas and favors grasslands, deserts, and other semi-open habitats.	**Habitat:** A true grassland species that is found throughout much of the Great Plains Level I Ecoregion. Also occurs in desert grassland habitats in the Chihuahuan Desert Level III Ecoregion.
Breeding: Young snakes are born in late summer or early fall about a year after breeding. Females will produce young only every other year. Average litter is 6 to 12.	**Breeding:** Females give birth in late summer and will remain in the vicinity of their brood for several days. As many as two dozen young may be produced by large females.	**Breeding:** Young are born in late summer or early fall. Average litter is about 10 to 12 but as many as 25 young have been recorded. Larger females produce larger litters.
Natural History: This is one of the largest rattlesnake species in America and their bite is quite capable of killing a human. Fortunately, they are peace-loving animals that only strike as a last resort. These large snakes feed mostly on mammals, with squirrels and chipmunks being a favorite food. They are known to lie in ambush beside fallen logs that are frequently traveled by ground foraging chipmunks and squirrels. Almost any type of small mammal can be food and many types of mice and voles are eaten. Nestlings of ground dwelling birds can also be prey. Mice are probably the main food for the young and even a newborn Timber Rattlesnake is large enough to swallow a young mouse.	**Natural History:** If the state of Texas had a "state rattlesnake," it would be this iconic species. Not only is the Western Diamondback the largest of the state's venomous snakes, it is also the most common venomous snake in most areas. It is an easily provoked species that is responsible for many snakebites and for more snakebite deaths than any other Texas snake. A fully aroused snake in a defensive posture presents an intimidating picture, raising the forepart of the body and rattling loudly. The food of the adult snakes is mostly small mammals. Ground Squirrels, cottontails and Kangaroo Rats are favorite food items and a large adult can swallow a fully grown cottontail. Young snakes feed on mice, voles, and probably some lizards.	**Natural History:** The name Prairie Rattlesnake is very appropriate for this species since it ranges throughout the short-grass prairie regions of North America from southern Canada to northern Mexico. Its range in Texas is restricted to the Panhandle and the Trans-Pecos region of western Texas. The venom of this species is quite toxic and several fatalities are recorded from its bite. Food is mostly small mammals like mice and ground squirrels. In many areas of its range this species ascends into the higher elevations of mountains where it can be found in canyons, high mountain meadows and talus slopes. In Texas it has been found as high as 5,000 feet (from the book *Texas Snakes, A Field Guide* by Dixon and Werler).

Class—**Reptilia** (reptiles)

Order—**Squamata** (lizards & snakes)

Family—**Viperidae** (vipers)—subfamily—**Crotalinae** (pit vipers)

Eastern Black-tailed Rattlesnake	Mohave Rattlesnake	Rock Rattlesnake
Crotalus ornatus	*Crotalus scutulatus*	*Crotalus lepidus*

Subspecies lepidus
Mottled Rock Rattle Snake

Subspecies klauberi
Banded Rock Rattle Snake

Size: Averages 2.5 feet. Record 52 inches.

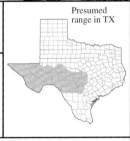
Presumed range in TX

Size: Averages about 2.5 feet. Record 48 inches.

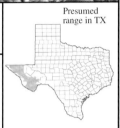
Presumed range in TX

Size: Averages about 18 inches. Record 33.6.

Presumed range in TX

Abundance: Common in Big Bend, fairly common elsewhere.

Abundance: Fairly common in the Trans-Pecos region of western Texas.

Abundance: Uncommon in Texas. Found only in the western end of the state.

Variation: Varies from greenish gray to bluish gray.

Variation: Varies from greenish gray to greenish brown.

Variation: There are two subspecies in Texas. See Natural History below.

Habitat: Rocky canyons and rugged plateaus with rocky ridges and steep, rocky slopes. Ascends desert mountains to over 7,000 feet.

Habitat: This is a desert species that avoids the mountains. Rather it lives in desert basins between the mountain ranges. Associates with Creosote Bush.

Habitat: Rocky areas. Canyons, steep rocky hillsides, boulder piles, and talus slopes in mountainous areas. At lower elevations found in rocky canyons.

Breeding: Average litter size is a half dozen. But as many as 16 has been recorded.

Breeding: An average of 6 to 8 young with a maximum of 13. Young snakes are about 8 inches at birth.

Breeding: Typically produces small litters of 4 to 6 young. Baby snakes are about 7 inches in length.

Natural History: This rattlesnake species is most common in Big Bend National Park where it can be found in canyons, rocky slopes and talus slopes below the highest peaks of the Chiso Mountains. It is a relatively mild mannered species that is less inclined to rattle or assume a defensive stance that many other rattlesnake species. When threatened and sufficiently aroused, however, it will defend itself vigorously and rattle profusely. The venom of this snake is reportedly less toxic than that of the Western Diamondback and most victims of bites by this species survive, but it is regarded as being capable of killing a human. Small mammals make up the bulk of the diet for adult snakes. Many rodents are eaten as are rabbits and occasionally birds. Young snakes will eat lizards.

Natural History: The venom some Mohave Rattlesnakes contains powerful neurotoxins and it is the most toxic of any rattlesnake species in Texas. Many experts consider it to be one of North America's most dangerous serpents and a high percentage of bites by this snake are fatal. These snakes are easily provoked and quick to strike if molested or threatened. They are easily confused with the Western Diamondback and some believe that many of the deaths attributed to the Western Diamondback over the years were actually bites by this species. Although they are not a common snake in Texas they can be found throughout most of the Trans-Pecos region. Small mammals are the main food item of adults and may make up as much as 90 percent of the diet. Baby snakes probably feed on lizards.

Natural History: There are two subspecies of this small rattlesnake and both can be found in Texas. Most Texas specimens belong to the subspecies *lepidus* (the Mottled Rock Rattlesnake). In the extreme western tip of the state in the vicinity of El Paso and the Franklin Mountains can be found the subspecies *klauberi* (Banded Rock Rattlesnake). Both subspecies are variable in color and tend to match the color of the substrate or dominant rocks in their habitat. In habits they are crepuscular and nocturnal. Lizards are the main food for this species. Lizards are very common in this snakes habitat with several species of the family Phrynosomatidae (the Spiny, Earless, Tree, Side-blotched, and Brush Lizards) being among the most common and thus they are the main food of this species.

CHAPTER 9

THE AMPHIBIANS OF TEXAS

TABLE 6

— THE ORDERS AND FAMILIES OF TEXAS AMPHIBIANS —

Class—**Amphibia** (amphibians)

Order—**Anura** (frogs & toads)

Family	**Ranidae** (true frogs)
Family	**Hylidae** (tree frogs)
Family	**Leptodactylidae** (leptodactylid frogs)
Family	**Craugastoridae** (northern rainfrogs)
Family	**Eleutherodactylidae** (rainfrogs)
Family	**Rhinophrynidae** (burrowing toads)
Family	**Microhylidae** (narrowmouth toads)
Family	**Scaphiopodidae** (spadefoots)
Family	**Bufonidae** (true toads)

Order—**Caudata** (salamanders)

Family	**Ambysotmatidae** (mole salamanders)
Family	**Salamandridae** (newts)
Family	**Plethodontidae** (lungless salamanders)
Family	**Proteida** (mudpuppies)
Family	**Cryptobranchidae** (hellbenders)
Family	**Amphiumidae** (amphiumas)
Family	**Sirenidae** (sirens)

THE AMPHIBIANS OF TEXAS

PART 1: FROGS AND TOADS

Class—**Amphibia** (amphibians)

Order—**Anura** (frogs & toads)

Family—**Ranidae** (true frogs)

Rio Grande Leopard Frog *Lithobates berlandieri*	Southern Leopard Frog *Lithobates sphenocephala*	Plains Leopard Frog *Lithobates blairi*
	Green morph Brown morph	

Size: Average 3 inches. Max 5.5 inches. 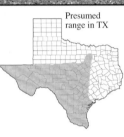 Presumed range in TX	**Size:** Average 3 inches. Record 5 inches.  Presumed range in TX	**Size:** To 3.75 inches. Record 4.375.  Presumed range in TX
Abundance: Fairly common in aquatic situations within range.	**Abundance:** Very common. One of the most common frogs in Texas.	**Abundance:** Common in the Panhandle and northern plains of TX.
Variation: The skin color between the spots varies from brown, tan, olive green or bright green. Females are apparently smaller than males.	**Variation:** Individuals vary from bright green to light tan (see photos above). Very similar to the preceding species but without a spot on the snout.	**Variation:** Ground color (skin color between the spots) varies from tan to brown or greenish. There are no subspecies.
Habitat: Grasslands, savanna, semi-arid brushlands, and desert regions, where it is associated with stream courses mainly. Also in stock ponds and canals.	**Habitat:** Found in virtually all aquatic habitats within its range. Like the Northern Leopard Frog they often wander in to grassy fields far from water.	**Habitat:** Mainly a prairie species. Occupies lowlands, river valleys, and remnant prairie. Always found near water.
Breeding: Breeds in both spring and fall in Texas. Egg laying and tadpole development is assumed to be the same as for the other North American Leopard Frog species.	**Breeding:** Breeds mostly in April and May. Breeding localities are ponds, ditches, marshes, and swamps. Lays up to 5,000 eggs in several clumps. Young frogs emerge in mid-summer.	**Breeding:** Breeds in March and April. Lays up to 6,500 eggs. Tadpoles transform into froglets by mid to late summer. Emerging froglets can be extremely common in early fall.
Natural History: Although this species inhabits much of the arid and semi-arid regions in Texas, it is always found in close proximity to a permanent water source, and is usually associated with rivers and creeks. They are primarily nocturnal in habits and the food is mainly insects. The range of the Rio Grand Leopard Frog extends southward well into tropical regions of Mexico. In fact the species is sometimes referred to as the "Mexican Leopard Frog." The species name honors an early French-born naturalist (Jean Louis Berlandier) who did much field work in northern Mexico and, among other things, discovered the Texas Tortoise (*Gopherus berlandieri*).	**Natural History:** These frogs are frequently found some distance from permanent water sources in meadows and overgrown fields. They can even be seen in rural lawns on occasion, especially in late summer. Southern Leopard Frogs can be told from their northern cousin by the lack of a dark spot on the snout. They are easily discerned from the Pickerel Frog by their round rather than squarish spots; while the Northern Crayfish Frog is much stouter with a more rounded snout. A wide variety of insects, spiders, and other invertebrates are eaten. Like most frogs, they spend the winter in the mud at the bottom of a pond, creek, or other permanent water.	**Natural History:** The bulk of this frog's range is far to the north in the Great Plains region. There it can be a common species. It was perhaps once more common in Texas before the state's extensive prairies went under the plow. Loss of many small ponds that once dotted the prairie landscape in the days of subsistence farming has also probably impacted this and other frog species. Todays large crop fields can be deserted of wildlife, especially amphibians. In places, it shares its range with the more common Southern Leopard Frog and hybrids between the two species are known. Food is mostly insects and other invertebrates.

Class—**Amphibia** (amphibians)
Order—**Anura** (frogs & toads)
Family—**Ranidae** (true frogs)

Pickerel Frog *Lithobates palustris*	**Crayfish Frog** *Lithobates areolatus*	**Green (Bronze) Frog** *Lithobates clamitans*

Size: Average about 3 inches. Record 3.75.  Presumed range in TX	**Size:** Record length 4.5 inches.  Presumed range in TX	**Size:** Average 3 inches, maximum of 4.25.  Presumed range in TX
Abundance: Uncommon to rare. Range restricted to eastern Texas.	**Abundance:** Uncommon to rare and declining in Texas.	**Abundance:** Common to very common in the Piney Woods of eastern Texas.
Variation: Ground color varies from tan to brown. There are no subspecies of this frog.	**Variation:** There are two subspecies, but only *L. a. areolatus*, the Southern Crayfish Frog, occurs in Texas.	**Variation:** There are two color morphshs. Texas frogs are invariably the Bronze morph shown above.
Habitat: Prefers spring-fed streams and clear, cool waters in woodland areas. Texas range is mostly in the Piney Woods region.	**Habitat:** Floodplains, bottomland fields, and other low-lying areas with mesic substrates supporting crayfish. Found mainly in wet meadows.	**Habitat:** Found in virtually every aquatic habitat within their range, from small ponds and large lakes to streams and wetlands.
Breeding: Breeds in ponds, ditches or permanent streams. Lays 2,000 to 4,000 eggs. Tadpoles transform in about three months.	**Breeding:** An early breeder. Most breeding apparently occurs during periods of heavy rainfall in March. Up to 7,000 eggs may be laid.	**Breeding:** Up to 4,000 eggs may be deposited. Males clasp onto females back and release sperm onto eggs as they are extruded from the female.
Natural History: Pickerel Frogs are distinguished from Leopard Frogs by their square rather than round spots. These frogs secrete a toxin from the skin that protects them from many predators and is strong enough to kill other frogs kept with them in a small container. Among the predators that are able to eat them, however, is another frog species, the Bullfrog. Pickerel Frogs show a preference for clean water and an intolerance for pollution. In this respect, the Pickerel Frog may be an indicator species that can provide an early warning regarding environmental threats like water pollution. Sadly for those who appreciate nature, populations of this frog, (and in fact frogs in general) are declining in many areas.	**Natural History:** This frog's name is derived from their habit of utilizing crayfish burrows as a home. They are quite secretive and are rarely observed except during the breeding season when they will travel overland in search of suitable breeding ponds or pools in wetland areas. Crayfish, other amphibians, small reptiles, and of course insects are food items. This frog is a species in sharp decline. Modern agricultural practices such as tiling of wetland meadows to remove water and thus enable row cropping, along with the filling of small isolated ponds is possibly the cause of this decline. The range map above indicates the presumed historical range in Texas. It is today probably absent from much of this area.	**Natural History:** A drive through a wetland on a rainy night in late summer when the tadpoles of *Lithobates clamitans* are emerging onto land will reveal astounding numbers of small frogs crossing the roadway as they disperse into new territories. Adult frogs feed on insects primarily but other arthropods including small crayfish are frequently eaten. Minnows and other small aquatic vertebrates are also potential prey. These frogs are easily confused with the much larger Bullfrog, but are distinguished by the presence of a fold of skin (known as a dorso-lateral fold) that runs along each side of the back. Like other aquatic frogs they sometimes wander away from water on rainy nights to forage for insects in grassy areas.

Class—**Amphibia** (amphibians)

Order—**Anura** (frogs & toads)

Family—**Ranidae** (true frogs)

Bullfrog *Rana catesbeianus*	**Pig Frog** *Rana gyrlio*

Green morph — Brown morph

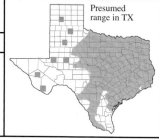

Size: Record 8 inches (snout to vent length). Averages 4 to 5 inches.

Abundance: Very common.

Variation: Dorsal color varies from green to brown. Ventral color varies from nearly white with grayish mottling to pale gray with heavy, charcoal gray mottling. Males have a larger tympanum (ear membrane) than females and grow to a larger size.

Presumed range in TX

Size: Max size 6.5 inches.

Abundance: Rare in Texas.

Variation: Greenish or gray to olive brown.

Presumed range in TX

Habitat: Found in virtually every aquatic habitat type within its rang in the state, from small ponds and large lakes to streams. Also common in wetlands such as marsh and swamp.

Habitat: Most freshwater habitats are inhabited. Wet prairies and marshes are a favorite habitat.

Breeding: Breeding and egg laying occurs from late spring through mid-summer. Several thousand eggs (as many as 10,000) can be laid and two clutches per year is not uncommon. The eggs are encased in a mass of a clear jelly-like substance. Always breeds in permanent water since tadpole development is very prolonged. Tadpole metamorphosis in the Bullfrog does not occur until the following summer or in northern populations metamorphosis may not occur until the third year.

Breeding: Large masses of up to 8 to 10 thousand eggs are laid in summer amid aquatic vegetation in permanent water. Tadpole stage lasts through the winter. Will breed all summer in southern parts of its range.

Natural History: These are the largest frogs in America. Their hind legs are considered to be a delicacy by many. They are regarded as a game animal and are hunted for food during the annual "frog season." In some places they are raised commercially for food and for research or teaching laboratories. They may venture far from water and will travel from pond to pond during rainy weather. The ability to traverse long distances on rainy nights allows them to colonize newly constructed ponds and lakes. Insects are important food items for young frogs and are also eaten by adults. Crayfish are another important food item. The list of animals known to be consumed by these voracious predators includes almost any animal small enough to be swallowed, including other frogs. There is even a record of a large Bullfrog eating a baby rattlesnake! The original range of the Bullfrog was the eastern half of America. But they have been widely introduced across the continent and even into many foreign countries. Introduced populations of Bullfrogs have become a threat to other frog species in some areas, especially in the desert southwest where small pockets of wetland habitats can be over run by Bullfrogs. The original frog residents are often endemic species with limited distributions. The much smaller native frogs become food for the larger Bullfrog and are rapidly decimated. The bellowing call of the Bullfrog will carry for long distances and is a familiar nocturnal sound in summer in rural regions of Texas. In color they can vary from very dark green to lighter green or brown. Sometimes with a dark mottled pattern. Breeding male Bullfrogs develop a bright yellow throat, which can distinguish them from the females.

Natural History: Very similar to the Bullfrog and like that species, the Pig Frog is hunted for its legs which are regarded as quite tasty. The name comes from its call which sounds a bit like the grunting of a pig. This species appears to be in decline in some areas of its range but it is also known to exhibit a tendency towards cyclical populations. As with many amphibians, severe droughts can drastically reduce the population, while several years of adequate moisture can cause a population boom. These are reportedly highly aquatic frogs that rarely leave the water except during periods of heavy rainfall. Distinguishing between this species and the Bullfrog and Green Frog can be challenging. The Pig Frog has a more pointed snout than the Bullfrog and lacks the dorso-lateral fold of the Green Frog.

Class—**Amphibia** (amphibians)

Order—**Anura** (frogs & toads)

Family—**Hylidae** (tree frogs)

Blanchard's Cricket Frog *Acris blanchardi*	**Spring Peeper** *Pseudacris crucifer*	**Spotted Chorus Frog** *Pseudacris clarkii*

Size: Tiny, usually less than 1 inch. 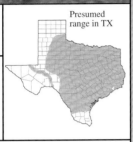 Presumed range in TX	**Size:** About 1 inch. Record 1.5 inches. 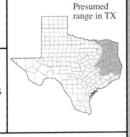 Presumed range in TX	**Size:** About 1 inch. Record 1.25 inches.  Presumed range in TX
Abundance: Very common throughout eastern and central Texas.	**Abundance:** Common, especially in wetlands but will breed in roadside ditches.	**Abundance:** Fairly common. Ranges throughout central Texas.
Variation: Varies from brown to reddish brown or tan. May also be green. Many will have markings on the back that may be greenish or brownish.	**Variation:** Ground color varies. Usually tan or brown. Sometimes grayish or reddish. Always has a darker "X" shaped marking on the back.	**Variation:** Skin between spots is usually some shade of brown, tan, olive gray or greenish brown. Cold specimens tend to be darker.
Habitat: Shorelines of ponds, along creeks, temporary pools, marshes, swamps, wet meadows, and uplands.	**Habitat:** Woodlands and thickets, usually near water. Most common in lowlands (swamps, marshes, etc).	**Habitat:** This is an open country species that favors grassland habitats. Can be found in pastures or natural meadow.
Breeding: Breeds from spring through late summer. Up to 400 eggs are laid in small clusters of 10 to 15 per cluster. Tadpoles and froglets are tiny.	**Breeding:** Spring Peepers begin breeding activity as early as late winter and continue into early spring. Several hundred eggs are laid in shallow water.	**Breeding:** May breed at any time of the year during periods of heavy rainfall, sometimes in the late summer. Lays up to 1000 eggs.
Natural History: These diminutive frogs are most commonly seen along the receding shorelines of ponds and lakes in late summer or early fall. When startled by a passing human they will often jump into the water and then immediately swim back to shore. This may be an "out of the frying pan into the fire" behavior intended to keep them from the jaws of hungry fish. They are often seen far from water in fields and woodlands, but are always more common in wetland habitats and permanently damp areas. Their name comes from their call which resembles that of a cricket, but is more accurately described as sounding like two small stones being rapidly clicked together. This is one of the most common frog species in the US, but they are more often heard than seen.	**Natural History:** Another tiny frog that is heard more often than seen. The name comes from the sound made when breeding frogs are calling. The call is a rapidly repeated "peep, peep, peep." Despite being members of the tree frog family they live mostly on the ground. The species name *"crucifer"* is Latin for "cross bearer" and refers to the x-shaped mark that is always present on this frogs back. These little frogs, along with their cousins the Chorus Frogs, are a true harbinger of spring throughout much of the United States. They may breed in the same flooded field pools with Chorus Frogs or even in the same pool. They are widely distributed throughout the Eastern Temperate Forest Level I Ecoregion and in Texas they can be found throughout the Piney Woods region.	**Natural History:** In some respects this is the western version of the more widespread Spring Peeper, from which it is easily distinguished by the presence of dorsal spots. While they may occur in many semi-arid areas they are usually near some source of permanent water. Adults will wander far from water but always return to ponds, lakes, flooded ditches, etc. to breed. Most frog species are in decline but there is no information indicating that this species is not thriving. These frogs tend to do well in pastures that are not overgrazed. Their biggest threat in Texas is probably loss of habitat to row crop agriculture. The food is very small, invertebrates captured on the ground amid grasses. They are rarely seen during dry periods or droughts.

Class—**Amphibia** (amphibians)

Order—**Anura** (frogs & toads)

Family—**Hylidae** (tree frogs)

Cajun Chorus Frog *Pseudacris fouquettei*	Strecker's Chorus Frog *Pseudacris streckeri*	Mexican Tree Frog *Smilisca baudini*
		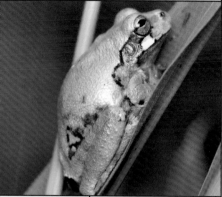

<table>
<tr>
<td>Size: About 1 inch. Record 1.1875 inches.</td>
<td>
Presumed range in TX</td>
<td>Size: About 1.5 to 2 inches. Record 1.87 inches.</td>
<td>
Presumed range in TX</td>
<td>Size: About 2.5 inches. Record 3.5.</td>
<td>
Presumed range in TX</td>
</tr>
<tr>
<td>Abundance: Common within its range in easternmost Texas.</td>
<td></td>
<td>Abundance: Uncommon. USFWS lists it as a Species of Special Concern.</td>
<td></td>
<td>Abundance: Rare in Texas. Regarded as Threatened Species.</td>
<td></td>
</tr>
</table>

Variation: Light brown to very dark brown. Stripes on back sometimes broken in dashes.	**Variation:** Some experts recognize two subspecies but there is no definitive variation in Texas populations.	**Variation:** Changes color to match its habitat. Gray, various shades of brown, greenish, yellowish or reddish.
Habitat: Found in a variety of habitats across central Texas. Woodland, fields, and especially wetlands.	**Habitat:** Woodlands and grassy fields, usually near water. Prefers sandy soils for ease in burrowing.	**Habitat:** Humid and subhumid environments mostly but also occasionally found in semi-arid habitats near water.
Breeding: Breeds as early as February in Texas. Several hundred eggs are laid. Tadpoles transform within 2 months.	**Breeding:** Breeds in ephemeral pools in flooded fields and roadside ditches. Breeding occurs in early spring.	**Breeding:** As many as 3,500 eggs are laid in a film on the surface of the water. Tadpoles may transform in 2 to 3 weeks.
Natural History: The taxonomy of the common and widespread Chorus Frogs in America has recently undergone significant revision. One result of those studies has been to assign the former Western Chorus Frog population in Texas to a new species (Cajun Chorus Frog). In appearance this new species is largely indistinguishable from other Chorus Frog populations that were formerly assigned to the species *triseriata* (Western Chorus Frog). The new species designation for Texas populations is based on the difference in DNA and in their breeding calls; which prevents interbreeding with other Chorus Frog species within its range. Each species will respond only to the breeding call of their species. In some specimens the longitudinal stripes on the back can be broken and resemble spots similar to the Spotted Chorus Frog.	**Natural History:** This species is unique among frogs in the Hylidae family in a number of respects. First, it is a tree frog that actually looks and acts more like a toad than a tree frog. It is a burrowing species, but unlike other burrowing anurans such as the spadefoots and the toads which burrow using the hind feet and enter the soil backwards, this species burrows in head first. The range of this frog in Texas is relatively contiguous, but in other regions its populations are disjunct and widely scattered. In the adjoining states of Arkansas and Louisiana it is regarded as a Species of Special Concern. The Texas and Oklahoma populations of this frog are probably the most stable. Disjunct populations occurring in southeast Missouri and in west-central Illinois are regarded by some experts as a separate and distinct species.	**Natural History:** The *Smilisca* genus of tree frogs is mostly a Latin American genus consisting of only eight species. The Mexican Tree Frog, as its name implies, is found mostly in Mexico (and in northern Central America). Its range barely extends into Texas along the lower Rio Grande River Valley. At over 3 inches in length for a large adult, it is the largest native tree frog in the US. These frogs are much more common south of Texas and they can be found as far south as Costa Rica. They will aestivate during dry seasons, usually taking refuge in hollows or beneath tree bark. Like many tree frogs, the Mexican Tree Frog has the ability to change colors rapidly to match their substrate. This species is named after the French naturalist and explorer Nicolas Baudin who collected plant and animal specimens in the Caribbean in the late 1700s.

Class—**Amphibia** (amphibians)

Order—**Anura** (frogs & toads)

Family—**Hylidae** (tree frogs)

Canyon Tree Frog *Hyla arenicolor*	**Green Tree Frog** *Hyla cinerea*	**Squirrel Tree Frog** *Hyla squirella*

Size: Average 1.75 inches. Record 2.25.  Presumed range in TX	**Size:** Record size 2.5 inches.  Presumed range in TX	**Size:** Record size 1.75 inches.  Presumed range in TX
Abundance: Uncommon to rare in Texas. Restricted to the Big Bend.	**Abundance:** Fairly common in the Piney Woods Ecoregion.	**Abundance:** Fairly common in the upper Coastal Plain.
Variation: May be uniformly colored or have a profusion of dark spots. Ground color variable, gray, brown, or olive.	**Variation:** Varies in the amount of yellow spots on the back. May have several or none at all.	**Variation:** Can change from green to grayish brown. Lighter color occurs with warmer temperatures.
Habitat: A desert-adapted species. In Texas found only in Big Bend region where it inhabits rocky canyons with permanent water.	**Habitat:** This is a lowland animal that is found in swamps and marshes mostly. Range in Texas is mostly in the Piney Woods and Western Gulf Coastal Plain.	**Habitat:** Woodlands. Endemic to the Coastal Plain. Common around homes and buildings having dense vegetation. Likes being near water.
Breeding: Breeds in warmer months during periods of heavy rainfall. Little information is available regarding number of eggs or tadpole development.	**Breeding:** Breeds in early to mid-summer. Lays up to 1,500 eggs in shallow waters of swamps or marshes. Multiple clutches may be produced in a summer.	**Breeding:** Female will lay up to 800 eggs in ponds, canals or ephemeral waters such as ditches. Tadpoles will transform in about two months.
Natural History: This is the only tree frog species found in the Big Bend region. Its range also includes most of the southwestern US and much of the Sierra Nevada Occidental and central plateaus of western Mexico. Although mainly nocturnal, they will bask in the in the morning on boulders out in the open. Unlike most *Hyla* species these frogs are rarely seen in trees but rather use boulders and rock faces as their primary habitat. Their cryptic color and pattern will match the surface of the rock perch perfectly and render them almost invisible. These frogs are most likely to be seen during monsoon season in west Texas. In drier periods they will aestivate deep inside rock crevices where the humidity remains slightly higher and they can avoid dessication.	**Natural History:** One of this frogs favorite daytime perches are the stems of cattails and sedges where its deep green color renders it almost invisible. Its primary prey consists of caterpillers, spiders, grasshoppers, and other insects. Green Tree Frogs are primarily nocturnal in habits but they are sometimes seen during the day, especially during rainy weather. As with most other tree frogs of the genus *Hyla* this is a mainly southern species. Its range extends northward up the Mississippi Valley as far as southern Illinois where the Gulf Coastal Plain Province reaches its northernmost extension. In Texas it is found only in the eastern portion of the state. In cold weather, individuals will turn from bright green to dark brown but turn back to green with warming.	**Natural History:** This little frog can rapidly change its color back and forth from brown to green (and every shade in between) to match a tree trunk or green foliage. These frogs will typically call from their perch in trees during rains and another common name for this species in the southern US is "Rain Frog." The name Squirrel Tree Frog is derived some the sound of their call, which sounds a little like a Gray Squirrels call. Although they are quite arboreal they can also be found low to the ground or on the ground and they will take refuge under bark, logs or within rotted stumps. In older neighborhoods with large trees Squirrel Tree Frogs are common around the gutters and eaves of houses. Here they are often seen on windows at night as they hunt insects drawn to lights.

Class—**Amphibia** (amphibians)

Order—**Anura** (frogs & toads)

Family—**Hylidae** (tree frogs)	Family—**Leptodactylidae**
Gray Tree Frog complex *Hyla chrysoscelis & Hyla versicolor*	**Mexican White-lipped Frog** *Leptodactylus fragilis*

Gray phases / Green phase

Size: Averages about 2 inches. Maximum of just under 2.5 inches.	 Presumed range of the Cope's Gray Tree Frog  Presumed range of the Gray Tree Frog
Abundance: Fairly common to common.	
Habitat: Habitat is chiefly woodlands. They can be found far from water in dry upland woods.	

Size: To 1.75 inches.	 Presumed range in Texas
Abundance: Rare in Texas. This is mainly a Mexican species that is found in Texas only in the lower Rio Grande valley.	

Variation: There are actually two identical species in the Gray Tree Frog complex. They can only be reliably differentiated by the sound of their call or by laboratory examination of the number of cell chromosomes. The two species are known as the Cope's Gray Tree Frog (*Hyla chrysoscelis*), and the Gray Tree Frog (*Hyla versicolor*). Both species have the ability to change color from gray to green. Additionally, the shade of gray can range from a dark sooty gray to a light smoky gray (see photos above).

Variation: Ground color varies from gray to brown or dark brown. Amount of dark spots is also variable.

Habitat: In Texas it can be found in ditches, oxbows and similar aquatic habitats along the Rio Grande

Breeding: Breeds from late spring through summer in small bodies of water ranging from small ponds to roadside ditches. Up to 2,000 eggs are laid.

Breeding: Lays eggs in a foam created from skin secretions

Natural History: These highly arboreal tree frogs are rarely seen on the ground and they often climb high into treetops to forage for insects. They are mainly nocturnal but they may be active by day on cloudy or rainy days or in cooler weather. They shelter by day in small hollows in tree trunks or limbs and have been known to take up residence in small bird nest boxes such as a wren box or bluebird box. They will also live in the rain gutters of house roofs. They can sometimes be seen sitting in the opening of their hiding place with the head and front feet exposed. They possess remarkable camouflage abilities and the gray, lichen like pattern of their skin will perfectly match the bark of the tree they occupy. They can produce a natural anti-freeze in the blood which allows them to hibernate in tree hollows above the ground, or in leaf litter on the forest floor. Most members of the genus *Hyla* are southern animals, but these frogs range far into the northern states and even into parts of southern Canada. Food items are small insects and arthropods. Both of these species can be found in eastern Texas and their ranges overlap to some degree (see range maps above). Differentiating between these two species is very difficult and nearly impossible in the field. Those with a "good ear" can tell the difference between their calls. Other researchers must resort to a laboratory analysis of chromosomes. Cope's Gray Tree Frog has a the typical diploid set of chromosomes (two chromosomes) while the Gray Tree Frog is tetraploid, having four chromosomes in its chromosome count.

Natural History: This is the only member of the Leptodactylidae family of frogs that ranges into the United States. These frogs are unique in that many species build foam nests in a branch overhanging water or on the ground in a floodplain into which they lay their eggs. The tadpoles begin life in the foam until the rains create the opportunity access pools to continue their development. Their are approximately 200 species of Leptodactylid frogs ranging throughout Mexico, Central America and South America. The climate of the lower Rio Grande Valley is semi-tropical and this region supports many species of plants and animals from tropical regions that cannot be found anywhere else in the United States.

Class—**Amphibia** (amphibians)		
Order—**Anura** (frogs & toads)		
Family—**Craugastoridae**	Family—**Eleutherodactylidae** (rain frogs)	
Barking Frog *Craugastor augusti*	**Rio Grande Chirping Frog** *Eleutherodactylus cystignathoides*	**Cliff Chirping Frog** *Eleutherodactylus marnockii*

Size: Record size 3.75 inches.	Presumed range in TX	**Size:** Maximum size 1 inch.	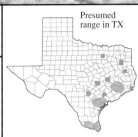Presumed range in TX	**Size:** Maximum size 1.25 inches.	Presumed range in TX
Abundance: Rare in Texas but fairly common south into Mexico.		**Abundance:** Uncommon to rare but spreading in Texas cities.		**Abundance:** Probably fairly common within its range.	

Variation: Varies from light brown to greenish. Variable amounts of red/pink.

Habitat: Rocky canyons and cliff faces with deep fissures and caves. In Texas found in parts of the Chihuahuan Desert and Edwards Plateau Ecoregions.

Breeding: Females lay their eggs in deep rock crevices where the humidity is higher. The eggs hatch into fully formed frogs.

Natural History: This species skips the tadpole stage and baby frogs emerge fully formed from the egg. An unusual reproductive trait shared with the frogs of the Eleutherodactylidae family (next 4 species). They spend most of their lives in hibernation (during winter) or in aestivation (during hot dry weather). Their peak activity above ground is apparently during the brief monsoon season in late summer. Nothing is known about their habits or life history during the extended periods spent in crevices and caves. Do they feed on troglodytic invertebrates while in caves and crevices? Or are they in a state of low metabolic activity for months at a time? The name comes from the sound made by this frogs calls, which resemble that of a dog barking. Although rare in Texas, this is a common frog farther south in Mexico.

Variation: Ground color varies from brown to grayish or olive.

Habitat: Native habitat in Texas is riparian areas in the lower Rio Grande valley. Now found in lawns and gardens in many urban areas of the state.

Breeding: Females lay a maximum of a dozen eggs in moist environments in the soil. Tadpoles metamorphosis in the egg and emerge as fully formed froglets.

Natural History: Originally found in Texas only in the lower Rio Grande valley this species has spread to many cities across the state. The method of dispersal is believed to be potted nursery plants shipped to cities and towns across Texas. They are mainly restricted to areas in the Western Gulf Coastal Plain (including Houston), but they have been recorded as far north as Ft. Worth. The name "Chirping" Frog comes from the sound of their call that is described as a "high pitched chirp," "insect-like," "bird-like," or like the sound of a squeaky shoe. The ventriliquist call coupled with their tiny size makes them almost impossible to locate. A very similar non-native species (the **Greenhouse Frog**, *E. planirostris*) has recently become established and is spreading in the area of Galveston Bay.

Variation: Ground color varies from brown to greenish.

Habitat: Inhabits rock fissures, caves and rock piles in canyons and escarpments within the Edwards Plateau Level III Ecoregion (Hill Country).

Breeding: As with other Eleutherodactylid frogs, tadpole development occurs in the egg and babies hatch fully developed.

Natural History: To the average Texan, the *Eleutherodactylus* frogs are probably some of the least known of Texas's frog species. They are tiny, mostly nocturnal, and secretive frogs that spend most of their time hidden beneath rocks or in rock crevices. They are rarely observed except by professional herpetologists who seek them out caves and other daytime hiding places. Little is known about breeding in most members of the *Eleutherodactylus* genus in Texas. It is known that the eggs are not laid in water as with most amphibians and the tadpole stage occurs within the egg. In this regard, these interesting little frogs are pushing the definition of the term "Amphibian," as they no longer are tied to water for successful reproduction. The eggs are laid in moist terrestrial environments during periods of rainfall.

Class—**Amphibia** (amphibians)

Order—**Anura** (frogs & toads)

Family—**Eleutherodactylidae** (rain frogs)	Family—**Rhinophrynidae** (burrowing toads)	Family—**Scaphiopodidae** (spadefoots)
Spotted Chirping Frog *Eleutherodactylus guttilatus*	**Burrowing Toad** *Rhinophrynus dorsalis*	**Couch's Spadefoot** *Scaphiopus couchii*

Size: Maximum size of 1.25 inches.

Abundance: Very rare. Only a few known localities in TX.

Size: Can reach a maximum of 3.75 inches.

Abundance: Rare and very restricted in range in Texas.

Size: Average about 2.5 inches.

Abundance: Common. More common in western Texas.

Variation: Ground color varies from light brown to yellowish brown.

Variation: Somewhat sexually dimorphic with females being larger.

Variation: Females are larger and have more pronounced dark reticulations.

Habitat: Habitat in Texas is along rock faces on cliffs and in ravines and canyons. Also in road cuts and man-made stone walls.

Habitat: Found mainly in floodplain areas in tropical dry forests, brushland scrub and semi-arid grassland. In Texas only in the lower Rio Grande Valley.

Habitat: Most common in desert scrub and semi-desert grasslands. Less common in dry upland woods. May be found far from permanent water.

Breeding: As with other Eleutherodactylid frogs, tadpole development occurs in the egg and babies hatch fully developed.

Breeding: An explosive breeder that emerges from burrows to breed during periods of heavy rainfall. Eggs hatch within days and tadpoles grow rapidly.

Breeding: A true explosive breeder. These frogs emerge in huge numbers during the monsoon season and lay up to 3000 their eggs in ephemeral pools

Natural History: This species of chirping frog was once regarded as being conspecific with the Cliff Chirping Frog (previous species), and some still consider that to an accurate designation. Small invertebrates are eaten, with termites possibly constituting a significant part of the diet. This species has a very limited range in Texas but it is also found in Mexico where it is probably more common and widespread. It is apparently a species of the Sierra Madre Occidental mountain range in Mexico and ranges northward into the desert mountains of Texas at least as far as the Davis Mountains and they are reportedly common in Big Bend National Park. Although they have a restricted range in Texas, the areas where they occur are remote and relatively undisturbed. Thus there appears to be little threat to the species.

Natural History: This bizarre looking anuran is mainly a Mexican species whose range barely extends into the US along the lower Rio Grande valley. With its narrow head, pointed snout, and rotund body it presents an almost cartoonish image of a toad. It is not only unique in its appearance, but also in its phylogeny. In fact, this is the only species in its genus and the only genus within its family, making it one of the most unique animal species on earth. Even more amazing is their ability to spend several years in a dormant state underground during prolonged drought periods. Even during wetter periods they are nocturnal animals that spend most of their time in underground burrows and are thus rarely observed. The small mouth of this toad precludes an ability to eat anything other than very small prey such as ants and termites.

Natural History: This is the most desert-adapted amphibian in America. They have been known to spend several years aestivating underground during periods of prolonged drought. With the arrival of desert thunderstorms the males emerge and gather in large numbers in temporary pools. Females respond to the calling of the males and breeding commences almost immediately. The eggs can hatch within 24 hours. Tadpoles are capable of transforming in less than two weeks if their pool is drying but they can prolong the tadpole stage as long as their temporary pool still holds water. Tadpoles that are able to grow longer produce larger toadlets and have a higher survival rate. It is believed by many that spadefoots are aroused from aestivation by the low frequency sounds of thunder and/or the sound of rain drops striking the hard, dry desert soil.

Class—**Amphibia** (amphibians)

Order—**Anura** (frogs & toads)

Family— **Scaphiopodidae** (spadefoot toads)

Hurter's Spadefoot *Scaphiopus hurterii*	Plains Spadefoot *Spea bombifrons*	New Mexico Spadefoot *Spea multiplicata*

Size: Average about 2 inches. Maximum 3.25. 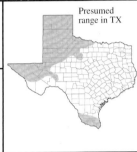Presumed range in TX	**Size:** About 2 inches. Maximum 2.5. Presumed range in TX	**Size:** Average about 2 inches. Presumed range in TX
Abundance: Uncommon, but can be very common locally.	**Abundance:** No data is available on abundance in Texas.	**Abundance:** Generally uncommon, can be locally common.
Variation: Varies from greenish gray to very dark brown.	**Variation:** Gray or brown, sometimes with an overall greenish wash.	**Variation:** Can be grayish, greenish, brownish or very dark, chocolate brown.
Habitat: Mesic woodlands are the primary habitat. Requires sandy or loamy soils that facilitate burrowing.	**Habitat:** An open ground, prairie species. Uses short grass prairie and desert grassland. Avoids wooded areas.	**Habitat:** Arid grasslands, sagebrush communities, creosote flats, desert scrub, and semi-desert brushlands.
Breeding: Breeds during torrential rains from late winter through summer. Eggs are laid in long strings. Tadpoles may cannibalize their siblings.	**Breeding:** Breeding is similar to other spadefoots. Explosive and occurring during rainy periods. In Texas it does not breed in years when monsoons fail.	**Breeding:** Breeds during summer monsoons. Explosive breeding may last only a few days. Eggs hatch within two days and tadpoles transform in 3 weeks.
Natural History: The name "Spadefoot" come from a sickle-shaped horny structure present on the hind feet of all spadefoot species that is used for digging into the ground. The genus name "*Scaphiopus*" is latin for "shovel foot." Spadefoots spend much of their lives in burrows only a few inches deep and emerge on rainy nights. During dry weather they may spend weeks in the burrow without feeding. They all secrete a toxic substance which is highly irritant to mucus membranes, thus making these anurans unpalatable to many potential predators. Touching the face or other sensitive skin after handling a spadefoot will result in an uncomfortable burning sensation. Although this species is spottily distributed throughout much of its range, in some regions it can be remarkably plentiful.	**Natural History:** In addition to burrowing into the soil rear end first using the "spades" present on the hind feet, Plains Spadefoots will also utilize burrows of other species such as gophers and ground squirrels. Like other spadefoots, this is a secretive and nocturnal species. Hybrids are known from areas where the range overlaps that of the New Mexico Spadefoot. Most spadefoot are southern animals but the Plains Spadefoot ranges as north as the prairies of Canada. The biggest threat to this species today has been the conversion of prairie grassland to crop fields. Climate change could have a significant impact on this and all other amphibian species inhabiting the more arid regions of North America. If climate models are correct there will likely be more extreme periods of extended drought in the west.	**Natural History:** Nocturnal and secretive, this species spends most of its time in underground burrows and is usually only observed during rainy periods. But they may sometimes be seen on roadways at night as they forage for small terrestrial arthropods. Interestingly males have been known to begin calling from within their burrow at the sound of thunder from gathering storms. This species also goes by the name "Mexican Spadefoot." Either name would seem appropriate since they are widespread in Mexico and are also found throughout the state of New Mexico. Their range in Texas is restricted to the more xeric regions in the western end of the state. This species was only recently elevated to full species level, having been previously regarded as a subspecies of the Western Spadefoot.

Class—**Amphibia** (amphibians)

Order—**Anura** (frogs & toads)

Family-**Microhylidae** (narrow-mouthed frogs)

Sheep Frog *Hypopachus variolosus*	Eastern Narrow-mouth Toad *Gastrophryne carolinensis*	Western Narrow-mouth Toad *Gastrophryne olivacea*

Size: Average about 1.25 inches.	 Presumed range in TX	**Size:** Average about one inch. Record 1.5.	 Presumed range in TX	**Size:** Average about one inch. Record 1.75.	 Presumed range in TX
Abundance: A rare and threatened species in TX.		**Abundance:** Uncommon. Possibly declining in Texas.		**Abundance:** Probably fairly common in much of Texas.	

Sheep Frog	Eastern Narrow-mouth Toad	Western Narrow-mouth Toad
Variation: May be tan, brown, or reddish brown. Mid-dorsal stripe varies from yellow to reddish.	**Variation:** Dark gray to light gray or frequently rusty brown. Color tends to match the habitat.	**Variation:** Very little variation. Ground color may be gray or greenish gray. Young are a mottled dark brown.
Habitat: Found along the southern portion of the Western Coastal Plain. In semi-arid thorn-scrub habitats mostly. Micro-habitat is underground burrows.	**Habitat:** Can be found both in dry uplands and in more mesic bottomlands. In dry uplands usually seeks refuge in moist micro-habitats such as rotted logs.	**Habitat:** Semi-arid grasslands, dry upland woods, and lowland woods. Usually in the vicinity of water and probably most common in flood plains.
Breeding: Up to 700 eggs are laid, usually in ephemeral pools. Eggs hatch within a day and turn into frogs within a month.	**Breeding:** From 500 to 800 eggs are laid in late spring or summer. Eggs hatch in two days. Tadpoles transform in 2 to 4 weeks.	**Breeding:** An explosive breeder. Breeding occurs during periods of rainfall in spring and summer. Up to 2000 eggs can be laid.
Natural History: Much of this tiny frog's range is in Mexico and northern Central America, where it can be a common species. Like other members of its specialized family (Microhylidae) it has a very narrow snout and a tiny mouth. Its food is restricted to the smallest invertebrates like ants and termites. All species of Microhlidae frogs are secretive and spend much of their time hidden in burrows or beneath logs, rocks or leaf litter. There is a fold of skin across the top of the head just behind the eyes. It is thought that this skin fold can be moved forward to protect the eyes when the frogs are feeding on ants. Like many frogs and toads the Microhylidae have skin secretions that may offer some protection from potential predators, either by making them distasteful or by irritating mucus membranes.	**Natural History:** Narrow-mouth Frogs are confirmed burrowers that are occasionally found hiding beneath flat rocks, boards, etc. Their call is a nasal "baaaa" and sounds like the cry of a young lamb. Ants and termites are recorded as prey and it is likely that other diminutive insects and other arthropods are eaten. The tiny mouth on this frog precludes eating anything larger than the average termite. Despite their name, they are not true frogs but are the representatives in the United States of a specialized family known as Microhylidae. Microhylidae frogs are much more common in more tropical regions. Their are over 300 species in the family and they can be found on every major continent except Europe and Antarctica. In Texas this species is found mainly in the Piney Woods and the Gulf Coastal Plain.	**Natural History:** Hidden for most of the year in underground burrows, these little toads emerge in huge numbers during periods of heavy rainfall and entire populations in a given area will all converge. In a unique breeding behavior the male secretes a sticky substance to glue himself to back of the female during breeding, releasing sperm onto the eggs as they are extruded. Perhaps the most fascinating thing about this species is its symbiotic relationship with Tarantulas. Western Narrow-mouth Toads are known to live in the Tarantula burrows with Tarantulas. For some reason, the Tarantulas do not eat the toads. The toads probably receive some protection from predators while in the burrow. It has been suggested that the Tarantula may benefit from having the toads to keep ants out of the burrow.

Class—**Amphibia** (amphibians)

Order   Anura (frogs & toads)

Family—**Bufonidae** (true toads)

(Dwarf) American Toad *Anaxyrus americanus*	**Great Plains Toad** *Anaxyrus cognatus*	**Woodhouse's Toad** *Anaxyrus woodhousii*

| **Size:** About 2.5 inches. Record 4 inches.

 Abundance: Uncommon in Texas. Found only in NE corner of state. |  Presumed range in TX | **Size:** 2 to 3 inches. Record 4 inches.

 Abundance: Common in the Panhandle. Less so in desert areas. | 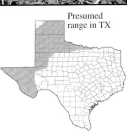 Presumed range in TX | **Size:** 3 to 4 inches. Record 5 inches.

 Abundance: Fairly common except in desert areas and south TX. |  Presumed range in TX. Typical Woodhouse's Toad / Hybrid Zone |

Variation: There are two subspecies of this toad. The Dwarf American Toad (*B. a. charlesmithi*) occurs in Texas. This is a much smaller subspecies.

Variation: Ground color various shades of browns, grays, and olive or greenish. Dark blotches vary from nearly black to brownish or olive.

Variation: Specimens from easternmost Texas are regarded as constituting a hybrid population with the more easterly occurring Fowler's Toad (*B. fowleri*).

Habitat: Uses a wide variety of habitats from woodlands and fields to urban lawns and gardens.

Habitat: The Great Plains and the desert southwest. Less common in desert regions than in grasslands.

Habitat: Found in virtually every type of habitat in Texas. In arid regions tends to occur mainly in riparian zones.

Breeding: Breeds as early as March. Eggs are laid in long strings of clear gelatinous material. Breeds in small ponds, water filled ditches, or temporary pools in seasonally flooded lowlands.

Breeding: Breeds from spring through fall. In the Great Plains breeding occurs during heavy spring rainfall events. Well over 10,000 eggs have been documented from a female.

Breeding: Breeds mainly in the spring and summer in eastern and central Texas. In the arid region of the Chihuahuan Desert its breeding may be tied to seasonal monsoons.

Natural History: American Toads eat a wide variety of insects and other small arthropods. They are adept burrowers and like other toads possess hardened spade-like structures on the hind feet that are used for digging. These toads can be told from the similar Woodhouse's Toad by the their larger and less numerous warts on the body. The similar Woodhouse's Toad has much smaller and more numerous warts. The American Toad also has dark splotches on the chest. Although they are sometimes active by day, these toads are primarily nocturnal in habits. When attacked by a predator they will inflate their bodies by gulping air. This tactic may work if the predator is an animal like a snake that must swallow its food whole.

Natural History: This is mainly a grassland species and it is very common in the northern Great Plains region, ranging as far north as southern Canada. They also range well down into Mexico. The range in Texas includes the entire Panhandle region and the Big Bend region. In habits they are mainly nocturnal but they are sometimes active at dawn and dusk or during the day on rainy days. Like most toads, they are confirmed burrowers and they can dig their way deep into the ground during hot, dry weather or to escape freezing. Mortality can be high during winter hibernation. Between long winter hibernation periods and avoidance of hot, dry summers in some years they may spend three-fourths of the year underground.

Natural History: The taxonomy of this toad in eastern Texas has been a puzzle for herpetologists. The population in eastern Texas has variously been assigned by different experts to the species *B. fowleri* (i.e the Fowler's Toad of the eastern US); and it was is regarded by some as a unique species called the East Texas Toad (*B. velatus*). Additionally it has been assigned as a subspecies of the Woodhouse's Toad. At present, the determination is that the east Texas populations represent a hybrid between the Woodhouse's Toad and the Fowler's Toad, but that designation may be reconsidered in the future. The Woodhouse's Toad does seem prone to hybridize with other *Bufo* species with which its range is sympatric.

Class—**Amphibia** (amphibians)
Order—**Anura** (frogs & toads)
Family—**Bufonidae** (true toads)

Houston Toad *Anaxyrus houstonensis*	**Red-spotted Toad** *Anaxyrus punctatus*	**Texas Toad** *Anaxyrus speciosus*

Houston Toad
Anaxyrus houstonensis

Size: Average 2 to 3 inches. Record 3.75.

Abundance: Very rare. A federally endangered species.

Presumed range in TX

Variation: Varies from mottled browns and grays to reddish or even greenish gray. No subspecies.

Habitat: Coastal prairies and mesic woodlands with sandy soils. Usually in the vicinity of aquatic situations.

Breeding: Breeding takes place in late winter or early spring. Several thousand eggs are laid in long strands.

Natural History: This is a critically endangered species that has always had a very restricted range in southeastern Texas. It is already extirpated from many areas of its former range which at one time included the Houston area. It is believed that there may be only a few thousand of these toads left in the wild today and efforts to save this species have been underway for many years. Breeding in captivity and releasing young toads by zoos has helped. Continued threats include natural events such as droughts or hybridization with Woodhouse's Toad. The major threats are man-made and include loss of habitat to urbanization, agriculture, introduced fire ants (that kill baby toads) and resource extraction (mining or logging). The range map above shows where this toad may still exist, but its only remaining stronghold is in Bastrop County.

Red-spotted Toad
Anaxyrus punctatus

Size: About 2 to 2.5 inches. Record 3.

Abundance: Generally a fairly common species in Texas.

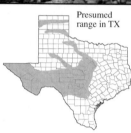
Presumed range in TX

Variation: Varies from pale gray to tan, brown, or reddish brown. Some specimens may lack red spots.

Habitat: An southwestern desert and arid land toad that ranges eastward into the western half of Texas.

Breeding: Populations in west Texas breed during summer monsoons. Elsewhere in Texas breeds during spring rains.

Natural History: This toad species is usually easily recognized by the numerous small red spots on the body. However some specimens from the "Hill Country" may lack these characteristic red spots (from *Texas Amphibians, A Field Guide*). All Red-spotted Toads can be distinguished by their parotoid glands which are round rather than elongate and are also quite small (no bigger than the toads eye). These are nocturnal animals that hide by day under rocks or other shelter where they are protected from the sun and dessication. They are rarely seen abroad in daylight. But they can be quite common on roadways at night during rainy weather. They are able to absorb water directly through the skin during periods of heavy rainfall. Like most anurans, they will feed on a wide variety of arthropod prey, as well other, smaller toads.

Texas Toad
Anaxyrus speciosus

Size: Record size is nearly 5 inches.

Abundance: Common. One of the states most common toad species.

Presumed range in TX

Variation: Brown to reddish brown or sometimes very dark brown. Some specimens may be olive or grayish.

Habitat: Usually near water in woodland, mesquite thickets, prairies and desert grasslands. Likes sandy soils.

Breeding: Breeds in rainy seasons and often lays its eggs in ephemeral pools. Tadpole stage lasts 3 to 8 weeks.

Natural History: The range of this frog encompasses most of Texas west of the "Piney Woods" region. It also ranges southward well into Mexico. It is a common toad in most of its range. It is a rather nondescript toad that can be distinguished from the Woodhouse's and Great Plains Toads by the lack of a light stripe down the middle of the back. It also resembles the non-spotted morph of the Red-spotted Toad but the Texas Toad has elongated rather than round parotoid glands. As with other toad species that inhabit desert regions, Texas Toad populations in arid regions are prone to aestivate during hot, dry periods and will emerge during monsoons or periodic thunderstorms. While this is a common species in Texas, they do appear to be vulnerable to habitat destruction and widespread pesticide use in areas of intensive agriculture.

Class—**Amphibia** (amphibians)

Order—**Anura** (frogs & toads)

Family—**Bufonidae** (true toads)

Green Toad *Anaxyrus debilis*	**Cane Toad** *Rhinella marina*	**Gulf Coast Toad** *Incilius nebulifer*

<table>
<tr>
<td>

Size: Can reach a maximum of 2.15 inches.

</td>
<td>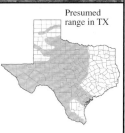
Presumed range in TX</td>
<td>

Size: About 5 or 6 inches. Record size 9.4 inches.

</td>
<td>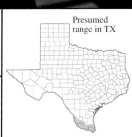
Presumed range in TX</td>
<td>

Size: Average 4 inches. Maximum 5.12 inches.

</td>
<td>
Presumed range in TX</td>
</tr>
</table>

Abundance: Uncommon but apparently secure in Texas.	**Abundance:** Rare in Texas. Restricted range in state.	**Abundance:** Common in the Coastal Plain Province.
Variation: There are two subspecies in Texas, the Eastern (subpecies *debilis*) and Western (subspecies *insidior*) Both are very similar in appearance.	**Variation:** Little variation in this species but females attain a larger size. The largest specimens occur in tropical environments.	**Variation:** Ground color variable but usually some shade of brown or tan. The prominence of the dark lateral stripe varies from distinct to vague.
Habitat: Deserts and arid to semi-arid regions. Dry grasslands, Short-grass Prairie, Mesquite woodlands, and scrub.	**Habitat:** Texas habitat includes most mesic and aquatic habitats present in the lower Rio Grande valley.	**Habitat:** Found in a variety of mesic habitats including lawns and gardens in both rural and suburban areas.
Breeding: Breeds from spring though summer during rainy periods. Eggs hatch quickly and tadpoles may transform with 10 days if pool is drying up.	**Breeding:** Breeds in canals and ditches where females may lay as many as 20,000 eggs. The tadpoles are jet black above and whitish below.	**Breeding:** May breed anytime from late winter through fall. As many as 20,000 eggs have been reported (herpedia.com). Breed in permanent and temporary waters.
Natural History: This species is also referred to as the "Chihuahuan Green Toad." That name is somewhat meaningful as this species does occur throughout the Chihuahuan Desert region. But their range extends well beyond the Chihuahuan Desert into central and southern Texas as well as northward into the portions of the Panhandle in the southern High Plains. There is even an isolated population as far north as southwestern Colorado. The name Green Toad is appropriate as individuals are always some shade of green. They may be yellowish, "Pea Green," or pure green. These are the smallest *Anaxyrus* species in Texas and most are under 2 inches when fully grown. Nocturnal. Seen above ground only during rains.	**Natural History:** Introduced. This huge toad also goes by the name "Marine Toad." Although some individuals from the neotropics have exceeded 9 inches in length, in the US most are under 6 inches at maturity. In addition to insects they will eat virtually anything they can swallow, and they probably pose a threat to many native small vertebrates in the state. They are also a threat to larger animals due to the toxic secretions from parotoid glands. All toads probably have the ability to secrete "bufotoxins" from these glands, but the large size of the Cane Toad means it can produce prodigious amounts of toxin, enough to kill a raccoon, an opossum, or a dog. They have been intentionally (and wrongly) introduced in many places.	**Natural History:** This species is characterized by a irregular, broad dark stripe along the side with a much lighter irregularly shaped stripe above it. They also have a prominent mid-dorsal stripe down the middle of the back. Some specimens are more uniformly colored and these stripes are less evident. As with other toads they secrete a noxious "toxin" from the parotoid glands that protects them from some types of predation. This defense is apparently not effective against many toad-eating snakes, especially those of the Natricidae family (water, garter, and ribbon snakes). No doubt they are also eaten by Hog-nosed Snakes. These toads are most common in Texas in the Coastal Plain physiographic province.

THE AMPHIBIANS OF TEXAS

PART 2: SALAMANDERS

Class—**Amphibia** (amphibians)

Order— **Caudata** (salamanders)

Family—**Ambystomatidae** (mole salamanders)

Spotted Salamander *Ambystoma maculata*	**Western (Barred) Tiger Salamander** *Ambystoma mavortium*	**Eastern Tiger Salamander** *Ambystoma tigrinum*

Size: Average 6 inches. Maximum 9 inches.	 Presumed range in TX	**Size:** Average 6 inches. Maximum 13.	 Presumed range in TX	**Size:** Average about 8 inches. Maximum 14.	 Presumed range in TX
Abundance: Fairly common in woodland habitats in eastern Texas.		**Abundance:** No information is available on abundance in Texas.		**Abundance:** An uncommon species with a limited range in Texas.	

Variation: The spots on the Spotted Salamander may be yellow or orange. The number of spots varies widely. On rare individuals spots may be absent.

Variation: There are five subspecies of this widespread species. Only one occurs in Texas. The subspecies *mavortium*, the Barred Tiger Salamander.

Variation: Light markings can appear as irregular spots, blotches, or stripes. The color of light pigments may be yellow, orange, or greenish.

Habitat: Primarily woodland areas but also found in overgrown fields.

Habitat: Found in nearly all habitat types but usually near water.

Habitat: Woodlands and fields, in both upland an lowland areas.

Breeding: Breeds during periods of heavy rainfall in late winter. Eggs are deposited in large gelatinous masses in ponds or wetland pools. Larva transform in two to four months. Like all other amphibians, eggs are fertilized externally. The males clasp onto the female and release sperm onto the eggs as they are laid, rather like a fish.

Breeding: Breeding can take place from late winter in warmer climate or in the spring in cooler regions. Adults migrate to small ponds, streams, prairie potholes and other permanent water sources and deposit several hundred eggs. Larval salamanders may take up to two years to develop and transform at lengths of 3 to 5 inches.

Breeding: Breeds in small bodies of water like stock ponds, vernal pools and "borrow pits." Breeding occurs in mid-winter a few hundred to several thousand eggs produced by the female. Males meet females in breeding ponds and fertilize the eggs as they are laid. Eggs are encased in a ball of jelly-like material and hatch in about a month.

Natural History: Primarily subterranean in habits. Lives in underground burrows and beneath rocks, logs, or leaf litter on the forest floor. During periods of hot dry weather retreats deeper underground or stays in the vicinity perennially wet areas. Feeds on a wide variety of insects and invertebrates as well as a few small vertebrates. This is one of the most common members of the "mole salamander" group in the eastern US, but they are less common in Texas. In the late winter breeding season they are easily observed on rural roads at night during rainy weather, as they make the migration to breeding ponds.

Natural History: This salamander has the largest geographical distribution of any North American salamander. They range from the lower Rio Grande River to central Saskatchewan. Their range encompasses all of the Great Plains Level I Ecoregion plus much of the Rocky Mountain and desert southwest regions. Additionally there are isolated, widely scattered populations all the way to the Pacific. There is little information available on population trends for this species in Texas. The building of ponds for watering livestock may help provide breeding locales. Conversely, expansive row crop fields destroy habitat.

Natural History: The large size of the Tiger Salamander allows it to feed on much larger prey than most salamander species. Although invertebrates such as earthworms and insect larva are the major foods, small vertebrates may also be eaten and captive specimens will eat baby mice. Despite their large size, Tiger Salamanders are rarely seen except during the late winter breeding season when they make their nocturnal overland treks to breeding ponds. At this time, they can sometimes be seen on rural roadways on stormy nights. These uncommon salamanders occur only sporadically in the area shown on map.

Class—**Amphibia** (amphibians)

Order—**Caudata** (salamanders)

Family—**Ambystomatidae** (mole salamanders)

Mole Salamander *Ambystoma talpoideum*	**Small-mouthed Salamander** *Ambystoma texanum*	**Marbled Salamander** *Ambystoma opacum*

Size: Average 4 inches. Record nearly 5 inches.  Presumed range in TX	**Size:** Average 4 to 5 inches. Record 7.5 inches.  Presumed range in TX	**Size:** 3 to 4 inches. Record 5.25 inches.  Presumed range in TX
Abundance: Uncommon and restricted in range in Texas.	**Abundance:** Fairly common but declining in urban regions.	**Abundance:** Fairly common in pristine habitat.
Variation: Some are uniformly dark gray. Others have a significant amount of light gray or silvery flecking on the sides.	**Variation:** Varies in color from uniform dark gray to blue-gray with varying amounts of silver or light gray flecking. Some have no light flecking.	**Variation:** Sexually dimorphic. Light colors are grayish or silver in the female and whiter in the male. Females are a bit larger.
Habitat: Swamps, marshes and bottomland woods prone to seasonal flooding. Less commonly in upland woods.	**Habitat:** Found in a variety of habitats from woodlands to grassy meadows. Found in both lowland and upland areas.	**Habitat:** Most fond of bottomlands (especially during breeding) but also common in upland woods.
Breeding: Breeding occurs in late fall or early winter and overland treks to breeding areas are made. Eggs are laid in the waters of swamps and marshes. After a few months the gill breathing, larva develop into air breathing adults.	**Breeding:** Breeds in late winter or very early spring. May lay up to several hundred eggs in large clumps. Ponds, wetland pools or flooded roadside ditches may be used for egg deposition. Larva transform in about 6 to 8 weeks.	**Breeding:** Breeds in the fall during rainy weather. Overland migration is common. Eggs are laid on land under rocks, logs, etc., in low lying areas subject to flooding. Hatching is delayed until eggs are flooded by fall rains.
Natural History: This decidedly fossorial salamander is the namesake of the "mole salamander" family. This species is rarely seen above ground except during the breeding season when they will emerge on rainy nights and travel to areas of breeding congregations. They can sometimes be turned up beneath logs or other objects in low, perennially moist areas. These salamanders have a stout-bodied appearance and a large head which distinguishes them from the similarly colored Small-mouthed Salamander. When captured they will sometimes assume a defensive posture that consists of raising the body off the ground while lowering the head. Seen only in the Piney Woods region in Texas.	**Natural History:** Like other members of its genus the Smallmouth Salamander spends most of its time in underground burrows or beneath rocks, logs, or leaf litter. They will emerge on rainy nights to forage above ground. Feeds on a wide variety of soft bodied invertebrate prey such as earthworms, slugs, and grubs. The Smallmouth Salamander is very similar in appearance to the Mole Salamander but is less "stocky" and has a smaller head. Both can be uniformly colored or have varying amounts of whiteish, silver, or light gray "freckles" on the body. The light colored pigment usually takes on a lichen-like pattern and is often more prominent on the sides.	**Natural History:** This is one of the few salamanders to exhibit sexual dimorphism. The light markings are wider and whiter on the male and narrower and more silver or grayish on the female. Like other members of the "mole salamander" family, Marbled Salamanders are fossorial in habits. In fact, this species may be even more secretive than many of its kin. Thus, though they are fairly common they are not readily observed. They can reportedly produce a noxious secretion from the tail which may help to ward off some predators. Adults probably feed on most any small animal they can swallow, mostly invertebrates. Larva have been known to eat the eggs of small frogs.

Class—**Amphibia** (amphibians)

Order—**Caudata** (salamanders)

Family-**Amphiumidae** (amphiumas)	Family-**Sirenidae** (sirens)	Family-**Proteidae** (mudpuppies)
Three-toed Amphiuma *Amphiuma tridactylum*	**Lesser Siren** *Siren intermedia*	**Gulf Coast Waterdog** *Necturus beyeri*

Size: Average 2 to 3 feet. Record length is 42 inches.  Presumed range in TX	**Size:** Average 12 to 16 inches. Maximum 20 inches.  Presumed range in TX	**Size:** Maximum 8.75 inches. Most are smaller.  Presumed range in TX
Abundance: Common in swamps in eastern Texas.	**Abundance:** Common in wetlands in eastern Texas.	**Abundance:** Uncommon with restricted range in Texas.
Variation: There is no variation among adults. The larval stage possesses external gills.	**Variation:** There are two subspecies and both occur in Texas. Differences between subspecies are very slight.	**Variation:** Various shades of brown with varying amounts of dark spots and lighter brown or tan flecking.
Habitat: Swamps, oxbows, flooded roadside ditches, and ponds in low, swampy regions.	**Habitat:** Swamps, marshes, oxbows, sloughs, slow moving streams and low lying areas along stream courses.	**Habitat:** Blackwater streams and associated wetlands. May inhabit very small streams only a few feet wide.
Breeding: Slithers onto land at night to lay eggs above the waterline. Fall rains inundate the eggs and stimulate development. There is a larval stage that has external gills.	**Breeding:** Lays several hundred eggs in a nest hollowed out in the mud. Probably breeds in late winter or early spring. Larval stage typically lasts up to nine months.	**Breeding:** Very little is known about the reproduction of this species since it was recently differentiated as a full species from the Alabama Waterdog. Believed to breed in late fall to winter.
Natural History: This is a large, eel-like salamander that is often mistaken for an eel. Close examination will reveal the presence of tiny, vestigial limbs. Amphiumas are totally aquatic in habits but have lungs for breathing air and they can survive out of water as long as there is enough moisture to prevent dessication. During droughts they can aestivate in chambers hollowed out in the mud or within crayfish burrows. They feed on earthworms, small fish, snails, insects and crayfish. In Louisiana they often end up in crayfish traps where they will stuff themselves with those crustaceans. The legs of the Amphiuma are vestigial and so small that they are easily overlooked. There are three tiny toes on the legs, hence the name "Three-toed Amphiuma."	**Natural History:** A completely aquatic salamander that breathes through external gills that are easily visible just in front of the forelimbs. Known food items include insects, crustaceans, mollusks, and worms, as well as some plant material such as algae. Capable of surviving drought periods by secreting slime which hardens into a cocoon-like structure, creating a sealed chamber in the mud. Like many wetland species the Lesser Siren has been negatively impacted by the conversion of wetlands to agricultural land. Both the Lesser Siren and the Amphiuma are preyed upon by the Mud Snake, a snake species which specializes in feeding on aquatic salamanders. Sirens have elongated bodies with very small front legs and lack hind limbs completely.	**Natural History:** The Proteidae family of salamanders are a totally aquatic group that breathe through well developed external gills. The northernmost representative of the group is the widespread Mudpuppy of the northern US. These salamanders are an example of a condition known to biologists as "neotony" (the retaining of juvenile characteristics into adulthood). Many salamanders have larva stages in which the developing salamanders live in water and breathe through gills before transfoming into air breathing adults. This is exactly the same type of life cycle exhibited by frogs and toads with their well-known "tadpole" stage. In the Proteidae salamanders the animal never metamorphosis into a terrestrial air breather but instead retains the gills.

Class—**Amphibia** (amphibians)

Order—**Caudata** (salamanders)

Family—**Plethodontidae** (lungless salamanders)

Spotted Dusky Salamander *Desmognathus conanti*	**Western Slimy Salamander** *Plethodon albagula*	**Dwarf Salamander** *Eurycea quadridigitata*

Size: Average 3 inches. Record length is 5 inches.

Presumed range in TX

Abundance: Rare and in decline in its range in Texas.

Variation: Color varies through many shades of brown. Dorsum may have spots or a broad dorsal stripe.

Habitat: Springs, seeps, and spring-fed brooks in wooded areas. Beneath rocks, detritus or in the muck of forest streams. Has a strong affinity to springs or seeps.

Breeding: Eggs are laid under rocks in the vicinity of streams. The eggs (average 15–30) are laid in clusters of individual eggs.

Natural History: Texas populations were once placed in a different species but then re-assigned later to the original designation of *D. conanti*. Populations of this species in Texas are disjunct many miles from any other populations and need further study. Unfortunately, they appear to be disappearing from many areas of the state. The *Desmognathus* salamanders are a wide ranging group in the eastern US and there are eighteen species in the genus. The vast majority live east of the Mississippi River and reach their greatest diversity in the southern Appalachians. This is the only species that is found in Texas and it represents the westernmost extent of the range for the genus. In many areas within their range, they sometimes go by the name "Spring Lizards."

Size: Average 4 to 5 inches. Record length is 8.1 inches.

Presumed range in TX

Abundance: Fairly common within their range.

Variation: Significant variation in the amount of silvery, lichen-like speckling on the body.

Habitat: A decidedly woodland species. More common in upland woods and hillsides than in bottomlands, but always seeks mesic micro-habitats.

Breeding: 12 to 15 eggs seems to be the average. In all members of the genus *Plethodon* Salamanders, young hatch from the egg fully formed.

Natural History: The name "Slimy" is derived from the fact that these salamanders exude a thick, sticky mucus from the skin when handled. This material is difficult to wash off and once dried becomes black and crusty. Herpetologists capturing slimy salamanders sometimes wear the residue of salamander mucus on their hands for days before it finally wears off. The food of these woodland species is undoubtedly a wide variety of soft bodied insects, insect larva, annelids, small crustaceans and other tiny invertebrate life found among the leaf litter on the forest floor. Until the advent of DNA technology there was only one ubiquitous species of Slimy Salamander that ranged across most of the eastern United States. There are now over dozen individual species.

Size: Average less than 3 inches. Record 4.32 inches.

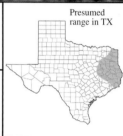
Presumed range in TX

Abundance: May be locally common. Possibly in decline.

Variation: Brown, tan or yellowish. With or without dark dorso-lateral stripes that may or may not be broken.

Habitat: Low-lying mesic woodlands, ponds, streams and sphagnum bogs. Sometimes found in the water amid plants such as Water Hyacinth.

Breeding: Eggs are laid in the water among mats of vegetation or near the shore in wet moss or other detritus. Clutch size can number several dozen.

Natural History: Aptly named, these tiny salamanders rarely exceed 3 inches in length and they are quite slender. They are often confused with the Southern Two-lined Salamander but that species has five toes on the hind foot (Dwarf Salamander has only four). This is the most southerly ranging of the Plethodontidae salamanders. They reportedly are mainly nocturnal. During the day they shelter in small animal burrows or in mats of floating vegetation if in the water. Sphagnum Moss is also a likely hiding place. They will wander abroad at night, especially during heavy rains and can sometimes be found on roadways on rainy nights. Many members of this genus are terrestrial but closely tied to streams and springs. Others are cave dwellers.

Class—**Amphibia** (amphibians)

Order—**Caudata** (salamanders)

Family—**Plethodontidae** (lungless salamanders)

Endemic Neotenic Brook Salamanders of Texas

Natural History: Although the southern Appalachian Mountains of western North Carolina and eastern Tennessee host the highest diversity of salamander species in North America, Texas has the highest number of endemic Brook Salamander species. Some of these species may be true troglodytes while others may exist within springs and seeps in the twilight zone of caves. These are neotenic salamanders that retain the gills and aquatic lifestyle typical of the larval stage of the typical terrestrial *Eurycea* species that are common in the eastern US. Many are small (less than 2 inches), while others can grow to twice that length (up to 4 inches.) Below is a list of these species with their respective range maps and a photos of sample species. For a more complete examination of these rare and unusual salamanders the reader is referred to the book *Texas Amphibians, A Field Guide*, by University of Texas Press. Black squares on maps below show approximate location of species populations.

Salado Salamander *Eurycea chisholmensis*	**Texas Salamander** *Eurycea neotenes*	**Jollyville Plateau Salamander** *Eurycea tonkawae*	**San Marcos Salamander** *Eurycea nana*
 Approximate range in Texas	 Approximate range in Texas	 Approximate range in Texas	 Approximate range in Texas
Cascade Caverns Salamander *Eurycea latitans*	**Georgetown Salamander** *Eurycea naugragia*	**Fern Bank Salamander** *Eurycea pterophila*	**Barton Springs Salamander** *Eurycea ssosorum*
Approximate range in Texas	Approximate range in Texas	Approximate range in Texas	Approximate range in Texas
Austin Blind Salamander *Eurycea waterlooensis*	**Blanco Blind Salamander** *Eurycea robusta*	**Texas Blind Salamander** *Eurycea rathbuni*	**Comal Blind Salamander** *Eurycea tridentifera*
Approximate range in Texas	Approximate range in Texas	Approximate range in Texas	Approximate range in Texas

Class—**Amphibia** (amphibians)

Order—**Caudata** (salamanders)

Family—**Plethodontidae**	Family—**Salamandridae** (newts)	
Valdina Farms Salamander *Eurycea troglodytes*	**Black-spotted Newt** *Notophthalmus meridionalis*	**Eastern Newt** *Notophthalmus viridescens*

Size: Adults are 2 to 3 inches in length.  Presumed range in TX	**Size:** Adults reach 4.1 inches. Efts are smaller.  Presumed range in TX	**Size:** Adults reach 5 inches. Efts are about 3 inches.  Presumed range in TX
Abundance: Uncommon to rare. Some populations extirpated.	**Abundance:** Rare. A threatened species in Texas.	**Abundance:** Still fairly common but appears to be in decline in Texas.
Variation: There are two morphs, a surface morph and a cave morph. It has been suggested that this salamander may actually be a complex of species.	**Variation:** Skin color between black spots is olive green, or reddish brown. Some individuals have rows of pale yellowish spots along the back	**Variation:** Two subspecies in exist. Only one, the Central Newt (*louisianensis*) occurs in Texas. Significant ontogenetic variation.
Habitat: Associates with springs and seeps that emanate from rock canyons in the southern portion of the Edwards Plateau. Also in caves in same locale.	**Habitat:** Inhabits brushy thorn scrub in the southern portion of the Western Gulf Coastal Plain. Usually in areas where there is poor soil drainage.	**Habitat:** Adults are found in ponds, swamps, or other permanent water. Eft stage is a terrestrial animal inhabiting woodlands.
Breeding: Almost nothing is known about breeding in these salamanders. No data is available on clutch size or where eggs are laid. It is believed that adults become sexually mature at 2 years of age.	**Breeding:** Breeds in small ponds, flooded ditches and swamps. Up to 300 eggs are laid. Breeding may coincide with periods of rainfall but can occur at any time of the year. The eft stage may be shorter than in other newts.	**Breeding:** Breeds in spring. Males deposit packages of sperm which are taken up by the female into the cloaca where fertilization occurs internally before eggs are then laid. Hatchlings metamorph into efts in 4 to 5 months.
Natural History: This is the most widespread example of the neotenic brook salamanders of central Texas. They are aquatic salamanders that breathe through external gills. The phylogeny and taxonomy of this species is still not completely understood. It is possible that these salamander arose from the hybridization of other similar species, and that 'back-crossing" hybridization may exist. It is also possible that there may be a "species complex" of as yet undescribed "cryptic species." To add to the confusion, apparently some individuals are cave dwelling and some will live under rocks on the surface near the mouths of caves and in springs emanating from caves.	**Natural History:** The bulk of this salamanders range in along the gulf coastal plain of Mexico. They will aestivate during periods of hot, dry weather or to survive droughts. Sometimes when threatened they will contort their body into an "S" shape and roll onto the back revealing the bright yellow-orange "warning colors" on the belly. As with other newts, they secrete a toxin from the skin to deter predators. Probably because of this toxin, newts seem to have few predators. Among the animals that likely eat them are water, garter and ribbon snakes. Common Snapping Turtles are listed by some sources as predators along with Bullfrogs and fish. Food is a variety of small invertebrates.	**Natural History:** Newts are unique among Texas salamanders in having an extra stage in their life cycle. Following hatching the young spend the summer as gill breathing larva then undergo a transformation to an air breathing semi-adult that lives on land for up to three years. Newts in this terrestrial stage are call "efts." After one to three years the eft returns to the water and undergoes another metmorphosis into a totally aquatic adult. After returning to the water the coarse skin of the eft becomes smooth and the round tail flattens vertically to become fin-like. They can live up to fifteen years. They produce a neurotoxin in their skin that probably protects them from predators.

CHAPTER 10

RIVERS AND STREAMS OF TEXAS

As a preface to the next chapter (Chapter 11, The Freshwater Fishes of Texas), this short chapter is intended to provide a brief introduction into the waterways of Texas, which are home to the state's freshwater fish species.

There are fourteen major rivers in Texas. If the many miles of small tributaries are taken into account, the total number of miles of drainages in Texas is just over 191,000 miles. Of this total, only about 21 percent are

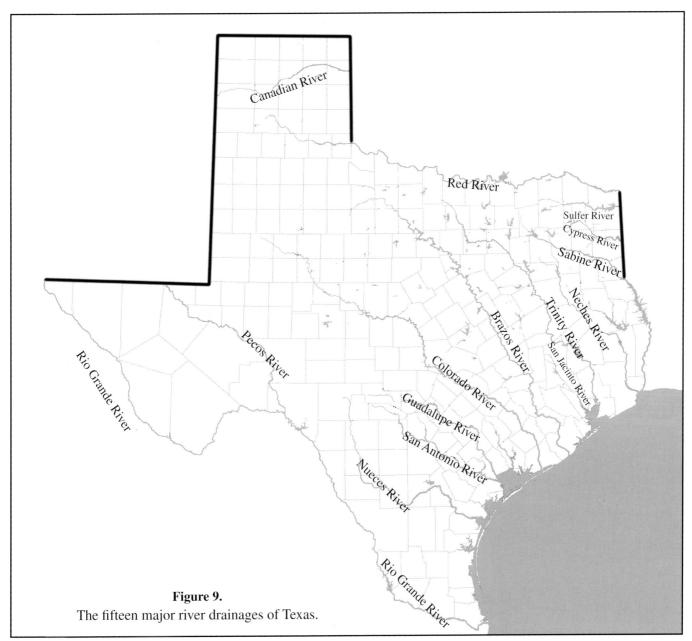

Figure 9.
The fifteen major river drainages of Texas.

perennial streams that flow year-round. Most of the drainages in Texas are actually intermittent streams that are dry for some portion of the year. Most streams in the eastern portion of the state are perennial, as are the main channels of the larger rivers in the state. But many of the smaller drainages in the western and west-central parts of the state are intermittent.

The map below (Figure 9) shows the main channels of the fourteen largest drainages in Texas. Also evident on this map are a few of the larger of Texas's two hundred odd reservoirs and impoundments.

Each of the rivers shown on the map in Figure 9 are a representation of the main river channel (called a river Mainstem). Each Mainstem is fed by a series of smaller river tributaries, which are in turn fed by a series of smaller and smaller creeks and brooks. The map below

(Figure 10), shows the larger tributaries of the state's major river systems and demonstrates how widely Texas is dissected by drainages. Many of the drainages shown in Figure 10 are intermittent streams that flow only during wet periods. In Texas, intermittent streams are common in the western half of the state.

Of the fourteen major river systems in Texas, the Rio Grande is the longest, stretching 1400 miles from its headwaters in the mountains of Colorado to its mouth at the Gulf of Mexico. The Colorado River is often referred to as the longest river in Texas that begins and ends in entirely within the state. But technically its drainage area includes a small portion of southeastern New Mexico, as does the headwaters of the Brazos River. The Pecos River also extends well into eastern New Mexico. The Red River, Canadian River, and Sabine River are the only

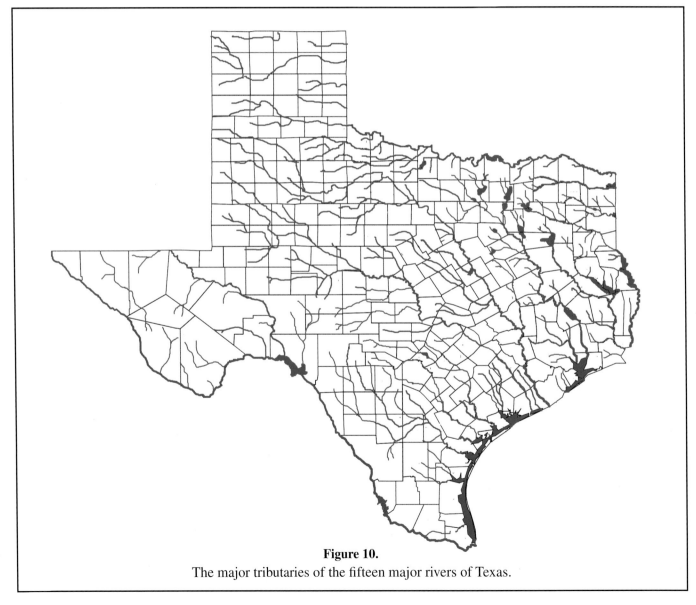

Figure 10.
The major tributaries of the fifteen major rivers of Texas.

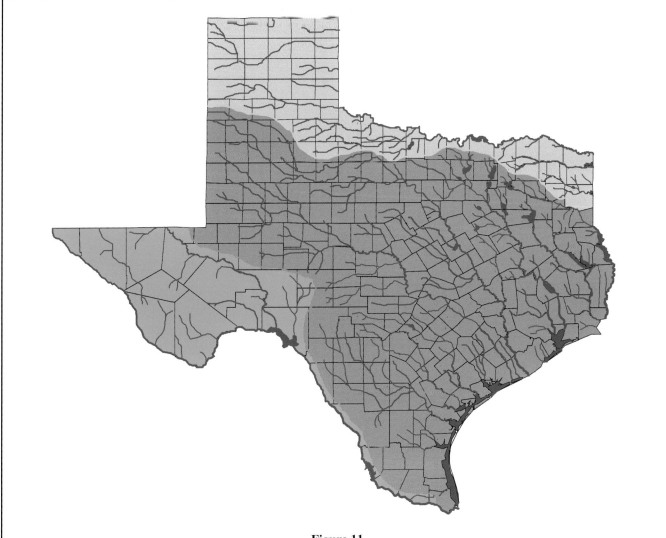

Figure 11.
The Level I Watersheds of Texas.
On the map above, the Mississippi River Watershed is in gray. The Rio Grande Watershed is green. The brown shaded region represents all the other watersheds in Texas. All the rivers in the brown area are rivers that originate within the borders of Texas. All the waterways in Texas ultimately flow into the Gulf of Mexico.

other Texas rivers that have their portions of their drainages outside the state of Texas.

The land area drained by a stream is known as the streams "basin." The term "watershed" is also frequently used interchangeably to define the land area drained by a particular stream.

The map in Figure 11 shows the rivers and the major watershed regions that impact the state of Texas. These large watersheds can be subdivided into smaller "sub-watersheds" (also called sub-basins). The map shown in Figure 12 shows the sub-watersheds of the three major watersheds affecting Texas.

Some appreciation of the drainage basins (or watersheds) shown in Figures 11 and 12 can provide insight into the distribution of the states fish species. More importantly, conservation organizations can monitor these various watersheds for pollution and other factors that may impact upon the health of fish populations contained within them.

The distribution of most fish populations in the state will be determined by the largest watersheds. Some more widespread species like the Largemouth Bass may inhabit several large watersheds. Meanwhile other species like the Guadalupe Bass may have much smaller distributions that are contained in the smaller sub-watersheds. Thus an awareness of the delineation of watersheds and sub-watersheds can be helpful in understanding the biology of the state's freshwater fishes.

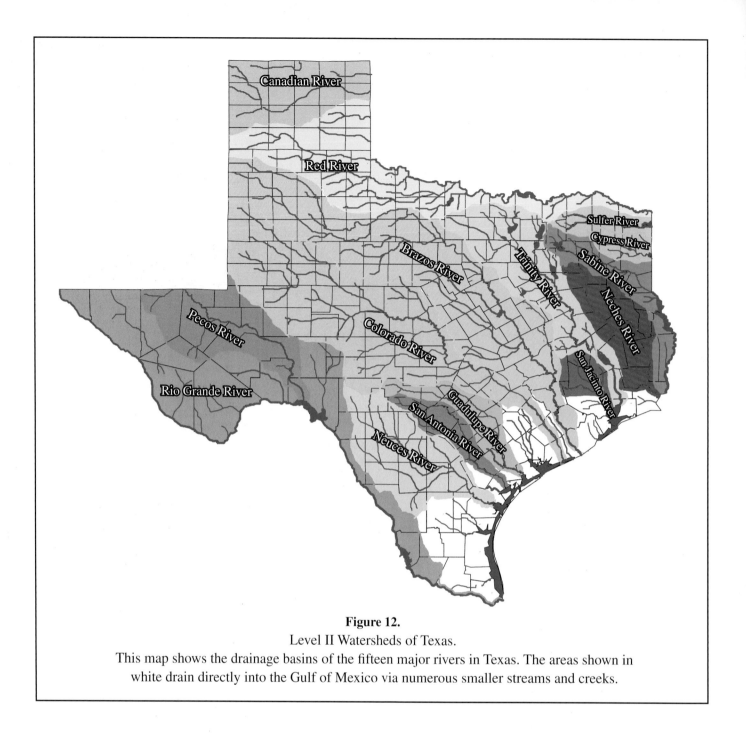

Figure 12.
Level II Watersheds of Texas.
This map shows the drainage basins of the fifteen major rivers in Texas. The areas shown in white drain directly into the Gulf of Mexico via numerous smaller streams and creeks.

Scientists engaged in the study of aquatic ecosystems use a number of different schemes to classify streams depending on the goal and what is being studied. One frequently used classification scheme is based on the size of the stream. This classification system (called the "Stream Order System") uses the term "Order" to define the size of a stream. In this system, a first order stream is the smallest and a twelfth order the largest. First order streams are tiny and often seasonally dry.

When two first order streams converge, the drainage becomes a second order stream, two second order streams merging constitutes a third order stream; etc. As more drainages converge, the stream order increases.

First through third order streams are what are known as "headwater" streams because they are the origins of the much larger rivers which they feed. The term "brook" is another common name used to delineated these smaller streams. Streams in the fourth through sixth order are usually called creeks, while larger orders (seventh through twelfth) are referred to as rivers. Under this classification system, the Rio Grande River is a seventh order stream. For comparison the Mississippi River is a tenth order stream and the mighty Amazon (the world's largest river) is a twelfth order stream.

Although Texas still boasts an abundance of fresh water fish species inhabiting its streams, one species was recently declared extinct and a total of thirty-four more are now regarded as endangered or threatened. Like all other habitat types within the United States, many of the waterways of Texas have been highly altered by man. There are some two hundred impoundments on the state's drainages that serve to help control flash floods and provide the state with a source of fresh water. These impoundments are also important as a source of recreation for the state's human population. The impact of impoundments on native fishes can be either good or bad, depending on the fish species.

Direct pollution from industry and resource extraction can be an important source of stream degradation in the state. But of equal importance is indirect contamination from agriculture. Agricultural related pollution and stream degradation can come in the form of chemical runoff or the destruction of vegetated buffer zones by farmers needing to maximize the production area of their land.

Erosion and siltation from row cropping operations can also have a negative impact. To a lesser extent, livestock operations statewide can also be detrimental as cattle destroy creek banks and stir up silt from stream bottoms.

The series of maps shown on the preceding pages gives a good representation of how smaller streams and their watersheds are integrated into larger streams and larger watersheds. What also becomes apparent from these maps is that when it comes to water, everything (and everyone) downstream is affected by the quality of the water and the overall environmental health of the waters upstream. The environmental quality of that tiny creek in your backyard or on your farm or ranch affects not only the life of organisms living within that stream, but also organisms within the larger streams into which it flows. And ultimately, the wildlife living in the state's coastal marshes, the fishes living in the depths of the Gulf of Mexico, and the magnificent coral ecosystems of the great reefs of the Caribbean.

Some of the states, rivers and streams no longer support the high diversity of fish and other aquatic species that once were abundant within their banks and the future for many of Texas's fish species is in doubt. At least seven species that once swam in Texas waterways are no longer found in the state. If we regard this fact as a warning sign relating to the health of our aquatic ecosystems, and surely they are just that, then all Texans should be acutely concerned about the future of the state's waterways. We often hear reasonable people argue against stringent protections of our environment. But few things are more important than these protections. Humans can survive for a maximum of four minutes without air and maximum of four days without water. It follows then that our paramount priorities should be to ensure that we all always have clean air to breathe and pure water to drink!

This author is old enough to remember the days before congress passed the landmark environmental legislation in the early 1970s. Before the Clean Water Act, some rivers in America had become so polluted that one river in Ohio actually caught fire and burned! Prior to the passage of the Clean Air Act just breathing the air in some of our heavily industrialized cities was the equivalent of smoking two packs of cigarettes a day!

CHAPTER 11

THE FRESHWATER FISHES OF TEXAS

TABLE 7

— THE ORDERS AND FAMILIES OF TEXAS FISHES —

Class—**Actinopterygii** (ray-finned fishes)

Order—**Perciformes** (typical fishes)

Family	**Centrarchidae** (sunfishes)
Family	**Elassomatidae** (pygmy sunfishes)
Family	**Moronidae** (true basses)
Family	**Percidae** (perches & darters)
Family	**Scianidae** (drums)
Family	**Chichlidae** (chiclids & tilapia)

Order—**Esociformes** (pikes & mudminnows)

Family	Esocidae (pikes)
Family	Umbridea (mudminnows)

Order—**Amiiformes** (bowfin)

Family	**Amiidae** (bowfin)

Order—**Lepisosteiformes** (gar)

Family	**Lepisosteidae** (gars)

Order—**Acipenseriformes** (primitive fishes)

Family	**Acipenseridae** (sturgeons)
Family	**Polyodontidae** (paddlefish)

Order—**Salmoniformes**

Family	**Salmonidae** (salmonids)

Order—**Anguilliformes** (eels)

Family	**Anguillidae** (freshwater eels)

Order—**Percopsiformes** (pirate perch & cavefish)

Family	**Aphredoderidae** (pirate perch)

Order—**Characiformes**

Family	**Characidae** (tetras)

Order—**Siluriformes** (catfishes)

Family	**Ictaluridae** (american catfishes)

Order—**Hiodontiformes**

Family	**Hiodontidae** (moooneyes)

Order—**Clupeiformes** (sardines, herrings, & shads)

Family	**Alosidae** (herring)
Family	**Dorosmatidae** (herring)

Order—**Cypriniformes** (minnows & suckers)

Family	**Catastomidae** (suckers)
Family	**Cyprinidae** (minnows)

Order—**Cyprinodontiformes** (topminnows & livebearers)

Family	**Fundulidae** (topminnows)
Family	**Cyprinidontidae** (pupfishes)
Family	**Poeciliidae** (livebearers)

Order—**Plueronectiformes** (flatfishes)

Family	**Paralichthyidae** (flounders)
Family	**Achiridae** (soles)

Order—**Beloniformes**

Family	**Belonidae** (needlefish)

Order—**Atheriniformes**

Family	**Atherinidae** (silversides)

Order—**Petromydontiformes** (lampreys)

Family	**Petrodontidae** (northern lampreys)

Class—**Actinopterygii** (bony fishes)

Order—**Perciformes** (typical fishes)

Family—**Centrarchidae** (sunfishes)

Largemouth Bass *Micropterus salmoides*	**Smallmouth Bass** *Micropterus dolomieu*

Size: May reach 38 inches and 22 pounds. The record size for Texas is 18 pounds, 2.8 ounces.

Abundance: Very common in all Level II watersheds. The most common *Micropterus* (Black Bass) species in America.

Presumed range in TX

Natural History: This is probably America's most popular freshwater game fish, pursued by anglers throughout the country. Indeed, an entire sporting industry has evolved around the pursuit of this fish. Found in virtually any body of water in the state, including streams and small farm ponds.

Size: Maximum of 11.95 pounds. Texas record size is 7 pounds, 15 ounces and 23 inches.

Abundance: Introduced. An uncommon species in Texas. Widely stocked in lakes across the state. Found mostly in streams in the Edwards Plateau.

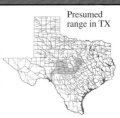

Presumed range in TX

Natural History: Prefers clearer, cooler, more highly oxygenated waters than the Largemouth Bass. Crayfish are a preferred prey, especially for stream dwelling bass. Like its cousin the Largemouth Bass, this is an important game species. It is renowned for its tenacious fighting abilities.

Spotted Bass *Micropterus punctulatus*	**Guadalupe Bass** *Micropterus treculii*

Size: Maximum of 8 lbs. Average adult is about 3 to 4 lbs. Texas record is 5.56 pounds and 21 inches.

Abundance: A fairly common species in the northeastern part of the state. Especially the Neches, Sabine, and Cypress Rivers.

Presumed range in TX

Natural History: Intermediate between the Largemouth Bass and Smallmouth Bass in both the size of the mouth and in its habitat preferences. Primarily a fish of flowing waters but can tolerate warmer conditions than the Smallmouth. Avoids the still waters favored by the Largemouth. The tongue of the Spotted Bass feels rough to the touch.

Size: Record size (both for Texas and the world record) is 3.71 pounds. Average about a pound.

Abundance: Uncommon to rare but recently increasing and benefiting from re-introduction into original habits and new streams.

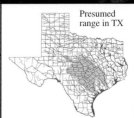

Presumed range in TX

Natural History: A Texas endemic, the Guadalupe Bass is the state fish of Texas. Populations of this fish have declined significantly from historical levels but in recent years re-introduction and conservation activities show promise. This is a species adapted to smaller streams and they are thus a smaller fish than their cousins.

Class—**Actinopterygii** (bony fishes)

Order—**Perciformes** (typical fishes)

Family—**Centrarchidae** (sunfishes)

Flier *Centrachus macropterus*	**Green Sunfish** *Lepomis cyanellus*	**Orange-spotted Sunfish** *Lepomis humilus*

| 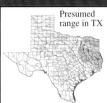 **Size:** Averages about 6 inches in length. World record is 5 pounds, 5.5 ounces. No records for Texas | 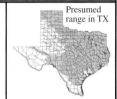 **Size:** Averages 6 to 8 inches, maximum 12. Record size (from Texas) 2 pounds 2.8 ounces. |  **Size:** Average adult is 2 to 3 inches. Maximum reported length is about 4 inches. No records for TX |

Presumed range in TX

Abundance: Fairly common in lentic waters in eastern Texas.	**Abundance:** Common. This is one of the most common sunfishes in America.	**Abundance:** Fairly common in still, lowland streams and swamps.
Natural History: The Flier is a lowland species that is usually found in natural lakes, oxbows, swamps, or sluggish streams. Most often occurs in waters with mud bottom and abundant aquatic vegetation. This fish has an unusually large anal fin that is as long as the dorsal fin.	**Natural History:** Though it can be found in ponds and lakes, its natural habitat is quite pools of slow moving streams. It is known to hybridize readily with other *Lepomis* sunfishes, especially the Bluegill. Tolerates warm, low oxygen, muddy waters better than many other sunfishes.	**Natural History:** Inhabits creeks and rivers where it favors quite water pools with cover in the form of brush. When it occurs in lakes and impoundments it is found in shallow bays. Nests in gravel. Eats mainly small aquatic insect larva and small crustaceans. Female is much less colorful than the male.

Bluegill *Lepomis macrochirus*	**Longear Sunfish** *Lepomis megalotis*	**Warmouth** *Lepomis gulosus*
 Male		

| 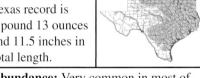 **Size:** Record of 4 pounds, 12 ounces. Texas record is 1 pound 13 ounces and 11.5 inches in total length. | 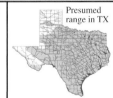 **Size:** World record size is 1 pound 12 ounces. Texas record is 0.84 pounds and length of 9.25 inches. | 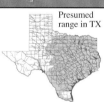 **Size:** Record of 2 pounds 7 ounces. Texas record is 1.3 pounds and 10.5 inches in total length. |

Abundance: Very common in most of eastern Texas. Sporadic in west Texas.	**Abundance:** Common and widespread. One of the most common sunfish in TX.	**Abundance:** Fairly common. More common in eastern portion of the state.
Natural History: The Bluegill is America's best known sunfish. This is the first fish caught on hook and line by many a young angler. It is an important game fish throughout the state. They are regularly stocked in new impoundments and are found in virtually every significant body of water in the state.	**Natural History:** Breeding males are one of the most brilliantly colored of the sunfishes. Clear streams with gravelly or sandy substrates are habitat. Breeding males of the Dollar Sunfish (next page) can look similar, but that species has a white margin on the opercle flap.	**Natural History:** A fish of lowland creeks and swamps, the Warmouth is most common in the southern United States. Although it occurs in Texas, it is sporadically distributed and may be absent from many areas. It prefers waters with thick growths of aquatic plants. Teeth are present on the tongue.

Class—**Actinopterygii** (bony fishes)

Order—**Perciformes** (typical fishes)

Family—**Centrarchidae** (sunfishes)

Dollar Sunfish *Lepomis marginatus*	**Bantam Sunfish** *Lepomis symmetricus*	**Spotted Sunfish** *Lepomis punctatus*

Size: Maximum 4.75 inches.

Abundance: An uncommon fish of sluggish, blackwater environments.

Presumed range in TX

Natural History: Mostly a fish of the lower coastal plain, the Dollar Sunfish reaches in westernmost distribution in eastern Texas. It inhabits pristine waters in swamps and slow moving, unpolluted streams in the eastern part of the Coastal Plain Province of Texas. Unfortunately for this interesting little sunfish, pristine waters are becoming increasingly rare within its range.

Size: Maximum 3.75 inches.

Abundance: Fairly common within its Texas range but rarely observed.

Presumed range in TX

Natural History: The smallest of Texas's *Lepomis* sunfishes, the Bantam Sunfish is an inhabitant of the lowlands of the Mississippi Valley and the Western Gulf Coastal Plain. Swamps, oxbows, and natural lakes with clean, clear water and ample aquatic vegetation are the favored habitats of this small sunfish. Frequently found in very shallow waters that are choked with aquatic plants.

Size: Maximum of 8 inches.

Abundance: Fairly common and widespread except west Texas.

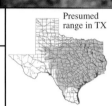
Presumed range in TX

Natural History: The Spotted Sunfish is mostly a fish of the southern lowlands where it inhabits swamps and slow moving streams. It often goes by the nickname "Stumpknocker," a reference to its affinity for submerged structure such as logs and stumps. Though relatively small for a game fish, it is popular with panfish anglers throughout the southern United States.

Redbreast Sunfish *Lepomis auritus*	**Redear Sunfish** *Lepomis microlophus*	**Rock Bass** *Ampbloplites rupestris*

Breeding male

Size: Texas record is 1.75 pounds and 12.5 inches.

Abundance: Introduced widely into lakes and rivers.

Presumed range in TX

Natural History: The natural range of the Redbreast Sunfish is the Atlantic Slope from Maine to Florida. Today this species has been widely introduced throughout the US including much of Texas. It now occurs in many of the state's impoundments and larger rivers. This is a popular game fish along the eastern seaboard where it is a common game fish species.

Size: Texas record is 2 pounds and 14 inches in length.

Abundance: Introduced widely into lakes and rivers.

Presumed range in TX

Natural History: These fish also go by the name "Shellcracker," a reference to their habit of eating small freshwater mollusks such small clams and especially aquatic snails. The natural distribution of this fish was originally the Coastal Plain of the southeastern United States. Today it has been widely introduced throughout many other regions, including central Texas.

Size: Record size 3 pounds. Texas record 1.3 pounds.

Abundance: Introduced species that is rare in Texas.

Presumed range in TX

Natural History: Also known as the "Goggle Eye," the Rock Bass is a fish of clear, cool waters. They are primarily a stream fish that is found in clear streams with good water quality mostly in the northern US. The natural distribution is from the Great Lakes region south into northern Alabama. They have been introduced into streams in central Texas and Lake Texoma.

Class—**Actinopterygii** (bony fishes)

Order—**Perciformes** (typical fishes)

Family—**Centrarchidae** (sunfishes)

Family—**Elassomatidae** (pygmy sunfish)

Black Croppie *Pomoxis nigromaculatus*	**White Croppie** *Pomoxis annularis*	**Banded Pygmy Sunfish** *Elassoma zonatum*

Size: Texas record 4 pounds, 17 inches.

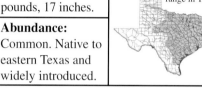
Presumed range in TX

Abundance: Common. Native to eastern Texas and widely introduced.

Natural History: The Black Croppie likes clearer waters than the White Croppie, though both are often found in the same waters. Popular game fishes, both species have been widely introduced across America. White Croppie is usually much lighter, but not always. Positive ID can be made by counting the stiff spines on the dorsal fin. White Croppie has only 6, Black has 7 or 8.

Size: Maximum 5 pounds, 3 ounces.

Presumed range in TX

Abundance: Common and widely distributed in lakes and streams.

Natural History: The White Croppie is more tolerant of turbid water conditions than the Black Croppie, though both are often found in the same waters. White Croppie is usually much lighter and typically has fewer black spots, but not always. The best way to make a positive ID is by counting the stiff spines on the dorsal fin. White Croppie has only 6, Black Croppie has 7 or 8.

Size: Maximum of 1.75 inches.

Presumed range in TX

Abundance: Fairly common in the eastern Coastal Plain of Texas.

Natural History: These tiny, secretive fishes are unknown to most Texans. They live in swamps, oxbows, and slow moving streams where their small size renders them unnoticeable to the average observer. This fish is an Coastal Plain endemic that ranges from the Carolinas to eastern Texas. The Banded Pygmy Sunfish exhibits sexual dimorphism (see photos above).

Family—**Moronidae** (true basses)

Yellow Bass *Morone mississipiensis*	**White Bass** *Morone chrysops*	**Striped Bass** *Morone saxatalis*

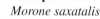

Size: Texas record is 3.76 pounds and 17.5 inches.

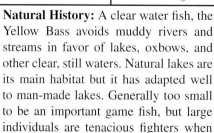
Presumed range in TX

Abundance: Fairly common in eastern Texas.

Natural History: A clear water fish, the Yellow Bass avoids muddy rivers and streams in favor of lakes, oxbows, and other clear, still waters. Natural lakes are its main habitat but it has adapted well to man-made lakes. Generally too small to be an important game fish, but large individuals are tenacious fighters when hooked.

Size: Texas record is 5.56 pounds and 20.75 inches.

Presumed range in TX

Abundance: Common in most lakes and rivers in Texas.

Natural History: These important game fish are famous for forcing schools of bait fish to the surface then attacking them in a feeding frenzy. Leaping bait fish indicate the presence of feeding bass. Savvy fishermen look for these eruptions of bait fish known as "jumps." This species prefers rivers and lakes with high turbidity.

Size: Texas record is 53 pounds and 48 inches.

Presumed range in TX

Abundance: Non-native and introduced. Uncommon.

Natural History: Striped Bass are anadromous fish that live in salt water but spawn in freshwater rivers. Widely stocked in lakes by wildlife agencies, they have adapted to a freshwater existence. Stocked in man-made lakes throughout the state, including many not shown on map above. Hybrid Striped/White Bass are known as "Rockfish."

Class—**Actinopterygii** (bony fishes)

Order—**Perciformes** (typical fishes)

Family—**Percidae** (perch & darters)

Yellow Perch *Perca flavescens*	Walleye *Sander vitreus*	Western Sand Darter *Ammocrypta clara*

Size: World record 4 pounds 3 ounces. Averages less than a pound.

Abundance: Rare in Texas.

Presumed range in TX

Natural History: Native to the northern and eastern United States, Yellow Perch have recently expanded their range into more southerly regions. They are a popular pan fish in the north. In Texas they are found in at least two man-made lakes, Meridith Reservoir and Greenbelt Reservoir. Also found in the Rio Grande River near El Paso. May be found in other lakes and rivers in the state.

Size: Record 25 pounds. Texas record 11.9 pounds, 31.75 inches.

Abundance: Rare in Texas.

Presumed range in TX

Natural History: Walleye live in larger rivers, impoundments, and natural lakes where deep water provides the cool temperatures these fish require. They are regarded as one of the most palatable of the game fishes. The range map above may not represent all the places where it may occur. Breeds in only a handful of lakes in Texas. Stocked in additional lakes in Texas.

Size: Maximum size for both species is 2.75 inches total length.

Abundance: Uncommon in Texas.

Combined range in TX

Natural History: Though nearly identical, Sand Darters are associated with sandy substrates of medium to large streams. When not swimming about in search of food or a mate they stay buried in the sand except for the top of head. Their translucent-colored bodies render them effectively invisible. Two species occur in eastern Texas, the other is the **Scaly Sand Darter** (*Ammocrypta vivax*).

Logperch *Percina caprodes*	Texas Logperch *Percina carbonaria*	Bigscale Logperch *Percina macrolepida*

Size: Average 3 to 5 inches. Maximum of 7 inches.

Abundance: Rare with limited distribution in Texas.

Presumed range in TX

Natural History: Although common and widespread in the north central US, this fish is rare in Texas, being found only along the Red River and the northeastern corner of the state. The long snout of the logperches (*Percina*) is used to "root around" hog-like in the substrate of streams. Their food is small aquatic inverbrates including large amounts of larva of midges and blackflies.

Size: Average 3 to 4 inches. Maximum of 4.5 inches.

Abundance: Fairly common in unpolluted streams.

Presumed range in TX

Natural History: This fish inhabits creeks and small to medium rivers. For a microhabitat it shows a preference for shallow riffle areas and flowing waters. Like most *Percina* fishes it requires clean, clear waters and is vulnerable to stream pollution. Feeds on tiny benthic organisms it digs from the gravel or sandy substrates using its elongated snout. A Texas endemic. Population is stable.

Size: A small *Percina*, maximum of 3.8 inches.

Abundance: Fairly common and widespread.

Presumed range in TX

Natural History: In addition to being found in small to medium-size rivers, this fish can also occur in impoundments. Its micro-habitat in streams includes deep channels with little current as well as pools. Most *Percina* fishes are stream reliant and many cannot persist in impoundments. The Bigscale Logperch however can thrive in lakes. It prefers sandy or silty substrates.

Class—**Actinopterygii** (bony fishes)

Order—**Perciformes** (typical fishes)

Family—**Percidae** (perch & darters)

Slenderhead Darter *Percina phoxocephala*	**River Darter** *Percina shumardi*	**Guadalupe Darter** *Percina apristis*

Size: Maximum of 3.75 inches.

Abundance: Very rare in Texas. Only a few records from the Red River in northeast Texas.

Presumed range in TX

Natural History: Inhabits large creeks and small to medium-size rivers. Over gravel bottoms in relatively swift current. Migrates upstream into shallower waters in the spring and downstream into deeper waters in winter. Range in Texas is restricted to the Red River.

Size: Maximum length 3 inches.

Abundance: Fairly common in streams where it occurs, mostly in northeastern Texas.

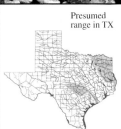

Presumed range in TX

Natural History: Unlike most darter that favor smaller streams, the River Darter is a fish of larger rivers. It does occur in small rivers and the mouths of creeks where they join larger streams. Utilizes deeper water than many darters, but may move into shallows at night.

Size: Maximum of 4.5 inches.

Abundance: Uncommon. Restricted to the Guadalupe River basin where it is fairly common.

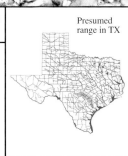

Presumed range in TX

Natural History: Found in gravelly riffles and around or under large rocks within the current. This species is very similar to the Dusky Darter and is apparently a close relative of that species. Along with the Texas Logperch it is a Texas endemic.

Blackside Darter *Percina maculata*	**Dusky Darter** *Percina sciera*

Size: Maximum of 4.5 inches.

Abundance: Although this is a widespread species that is common in much of its range throughout the midwest and mid-south, it is an uncommon fish in Texas and is regarded as a Threatened species by the Texas Parks & Wildlife Dept.

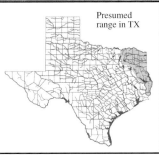

Presumed range in TX

Natural History: Generally regarded as being a fish of small to medium rivers, but it has been taken in large creeks. Young individuals like sandy riffles but larger fish tend to be in quieter pools with little or no current.

Size: Maximum of 5 inches.

Abundance: Apparently a fairly common species in Texas. It is one of the most geographically wide-ranging *Percina* species in Texas. It is probably most common in the Brazos River basin and in streams in easternmost Texas.

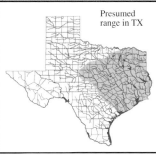

Presumed range in TX

Natural History: Seems to prefer clear, slow moving streams. Usually found over sandy or gravelly substrates and may associate with structure such as fallen trees and piles of twigs, leaves, and other detritus.

Class—**Actinopterygii** (bony fishes)

Order—**Perciformes** (typical fishes)

Family—**Percidae** (perch & darters)

Genus—**Etheostoma** (true darters)

Natural History: With at least 148 species distributed across North America, this genus boasts more species than any other genus of freshwater fish in the US. Among them are some of America's rarest fish and some of our most common. In coloration they range from a cryptic mottled brown to remarkably colorful. In many species the breeding males rival the most colorful of tropical aquarium fishes. Most species are strongly sexually dimorphic, with the females being more subdued in color and sometimes outright drab. The stunning breeding color of the male is temporary and replaced by a much more faded appearance through the rest of the year following spring breeding. The females of these fishes are often so similar that even expert ichthyologists can have difficulty identifying them. New species have been recently described and there are most likely new species yet to be discovered. Unlike most fishes, they lack air bladders for flotation and they are mostly bottom dwellers that hug the sand and gravel bottoms of flowing streams. When startled they will move in quick, short dashes, hence the common name "darter." Texas boasts 13 species of *Etheostoma*. All but three are found exclusively in the easternmost portion of the state. There, their habitats collectively include almost every drainage within the region and they are found in waterways ranging from swamps to large rivers to small creeks. Darters feed on a wide variety of small invertebrate prey. Copepods and other small crustaceans, mosquito larva and other small aquatic insects (both larval and adult) are eaten. In fact almost any invertebrate small enough to swallow may become prey. In recent years darters have become a favorite species of many aquarists in America. Their wonderful colors and wide variety of species make them an appealing group of fishes to observe and study in an aquarium. In recent years the keeping of native freshwater fish species has grown into a significant hobby. In fact, today there is an organization of individuals who keep and study native fishes in home aquariums. The North American Native Fish Association is a national organization with a newsletter and regularly scheduled conventions and field/collecting trips. The states east of the Mississippi River have the most darter species, with states like Kentucky and Tennessee boasting in excess of 50 species. There are 13 species that can be found in Texas, but the range of one of these in Texas is restricted to the Red River (Orangebelly Darter-*Etheostoma radiosum*). Most Texas darters are found in the eastern part of the state. Many darter species require pristine water conditions and these fish can be a barometer to help determine the quality of waterways. Like "the canary in the coal mine" they are often the first fishes to suffer from the effects of water pollution, siltation, and other forms of stream degradation. Nationwide many are regarded as endangered, threatened or are considered species of concern. Of the Texas darters there is one that is an Endangered Species (*Etheostoma fonticola*, the fountain darter) and one other that is a Threatened Species (Rio Grande Darter-*Etheostoma grahami*).

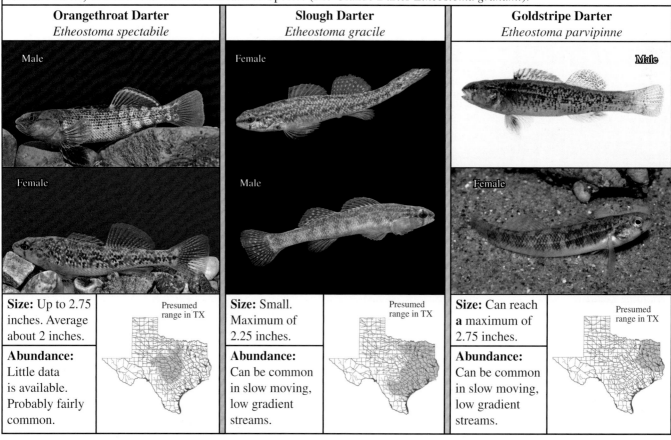

Orangethroat Darter *Etheostoma spectabile*	**Slough Darter** *Etheostoma gracile*	**Goldstripe Darter** *Etheostoma parvipinne*
Male / Female	Female / Male	Male / Female
Size: Up to 2.75 inches. Average about 2 inches.	**Size:** Small. Maximum of 2.25 inches.	**Size:** Can reach a maximum of 2.75 inches.
Abundance: Little data is available. Probably fairly common.	**Abundance:** Can be common in slow moving, low gradient streams.	**Abundance:** Can be common in slow moving, low gradient streams.

Presumed range in TX

Class—**Actinopterygii** (bony fishes)

Order—**Perciformes** (typical fishes)

Family—**Percidae** (perch & darters)

Genus—**Etheostoma** (true darters)

Fountain Darter *Etheostoma fonticola*	**Greenthroat Darter** *Etheostoma lepidum*	**Bluntnose Darter** *Etheostoma chlorosoma*

Size:: Tiny. Maximum of only 1.4 inches.

Abundance: Very rare. Found in only two locations in central Texas.

Presumed range in TX

Size: Can reach a maximum of 2.5 inches.

Abundance: Uncommon. Found in spring fed streams in the Hill Country.

Presumed range in TX

Size: Small. Maximum of 2.25 inches.

Abundance: Common. One of the more common darters in the state.

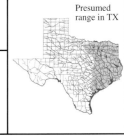
Presumed range in TX

Redspot Darter *Etheostoma artesia*	**Cypress Darter** *Etheostoma proeliare*	**Harlequin Darter** *Etheostoma histrio*

 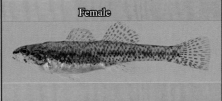 

Female

Size: Can reach a Maximum of 3 inches.

Abundance: Can be common in slow moving, low gradient streams.

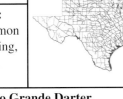
Presumed range in TX

Size: Small. Maximum of only 2 inches.

Abundance: Uncommon in Texas but not threatened or endangered.

Presumed range in TX

Size: Can reach a maximum of 3 inches.

Abundance: Apparently fairly common within its range in eastern Texas.

Presumed range in TX

Rio Grande Darter *Etheostoma grahami*	**Swamp Darter** *Etheostoma fusiforme*	**Mud Darter** *Etheostoma asprigne*

Size: Small. Maximum of 2.25 inches.

Abundance: Rare. Found only in the vicinity of the lower Pecos.

Presumed range in TX

Size: Small. Maximum of 2.25 inches.

Abundance: Rare in Texas. Restricted to the Cypress River in northeast Texas.

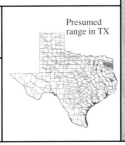
Presumed range in TX

Size: Can reach a maximum of 2.75 inches.

Abundance: Apparently fairly common within its range in eastern Texas.

Presumed range in TX

Class—**Actinopterygii** (bony fishes)

Order—**Perciformes** (typical fishes)

Family—**Sciaenidae** (drums)

Family—**Cichlidae** (cichlids)

Freshwater Drum *Aplondinotus grunniens*	**Rio Grande Cichlid** *Cichlasoma cyanoguttatum*	**Blue Tilapia** *Oreochromis aurea*

Male

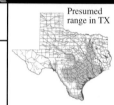

Size: World record 54 pounds.

Presumed range in TX

Abundance: Common. Most common in larger streams and lakes.

Size: Texas record is 2 pounds.

Presumed range in TX

Abundance: Common and recently expanding its range in Texas.

Size: Record 10 pounds, 21 inches.

Presumed range in TX

Abundance: Common. Can be very common in localized habitats.

Natural History: This is the only member of the drum family that lives in fresh water. Most are saltwater fishes and several are important food and sport fishes. By contrast, the Freshwater Drum is not highly regarded by sport anglers despite the fact that they obtain an impressive size. The name Drum is derived from their habit of producing a deep thudding sound similar to a drum.

Natural History: This species is originally native to the Rio Grande River and northeastern Mexico. It has been widely introduced into more northern regions of the state and has also spread northward along the Gulf Coast. It is intolerant of cold temperatures (below 56 degrees F), but can survive in warm, spring fed waters and in warm waters around power plants. Tolerates polluted waters.

Natural History: An introduced, invasive species that competes with native fish species and has been shown to have a very detrimental impact on populations of sunfishes, black basses, catfish, and even minnows. Inhabits mainly freshwater environments but can use brackish waters. They can be subject to winter die-offs if caught in areas where they can't move into warmer waters.

Order—**Esociformes** (pikes & mudminnows)

Order—**Amiiformes**

Family—**Esocidae** (pikes)

Family—**Amidae** (bowfin)

Chain Pickerel *Esox niger*	**Grass Pickerel** *Esox americanus*	**Bowfin** *Amia calva*

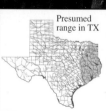

Size: Record size 9 pounds 6 ounces. Texas record is 4.5 pounds.

Presumed range in TX

Abundance: Fairly common.

Size: Average 8 to 10 inches. Maximum length 14 inches.

Presumed range in TX

Abundance: Fairly common.

Size: Record size 21.5 pounds. Texas record is 17.5 pounds.

Presumed range in TX

Abundance: Fairly common.

Natural History: The Chain Pickerel is a fish of clear waters with abundant aquatic vegetation. Like all members of the pike family it is a highly carnivorous ambush predator with a very large mouth. The jaws are equipped with rows of sharp, barracuda-like teeth.

Natural History: Inhabits swamps and streams. In smaller creeks it usually is found in quiet pools. This fish likes clear waters and avoids muddy streams. This is the smallest of the pike family and thus feeds on smaller prey. Minnows and other small fish are prey.

Natural History: This is the only surviving species of an ancient family of primitive fishes that dates back to the age of the dinosaurs. Found in swamps and oxbow lakes. They often go by the nickname "Grinnel." They can survive for long periods out water.

Class—**Actinopterygii** (bony fishes)

Order—**Lepisostiformes** (gar)

Family—**Lepisosteidae**

Longnose Gar *Lepisosteus osseus*	**Shortnose Gar** *Lepisosteus platostomus*	**Spotted Gar** *Lepisosteus*

Longnose Gar
Lepisosteus osseus

Presumed range in TX

Size: Record 50 pounds (6 feet).

Abundance: Common. In every major river and most impoundments

Natural History: America's most widespread gar species, the Longnose Gar can be found in both large and medium-size rivers as well as large creeks. Also common in natural lakes and oxbows and in man-made impoundments. Females average larger than males and can live over twenty years. Feeds mostly on shad and other forage fishes.

Shortnose Gar
Lepisosteus platostomus

Presumed range in TX

Size: Up to about 5 lbs and 33 inches.

Abundance: Uncommon in Texas. Red and Sulphur Rivers only.

Natural History: An inhabitant of quite pools and floodplains of rivers and large creeks. Also found in swamps and oxbows and can tolerate waters with high turbidity. During periods of severe drought can survive for days in the mud of drying pools. In addition to fish, also eats insects and crayfish. Range in Texas restricted to Red and Sulphur Rivers.

Spotted Gar
Lepisosteus

Presumed range in TX

Size: Maximum about 3.5 feet.

Abundance: Common. Most common in eastern Texas.

Natural History: Habitat is swamps, sloughs, oxbows, natural lakes and slow moving creeks. They are most common in the Coastal Plain. This gar prefers clearer waters with less siltation than the similar Shortnose Gar. Heavily vegetated waters are preferred. Best differentiated from the Shortnose Gar by the presence of dark spots on the snout.

Alligator Gar
Atractosteus spatula

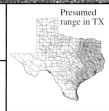

Presumed range in TX

Size: Can reach 10 feet and 300 pounds.

Abundance: Uncommon to rare but increasing.

Natural History: Alligator Gar once ranged well up the Ohio and Mississippi Rivers and their major tributaries into Illinois, Missouri, and southern Indiana and southern Ohio. Today this is a highly endangered fish and efforts to restore the species are being undertaken. Adult Alligator Gars are highly predaceous and known to eat small mammals and birds as well as fish and even carrion.

Order—**Acipenseriformes** (paddlefish & sturgeons)

Family—**Polydontidae**	Family—**Acipenseridae**
Paddlefish *Polyodon spathula*	**Shovelnose Sturgeon** *Sacphirhynchus platorynchus*

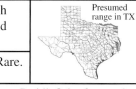

Presumed range in TX

Size: Can reach 180 pounds and over 7 feet.

Abundance: Rare.

Natural History: Paddlefish often go by the name "Spoonbill Catfish," but in fact they are not related to the catfishes. They are a member of a very small, primitive order of fishes that contains only two species (the other is a giant found in China that can reach lengths of over 20 feet). Paddlefish have skeletons that are mostly cartilage.

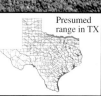

Presumed range in TX

Size: Maximum of 43 inches. No records for Texas.

Abundance: Rare.

Natural History: Lives in the deep channels of the Mississippi, Ohio, Missouri, Tennessee, Arkansas, and Red Rivers. In Texas this species is found only in the main channel of the Red River. Historically occurred in the Rio Grande, but apparently extirpated from that river. Now a threatened species in Texas. Not found in lakes.

Order—**Salmoniformes** (salmon)

Family—**Salmonidae**

Rainbow Trout
Oncorhynchus mykiss

Size: Record size 42 pounds 2 ounces.

Abundance: Very rare. A single self-sustaining population in Texas.

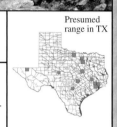
Presumed range in TX

Natural History: The Rainbow Trout was originally native to Pacific drainages of the northwest. Today they have been widely introduced across much of America. They require cold, clear waters and thus are limited in distribution in Texas. Although they are widely stocked in lakes across the state, the only self sustaining population in Texas is in the Guadalupe Mountains.

Order—**Anguiliformes** (eels)

Family—**Anguilidae**

American Eel
Anguilla rostrata

Size: The maximum recorded length is 60 inches.

Abundance: Fairly common but declining in upstream regions.

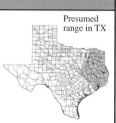
Presumed range in TX

Natural History: Eels have one of the most remarkable life cycles of any fish. After hatching far out in the Atlantic Ocean tiny larva migrate to the coast and swim hundreds of miles upstream in inland rivers. After as many as fifteen years later, adults return to the sea to spawn and die. Dams can hinder migrations and today they no longer occur in most rivers in western and central Texas.

Order—**Percopsiformes**

Family—**Aphredoderidae**

Pirate Perch
Aphredoderus sayanus

Size: Maximum 5.5 inches. Average 3 to 4.

Abundance: Locally common in suitable aquatic habitats.

Presumed range in TX

Natural History: The Pirate Perch lives in swamps and spring-fed wetlands among heavy aquatic vegetation. May also be found in backwaters of large creeks and small rivers. Although they are small fishes, they have rather large mouths and they are quite predaceous on insects, crustaceans, and small fishes. They are unique among Texas fishes in that their anus is situated in the throat!

Order—**Characiformes**

Family—**Characidae**

Mexican Tetra
Astyanax mexicanus

Size: Maximum length of 4.5 inches.

Abundance: Common. Introduced into the Edwards Plateau.

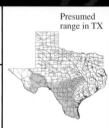
Presumed range in TX

Natural History: The only member of the Characidae family in North America, the Mexican Tetra is a cousin of the infamous South American Pirhana. It is intolerant of cold and will move towards springs and seeps to survive cold snaps. Highly insectivorous.

Order—**Siluiformes** (catfishes)

Family—**Loricariidae** (armored catfish)

Suckermouth Catfish
Hypostomus plecostomus

Size: Maximum length of about 18 inches.

Abundance: Introduced. Increasingly common along the Gulf Coast.

Presumed range in TX

Natural History: Native to Central and South America this popular aquarium fish has become well established in much of the southern US. There are probably several species of this genus now living in Texas. The species shown above is likely the most common.

Family—**Ictaluridae** (American catfish)

Toothless & Widemouth Blindcats
Trogloglanis pattersoni & Satan eurystomus

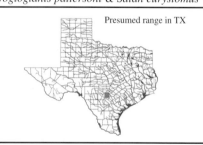
Presumed range in TX

Size: Maximum lengths of 4 and 5.25 inches.

Abundance: Both species are quite rare found in a few localities around San Antonio.

Natural History: These blind cavefishes are native to five closely associated artesian springs in the vicinity of San Antonio. How far they may range in underground waterways is unknown. Both species are similar in appearance and lack eyes and skin pigments. Few photos of these rare fishes exist and most are of preserved specimens.

Class—**Actinopterygii** (bony fishes)

Order—**Siluriformes** (catfishes)

Family—**Ictaluridae** (American catfishes)

Yellow Bullhead *Ameiurus natalis*	**Black Bullhead** *Ameiurus melas*	**Headwater Catfish** *Ictalurus lupus*

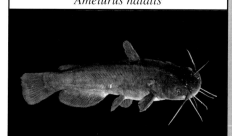  

Size: Maximum of 19 inches. Record weight 3 pounds 10 ounces.

Abundance: Common.

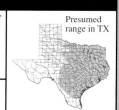 Presumed range in TX

Natural History: Widespread, common, and easily caught on hook and line the Yellow Bullhead is a familiar fish to many Texans. They are often known by the nickname "Mudcat." Ranges from the east coast to the central Great Plains, including much of Texas. Told from the Black Bullheads by its yellow-colored chin barbels.

Size: Record weight is 8 pounds but few will ever exceed 3 pounds.

Abundance: Fairly common.

 Presumed range in TX

Natural History: Black Bullheads are mainly nocturnal fishes that do not feed during the day. They live in still water pools in streams or in natural lakes and man-made impoundments. Like the Yellow Bullhead they are easily caught on hook and line. They can be distinguished from the Yellow Bullhead by their dark chin barbels.

Size: Maximum is about 19 inches. Not listed in state fishing records.

Abundance: Uncommon, declining.

 Presumed range in TX

Natural History: Consumes more plant material that other catfishes, with algae being an important element in the diet at times. Otherwise an opportunistic predator of benthic invertebrates, insects and crustaceans. This is a declining species in Texas that was once found in many streams in the Gulf Coastal Plain.

Channel Catfish *Ictalurus punctatus*	**Blue Catfish** *Ictalurus furcatus*	**Flathead Catfish** *Plylodictus olivaris*

Size: Maximum of about 65 pounds. Texas record 36.5 pounds and 38 inches.

Abundance: Common.

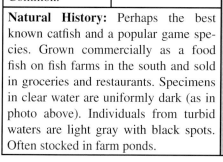 Presumed range in TX

Natural History: Perhaps the best known catfish and a popular game species. Grown commercially as a food fish on fish farms in the south and sold in groceries and restaurants. Specimens in clear water are uniformly dark (as in photo above). Individuals from turbid waters are light gray with black spots. Often stocked in farm ponds.

Size: Maximum size 150 lbs. and 5 feet. Texas record 121.5 pounds and 58 inches.

Abundance: Fairly common.

 Presumed range in TX

Natural History: This is America's largest catfish and old reports of specimens in excess of 300 pounds exist, though their reliability is questioned. This is an important game fish and also important commercially. Most common in large rivers and the lower reaches of major tributaries. Probably the least common of the three large catfish.

Size: Maximum of about 100 pounds. Texas record 98.5 pounds and 53 inches in length.

Abundance: Fairly common.

 Presumed range in TX

Natural History: Second in size only to the Blue Catfish. Found mostly in rivers and in impoundments of larger rivers. Adults are mainly nocturnal and spend the day hidden among submerged structure such as logs or rocks. In river environments uses deep pools. Often hides in caves in river banks. More predaceous than our other large catfish.

Class—**Actinopterygii** (bony fishes)

Order—**Siluriformes** (catfishes)

Family—**Ictaluridae** (American catfishes)

Tadpole Madtom *Noturus gyrinus*	**Freckled Madtom** *Noturus nocturnus*

Size: Maximum of 5 inches. Average 3.5.

Abundance: Fairly common in eastern Texas.

Presumed range in TX

Natural History: The madtoms (genus *Noturus*) are a group of small catfishes that consists of a total of 30 species nationwide. They are represented in Texas by only two species. Like other American catfishes the Madtoms have spiny dorsal and pectoral fins that produce a mild venom. A puncture from one of these spines can result in a significant amount of pain and swelling, but it is not life threatening.

Size: Maximum of 5.5 inches. Average 3.5.

Abundance: Fairly common in northeast Texas.

Presumed range in TX

Natural History: Madtoms are stream fishes that can be found in habitats ranging from small creeks to large rivers. They have a fleshy fin between the dorsal fin and the tail known as an "adipose fin." In most madtoms this fin connects to the caudal (tail) fin, a character that immediately separates the madtoms from the rest of the catfish family. These small catfish have been known to spawn in an old soda can.

Order—**Hiodontiformes**

Family—**Hiodontidae** (mooneyes)

Goldeye
Hiodon alosoides

Size: Reaches 20 inches and 3 pounds.

Abundance: Rare in Texas. Found in the Red River only.

Presumed range in TX

Natural History: The Goldeye is one of only two species in the family Hiodontidae. They live in large rivers and lakes and feed on a wide variety of invertebrate and small vertebrate prey. Goldeye is found in rivers with high turbidity and does not thrive in impoundments, but does exist in natural lakes and backwaters of large rivers. It is an important food fish in parts of Canada, where it is eaten smoked.

Order—**Clupeiformes** (herrings & shads)

Family—**Alosidae** (herrings)

Skipjack Herring
Alosa chrysochloris

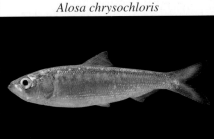

Size: Can get to 3.75 pounds.

Abundance: Fairly common along gulf coast, also in Red River.

Presumed range in TX

Natural History: The Skipjack Herring is a species that lives in saltwater and returns to freshwaters to spawn. This condition is known as being an "anadromous" species. In some places they are now mostly landlocked due to the presence of dams on major rivers.

Family—**Dorosomatidae** (shads)

Gizzard Shad *Dorosoma cepedianum*	**Threadfin Shad** *Dorosoma petenense*

Size: Can reach 3.5 pounds.

Abundance: Common. Found in all major rivers in Texas.

Presumed range in TX

Natural History: Shad are plankton feeders that filter tiny organisms from the water through specialized gill rakers. They occur in major rivers and their large impoundments throughout the eastern United States and they are an important food for many game fishes.

Size: Maximum of about 9 inches.

Abundance: Common but less widespread in than the Gizzard Shad.

Presumed range in TX

Natural History: Threadfin Shad occur in large schools and they are a major food for many important game fishes in America. They are southern fish and not very tolerant of cold temperatures and severe winter cold fronts can cause major die-offs.

Class—**Actinopterygii** (bony fishes)

Order—**Cypriniformes** (minnows & suckers)

Family—**Catastomidae** (suckers)

Blue Sucker *Cycleptus elongatus*	**Highfin Carpsucker** *Carpiodes velifer*	**River Carpsucker** *Carpiodes carpio*

Size: Current world record is 18 pounds, 14 ounces.

Abundance: Uncommon to rare in Texas.

Presumed range in TX

Natural History: A unique member of the sucker family. Although its range includes all of the Mississippi and western gulf coastal rivers, this is today a rare fish throughout most of its range. It prefers fast flowing channels over hard bottom. Dams and siltation impact it negatively. The Rio Grande River population may represent a new species.

Size: Can reach about 15 inches and up to 2 pounds.

Abundance: Rare in Texas. Lower Red River only.

Presumed range in TX

Natural History: This is the smallest of the Carpsuckers and is therefore not highly valued by commercial fishermen. An inhabitant of medium to large rivers and favors clearer waters with some gravel substrates. Highfin Carpsukers are less common than America's other two *Carpoides* species. Siltation and lake impoundments may be to blame.

Size: Maximum 25 inches. Record weight 10 pounds.

Abundance: Fairly common. Found mostly in large rivers.

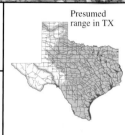

Presumed range in TX

Natural History: Found in the larger rivers and their reservoirs. Favors slow moving waters and silt or sand substrates. The most common of the large suckers found in Texas. A bottom feeder. Food is tiny invertebrates sucked from mud of the bottom of a river or lake. Known to live at least ten years. Valued as a commercial food fish.

Smallmouth Buffalo *Ictiobus bubalus*	**Largemouth Buffalo** *Ictiobus cyprinellus*	**Black Buffalo** *Ictiobus niger*

Size: Texas record is 82.2 pounds and 43.5 inches.

Abundance: Common in larger rivers and reservoirs.

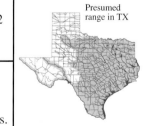

Presumed range in TX

Natural History: A river fish that also thrives in lakes and impoundments. Less likely to be found in turbid water than the Largemouth Buffalo and also is more fond of waters with some current. Feeds on bottom dwelling invertebrates and plants. Like other *Ictiobus* (buffalo fishes), a commercially valuable fish.

Size: Can reach a maximum of 80 pounds.

Abundance: Uncommon in Texas. Limited distribution.

Presumed range in TX

Natural History: Largemouth Buffalo are important commercial food fishes. Found in large rivers and their backwaters and in impoundments and is more accepting of silt laden waters than others of its genus. Breeds during spring in flooded fields and backwaters. Dams restrict movement.

Size: Texas record 34.8 pounds, 39.5 inches.

Abundance: Uncommon in Texas. Limited distribution.

Presumed range in TX

Natural History: Least common of the Buffalo fishes and regarded as a species of concern in some states. Morphologically somewhat intermediate between the two previous species. In habits, feeding, etc., it is most similar to the Smallmouth Buffalo. Found in large and medium-size rivers.

Class—**Actinopterygii** (bony fishes)

Order—**Cypriniformes** (minnows & suckers)

Family—**Catastomidae** (suckers)

Golden Redhorse *Moxostoma erythrurum*	**Blacktail Redhorse** *Moxostoma poecilurum*	**Gray Redhorse** *Moxostoma congestum*

Golden Redhorse
Moxostoma erythrurum

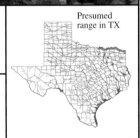

Size: Maximum 30 inches. No records for Texas.

Abundance: Rare in Texas. Found in Red River only.

Natural History: The Redhorse Suckers are the most diverse group within the sucker family (Catastomidae). There are at least 21 species in North America. The Golden Redhorse is widespread in the eastern US but barely ranges into Texas in the lower portion of the Red River. It inhabits rivers and large creeks but will survive in impoundments.

Blacktail Redhorse
Moxostoma poecilurum

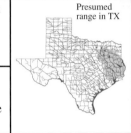

Size: Maximum 20 inches. No records for Texas.

Abundance: Fairly common in streams in the Piney Woods.

Natural History: The Blacktail Redhorse is one of the more southerly ranging members of the Moxostoma genus. Originally an inhabitant of slow moving rivers and creeks, it adapts well to impoundments and can tolerate brackish water. All the Redhorse Suckers have been utilized as a food fish. The flesh is described as good but boney.

Gray Redhorse
Moxostoma congestum

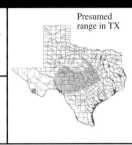

Size: Maximum 20.5 inches. No records for Texas.

Abundance: Uncommon. Has declined significantly.

Natural History: This redhorse species is native to streams of the Edwards Plateau. It inhabits deep runs and pools of gravel or sandy bottomed creeks and migrates to smaller streams to spawn. A very similar species, the **Mexican Redhorse** (*Moxostoma austrunum*) is found in the US only in the Big Bend region of Texas (shaded square on map above).

Spotted Sucker
Minytrema melanops

Size: Maximum of about 18 inches.

Abundance: Uncommon, declining.

Natural History: Lives in pools and slow moving waters of large and small rivers, as well as larger creeks and impoundments. Moves into smaller creeks in spring to spawn over gravel or rocks. Feeds on small aquatic invertebrates. Although fairly widespread, this is not a common fish and it may be decreasing in much of its range as water quality declines. Stream siltation is probably the biggest cause of declines.

Lake Chubsucker
Erimyzon sucetta

Size: Maximum about 15 inches in total length.

Abundance: Presumably fairly common.

Natural History: The Lake Chubsucker as its name implies inhabits natural lakes and slow moving streams that connect with wetlands. They are also found in a few man-made impoundment lakes. They are very similar to and difficult to distinguish from the Western Creek Chubsucker. But the Lake Chubsucker tends to avoid lentic waters and is found mostly in natural lakes, swamps and slow moving creeks within wetlands.

Western Creek Chubsucker
Erimyzon claviformis

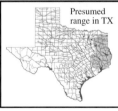

Size: Maximum of about 15 inches.

Abundance: Presumably fairly common.

Natural History: The Creek Chubsucker is widespread throughout the mid-south and ranges as far north as the Great Lakes region. It is fairly common in small and large creeks in areas with sand or gravel substrate. They eat tiny crustaceans, insects and algae. Very similar in appearance to the Lake Chubsucker, which has 11 or 12 dorsal fin rays as opposed to 9 or 10 in the Creek Chubsucker.

Class—**Actinopterygii** (bony fishes)

Order—**Cypriniformes** (minnows & suckers)

Family—**Cyprinidae** (minnows)

Grass Carp *Ctenopharyngodon idella*	**Silver Carp** *Hypophthalmichthys molitrix*	**Bighead Carp** *Hypophthalmichthys nobilis*

Grass Carp — **Size:** 4 feet and 100 pounds.

Abundance: Introduced to control aquatic plants.

 Presumed range in TX

Natural History: Inhabits pools and backwaters of large rivers and both man made and natural lakes. Introduced into the United States from Asia to control aquatic plant growth in commercial minnow ponds. As with most alien species, the Grass Carp probably does more harm than good to the environments where it has become established.

Silver Carp — **Size:** Can reach 60 pounds.

Abundance: Introduced. Still rare but likely increasing.

 Presumed range in TX

Natural History: Native to China, the Silver Carp has become established in the larger rivers of the eastern United States. These fish consume tiny zooplankton and algae that is filtered from the flowing water of large river channels. Originally imported into Arkansas along with the Bighead Carp to control algae blooms in fish ponds.

Bighead Carp — **Size:** Up to 90 pounds.

Abundance: Introduced. Still rare but increasing.

 Presumed range in TX

Natural History: Like the previous species this fish is native to China. Now widespread in the major rivers of the eastern US. This is a filter feeder that inhabits the flowing waters of large river channels. Though both species of *Hypophthalmichthys* were intentionally introduced, they are now regarded as environmentally harmful aliens.

Common Carp *Cyprinus carpio*	**Goldfish** *Carassius auratus*	**Golden Shiner** *Notemigonus crysoleucas*

Common Carp — **Size:** Angling record is 55 pounds.

Abundance: Common. Found statewide in Texas waters.

Presumed range in TX

Natural History: Many people are surprised to learn that the Common Carp is an invasive species in America. Native to Eurasia, they were first brought to the US in the early 1800s. They are now widespread and common in most aquatic habitats in America. A benthic feeder that "roots" like a hog in muddy bottoms and increases water turbidity. These widespread aliens are today presumed to occur statewide in Texas.

Goldfish — **Size:** Maximum 20 inches and up to 5 pounds.

Abundance: Uncommon but widely distributed across US.

Presumed range in TX

Natural History: Native to Asia, the Goldfish is now widely established across most of North America. The gaudy colors commonly seen in fish ponds and pet stores rarely survive in wild populations. Found in most rivers and lakes and can survive in tiny ponds. More tolerant of pollution and siltation than many native species. Although sporadically distributed, they may presumably be seen statewide in Texas.

Golden Shiner — **Size:** Up to 14.5 inches. Average 8 inches.

Abundance: Common and widespread across US.

 Presumed range in TX

Natural History: This minnow is well-known among fishermen and is sold as a bait fish in many regions of the US. In their natural habitat they are fish of still water pools of streams and backwaters of rivers. They will also thrive in impoundments and small farm ponds. Millions are raised commercially each year to be sold in bait stores. As with most bait minnows, they have been distributed widely in the US.

Class—**Actinopterygii** (bony fishes)

Order—**Cypriniformes** (minnows & suckers)

Family—**Cyprinidae** (minnows)

Rudd *Scardinius erythropthalmus*	**Central Stoneroller** *Campostoma anomalum*	**Mexican Stoneroller** *Campostoma ornatum*

Size: Maximum length of 19 inches.

Abundance: Rare. Introduced into a few lakes in Texas.

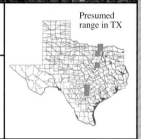
Presumed range in TX

Natural History: The Rudd is a Eurasian species resembling the Goldfish that is sometimes sold as a bait species in the US. As a result of bait bucket releases, it has become established in some waterways across America and has been documented from a half dozen lakes in the state of Texas (fishesoftexas.org.)

Size: Maximum length of 6.75 inches.

Abundance: Common. Can be very common in some streams in central Texas.

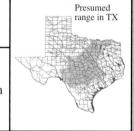
Presumed range in TX

Natural History: The Stonerollers have a hard cartilaginous lower lip which they use to scrape algae from rocks and logs. Their name comes from their habit of aggressive bottom feeding in gravelly bottomed streams which rolls small pebbles in the process. Five species occur in the US, two in Texas.

Size: Maximum length of 6.25 inches.

Abundance: A rare fish in Texas. More common in Mexico.

Presumed range in TX

Natural History: The Mexican Stoneroller is the Chihuahuan Desert version of the Stonerollers. The bulk of its range is in Mexico. It enters the US in a few streams in the Big Bend region of Texas. This fish appears to have declined from historical numbers and is now regarded as a Threatened Species.

Creek Chub *Semotilis atromaculatus*	**Long-nosed Dace** *Rhinichthyes cataractae*	**Flathead Chub** *Platygobio gracilis*

Breeding male

Size: Maximum length 12 inches.

Abundance: Common but not wide ranging in Texas.

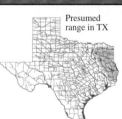
Presumed range in TX

Natural History: One of the most widespread and common creek fishes in America, but found in Texas only in the Piney Woods region. Like many minnows, breeding males develop tubercles on the head and snout, leading to the common nickname "Hornyhead." In the days when most Americans lived on the farm, fishing in small creeks for Creek Chubs was commonplace entertainment for many rural youngsters.

Size: Maximum length 6.25 inches.

Abundance: Fairly common in the upper Rio Grande River.

Presumed range in TX

Natural History: This is a widespread fish across the northern portions of North America. In fact it is one of the most widespread minnows in North America and it can be found from coast to coast in the northern tier of states. Its range also extends into most of Canada as far north as the Yukon and Northwest Territory. Though most of its range is far to the north, it can be found in Texas in the upper Rio Grande River.

Size: Maximum length of 12.5 inches.

Abundance: Uncommon in Texas. Upper Panhandle only.

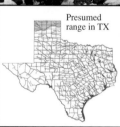
Presumed range in TX

Natural History: The northernmost potion of the Texas Panhandle represents the southernmost extension of the range in the Great Plains for this mainly northern fish. The Flathead Chub has one of the greatest north/south distributions of any North American fish, ranging all the way to the Arctic Circle. It lives in large rivers with high turbidity and prefers areas with significant current.

Class—**Actinopterygii** (bony fishes)

Order—**Cypriniformes** (minnows & suckers)

Family—**Cyprinidae** (minnows)

Genus *Cyprinella*—carp minnows (5 species in Texas)

Size: Prosepine Shiner, Plateau Shiner and Nueces River Shiner can reach 3 inches. Red Shiner 3.5 inches. The Blacktail Shiner is the largest of the group with a maximum of 7.5 inches.

Abundance: Prosepine Shiner is a threatened species by TPWD. Plateau Shiner and Nueces River Shiner are regarded as Critically Imperiled by the Nature Conservancy. Blacktail Shiner is common. Red Shiner is quite common and is the most widespread member of the genus in Texas. Plateau Shiner and Neuces River Shiner have restricted distribution.

Natural History: These minnows are very similar to the *Notropis* shiners (next page) and many species were once included in that group. This is a fairly large genus with 27 total species ranging throughout the eastern half of North America from southern Canada to northern Mexico. The groups common name "Carp Minnows" comes from the genus name (*Cyprinella*) which translates as "little carp." Like many minnows, immatures and females can pose a difficult identification challenge, especially for non-professionals. The adult males (especially in breeding colors) are often fairly distinctive in color and morphology and much easier to recognize. The preferred habitat of many *Cyprinella* species is sandy bottomed streams. This habitat has been greatly reduced by siltation in many regions leading to a decline in some species. The Red Shiner, on the other hand, is much more tolerant of siltation and water turbidity and is a fairly abundant fish. All *Cyprinella* are mainly insectivorous but some plant material is also eaten. Some species are quite opportunistic and larger invertebrates or even tiny fish fry are taken on occasion. Hybridization can be common among these minnows where their ranges overlap, adding to the already difficult task of identification. The Plateau Shiner has recently been divided into two species. The newest addition to the *Cyprinella* in Texas is commonly called the Nueces River Shiner (not pictured). The name is a reflection of the fact that it is endemic to the Nueces River. No scientific name has been assigned to this species as yet. The remaining population of the Plateau Shiner meanwhile is endemic to the Frio River.

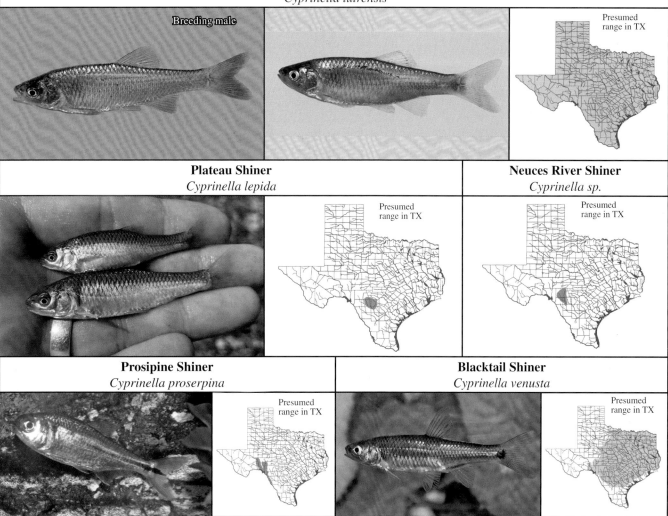

Red Shiner
Cyprinella lutrensis

Plateau Shiner
Cyprinella lepida

Neuces River Shiner
Cyprinella sp.

Prosipine Shiner
Cyprinella proserpina

Blacktail Shiner
Cyprinella venusta

Class—**Actinopterygii** (bony fishes)

Order—**Cypriniformes** (minnows & suckers)

Family—**Cyprinidae** (minnows)

Genus—*Notropis*—true minnows (21 species in Texas)

Size: For the most part, these are small minnows. Some will not exceed 2.5 inches in length. A few of the larger species can reach 5.5 inches.

Abundance: This group of minnows ranges from being very common to very rare.

Natural History: In the sense that most people think of minnows as being tiny fishes, these are the "true minnows." Members of this genus are among the smallest of America's fishes. Several *Notropis* are quite diminutive with a maximum length of only about 2.5 inches. The largest species will barely exceed 5.5 inches. *Notropis* is largest genus of Cyprinidae fishes in North America with at least 75 species across the continent. In fact, this is the second largest generic group of fishes in North America, surpassed only by the darters of the *Etheostoma* genus. The exact status some species included in this genus is problematic and taxonomic changes occur frequently within the group, with occasional species being re-assigned to another genus and some being added from other genera. Their distribution is generally east of the Rocky Mountain Continental Divide, and most species occur within the Gulf of Mexico Drainage Basin. There are twenty species in Texas but one is regarded as endangered in the state and at least two others are threatened. In addition, four species that once occurred in Texas are no longer found in the state. Collectively, the Shiner Minnows are found in virtually all aquatic habitats within the state and their combined ranges encompass all of Texas. The breeding males of many *Notropis* species are quite colorful. Even those species that don't acquire significant color on the body will typically acquire yellow, orange or red color in the fins of nuptial males. At least one species, the Emerald Shiner (*Notropis atherinoides*) is widely used as a bait minnow.

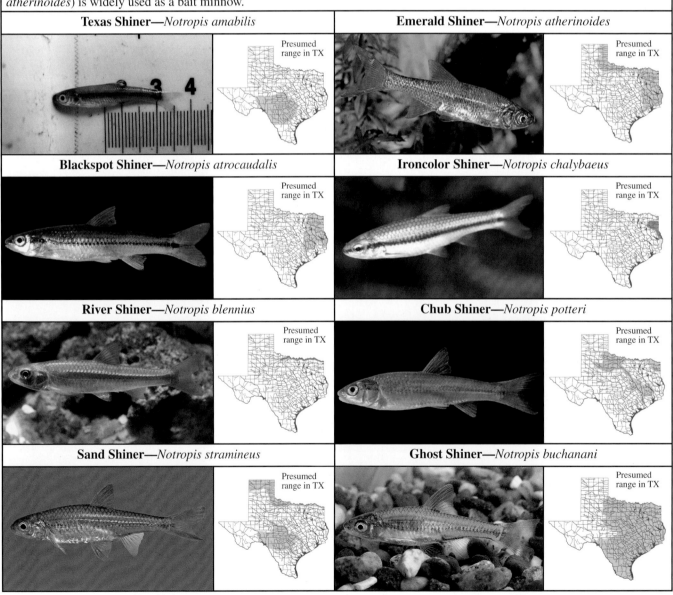

Texas Shiner—*Notropis amabilis*

Emerald Shiner—*Notropis atherinoides*

Blackspot Shiner—*Notropis atrocaudalis*

Ironcolor Shiner—*Notropis chalybaeus*

River Shiner—*Notropis blennius*

Chub Shiner—*Notropis potteri*

Sand Shiner—*Notropis stramineus*

Ghost Shiner—*Notropis buchanani*

Class—**Actinopterygii** (bony fishes)	
Order—**Cypriniformes** (minnows & suckers)	
Family **Cyprinidae** (minnows)	
Genus—*Notropis*—true minnows	

Weed Shiner—*Notropis texanus*	Mimic Shiner—*Notropis volucellus*

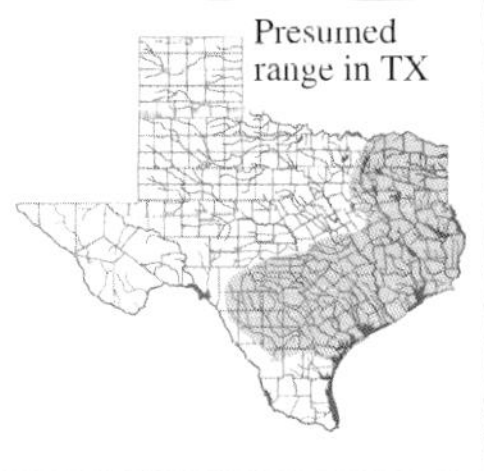

Presumed range in TX

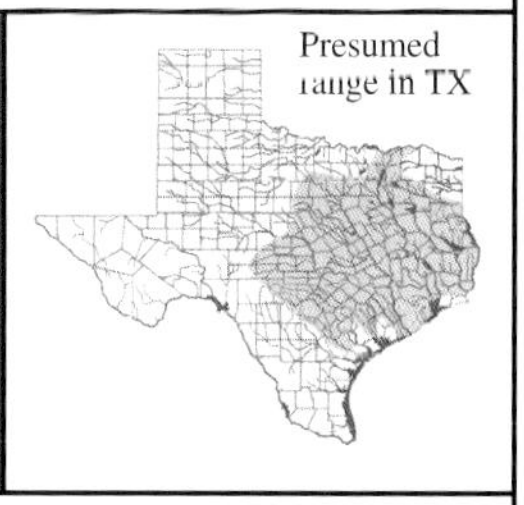

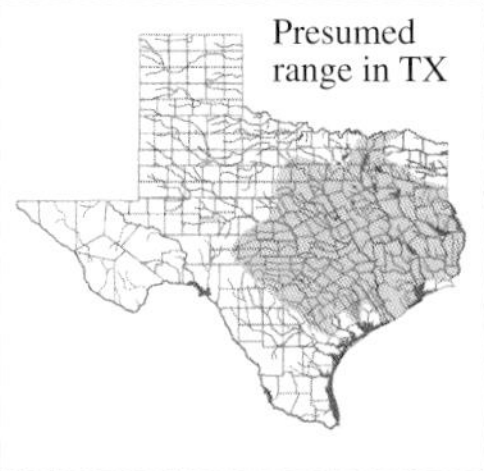

Presumed range in TX

Mimic Shiner—*Notropis volucellus*	Sabine Shiner—*Notropis sabinae*

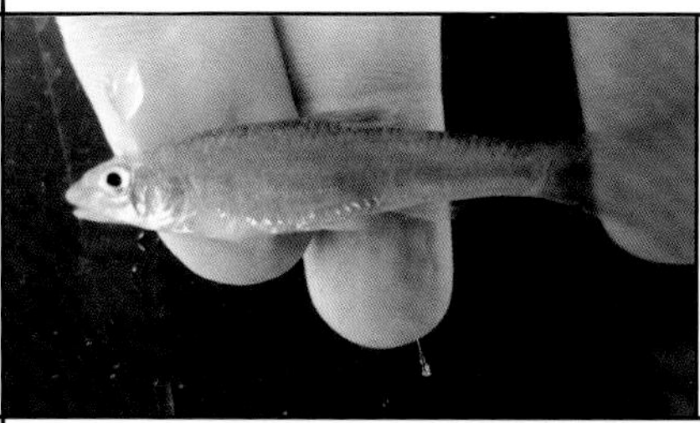

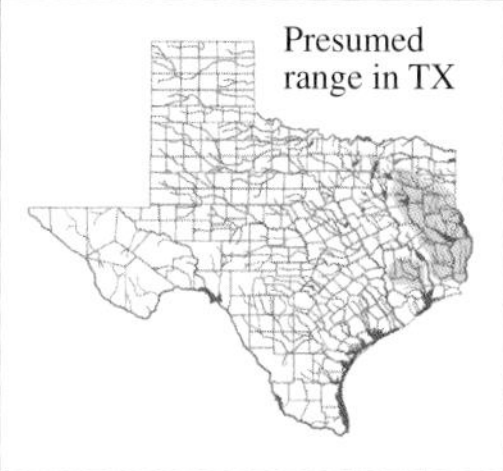

Presumed range in TX

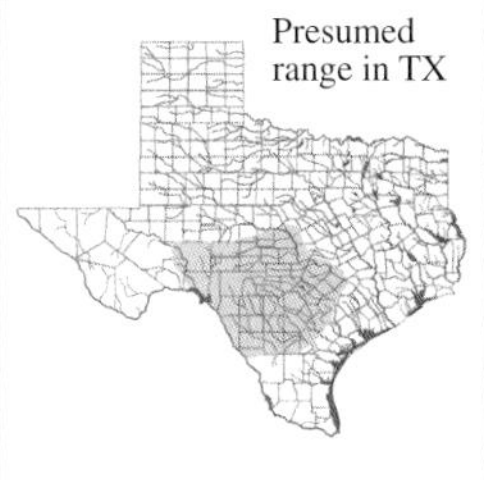

Presumed range in TX

Texas Shiner—*Notropis amabilis*	Tamaulipas Shiner—*Notropis braytoni*

Presumed range in TX

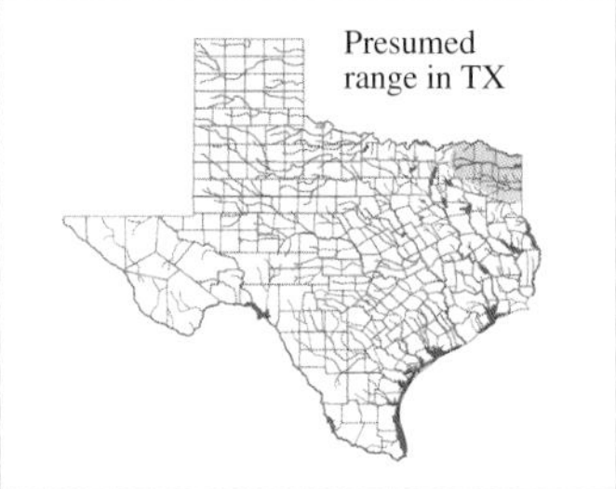

Presumed range in TX

Taillight Shiner *Notropis maculatus*	**Silverband Shiner** *Notropis shumardi*	**Sharpnose Shiner** *Notropis oxyrhynchus*	**Red River Shiner** *Notropis bairdi*
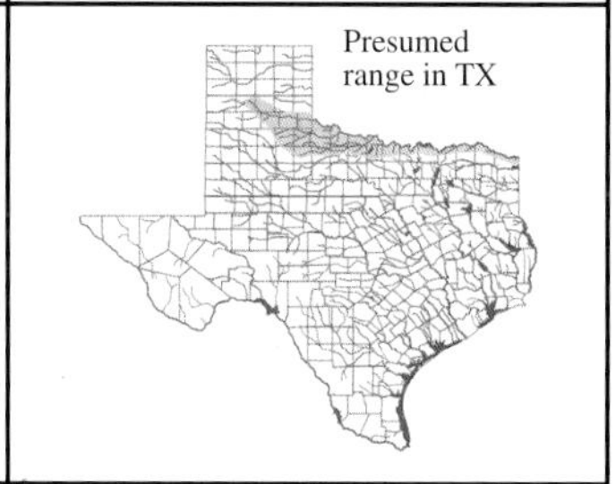 Presumed range in TX	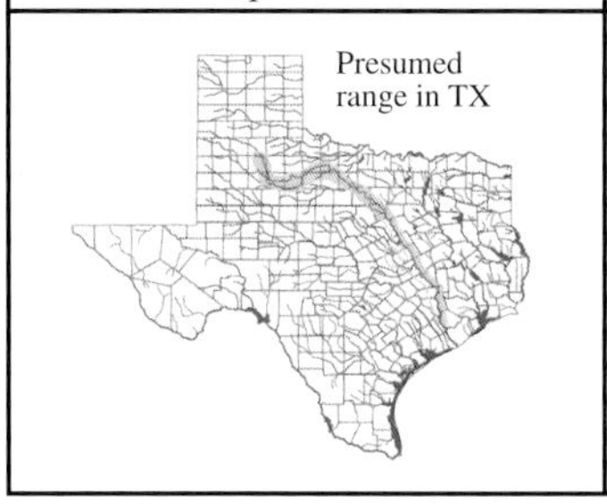 Presumed range in TX	Presumed range in TX	Presumed range in TX
Smalleye Shiner *Notropis buccala*	**Arkansas River Shiner** *Notropis giriardi*	**Rio Grande Shiner** *Notropis jemezanus*	**Chihuahua Shiner** *Notropis chihuahua*
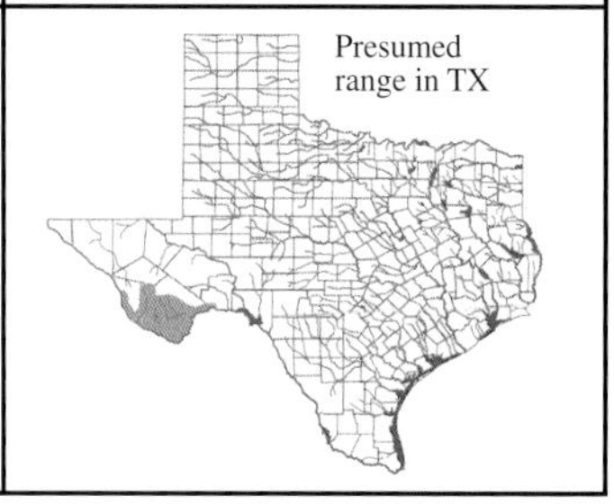 Presumed range in TX	Presumed range in TX	Presumed range in TX	Presumed range in TX

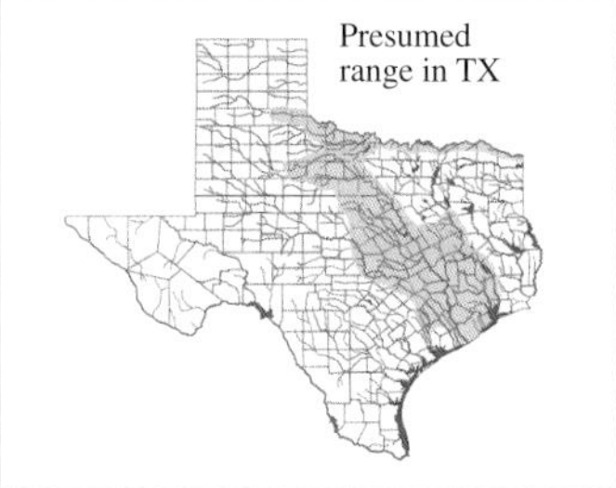

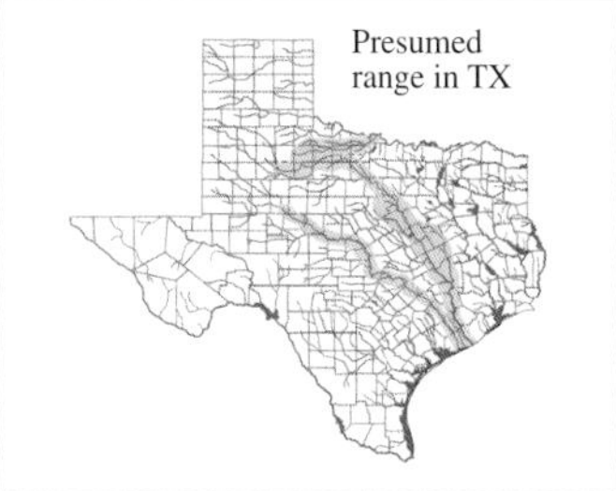

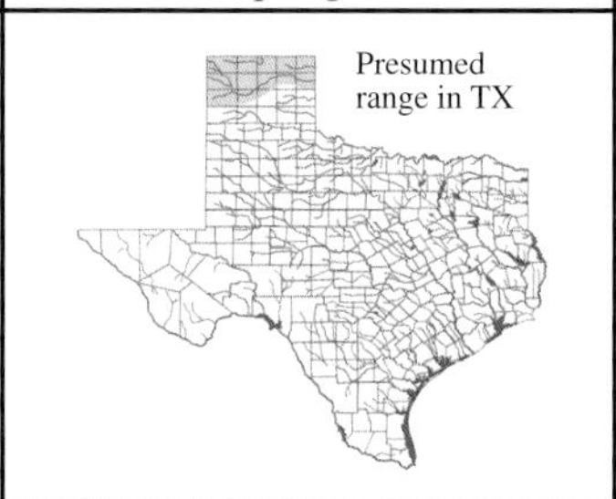

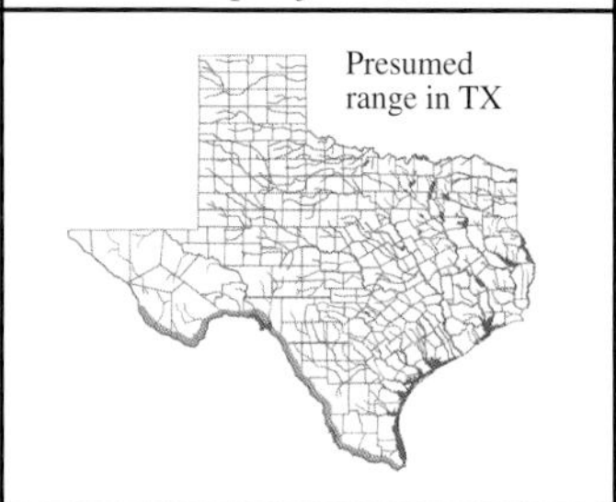

Class—**Actinopterygii** (bony fishes)

Order—**Cypriniformes** (minnows & suckers)

Family—**Cyprinidae** (minnows)

Redfin Shiner	**Ribbon Shiner**	**Striped Shiner**
Lythrurus umbratilis	*Lythrurus fumeus*	*Luxilus chrysocephalus*

Breeding male

Size: Maximum length of 3.5 inches.

Presumed range in TX

Abundance: Widespread in the central US but less common in Texas.

Size: Maximum length is 2.5 inches.

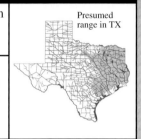
Presumed range in TX

Abundance: Fairly common in low gradient streams in the Coastal Plain.

Size: Can reach a maximum of 8 inches.

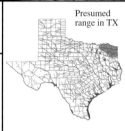
Presumed range in TX

Abundance: Uncommon in Texas. Restricted to northeast corner of state.

Natural History: Habitat is the middle and upper reaches of small and medium-size creeks. Found in creeks with flowing waters, but not necessarily swift currents. This species tolerates turbid waters and in fact shows a preference for low gradient streams that are subject to periodic siltation and muddy waters.

Natural History: The Ribbon Shiner is mostly a lowland species of the lower Gulf Coastal Plain that ranges north as far as southern Illinois. Inhabits creeks and small rivers over mud or sandy substrates. Habitats include a wide variety of streams from still water oxbows to fast flowing mountain creeks.

Natural History: As with many minnow species, the color and pattern of the Striped Shiner can change with age and significant sexual dimorphism also occurs (shown above is a mature male). Habitat is small creeks with sand or gravel bottoms. Found in triburtaries of the Red, Sulphur and Cypress Rivers.

Fathead Minnow	**Bullhead Minnow**	**Bluntnose Minnow**
Pimaphales promelas	*Pimaphales vigilax*	*Pimephales notatus*

Size: Can reach 4 inches long.

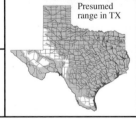
Presumed range in TX

Abundance: Common and widespread in Texas.

Size: Can reach 3.5 inches in length.

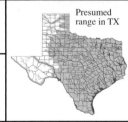
Presumed range in TX

Abundance: Common and widespread in Texas.

Size: Can reach 4.25 inches in length.

Presumed range in TX

Abundance: Rare in scattered populations in Texas.

Natural History: These are very common minnows that may be found in rivers, creeks, reservoirs, and even ponds occasionally. They are tough little fishes that can survive warm, low oxygen waters and waters with high turbidity. Their resilience, rapid reproductive capacity, and ease in rearing in captivity has led to their being widely used as bait minnows, where they are often sold under the nickname "Tuffy."

Natural History: Another minnow that is commercially raised on fish farms for sale as a bait minnow. Because of their prolific use for bait, these minnows have become widely established across the United States and Canada and they are today perhaps the most common fish species in North America. They are mostly bottom feeders that eat both tiny invertebrates as well as algae. Habitat is low gradient, slow moving streams

Natural History: Probably not native to Texas except perhaps in the Red River. However this minnow has been widely introduced across much of the eastern half of America and it can likely be found in scattered locations in Texas. Can be found in lakes, streams and sometimes ponds and has a preference for clear waters and sandy substrates. One of the most common fishes in the eastern United States.

Class—**Actinopterygii** (bony fishes)

Order—**Cypriniformes** (minnows & suckers)

Family—**Cyprinidae** (minnows)

Roundnose Minnows—genus *Dionda* (5 similar species in Texas)

Manantial Roundnose Minnow *Dionda argentosa*	**Devils River Minnow** *Dionda diaboli*	**Guadalupe Roundnose Minnow** *Dionda nigrotaeniata*

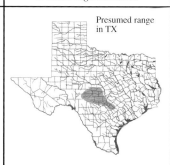

Size: The *Dionda* are small minnows. Most can reach 3 inches. The smallest at 2.5 inches is the Devil's River Roundnose Minnow.

Abundance: Although they may be quite common within their limited range, their restricted distribution makes all these species vulnerable.

Roundnose Minnow *Dionda argentosa*	**Nueces Roundnose Minnow** *Dionda serena*

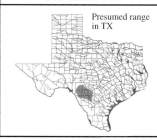

Natural History: All five species of *Dionda* minnows are similar in appearance to the Mannantial Roundnose Minnow shown in the photo above. Most species occur in different drainage basins and thus the easiest way to make an identification is to note the stream from which the specimen is obtained. All species are found in flowing, spring fed headwater streams.

Pallid Shiner *Hybopsis amnis*	**Pugnose Minnow** *Osopoeodus emiliae*	**Bluehead Shiner** *Pteronotropis hubbsi*

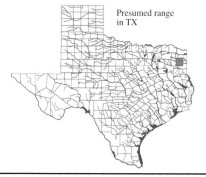

Size: Maximum of 3.25 inches.

Abundance: Has a significant range but some populations have declined.

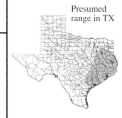

Size: Maximum of 2.5 inches.

Abundance: Common in Coastal Plain streams, fairly common elsewhere.

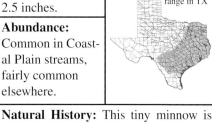

Size: Maximum of 2.25 inches.

Abundance: Rare. A Threatened Species. Very small range in the state.

Natural History: Lives in smaller rivers of eastern Texas where its habitat is quite pools with sand or silt substrate. This species is intolerant of siltation and many populations in Texas may be vulnerable to water quality degradation. Very little is known about the biology of this species. For instance there is little information available of food preferences or breeding.

Natural History: This tiny minnow is widespread across the southeast from South Carolina to eastern Texas. It also ranges northward up the Mississippi and Ohio drainages as far as the southern Great Lakes. Habitat is backwaters and pools of low gradient streams having some aquatic vegetation. Also in swamps and oxbow lakes as well as man-made lakes.

Natural History: The *Pteronotropis* genus of minnows contains nine total species. Males of this genus develop bright breeding colors and enlarged dorsal fins. Most members of this genus live in low gradient, slow moving "blackwater" streams along the lower gulf coast. In Texas the species is known only from the Cypress River basin in northeastern Texas.

Class—**Actinopterygii** (bony fishes)

Order—**Cypriniformes** (minnows & suckers)

Family—**Cyprinidae** (minnows)

Mississippi Silvery Minnow *Hybognathus nuchalis*	**Plains Minnow** *Hybognathus placitus*	**Cypress Minnow** *Hybognathus hayi*

Size: Maximum length of 7 inches.

Presumed range in TX

Abundance: Fairly common in streams in the Piney Woods region.

Natural History: As with the other members of its genus, the Mississippi Silvery Minnow is a bottom feeder that ingest tiny algae and detritus from the silt of sloughs and backwaters. The habitat is low gradient streams ranging from large creeks to rivers but it is probably more common in river tributaries.

Size: Maximum length of 5 inches

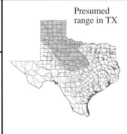
Presumed range in TX

Abundance: Can be quite common in some prairie streams.

Natural History: Although this is still a fairly common minnow in much of the Great Plains Ecoregion, it does face threats. Conversion of grasslands to row crops and the loss of riparian habitat, alterations to natural stream flows, construction of dams, and introduction of predatory fishes pose challenges.

Size: Maximum length of 4.5 inches.

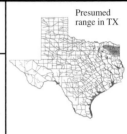
Presumed range in TX

Abundance: Uncommon in Texas with a limited distribution in Texas.

Natural History: This is a lowland species that is found in low gradient streams, backwaters and swamps. It is primarily a southern species but does range northward up the Mississippi Valley as far as southern Illinois. Northern populations in Illinois and Missouri are in decline.

Rio Grande Chub *Gila pandora*	**Suckermouth Minnow** *Phenocobius mirabilis*

1 cm

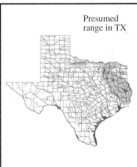
Presumed range in TX

Size: Maximum length of 7 inches.

Presumed range in TX

Abundance: Very rare. Found in a single creek.

Natural History: The range of this fish in Texas is restricted to a single creek in the Davis Mountains. Additional populations exist in New Mexico in portions of the Rio Grande and Pecos River basins. This species requires cool, clear streams with significant current and sandy or gravelly substrates. It is the only member of the *Gila* genus found in Texas. The genus is widespread in the southern Rocky Mountain states.

Size: Averages 4 to 4.25 inches, maximum of 4.75 inches.

Abundance: Generally a fairly common and widespread minnow throughout the Midwest. But it is an uncommon species in Texas. The map above is based on fishes oftexas.org, but it may not occur in many areas shown on the map.

Natural History: Found in streams ranging from creeks to rivers. Inhabits riffle areas with sandy or gravelly substrates. Can withstand periodic turbidity associated with precipitation events. Needs flowing waters to keep riffle areas free of siltation. A bottom feeder that in both habits and appearance resembles a member of the sucker family (family Catostomidae), but it is in the minnow family (family Cyprinidae). It feeds in sucker-like fashon on bottom dwelling invertebrate organism that may be sucked from the stream substrate of sand or gravel. The aquatic larval forms of Caddisflies and Mayflies are reported to be important elements in the diet. May be more widespread in Texas than range map shows. Possibly occurs in the Panhandle and in the lower Colorado River.

Class—**Actinopterygii** (bony fishes)

Order—**Cyprinodontiformes** (topminnows & livebearers)

Family—**Fundulidae** (topminnows)

Blackspotted Topminnow *Fundulus olivaceus*	Blackstripe Topminnow *Fundulus notatus*	Western Starhead Topminnow *Fundulus blairae*
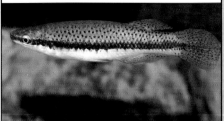		

Blackspotted Topminnow
Fundulus olivaceus

Size: Maximum of 3.75 inches.

Abundance: Common in small, streams in eastern part of Texas.

Presumed range in TX

Natural History: The topminnows get their name from the fact that they are always seen right at the water's surface. They have a white spot on the top of the head that is easily visible from above. They feed on both aquatic insects and tiny terrestrial insects that fall or fly onto the water. Nearly identical to the next species but has larger spots than the similar Blackstriped Topminnow.

Blackstripe Topminnow
Fundulus notatus

Size: Maximum of 3 inches.

Abundance: Common in creeks in eastern part of Texas.

Presumed range in TX

Natural History: This is one of the few *Fundulus* species to occupy upland streams. Most are lowland fishes. Although they are found in flowing streams, all prefer quite pools and backwaters for a microhabitat, including beaver ponds, swamps, and low gradient streams throughout their range. Nearly identical to the preceding species but black spots are much smaller.

Western Starhead Topminnow
Fundulus blairae

Size: Maximum of 3 inches.

Abundance: Common in still and slow moving water in east Texas.

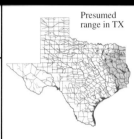
Presumed range in TX

Natural History: Like most *Fundulus* species, this fish likes still waters in swamps, beaver ponds, oxbows, and small, slow moving creeks. It can also be found in shoreline shallows of man-made lakes. Enjoys clear waters with abundant vegetation. The name "Starhead" Minnow comes from the light spot on the top of the head that is characteristic of the *Fundulus* genus.

Golden Topminnow
Fundulus chrysotus

Size: Maximum length of 3 inches.

Abundance: Fairly common in eastern Texas.

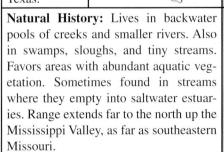
Presumed range in TX

Natural History: Lives in backwater pools of creeks and smaller rivers. Also in swamps, sloughs, and tiny streams. Favors areas with abundant aquatic vegetation. Sometimes found in streams where they empty into saltwater estuaries. Range extends far to the north up the Mississippi Valley, as far as southeastern Missouri.

Gulf Killifish
Fundulus grandis

Size: Maximum of 5.8 inches.

Abundance: Common in coastal streams.

Presumed range in TX

Natural History: A saltwater marsh and estuarine species that can be found along the coast from southern Florida to Veracruz, Mexico. They will enter freshwater rivers and populations exist hundreds of miles inland. Inland populations in Texas occur in the Rio Grande, Pecos, and Brazos Rivers as well as the mouths of all streams in coastal areas.

Northern Plains Killifish
Fundulus kansae

Size: Maximum length of 4 inches.

Abundance: Uncommon. Has a small range in Texas.

Presumed range in TX

Natural History: Adapted to the murky waters common in streams in much of the northern Great Plains. This species was recently split from the Plains Killifish based on DNA studies. All Plains Killifish north of the Red River drainage are now regarded as being *kansae* and all south of the Canadian River in Texas are *zebrinus*.

Class—**Actinopterygii** (bony fishes)

Order—**Cyprinodontiformes** (topminnows & livebearers)

Family—**Fundulidae** (topminnows)

Plains Killifish *Fundulus zebrinus*	**Rainwater Killifish** *Lucania parva*	**Bluefin Killifish** *Lucana goodei*

Size: Maximum length of 4 inches.

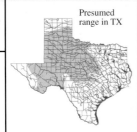
Presumed range in TX

Abundance: Common but some populations extirpated in Texas.

Natural History: The Plains Killifish is adapted to the rather harsh conditions that can be common in streams in arid regions. This fish can withstand waters with low oxygen and high salinity or alkalinity, a common stream condition in some regions of its range in western Texas. Favors streams with sandy substrates ranging in size from small creeks to small rivers.

Size: Maximum of 2.75 inches.

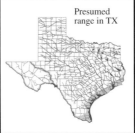
Presumed range in TX

Abundance: Common, especially in coastal streams.

Natural History: This is a saltwater marsh and estuarine species that can be found along the coast from southern New England to northern Mexico. They will enter freshwater rivers and are known to ascend upstream for hundreds of miles. Permanently freshwater populations exist in Texas in the Rio Grande and Pecos Rivers as well as all streams in coastal areas.

Size: Maximum length of 2 inches.

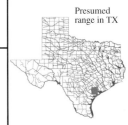
Presumed range in TX

Abundance: Very rare. Introduced in the lower Guadalupe basin.

Natural History: A tiny but gorgeous little fish that is prized by native fish enthusiasts and aquarists. Found in all types of quiet waters including in backwaters and pools of streams from tiny creeks to medium-size rivers. Favors waters with abundant vegetation. Reportedly can be common in springs. Breeding males acquire a rainbow of colors in the dorsal and caudal fins.

Family—**Cyprinidontidae** (pupfishes)

Sheepshead Minnow *Cyprinodon variagatus*	**Inland Pupfishes**—genus *Cyprinodon*

Inland Pupfishes—genus *Cyprinodon*

Size: These are small fishes, most are only 2.25 inches in length. The Comanche Springs Pupfish is the largest at 2.5 inches.

Abundance: All but Red River Pupfish are rare with limited distribution.

Natural History: These fishes live mostly in springs and spring runs in the arid regions of west Texas. They are highly vulnerable and all but the Red River Pupfish are regarded as threatened or endangered. All the Pupfishes are similar in appearance to the Sheepshead Minnow.

Size: Maximum length about 3 inches.

Abundance: Fairly common along the coast.

Natural History: A marine species that follows rivers and streams well inland into freshwater environments. Populations in inland areas such as in the Trans-Pecos region are apparently the result of introductions by man.

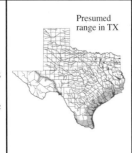
Presumed range in TX

Pecos Pupfish *Cyprinodon pecosensis*

Conchos Pupfish *Cyprinodon eximus*

Red River Pupfish *Cyprinodon rubrofluviatilis*

Leon Springs Pupfish *Cyprinodon bovinus*

Comanche Springs Pupfish *Cyprinodon elegans*

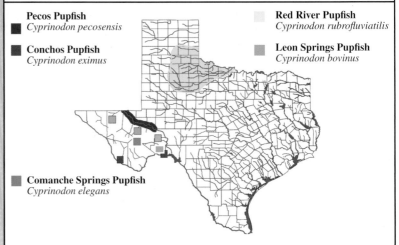

Class—**Actinopterygii** (bony fishes)

Order—**Cyprinidontiformes** (topminnows & livebearers)

Family—**Poeciliidae** (livebearers)

Sailfin Molly *Poecilia latpinna*	**Amazon Molly** *Poecilia formosa*	**Least Killifish** *Heterandria formosa*

Size: Maximum of 6 inches.

Abundance: Common. Found in both freshwaters and brackish coastal waters.

Presumed range in TX

Natural History: Named for the exceptionally large dorsal fin of the male. Inhabits the lower coastal plain from South Carolina to northern Mexico, including much of the Texas coastal plain. Lives in still waters. Mainly a freshwater species but also inhabits brackish waters. Can be common near springs and inland populations exist in Texas.

Size: Maximum of 3.5 inches.

Abundance: Fairly common. Always occurs in regions with other Molly species.

Presumed range in TX

Natural History: This is an all female species that mates with males from another related species (often the Sailfin Molly) but does not incorporate the genetic material from the sperm into the egg. Instead the sperm merely stimulates the egg to begin to divide and ultimately produces a genetic clone of the female (process is known as Gynogenesis).

Size: Maximum under 1.5 inches.

Abundance: Common and widespread. Found throughout most of the state.

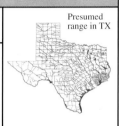
Presumed range in TX

Natural History: This is one of North America's smallest fish species. It ranges throughout much of the gulf coast region all the way to Florida. In Texas it is restricted to the eastern gulf coast. It inhabits quite waters of all types and favors areas with heavy vegetation. Mainly a freshwater species but sometimes can be found in slightly brackish waters.

Western Mosquitofish *Gambusia affinis*	**Rare Texas Mosquitofishes**—genus *Gambusia* 9 species in Texas

Male
Female

Size: Maximum 2.5 inches.

Abundance: Very common in swamps and backwaters.

Presumed range in TX

Natural History: True to their name, these tiny fish eat large numbers of mosquito larva. Like other members of their family they give birth to fully formed young. They live in the shallows of swamps and backwaters and will forage in water less than an inch deep.

Size: Tiny. Most can reach a maximum of 2.25 inches. The smallest is the San Felipe Gambusia at 1.5 inches. Females reach a larger size than males.

Abundance: All are rare with very finite distributions. Six of the species below are listed as Threatened or Endangered.

Natural History: All the rare Mosquitofish shown on the map below are nearly indistinguishable from the Western Mosquitofish. But these populations are distinct and often isolated. Some are restricted to a single creek or spring run.

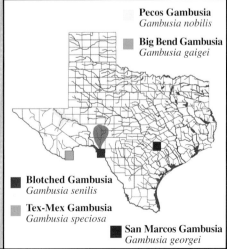

Pecos Gambusia
Gambusia nobilis

Big Bend Gambusia
Gambusia gaigei

Blotched Gambusia
Gambusia senilis

Tex-Mex Gambusia
Gambusia speciosa

San Marcos Gambusia
Gambusia georgei

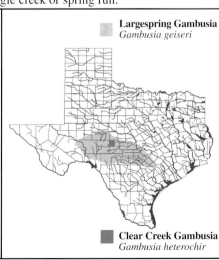

Largespring Gambusia
Gambusia geiseri

Clear Creek Gambusia
Gambusia heterochir

Class—**Actinopterygii** (bony fishes)

Order—**Plueronectiformes** (flatfishes)

Family—**Paralichthyidae** (flounders)

Southern Flounder
Paralichthys lethostigma

Size: Can reach a maximum of 30 inches in length.

Abundance: Uncommon in fresh water. Common in marine habitat.

Presumed range in TX

Natural History: Members of this genus are often known as "Sand Flounders." Sand flounders are highly specialized fish bottom fish that can change their colors to match the color of the substrate in their location.

Family—**Achiridae** (soles)

Hogchocker
Trinectes maculatus

Size: Can reach a maximum of 8 inches in length.

Abundance: Uncommon in fresh water. Common in marine habitat.

Presumed range in TX

Natural History: Found in both salt and fresh waters in Texas. Ascends rivers well inland and may be more widespread inland than indicated by the map above. Favors clear waters with sandy substrates.

Order—**Beloniformes**

Family—**Belonidae** (needlefish)

Atlantic Needlefish
Strongylura marina

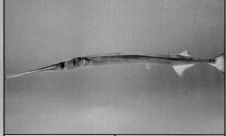

Size: Maximum 27 inches, average about 18.

Abundance: Uncommon in fresh water. Common in marine habitats.

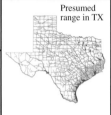
Presumed range in TX

Natural History: In addition to the Atlantic Needlefish, one other needlefish occurs in Texas waters. The **Redfin Needlefish** (*S. notata*), is rather rare in freshwater habitats, but can be found in the mouths of rivers and estuaries.

Order—**Atheriniformes**

Family—**Atherinopsidae** (silversides)

Brook Silverside
Labidesthes sicculus

Size: Maximum of 4.75 inches.

Abundance: Fairly common.

Natural History: Found in creeks and stream backwaters. Usually in schools and nearly always near the surface, usually within a few inches.

Presumed range in TX

Mississippi Silverside
Menidia audens

Size: Maximum length about 5 inches.

Abundance: Fairly common.

Natural History: Silversides travel in large schools near the surface of lakes and rivers and they area an important prey for many game fish species.

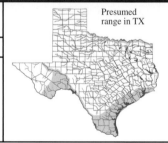
Presumed range in TX

Inland Silverside
Menidia berryllina

Size: Maximum size 5 inches.

Abundance: Common.

Natural History: Travels in large schools near the surface of lakes, rivers, and coastal waterways. Seems to favor sand or gravel substrates.

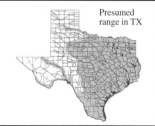
Presumed range in TX

Rough Silverside
Membras martinica

Size: To 4.75 inches.

Abundance: Fairly common.

Natural History: Found mainly in coastal waters. Introduced populations in Falcon Reservoir and Amistad Reservoir (fishesoftexas.org).

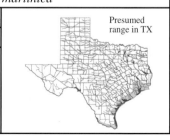
Presumed range in TX

Class—**Agnatha** (jawless fishes)

Order—**Petromyzontiformes** (lampreys)

Family—**Petromyzontidae** (northern lampreys)

Southern Brook Lamprey *Ichthyomyzon gagei*	**Chestnut Lamprey** *Ichthyomyzon castaneus*

Size: Maximum of 6.8 inches in length.	**Size:** Can reach a maximum of 15 inches in length.
Abundance: Fairly common in east Texas streams.	**Abundance:** Fairly common in east Texas streams.

| **Natural History:** The lampreys are so different from all other Texas fishes that they are in their own class of animals. They lack jaws and bones (instead have cartilaginous skeletons). They also lack scales and pectoral and pelvic fins. They live in streams throughout North America. | 
Presumed range in TX | **Natural History:** Among their many differences from the typical fishes, the lampreys have a larval stage in their life cycle. Known as ammocytes, the eyeless larva persist for several years before developing eyes and changing into adults. The Chestnut Lamprey is parasitic on other fishes as an adult. | 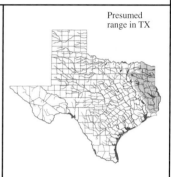
Presumed range in TX |

REFERENCES

Chapter 1: The Face of the Land & Chapter 2: Ecoregions and Habitats of Texas

Print

Bailey, Robert G. 2009. *Ecosystem Geography, From Ecoregions to Sites.* Springer Science & Business Media, New York, NY.

Hunt, Charles B. 1974. *Natural Regions of the United States and Canada.* W.H. Freeman and Company, San Francisco, CA.

Ricketts, Taylor, H., Eric Dinerstein, David M. Olson, and Col J Loucks, et al. 1999. *Terrestrial Ecoregions of North America.* World Wildlife Fund and Island Press. Washington, DC.

Internet

Commission for Environmental Cooperation—cec.org

The Encyclopedia of Earth—eol.earth.org

One Earth—oneearth.org

The Texas Handbook Texas/State Historical Society—tshaonline.org

Texas Alamanac—texasalmanac.com

Trees of Texas by Texas A&M—texastreeid.tamu.edu

Texas Parks and Wildlife Department—tpwd.texas.gov

US Environmental Protection Agency/Ecoregions of North America—epa.gov/wed/pages/ecoregions.htm

USGS—usgs/science/geology/regions

Chapter 3: Wildlife Conservation in Texas

Internet

Texas Parks and Wildlife Department—tpwd.texas.gov

Texan by Nature—texanbynature.org

International Union for Conservation of Nature—iucnredlist.org

Nature Serve Explorer—natureserve.org

Smithsonian National Museum of Natural History—mnh.si.edu

Mammalian Species, American Society of Mammalogists species accounts—science.smith.edu

Chapter 4: The Mammals of Texas

Print

Barbour, Roger W. and Wayne Davis. 1974. *Mammals of Kentucky.* University Press of Kentucky. Lexington, KY.

Bauer, Erwin A. and Peggy Bauer. 1993. *Whitetails: behavior, ecology and conservation.* Voyageur Press, Inc., Stillwater, MN.

Bowers, Nora, Rick Bowers and Kenn Kafuman. 2004. *Mammals of North America.* Houghton Mifflin Company. NY, NY.

COSEWIC. 2009. Assessment and update status report on the Swift Fox Vulpes velox in Canada. Committee on the Status of Endangered Wildlife in Canada. Ottawa. v+44pp.

Feldhamer, George A. 1980. "Cervus nippon." Mammalian Species 128: 1–7.

Gonzales, Laurie Lomas and Krysta D. Demere. 2018. "A Noteworthy Longevity Record for Rafinesque's Big-eared Bat (*Corynorhinus rafinesquii*)." *Bat Research News* Vol.58: No.3. Hall, E.R. 1951.

Hall, E.R. 1951. *American Weasels.* University of Kansas Museum of Natural History. Vol.4: 1‑466.

Jefferson, Kamren P,. S. Leigh Ann Garcia, Dianna M. Krejsa, J. Clint Perkins, Skyler Stevens, Ramyond S. Matlack and Robert C. Dowler. "Noteworthy Records, Range Extensions, and Conservation Status of Skunk Species in Texas." Occasional Papers, Museum of Texas Tech University 384:1–13.

Kays, Roland W. and Don. E. Wilson. 2009. *Mammals of North America.* Princeton University Press. Princeton, NJ.

Light, Jessica E., Marcy O. Ostroff, and David J. Haffner. 2016. "Phylogeographic Assessment of the Northern Pygmy Mouse, *Baiomys taylori.*" *Journal of Mammalogy*, Vol. 97, Issue 4. 1081–1094.

Matthew E. Gompper. 1996. "Sociality and asociality in White-nosed Coatis (Nasua narica): foraging costs and benefits." *Behavioral Ecology*, Vol 7, Issue 3.

McDonough, Molly M., Adam W. Ferguson, Robert C. Dowler, Matthew E. Gompper and Jesus E. Maldonado. "Phylogenomic systematics of the spotted skunks (Carnivora, Mephitidae, Spilogale): Additional species diversity and Pleistocene climate change as a major driver of diversification." bioRxiv doi:10.1101/2020.10.23.353045

McKinney, Billy Pat. 1996. "A Field Guide to the Mountain Lions of Texas." Texas Parks and Wildlife Department. Austin, TX; Schmidly, David J. and Robert D. Bradley. 2016. *The Mammals of Texas*, Seventh Edition. The University of Texas Press.

Schmidly, David J. and Robert D. Bradley. 2016. *The Mammals of Texas Seventh Edition.* The University of Texas Press, Austin, TX.

Trani, Margaret K., Mark Ford and Brian R. Chapman. 2007. *The Land Manager's Guide to Mammals of the South.* The Nature Conservancy, Southeast Region. Durham, NC.

Walker, E.P. 1983. *Walkers Mammals of the World.* The John's Hopkins University Press. Baltimore, MD.

Whitaker, John O. Jr. and W. J. Hamilton Jr. 1998. *Mammals of the Eastern United States.* Cornell University Press. Ithaca, NY.

Whitsett, Juliet. 2021. *The Complete Threatened and Endangered Species of Texas List.* Austin, TX.

Wilson, Don E. and Sue Ruff. 1999. *North American Mammals.* Smithsonian Institution.

Yancy, Franklin D, Richard W. Manning, Jim R. Goetze, Laramie L. Lindsey, Robert D. Bradley, and Clyde Jones. "The Hooded Skunk (Mephitis macroura) from the Davis Mountains of West Texas: Natural History, Morphology, Molecular Characteristics, and Conservation Status." *Texas Journal of Science* 69: 87–95.

Zabriskie, James E., Patricia L. Cutler and James N. Stuart. 2019. "Range Extension of the Western Yellow Bat (Dasypterus xanthinus) in New Mexico." *Western Wildlife* 6: 1–4.

Internet

American Society of Mammalogists—mammalogy.org

Animal Diversity Web—animaldiversity.org

Encyclopedia of Life—eol.org

Florida Bat Conservancy—floridabats.org

International Union for Conservation of Nature—iucnredlist.org

Kentucky Bat Working Group—biology.eku.edu/bats

Mammalian Species, American Society of Mammalogists species accounts—science.smith.edu

Nature Serve Explorer—natureserve.org

Smithsonian National Museum of Natural History—mnh.si.edu

Texas Parks and Wildlife Department—tpwd.texas.gov

The Swift Fox in Texas—tpwd.texas.gov/publications/pwdpubs/media/pwd_br_w7000_0032.pdf

U.S. Fish and Wildlife Service—fws.gov

West Texas Bat Group—westtexasbats.org

Chapter 5: The Birds of Texas

Print

Bryan, K. et al. 2003. *A Checklist of Texas Birds.* Texas Parks and Wildlife. PWD BK P4000-000M (1-03.

Benson, K.L.P. and K.A. Arnold. 2001. *Texas Breeding Bird Atlas.* Texas A&M University System, College and Corpus Christi, TX.

Clark, William S. and Brian K. Wheeler. 1987. *A Field Guide to Hawks-North America.* Peterson Field Guides, Houghton Mifflin Co. Boston, MA.

Dunn, John L., Kimball Garret, Thomas Shultz, and Cindy House. *A Field Guide to Warblers of North America.* Peterson Field Guides, Houghton Mifflin Co. Boston, MA.

Farrand, John, Jr. 1998. *An Audubon Handbook, Eastern Birds.* McGraw Hill Book Co. New York, NY.

Floyd, Ted. 2008. *Smithsonian Field Guide to the Birds of North America.* Harper Collins Publishers. New York, NY.

Johnsgard, Paul A. 1988. *North American Owls, Biology and Natural History.* Smithsonian Institution Press, Washington, DC.

Kaufman, Ken. 2000. *The Birds of North America.* Houghton Mifflin Co., New York, NY.

Lockwood, Mark. 2008. *Birds of the Edwards Plateau, a field checklist.* Texas Parks and Wildlife, Austin, TX.

Peterson, Roger T. 1980. *A Field Guide to the Birds, Eastern Birds.* Houghton Mifflin Co., Boston, MA.

Mengel, Robert M. 1965. *The Birds of Kentucky.* American Ornithologist's Union Monogram, no. 3. The Allen Press, Lawrence, KS.

National Geographic Society. 1999. *Field Guide to the Birds of North America.* National Geographic Society, Washington, DC.

Olberholser, H. C. 1974. *The Bird Life of Texas.* University of Texas Press, Austin, TX.

Shackleford, Clifford E. and Mark W. Lockwood. 2000. *The Birds of Tesas: Occurrence and Seasonal Movements.* Texas Parks and Wildlife.

Sibley, David Allen. 2003. *Field Guide to Birds of Western North America.* Alfred A. Knopf Chanticleer Press, New York, NY.

Vanner, Micheal. 2003. *The Encyclopedia of North American Birds.* Parragon Publishing, Bath, UK.

Whitsett, Juliet. 2021. *The Complete Threatened and Endangered Species of Texas List.* Austin, TX.

Internet

Audubon Guide to North American Birds—audubon.org

American Bird Conservancy—abcbirds.org

Cornell University Lab of Ornithology-Birds of North America Online—birds.bna.cornell.edu.bna/species.

Ebird—ebird.org

Encyclopedia of Life—eol.org

Environment Canada—ec.gc.ca

Houston Audubon Society—houstonaudubon.org

McGill Bird Observatory—migrationresearch.org

NatureServe Explorer—natureserve.org

Waterfowl Hunting Management in North America—flyways.us

Merlin Bird Guide

National Wild Turkey Foundation—nwtf.org

U.S. Fish and Wildlife Service—fws.gov

Chapter 6: The Turtles of Texas

Print

Ashton, Ray E. Jr. and Patricia Sawyer Ashton. 1985. *Handbook of Reptiles and Amphibians of Florida, Part Two—Lizards, Turtles and Crocodilians.* Windward Publishing, Miami, FL.

Bartlett, R.D. and Patricia Bartlett. 1999. *A Field Guide to Florida Reptiles and Amphibians.* Gulf Publishing Co., Houston, TX.

Buhlmann, Kurt. Tracey Tuberville, and Whit Gibbons. 2008. *Turtles of the Southeast.* The University of Georgia Press, Athens, GA.

Carr, Archie and Coleman J. Goin. 1955 *Guide to the Reptiles, Amphibians and Fresh Water Fishes of Florida.* University of Florida Press, Gainesville, Florida.

Collins, Joseph T. and Travis W. Taggart. 2009. *Standard Common and Scientific Names for North American Amphibians, Turtles, Reptiles & Crocodilians.* The Center for North American Herpetology, Hays, KS.

Conant Roger, and Joseph T. Collins. 1998. *Reptiles and Amphibians of Eastern/Central North America.* Houghton Mifflin Co., Boston-New York.

Ernst, Carl H., Jeffrey E. Lovich, and Roger W. Barbour. 1994. *The Turtles of the United States and Canada.* Smithsonian Institute Press. Washington and London.

Hibbets, Troy D. and Terry L. Hibbets. 2016. *Texas Turtles and Crocodilians, A Field Guide.* University of Texas Press, Austin, Texas.

Niemiller, Matthew L., R. Graham Reynolds, and Brian T. Miller. 2013. *The Reptiles of Tennessee.* The University of Tennessee Press, Knoxville, TN.

Trauth, Stanley E., Henry W. Robison, and Michael V. Plummer. 2004. *The Amphibians and Reptiles of Arkansas.* The University of Arkansas Press, Fayetteville, AR.

Turtle Taxonomy Working Group (Rhodin, A.G.J., Iverson, J.B., Bour, R., Fritz, U., Georges, A., Shaffer, H.B., and van Duk,P.P. 2021. *Turtles of the World: Annotated Checklist and Atlas of Taxonomy, Synonymy,*

Distribution, and Conservation Status (9th Ed.). In: Rhodin, A. G. J., Iverson, J.B., van Dijk, P.P., Stanford, C. B., Goode, E.V., Buhlmann, K.A. and Mittermeier, R. A. (Eds.). "Conservation Biology of Freshwater Turtles and Tortoises: A Compilation Project of the IUCN/SSC Tortoise and Freshwater Turtle Specialist Working Group." Chelonian Research Monographs 8:1–472. doi:10.3854/crm.8checklist.atlas.v9.2021.

Whitsett, Juliet. 2021. *The Complete Threatened and Endangered Species of Texas List.* Austin, TX.

Internet

NatureServe Explorer—natureserve.org

iNaturalist—inaturalist.org

International Union of Concerned Naturalists—iucnredlist.org

Kingsnake.com—kingsnake.com

Texas Parks and Wildlife Department—tpwd.texas.gov

Texas Turtles—texasturtles.org

Chapter 7: The Crocodilians of Texas

Print

Ashton, Ray E. Jr. and Patricia Sawyer Ashton. 1985. *Handbook of Reptiles and Amphibians of Florida, Part Two—Lizards, Turtles and Crocodilians.* Windward Publishing, Miami, FL.

Bartlett, R.D. and Patricia Bartlett. 1999. *A Field Guide to Florida Reptiles and Amphibians.* Gulf Publishing Co., Houston, TX.

Hibbets, Troy D. and Terry L. Hibbets. 2016. *Texas Turtles and Crocodilians, A Field Guide.* University of Texas Press, Austin, Texas.

Jones, Lawrence L.C. and Robert E. Lovich. 2009. *Lizards of the American Southwest, A Photographic Field Guide.* Rio Nuevo Publishers, Tucson, AZ.

Internet

iNaturalist—inaturalist.org
Texas Parks and Wildlife Department—tpwd.texas.gov

Chapter 8: The Reptiles of Texas

Print

Boundy, Jeff and John L. Carr. 2017. *The Amphibians and Reptiles of Louisiana, An Identification and Reference Guide.* Louisiana State University Press. Baton Rouge, Louisiana.

Camper, Jeffrey D. and James R. Dixon. 2002. "Clutch and Ovum Sizes of Three Species of Whipsnakes (Masticophis, Colubridae)." *The Southwest Naturalist.* Vol. 47, No.3 pp467–471.

Collins, Joseph T. and Travis W. Taggart. 2009. *Standard Common and Scientific Names for North American Amphibians, Turtles, Reptiles & Crocodilians.* The Center for North American Herpetology, Hays, KS.

Conant Roger, and Joseph T. Collins. 1998. *Reptiles and Amphibians of Eastern/Central North America.* Houghton Mifflin Co., Boston-New York.

Degenhardt, William G., Charles W. Painter and Andrew H. Price. 1996. *Amphibians and Reptiles of New Mexico.* University of New Mexico Press. Albuquerque, New Mexico,

Dixon, James R. 1987. *Amphibians and Reptiles of Texas.* Texas A & M University Press, College Station, Texas.

Dixon, James R. and John E. Werler. 2000. *Texas Snakes, A Field Guide.* University of Texas Press, Austin, Texas.

Dundee, Harold A. and Douglas A. Rossman. 1989. *The Amphibians and Reptiles of Louisiana.* Louisiana State University Press. Baton Rouge, Louisiana.

"Food habits of three species of striped whipsnakes (Serpentes, Colubridae)." The Free Library. 2000. Texas Academy of Science 13 Sept. 2023.

Goldberg, Stephen R. 2004. "Reproductive Cycle of Smith's Blackheaded Snake *Tantilla hobartsmithi* (Serpentes: Colubridae), in Arizona." Western North American Naturalist 64 (1) pp141–143.

Javier, Rodriguez A. and Harry W. Green. 1999. Food habits of the long-nosed snake (*Rhinocheilus lecontei*) *Journal of the Zoological Society of London.* 248 pp 489–499.

Johnson, Tom R. 2000. *The Amphibians and Reptiles of Missouri.* Missouri Department of Conservation. Jefferson City, MO.

Jones, Lawrence L.C. and Robert E. Lovich. 2009. *Lizards of the American Southwest, A Photographic Field Guide.* Rio Nuevo Publishers, Tucson, AZ.

McBride, Dustin L. 2009. "Distribution and Status of the Brazos Water Snake (*Nerodia harteri harteri*)." Masters Thesis, Tarleton State University.

Middendorf, George A. and Wade C. Sherbrooke. 1992. "Canid Elicitation of Blood Squirting in a Horned Lizard (*Phrysoma cornutum*)." Copeia. Vol. 1992, No. 2, pp 519–527.

Powell, Robert, Roger Conant and Joseph T. Collins. *Field Guide to Reptiles and Amphibians of Eastern/Central North America. 2016.* Houghton, Miflin, Harcourt. Boston, New York.

Shupe, Scott. 2005. *US Guide to Venomous Snakes and Their Mimics.* Skyhorse Publishing, New York, NY

Shupe, Scott. Editor. 2012. *Venomous Snakes of the World, A Manual for US Amphibious Forces.* Skyhorse Publishing, New York, NY.

Sievert, Greg and Lynnette Sievert. 2005. *Field Guide to Oklahoma's Amphibians and Reptiles.* Oklahoma Department of Wildlife Conservation. Oklahoma City, Oklahoma.

Stebbins, Robert C. *Western Reptiles and Amphibians.* 2003. Houghton Miflin Company, Boston-New York

Trauth, Stanley E., Henry W. Robinson and Micheal V. Plummer. 2004. *The Amphibians and Reptiles of Arkansas.* University of Arkansas Press. Fayetteville, Arkansas.

Internet

Brazos River Authority—brazos.org
California Herps.com—herpedia.com
Center for Biological Diversity—biologicaldiversity.org
Clinical Toxinology Resources—toxinology.com
Herpedia.com—herpedia.com
HerpsofArkansas.com—herpsofarkansas.com
iNaturalist—inaturalist.org
Nature Serve Explorer—explorer.natureserve.org
Repfocus, A Survery of the Reptiles of the World—repfocus.dk
The Reptile Database—reptiledatabase.org
Texas Invasive Species Institute—tsusinvasive.org
Texas Parks and Wildlife Department—tpwd.texas.gov
Wild Herps—wildherps.com

Chapter 9: The Amphibians of Texas

Print

Boundy, Jeff and John L. Carr. 2017. *The Amphibians and Reptiles of Louisiana, An Identification and Reference Guide.* Louisiana State University Press. Baton Rouge, Louisiana.

Collins, Joseph T. and Travis W. Taggart. 2009. *Standard Common and Scientific Names for North American Amphibians, Turtles, Reptiles & Crocodilians.* The Center for North American Herpetology, Hays, KS.

Conant Roger, and Joseph T. Collins. 1998. *Reptiles and Amphibians of Eastern/Central North America.* Houghton Mifflin Co., Boston-New York.

Degenhardt, William G., Charles W. Painter and Andrew H. Price. 1996. *Amphibians and Reptiles of New Mexico.* University of New Mexico Press. Albuquerque, New Mexico,

Dixon, James R. 1987. *Amphibians and Reptiles of Texas.* Texas A & M University Press, College Station, Texas.

Dodd, C. Kenneth. 2013. *Frogs of the United States and Canada.* Johns Hopkins University Press, Baltimore, MD.

Dundee, Harold A. and Douglas A. Rossman. 1989. *The Amphibians and Reptiles of Louisiana.* Louisiana State University Press. Baton Rouge, Louisiana.

Johnson, Tom R. 2000. *The Amphibians and Reptiles of Missouri.* Missouri Department of Conservation. Jefferson City, MO.

Powell, Robert, Roger Conant and Joseph T. Collins. *Field Guide to Reptiles and Amphibians of Eastern/Central North America. 2016.* Houghton, Miflin, Harcourt. Boston, New York.

Sievert, Greg and Lynnette Sievert. 2005. *Field Guide to Oklahoma's Amphibians and Reptiles.* Oklahoma Department of Wildlife Conservation. Oklahoma City, Oklahoma.

Stebbins, Robert C. *Western Reptiles and Amphibians.* 2003. Houghton Miflin Company, Boston-New York

Tipton, Bob L., Terry L. Hibbetts, Troy D. Hibbitts, Toby J. Hibbetts, and Travis J. Laduc. 2012. *Texas Amphibians, A Field Guide.* Univerisity of Texas Press, Austin, Texas.

Trauth, Stanley E., Henry W. Robinson and Micheal V. Plummer. 2004. *The Amphibians and Reptiles of Arkansas.* University of Arkansas Press. Fayetteville, Arkansas.

U.S. Fish and Wildlife Service. 2020. "Habitat Characteristics of the Houston Toad (*Anaxyrus = Bufo houstonensis*)" September 2020 (version 1.0) U.S. Fish and Wildlife Service, Region 2. Albuquerque, New Mexico.

Internet

Amphibia Web—amphibiaweb.org
Herpedia—herpedia.com
Texas Parks and Wildlife Department—tpwd.texas.gov

Chapter 10: The Rivers and Streams of Texas

Print

Texas Watersheds. Summer 2012. *Texas Watersheds, Conservation News From Headwaters to the Coast.* Texas Parks and Wildlife, Austin, Texas.

Internet

Texas Parks and Wildlife Department—tpwd.texas.gov

Chapter 11: The Freshwater Fishes of Texas

Print

Goldstein, Robert J. with Rodney Harper and Richard Edwards. 2000. *American Aquarium Fishes.* Texas A&M University Press, College Station, TX.

Etnier, David A. and Wayne C. Starnes. 1993. *The Fishes of Tennessee.* The Univeristy of Tennessee Press, Knoxville, Tennessee.

Hendrickson, Dean and Adam E. Cohen. 2022. Fishes of Texas Project Database (Version 3.) http://doi.org/10.17603/C3WC70. Accessed 11/17/23.

Hubbs, C., R.J. Edwards and G.P. Garrett. 2008. "An annotated checklist of the freshwater fishes of Texas, with keys to identification of species." Texas Academy of Science. Available from: http://www.texasacademyofscience.org.

Miller, Rudolph J. 2004. *The Fishes of Oklahoma.* The University of Oklahoma Press, Norman, OK.

Page, Lawrence M. and Brooks M. Burr. 2011. *Peterson Field Guide to Freshwater Fishes of North America North of Mexico.* Houghton Mifflin Harcourt, Boston—New York.

Pflieger, William L. 1975. *The Fishes of Missouri.* Missouri Department of Conservation, Springfield, MO.

Thomas, Chad, Timothy H. Bonner, & Bobby G. Whiteside. 2007. *Freshwater Fishes of Texas, A Field Guide.* Texas A&M University Press, College Station, Texas.

Internet

FishBase—fishbase.org

FishMap—FishMap.org

Fishes of Texas—Fishesoftexas.org

International Union for Conservation of Nature—ww.iucn.org

North American Native Fish Association—nanfa.org

National Fish Habitat Action Plan—fishhabitat.org

NatureServe Explorer—natureserve.org

USGS Fact Sheets—search.usgs.gov

Encyclopedia of Life—eol.org

Land Big Fish—landbigfish.com

Texas Parks and Wildlife Department—tpwd.texas.gov

Nature Serve Explorer—explorer.natureserve.org

GLOSSARY

Aestivate/Aestivation	Dormant state of inactivity usually brought on by hot, dry conditions. Common in reptiles and amphibians.
Amphipod	A Crustacean of the order Amphipoda. Includes the freshwater shrimps.
Anadromous	Ascending into freshwater rivers to spawn.
Annelid/Annelida	A class of invertebrate organisms commonly known as worms.
Annuli	Ring-like structures, bands around body.
Anuran	A member of the amphibian order Anura (the frogs & toads).
Arboreal	Pertaining to trees.
Arthropod	A member of the invertebrate phylum Arthropoda.
Aspen Parkland	An open or semi-open area (usually grassland) that is intermingled with groves of Aspen.
Autotomy	Self-amputation of the tail, common in some lizards and salamanders when attacked.
Barbel	A long "whisker-like" appendage originating near the mouth of fishes, often sensory.
Barrens	Open areas within normally forested or brushy habitats.
Benthic	Pertaining to the bottom of a stream or lake.
Bivalve	An organism of the phylum Molluska (mollusks) or Branchiopoda having a shell consisting of two halves.
Boreal	Northern.
Buteo	A hawk belonging to the genus Buteo. Also known as the "Broad-winged Hawks."
Brumation	A period of inactivity in a dormant state during cold seasons. Common in reptiles
Cache	The act of storing or hiding food for future use.
Carapace	The top half of the shell of a turtle.
Carnivore	A meat eater.
Caudal	Pertaining to the tail.
Cere	Featherless area at the base of the bill on some birds.
Chromosome	Long strand of proteins and DNA found within the nucleus of a cell.
Circumpolar	Literally, around the poles. Usually used in reference to the geographic range of an organism, that is found throughout the northern hemisphere.
Cloaca	A common opening for reproductive and excretory functions in an organism. Typical for all animals except mammals.
Congeneric	Belonging to the same genus.
Conspecific	Belonging to the same species.
Contiguous	In contact with or adjoining.

Copepod	A group of tiny crustaceans belonging to the suborder Copepoda. Many are microscopic and aquatic and are important food for tiny fishes and other small aquatic organisms.
Covey	A group of quail. Usually a family unit consisting of parents and young of the year. Family stays together through the winter and breaks up in spring when survivors pair up to breed with survivors of other nearby coveys.
Crepuscular	Pertaining to dawn and dusk. Usually used in reference to an organism's activity period.
CRP	Conservation Reserve Program.
Crustacean	A member of the class Crustacea. A class of Arthropod organisms that includes the crayfish, lobsters, crabs, shrimps, barnacles, copepods, and water fleas.
Cryptic	Hidden. Pertains to colors and patterns that blend with the environment and render an organism hard to see.
Cryptic species	A species that is so similar to another known species that it goes undetected as being a different species.
Desert Pavement	A soil type common in desert environments, characterized by hard packed sand, gravel, and clay material that is tightly compressed into a "pavement"-like material.
Dessicate/Dessication	Dry out.
Detritus	Literally means trash but in most contexts refers to organic material such as leaves, twigs, etc.
Dipteran	An insect of the order Diptera. Includes flies, mosquitoes, gnats, and midges.
Disjunct	Not attached to or not adjoining.
Diurnal	Pertaining to day. Being active by day.
Dorsal	The top or back of an organism.
Dorso-lateral	Pertaining to the region of the body where the back meets the sides.
Dorso-lateral fold	A ridge of raised skin on the upper side of frog that runs from the tympanum to the groin.
Dorso-ventral	The region between the side and the belly of an organism, or along the lower side adjacent to the belly.
Echolocate/echolocation	The use of sound waves to navigate or move about. As in bats.
Ecoregion	A large unit of land or water containing a geographically distinct assemblage of species, natural communities, and environmental conditions.
Ecotone	The region where one or more habitats converge.
Embryo	A young animal that is developing from a fertilized egg. Embryonic stage ends at birth or hatching.
Endemic	Native to a particular area.
Endotherm/Endothermic	An organism that regulates its body temperature internally. Warm-blooded.
Ephemeral	Temporary, fleeting.
Estrous	In mammals the condition of the female being receptive to breeding and capable of conceiving.
Estuary/Estuaries	The region where a river or stream meets the sea.
Explosive breeder	Pertains to the breeding habits of some toads in which all individuals within a local population will gather to breed at the same time. Explosive breeding is of short duration, often only a few days.
Extant	Still present. Opposite of extirpated.

Extirpated	No longer found within a given area.
Fecund/Fecundity	Capable of producing abundant offspring.
Fin rays	The bony structures that support the membranes of a fish's fin.
Fledge	The act of young birds leaving the nest.
Fledgling	A young bird that has recently left the nest.
Fossorial	Burrowing or living in underground burrows.
Gastropod	A class of the animal phylum Molluska. Includes snails and slugs.
Gorget	The brilliantly colored patch of feathers on the throat of most hummingbirds.
Gynogenesis	A reproductive mode in fishes in which the female of a gynogenic species mates with a male of another species but does not incorporate the sperms genetic material into the egg. The sperm of the male merely acts to stimulate the egg to begin to replicate genetic material and begin cell divisioin to ultimately produce a genetic clone of the female. Thus all Gynogenic individuals are female.
Herbaceous	A type of flowering plant which does not develop woody tissue.
Hermaphroditic	Possessing both male and female sexual characteristics.
Heterocercal	Pertains to the shape of the caudal fin of a fish in which the upper lobe is longer than the bottom lobe and often has and extension of the spine into the upper lobe of the fin.
Holarctic	The circumpolar region that includes polar regions of North America, Europe, and Asia.
Homogeneous	Of the same kind.
Humus	Decayed or decaying plant material.
Insectivorous	Insect eating.
Intergrade	An organism which possesses morphological characteristics that are intermediate between two distinctly different forms.
Invertivorous	Feeding on invertebrates.
Irruptive	The sudden movement of animals from one portion of their range to another, often very distant portion of their range. As in when Snowy Owls occasionally move down from the Arctic region into the southern half of North America.
Isopod	An order of Crustaceans that includes the familiar pillbugs.
IUCN	The International Union for Conservation of Nature.
Keeled Scales	The presence of a small ridge down the middle of the dorsal scales on snakes.
Kettle	A flock of raptors. Usually used to refer to large flocks of migrating hawks or vultures.
Keystone species	A species that is vital to an ecosystem because many other species benefit in some way from its presence in the ecosystem.
Lentic	Slow-moving or still bodies of water, such as lakes, swaps, ponds, etc.
Mandible	The lower jaw of an animal or the bill of a bird.
Marine	Pertaining to living in a saltwater environment.
Mast	Seeds produced by plants in a deciduous forest. Usually means the cumulative production of acorns, nuts, berries, seeds, etc., which are widely utilized by wildlife as food.
Melanistic	A predominance of the dark pigment known as melanin. The opposite of Albinistic.
Mesic	Damp or moist.

Metabolic/Metabolism	The sum of the chemical activity that occurs within a living organism. Usually relates to the digestion of food and utilization of food compounds within the body.
Metamorphose	Change of the body. Usually refers to the change from an immature stage to a more mature stage (as in a tadpole to a frog).
Metamorphosis	Abrupt physical change of body form.
Millinery Trade	The sale of bird feathers.
Molt	The shedding of and renewal (replacement) of skin, hair, or feathers.
Monotypic species	A species that does not have any subordinate taxons (i.e. subspecies).
Moraine	Large mass of earth, sand, gravels, and rock bulldozed by glacial movement. Moraines usually accumulate along the sides and in the front of glaciers.
Morph	Short for morphological, in this book used to described different color and pattern variations within a species, as in "red morph," "dark morph," etc.
Morphological	Pertain to morphology.
Morphology	The study of the body form, shape, and structure of organisms, including colors or patterns.
Muskeg	A Sphagnum bog occurring in the boreal (northern) regions of North America.
Nape	The back of the neck.
Neonate	A newborn (or newly hatched) young.
Neotony/Neotenic	The condition of retaining juvenile characteristics into adulthood.
Neotropic/Neotropical	The zoogeographical region comprised of Central and South America, the tropical regions of Mexico, and the Caribbean.
Nuptial	Pertaining to breeding.
Obligate	In biology, means occurring within a restricted environment.
Omnivore	Eats both plant and animal matter.
Ontogenetic	Related to the development or age of an organism.
Opercle flap	The bony structure on the side of a fish's head that covers the gills. Also sometimes called gill cover.
Organism	A living thing.
Orthopteran	A member of the insect order Orthoptera. Includes such well-known insects as crickets and grasshoppers.
Ossification	The formation of bone.
Palearctic	The geographic region that includes Europe and northern Asia.
Parotoid Gland	The large lump on each side of the head of toads.
Parthenogenesis	The development of an ovum (egg) without fertilization.
Passage Migrant	Refers to birds that merely migrate through an area without staying any appreciable amount of time.
Pectoral	Pertain to or located in the chest area.
Pelage	Fur.
Pelagic	Pertaining to deep ocean waters far offshore.
Pelvic	Pertaining to or located in the region of the pelvis (hips).
Perennial	Continually occurring.
Phylogeny	The evolutionary relationships and/or evolutionary history of organisms.
Physiography	Refers to the natural features of a landscape, i.e. mountains, rivers, plains, etc.

Pinnae	A projecting body part. Often refers to feathers on birds that extend well beyond the body.
Piscivorous	Fish eating.
Plastron	The ventral (bottom) portion of a turtle's shell.
Plumage	The feathers of a bird.
Polychaete worms	Annelid worms (Phylum Annelida) belonging to the class Polychaeta. Mostly marine but some are fresh water.
Precocious	Having adult (or highly developed) characteristics in the young. Precocial being highly precocious.
Predaceous	Feeding on other animals, being a predator.
Prehensile	Grasping. As in a prehensile tail that is able to wrap around and grasp a tree limb.
Psitticine	Pertaining to the parrot family (Psittacidae).
Puddle Duck	Ducks belonging to the genus *Anas*.
Regenerative	Refers to the ability to repair or replace damaged or destroyed tissues or structures.
Riparian	Pertaining to the bank of a stream or river.
Seasonal Migrant	A migrant that appears during a particular season (usually spring and/or fall in the case of neotropical migrant birds).
Sedentary	Inactive, stationary. Refers to animals that don't move around a lot.
Sexual Dimorphism	Morphological differences between the sexes.
Sky Islands	A particular habitat of the desert southwest where many indigenous species exist in the cooler, wetter habits of higher elevations in mountain ranges surrounded by low desert. These habitats are surround and isolated by hot, dry, desert basins, thus the mountain tops have become "islands" in the desert.
Species of Concern	A species or subspecies which might become threatened under continued or increased stress.
Spermatophore	An encapsulated package of sperm deposited in the environment by the male that is then picked up by the female.
Steppe	Grassland.
Successional Woodlands/Areas	Landscape areas (usually woodlands) that are undergoing change from an early stage of development to an older stage. As in woodlands regenerating following logging operations.
Sympatric/Sympatrically	A condition where more than one species occurs in the same or overlapping area or habitat.
Taiga	A type of forest occurring in the far north. Usually dominated by dwarfed spruces.
Talus	The piles of rocks that accumulate at the base of cliffs or steep mountain slopes.
Tannins	Dark-colored compounds that are found in plants. Decaying plant material releases tannins that are responsible for the "tea colored" waters seen in swamps and "black water" streams.
Tetraploid	Possessing four chromosomes.
Topography	The configuration of the land surface. Literally, "the lay of the land."
Torpor	A period of inactivity.
Troglodyte/Troglodyitc	Cave dweller.
Turbid/Turbidity	Refers to waters with high silt content, i.e. muddy water.

Tympanum	The circular ear structure on the side of the head of frogs and toads.
TWPD	Texas Parks and Wildlife Department.
Ungulate	A hooved mammal. Once regarded as an order (Ungulata) in the taxonomy of mammals, now split into two orders; the Artiodactyla, which are the even toed ungulates (deer, pigs, cattle, etc.) ; and the Perrisodactyla, which are the odd-toed ungulates (horses, tapir, rhinoceroses).
USFWS	United States Fish and Wildlife Service.
Ventrolateral	Pertaining to the region of the body where the sides meet the belly.
Vernal	Pertaining to spring. Also frequently used to describe temporary ponds and pools that hold water only during the wet season.
Vestigial	A rudimentary structure. Usually a remnant, degenerative structure that was once (in the evolutionary history of the organism) a fully functioning structure.
Xeric	Dry.
Zygote	A fertilized egg that has not yet begun to divide.

INDEX

PHOTO CREDITS

Robby Deans

Western Harvest Mouse, Merriam's Pocket Mouse, Texas Map Turtle, Texas River Cooter, Rio Grande Cooter, Big Bend Slider, Texas Tortoise, Reticulated Collared Lizard, Plateau Earless Lizard, Keeled Earless Lizard, Graphic Spiny Lizard, Eastern Side-blotched Lizard, Four-lined Skink, Great Plains Skink, Many-lined Skink, Texas Alligator Lizard, Mediterranean House Gecko, Northern Cat-eyed Snake, Rio Grande Leopard Frog, Spotted Chorus Frog, Cajun Chorus Frog, Mexican Tree Frog, Mexican White-lipped Frog, Barking Frog, Rio Grande Chirping Frog, Cliff Chirping Frog, Sheep Frog, Valdini Farms Salamander, Jollyville Plateau Salamander, San Marcos Salamander, Guadulupe Darter, Mexican Stoneroller, Plains Killifish, Rio Grande Darter.

John Dickson

Bell's Vireo, Black-capped Vireo, Gray Vireo, Hutton's Vireo, Sedge Wren, Virginia's Warbler, Lucy's Warbler, Black-throated Gray Warbler, Golden-cheeked Warbler, Grace's Warbler, Mourning Warbler, McGillvray's Warbler, Varied Bunting, Cassin's Sparrow, Chestnut Collared Longspur, Thick-billed Longspur, Green Kingfisher, Green Parakeet, Lucifer Hummingbird, White-throated Swift, Common Paraque, Ferrignous Pygmy Owl, Elf Owl, Zone-tailed Hawk, Least Grebe, Mexican Duck.

Dave Neely

Ribbon Shiner, Cypress Minnow, Blacktail Redhorse, Gray Redhorse, Headwater Catfish, Texas Logperch, Brook Silverside, Bigscale Logperch, Blackspot Shiner, Chub Shiner, Plateau Shiner, Northern Plains Killifish, Chestnut Lamprey, Southern Brook Lamprey.

Matthew R. Thomas

Mississippi Silvery Minnow, Pugnose Minnow, Bullhead Minnow, Mimic Shiner, Threadfin Shad, Skipjack Herring, Goldeye, Tadpole Madtom, Mud Darter, Harlequin Darter, Cypress Darter, Bluntnose Darter.

C. K. Kelly

Gray-footed Chipmunk, Texas Antelope Squirrel, Yellow-faced pocket Gopher, Smith's Black-headed Snake, Hurter's Spadefoot, Western Narrowmouth Toad, New Mexico Spadefoot, Texas Spiny Lizard, Round-tailed Horned Lizard, Western Spotted Skunk.

John R. McGregor

Golden Mouse, Rafinesque's Big Eared Bat, Hoary Bat, Eastern Red Bat, Silver-haired Bat, Slender Glass Lizard.

Don Martin

Ruby-crowned Kinglet (M), American Tree Sparrow, Henslow's Sparrow, LeConte's Sparrow, Red-cockaded Woodpecker, Clay-colored Sparrow.

Konrad Schmidt

Ghost Shiner, River Shiner, Flathead Chub, River Darter, Western Sand Darter, Pallid Shiner.

Peter Paplanus

Lined Snake, Flat-headed Snake, Western Slimy Salamander, Dusty Hog-nosed Snake, Razorback Musk Turtle.

Tim Leppek

Swift Fox, Spotted Ground Squirrel, Flammulated Owl, Common Poorwill, Mountain Plover, Lesser Earless Lizard, Greater Short-horned Lizard.

Cundy McNamee

Monk Parakeet, Sprague's Pipit, Red-crowned Parrot, Yellow-headed Parrot, Masked Booby, Central American Indigo Snake, Sprague's Pipit.

Romey Swanson

Mexican Racer, Mexican Hog-nosed Snake, Brazos Water Snake, Concho Water Snake, Mexican Burrowing Toad, Fern Bank Salamander, Texas Salamander.

Brian Zimmerman

Rainwater Killifish, Lake Chubsucker, Highfin Carpsucker, Swamp Darter.

Florida Wildlife Commission

Northern Yellow Bat, Leatherback Sea Turtle, Hogchocker, Brazilian Free-tailed Bat.

Fishes of Texas Project Team

Plains Minnow, Amazon Molly, Mimic Shiner, Sabine Shiner, Texas Shiner, Tamaulipas Shiner.

Michael Price

Spotted Chorus Frog, Reticulated Gecko, Rough-tailed Gecko.

Scott Wahlberg

Speckled Racer, Louisiana Pine Snake, Houston Toad.

Clint Guardiana

Tamaulipan Hook-nosed Snake, Tamaulipan Milk Snake, Black-spotted Newt.

Dr. Edmund Zimmerer

Glossy Swamp Snake, Mediterranean Gecko.

U. S. Fish and Wildlife Service

Hawksbill Sea Turtle, Long-tongued Bat.

James Kiser

Seminole Bat, Southeastern Bat.

Cyrus Allen

Plains Pocket Gopher, Plains Thread Snake.

Corey Raimond

Dwarf Salamander, Rough Earth Snake

Pete Siminski

Hooded Skunk, Botta's Pocket Gopher.

NOAH

Atlantic Needlefish.

Tim Johnson

Feral Hog.

Greg Schechter

Southern Short-tailed Shrew.

John Williams

Eastern Woodrat.

Alan Cressler

Cuban Flat-headed Frog.

Margaret Novak

Rudd.

Allison Holdorf

Hispid Pocket Mouse.

USFWS Bill Shreve

Chuck-wills-widow.

USFWS Lisa Hupp

Smith's Longspur—https://creativecommons.org/publicdomain/mark/1.0/

Nicole Montoya BLM NM

Dunes Sagebrush Lizard—https://creativecommons.org/licenses/by/2.0/

American Society of Mammalogists

Chihuahuan Grasshopper Mouse—https://upload.wikimedia.org/wikipedia/commons/2/2e/Chihuahuan_grasshopper_mouse.jpg

National Park Service

Western Small-footed Bat.

NPS, White Sands National Park

Pallid Bat—https://creativecommons.org/publicdomain/mark/1.0/

Alex Borisenko, Biodiversity Institute of Ontario

Ghost-faced Bat—CC BY-SA 3.0 <https://creativecommons.org/licenses/by-sa/3.0>, via Wikimedia Commons

Bob Johnson

American Parastrelle—CC BY-SA 4.0 <https://creativecommons.org/licenses/by-sa/4.0>, via Wikimedia Commons

Conner Long

Common Poorwill—CC BY-SA 4.0 <https://creativecommons.org/licenses/by-sa/4.0>, via Wikimedia Commons

Mario Suarez Porras

Buff Breasted Sandpiper—CC BY-SA 3.0 <https://creativecommons.org/licenses/by-sa/3.0>, via Wikimedia Commons

Hector Bottai

Black Rail—CC BY-SA 4.0 <https://creativecommons.org/licenses/by-sa/4.0>, via Wikimedia Commons

Dominic Sherony

Yellow Rail—CC BY-SA 2.0 <https://creativecommons.org/licenses/by-sa/2.0>, via Wikimedia Commons

Bret Albanese, Georgia Department of Natural Resources

Southern Flounder.

Sapphosyne

Prairie Skink—CC BY-SA 3.0 <https://creativecommons.org/licenses/by-sa/3.0>, via Wikimedia Commons

Nick Loveland

Plateau Shiner—https://commons.wikimedia.org/wiki/File:Plateau_Shiner_imported_from_iNaturalist_photo_187972116_on_24_October_2023.jpg no rights reserved, CC0, via Wikimedia Commons

Llussier

Western Hook-nosed Snake—https://commons.wikimedia.org/wiki/File:Gyalopion_canum.jpg

Clinton & Charles Robertson

Rio Grande Shiner, Guadulupe Darter—https://commons.wikimedia.org/wiki/File:Percina_apristis_(3628005726).jpg, https://commons.wikimedia.org/wiki/File:Etheostoma_grahami.jpg

Sophia Osho

Author photo.

ABOUT THE AUTHOR

Photo by Sophia Osho

Naturalist Scott Shupe began his professional career in the early 1970s at the famed Ross Allen Reptile Institute and Venom Laboratory in Silver Springs, Florida, where he served as a lecturer and curator and extracted venom from captive snakes in that facility's venom laboratory. He later performed similar duties at the St. Augustine Alligator Farm in St. Augustine, Florida, and in the 1980s engaged in a contract to train raptors and perform the Birds of Prey Show at Reptile Gardens in Rapid City, South Dakota.

During his eclectic career as a freelance naturalist he has hosted a nature-oriented television series for the Outdoor Channel, produced a life-science instructional video series marketed to public schools nationwide, served as director of a private zoo/nature center in his home state of Kentucky, and founded a school assemblies company that provided wildlife education programs to schools in over 30 states; as well as contracting interpretive naturalist services with state parks, US Forest Service, and US Army Corps of Engineers facilities. He has enjoyed a longtime personal and professional relationship with the Kentucky Reptile Zoo and Venom Laboratory in Slade, Kentucky, where he previously served as Outreach Ambassador for Educational Programming.

He has twice been recognized by the U.S. Fish and Wildlife Service for his contribution to conservation efforts, been named naturalist of the year by the Kentucky Society of Natural History, and was awarded the Environmental Stewardship Award by the Kentucky Environmental Quality Commission. In 1996, he was awarded the Jesse Stuart Media Award by the Kentucky School Library Association for his educational life science video products and won that award a second time in 2018 for the book *Kentucky Wildlife Encyclopedia.*

Since his semi-retirement in 2018, he has focused on eco-travel, wildlife photography, and writing natural history reference books for the lay public, while occasionally taking temporary contracts with various conservation organizations. Among his most recent contract endeavors are consulting for the Birds of Prey Program at Reptile Gardens in Rapid City, South Dakota, completing a term as On-site Naturalist at the Desert Tortoise Research Natural Area in California's Mojave Desert, guiding birdwatching groups in Nebraska and Kansas for Audubon of Kansas, and serving as Naturalist Instructor for the Road Scholar program taking groups on tours of Yosemite, Kings Canyon, and Sequoia National Parks.

The *Texas Wildlife Encyclopedia* is the seventh book in a series of state-by-state wildlife encyclopedias produced for Skyhorse Publishing, having previously authored encyclopedias for the states of Kentucky, Ohio, Illinois, New York, Florida, and Indiana. He has also authored for the same publisher *U.S. Guide to Venomous Snakes and Their Mimics* and served as the editor for the military manual *Venomous Snakes of the World, A Manual for US Amphibious Forces.*

Contact Scott Shupe at kscottshupe@gmail.com.